QUR'ĀNIC CHRISTIANS

An analysis of classical and modern exegesis

QUR'ĀNIC CHRISTIANS

AN ANALYSIS OF CLASSICAL AND MODERN EXEGESIS

JANE DAMMEN McAULIFFE
Emory University

The right of the University of Cambridge to print and sell all manner of books was granted by Henry VIII in 1534. The University has printed and published continuously since 1584.

CAMBRIDGE UNIVERSITY PRESS
CAMBRIDGE
NEW YORK PORT CHESTER MELBOURNE SYDNEY

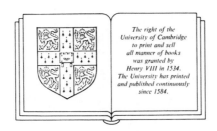

Published by the Press Syndicate of the University of Cambridge
The Pitt Building, Trumpington Street, Cambridge CB2 1RP
40 West 20th Street, New York, NY 10011, USA
10 Stamford Road, Oakleigh, Melbourne 3166, Australia

First published 1991

Printed in the United States

Library of Congress Cataloging-in-Publication Data

McAuliffe, Jane Dammen.

Qurʾānic Christians : an analysis of classical
and modern exegesis / Jane Dammen McAuliffe.

p. cm.

Includes bibliographical references.

ISBN 0-521-36470-1

1. Christianity in the Koran. 2. Koran – Commentaries –
History and criticism. I. Title.
BP134.C45M35 1991
297′. 1228 – dc20 90-34284
CIP

British Library Cataloguing in Publication Data

McAuliffe, Jane Dammen

Qurʾānic Christians : an analysis of
classical and modern exegesis.

1. Title

297.1228

ISBN 0-521-36470-1 hardback

For
DENNIS

Contents

Acknowledgments

Preparing this book for publication concludes with the pleasant task of thanking those who helped to bring it to fruition. Colleagues, both Canadian and American, have read and commented upon drafts of this work at various stages in its development. Among Canadian scholars, I am grateful to Professors Roger Savory, Ronald Sweet, John Revell, and Michael Marmura of the University of Toronto and to Professor Charles Adams of McGill University.

American colleagues to whom I owe a debt of gratitude include Professors Gerhard Böwering, Yale University; Yvonne Haddad, University of Massachusetts at Amherst; Frederick Denny, University of Colorado at Boulder; John Esposito, College of the Holy Cross; and Michael Carter, New York University.

Institutional support has been provided by the Social Sciences and Humanities Research Council of Canada, the Emory University Research Fund and the librarians of Robarts Library at the University of Toronto, the Pontificio Istituto di Studi Arabi e d'Islamistica, and the Pitts Theology Library of Emory University. *Alif: Journal of Comparative Poetics* has graciously granted permission for reproduction of material from my article "Ibn al-Jawzī's Exegetical Propaedeutic: Introduction and Translation," *Alif* 8 (1988): 101–13.

I am particularly grateful to Dean Jim L. Waits of the Candler School of Theology for his persistent encouragement and support and to my colleagues at Candler, especially Professor Hendrikus Boers, who sustain an academic environment of warm collegiality and who ask good questions.

Finally, I would like to offer heartfelt thanks to the man who introduced me to the field of Islamic studies, who directed this work in its early stages, and whom I esteem as an epitome of elegant and incisive scholarship, University Professor Emeritus George Michael Wickens of the University of Toronto.

Abbreviations

Approaches	*Approaches to the History of the Interpretation of the Qurʾān*, edited by Andrew Rippin (Oxford: Clarendon Press, 1988).
AT	*Analyses, théorie*
BEO	*Bulletin d'études orientales*
BRISMES	*British Society for Middle Eastern Studies Bulletin*
BSOAS	*Bulletin of the School of Oriental and African Studies*
EI[1]	*The Encyclopedia of Islam*, 8 vols. and supplement (1913–38; reprint, Leiden: E.J. Brill, 1987).
EI[2]	*The Encyclopedia of Islam*, new edition (Leiden: E.J. Brill, 1954–).
GAL	Carl Brockelmann, *Geschichte der arabischen Litteratur*, 2 vols. and 3-vol. supplement (Leiden: E.J. Brill, 1937–49).
GAS	Fuat Sezgin, *Geschichte des arabischen Schrifttums, Band 1: Qurʾān wissenschaften, Ḥadīth, Geschichte, Fiqh, Dogmatik, Mystik bis ca. 430 H.* (Leiden: E.J. Brill, 1967).
IC	*Islamic Culture*
IJMES	*International Journal of Middle East Studies*
IQ	*Islamic Quarterly*
IS	*Islamic Studies*
ISC	*Islam, storia e civiltà*
Islamo	*Islamochristiana*
JA	*Journal asiatique*
JAOS	*Journal of the American Oriental Society*
JESHO	*Journal of the Economic and Social History of the Orient*
JNES	*Journal of Near Eastern Studies*
JSAI	*Jerusalem Studies in Arabic and Islam*

JSS	*Journal of Semitic Studies*
MIDEO	*Mélanges de l'Institut Dominicain d'Études Orientales du Caire*
MW	*The Muslim World*
Prédication	*Prédication et propagande au Moyen Age* (Paris: Presses Universitaires de France, 1983).
Quest	*In Quest of an Islamic Humanism: Arabic and Islamic Studies in Memory of Mohamed al-Nowaihi*, edited by A.H. Green (Cairo: The American University in Cairo Press, 1984).
Qurʾān Congress	*International Congress for the Study of the Qurʾān, Australian National University, Canberra, 8–13 May 1980*, edited by A.H. Johns, 2nd ed. (Canberra: Australian National University, n.d.).
REI	*Revue des études islamiques*
RHR	*Revue de l'histoire des religions*
RS	*Religious Studies*
SI	*Studia Islamica*
Studia Arabica	*Studia Arabica et Islamica: Festschrift for Iḥsān ʿAbbās on his Sixtieth Birthday*, edited by Wadād Qāḍī (Beirut: American University of Beirut, 1981).
UEAI 9	*Proceedings of the Ninth Congress of the Union Européenne des Arabisants et Islamisants, Amsterdam 1978*, edited by Rudolph Peters (Leiden: E.J. Brill, 1981).
UEAI 10	*Proceedings of the Tenth Congress of the Union Européenne des Arabisants et Islamisants, Edinburgh 1980*, edited by Robert Hillenbrand (Edinburgh: n.p., 1982).
WI	*Die Welt des Islams*
ZAL	*Zeitschrift für arabische Linguistik*
ZDMG	*Zeitschrift der Deutschen Morgenländischen Gesellschaft*

Introduction

The question of religious self-definition and that of interreligious understanding continue to intrigue contemporary historians of religions. The first seeks to determine how particular religious traditions have defined themselves at various periods in their histories. The second inquires about ways in which one tradition perceives, or has perceived, another. Self-reflective concerns cede prominence to external investigations. The lines cross, of course, at those points where one tradition attempts to distinguish itself from another. In such instances interreligious understanding, by a kind of *via negativa*, becomes self-definition.

The focus of the present study will be this question of interreligious understanding as undertaken within a Muslim context. In particular, the Islamic understanding of Christians will be probed. As the youngest of the three "Abrahamic" faiths, Islam from its inception developed in both confrontation and conversation with Jews and Christians. The gradual clarification of differences among these traditions generated a vast polemical literature on all three fronts. This literature, in turn, bases itself upon and draws its lines of argument from a rich scriptural heritage.

The primary source for the Muslim understanding of Christianity is the revelation vouchsafed to Muḥammad, the Qurʾān. While the still-vigorously debated questions of the Qurʾān's compilation and early exegesis will be discussed later, it is important at the outset to clarify that conception of the Qurʾān which undergirds this study. For the committed Muslim, the Qurʾān represents the word of God as revealed, or 'sent down', to His prophet, Muḥammad. It is not, then, for Muslims, a book like other books, or a mere part – even if an obviously important part – of their religious literature. Rather it is a revelation, a divine disclosure, to which special, even unique, treatment must be accorded. As God's own word, Qurʾānic statements are normative for the thought and behavior of Muslims. Any effort to comprehend the Islamic understanding of Christians and Christianity must begin therein.

Within the Qurʾān may be found two general categories of statements relative to Christianity. The first speaks of the Christians (under various designations) as a particular religious group. The second includes allusions to Christian figures, especially Jesus and Mary, and to the theological indictments that have fueled the long-standing quarrel of Muslim-Christian polemic. Much has been written and continues to be written about this polemic and its principal theological preoccupations.[1] What Christians term the doctrines of the Incarnation and the Trinity, but what Muslims have frequently excoriated as the blasphemies of divine reproduction and tritheism, remain but the most prominent of these. There has also been no lack of studies on the Qurʾānic depiction of Jesus (and of Mary), some clearly motivated by a desire for Muslim-Christian rapprochement.[2] The place that Jesus occupies in Muslim piety and eschatology is a further development of this Qurʾānic prominence and has been studied by both Muslim and Christian scholars. No commensurate degree of attention, however, has been paid to those statements in the Qurʾān that refer to Christians as a social and religious group.

The number of such references is surprisingly large. Calculation of the precise sum depends upon issues of interpretation, for a variety of phrases

1 The most comprehensive bibliographic source for Muslim writings on Christianity and Christian writings on Islam may be found in the journal issued in Rome by the Pontifical Institute for Arabic and Islamic Studies, *Islamochristiana*. These have been published by Robert Caspar and his collaborators under the title "Bibliographie du dialogue islamo-chrétien" in the following volumes: 1 (1975): 125–81; 2 (1976): 187–249; 3 (1977): 255–86; 4 (1978): 247–67; 5 (1979): 299–317; 6 (1980): 259–99; 7 (1981): 299–307; 10 (1984): 273–92.

2 The Qurʾānic depiction of Jesus has been studied by a number of authors. Significant monographs include: Henri Michaud, *Jésus selon le Coran* (Neuchatel: Éditions Delachaux et Niestlé, 1960); Geoffrey Parrinder, *Jesus in the Qurʾān* (New York: Barnes and Noble, 1965); Donald Roland Rickards, "A Study of the Quranic References to ʿĪsā in the Light of *Tafsīr* and *Ḥadīth*," Ph.D. diss., Hartford Seminary Foundation, 1969; Heikki Räisänen, *Das Koranische Jesusbild: ein Beitrag zur Theologie des Korans* (Helsinki: Missiologian ja Ekumeniikan, 1971); Olaf H. Schumann, *Der Christus der Muslime: christologische Aspekte in der arabisch-islamischen Literatur* (Gütersloh: Gütersloher Verlagshaus Gerd Mohn, 1975); Kenneth Cragg, *Jesus and the Muslim* (London: George Allen and Unwin, 1985). Don Wismer has produced a book-length bibliography entitled *The Islamic Jesus: An Annotated Bibliography of Sources in English and French* (New York: Garland Publishing, 1977). Miguel Asín Palacios has collected the sayings attributed to Jesus that can be found in the works of Muslim authors of the classical period such as Abū ʿUmar b. ʿAbd Rabbih (d. 328/940), Abū al-Layth al-Samarqandī (d. 373/983–84), and Abū Ṭālib al-Makkī (d. 386/998). See his "Logia et Agrapha Domini Jesu apud Moslemicos Sciptores," *Patrologia Orientalia* 13 (1919): 332–432 and 19 (1926): 529–624.

Studies on Mary have been fewer. Useful information is presented in Jean Abd el-Jalil, *Marie et l'Islam* (Paris: Beauchesne, 1950); Nilo Geagea, *Mary of the Koran: A Meeting Point Between Christianity and Islam*, trans. and ed. by Lawrence T. Fares (New York: Philosophical Library, 1984); and my "Chosen of All Women: Mary and Fāṭima in Qurʾānic Exegesis." *Islamo* 7 (1981): 19–28. David Kerr has drawn upon these works and others in his recent "Mary, Mother of Jesus, in the Islamic Tradition: A Theme for Christian-Muslim Dialogue," *Newsletter of the Office on Christian-Muslim Relations* 39 (1988): 1–9.

are used to designate the Christians both separately and in combination with the Jews.[3] Most obvious is, of course, the Arabic noun *al-naṣārā*, the common Qurʾānic term for Christians, which is found seven times in *sūrat al-baqarah* (2), five times in *sūrat al-māʾidah* (5), and once each in *sūrat al-tawbah* (9) and *sūrat al-ḥajj* (22).[4] Less direct designations are those that highlight the common scriptural heritage of Jews, Christians, and Muslims. Of most frequent occurrence is the phrase *ahl al-kitāb* ('people of the book'), which is found more than thirty times in the Qurʾān. This ordinarily signifies, unless otherwise qualified, both Christians and Jews. Other phrases that bear such dual signification also indicate in various ways the reception of divinely inspired scripture. Examples include: "those who were given the book (*alladhīna ūtū al-kitāb*)," "those to whom We gave the book (*alladhīna ātaynāhum al-kitāb*)," "those who were given a portion of the book (*alladhīna ūtū naṣīban min al-kitāb*)," and "those who read the book before you (*alladhīna yaqraʾūna al-kitāb min qablika*)." An additional category of designation – and one more unambiguously applicable to the Christians – includes the verses that refer to Jesus and then subsequently mention his 'followers' by such phrases as "those who follow you (*alladhīna ittabaʿūka*)" or "those who follow him (*alladhīna ittabaʿūhu*)." Such are certain to bedevil scholars who rely only on concordances to collect all relevant citations for a subject; as would also another group that includes only associative references to Christians. An example of the latter is to be found in *sūrat al-māʾidah* (5):66 and will be treated at length in Chapter 6. In this instance reference to the Torah and Gospel is associated with the approbatory label, "a balanced people (*ummatun muqtaṣidatun*)."

Given the state of reference materials in the field of Islamic studies, collecting all of the verses that refer to the Christians involves a combination of several tasks. These include careful reading of the Qurʾānic text itself, use of the available concordances and indices, and – as will become clear in this study – repeated reference to the major products of the Islamic exegetical tradition.[5] Once collected, the verses or groups of verses begin

3 Various indices to the Qurʾān are surveyed in Willem A. Bijlefeld, "Some Recent Contributions to Qurʾānic Studies: Selected Publications in English, French and German, 1964–1973," *MW* 64 (1974): 79–102.

4 As Muslim writers generally cite the divisions of the Qurʾān by name rather than number, that convention will be respected in this book, with the numerical designation placed afterward in parentheses. Except for some minor modification, transliteration of Arabic and Persian follows the system adopted by the Library of Congress.

5 The most useful concordance to the Qurʾān is that of Muḥammad Fuʾād ʿAbd al-Bāqī entitled *al-Muʿjam al-mufahras li-alfāẓ al-Qurʾān al-karīm* (Beirut: Dār Iḥyāʾ al-Turāth al-ʿArabī, n.d.), which reproduces the full phrase in which a word is found. A popular, earlier work that gives only sūrah and verse citation for each entry is that of Gustav Flügel, *Concordantiae Corani Arabicae* (Leipzig: C. Tauchnit, 1842). Hanna E. Kassis has

to fall into several categories. (Again, it must be noted that Christians are frequently mentioned in combination with reference to the Jews and others through the use of such inclusive phrases as "people of the book [*ahl al-kitāb*]," "those who were given the book [*alladhīna ūtū al-kitāb*]," etc.) Direct or indirect criticism of Christians constitutes the largest category.[6] Persistent charges condemn Christians for being untrustworthy and internally divisive. Further accusations censure them for boasting, for deliberately or inadvertently corrupting their scripture, for trying to lead Muslims astray, and for being unfaithful to Jesus' message. A second grouping can be made of those verses that seek to prescribe Muslim behavior toward Christians both socially and economically, such as reference to the collection of a special tax, the *jizyah*, levied on the Christians (and others of the *ahl al-kitāb*), and reference to the protection of existing churches and cloisters. Verses that make ostensibly positive remarks about the Christians compose the final category and the focus of this investigation.

These positive allusions to the Christians are scattered throughout the Qur'ān and a number have been persistently extracted to serve as proof-texts of Muslim religious tolerance. Several contemporary examples should suffice to convey the range of such efforts. One traces Islam's "age-old tolerance to Christian and Jewish communities" to the Qur'ānic praise of Christians in *sūrat al-mā'idah* (5):82.[7] Another remarks that there are "certain passages in the Qur'ān which might be regarded as conciliatory towards Christians."[8] Two Muslim scholars draw upon these verses to emphasize

recently published a handsomely produced English concordance keyed to A.J. Arberry's translation of the Qur'ān. See *A Concordance of the Qur'ān* (Berkeley: University of California Press, 1983). An ingenious, thematic index to the Qur'ān is that of Michel Allard, which consists of 430 punched cards with accompanying code and commentary. See *Analyse conceptuelle du Coran sur cartes perforées* (Paris: Mouton, 1963). This project receives theoretical reconsideration in G. Laroussi, "Enonciation et stratégies discursives dans le Çoran," *AT* 2/3 (1982): 121–71.

6 For a list of such Qur'ānic criticism see Abdelmajid Charfi, "Christianity in the Qur'ān Commentary of Ṭabarī," *Islamo* 6 (1980): 134–38. This article is a translation by Penelope C. Johnstone from *Revue Tunisienne des Sciences Sociales* 58/59 (1979): 53–96. A French translation by Robert Caspar was published in *MIDEO* 16 (1983): 117–61.

7 William Stoddart, *Sufism: The Mystical Doctrines and Methods of Islam* (Wellingborough, England: Thorsons Publishers, 1976), 35. Stoddart omits from his citation of this verse – with no indication that he is doing so – the condemnatory statement about the Jews, presumably because to include it would contradict his interpretation of the verse. Drawing upon the work of Rudi Paret, Josef van Ess distinguishes between the Qur'ānic condemnation of the Jews for moral reasons and of Christians on dogmatic grounds. With this in mind, he finds in 5:82 an instance where "the actual behavior of Christians comes close to being praised." See "Islamic Perspectives," in *Christianity and the World Religions: Paths of Dialogue with Islam, Hinduism, and Buddhism (Christentum und Weltreligionen)*, ed. by Hans Küng et al., trans. by Peter Heinegg (Garden City: Doubleday and Company, 1986), 101.

8 Kenneth Cragg, *The Call of the Minaret* (New York: Oxford University Press, 1956),

that "the tolerant spirit of Islam is apparent in its recognition of other religions" and that in "times of prosperity and security from external dangers, this tolerant attitude was the hallmark of Muslim-Christian relations."[9]

A final instance proves yet more emphatic: "These passages recognize the worth of other religions, if they had scriptures and believed in one God. They have been valuable in inculcating tolerance among Muslims in the past, and in modern times they have guided thought and action in the closer relationships that now obtain between all religions."[10]

Such claims for a Qur'ānic message of religious tolerance, whether made by Muslims or by those presenting Muslims' views, find their correlate in a predominantly Christian use of this same body of material. A contemporary Christian scholar has noted: "A number of well-known Qur'ānic texts, quoted frequently especially by Christians, seem to point in a different direction, as they supposedly substantiate the thesis that – using intentionally non-Qur'ānic terminology – Christianity remains a way of salvation even after the coming of the Seal of the Prophets."[11] Nor is such Christian use of these Qur'ānic texts of but recent vintage. Classical sources attest to its longevity. The fourteenth-century theologian and jurisconsult Taqī al-Dīn b. Taymīyah (d. 728/1328)[12] saw fit to refute such Christian Qur'ānic interpretation in his treatise *al-Jawāb al-ṣaḥīḥ li-man badala dīn al-masīḥ* (The Correct Response to Those Who Have Changed the Religion of the Messiah).[13]

260. This statement is reproduced with a minor reworking and a more gender-inclusive translation of the accompanying Qur'ānic example in the 2nd edition (Maryknoll: Orbis, 1985), 234.

9 Abdul Ali, "Tolerance in Islam," *IC* 56 (1982): 110; Mahmoud M. Ayoub, "Roots of Muslim-Christian Conflict," *MW* 79 (1989): 31.

10 Parrinder, *Jesus*, 154.

11 Bijlefeld, "Some Recent Contributions," 94. More recently Simon Jargy has drawn upon such texts to argue that the *ahl al-kitāb* have not been excluded from "l'économie du salut." See *Islam et chrétienté: les fils d'Abraham entre la confrontation et le dialogue* (Geneva: Labor et Fides, 1981), 62. Similarly, Charles Kimball cites *sūrat al-baqarah* (2):62 to support the assertion that "the Qur'ān makes clear the salvific value inherent in at least some of the religious traditions." "Striving Together in the Way of God: Muslim Participation in Christian-Muslim Dialogue," (Ph.D. thesis, Harvard Divinity School, 1987), 31.

12 Names are given in their longer form and death dates are supplied only at the first mention of individuals, whether that be in the text or the notes. The exceptions to this procedure involve the ten Qur'ānic commentators whose biographies are treated at length.

13 4 vols. (Cairo: Maṭbaʿat al-Nīl, 1322/1905). Thomas F. Michel, S.J., has published a study and partial translation in his *A Muslim Theologian's Response to Christianity* (Delmar, New York: Caravan Books, 1984). This treatise is, in large measure, a response to one by Paul of Antioch, a twelfth-century Melkite bishop of Sidon (now in Lebanon). The

The verses that generate such divergent assessments have been selected by following the procedure outlined above. Some were obvious candidates simply from a straightforward reading of the Qurʾānic text, while others were added after cross-checking the major concordances and indices. The conclusive test, however, of a verse's inclusion in this third category remains the testimony of Islamic exegesis (*tafsīr*).[14] The final collection contains seven citations, to each of which a chapter of this book is devoted. Presented here in their textual order, the verse translations are offered as provisional renderings, for in some instances a considerable degree of Muslim exegetical effort has been expended through the centuries in an attempt to secure the precise meaning of a particular word or phrase. As any translation necessarily prejudges the results of such endeavor, those recorded herein should be read as tentative and subject to emendation in light of the full commentary tradition:

sūrat al-baqarah (2):62

Truly those who believe and those who are Jews, the Christians and the Ṣābiʾūn, whoever believes in God and the Last Day and does right, for them is their reward near their Lord; they will have no fear, neither will they grieve.

sūrah Āl ʿImrān (3):55

When God said, "O Jesus, I am the One who will take you and raise you to Me and cleanse you of those who disbelieve and place those who follow you over those who disbelieve until the Day of Resurrection. Then to Me is your return. I shall judge between you in that about which you disagree."

sūrah Āl ʿImrān (3):199

Truly among the people of the book are those who believe in God and what was

text and translation of Paul's work may be found in Paul Khoury, *Paul d'Antioche* (Beirut: Imprimerie Catholique, 1964).

14 Through a combination of the search procedures that have been mentioned, the following verses came to notice as potential candidates for inclusion in the category of positive allusions to the Christians: *sūrat al-baqarah* (2):121 and 253; *sūrah Āl ʿImrān* (3):75–76, 110, and 113–15; *sūrat al-māʾidah* (5):46–47 and 84–85; *sūrat al-aʿrāf* (7):181; *sūrah Yūnus* (10):94; *sūrat al-isrāʾ* (17):107–09; and *sūrat al-malāʾikah* (35):32. In all cases recourse to the exegetical literature, particularly al-Ṭabarī and Ibn al-Jawzī, revealed no sustained reference to the Christians as the principal interpretive focus for the relevant phrase of the verse. In most cases no mention at all was made of the Christians; in a few instances there was one short reference to the *ahl al-kitāb*.

The one passage for which a full exegetical survey was made is *sūrah Āl ʿImrān* (3):113–15, which begins: "They are not alike; among the *ahl al-kitāb* there is an upright people (*ummatun qāʾimatun*) who recite the verses of God in the night and they prostrate." Almost uniformly this was taken as an allusion to the Jews. The one exception is Fakhr al-Dīn al-Rāzī who records, among a number of *ḥadīth*s, a single one that refers to people from Najrān, Abyssinia, and Rūm. Although al-Rāzī does not name them as Christians in his exegesis of this verse, in the rest of the verses examined in this work such a reference has always been taken to mean the Christians. However, in this instance, as in the others, there was not sufficient exegetical evidence to view these as unequivocal allusions to the Christians.

sent down to you and what was sent down to them, submissive before God. They do not sell the verses of God for a small price. For them is their reward near their Lord. Surely God is quick to reckon.

sūrat al-māʾidah (5):66

If they had adhered to the Torah and the Gospel and what was sent down to them from their Lord, they would have eaten from above them and from beneath their feet. Among them is a balanced people but many of them are evildoers.

sūrat al-māʾidah (5):82–83

You will find the people most intensely hostile to the believers are the Jews and the idolaters. You will surely find those closest in friendship to those who believe to be those who say "We are Christians." That is because among them are priests and monks and because they are not arrogant. (82)
When they heard what was sent down to the Messenger their eyes overflowed with tears because of what they recognized as the truth. They say, "Our Lord, we believe, so write us with those who testify." (83)

sūrat al-qaṣaṣ (28):52–55

Those to whom We gave the book before it/him believe in it/him. (52)
And when it was recited to them they said, "We believe in it/him. Certainly it is the truth from our Lord; truly we were Muslims before it." (53)
These will be given their reward twice because of that in which they have persisted. They turn back evil with good. From what We have given them, they spend. (54)
When they hear idle chatter, they turn away from it and say, "To us, our deeds and to you, your deeds. Peace be upon you; we do not desire ignorant people." (55)

sūrat al-ḥadīd (57):27

Then We caused Our messengers to follow in their footsteps. We sent Jesus, son of Mary, to follow and We gave him the Gospel. We placed in the hearts of those who followed him compassion and mercy and monasticism which they invented; We did not prescribe it for them except as the seeking of God's acceptance. But they did not observe it correctly. So We gave to those of them who believed their reward but many of them are sinners.

These verses prompt several central questions: How have Muslims understood this apparent divine praise of Christians? What have these verses meant to Muslims in both the classical and modern periods of Islamic history? Do these verses justify the assertions and claims made on their behalf? The most comprehensive answer to such queries lies in a close examination of that body of Islamic literature to which allusion has already been made, Qurʾānic commentary (*tafsīr*). Each generation of Muslims has felt the need and the desire for an ever more profound appreciation of the Qurʾān. To meet such a need and to fulfill such a desire there developed within the Islamic religious sciences the particular study and activity known as *tafsīr al-Qurʾān*. The results of this activity number in the thousands of volumes. Not only is any individual *tafsīr* likely to be a multi-volume work, but the span of Islamic exegetical activity now amounts to over thirteen centuries. Nor has the production of commentaries been limited to the "canonical" language of Islam, Arabic. Commentaries (*tafāsīr*) have been written in Persian, Turkish, Urdu – in fact, in virtually every language to which the Islamic missionary call (*daʿwah*) has accommodated itself.[15] The sheer size and linguistic coverage of this religious science clearly indicate its centrality and significance for charting the development of Islamic intellectual history. As Charles Adams, in his survey of the field of Islamic studies, has remarked: "There is probably no richer or more important key to the basic but always evolving significance of the Qurʾān in the Muslim religious consciousness than this tradition of *tafsīr* writings."[16]

It is precisely the attempt to chart the "evolving significance" of these Qurʾānic references to Christians that this book explores by tracing the interpretation of these verses through a series of Qurʾān commentaries chosen to provide both chronological and sectarian coverage. While the full range of exegetical issues raised by each verse is presented, special attention is paid to the phrases most pertinent to this investigation. A dual query animates this effort: Are these verses, as understood by generations of Muslim exegetes, indeed proof-texts for claims about Muslim religious tolerance? Alternately, are interpretations that find in these texts warrants for Christian salvific assertions justified within the broad scope of Islamic exegetical history? Beneath both concerns lies the fundamental question of whether the Muslim understanding of the term "Christian" is consonant with the self-understanding of those who so define themselves. To return to the categories with which this inquiry began: Does Christian self-def-

15 Bibliographic interest in the range of Qurʾānic commentary and translation is increasing. See, for example, Maulana Ghulam Mustafa Qassmi, "Sindhi Translations and Tafsirs of the Holy Quran," trans. by Sayid Ghulam Mustafa Shah, *Sind Quarterly* 5 (1977): 33–49; Jin Yijiu, "The Qurʾān in China," *Contributions to Asian Studies* 17 (1983): 95–101; Hassan A. Ma'ayergi, "History of the Works of Qurʾānic Interpretation (*Tafsir*) in the Kurdish Language," *Journal: Institute of Muslim Minority Affairs* 7 (1986): 268–74. In a work edited by Christian W. Troll may be found articles on Qurʾān renderings in various languages of the Indian subcontinent, such as Tamil, Telugu, Kannada, and Gujarati: *Islam in India: Studies and Commentaries* (New Delhi: Vikas, 1982). A recently published volume lists translations of the Qurʾān in sixty-five languages, ranging from Afrikaans to Yoruba: Ekmeleddin Ihsanoglu, ed., *World Bibliography of Translations of the Meanings of the Holy Qurʾān: Printed Translations 1515–1980* (Istanbul: Research Centre for Islamic History, Art and Culture, 1406/1986).

16 Charles J. Adams, "Islamic Religious Tradition," in Leonard Binder, ed., *The Study of the Middle East: Research and Scholarship in the Humanities and Social Sciences* (New York: John Wiley, 1976), 65. Yet more specifically Jacques Waardenburg counts the Qurʾān and its exegetical literature as the first source of information on Muslim assessments of other religious traditions. See "Types of Judgment in Islam About Other Religions," in Graciela de la Lama, ed., *Middle East: 30th International Congress of Human Sciences in Asia and North Africa, Mexico City 1976* (Mexico City: El Colegio de México, 1982), 137–38.

inition match the Muslim understanding of Christians? A useful exercise for the preparation of a response would be to "bracket" all previous conceptions of Christianity, or mentally to erase all prior knowledge of the religious community known as Christians. The reader is then encouraged to approach the information offered by these commentators, as they address the Qur'ānic verses under consideration, as if it were the only available data on this group.[17] The merits of such an approach are commensurate with the degree of clarity and comprehension it provides. Such mental "reservation" serves as an indispensable propaedeutic to any adequate appreciation of the centuries of Islamic scholarship herein discussed. For Muslim exegetes, as for other Muslims, the Qur'ān is God's own word. It is the ultimate source of truth on all matters, including other religions. Only if this is clearly understood will the testimony of Islamic exegesis be comprehensible, will a faithful understanding of Qur'ānic Christians emerge.

17 Roger Arnaldez followed such an approach in his presentation of the Qur'ānic Jesus: "Nous laisserons se dessiner le portrait du Messie sur un fond purement coranique et islamique et nous parlerons de lui comme d'un prophète de l'Islam, exactement comme si le Coran avait été le premier et le seul livre révélé qui parle de lui." *Jésus: fils de Marie, prophète de l'Islam* (Paris: Desclée, 1980), 16–17.

PART I

Qurʾānic commentary and commentators

1

Text and *tafsīr*

Systematic scholarship on Qurʾānic *tafsīr* (commentary) is a matter of growing interest for Muslim and non-Muslim scholars alike. While the subject of *tafsīr* has benefited from the increased attention to Qurʾānic studies generally, it has also been the focus of more specific concern.[1] For the purposes of a brief presentation, the history of *tafsīr* may conveniently be divided into three periods: formative, classical, and modern. This study, for reasons that will be explained, concentrates on the latter two stages. However, the earliest period deserves some consideration not only for its intrinsic importance as prelude to all subsequent exegetical endeavor but also for the prolonged scholarly attention that it has attracted.

THE FORMATIVE PERIOD OF QURʾĀNIC *TAFSĪR*

If one accepts Muḥammad (d. 9/632) as the Qurʾān's first interpreter, then the formative period may be said to extend from his lifetime to the early years of the tenth century, the era that saw both the appearance of Abū Jaʿfar Muḥammad b. Jarīr al-Ṭabarī's commentary and the consensual establishment of an accepted range of Qurʾānic textual variation.[2] It is this

1 An indication of this may be seen in two bibliographic surveys separated by a period of twenty-five years. While Arthur Jeffery's 1957 article "The Present Status of Qurʾānic Studies" contained a section on *tafsīr*, in 1982 Andrew Rippin devoted an entire article to that alone. See Rippin's "The Present Status of *Tafsīr* Studies," *MW* 72 (1982): 224–38. The Jeffery article is in *Report on Current Research on the Middle East* (Washington, D.C.: The Middle East Institute, Spring, 1957), 1–16.

2 This is also, roughly, the period in which Islamic jurisprudence was defined, culminating in Abū ʿAbdallāh Muḥammad al-Shāfiʿī's (d. 204/820) identification of the sources of legal knowledge (*uṣūl al-fiqh*) as Qurʾān, *sunnat al-nabī* (preserved in *ḥadīth*), *ijmāʿ*, and *qiyās*. So strong was al-Shāfiʿī's emphasis on the *sunnat al-nabī* that according to Joseph Schacht "traditions from the Prophet could not even be invalidated by reference to the Koran. Shāfiʿī took it for granted that the Koran did not contradict the traditions from the Prophet, and that the traditions explained the Koran; the Koran had therefore to be interpreted in the light of the traditions, and not vice versa." *An Introduction to Islamic Law* (Oxford: Clarendon Press, 1964), 47.

span of slightly less than three hundred years that is the object of considerable controversy. Comprehension of the main lines of debate would be impossible without some notion of the traditional Muslim view of the Qurʾān's textual history. While accounts of the formation of the Qurʾānic canon are by no means uniform, most cite the period immediately following Muḥammad's death as critical. How much of the revelation, if any, had been written down by that time and how much was a purely oral transmission is still a moot question. The only point on which the tradition is unanimous is that the canon was not closed before the death of the Prophet.[3] After his death, however, and the consequent cessation of revelation, efforts at consolidating the Qurʾānic corpus accelerated. These efforts, which are commonly dated to the caliphate of Abū Bakr (d. 13/634), prominently feature Muḥammad's principal secretary, Zayd b. Thābit (d. 45/665–66). Motivation for such activity usually surfaces as a concern that some of the Qurʾān was in danger of being lost because of the great number of its oral transmitters or 'reciters (*qurrāʾ*)' who had been killed in the wars of apostasy (*riddah*) after the death of Muḥammad, particularly the battle of Yamāmah in 12/634.

But the transcription of oral reports and the collection of any written fragments posed but the first stage of the Qurʾān's textual canonization. Furthermore, it was evidently an activity not limited to one person. During the period in which Zayd was busy with his compilation (which was subsequently given to the second caliph, ʿUmar b. al-Khaṭṭāb [d. 23/644], and then to ʿUmar's daughter, Ḥafṣah) others were similarly occupied. While there is no surviving textual evidence for multiple codices, the traditional accounts of the Qurʾān's formation presume their existence. The most frequently mentioned are those attributed to Ubayy b. Kaʿb (d. 29/649), ʿAbdallāh b. Masʿūd (d. 32/652–53). ʿAlī b. Abī Ṭālib (d. 40/660), and Abū Mūsā ʿAbdallāh al-Ashʿarī (d. 42/662), among several others. Various of these gained favor in the leading metropolitan areas of seventh-century Islam, and it is the resultant diversity of Qurʾānic recitation that is said to have precipitated the next stage of Qurʾānic canonization.

This is the point, according to traditional Muslim accounts, that saw the proclamation of the ʿUthmānic recension as the authorized text. Spurred on by reports of disputes arising over the proper recitation (*qirāʾah*) of the revelation, the third caliph, ʿUthmān b. ʿAffān (d. 35/656), appointed what one contemporary Muslim scholar has dubbed the "Zayd Commission"

3 The most comprehensive Western study of the textual history of the Qurʾān is that by Theodor Nöldeke, *Geschichte des Qorans* (Göttingen: Verlag der Dieterichschen Buchhandlung, 1860). This was re-edited as Volumes 1 and 2, revised by Friedrich Schwally (Leipzig: Dieterich'sche Verlagsbuchhandlung, 1909), and Volume 3, revised by G. Bergsträsser and O. Pretzl (Leipzig: Dieterich'sche Verlagsbuchhandlung, 1926).

to achieve a standardized text.[4] Under the terms of his second mandate, Zayd b. Thābit was to examine all available material, decide – in concert with a few others – what was genuine, and record the result in the Quraysh dialect of Mecca. The dominant versions of this account then state that ʿUthmān circulated copies of the result to the major metropolitan areas and ordered all other written Qurʾānic material to be destroyed.[5]

This, nonetheless, did not conclude the extended process of textual canonization. As Arthur Jeffery has noted in describing the ʿUthmānic recension: "The text that ʿUthmān canonized, however, was a bare consonantal text, with marks to show verse endings, but no points to distinguish consonants, no marks of vowels, and no orthographic signs of any kind."[6] What made such a *scriptio defectiva* workable was, of course, the continuous oral tradition of Qurʾān memorization. Nevertheless over the next hundred years enough variation developed in the vocalization and consonantal identification of the text to precipitate the final stage of Qurʾānic textual development. Following an extended period of 'choice (*ikhtiyār*)' during which a number of regional recitation systems developed, Abū Bakr b. Mujāhid

4 M.O.A. Abdul, "The Historical Development of Tafsīr," *IC* 50 (1976): 141. The process of Muslim and Christian scriptural transmission and fixation are compared in Sarwat Anis Al-Assiouty, *Théorie des sources: évangiles et corans apocryphes, logia et hadîths forgés* (Paris: Letouzey et Ané, 1987). In a further comparative effort, Claus Schedl seeks to draw a connection between *sūrah* enumeration and the structure of the Nag Hammadi *Gospel of Thomas*. "Die 114 Suren des Koran und die 114 Logien Jesu im Thomas-Evangelium," *Der Islam* 64 (1987): 261–64.

5 To explain reports that Ibn Masʿūd refused to accept this edict, Alford Welch has suggested that "the accounts saying that when the ʿUthmānic text was made official, Ubayy destroyed his codex while Ibn Masʿūd refused to do so may be examples of historical telescoping, meaning that the people of Syria (possibly over a period of many years) gave up their distinctive reading (i.e. that of Ubayy), while the people of Kūfa refused to give up theirs (i.e. that of Ibn Masʿūd)." "al-Ḳurʾan," *EI*² 5:406. For the debate on the early meaning of the designation *qurrāʾ*, a common plural for *qāriʾ* (Qurʾān reciter), see G.H.A. Juynboll, "The Qurrāʾ in Early Islamic History," *JESHO* 16 (1973): 13–29; his "The position of Qur'an Recitation in Early Islam," *JSS* 19 (1974): 240–51; and T. Nagel, "Ḳurrāʾ," *EI*² 5:499–500.

6 Arthur Jeffery, "The Textual History of the Qurʾān," in his *The Qurʾān as Scripture* (New York: Russell F. Moore, 1952), 97. Following his discovery of a manuscript of *Kitāb al-maṣāḥif* by Ibn Abī Dāwūd (d. 316/929), Arthur Jeffery compiled a collection of textual variants (*qirāʾāt*) found in the non-ʿUthmānic codices: *Materials for the History of the Text of the Qurʾān* (Leiden: E.J. Brill, 1937). This can be used most efficiently when supplemented by his *Index of Qurʾānic Verses to the English Part of 'Materials for the History of the Text of the Qurʾān'* (Leiden: E.J. Brill, 1951). For further on the debate surrounding the relation of early Qurʾānic orthography and the spoken language that it strove to transcribe see Michael Zwettler, *The Oral Tradition of Classical Arabic Poetry: Its Character and Implications* (Columbus: Ohio State University Press, 1978), 122–25. A succinct overview of the range of Islamic languages and scripts is offered by Gerhard Endress as an appendix to *An Introduction to Islam (Einführung in die islamische Geschichte)*, trans. by Carole Hillenbrand (New York: Columbia University Press, 1988), 138–49.

(d. 324/936) is credited with the final textual stabilization. He did this by canonizing several well-established systems of readings on the basis of a Prophetic *ḥadīth* in which Muḥammad says that "the Qurʾān was sent down according to seven letters (*aḥruf*)."[7] This solution, which was promulgated during the vizierates of Ibn Muqlah and Ibn ʿĪsā in 322/934, as well as the development of a *scriptio plena*, amounted to a virtual closure of the canon.[8]

Coextensive with the textual history of the Qurʾān stands the history of its early explication. Once again, the outlines of the traditional Muslim view of this history must be sketched in order to make the debate about it comprehensible. Both during, but especially after, Muḥammad's lifetime a need was felt for an explanation of obscure terms or references.[9] Muslims would insist that the motivating impulse was far more than intellectual curiosity: "The search was rooted in the desire to understand fully every aspect of the text; the better to fulfill its commandments, the more completely to submit to the will of God."[10] In the succinct and well-ordered

7 Abū Jaʿfar Muḥammad b. Jarīr al-Ṭabarī, "*Muqaddimat al-tafsīr*," in *Jāmiʿ al-bayān ʿan taʾwīl āy al-Qurʾān*, ed. by Maḥmūd Muḥammad Shākir and Aḥmad Muḥammad Shākir (Cairo: Dār al-Maʿārif, 1374/1954), 1:22. Al-Ṭabarī has here (pp. 21–67) collected fifty-nine *ḥadīth*s on the subject of the seven readings. For an extended analysis of this tradition see Claude Gilliot, "Les sept 'lectures', corps social et écriture révélée," *SI* 61 (1985): 5–25 and *SI* 63 (1986): 49–62.

8 The extra-canonical readings that remained in circulation raised to ten and sometimes fourteen the number to which scholars referred. These additions became known as the "three after the seven" and the "four after the ten." Further breakdown according to 'version (*riwāyah*)' and 'way (*ṭarīq*)' produced even more subtle distinctions. On p. 49 of his revision of *Bell's Introduction to the Qurʾān* (Edinburgh: University Press, 1970), W. Montgomery Watt has tabulated the versions for the seven readings authorized by Ibn Mujāhid. For a full list of the *riwāyāt* and *ṭuruq* of the seven of Ibn Mujāhid plus the "three after the seven" see Labib as-Said, *The Recited Koran*, trans. and adapted by Bernard Weiss, M.A. Rauf, and Morroe Berger (Princeton: The Darwin Press, 1975), 127–30. Classical *qirāʾāt* literature is surveyed by Angelika Neuwirth, "Koranlesung zwischen islamischem Ost und West," *Islamo e arabismo na península ibérica: actas do XI congresso da União europeia de arabistas e islamólogos* (Évora-Faro-Silves, 29 set. – 6 out. 1982) (Évora: Universidade de Évora, 1986), 305–17. The two printed Qurʾānic transmissions are compared by Adrian Brockett, "The Value of the Ḥafṣ and Warsh Transmissions for the Textual History of the Qurʾān," in *Approaches*, 31–45.

9 For an instance of the Prophet as *mufassir* see Jalāl al-Dīn al-Suyūṭī (d. 911/1505), *al-Itqān fī ʿulūm al-Qurʾān*, ed. by Muḥammad Abū al-Faḍl Ibrāhīm (Cairo: Dār al-Turāth, 1405/1985), 4:170. John Wansbrough discusses the development of Qurʾānic lexicography under the rubric of "Masoretic exegesis." *Quranic Studies: Sources and Methods of Scriptural Interpretation* (Oxford: Oxford University Press, 1977), 202–27. Andrew Rippin builds upon this in his "Lexicographical Texts and the Qurʾān," in *Approaches*, 158–74. For more specialized consideration of lexicographical texts traditionally ascribed to ʿAbdallāh b. ʿAbbās, see Rippin's "Ibn ʿAbbās's *al-Lughāt fīʾl-Qurʾān*," *BSOAS* 44 (1981): 15–25 and "Ibn ʿAbbās's *Gharīb al-Qurʾān*," *BSOAS* 46 (1983): 332–33.

10 Ilse Lichtenstädter, "Quran and Quran Exegesis," *Humaniora Islamica* 2 (1974): 7.

introduction of his commentary, Ismāʿīl b. Kathīr, the fourteenth-century exegete whose views will form a part of this study, offers a good summary of the early stages of Qurʾānic *tafsīr*.

Ibn Kathīr proposed to outline the principles of Qurʾānic exegesis, the proper progression that should be followed in explicating a particular passage. The stages in this progression nicely parallel the traditional Islamic view of the history of *tafsīr*. Thus, the first step is to let the Qurʾān interpret itself, to let one part of the revelation clarify the obscurities of another part.[11] If no such clarification can be found, recourse may be had to the *sunnah*, the normative remembrance of Muḥammad's words and deeds, at least to that part of it which contains the exegetical remarks of the Prophet. If such a search is greeted with Prophetic silence, the next step – both hermeneutically and historically – is reference to the Companions of the Prophet. Ibn Kathīr here singles out two figures for special approbation, ʿAbdallāh b. Masʿūd and ʿAbdallāh b. ʿAbbās (d. 68/687–88), with particular praise for the latter.

The exegetical involvement of these Companions, and others, did not begin until after Muḥammad's death. As Ṣubḥī al-Ṣāliḥ forthrightly puts it, "They would not dare explain the Qurʾān while he (Muḥammad) was among them."[12] But after his death the exegetical burden passed to those, like Ibn ʿAbbās and Ibn Masʿūd, whose association with him had been both close and enduring. Ibn Masʿūd was apparently well aware of his own expertise, as he is reported to have said: "If I knew someone more knowledgeable in the Book of God than I, who brings to it the appropriate equipment (*maṭāyā*), I would go to him."[13] However, by far the greatest number of exegetical *ḥadīths* are ascribed to Ibn Masʿūd's younger contemporary, ʿAbdallāh b. ʿAbbās.

The father of modern Western studies on *tafsīr*, Ignaz Goldziher, has conveyed Muslim estimations of this figure by titling him the "superman" (*Übermensch*) of *tafsīr*.[14] Although still a youth at the time of Muḥammad's death, Ibn ʿAbbās is reported to have been the beneficiary of a Prophetic

11 ʿImād al-Dīn Abū al-Fidā Ismāʿīl b. Kathīr, *Tafsīr al-Qurʾān al-ʿaẓīm* (Cairo: Maṭbaʿah Muṣṭafā Muḥammad, 1356/1937), 1:3. The stages of this hermeneutical sequence are discussed at some length by Ismāʿīl Sālim ʿAbd al-ʿĀl, *Ibn Kathīr wa-manhajuhu fī al-tafsīr* (Cairo: Maktabat al-Malik Fayṣal al-Islāmīyah, 1404/1984). 277–358. For a comparison of Ibn Kathīr with al-Ṭabarī see my "Quranic Hermeneutics: The Views of al-Ṭabarī and Ibn Kathīr," *Approaches*, 46–62. Standard topics of classical *tafsīr* introduction are exemplified in my "Ibn al-Jawzī's Exegetical Propaedeutic: Introduction and Translation," *Alif: Journal of Comparative Poetics* 8 (1988): 101–13.

12 Ṣubḥī al-Ṣāliḥ, *Mabāḥith fī ʿulūm al-Qurʾān* (Beirut: Dār al-ʿIlm lil-Malāyīn, 1969), 289.

13 Ibn Kathīr, *Tafsīr al-Qurʾān al-ʿaẓīm*, 1:3. J.-C. Vadet, "Ibn Masʿūd," *EI*² 3:873–75.

14 Ignaz Goldziher, *Die Richtungen der islamischen Koranauslegung* (Leiden: E.J. Brill, 1920), 65.

prayer: "O God, give him understanding in religion (*dīn*) and teach him interpretation (*ta'wīl*)."[15] Ibn Kathīr enthuses about the relatively greater degree of knowledge available to this younger Qur'ānic scholar. After noting that Ibn Masʿūd died in 32/652, he adds that Ibn ʿAbbās lived thirty-six more years, "so just think what kind of knowledge he acquired after Ibn Masʿūd!"[16]

With the death of the first Islamic generation the torch of Qur'ānic studies passed to the Followers (*al-tābiʿūn*).[17] Pupils of Ibn Masʿūd, Ibn

15 Ibn Kathīr, *Tafsīr al-Qur'ān al-ʿaẓīm*, 1:3. Although apparently synonymous in the earliest period, the significations of *tafsīr* and *ta'wīl* began to diverge as the Qur'ānic sciences developed in the classical period. *Tafsīr* remained the term of more limited denotation, often restricted largely to philological exegesis, while *ta'wīl* connoted hermeneutical approaches that sought to uncover deeper meanings in the text or to align the text with particular theological or philosophical orientations. The editors of Abū Manṣūr al-Māturīdī's (d. 333/944) commentary ascribe to him a definition of these terms that draws the distinction between one meaning authoritatively transmitted (*tafsīr*) and the several possible meanings (*ta'wīl*) that a verse may bear. *Ta'wīlāt ahl al-sunnah*, ed. by Ibrāhīm and al-Sayyid ʿAwadayn (Cairo: Lajnat al-Qur'ān wa-al-sunnah, 1391/1971), 1:23 (of the introduction). Al-Māturīdī's commentary is discussed in M. Götz, "Māturīdī und sein *Kitāb Ta'wīlāt al-Qur'ān*," *Der Islam* 41 (1965): 27–70 and in Ahmad Mohmed Ahmad Galli, "Some Aspects of al-Māturīdī's Commentary on the Qur'ān," *IS* 21 (1982): 3–21. For a comparative study, see the use of these terms by Saʿadyah Gaon (d. 942), a contemporary of al-Ṭabarī and al-Māturīdī, in his Arabic translation of the Hebrew Bible. Andrew Rippen, "Saʿadya Gaon and Genesis 22: Aspects of Jewish–Muslim Interaction and Polemic," in William M. Brinner and Stephen D. Ricks, eds., *Studies in Islamic and Judaic Tradition* (Atlanta: Scholars Press, 1986), 33–36. A recent analysis of *tafsīr/ta'wīl* and related exegetical vocabulary is Jaroslav Stetkevych's "Arabic Hermeneutical Terminology: Paradox and the Production of Meaning," *JNES* 48 (1989): 81–96.

16 Ibn Kathīr, *Tafsīr al-Qur'ān al-ʿaẓīm*, 1:4. For an evaluation of the authenticity of the *tafsīr* attributed to Ibn ʿAbbās, see Goldziher, *Die Richtungen*, 76–77. As a corrective to Goldziher's accusation that the *isnād*s leading back to Ibn ʿAbbās are "concocted (*geschmiedet*)," Harris Birkeland emphasizes the motives of the transmitters, especially Muḥammad b. Saʿd (d. 230/844–45), who transmitted more than fifteen hundred traditions attributed to Ibn ʿAbbās. According to Birkeland, Ibn Saʿd "certainly believed that Ibn ʿAbbās shared the opinion expressed in the traditions. He did not lie or fabricate anything. For he was living in a traditionalistic social group, in which every current religious opinion was held to have its origin in an authority generally accepted by that group." *The Lord Guideth: Studies on Primitive Islam* (Oslo: I Kommisjon Hos H. Aschehoug, 1956), 7. Isaiah Goldfeld has made a study of the transmission history of the material ascribed to Ibn ʿAbbās and circulated as his *tafsīr*, frequently under the title *Tanwīr al-Miqbās*. "The '*Tafsīr*' of ʿAbdallāh b. ʿAbbās," *Der Islam* 59 (1982): 125–35. In the present era, the controversial Qur'ānic reflections of Muṣṭafā Maḥmūd, a man without the scholastic training required of a *mufassir*, have been defended on the grounds that Ibn ʿAbbās had no formal theological education either. J.J.G. Jansen, "Polemics on Mustafa Mahmud's Koran Exegesis," *UEAI 9*, 110.

17 While Ibn ʿAbbās's political involvement and his changing relation with the fourth caliph, ʿAlī, are a matter of historical debate, the latter figures in a story about the extent of this man's exegetical talents. As reported by Ibn Kathīr, "ʿAlī appointed

ʿAbbās, and others continued the tradition in such major metropolitan centers as Mecca, Medina, Baṣrah, and Kūfah.[18] In all likelihood exegetical activity was still principally an oral exercise at this stage. While some of the *tābiʿūn* may have compiled proto-*tafsīr*s, there is no extant textual evidence to support such an assertion.[19] What does seem clear is that exegesis

ʿAbdallāh b. ʿAbbās at the *ḥajj* festival to preach to the people. In his sermon he recited *sūrat al-baqarah* and, according to one account, *sūrat al-nūr*. He interpreted so well that if the Byzantines, Turks and Daylamites had heard it, they would have become Muslims." *Tafsīr al-Qurʾān al-ʿaẓīm*, 1:4. Claude Gilliot offers a semiotic analysis of the biographical *akhbār* about Ibn ʿAbbās to be found in Ibn Saʿd's *al-Ṭabaqāt al-kubrā*. "Portrait 'mythique' d'Ibn ʿAbbās," *Arabica* 32 (1985): 127–83.

18 Ibn Kathīr states very clearly that the pronouncements of the *tābiʿūn* do not carry the same authority as those from the Companions. If the former agree upon something, this consensus may be taken as authoritative. However, if they are in disagreement, one may not be preferred over another, nor may the view of a Follower gain precedence over that of a Companion. See *Tafsīr al-Qurʾān al-ʿaẓīm*, 1:4.

19 The question of oral and/or written transmission is nicely caught in reports about one of Ibn ʿAbbās's most respected disciples, Mujāhid b. Jabr (d. 104/722). In one instance he is quoted as saying: "I presented the *muṣḥaf* to Ibn ʿAbbās three times, from the *Fātiḥah* to the end of it, stopping him at every verse of it and asking him about it." In another case it was reported from Ibn Abī Malīkah: "I saw Mujāhid ask Ibn ʿAbbās about the *tafsīr* of the Qurʾān, having his writing tablets (*alwāḥ*) with him. Ibn ʿAbbās kept saying to him 'Write' until Mujāhid had asked him about every bit of *tafsīr*. Because of this Sufyān al-Thawrī says 'When the *tafsīr* on the authority of Mujāhid comes to you, it suffices for you.' " Ibn Kathīr, *Tafsīr al-Qurʾān al-ʿaẓīm*, 1:4–5.

After studying manuscript evidence F. Leemhuis concludes that the work published as *Tafsīr Mujāhid* is a recension by Abū Bishr Warqāʾ b. ʿUmar (d. 160/776) of Ibn Abī Najīḥ's (d. 131-32/749–50) transmission of Mujāhid's *tafsīr*. "MS. 1075 Tafsīr of the Cairene Dār al-Kutub and Mujāhid's *Tafsīr*," in *UEAI* 9, 169–80. For further consideration of this see his "Origins and Early Development of the *tafsīr* Tradition," in *Approaches*, 13–30. In both articles Leemhuis directs readers to the doctoral dissertation by G. Stauth, "Die Überlieferung des Korankommentars Mujāhid b. Jabrs. zur Frage der Rekonstruktion der in den Sammelwerken des 3. Jh. D. H. benutzten frühislamischen Quellenwerke" (Justus-Liebig-Universität, Giessen, 1969). The printed text is *Tafsīr Mujāhid*, ed. by ʿAbd al-Raḥmān al-Ṭāhir b. Muḥammad al-Sūrtī, 2 vols. (Islamabad, n.d.; reprint, Beirut: al-Manshūrāt al-ʿIlmīyah, n.d.). For a wide-ranging survey of issues related to early transmission history which addresses the work of Leemhuis and Stauth, among others, see Gregor Schoeler, "Die Überlieferung der Wissenschaften im frühen Islam," *Der Islam* 62 (1985): 210–30.

Contemporary with Warqāʾ b. ʿUmar is the work of Muqātil b. Sulaymān (d. 150/767). Isaiah Goldfeld has edited his *Tafsīr al-khams miʾat āyah min al-Qurʾān* (Shefarʿam: Dār al-Mashriq, 1980) and has written an introductory study: "Muqātil Ibn Sulāyman," *Arabic and Islamic Studies (Bar-Ilan)* 2 (1978): xiii–xxx. The first volume of Muqātil's larger *tafsīr* has been published as *Tafsīr Muqātil b. Sulaymān*, ed. by ʿAbdallāh Maḥmūd Shiḥātah (Cairo: al-Hayʾah al-Miṣrīyah al-ʿĀmmah lil-Kitāb, n.d.).

For Sufyān al-Thawrī (d. 161/778) see M. Plessner, "Sufyān al-Thawrī," *EI*[1] 7:500–02. An edition of the *tafsīr* attributed to him has been published from a manuscript in the Riḍā Library of Rāmpūr: *Tafsīr Sufyān al-Thawrī*, ed. by Imtiyāz ʿAlī ʿArshī (Beirut: Dār al-Kutub al- ʿIlmīyah, 1403/1983). Gérard Lecomte accepts the attribution but questions the editor's dating of his manuscript. "Sufyān al-Thawrī: quelques rem-

was increasingly constrained by the developing science of *ḥadīth* collection and evaluation. The very name by which it was subsequently designated, *al-tafsīr bi-al-ma'thūr*, that is, interpretation by the received tradition, is an indication of this. That the prevailing tendency was conservative is undeniable. Preservation and transmission of applicable *ḥadīth*s and verification of their trains of transmission (*isnād*s) were of paramount importance. Almost universally disparaged was the free play of (arbitrary) personal opinion known as *al-tafsīr bi-al-ra'y*. The Prophet is reported to have stated flatly: "Whoever talks about the Qur'ān on the basis of his personal opinion (*ra'y*) or from a position of ignorance, will surely occupy his seat in the Fire!"[20] As other *ḥadīth*s indicate, the Prophetic denunciation extends even to those instances where the interpretation chances to be correct. Here the emphasis is on venturing into such matters inadequately prepared rather than on the actuality of faulty exegesis.[21]

Not only was *al-tafsīr bi-al-ra'y* proscribed but in the eyes of some Muslims any attempt at all to interpret the Book of God verged on blasphemy. The fear of inadvertent error was strong. Certainly the most famous expres-

arques sur le personnage et son oeuvre," *BEO* 30 (1978): 51–60. Another recent edition is the *tafsīr* of Sufyān's disciple, Sufyān b. ʿUyaynah (d. 196/811). *Tafsīr Sufyān b. ʿUyaynah*, ed. by Aḥmad Ṣāliḥ Maḥāyirī (Riyadh: Maktabah Asāmah, 1403/1983).

A recent study that draws upon the exegesis attributed to Mujāhid, Muqātil, and Sufyān al-Thawrī, among others, is Wadād al-Qāḍī, "The Term 'Khalīfa' in Early Exegetical Literature," *WI* 28 (1988): 393–411.

20 Ibn Kathīr, *Tafsīr al-Qur'ān al-ʿaẓīm*, 1:5. In a section of the introduction to his *tafsīr* al-Ṭabarī has collected variants on this Prophetic denunciation of *al-tafsīr bi-al-ra'y*. See his *Jāmiʿ al-bayān* 1:77–79. In presenting a similar *ḥadīth* recorded in the introduction to the anonymous *Kitāb al-mabānī* (p. 172), Vincent Cornell has apparently missed the crucial negative in his rendering: "He who interprets the Qur'ān according to his insight will gain a recompense never before seen [*man fassara al-qur'ān bi-ra'yihi in aṣāba lam yu'jar*]; but if he errs he will surely find his place in the Fire quickly advancing. . . ." "*Ilm al-qur'an* in al-Andalus: the *tafsir muharrar* in the Works of Three Authors," *Jusūr* 2 (1986): 69. The *Kitāb al-mabānī* is printed in Arthur Jeffery, *Two Muqaddimas to the Qur'ānic Sciences*, 2nd ed. (Cairo: Brothers al-Khaniji, 1972). Aron Zyson, following upon the work of Josef van Ess, suggests a Karrāmī attribution for *Kitāb al-mabānī*. "Two Unrecognized Karrāmī Texts," *JAOS* 108 (1988): 577–87.

21 Ibn Kathīr, *Tafsīr al-Qur'ān al-ʿaẓīm*, 1:5. That such is not an uncommon view even in the later, classical period is confirmed by G.M. Wickens's work on Naṣīr al-Dīn Ṭūsī (d. 672/1274). In his introductory remarks on the *Akhlāq-i Nāṣirī*, Wickens notes that Naṣīr al-Dīn, "in keeping with 'mediaeval' attitudes in general, and repugnantly to the 'modern' mind . . . treats nothing in isolation, or relatively, or subjectively, or from a purely pragmatic standpoint. He admits no disparity between the rules laid down or elicited for Man's conduct, the courses of the planets, and the laws of mathematics: all are interdependent, all absolute, right and real. Theory must precede practice: whatever is soundly thought out will be effective, but what may seem at any moment to work must not be adopted as right merely for that reason." *The Nasirean Ethics*, trans. by G. M. Wickens; UNESCO Collection of Representative Works: Persian Series, (London: George Allen and Unwin, 1964), 10–11.

sion of this is an exclamatory question attributed to the first caliph, Abū Bakr: "What earth would bear me up, what heaven would overshadow me (protectively), were I to speak about the Book of God what I know not?"[22] An echo of this may be found in a dialogue traced to Ibn ʿAbbās:

> A man asked Ibn ʿAbbās about the Qurʾānic mention of "a day whose length would be reckoned as a thousand years" (32:5). Ibn ʿAbbās responded: "What is 'the day whose length would be reckoned as fifty thousand years' (70:4)?" The man, in turn, retorted: "I asked you only so that you would tell me." Ibn ʿAbbās then replied: "They are two days which God mentioned in His Book. God is all-knowing." Ibn ʿAbbās was loath to speak about the Book of God what he did not know.[23]

Other *ḥadīth*s that Ibn Kathīr cites are even more sweeping in their condemnation. It would seem that for some pious Muslims the only acceptable activity remained recitation. Explication of the text was unnecessary and to be avoided.

Nevertheless, exegetical activity, particularly in the form of *al-tafsīr bi-al-maʾthūr,* continued to spread and reached a point of culmination in the encyclopedic work of Abū Jaʿfar b. Jarīr al-Ṭabarī, *Jāmiʿ al-bayān ʿan taʾwīl āy al-Qurʾān*. With the arrival of al-Ṭabarī's commentary the early, formative period of *tafsīr* history came to a close. His work inaugurated the classical era of Qurʾānic exegesis, a period that will be a primary focus of this study.[24] No satisfactory prelude to such a study, however, can neglect the challenges that Western scholarship has raised to this traditional Muslim understanding of the Qurʾān's formation and early exegesis.

Twentieth-century Western scholarship on the Qurʾān has been particularly preoccupied with the interrelated issues of textual criticism and the

22 Ibn Kathīr, *Tafsīr al-Qurʾān al-ʿaẓīm*, 1:4. Kenneth Cragg cites the continuing vitality of accusations of *al-tafsīr bi-al-raʾy* and notes that, as ever, "it is sometimes hard for those who decry this in others to absolve themselves convincingly of the same charge." *The Pen and the Faith: Eight Modern Muslim Writers and the Qurʾān* (London: George Allen and Unwin, 1985), 9. His comment nicely echoes Birkeland's remark which is set against the background of eighth-century Muslim intellectual life: "The orthodox position that their own view was not based on *tafsīr* was a fiction and impossible to maintain in the long run." *Old Muslim Opposition Against Interpretation of the Koran* (Oslo: I Kommisjon Hos Jacob Dybwad, 1955), 30.

23 Ibn Kathīr, *Tafsīr al-Qurʾān al-ʿaẓīm*, 1:5–6. According to Birkeland, a general unease at the possibilities for ideological manipulation and justification that scriptural interpretation present eventually crystallized into the dichotomy of *al-tafsīr bi-al-raʾy* and *al-tafsīr bi-al-ʿilm*, with *ʿilm* understood as "reliable knowledge in the form of *traditions*." *Old Muslim Opposition*, 28.

24 As exemplification of the two exegetical trajectories, *al-tafsīr bi-al-maʾthūr* and *al-tafsīr bi-al-raʾy*, Guy Monnot presents translations from al-Ṭabarī's *Jāmiʿ al-bayān* and Niẓām al-Dīn al-Ḥasan b. Muḥammad al-Qummī al-Nīsābūrī's (d. 728/1327) *Gharāʾib al-Qurʾān wa-raghāʾib al-furqān* on *sūrat al-baqarah* (2): 255. "Le verset du Trône," *MIDEO* 15 (1982): 119–44.

historicity of *ḥadīth*. The latter came to prominence in the seminal study of Ignaz Goldziher which questioned Muslim belief in an extrascriptural source of authority dating from the lifetime of the Prophet. After extensive research in the *ḥadīth* literature, Goldziher decided that the *ḥadīth*s that faithfully recorded the words of Muḥammad or reported his behavior were very rare. Rather than being a record of the first Islamic generations, "by far the greater part of it" should be considered "the result of the religious, historical and social development of Islam during the first two centuries. The *ḥadīth* will not serve as a document for the history of the infancy of Islam, but rather as a reflection of the tendencies which appeared in the community during the maturer stages of its evolution."[25] Goldziher was, of course, well aware of the fact that Muslim scholars in the early centuries were not ignorant of the circulation of fabricated *ḥadīth*s (*awḍā*ᶜ). Whether for pious or for political motives thousands of statements were attributed to the Prophet and his Companions that (because, for example, of anachronistic elements) they could not possibly have made. In response to such a situation, Muslim scholars developed the religious science of *ᶜilm al-ḥadīth*. In Goldziher's eyes, one of the most remarkable results of this effort to combat forged *ḥadīth*s was the invention of new *ḥadīth*s: "With pious intention fabrications were combated with new fabrications, with new *ḥadīth*s which were smuggled in and in which the invention of illegitimate *ḥadīth*s were [*sic*] condemned by strong words uttered by the Prophet."[26]

Some sixty years later Joseph Schacht applied these insights to the historical development of Islamic legal material. Doubtless his most famous conclusion is that "*isnād*s have a tendency to grow backwards, that after going back to, say, a Successor to begin with, they are subsequently often carried back to a Companion and finally to the Prophet himself; in general we can say: the more perfect the *isnād*, the later the tradition."[27] Schacht

25 Ignaz Goldziher, *Muslim Studies (Muhammedanische Studien)*, ed. by S.M. Stern, trans. by C.R. Barber and S.M. Stern (London: George Allen and Unwin, 1971), 2:19. (German edition first published in 1889–1890.) In a later work Goldziher summarized the range of *ḥadīth* proliferation: "It soon became evident that each point of view, each party, each proponent of a doctrine gave the form of ḥadith to his theses, and that consequently the most contradictory tenets had come to wear the garb of such documentation. There is no school in the areas of ritual, theology, or jurisprudence, there is not even any party to political contention, that would lack a hadith or a whole family of hadiths in its favor, exhibiting all the external signs of correct transmission." *Introduction to Islamic Theology and Law (Vorlesungen über den Islam)*, trans. by Andras and Ruth Hamori (Princeton: Princeton University Press, 1981), 39. The German original was published in 1910.

26 Goldziher, *Muslim Studies*, 2:127.

27 Joseph Schacht, "A Revaluation of Islamic Traditions," *JRAS* n.v. (1949): 147. For an exemplification of Schacht's theory see Michael Cook's chapter on "The Dating of Tradition" in his *Early Muslim Dogma: A Source-critical Study* (Cambridge: Cambridge University Press, 1981), 107–16.

credits the jurisprudent al-Shāfiʿī with providing much of the motivation for this backward progression by his emphasis on the *sunnah* of the Prophet among the fundamental sources of Islamic law (*uṣūl al-fiqh*). The results of Schacht's study amounted to almost complete disavowal of Muḥammad as a historically valid source of Islamic law: "Every legal tradition from the Prophet, until the contrary is proved, must be taken not as an authentic or essentially authentic, even if slightly obscured, statement valid for his time or the time of the Companions, but as the fictitious expression of a legal doctrine formulated at a later date."[28]

The studies of Goldziher and Schacht have not gone unchallenged. N. J. Coulson, another Western scholar of Islamic jurisprudence (*fiqh*), questions the logic of Schacht's evaluation:

> He translated the negative proposition that the evidence of legal *Ḥadīth* does not take us back beyond the second century of Islam into the positive statement that legal development began only in late Umayyad times. This creates an unacceptable void in the picture of law in the early Muslim community; for it is unrealistic to assume that legal problems created by the terms of the Qurʾān itself were ignored for a century or more.[29]

Attempts to rehabilitate or to draw closer to the standard Muslim position have also been made by Nabia Abbott and Fuat Sezgin. Both have taken a paleographic approach by examining and cataloguing a large number of early *ḥadīth* and *tafsīr* works, or parts thereof. Abbott seeks to provide evidence of the early and continuous written transmission of *ḥadīth* and its – at that historical stage – subcategory, *tafsīr*. As evidence she presents a collection of fourteen papyri dating from the mid-eighth to the mid-ninth centuries.[30] Fuat Sezgin's extensive manuscript supplementation of Carl Brockelmann's *Geschichte der arabischen Litteratur* also argues for a much

28 Joseph Schacht, *The Origins of Muhammadan Jurisprudence*, 3rd corrected impression (Oxford: Clarendon Press, 1959). Aharon Layish has written an appreciation of Schacht's work: "Notes on Joseph Schacht's Contribution to the Study of Islamic Law," *BRISMES* 9 (1982): 132–40.

29 N.J. Coulson, "European Criticism of Ḥadīth Literature," *Arabic Literature to the End of the Umayyad Period*, ed. by A.F.L. Beeston, T.M. Johnstone, R.B. Serjeant, and G. R. Smith (Cambridge: Cambridge University Press, 1983), 320–21. Coulson is willing to accept that an *isnād* may have been fabricated but sees no compelling historical reason to question that the *matn* represents a valid Prophetic judgment. On the other hand, he frankly admits the unbridgeable disparity between traditional Islamic legal theory and the historical criticism of such as Goldziher and Schacht: "Between the dictates of religious faith on the one hand and secular historical criticism on the other there can be no middle way of true objectivity." *Ibid.*, 321. For the considered response of a contemporary Muslim scholar see Fazlur Rahman, *Islam* (Chicago: University of Chicago Press, 1966) and "Sunnah and Hadith," *IS* 1 (1962): 1–36.

30 Nabia Abbott, *Studies in Arabic Literary Papyri, Vol. 2: Qurʾānic Commentary and Tradition* (Chicago: University of Chicago Press, 1967).

earlier written tradition than has customarily been credited by Western scholars.[31] His effort to document a virtually uninterrupted written conveyance from the first years after the Prophet's death attempts to strengthen the traditional Muslim claim for the authenticity of *ḥadīth* transmission. The more recent work by G.H.A. Juynboll takes a mediating position between the theories of Goldziher/Schacht and those of Abbott/Sezgin. While acknowledging that it is difficult to accept the historical truth of "all those early reports," Juynboll maintains that "*taken as a whole*, they all converge on a description of the situation obtaining in the period of history under scrutiny which may be defined as pretty reliable."[32]

Two additional contributions to the debate, however, align themselves with the critiques of Goldziher and Schacht but come to startlingly different conclusions. John Burton argues that traditional accounts of the Qurʾān's textual history are a fabrication. The motive for this fabrication he finds in a close analysis of the legal theory of Qurʾānic abrogation (*naskh*). The idea that the words of a particular verse but not the ruling contained therein (*naskh al-tilāwah dūna al-ḥukm*) could be abrogated is conceivable only if someone other than Muḥammad was responsible for the final compilation of the Qurʾān. The most frequently cited example of this legal phenomenon is the penalty of stoning for adultery. Burton, therefore, judges the accounts that attribute this collation to the first and third caliphs to be backward projections by later jurisprudents to justify this category of *naskh*. The historical truth, according to Burton, is that

> the single vigorous Qurʾān text that throughout the ages has successfully withstood the assaults of both the exegetes and the *uṣūlīs*, stoutly retaining its textual identity in the face of countless attempts to insinuate interpolations through exploitation of the alleged codex of this or that Companion, is none other than the unique text of the revelations whose existence all their tricks betoken, the text which has come down to us in the form in which it was organized and approved by the Prophet.[33]

31 Fuat Sezgin, *Geschichte des arabischen Schrifttums, Band 1: Qurʾānwissenschaften, Ḥadīth, Geschichte, Fiqh, Dogmatik, Mystik bis ca. 430 H.* (Leiden: E.J. Brill, 1967). Carl Brockelmann, *Geschichte der arabischen Litteratur*, 2nd ed. of 2 vols. and 3-vol. supplement (Leiden: E.J. Brill, 1943–49 and 1937–42).

32 G.H.A. Juynboll, *Muslim Tradition: Studies in Chronology, Provenance and Authorship of Early Ḥadīth* (Cambridge: Cambridge University Press, 1983), 6. A welcome note in Juynboll's work is its consciously irenic tone. After gently chiding Schacht for a style that is "somewhat supercilious and definitely too apodictical for Muslim ears" the author remarks that despite the debt owed to one's intellectual predecessors "we need not necessarily express ourselves in the same tone of voice." *Ibid.*, 3–4. For an extended response to Juynboll, consult R.G. Khoury, "Pour une nouvelle compréhension de la transmission des textes dans les trois premiers siècles islamiques," *Arabica* 34 (1987): 181–96. A recent entry in the continuing conversation on this issue is David S. Powers, "On Bequests in Early Islam," *JNES* 48 (1989): 185–200.

33 John Burton, *The Collection of the Qurʾān* (Cambridge: Cambridge University Press, 1977), 239.

John Wansbrough, on the other hand, comes to a contrary conclusion. Not only was the canon not closed by the Prophet or the early caliphs, it remained open and in the process of formation until the early ninth century. He speaks in terms of an extensive corpus of prophetical *logia*, orally transmitted, that took generations to achieve the form in which it is now known. Wansbrough's analysis is primarily structural. In the spirit of Biblical *Formgeschichte* he has isolated various literary types within the Qur'ānic materials and then

> attempted to show that the structure itself of Muslim scripture lends little support to the theory of a deliberate edition. Particularly in the *exempla* of salvation history, characterized by variant traditions, but also in passages of exclusively advisory or eschatological content, ellipsis and repetition are such as to suggest not the carefully executed project of one or of many men, but rather the product of an organic development from originally independent traditions during a long period of transmission.[34]

Therefore, not only are the *ḥadīth*s that underlie the textual history of the Qur'ān a fabrication, but the structure of the Qur'ān itself bears witness against them.

As even this brief outline makes clear, these major concerns of contemporary Western scholarship on the Qur'ān and its exegesis, namely, textual criticism and the historicity of *ḥadīth*, are not unrelated to each other. It is *ḥadīth* that supports the tradition of textual variants, particularly in the very early period for which there is little or no manuscript evidence. The whole history of the text and its canonization, as understood by Muslim scholarship, depends upon the historical authenticity of accepted *ḥadīth*s. Such, too, is the case with the Muslim understanding of the history of exegetical activity. The interpretations of such early commentators as Ibn ʿAbbās and Ibn Masʿūd are all in the form of carefully documented *ḥadīth*s. In fact, the formative period of Qur'ānic *tafsīr* amounts to little more than a compilation and classification of the relevant explanatory *ḥadīth*s. By attacking the orthodox Islamic understanding of *ḥadīth*, Western scholars, such as some of those discussed above, have thrown the issues of the Qur'ān's canonization and its early exegesis open to question. Furthermore, since exegesis based on *ḥadīth* (*al-tafsīr bi-al-ma'thūr*) remains the backbone of all subsequent Qur'ānic interpretation, this latter is equally jeopardized.

34 John Wansbrough, *Quranic Studies*, 46–7. Wansbrough divides early *tafsīr* into categories derived from Jewish exegesis, e.g., haggadic, halakhic, masoretic, etc. For further explanation, see Andrew Rippin, "Literary Analysis of *Qur'ān, Tafsīr* and *Sīra*: The Methodologies of John Wansbrough" in *Approaches to Islam in Religious Studies*, ed. by Richard C. Martin (Tucson: The University of Arizona Press, 1985), 151–63. A more specialized study that draws upon Wansbrough's theses is Rippin's "Al-Zuhrī, *Naskh al-Qur'ān* and the Problem of Early *Tafsīr* Texts," *BSOAS* 47 (1984): 22–43.

In fact, the basic Muslim belief, as reiterated above by the late medieval writer Ibn Kathīr, that the Prophet is the principal (non-Qur'ānic) interpreter of the Qur'ān is, for such scholars, a piece of historical nonsense.

There seems no immediate resolution to this cluster of problems that confound Western scholarship on the formative period of Qur'ānic *tafsīr*. As long as the historicity of *ḥadīth* is questioned and in the absence of sufficient textual evidence for the very early period, scholarship in this area will continue to be a matter of individual interpretation or an *argumentum ex silentio*. Western studies in this area now find themselves at a more or less inevitable impasse. Having abandoned the results of traditional Muslim historiography, they have very little certitude with which to replace it. So far their negative judgments far outweigh their positive contributions.

Of what use, then, is any further consideration of a literature whose historical basis is so questionable? Is there anything to be gained from perusing works, such as those of al-Ṭabarī and Ibn Kathīr, whose necessary aim is, at least in part, the continued transmission of relevant exegetical *ḥadīth*? It is, of course, an aim not restricted to those two commentators but one shared by virtually all of the exegetes treated in this study. The answer to these questions must be found in the purposes for which such a literature was created and the uses to which it can be put.

To take the latter first: if the chief function is that of textual studies or historical verification, then the results will be problematic at best. Such, indeed, would seem to be the use intended by those who seek to find the original meaning of the text. In the introduction to a volume of essays on Qur'ān and *tafsīr*, Alford Welch has divided the field of Qur'ānic studies into three basic areas: "(1) exegesis, or the study of the text itself, (2) the history of its interpretation (*Tafsīr*), and (3) the roles of the Qur'ān in Muslim life and thought (in ritual, theology, etc.)."[35] For Welch, this first

35 Alford Welch, "Introduction: Qur'anic Studies–Problems and Prospects," in *Studies in Qur'an and Tafsir: Journal of the American Academy of Religion,* Thematic Issue 47 (1979): 630. The third category, that of the function of the Qur'ān in Muslim life, has recently come under renewed consideration. Richard Martin argues that for historians of religion who concern themselves with religious texts the "primary problematic" is "to determine how textual communities use texts to get things done in the world." "Text and Contextuality in Reference to Islam," *Semeia* 40 (1987): 142.

The predominantly oral experience of the Qur'ān is the focus of Kristina Nelson, *The Art of Reciting the Qur'ān* (Austin: University of Texas Press, 1985); William A. Graham, *Beyond the Written Word: Oral Aspects of Scripture in the History of Religion* (Cambridge: Cambridge University Press, 1987); Frederick M. Denny, "Exegesis and Recitation: Their Development as Classical Forms of Qur'ānic Piety," in *Transitions and Transformations in the History of Religions: Essays in Honor of Joseph M. Kitagawa*, ed. by Frank E. Reynolds and Theodore M. Ludwig (Leiden: E.J. Brill, 1980), 91–123; Denny's "Qur'ān Recitation Training in Indonesia: A Survey of Contexts and Handbooks," in *Approaches*, 288–306; and Denny's "The *Adab* of Qur'ān Recitation," in *Qur'ān*

category involves trying "to understand the ideas of the Qurʾān itself and what they meant to its first hearers."[36] To pursue such an endeavor, the scholar must first take a stand on the historicity of the materials at his disposal and is thus propelled into the very problems just discussed. Even more basic, however, are the philosophical implications of such a stated effort, considerations to which the entire present-day discussion of hermeneutics generally is devoted.[37]

To say this is not to question the importance of such undertakings or to demean their results. But it is to draw attention to the fact that research of this sort forms but one facet of the total complex of Qurʾānic studies. Another equally important aspect is that which treats of the Qurʾān's place in the intellectual life of Muslims for over a thousand years, that is, for what have here been called the classical and modern periods. The primary filter, in each of these centuries, for the accumulated, communal understanding of the Qurʾān is *tafsīr*. Classical and modern *tafsīr*, therefore, may validly be treated as a window looking into the Islamic *Weltanschauung* of any given generation. It provides the historian of religions with a wide perspective from which to survey Islamic self-definition and interreligious understanding at particular points in its history.

Nor does such an approach do violence to Muslim attitudes toward their scriptural heritage. Because the Qurʾānic revelation, as the eternal word of God, is ontologically timeless, it may and must be reappropriated by every generation. It is addressed not to one group of Muslims but to all, and ever renews itself on the lips and in the hearts of each new age. William Graham has aptly phrased this:

> The most crucial kind of "authenticity" of a scripture or anything else of religious significance is, in the final analysis, its absolute authenticity in the understanding and faith of a particular individual or a particular group in a particular age. What a person or community recognizes as true, has faith in as true, is as legitimate an object of scholarly concern as the equally elusive genesis or "original source" of an idea, an image, a myth, or even a text; and certainly it is more important than the latter [i.e., the genesis or "original source"] in seeking to understand the person or group involved.[38]

Congress, 143–60. Michael Gilsenan has elegantly sketched the ambiguities of literacy and orality within Islamic culture generally in his "Sacred Words," in *The Diversity of the Muslim Community: Anthropological Essays in Memory of Peter Lienhardt*, ed. by Ahmed Al-Shahi (London: Ithaca Press, 1987), 92–98.

36 Welch, "Introduction," 629. An earlier version of this is to be found in the statement by Arthur Jeffery in which he assigns to "critical scholarship . . . the task of ascertaining as accurately as possibly what the message meant to the original hearers." "The Present Status of Qurʾānic Studies," 12.

37 Richard C. Martin has taken account of some of these implications in his article entitled "Understanding the Qurʾān in Text and Context," *History of Religions* 21 (1982): 361–84.

38 William A. Graham, *Divine Word and Prophetic Word in Early Islam: A Reconsideration*

It is within such an intellectual horizon that the present study is undertaken. The commentators whose work is here discussed will be addressed with these considerations in mind.

CLASSICAL *TAFSĪR* AND MODERN *TAFSĪR*

Classical and modern *tafsīr* represents, to a large extent, a coherent and internally consistent body of literature. It has developed within the confines of a limited number of hermeneutical principles. It is a remarkably uninterrupted craft, whose contemporary practitioners are fully conversant with their tenth-, twelfth-, and fourteenth-century counterparts. Rare is the modern Biblical scholar who is on easy terms with Rabanus Maurus (d. 856), Hugh of St. Victor (d. 1144), and Nicholas of Lyra (d. 1349). Yet just as uncommon would be the modern Muslim exegete who were *not* thoroughly familiar with al-Ṭabarī (d. 923), al-Zamakhsharī (d. 1144), and Ibn Kathīr (d. 1373).

The reason for this discrepancy lies in the very different activities that constitute contemporary Biblical criticism on the one hand and most of both classical and twentieth-century Qur'ānic *tafsīr* on the other. Although both fields are manifestly engaged in the task of exegesis or interpretation, they ask quite different questions of their respective texts. One who has even a superficial acquaintance with the goals and methods of nineteenth- and twentieth-century Biblical scholarship will very likely find the writings of Qur'ānic commentators puzzling or peculiar to a degree.

The disparity revolves around the question of authorship. For contemporary Biblical scholars the Bible may well be in some sense a divine disclosure; but it is also a human document. As such, it is amenable to textual study, to tracing the changes that have accrued through transmission. It is open to such questions as literary criticism might raise about the structure, date, and authorship of its composite documents. The materials, both oral and written, from which such documents were formed, and the motives that guided their final shape, are legitimate areas of inquiry. Questions of cultural borrowings, of indirect influence, and of historical reliability may be justly entertained. Such is not the case with a scripture understood to be the "uncreated Word of God." In straightforward fashion R. C. Zaehner fastened upon the distinction: "For once, then, God had spoken plainly in the full light of history: it did not take some four hundred years for the faithful to decide what was Holy Writ and what was not, as in the case of the Christians, whose task was made the more difficult by the fact that their Founder left nothing at all in writing."[39] For the Qur'ānic commen-

of the Sources with Special Reference to the Divine Saying or Ḥadīth Qudsī (The Hague: Mouton, 1977), 2.

39 R.C. Zaehner, "Why Not Islam?," *RS* 11 (1975), 177. William Graham provides a

tator who believes that he is possessed of God's own words, the exegetical imperative is quite straightforward.

He will seek to clarify words and phrases that carry an uncommon signification. He will make explicit the grammatical relationships within the verse and suggest connectives where the passage is elliptical or paratactic. Any apparent irregularities of morphology, syntax, or word order will be discussed within the framework of classical Arabic grammar, itself drawn substantially from the evidence of Qurʾānic usage.[40] If the collective memory of the community, as enshrined in *ḥadīth*, can offer a historical context for the revelation (*sabab al-nuzūl*), this will be cited. Any relevant insights recorded from the Prophet or his Companions will be included, as will parallel words and phrases from elsewhere in the Qurʾān itself.

Beyond these basics, an individual commentator may choose to draw attention to the legal and moral implications of the passage. He may consider philosophical issues raised therein and/or express the mystical insights to which he perceives some allusion. Some commentators will try to place the verse within the total structure of Qurʾānic revelation, establishing connections among verses and, occasionally, among *sūrah*s. Others will draw on such noncanonical material as historical narratives, collections of classical poetry, and that class of *ḥadīth* known as *isrāʾīlīyāt*.[41]

contrastive overview of Muslim and non-Muslim Qurʾānic scholarship in "Those Who Study and Teach the Qurʾān," in *Qurʾān Congress*, 9–28.

40 Ira Lapidus has succinctly sketched the interrelated development of Qurʾānic studies and Arabic literary interests in *A History of Islamic Societies* (Cambridge: Cambridge University Press, 1988), 89–91.

41 This is a term applied to a body of material found in a broad range of Islamic sources, including early histories and *tafāsīr*, that purports to give supplementary information about figures, especially ancient prophets, mentioned in the Qurʾān. Because it was largely derived from non-Islamic, especially Jewish, sources it was frequently condemned by the more conservative scholars. See G. Vajda, "Isrāʾīliyyāt," EI^2 4:211–12; Gordon D. Newby, "Tafsir Israʾiliyat," *Studies in Qurʾan and Tafsir: Journal of the American Academy of Religion*, Thematic Issue 47 (1979): 685–97. An extended bibliography is to be found in Haim Schwarzbaum, *Biblical and Extra-Biblical Legends in Islamic Folk-Literature* (Walldorf-Hessen: Verlag für Orientkunde Dr. H. Vorndran, 1982), 178–209. Much of the support for the use of such extra-Qurʾānic material came from a *ḥadīth* in which the Prophet permitted and encouraged transmission on the authority of the Banū Isrāʾīl. M.J. Kister has studied this *ḥadīth* and the interpretations of it in "Ḥaddithū ʿan banī isrāʾīla wa-lā ḥaraja," *Israel Oriental Studies* 2 (1972), 215–39. For the modernist rejection of the use of *isrāʾīlīyāt* see H.A.R. Gibb, *Modern Trends in Islam* (Chicago: University of Chicago Press, 1947), 73–74 and Daud Rahbar, "Reflections on the Tradition of Qurʾanic Exegesis," *MW* 52 (1962): 304.

One genre of *isrāʾīlīyāt* are the works known as 'stories of the prophets (*qiṣaṣ al-anbiyāʾ*)'. T. Nagel, "Ḳiṣaṣ al-anbiyāʾ," EI^2 5:180–81. An early example of this, which was preserved on papyrus and entitled *Ḥadīth Dāwūd*, has been transcribed and translated by R.G. Khoury in his study on Wahb b. Munabbih. This is a two-volume work of which the second volume comprises photographs of the damaged manuscript from

What the classical and modern exegetes, as discussed in this study, will not do is to consider a word or passage as incomplete or corrupt, a victim of scribal transmission.[42] They will not entertain theories about cultural borrowing or extra-Islamic influence. Qurʾānic passages that appear to echo versions of Biblical narratives are not examined in order to discover their possible lines of transmission and the various shapings undergone along the way. In fact, most of the questions that fuel the historical-critical method of the Biblical scholar are, for his or her Qurʾānic counterpart, non-questions or even blasphemies. This is not to say that no one has ever subjected the Qurʾān to this kind of interrogation. There is at least a century of Western scholarship on the Qurʾān that employs such methodology, examples of which were discussed above. In the last fifty years scattered instances of this approach have appeared in the Islamic world.[43] Such efforts have been

which Khoury reconstructed his text. *Wahb B. Munabbih* (Weisbaden: Otto Harrassowitz, 1972). For corrections to this publication see M.J. Kister, "On the Papyrus of Wahb b. Munabbih," *BSOAS* 37 (1974): 545–71. An English translation of one prominent work in this class has been produced by W.M. Thackston, Jr., *The Tales of the Prophets of al-Kisaʾi* (Boston: Twayne, 1978).

42 Muslim belief in the textual perfection of the Qurʾān is expressed in the doctrine of the inimitability of the Qurʾān, *iʿjāz*, a word whose non-technical meaning is 'to incapacitate'. A standard classical source is Abū Bakr Muḥammad b. al-Ṭayyib al-Bāqillānī (d. 403/1013), *Iʿjāz al-Qurʾān*, ed. by Aḥmad Ṣaqr (Cairo: Dār al-Maʿārif, 1401/1981). For a brief overview of the subject, see the introductory material provided by Claude-France Audebert in *Al-Khaṭṭābī et l'inimitabilité du Coran: traduction et introduction au Bayān iʿjāz al-Qurʾān* (Damascus: Institut Français de Damas, 1982). An early stylistic challenge to this dogma is analyzed by Josef van Ess, "Some Fragments of the *Muʿāraḍat al-Qurʾān* Attributed to Ibn al-Muqaffaʿ," in *Studia Arabica*, 151–63.

43 In a response to the article by Zaehner cited earlier, Kenneth Cragg notes a few of the "voices within Islam which press for an intellectually responsible possession of the Qurʾān." See "How Not Islam?," *RS* 13 (1977): 391. The late Fazlur Rahman has called upon Muslims "to distinguish clearly between normative Islam and historical Islam." This, he feels, can only be done through "studying the Qurʾān in its total and specific background (and doing this study systematically in a historical order), not just studying it verse by verse or passage by passage with an isolated 'occasion of revelation' (*sha'n al-nuzūl*)." *Islam and Modernity: Transformation of an Intellectual Tradition* (Chicago: University of Chicago Press, 1982), 141 and 145. The writings of Mohammed Arkoun address Qurʾānic materials from the perspective of such contemporary intellectual concerns as semiotic analysis and intertextuality. A published lecture, "The Notion of Revelation: From Ahl al-Kitāb to the Societies of the Book," *WI* 28 (1988): 62–89, offers an accessible entrée to the elaboration of Arkoun's thought as collected in his volumes of essays. See especially *Lectures du Coran* (Paris: Éditions Maisonneuve et Larose, 1982) and *Pour une critique de la raison islamique* (Paris: Éditions Maisonneuve et Larose, 1984). In a seminal essay Arkoun draws upon Jacques Derrida's notion of "clôture logocentrique" to suggest the grounds for a "*re*-lecture du Coran et, plus généralement, de tous les grands textes de la pensée islamique classique." "Logocentrisme et vérité religieuse dans la pensée islamique d'après *al-Iʿlām bi-manāqib al-Islām* d'al-ʿĀmirī," in his *Essais sur la pensée islamique*, 3rd ed. (Paris: Éditions Maisonneuve et Larose, 1984), 185. Reprinted from *SI* 35 (1972): 5–51.

vigorously opposed by conservative religious scholars (*ʿulamāʾ*), as has much Western scholarship in general.[44] (It should be noted, however, that comparing patristic and much medieval Biblical interpretation with classical Qurʾānic exegesis would produce far fewer differences. The earlier Christian understanding of scriptural authorship stands much closer to the Islamic position, as centuries of Biblical commentary bear witness.)

The differences here outlined should be borne in mind in approaching the body of this study. The evidence of exegetical traditionalism is undeniable. There is a great deal of repetition.[45] Many commentators seek to be comprehensive in their coverage, feeling, perhaps, that to delete is to deny. Yet for the student of this material, fascination lies in the diversity that emerges within the tight hermeneutical boundaries. Each of the ten scholars here studied has managed to fashion something new from the received tradition. Each has molded and reshaped it, enriching that tradition in the process. The biographical introductions to these creative figures in Chapter 2 will set the stage for an examination of their exegetical insights.

PRELIMINARY CONSIDERATIONS IN *TAFSĪR* ANALYSIS

Several matters should be noted as propaedeutic to the discussion of the passages chosen for this study. The first is the matter of Qurʾānic chronology. A significant proportion of nineteenth- and twentieth-century Western scholarship on the Qurʾān has been devoted to the problem of establishing the sequence of Qurʾānic revelation. Western scholars, frequently motivated by the desire to use the Qurʾān as a historical source, have applied various

44 In her work on Islamic historiography Yvonne Haddad discusses the case of Khalaf Allāh, an Egyptian scholar whose thesis on the historical authenticity of the Qurʾānic narratives caused a furor in the late 1940s. *Contemporary Islam and the Challenge of History* (Albany: State University of New York Press, 1982), 46–53. For further consideration of the discussion of Muslim and Western approaches to scripture see Tilman Nagel, "Gedanken über die europäische Islamforschung und ihr Echo im Orient," *Zeitschrift für Missionswissenschaft und Religionswissenschaft* 62 (1978): 21–39; and Peter Antes, "Schriftverständnis im Islam," *Theologische Quartalschrift* 161 (1981): 179–91.

45 It is and has been commonplace to hear Western scholars speak of *tafsīr* as repetitive, doctrinaire, defensive, dull, and irrelevant. Particularly is this said of post-twelfth-century works. One of the most blatant – but by no means the only – expression of such views is the statement by Harris Birkeland in which he complains about the "tiresome, uniform appearance" of Muslim commentaries and then goes on to assert categorically: "After aṭ-Ṭabarī, az-Zamakhsharī, and ar-Rāzī nothing essentially new has entered orthodox *tafsīr*. . . . It is absolutely superfluous to consult other commentaries than those mentioned, to obtain exhaustive information of the history of Muslim *tafsīr*." *The Lord Guideth*, 136. It should be noted that Birkeland has restricted his critique by the use of the word "orthodox." He later goes on to exclude "heretic" and "modernist" movements from his judgment.

critical methods to the text in an effort to establish the chronological order of the *sūrah*s and their constituent parts. Their results have often been at some variance with traditional Muslim dating, which is based primarily on *asbāb al-nuzūl*.

All systems make a distinction between Meccan and Medinan revelation, but beyond that their results differ, sometimes greatly. What must be stressed, however, is that considerations of dating form virtually no part of the classical and the modern *tafsīr* on these seven passages (and two parallels). That is, none of these commentators, from al-Ṭabarī to Ṭabāṭabāʾī, builds his exegesis of a verse on points of Qurʾānic chronology. (This, of course, would not have been the case, had the problem of abrogation (*naskh*) been a major element in any of the verses under discussion.[46]) However, some Western references to these verses are made against a background of one or more of the multiple dating systems. Therefore, it may be useful to list these Qurʾānic passages according to the principal chronologies so established. Those chosen for comparison are the systems of Theodor Nöldeke and Friedrich Schwally, J.M. Rodwell, Régis Blachère, and Richard Bell. These will be compared with the traditional Muslim dating as presented in the 'Egyptian standard edition' of the Qurʾān.[47]

The first three dating systems, those of Nöldeke-Schwally, Rodwell, and Blachère, are concerned with establishing the chronology of complete *sūrah*s. So, too, broadly speaking, is the traditional Muslim system. This latter system, as well, in its division of Meccan and Medinan material, does note interpolations of the former into the latter and conversely. There are six *sūrah*s of the Qurʾān from which passages have been drawn for this study. They are, in the order in which they are found in the Qurʾānic text,

46 For an example of chronology as an important interpretive issue see my "The Wines of Earth and Paradise: Qurʾānic Proscriptions and Promises," in *Logos Islamikos: Studia Islamica in Honorem Georgii Michaelis Wickens*, ed. by Roger M. Savory and Dionisius A. Agius (Toronto: Pontifical Institute of Mediaeval Studies, 1984), 160–74.

47 The epithet "Egyptian standard edition" has become, in the last fifty years, an increasingly common way to refer to an edition of the Qurʾān printed in Cairo in 1342/1923–24 under the aegis of King Fuʾād I. See Régis Blachère, *Introduction au Coran*, 1st ed. (Paris: G.P. Maisonneuve, 1947), xxxiv–v. This edition, based on the reading known as "Ḥafṣ ʿan ʿĀṣim" (i.e., the *qirāʾah* of ʿĀṣim b. Abī al-Najjūd [d. 128/745] in the *riwāyah* of Ḥafṣ b. Sulaymān [d. 180/796]), is, according to Alford Welch, "now regarded as the best of the Ḳurʾān so far available, although it was based on oral tradition and late *ḳirāʾāt* literature, and is not always consistent with the oldest and best sources." "al-Ḳurʾān," 5:409. J.J.G. Jansen, who states that "no other edition ever possessed such general authority," refers the reader to an article by G. Bergsträsser ("Koranlesung in Kairo," *Der Islam* 20 [1932]:1–42) which describes the publication history of "der amtliche Koran." *The Interpretation of the Koran in Modern Egypt* (Leiden: E.J. Brill, 1974), 3.

sūrat al-baqarah (2), *sūrah Āl ʿImrān* (3), *sūrat al-māʾidah* (5), *sūrat al-ḥajj* (22), *sūrat al-qaṣaṣ* (28), and *sūrat al-ḥadīd* (57). Of these, the only one that is traditionally designated as Meccan is *sūrat al-qaṣaṣ*. The traditional ordering of the other five, which are all considered Medinan, is as follows: 2, 3, 57, 22, 5. A survey of the above-named Western chronologies shows absolutely no disagreement with this ordering.[48] The only variant, in fact, is that of the traditional Muslim system, which views verses 52–55 of *sūrat al-qaṣaṣ* (the very ones pertinent to this study) as a later Medinan interpolation into this Meccan *sūrah*.[49]

Reviewing the system of Richard Bell produces less straightforward results. Bell, unlike his above-named predecessors, maintained that dating the Qurʾānic revelation involved analyzing not *sūrah*s as a whole but their constituent units, the individual pericopes. Therefore, he first divided the *sūrah*s into what he ascertained to be single units of revelation and then tried, by a variety of methods, to date these pericopes. The results are, in many cases, tentative and open to revision. With respect to the verses under consideration here, Bell's analysis sheds little light. Almost all of the relevant passages, including 28:52–55, are dated to the early Medinan period or identified as a "scrap of uncertain date." The only exceptions are 22:17, which is tagged a "later addition to an early Medinan address"; and 57:27, which is labeled a "late insertion" in an early Medinan *sūrah*.[50] Taken as

48 Nöldeke-Schwally, *Geschichte,* 1:ix–x; *The Koran*, trans. by J.M. Rodwell (London: J.M. Dent, 1909), xiv–xv; *Le Coran*, trans. by Régis Blachère (Paris: G.P. Maisonneuve, 1949), 2:xv.

49 *al-Qurʾān* (Cairo [Būlāq]: al-Maṭbaʿah al-Amīrīyah, 1344/1925), 506. This is the edition of the Qurʾān used in this study. Verse numbering follows this Egyptian edition rather than that of the nineteenth-century edition prepared by Gustav Flügel. Except for Kāshānī's division of the verse (199) in *sūrah Āl ʿImrān* into two verses (198 and 199), there was no significant difference in the Qurʾānic citations found in the Persian Shīʿī *tafsīr*s of Abū al-Futūḥ Rāzī and Mullā Fatḥ allāh Kāshānī, the Arabic Shīʿī *tafsīr* of Abū Jaʿfar al-Ṭūsī, and the rest of the Arabic *tafsīr*s. In discussing the development of Shīʿī acceptance of the ʿUthmānic text, E. Kohlberg remarks that "when the last of the great Imāmite theologians of the Buwayhid period, Abū Jaʿfar at-Ṭūsī, wrote the famous Qurʾān commentary, *at-Tibyān*, he had no doubts whatever about the integrity of all verses of the Qurʾān." He also mentions, however, that a secondary tradition, maintained by such scholars as Aḥmad b. ʿAlī al-Faḍl b. al-Ḥasan al-Ṭabarsī (d. 548/1153), continued to raise doubts about the ʿUthmānic *codex*. "Some Notes on the Imāmite Attitude to the Qurʾān," *Islamic Philosophy and the Classical Tradition* (R. Walzer *Festschrift*), ed. by S.M. Stern, Albert Hourani, and Vivian Brown (Columbia, S.C.: University of South Carolina Press, 1972), 217. It should be noted that Kohlberg's source for al-Ṭabarsī's views is the latter's *Iḥtijāj*, a work that, as the biographical sketch of Kāshānī in Chapter 2 observes, the latter translated into Persian. An earlier treatment of Imāmite views on the Qurʾān may be found in Joseph Eliash, "'The Shīʿite Qurʾān': A Reconsideration of Goldziher's Interpretation," *Arabica* 16 (1969): 15–24.

50 Richard Bell, trans., *The Qurʾān* (Edinburgh: T. and T. Clark, 1939), 2:562.

a whole, Bell's analysis of these verses does not differ significantly from either the traditional Muslim chronology or the classifications of Nöldeke-Schwally, Rodwell, and Blachère.

The second technical consideration concerns the format of the *tafsīrs* herein discussed and its hermeneutical implications. Each of the *tafsīrs* used for this study falls within the category of *tafsīr musalsal*, or 'chained' commentary. This means that each begins with the first *sūrah* of the Qurʾān and comments verse by verse on that *sūrah* and all subsequent ones. Exegetical chronology has, therefore, its own autonomy, following the sequence of text rather than that of revelation. There are, of course, anomalies – a verse passed over in silence or an unfinished work such as the *Tafsīr al-Manār*. Nevertheless, the standard procedure remains remarkably uniform. Within the *sūrah* each verse is quoted separately and then broken into exegetical units, what medieval Biblical scholars would call *lemmata*. Each passage, or *lemma*, is then analyzed separately and relevant comments are made about the verse as a whole, such as its *sabab al-nuzūl*. What is frequently absent is any extended consideration of the larger context. Occasionally, a connection will be made with the previous verse or, even more rarely, with more distant parts of the *sūrah*.[51]

The modern commentators, Muḥammad Rashīd Riḍā and Muḥammad Ḥusayn Ṭabāṭabāʾī, have paid somewhat more attention to problems of context and verse-grouping. Both have broken the *sūrahs* into coherent units and offered summarizations or digressions that take account of an individual *sūrah* as a whole. However, even with these two the coordination of such efforts with the analysis of individual verses remains perfunctory.[52] There is, therefore, among the exegetes here studied, very little of the attitude evinced by a scholar such as Irfan Shahid who has declared: "Koranic suras should be regarded, at least tentatively, as units of composition; and it is only after the failure of the most extensive exegesis to discover compositional unity that any particular sura can be declared disjointed."[53] This study

51 Some issues of contextuality are addressed in the two principal compilations of *ʿulūm al-Qurʾān*. The relationship between verses is the second topic entertained by Badr al-Dīn Muḥammad b. ʿAbdallāh al-Zarkashī (d. 794/1392), *al-Burhān fī ʿulūm al-Qurʾān*, ed. by Muḥammad Abū al-Faḍl Ibrāhīm (Cairo: Dār al-Turāth, n.d.), 1:35–52. The issue of correspondence as it relates to both verses and *sūrahs* is treated in Chapter 62 of al-Suyūṭī's *Itqān*, 3:322–38. Claude Gilliot notes the greater attention that Fakhr al-Dīn al-Rāzī devotes to contextual concerns and attributes this, in large part, to the refinement and elaboration of the doctrine of *iʿjāz*. "Parcours exégétiques: de Ṭabarī à Rāzī (Sourate 55)," *AT* n.v. (1983): 87–116.

52 Some modern *tafsīr* is deliberately opposed to such contextual issues as historical references and narrative development. For a summary of Khalaf Allāh's views on this, see Yvonne Haddad, *Contemporary Islam*, 46–53.

53 Irfan Shahid, "A Contribution to Koranic Exegesis," in *Arabic and Islamic Studies in*

attempts to reflect the weight, or lack thereof, accorded contextual considerations in the individual commentaries. Only when the *tafsīr*s herein discussed include references to coordinate verses or make connections with other verses and other *sūrah*s will these be recorded. To do otherwise would be to distort this presentation of Islamic exegesis by adding to it hermeneutical concerns of which the exegetes themselves were unaware or in which they displayed no interest.

A broader contextual issue must be addressed in any attempt to present faithfully the texture and teleology of Qur'ānic *tafsīr* as a genre of religious literature. Qur'ānic commentary, apart from some of its Ṣūfī manifestations, is a remarkably cohesive and continuous body of discourse, fully preoccupied with an established range of concerns and considerations. For over a millennium the conversation of classical and modern *tafsīr* has proceeded along well-prescribed paths, respecting a stable agenda of exegetical observations. Each stage of that conversation draws upon earlier discourse and in turn itself becomes a source for new partners who enter the deliberation. The eyes of the exegetes look back, focused upon seminal thoughts, figures, and incidents in the nascent period of Islam and their authoritative representation at subsequent historical stages. There is, however, little lateral vision. At least in the premodern period, the commentators exhibit virtually no concern with the contemporary context of their own work. They do not seek to draw into the discourse any allusions to the current political, social, or economic environment. The reader searches in vain for such reference. Aside from mention of the intellectual lineage to which an individual author pays respects, it is frequently difficult to determine from internal evidence alone whether a commentary was written in Anatolia or Andalusia, whether its *mufassir* (commentator) had ever seen a Mongol or a Crusader or had ever conversed with a Christian or conducted business with one.

Such features of his life simply do not figure in an author's exegetical enterprise. Contemporary context does not count as a hermeneutical element. When al-Ṭabarī writes about these verses, his glance does not light

Honor of Hamilton A.R. Gibb, ed. by George Makdisi (Leiden: E.J. Brill, 1965), 575. Irfan Shahid develops this in an article that argues for the compositional unity of two Meccan *sūrah*s. "Two Qur'ānic Sūras: al-Fīl and Quraysh," in *Studia Arabica*, 429–36. The structural integrity of Qur'ānic *sūrah*s is examined by Angelika Neuwirth in *Studien zur Komposition der mekkanischen Suren* (Berlin: Walter de Gruyter, 1981). Another contribution to this approach is the investigation (undertaken as a thesis at the University of Geneva) of the internal rhythmic structures of the Meccan *sūrah*s by regrouping the *sūrah*s "according to their metric affinities." Pierre Crapon de Caprona, *Le Coran: Aux sources de la parole oraculaire* (n.p.: Publications Orientalistes de France, 1981). A yet more comprehensive sense of the levels of Qur'ānic coherence as developed by the contemporary Pakistani exegete, Amīn Aḥsan Iṣlāḥī, in his eight-volume Urdu commentary, *Tadabbur-i Qur'ān*, is presented by Mustansir Mir in *Coherence in the Qur'ān* (Indianapolis: American Trust Publications, 1986).

upon the Christian community of late ninth-century Baghdād. Fakhr al-Dīn al-Rāzī never mentions the Christians of Herāt. Ibn Kathīr says nothing of the Christians in post-Crusader Damascus. Kāshānī shows no interest in the Christian population of Ṣafavid Persia. Only with the two twentieth-century commentators, Rashīd Riḍā and Ṭabāṭabā'ī, does the exegetical gaze expand sufficiently to prompt at least general reference to the contemporary context and the Christian component thereof.

These perspectives structure the content of this study. Much as one might wish to find in the centuries-long effort of Qur'ānic commentary a supplementary source for the social, political, and ecclesiastical history of Eastern Christianity, it simply does not serve that function. What it does offer is continuous testimony to the power of a formative tradition, a tradition that can attract and hold the unwavering gaze of its adherents, pushing to the periphery all immediate, ephemeral interests.

That tradition must be allowed to speak on its own terms, to reflect its own concerns and chronology. Therefore in the descriptive analysis of the exegetical deliberation on each of these verses, the chronological sequence of commentators will be respected. Each exegete who has joined the discussion of a particular hermeneutical issue will be presented in turn, with attention drawn to the points at which he concurs with or departs from his predecessors. Inevitably this will involve repetition. It would be tempting to collapse the chronology and present the various exegetical trajectories in more summary form. Certainly such concision would read more elegantly, but sacrificed would be the subtle variations among commentators, the ever-renewed reworkings and evolving nuances that have constituted the unfolding progression of Qur'ānic exegesis. Only after the full exegetical portrait has been painted for each verse may a concluding summarization be provided that does no violence to the integrity of Muslim commentary.

2

From Ṭabarī to Ṭabāṭabāʾī

Given the vast literature generated by centuries of Muslim exegetical effort, no topical study within that genre can aspire to comprehensive coverage. Inevitably some principle of selection must govern the choice of those works to be examined and discussed. In the present instance several intersecting concerns prompted the decision to concentrate upon the ten exegetes (*mufassirūn*) whose lives and commentaries are introduced in this chapter. Chronological considerations centered upon the desire to provide a spectrum of exegetical analysis ranging from the late ninth to the late twentieth century. That span of centuries commences in the classical period of Islamic thought with the foundational commentary of Abū Jaʿfar b. Jarīr al-Ṭabarī and concludes with the work of the recently deceased Iranian exegete, Muḥammad Ḥusayn Ṭabāṭabāʾī.

Sectarian inclusiveness forms a second, convergent spectrum. Four of the commentaries selected, two in Persian and two in Arabic, are by Shīʿī authors. This subcategory itself replicates the chronological span from classical to contemporary. The remaining six commentators may be loosely classed as Sunnī, yet this overriding designation shelters a variety of divergent perspectives. Theological orientations mark the Muʿtazilī identification of al-Zamakhsharī's commentary and Fakhr al-Dīn al-Rāzī's association with Ashʿarī thought, while legal representation, such as that of the Ḥanbalī *madhhab*, is provided by both Ibn al-Jawzī and Ibn Kathīr. A modernist agenda shapes issues addressed by Rashīd Riḍā in his *Tafsīr al-Manār* as well as by his younger contemporary, Ṭabāṭabāʾī. Although space restriction necessarily confined the ideal scope of this study, for contrastive purposes occasional allusion has also been made to a representative Ṣūfī *tafsīr*.[1] Among the most frequently reprinted and widely available of such

1 The study of Ṣūfī *tafsīr*, much of which remains in manuscript, is gaining momentum. Significant publications include Paul Nwyia, *Exégèse coranique et langage mystique: Nouvel essai sur le lexique technique des mystiques musulmans* (Beirut: Dar El-Machreq, 1970); and Gerhard Böwering, *The Mystical Vision of Existence in Classical Islam: The Qurʾānic Hermeneutics of the Ṣūfī Sahl At-Tustarī* (Berlin: Walter de Gruyter, 1980).

commentaries is the *Tafsīr al-Qur'ān al-karīm*, published under the name of Muḥyī al-Dīn b. al-ʿArabī (d. 638/1240) and popularly associated with him.[2]

Matters of popularity and accessibility were an additional factor operative in the selection decisions. The commentaries chosen for this study are, for the most part, among the most easily available in the Arabic-speaking world. A recent trip to Cairo confirmed this estimation, as copies of these texts could be found in a number of the bookstores that specialize in religious materials. Exceptions to this would be the Shīʿī commentaries, both Persian and Arabic, because recent events in both Iran and Iraq have disrupted normal patterns of book distribution. Nevertheless, these multivolume sets as well as their Sunnī counterparts may be counted among the best-known and most widely read products of the Muslim exegetical tradition.

Taken together, then, the commentaries selected provide representative coverage of the extraordinary productivity of Muslim exegetical activity. From the earliest to the most recent, these works and their authors remain part of a lively and continuing conversation. Frequent reprints and even new editions of them abound, attesting to their enduring vitality and their persistent importance within Muslim intellectual life. Each will now be presented in chronological turn, prefaced by a biographical sketch of its author.

AL-ṬABARĪ

Abū Jaʿfar Muḥammad b. Jarīr al-Ṭabarī was born during the years of ʿAbbāsid splendor but far from the center of that dynasty's power and culture. His early home was the province of Ṭabaristān, a mountainous region behind the southern coast of the Caspian Sea. Because its inaccessible outposts were difficult to conquer, Ṭabaristān was the last part of the Sassanian kingdom to accept Muslim domination and culture. His date of birth is usually given as 224 (838–39), but occasionally as 225 (839–40). Al-Ṭabarī is reported to have explained this discrepancy on the basis of a

2 This work, which is actually that of ʿAbd al-Razzāq al-Kāshānī (d. 730/1329), is often cited as a representative Ṣūfī *tafsīr*. Examples of such citation include the anthology of Helmut Gätje, *The Qur'ān and Its Exegesis: Selected Texts with Classical and Modern Muslim Interpretations* (Koran und Koranexegese), trans. and ed. by Alford T. Welch (London: Routledge and Kegan Paul, 1976), 40; and Mahmoud Ayoub's exegetical summary covering *sūrat al-fātiḥah* and *sūrat al-baqarah*, *The Qur'ān and Its Interpreters* (Albany: State University of New York Press, 1984), 6. An analysis of this *tafsīr* has been made by Pierre Lory in *Les Commentaires ésotériques du Coran d'après ʿAbd ar-Razzāq al-Qāshānī* (Paris: Les Deux Océans, 1980). For an assessment see James Morris's bibliographic essay, "Ibn ʿArabī and His Interpreters: Part II (Conclusion): Influences and Interpretations," *JAOS* 107 (1987): 101–06.

customary practice that related births to major events rather than dates. When, as an adult, he sought to discover the date by which his own birth was remembered, he fell victim to the fallibility of human memory.[3]

While al-Ṭabarī acquired an early education in his native city of Āmul, like most scholars of the classical period, he traveled far in his search for further learning. As a student he evinced precocity in that time-honored Muslim way, youthful memorization of the Qurʾān (in his case by the age of seven).[4] His early forays took him only as far south as Rayy but eventually he went on to Baghdād, using that city as a base for intellectual expeditions to such places as Baṣrah, Kūfah, Cairo, and parts of Syria.[5]

It was, however, to Baghdād, the center of the ʿAbbāsid universe, that al-Ṭabarī always returned and that remained his home until death. By the time he took up residence there, the Caliph had transferred to Sāmarrā where he and his successors would remain until near the end of the ninth century. Yet Baghdād continued to be the city of culture and learning, a magnet so powerful that its population at that time is estimated to have been a million and a half.[6] The city that al-Ṭabarī knew – that of the last quarter of the ninth and the first quarter of the tenth centuries – had survived the extended confrontation between the "rationalist" Muʿtazilīs and the traditionalist movement *ahl al-ḥadīth*. The triumph of the latter was due in large part to Aḥmad b. Ḥanbal (d. 241/855), "who weathered the persecution by sheer patience and pertinacity. Against the passive resistance of this pious man, the Muʿtazilī movement exhausted its political strength; it would never recover it."[7] Although al-Ṭabarī arrived in Baghdād too late to study with Ibn Ḥanbal, he could not escape this jurisconsult's enduring influence.[8] Biographers of al-Ṭabarī mention cases where his classes were disrupted and his students harassed by zealous Ḥanbalīs.[9] Doubtless, a major cause of this antagonism was al-Ṭabarī's introduction of a rival school of thought which became known as the Jarīrīyah.[10] Al-

3 Yāqūt b. ʿAbdallāh al-Ḥamawī al-Rūmī, *Irshād al-arīb ilā maʿrifat al-adīb*, ed. by D. S. Margoliouth (Cairo: Maṭbaʿah Hindīyah, 1925), 6:428–29.

4 Yāqūt, *Irshād*, 6:429–30.

5 Muḥammad b. ʿAlī b. Aḥmad al-Dāwūdī, *Ṭabaqāt al-mufassirīn*, ed. by ʿAlī M. ʿUmar (Cairo: Maktabah Wahbah, 1392/1972), 2:107–08.

6 A.A. Duri, "Baghdād," *EI*² 1:899.

7 George Makdisi, *The Rise of Colleges: Institutions of Learning in Islam and the West* (Edinburgh: Edinburgh University Press, 1981), 7.

8 Yāqūt, *Irshād*, 6:430.

9 al-Dāwūdī, *Ṭabaqāt*, 2:111; Yāqūt, *Irshād*, 6:425. A short theological treatise attributed to al-Ṭabarī develops some of the principal points of disagreement. Dominique Sourdel, who has reproduced and translated this text (save for the preamble in rhymed prose), notes the manifestation of al-Ṭabarī's historical consciousness in the thematic arrangement of this treatise, an arrangement that reflects the chronological emergence of major theological issues. "Une profession de foi de l'historien al-Ṭabarī," *REI* 2 (1968): 179.

10 Muḥammad al-Ṣabbāgh, *Lamaḥāt fī ʿulūm al-Qurʾān wa-ittijāhāt al-tafsīr* (Beirut: al-

though it gained considerable prominence, by the end of the eleventh century it had quite disappeared from Baghdād. The survival of the Ḥanbalī *madhhab* is evidence, according to George Makdisi, that al-Ṭabarī had "unsuccessfully impugned Aḥmad b. Ḥanbal's qualifications as a jurisconsult."[11]

Despite the demise of his school of law, al-Ṭabarī continues to be acknowledged as one of the great minds of his era. His biographers are unanimously impressed by the extent of his erudition and the magnitude of his written work. A statement by the eleventh-century jurisconsult al-Khaṭīb al-Baghdādī (d. 463/1071) sums up pages of laudation: "He had a degree of erudition shared by no one of his era."[12] Al-Ṭabarī put this vast knowledge at the disposal of his students and those who solicited his legal opinions. By all accounts, he sought no high offices for himself and refused those he was offered.

Biographical attestation to his rejection of such honors, as well as other rewards, appears with some frequency. In one account the Caliph al-Muktafī (289/902–295/908), wishing to establish a repository of teachings attributable to eminent Muslim scholars, had al-Ṭabarī brought before him. The latter dictated a book-length account in the presence of the court but refused any payment for it. When pressed, he simply requested that the Caliph not accept petitioners on the day of communal prayer, a request to which the Caliph reportedly acceded.[13] That such anecdotes serve a hagio-

Maktabah al-Islāmīyah, 1974), 185. Franz Rosenthal devotes considerable attention to the Jarīrī *madhhab* and al-Ṭabarī's relation with the Ḥanābilah in his Introduction to the English translation of al-Ṭabarī's *Taʾrīkh al-rusul wa-al-mulūk*. This multi-volume project is still under publication. See *General Introduction: From the Creation to the Flood, Volume 1 of The History of al-Ṭabarī* (Albany: State University of New York Press, 1989). In a recent survey Claude Cahen discusses al-Ṭabarī's stature within the full sweep of classical Muslim historiography. "L'historiographie Arabe des origines au viiᵉ s.H.," *Arabica* 33 (1986): 133–78. The most comprehensive bibliography of work on al-Ṭabarī and his history, covering supplementary studies as well as editions and translations, is that of Franz-Christoph Muth, *Die Annalen von at-Ṭabarī im Spiegel der europäischen Bearbeitungen* (Frankfurt-am-Main: Peter Lang, 1983). For a brief overview of al-Ṭabarī as historian see Claudio LoJacono, "Ṭàbari [*sic*], storiografo del primo Islàm," *ISC* 4 (1985): 91–99.

11 Makdisi, *The Rise of Colleges*, 8. See also Rudi Paret, "al-Ṭabarī," *EI*[1] 7:578. ʿIzz al-Dīn b. al-Athīr (d. 630/1233) recounts the standard grounds for Ḥanbalī dissatisfaction with al-Ṭabarī, the latter's dismissal of Aḥmad b. Ḥanbal as "merely a *muḥaddith*, not a *faqīh*." *Al-Kāmil fī al-taʾrīkh*, ed. by C. J. Tornberg (1851–74; reprint, Beirut: Dār Ṣādir lil-Ṭibāʿah wa-al-Nashr, 1965–67), 8:134.

12 al-Dāwūdī, *Ṭabaqāt*, 2:109. Muḥammad al-Ṣabbāgh, *Lamaḥāt*, 185. Occasionally the biographies of al-Ṭabarī verge on the miraculous. An instance of this is the account related by al-Dāwūdī in which al-Ṭabarī was suddenly presented with a bag of money at a point of destitution. See al-Dāwūdī, *Ṭabaqāt*, 2:109.

13 Shams al-Dīn Muḥammad b. Aḥmad al-Dhahabī, *Siyar aʿlām al-nubalāʾ*, ed. by Shuʿayb

graphical function is undeniable but by underscoring the purity of his intellectual motivation they also reinforce the impression of his professional life as one of persistent scholarship, dedicated teaching, and prolific writing.

The last-mentioned is no empty phrase. Even in an epoch where prodigious output – by present-day standards – was not uncommon, al-Ṭabarī's recorded corpus strains credulity. The wide range of subjects covered adds to this sense of amazement at the bulk itself. Apparently this commentator's productivity was a source of bemusement even to his own contemporaries. His biographers recount (perhaps apocryphal) conversations in which al-Ṭabarī's students beg him to condense both his historical and exegetical writings and he grudgingly agrees.[14] At a later date, his disciples are said to have divided his total output by his years of life to conclude that he wrote an average of fourteen pages a day.[15]

Al-Ṭabarī died in his adopted city of Baghdād in 310/923. It was a city whose days of political hegemony were numbered. Beset by financial and military difficulties, the caliphate suffered serious erosion of its power. Within less than fifteen years Ibn Rā'iq would assume the title of *amīr al-umarā'* (commander of commanders) and caliphal authority would cease to be much more than titular. Al-Ṭabarī's own life, then, drew to a close as the ʿAbbāsid sun was setting. Although well over eighty at the time of his death, his hair and beard remained full and black. He is further described by his biographers as tall, slender, and well-spoken.[16] While his burial place is uncertain, it is said that people prayed there day and night for months after his death.[17] His funeral procession was itself swelled by a "crowd which only God could count."[18] His student, Abū Muḥammad

al-Arna'ūt (Beirut: Mu'assasat al-Risālah, 1403/1983), 14:270. A variant of this tale on the authority of Abū Muḥammad al-Farghānī (d. 362/972–73) records more explicit praise accorded al-Ṭabarī. Ibid., 14:272.

14 al-Dāwūdī, *Ṭabaqāt*, 2:113.

15 Yāqūt, *Irshād*, 6:426. Yāqūt also mentions a report that has al-Ṭabarī producing as little as forty pages a year. *Irshād*, 6:424. Ibn Kathīr, in his own biography of al-Ṭabarī, corrects this to forty pages per day. *Al-Bidāyah wa-al-nihāyah* (Beirut: Maktabat al-Maʿārif, 1966), 11:145. See also al-Dhahabī, *Siyar*, 14:272.

16 Yāqūt, *Irshād*, 6:423. See also al-Dāwūdī, *Ṭabaqāt*, 2:114, and Ibn Kathīr, *al-Bidāyah*, 9:145.

17 Some sources maintain that he was interred in his home after nightfall, having incurred opposition sufficient to preclude his interment with full funeral honors. Henri Laoust, *La Profession de foi d'Ibn Baṭṭa* (Damascus: Institut Français de Damas, 1958), xxxv–vi. Yāqūt, for example, mentions and dismisses a report that al-Ṭabarī "was buried at night for fear of the masses because he was accused of being a Shīʿī." *Irshād*, 6:423. For Rosenthal's assessment of these sources see *Introduction*, 77–80.

18 Yāqūt, *Irshād*, 6:423.

al-Farghānī, eulogized him as "a scholar, a man of self-restraint, and an individual of virtue and piety."[19]

The principal legacy of this extraordinary man is to be found in his notional history of the world, *Taʾrīkh al-rusul wa-al-mulūk* (The History of Messengers and Kings), and in his commentary on the Qurʾān entitled *Jāmiʿ al-bayān ʿan taʾwīl āy al-Qurʾān* (The Comprehensive Clarification of the Interpretation of the Verses of the Qurʾān).[20] This latter work ushers in the classical period of Islamic exegetical activity. Therein is contained the compilation and methodical arrangement of the first two and a half centuries of Muslim exegesis. It has garnered praise for its clarity and comprehensiveness. Frequently cited is the encomium of Ibn Khuzaymah: "The *tafsīr* of Muḥammad b. Jarīr is clear; it is clear from beginning to end. I know no one on the face of the earth more knowledgeable than Muḥammad b. Jarīr."[21] His biographers never tire of repeating the remark laid to the credit of Abū Ḥāmid al-Isfarāʾīnī: "If a man were to travel to China so as to acquire the book of *tafsīr* of Muḥammad b. Jarīr, that would not be too far."[22] The immediate prominence of the work is underscored by the fact that the Sāmānid ruler of Transoxiana and Khurāsān, Abū Ṣāliḥ Mansūr b. Nūḥ (350/961–366/976), commissioned a Persian adaptation of it within fifty years of al-Ṭabarī's death.[23]

This *tafsīr* is noted primarily for the tremendous number of exegetical *ḥadīth*s that it incorporates.[24] As such, it is usually judged to be a par-

19 al-Dāwūdī, *Ṭabaqāt*, 2:114.

20 Fuat Sezgin points out that these were not the first attempts in Islamic literature at comprehensive documentation within their respective disciplines (*GAS* 1:323); they nevertheless remain the most noted and enduring.

21 al-Dāwūdī, *Ṭabaqāt*, 2:111. See also Yāqūt, *Irshād*, 6:425.

22 Yāqūt, *Irshād*, 6:424. See also Ibn Kathīr, *al-Bidāyah*, 9:146 and al-Dāwūdī, *Ṭabaqāt*, 2:109. J.J.G. Jansen (*Interpretation*, 56, note 5) has explained this remark not as praise but regret, i.e., that Abū Ḥāmid was unable to obtain a copy of the commentary.

23 In describing the circumstances of its genesis, C.A. Storey marks this translation as the "first definite landmark in the history of Persian Qurʾānic literature." *Persian Literature: A Bio-bibliographical Survey* (London: Luzac, 1927–71), 1:1. For further consideration of this translation, see ʿAlī Akbar Shahābī, *Aḥvāl va āthār-i Muḥammad Jarīr Ṭabarī* (Tehran: Intishārāt Dānishgāh-i Ṭihrān, 1335 [solar]/1957), 73-75.

24 Some idea of the magnitude of this compilation is to be found in a perusal of the most recent (and as yet unfinished) edition of the *tafsīr*. The editors have consecutively numbered the *ḥadīth*s that al-Ṭabarī incorporated. This edition has not gone beyond the commentary on *sūrah Ibrāhīm* (14):25 and yet the enumeration has reached 20, 787. Heribert Horst has done a detailed study of the *isnād*s in the *tafsīr* of al-Ṭabarī and, on the basis of it, suggested the likely sources, both complete and partial, upon which al-Ṭabarī drew: "So ist es möglich, dass ihm folgende vollständigen Bücher vorgelegen haben: der Tafsīr des ʿAlī b. a. Ṭalḥa, der Kommentar des Mujāhid, der Tafsīr des ʿAbdarraḥmān b. Zaid b. Aslam, das Kitāb al-Maġāzā des Ibn Isḥāq und vielleicht ein Werk, das ihm von Ibn Saʿd überliefert wurde." "Zur Überlieferung im Korankommentar aṭ-Ṭabarīs," *ZDMG* 103 (1953): 307.

ticularly important example of *al-tafsīr bi-al-ma'thūr*. It is not unusual for al-Ṭabarī to offer multiple *ḥadīth*s to support differing interpretations, carefully noting the *isnād* of each. Were he to have done no more than collect and compile this extant exegetical material, al-Ṭabarī would have performed an invaluable service.[25] Yet he went far beyond mere compilation and in so doing has, according to some, jeopardized his status as simply an exponent of *al-tafsīr bi-al-ma'thūr.*[26] The very act of choosing which *ḥadīth*s to include itself involves the exercise of personal opinion. In certain cases, al-Ṭabarī makes a forthright judgment among competing interpretations. At other times he more subtly reveals his preference by according one interpretation prominence of place and of additional supporting *ḥadīth*s.[27]

The fact that al-Ṭabarī was explicitly aware of the issues of method and hermeneutics receives clear attestation in the introductory material with which he begins his *tafsīr*. As befits a scholar of al-Ṭabarī's encyclopedic interests and abilities, the matters covered in this Introduction address a full range of exegetical concerns.[28] In addition to linguistic and lexical considerations (such as the commonly accepted "readings [*qirā'āt*]" of the Qur'ān), al-Ṭabarī discusses the problematic status of *al-tafsīr bi-al-ra'y*, the objections of those who oppose all exegetical activity, and the reputations of previous commentators, whether revered or denigrated in the passage of time.[29]

By the use of a number of formulaic expressions, al-Ṭabarī has organized

25 Speaking of al-Ṭabarī's *Ta'rīkh*, Stephen Humphreys takes issue with those who would rate him a "mere compiler." Based upon an understanding of classical Islamic notions of *'ilm*, Humphreys argues that "the historian's task was decisively *not* to interpret or evaluate the past as such; rather, he was simply to determine which reports about it (*akhbār*) were acceptable and to compile these reports in a convenient order." *Islamic History: A Framework for Inquiry* (Minneapolis: Bibliotheca Islamica, 1988), 72.

26 An example of this is the statement by Muḥammad al-Fāḍil b. 'Āshūr that those who place al-Ṭabarī's *Jāmi' al-bayān* in the "category of *al-tafsīr bi-al-ma'thūr* restrict their view of it to externals only, such as the mass of *ḥadīth*s and *isnād*s it contains. They do not take into consideration its method and objectives which are clarified in the citation of these carefully compiled, arranged and examined *isnād*s." *al-Tafsīr wa-rijāluhu* (Tunis: Dār al-Kutub al-Sharqīyah, 1966), 36.

27 In another instance David Powers notes that al-Ṭabarī's "arrangement of the material available to him serves to deflect the reader's attention from any statement that might constitute a potential challenge to the traditional understanding of the two verses." "The Islamic Law of Inheritance Reconsidered: A New Reading of Q. 4:12B," *SI* 55 (1982): 71.

28 The only extended treatment in Western languages of al-Ṭabarī's introduction to his *tafsīr* is to be found in an article published more than a hundred years ago by O. Loth entitled "Ṭabarī's Korankommentar," *ZDMG* 35 (1881):588–628.

29 As evidence of the fact that al-Ṭabarī himself has not ceased to be controversial see the study by Labīb Sa'īd that analyzes the exegete's attestations of variant readings (*qirā'āt*) and criticizes him for the inclusion of those now considered noncanonical. *Difā' 'an al-qirā'āt al-mutawātirah fī muwājahat al-Ṭabarī al-mufassir* (Cairo: Dār al-Ma'ārif, 1978).

the various sorts of exegetical material that may be applied to a particular verse. While he clearly aimed at comprehensiveness and was careful to include interpretations with which ultimately he did not agree, this commentator had very little patience with those who strayed too far from the literal sense. He was quick to discount such hypotheses as simply unsupported by the text. In similar fashion did he shy away from useless speculation about matters on which the text was silent. An example of the commonsensical approach that has won him such a central position in the history of Qur'ānic exegesis may be found in his treatment of *sūrat al-mā'idah* 5:114, the verse from which that *sūrah* derives its name "The Table." The verse is a prayer from Jesus, son of Mary, asking God "to send down on us a table from heaven which would be for us a feast. . . . " After citing numerous *ḥadīth*s that sought to discern the various delicacies the table might have held, al-Ṭabarī matter-of-factly states: "As for the correct view about what was on the table, it is said to be something to eat. Maybe it was fish or bread; maybe it was fruit from Paradise. There is no benefit in knowing and no harm in not knowing."[30]

Such reasoned insight has made al-Ṭabarī's work an indispensable reference for all subsequent exegetical endeavor. Not only has it been the source of various condensations and extracts, it has served as a major authority for more than a thousand years of Qur'ānic exegesis. A contemporary Muslim historian of *tafsīr*, Muḥammad al-Ṣabbāgh, has passed this judgment:

30 Abū Ja'far Muḥammad b. Jarīr al-Ṭabarī, *Jāmi' al-bayān 'an ta'wīl āy al-Qur'ān*, ed. by Maḥmūd Muḥammad Shākir and Aḥmad Muḥammad Shākir (Cairo: Dār al-Ma'ārif, 1374/1954), 11:232. This edition is complete through *sūrah Ibrāhīm* (14):27. For verses after that the following edition has been used: *Jāmi' al-bayān 'an ta'wīl āy al-Qur'ān*, 30 vols. in 15 (Beirut: Dār al-Fikr, 1405/1984). An earlier thirty-volume edition was published under the title *Jāmi'al-bayān fī tafsīr al-Qur'ān*, (Cairo: Maṭba'at al-Yamīnīyah, n.d.). An index keyed to the verse enumeration of Gustav Flügel has been published for this edition. Hermann Haussleiter, *Register zum Qorankommentar des Ṭabarī* (Strassburg: Karl J. Trübner, 1912). Efforts to translate abridged forms of this commentary into Western languages have begun. Three volumes of a beautifully bound French translation have appeared thus far: *Commentaire du Coran*, abridged, translated, and annotated by Pierre Godé (Paris: Éditions d'Art Les Heures Claires, 1983–). This production has been reviewed very negatively by Claude Gilliot, who criticizes Godé on a variety of grounds such as not using the Shākir edition and giving a false impression of exegetical consensus by the sort of abridgement he has done. "Traduire ou trahir at-Ṭabarī?" *Arabica* 34 (1987): 366–70. In this note Gilliot mentions that he has undertaken to complete the Shākir edition. *Ibid.*, 370. More recently, the first volume of an English translation has appeared: *The Commentary on the Qur'ān*, abridged, translated, and annotated by J. Cooper (Oxford: Oxford University Press, 1987). It is worth noting that abridgements of *Jāmi' al-bayān* are nothing new. One is credited to Abū Yaḥyā Muḥammad b. Ṣumādiḥ al-Tujībī (d. 419/1028), who died little more than a century after al-Ṭabarī. *Mukhtaṣar min tafsīr al-Imām al-Ṭabarī*, ed. by Muḥammad Ḥasan Abū al-'Azm al-Zufaytī (Cairo: al-Hay'ah al-Miṣrīyah al-'Āmmah lil-Ta'līf wa-al-Nashr, 1390–91/1970–71).

The literary and scientific character of Ibn Jarīr, his indications of what he considers the correct view among competing views and statements, his reliance on a sound, methodical procedure as well as scientific and lexical criteria create an unexcelled value for his book and give it a place not inferior to historical accounts and *ḥadīth* reports and traditions (*al-riwāyāt wa-al-āthār al-ḥadīthīyah*).[31]

AL-ṬŪSĪ

Muḥammad b. al-Ḥasan b. ʿAlī Abū Jaʿfar al-Ṭūsī was born in 385/995, some seventy-five years after the death of al-Ṭabarī. His birthplace in Ṭūs lies about 450 miles due east of al-Ṭabarī's natal city of Āmul.[32] That more easterly placement may be taken as a convenient symbol for the shift of power that had continued to occur in the intervening years. With the disintegration of caliphal authority, various power centers developed in the eastern lands of the ʿAbbāsid empire. The city of al-Ṭūsī's birth lived under the jurisdiction of one of these provincial regimes, the Sāmānids, whose court lay yet further east in Bukhārā. By the end of the tenth century the hegemony of this Sunnī dynasty had been considerably diminished by the Būyids (or Buwayhids) in the west and the Turkish nomads, the Qārākhānids (or Ilig Khans), in the east. When al-Ṭūsī was two years old, Sebüktigin, a Turkish slave commander who governed on behalf of the Sāmānids, gained independence from his overlords. His son, Maḥmūd of Ghaznah, who is most noted for his conquest of northwestern India and for his heavy-handed courtship of Firdawsī (d. 411/1020), Ibn Sīnā (d. 428/1037), and al-Bīrūnī (d. 442/1050), among others, solidified Ghaznavid control of Khurāsān, the province that includes the district of Ṭūs. Maḥmūd was a zealous Sunnī and the provinces he ruled may thus have become less tolerant of the Shīʿī heritage to which al-Ṭūsī laid claim.

In any event, al-Ṭūsī did not stay long in his native land but emigrated at the age of twenty-three to the more congenial environment of Baghdād. This city, which by 408/1017 had been under the authority of the Shīʿī Būyid dynasty for almost three-quarters of a century, was now the center of a Shīʿī intellectual renaissance. The historian Marshall Hodgson has called the interval between the closure of the lesser Ghaybah and the Saljūq occupation of Baghdād (940–1055) the "Shīʿī century" and has remarked that a "disproportionate number of the scholars and littérateurs of the time were Shīʿīs, even in fields other than the explicitly religious."[33] Al-Ṭūsī

31 Muḥammad al-Ṣabbāgh, *Lamaḥāt*, 188.

32 ʿAbbās al-Qummī in his biography of al-Ṭūsī includes a description of Ṭūs and its environs. See *Mashāhīr-i dānishmandān-i islām* (Tehran: Kitābfurūshī-yi Islāmīyah, 1350–51 [solar]/1972–73), 3:386.

33 Marshall G.S. Hodgson, *The Venture of Islam* (Chicago: University of Chicago Press,

himself, two of whose books number among the four canonical books (*al-kutub al-arbaʿah*) of the Shīʿīs, is a preeminent figure among these "scholars and littérateurs."

His early years in Baghdād, as might be expected, were those of student life. He first attached himself to Abū ʿAbdallāh Muḥammad b. Muḥammad al-Nuʿmān, known as al-Mufīd. This man was the most noted Shīʿī scholar and jurisconsult (*faqīh*) of his day; al-Ṭūsī studied with him for five years, until his death in 413/1022.[34] Intellectual leadership of the Shīʿī community in Baghdād then passed to al-Mufīd's student, al-Sharīf Abū al-Qāsim ʿAlī b. al-Ṭāhir al-Murtaḍā. That this scholar might well prove a suitable teacher for the future exegete is evident from some of the works ascribed to him, such as *Majāzāt al-Qur'ān* and *Kitāb maʿānī al-Qur'ān*.[35] Al-Ṭūsī's association with him was in fact a long and close one, lasting twenty-three years until al-Sharīf al-Murtaḍā's death in 436/1044.[36] The latter's interest in his young colleague extended beyond intellectual guidance to financial support. It is reported that al-Sharīf al-Murtaḍā "paid more attention to

1974), 2:37. The appropriateness of using the term "renaissance" to apply to this period of Islamic history has been debated, beginning with the publication of Adam Mez, *Die Renaissance des Islams* (1922; reprint, Hildesheim: G. Olms, 1968), English translation by Salahuddin Khuda Bukhsh and D.S. Margoliouth (London: Luzac, 1937). Roy Mottahedeh questioned the suitability of this epithet in *Loyalty and Leadership in an Early Islamic Society* (Princeton: Princeton University Press, 1980), 31. There he asks "what is being reborn?" but continues with the affirmation that "no one would deny the great flowering of culture of his period" [i.e., that studied by Mez]. More recently Joel L. Kraemer has argued at length in justification of its use. *Humanism in the Renaissance of Islam: The Cultural Revival During the Buyid Age* (Leiden: E.J. Brill, 1986).

34 R. Strothmann, "al-Mufīd," *EI*[1] 6:626; Martin J. McDermott, *The Theology of al-Shaikh al-Mufīd* (Beirut: Dar El-Machreq, 1978); Dominique Sourdel, *L'Imamisme vu par le Cheikh al-Mufīd* (Paris: Librairie Orientaliste Paul Guethner, 1974), which includes a translation of al-Mufīd's *Awā'il al-maqālāt fī al-madhāhib al-mukhtārāt*. Al-Mufīd is identified as a Shāfiʿī, and both al-Dāwūdī, (*Ṭabaqāt*, 2:126) and Jalāl al-Dīn al-Suyūṭī note that al-Ṭūsī issued *fatwā*s in accord with this *madhhab*. For al-Suyūṭī's remarks see his *Ṭabaqāt al-mufassirīn*, ed. by A. Meursinge (1839; reprint, Tehran: M.H. Asadi, 1960), 29. One of al-Ṭūsī's major works (and one of the two that he contributed to the "four books"), *Tahdhīb al-aḥkām*, forms a commentary to al-Mufīd's *al-Muqniʿah fī al-fiqh*.

35 C. Brockelmann, "al-Murtaḍā al-Sharīf," *EI*[1] 6:736.

36 Muḥammad Muḥsin Āghā Buzurg al-Ṭihrānī, "Ḥayāt al-Shaykh Ṭūsī," in Abū Jaʿfar Muḥammad b. al-Ḥasan al-Ṭūsī, *al-Tibyān fī tafsīr al-Qur'ān* (Najaf: al-Maṭbaʿah al-ʿIlmīyah, 1376/1957), 1: *jīm–dāl*. A Persian translation of Āghā Buzurg al-Ṭihrānī's biography of al-Ṭūsī has been published as *Zindagīnāmah-i Shaykh Ṭūsī*, trans. by ʿAlī Riḍā Mīrzā Muḥammad and Sayyid Ḥamīd Ṭabībīyān (Tehran: Jumhūr-i Islamī-yi Irān, 1360 [solar]/1982). Ḥasan al-Ṣadr marks this period as twenty-eight years and then contradicts this figure with the death dates he supplies for al-Mufīd and al-Murtaḍā. See Ḥasan al-Ṣadr, *Ta'sīs al-shīʿah li-ʿulūm al-Islām* (Baghdad: Sharikat al-Nashr wa-al-Ṭibāʿah al-ʿIrāqīyah al-Maḥdūdah, n.d.), 339.

him than to the rest of his pupils and earmarked for him each month twelve *dīnār*."[37]

Upon the death of al-Sharīf al-Murtaḍā, al-Ṭūsī assumed the leading intellectual position in the Baghdād Shīʿī community. He was then fifty-one years old. His house in the al-Karkh quarter of the city became an important destination for scholars both local and from afar. The extent of his influence is conveyed in biographical reports recounting how men learned in the religious sciences (*ʿulamāʾ*) and notables flocked to him to study and to hear him preach. His reputation was an international drawing card; students from far and wide sought him out. According to one account "he numbered three hundred Shīʿī authorities (*mujtahidūn*) among his students and an uncountable number of ordinary people."[38] So great was his renown that the caliph al-Qāʾim (422/1031–467/1075) appointed him to the chair of theology (*kalām*), an honor bestowed only on a scholar who had no equal: "At that time there was no one in Baghdād who outranked him or was more knowledgeable, so he was appointed to that honour."[39]

Al-Ṭūsī's relations with this caliph were not always so pleasant. On one occasion, the exegete was summoned before the caliph al-Qāʾim to answer charges that he had cursed some of the Companions, especially the first three caliphs. The evidence brought in support of this accusation was a prayer for the day of ʿĀshūrāʾ from al-Ṭūsī's *Kitāb al-miṣbāḥ* which asks God to curse "the first, second, third, fourth . . . and Yazīd as a fifth."[40] Called upon by the caliph to defend himself, al-Ṭūsī offered an inventive (if somewhat specious) response and thereby exonerated himself.[41] According to al-Shushtarī, the Caliph went so far as to award al-Ṭūsī a prize and to punish his slanderers.[42]

Shaykh al-Ṭāʾifah, as al-Ṭūsī is commonly called, enjoyed the prestige of his honors for little more than ten years. These represented the final years of Būyid domination and the last decade of the "Shīʿī century." For in 447/1055 the Saljūqs led by Tughril Beg "made a triumphant entry into

37 Āghā Buzurg al-Ṭihrānī, "Ḥayāt," 1: *jīm*.
38 Āghā Buzurg al-Ṭihrānī, "Ḥayāt," 1: *dāl*.
39 Āghā Buzurg al-Ṭihrānī, "Ḥayāt," 1: *dāl*.
40 Nūr Allāh al-Shushtarī, *Kitāb mustaṭab majālis al-muʾminīn* (Tehran: Kitābfurūshī-yi Islāmīyah, 1375/1956), 1:481.
41 al-Shushtarī, *Majālis*, 1:481-2. Al-Ṭūsī's response was a clever piece of extemporaneous exegesis. The first to be cursed was Qābīl (Cain) the killer of Abel, "who began murder on earth and opened the gateways of cursing upon himself." The second is identified as the one who in *sūrat al-aʿrāf* (7):77 hamstrung the she-camel of the prophet, Ṣāliḥ, while the third recalls the unnamed killer of Yaḥyā b. Zakarīyā (John the Baptist). Al-Ṭūsī concluded his listing with ʿAbd al-Raḥmān b. Muljam, the assassin of ʿAlī b. Abī Ṭālib.
42 al-Shushtarī, *Majālis*, 1:482. See also M. Hidayet Hosain, "al-Ṭūsī," *EI*[1] 8:982.

Baghdād, to free the caliph at last from the supremacy of the Shīʿī sectarians."[43] Civil disorder erupted and Shīʿī quarters of Baghdād were torched.[44] Al-Ṭūsī's house was plundered and burned, forcing him to flee the city.[45] In 448/1056 he settled in Najaf, wishing to live in the shadow of ʿAlī's tomb (and then to be buried nearby).[46] His biographers say little about the twelve years he spent there until his death in 460/1067.[47] Presumably he continued to teach and to write, the principal activities of his lifetime of scholarship.

Among those writings al-Ṭūsī's commentary on the Qur'ān, entitled *al-Tibyān fī tafsīr al-Qur'ān* (The Elucidation of the Interpretation of the Qur'ān), bulks large. In its most recent edition, it has been printed in ten volumes.[48] It is a comprehensive work, comparable in its breadth to that of al-Ṭabarī. Al-Ṭūsī, however, arranges his material in a somewhat different way. In a representative example, this exegete begins by mentioning any variant readings and next addresses issues of etymology and word signification. He then moves to a discussion of the meaning of particular words and phrases as they are used in the verse under examination. Matters of syntax are analyzed and, finally, *asbāb al-nuzūl* are offered where applicable. While the commentaries of al-Ṭabarī and al-Ṭūsī hold much in common, the latter's categorization of the diverse exegetical elements is a useful ex-

43 B. Spuler, "The Disintegration of the Caliphate in the East," in *The Cambridge History of Islam*, Vol. IA: *The Central Islamic Lands from Pre-Islamic Times to the First World War*, ed. by P.M. Holt, Ann K.S. Lambton, and Bernard Lewis (Cambridge: Cambridge University Press, 1970), 149.

44 For a fuller description of the events in Baghdād, including the destruction of the great Shīʿī library, see Muḥsin al-Amīn, *Aʿyān al-shīʿah* (Beirut: Maṭbaʿat al-Inṣāf, 1378/1959), 44:33f.

45 al-Shushtarī, *Majālis*, 1:480. Al-Dāwūdī mentions that several times his books were burned by a crowd in the courtyard of the Jāmiʿ al-Qaṣr. *Ṭabaqāt*, 2:127. See also Tāj al-Dīn Abū Naṣr ʿAbd al-Wahhāb al-Subkī, *Ṭabaqāt al-shāfiʿīyah al-kubrā* (Cairo: ʿĪsā al-Bābī al-Ḥalabī, 1384/1964), 4:126.

46 ʿAbbās al-Qummī notes that "his tomb is a famous place of pilgrimage in a mosque called *masjid-i Ṭūsī*." *Mashāhīr*, 3:385.

47 There is some doubt about al-Ṭūsī's death. Al-Dāwūdī gives the alternative possibility of 461/1068 and also mentions Kūfah (which lies a few miles east of Najaf) as the place of death. *Ṭabaqāt*, 2:127. Al-Subkī, also, gives Kūfah. See *Ṭabaqāt*, 4:127. The year most frequently cited, 460/1067, is famous as the founding date of the Niẓāmīyah *madrasah* in Baghdād by the Saljūq vizier, Niẓām al-Mulk; this was to be a major base for the next generation of Sunnī scholars. The great vizier was himself a native of Ṭūs.

48 Abū Jaʿfar Muḥammad b. al-Ḥasan al-Ṭūsī, *al-Tibyān fī tafsīr al-Qur'ān*, 10 vols. (Najaf: al-Maṭbaʿah al-ʿIlmīyah, 1376/1957). In his four-part chronological division of Shīʿī intellectual history, Henri Corbin places al-Ṭūsī in the second period, one noted principally for its summative theological work. *Histoire de la philosophie islamique* (Paris: Gallimard, 1964), 54. Mahmoud Ayoub provides a related chronology in "The Speaking Qur'ān and the Silent Qur'ān: A Study of the Principles and Development of Imāmī Shīʿī *tafsīr*," in *Approaches*, 184–86.

ercise. Although there is no slavish adherence to this methodology, al-Ṭūsī aims at comprehensive coverage throughout the entire work.[49] This factor has made the book a valuable source for later Shīʿī exegetes, such as those treated in this study, Abū al-Futūḥ Rāzī, Mullā Fatḥ Allāh Kāshānī, and Muḥammad Ḥusayn Ṭabāṭabā'ī.[50] In the case of the first two, reference to al-Ṭūsī has occasionally meant including portions of the latter's text – via Persian translation – into their own works. Another feature that has undoubtedly added to this *tafsīr*'s value for later scholars is its author's habit of introducing the discussion of a verse or a group of verses with a brief paraphrase or summary. A very useful exegetical handbook could be compiled from these synopses alone.

AL-ZAMAKHSHARĪ

Seven years after the death of al-Ṭūsī a man was born who moved the practice of Qur'ānic exegesis in a new direction. Abū al-Qāsim Maḥmūd b. ʿUmar al-Zamakhsharī was born in 467/1075 in the province of Khwārazm, a region just south of the Aral Sea. Al-Zamakhsharī's native city of Zamakhshar sits almost 500 miles due north of Ṭūs. By the eleventh century this area had become "like Khurāsān and Transoxiana, a bastion of Sunnī orthodoxy and scholarship."[51] It remained, however, one of the last, lingering strongholds of Muʿtazilī ideas, a school of thought with which al-Zamakhsharī was closely associated. At the time of his birth, Khwārazm had already passed from Ghaznavid to Saljūq domination. Al-Zamakhsharī spent the first eighteen years of his life as a subject of the great Saljūq sultan, Malik Shāh I.

These eighteen years were largely spent laying the educational foundation for his later achievements. Al-Zamakhsharī's earliest schooling occurred in his native city. Later he would travel to study with scholars in Bukhārā, Samarqand, and Baghdād. Probably his strongest intellectual influence was Maḥmūd b. Jarīr al-Ḍabbī al-Iṣbahānī, known as Abū Muḍar (d. 507/1113). This noted grammarian and philologist was deemed "unique in his era and time (*waḥīd dahrihi wa-awānihi*) in the sciences of lexicography,

49 Al-Ṭūsī's biographers frequently refer to this *tafsīr* as the first that incorporated all the sciences of the Qur'ān. See, for example, Ḥasan al-Ṣadr, *Ta'sīs*, 339 and Āghā Buzurg al-Ṭihrānī, "Ḥayāt," 1:*qāf*. As part of his 1974 thesis for the University of Baghdād, Ḥasan ʿĪsā al-Ḥakīm has studied *al-Tibyān* from the perspective of classical theological categories. *al-Shaykh al-Ṭūsī, Abū Jaʿfar Muḥammad b. al-Ḥasan* (Najaf: Maṭbaʿat al-Ādād, 1975).

50 The indebtedness of Abū ʿAlī al-Faḍl b. al-Ḥasan al-Ṭabarsī to al-Ṭūsī is discussed by Āghā Buzurg al-Ṭihrānī, "Ḥayāt," 1:*qāf*. For the estimations of *al-Tibyān* expressed by subsequent scholars, see al-Ḥakīm, *al-Shaykh al-Ṭūsī*, 310-12.

51 C.E. Bosworth, "Khwārazm," *EI*[2] 4:1063.

syntax, and medicine."[52] He was credited with introducing Muʿtazilī teaching to Khwārazm, where his proselytism was far-reaching.[53]

Al-Zamakhsharī's own profession of Muʿtazilism was open and forthright. He was in the habit of announcing himself, when making a call, by saying that "Abū al-Qāsim, the Muʿtazilī, is at the gate."[54] In line with the Muʿtazilī belief that the Qur'ān was created, this exegete is said to have begun his *tafsīr* with the phrase: "Praise be God who created (*khalaqa*) the Qur'ān." He was later persuaded to amend this to "Praise be God who made (*jaʿala*) the Qur'ān." According to Aḥmad b. Muḥammad b. Khallikān (d. 681/1282), who saw many copies of the work that began "Praise be God who sent down (*anzala*) the Qur'ān," this final modification was a scribal emendation and not from the pen of the author.[55]

By the time al-Zamakhsharī reached Baghdād, the golden days under the vizierate of Niẓām al-Mulk had ended. The Saljūq empire was feeling the strains of internecine rivalry. Yet the intellectual legacy of that era remained, continuing to attract students to Baghdād's *madrasah*s (study centers) and *masjid*s (mosques). While there al-Zamakhsharī received licentiates (*ijāzāt*) from some of that generation's leading scholars in *ḥadīth* and literary studies.[56]

From Baghdād he moved on to Mecca, where he settled for a while and to which he returned from subsequent travels. His tenure in that city was long enough to win him the cognomen of "God's neighbor (*jār Allāh*)."[57] It was on his second visit to Mecca that he wrote his commentary on the Qur'ān entitled *al-Kashshāf ʿan ḥaqā'iq ghawāmiḍ al-tanzīl wa-ʿuyūn al-aqāwīl fī wujūh al-ta'wīl* (Unveiler of the Real Meanings of the Hidden Matters of What Was Sent Down and the Choicest Statements About the Various Aspects of its Interpretation). This major work, completed in 528/1133, took al-Zamakhsharī only two years to write. In his Introduction to the *tafsīr* he notes that he had expected to spend more than thirty years on the task. The swiftness of its consummation he credits to the miraculous power of the Kaʿbah (*āyah min āyāt hādhā al-bayt al-muḥarram*) and the blessed influence (*barakah*) that emanates from it.[58]

52 Yāqūt, *Irshād*, 7:147.

53 Yāqūt, *Irshād*, 7:147.

54 Shams al-Dīn Aḥmad b. Muḥammad b. Khallikān, *Wafayāt al-aʿyān wa-anbā' al-zamān*, ed. by Iḥsān ʿAbbās (Beirut: Dār al-Thaqāfah, 1968), 5:170.

55 Ibn Khallikān, *Wafayāt*, 5:170.

56 al-Dāwūdī, *Ṭabaqāt*, 2:315; al-Suyūṭī, *Ṭabaqāt*, 41. A list of his more prominent students is provided by Lutpi Ibrahim, "Az-Zamakhsharī: His Life and Works," *IS* 19 (1980): 97–98.

57 al-Suyūṭī, *Ṭabaqāt*, 41.

58 Maḥmūd b. ʿUmar al-Zamakhsharī, *al-Kashshāf ʿan ḥaqā'iq ghawāmiḍ al-tanzīl wa-ʿuyūn al-aqāwīl fī wujūh al-ta'wīl* (Beirut: Dār al-Kitāb al-ʿArabī, 1366/1947), 1:*ghayn*.

Al-Zamakhsharī achieved considerable renown during his lifetime. Wherever he went students flocked to him in great numbers and sought to apprentice themselves.[59] Although born a Persian, his mastery of Arabic was (as with so many of his compatriots) exemplary. He taught in Arabic, refusing to speak to his students in Persian except for those who were absolute beginners.[60] His grammatical treatise, *al-Mufaṣṣal*, "became celebrated for its lucid and exhaustive exposition of the grammatical principles."[61]

The biographical material on al-Zamakhsharī strikes very few personal notes. An exception is the story surrounding a physical disability he suffered. As an adult, al-Zamakhsharī had a foot amputated. So that people he encountered would not assume that he had lost it in punishment for some crime, he carried with him a letter with many signatures attesting to the circumstances in which he was maimed.[62] With a touch of vanity, al-Zamakhsharī had a wooden foot made, over which he would throw a long cloak when out walking so that it could appear that he was merely lame.[63] In Baghdād, on one occasion, he was asked about the loss and explained it with an affecting tale. As a child, he answered, he had captured a sparrow and hobbled its leg. Frantic to escape, the bird snapped its fettered leg. His mother, who witnessed the sparrow's distress, begged God to treat her son likewise. Al-Zamakhsharī concluded by saying that in later years he fell from a horse on the road to Bukhārā and broke his foot.[64]

In 538/1144, at the age of seventy-one, al-Zamakhsharī died in Jurjānīyah, a town about twenty miles northwest of Zamakhshar.[65] His fame was such that Ibn Khallikān feels free to call him the "*imām* of his age," and al-Dāwūdī bestows upon him a string of superlatives.[66] A poem he

59 al-Suyūṭī, *Ṭabaqāt*, 41; al-Dāwūdī, *Ṭabaqāt*, 2:315.

60 Darwīsh al-Jundī, *al-Naẓm al-Qur'ānī fī Kashshāf al-Zamakhsharī* (Cairo: Dār Naḥḍah Miṣr lil-Ṭabʿ wa-al-Nashr, 1389/1969), 3.

61 Dionisius A. Agius, "Some Bio-bibliographical Notes on Abū 'l-Qāsim Maḥmūd b. ʿUmar al-Zamakhsharī," *Al-ʿArabiyya* 15 (1982): 109.

62 Ibn Khallikān, *Wafayāt*, 5:169.

63 Jalāl al-Dīn ʿAbd al-Raḥmān al-Suyūṭī, *Bughyat al-wuʿāh fī ṭabaqāt al-lughawīyīn wa-al-nuḥāh*, ed. by Muḥammad Abū al-Faḍl Ibrāhīm (Cairo: Maṭbaʿah ʿĪsā al-Bābī al-Ḥalabī, 1384/1965), 2:280.

64 Ibn Khallikān, *Wafayāt*, 5:170. In introducing this story Ibn Khallikān states that during one of the bitter winters in Khwārazm al-Zamakhsharī lost his foot from frostbite.

65 While most of al-Zamakhsharī's biographers agree on Jurjānīyah as his place of death, Abū al-Barakāt ʿAbd al-Raḥmān al-Anbārī (d. 577/1181) alludes to this only as "the capital (*qaṣabah*) of Khwārazm." *Nuzhāt al-alibbā' fī ṭabaqāt al-udabā'*, ed. by ʿAṭīyah ʿĀmir (Stockholm: Almquist and Wiksell, 1963), 232.

66 Ibn Khallikān, *Wafayāt*, 5:168; al-Dāwūdī, *Ṭabaqāt*, 2:315.

wrote to be engraved on his tombstone begs God to forgive him and, like a gracious host, to welcome this penitent guest.[67]

Another poem ascribed to him takes punning measure of his major work (and proves that he did not suffer from false modesty):

Truly *tafsīrs* in the world are uncounted,
But surely none among them is like my *Kashshāf*;
If you would seek guidance then constantly read it,
For ignorance is like disease and the *Kashshāf* like the cure (*wa-al-kashshāf ka-al-shāfī*).[68]

History justifies al-Zamakhsharī's pride in his *tafsīr*, among the most noted and most quoted of Qurʾānic commentaries. As Ibn Khallikān correctly observes, "Nothing like it had been written before."[69] Generations of readers have praised the *Kashshāf*; the noted fourteenth-century scholar ʿAbd al-Raḥmān b. Muḥammad b. Khaldūn (d. 808/1406) urged students to make use of its "remarkable and varied linguistic information."[70]

Yet Ibn Khaldūn's praise was tempered with caution, for he recognized that al-Zamakhsharī used verses of the Qurʾān to argue "in favor of the pernicious doctrines of the Muʿtazilah."[71] Although this does not destroy the value of the book for him, he warns that only the scholar who "is acquainted with the orthodox dogmas and knows the arguments in their defense" may safely use it.[72] (At least with respect to the verses examined for this study, there is very little that is obviously Muʿtazilī about the *Kashshāf*'s treatment.) The chief sin of which al-Zamakhsharī and other Muʿtazilī thinkers were accused is that of placing limitation on the divine. In their efforts to balance human freedom of the will and divine justice

67 al-Dāwūdī, *Ṭabaqāt*, 2:316.

68 al-Dāwūdī, *Ṭabaqāt*, 2:316. Muḥammad Ḥusayn Abū Mūsā has collected additional citations of al-Zamakhsharī's poetry relevant to the biographical information presented in the introduction to his *al-Balāghah al-Qurʾānīyah fī tafsīr al-Zamakhsharī* (Cairo: Dār al-Fikr al-ʿArabī, n.d.).

69 Ibn Khallikān, *Wafayāt*, 5:168.

70 Ibn Khaldūn, *The Muqaddimah*, 2nd revised ed., trans. by Franz Rosenthal (Princeton: Princeton University Press, 1967), 2:447; see also 3:338–39. Carl Brockelmann observes that Ibn Khaldūn's commendation notwithstanding, manuscripts of *al-Kashshāf* "are rarer in the west than in the east." "al-Zamakhsharī," *EI*[1] 8:1205.

71 Ibn Khaldūn, *The Muqaddimah*, 2:447. A nineteenth-century work on Ḥanafī biography underscores this assessment with a reference to the things that al-Zamakhsharī has slipped into (*dasāʾis*) his work with the consequence that "some of our jurisprudents have forbidden the study of his *tafsīr*." Abū al-Ḥasanāt Muḥammad al-Laknawī, *Kitāb al-fawāʾid al-bahīyah fī tarājim al-Ḥanafīyah*, ed. by Abū Firās al-Naʿsānī (Beirut: Dār al-Maʿrifah, n.d.), 20.

72 Ibn Khaldūn, *The Muqaddimah*, 2:447. For a discussion of al-Zamakhsharī's exegesis from the perspective of the five principles (*uṣūl*) of classical Muʿtazilī dogmatics, see Aḥmad Muḥammad al-Ḥūfī, *al-Zamakhsharī* (Cairo: Dār al-Fikr al-ʿArabī, 1386/1966), 112–66.

(ʿadl) they insisted that God could not (rather than would not) will evil. For orthodox Muslims such philosophical rationalism amounts to blasphemously limiting God's power.[73] The Muʿtazilī understanding of God's absolute oneness (*tawḥīd*), on the other hand, forced them to offer a metaphorical explanation for Qurʾānic anthropomorphisms and to assert the createdness of the Qurʾān.

The reliance on reason that such exegesis demanded runs counter to the more accepted form of that task, *al-tafsīr bi-al-maʾthūr*, and lands Muʿtazilī commentary, of which al-Zamakhsharī's is arguably the most famous example, squarely in the category of *al-tafsīr bi-al-raʾy*. This latter is occasionally tolerated but always distrusted as potentially misleading. Rashid Ahmad (Jullandri) summarizes the concern: "When reason exceeds its own limitations and tries to interpret the Qurʾān on its own terms, then the Qurʾān is relegated into a secondary place and commentary becomes more or less a collection of dialectical and theological views."[74]

As a mouthpiece for the dogmas of the *ahl al-ʿadl wa-al-tawḥīd* (People of [Divine] Justice and Unicity), as the Muʿtazilīs preferred to style themselves, the *Kashshāf* was frequently excoriated. However, as a study of Qurʾānic philology and syntax the work has been treasured since its composition.[75] Al-Zamakhsharī's analyses were felt to be so fruitful that many attempts were made to summarize his work and/or bowdlerize it of offending Muʿtazilī views. The most famous example is the *Anwār al-tanzīl wa-asrār al-taʾwīl* of ʿAbdallāh b. ʿUmar al-Bayḍāwī (d. 685/1286 or 692/1293). This extremely popular commentary has been described as "largely a condensed and amended edition of al-Zamakhsharī's *Kashshāf*," with heavy stress on linguistic questions.[76]

To understand al-Zamakhsharī's commentary entails acquaintance with the classical rules of Arabic grammar. On the basis of these rules, "al-Zamakhsharī analyzed the stylistic peculiarities of the Koran and gave reasons for the apparent irregularities in the text."[77] Deviations of word order

73 A contemporary Muslim writer has criticized the Muʿtazilah on the grounds that their "thinking on theological matters threatened to sacrifice religious interests to speculative consistency. What the Muʿtazilah ignored was that religion, as a system of faith and morals, is not amenable to purely discursive reasoning and metaphysics, because the motivations of the two are entirely different." Mazher ud-Din Siddiqi, "Some Aspects of the Muʿtazilī Interpretation of the Qurʾān," *IS* 3 (1963): 116.

74 Rashid Ahmad (Jullandri), "Qurʾānic Exegesis and Classical Tafsīr," *IQ* 12 (1968): 95.

75 Juan Vernet has even found an instance in which the commentary was used by an early sixteenth-century Spanish bishop in his sermons against Islam. See "Le *tafsīr* au service de la polémique antimusulmane," *SI* 32 (1970): 305–09.

76 J. Robson, "al-Bayḍāwī," EI^2 1:1129. ʿAbdallāh b. ʿUmar al-Bayḍāwī, *Anwār al-tanzīl wa-asrār al-taʾwīl*, ed. by H.O. Fleischer (1846–48; reprint, Osnabrück: Biblio Verlag, 1968).

77 J.J.G. Jansen, *Interpretation*, 63.

and of morphology are exhaustively explained. Unusual significations are justified, frequently by recourse to the corpus of classical poetry. Such syntactical and lexical idiosyncrasies are then lauded as marks of the Qur'ān's rhetorical preeminence. What begins as philological analysis becomes, in al-Zamakhsharī's hands, a paean to the doctrine of the Qur'ān's inimitability (*iʿjāz*).[78]

ABŪ AL-FUTŪḤ RĀZĪ

The second of the Shīʿī commentators to be discussed is a younger contemporary of al-Zamakhsharī known as Abū al-Futūḥ Rāzī. His full name is given as Jamāl al-Dīn Abū al-Futūḥ Ḥusayn b. ʿAlī b. Muḥammad b. Aḥmad Ḥusayn b. Aḥmad Khuzāʿī Naysābūrī Rāzī.[79] His biographers, who unanimously extol him as a scholar of *tafsīr* and *kalām* and even as a leading literary figure, trace his lineage back to the Companion of the Prophet, Nāfiʿ b. Budayl b. Warqā' al-Khuzāʿī, who fell in the battle of Ṣiffīn while fighting at the side of ʿAlī.[80] The Banū Khuzāʿah, "who were among the party (*shīʿah*) of the family of Muḥammad," are remembered as one of the "great Arab families who settled in foreign lands."[81] Abū al-Futūḥ's grandfather, his paternal great uncle, his son, and his nephew were all noted scholars and writers who have secured a place in Shīʿī intellectual history.[82]

Very little is known about this scholar's life although he is remembered as among the most noted intellectuals of his generation.[83] Even the dates of his birth and death are matters of conjecture. He is reported to have been a student of Abū ʿAlī Ḥasan al-Ṭūsī who died around 500/1106. Abū ʿAlī was the son of the Shīʿī exegete discussed earlier, Abū Jaʿfar Muḥammad b. al-Ḥasan al-Ṭūsī. On the basis of this date and those of some of Abū al-Futūḥ's students, Henri Massé has decided that this commentator was born around 480/1087 and lived until at least 525/1131.[84]

78 An analysis of al-Zamakhsharī's views on *iʿjāz al-Qur'ān* may be found in Muṣṭafā al-Sāwī al-Juwaynī's *Minhaj al-Zamakhsharī fī tafsīr al-Qur'ān wa-bayān iʿjāzihi* (Cairo: Dār al-Maʿārif, 1379/1959), 215–61.

79 Muḥammad Shafīʿī, *Mufassirān-i shīʿah* (Shiraz: Dānishgāh-i Pahlavī, 1349 [solar]/1970), 99.

80 al-Shushtarī, *Majālis*, 1:489. A recent edition of Abū al-Futūḥ Rāzī's *tafsīr* includes a genealogical chart for the author. *Rawḥ al-jinān wa-rūḥ al-janān* (Qum: Intishārat-i Kitāb, n.d.), 5:622.

81 Muḥammad Bāqir al-Mūsawī al-Khwānsārī, *Rawḍāt al-jannāt*, ed. by Asadallāh Ismāʿīlīyān (Tehran: Maktabat-i Ismāʿīlīyān, 1392/1972), 2:314–15.

82 Abū al-Ḥasan Shaʿrānī, "Muqaddimah," in Abū al-Futūḥ Rāzī's *Rawḥ al-jinān wa-rūḥ al-janān* (Tehran: Kitābfurūshī-yi Islāmīyah, 1382/1962), 1:2–19.

83 Ḥasan al-Ṣadr calls him "the leading shaikh of his era." *Ta'sīs*, 340.

84 Henri Massé, "Le *tafsīr* d'Abū 'l-Futūḥ Rāzī," in *Mélanges offerts à William Marçais*,

His *tafsīr* on the Qurʾān entitled *Rawḥ al-jinān wa-rūḥ al-janān* (The Cool Breeze of Paradise and [God's] Breath for the Soul) is "one of the earliest – if not the earliest – of the Shīʿite commentaries composed in Persian."[85] According to one biographer it "contains everything which minds desire and from which eyes derive delight."[86] The work itself is structured in a very methodical manner. A verse or group of verses is quoted with an interlinear Persian translation and then followed by a careful treatment of each individual phrase. Muḥammad Shafīʿī summarized the scope of this treatment by saying: "He brings out particularities of morphology (*ṣarf*) and syntax (*naḥw*) and stylistic matters (*adab*), issues concerning the occasion of revelation (*sabab al-nuzūl*), and differences about the reading of words, and also *ḥadīth* applicable to the subject."[87] Shafīʿī continues by noting that, when appropriate, Abū al-Futūḥ includes matters of *fiqh* and *kalām* as well as making reference, for lexical reasons, to authentic Arabic poetry.[88]

In the preface to his *tafsīr*, Abū al-Futūḥ outlines the intellectual preparation needed for one who would undertake the exegetical task and cautions those without the requisite background to forsake the challenge.[89] If such a one recklessly perseveres, the errors he is certain to make will unmask him and provide a proof of his ignorance (*ḥujjatī bāshad bar jahl-i ū*).[90] Before commencing the *tafsīr* proper, Abū al-Futūḥ includes in this introductory material a discussion of some general hermeneutical topics. He touches upon such matters as the various names by which the Qurʾān is known, the categories of verses it contains and the divine reward promised to those who recite it.[91]

A contemporary Persian study of the *Rawḥ al-jinān* by ʿAskar Ḥuqūqī praises, in particular, Abū al-Futūḥ's lucid prose style. Ḥuqūqī finds the lack of artificiality and excessive formality a refreshing change from much classical Persian prose.[92] He remarks upon this exegete's habit of inserting Arabic words and phrases in the midst of his Persian sentences and lists

ed. by Institut d'Études Islamiques de l'Université de Paris (Paris: G.P. Maisonneuve, 1950), 244. Massé (p. 245) reports that the earliest manuscript of the *tafsīr* that he saw was one (number 134) in the Library of Mashhad dated 556/1161.

85 Henri Massé, "Abū 'l-Futūḥ al-Rāzī," *EI*² 1:120. The title of this work is sometimes given as *Rawḍ al-jinān wa-rawḥ al-janān*.

86 ʿAbbās Qummī, *Mashāhīr*, 1:240.

87 Shafīʿī, *Mufassirān*, 100.

88 Shafīʿī, *Mufassirān*, 100.

89 Ḥusayn b. ʿAlī Abū al-Futūḥ Rāzī, *Rawḥ al-jinān wa-rūḥ al-janān* (Tehran: Kitābfurūshī-yi Islāmīyah, 1382/1962), 1:1–2.

90 Abū al-Futūḥ Rāzī, *Rawḥ al-jinān*, 1:2.

91 Abū al-Futūḥ Rāzī, *Rawḥ al-jinān*, 1:2–16.

92 ʿAskar Ḥuqūqī, *Taḥqīq dar tafsīr-i Abū al-Futūḥ Rāzī* (Tehran: Dānishgāh-i Ṭihrān, 1346 [solar]/1968), 1:58–60.

many examples of this.[93] For the convenience of contemporary readers, Ḥuqūqī includes a glossary of Abū al-Futūḥ's vocabulary with modern Persian equivalents.[94]

The number of scholars who are said to be indebted to this exegete include Fakhr al-Dīn al-Rāzī (d. 606/1210), al-Bayḍāwī, and Muḥammad Bāqir al-Majlisī (d. 1110/1698–99). Nūr Allāh al-Shushtarī (d. 1019/1610) notes in the *Majālis al-Muʾminīn* that al-Zamakhsharī was a contemporary of Abū al-Futūḥ and that some of the verses used in the *Kashshāf* were also used in the *Rawḥ al-jinān*. He insists, however, that Abū al-Futūḥ never saw a copy of the *Kashshāf*.[95] Fakhr al-Dīn al-Rāzī, on the other hand, is said to have borrowed the basis of his *al-Tafsīr al-kabīr* from this work of Abū al-Futūḥ's, simply including "his own misgivings (about particular points) within that basic structure in an effort to ward off any accusation that he was being presumptuous in so using it."[96]

Abū al-Futūḥ Rāzī is also credited with the production of an Arabic *tafsīr* but his biographers remain somewhat tentative about this because they confess to never having seen it. In fact, the size of this reputed work is the subject of some controversy between al-Shushtarī and al-Khwānsārī. Working from reports that this commentator wrote twenty volumes of *tafsīr*, al-Shushtarī speculates that, given the relatively few volumes of his Persian *tafsīr* (he does not mention a number), most of this output must be in Arabic.[97] Al-Khwānsārī retorts that there is no necessary correlation between the length of the composition and number of volumes into which it is divided.[98] His implication is that the Persian *tafsīr* may be as long as, or longer than, the Arabic.

Controversy erupts between these two biographers yet again over the subject of Abū al-Futūḥ's tomb. Because the birth and death dates of this exegete are unrecorded, it was customary for his early biographers to place him by mentioning the death date (588/1192) of his student Ibn Shahr-

93 Ḥuqūqī, *Taḥqīq*, 1:74–83.

94 Ḥuqūqī, *Taḥqīq*, 1:85–133.

95 al-Shushtarī, *Majālis*, 1:490. Henri Massé notes that Abū al-Futūḥ refers to al-Zamakhsharī several times in his *tafsīr*, even calling him "*al-imām*, our shaikh." Therefore, he argues, the absence of reference to the *Kashshāf* means either that the *Rawḥ al-jinān* was finished before the *Kashshāf* or, at least, before the *Kashshāf* reached Iranian lands. See Massé, "Le *tafsīr*," 245.

96 al-Shushtarī, *Majālis*, 1:490. Henri Massé judges this assessment "surprenante" and justifies his reservation with the remark: "Dans le *Rawḍ*, remarquable en général par sa clarté, l'on ne trouve ni l'attitude indécise à l'égard du muʿtazilisme ni les longues digressions philosophiques et métaphysiques qui caractérisent les *Mafātīḥ al-ghayb* de Fakhr al-Dīn." "Le *tafsīr*," 249.

97 al-Shushtarī, *Majālis*, 1:490.

98 al-Khwānsārī, *Rawḍāt*, 2:316–17.

āshūb.[99] Given this uncertainty about his personal history, it is not surprising that the place of his burial was also a matter of doubt. Al-Shushtarī reports that his tomb is in Iṣfahān.[100] Al-Khwānsārī, on the other hand, questions this on the basis that it is not so indicated in the customary sources.[101] The more recent biography by ʿAbbās Qummī states "the tomb of Abū al-Futūḥ is in the town of Rayy in the courtyard of Imām-Zādah Hamzah [i.e., his shrine], son of Mūsā b. Jaʿfar, in the vicinity of [Shāh] ʿAbd al-ʿAẓīm Ḥasanī."[102]

IBN AL-JAWZĪ

The life of Abū al-Faraj ʿAbd al-Raḥmān b. ʿAlī b. Muḥammad b. al-Jawzī spans most of the sixth/twelfth century. His was a public and politically active career with Baghdād as its stage. He was born there in 510/1116 at the end of the caliphate of al-Mustaẓhir.[103] Early twelfth-century Baghdād was a city buffeted from many sides. Continual internecine rivalry preoccupied the Saljūq dynasty in its declining years. The whole area of Iraq and western Persia suffered from the guerrilla warfare of the Ismāʿīlī Assassins. A further concern was the Crusaders' attacks on Palestine and the Levant. Although Baghdād itself was not under attack, it received urgent appeals for troops and other defensive support.

Ibn al-Jawzī was born into a family of some means and enjoyed an easeful and even pampered childhood.[104] His family were traders in brass (or copper) and for this reason he is sometimes cited as Ibn al-Jawzī al-Ṣaffār or simply as ʿAbd al-Raḥmān b. ʿAlī al-Ṣaffār.[105] Because his father died while he was still quite young, his mother and paternal aunt became responsible

99 al-Shaʿrānī, "Muqaddimah," *Rawḥ al-jinān*, 1:7–8; Qummī, *Mashāhīr*, 1:240.

100 al-Shushtarī, *Majālis*, 1:490.

101 al-Khwānsārī, *Rawḍāt*, 2:317.

102 Qummī, *Mashāhīr*, 1:241.

103 His birth date is a matter of disagreement. Al-Dāwūdī (*Ṭabaqāt*, 1:270) gives 508 as well as 510. In his biographical introduction to Ibn al-Jawzī's *tafsīr*, Muḥammad Zuhayr al-Shāwīs recounts a remark from the exegete to the effect that his father died in 514 and that his mother said he was about three years old at the time. On the basis of this al-Shāwīs offers a birth date of 511 or 512. See "Tarjamat al-muʾallif," *Zād al-masīr fī ʿilm al-tafsīr* (Beirut: al-Maktab al-Islāmī lil-Ṭibāʿah wa-al-Nashr, 1384/1964), 1:21. In H. Laoust, "Ibn al-Djawzī," EI^2 3:751, the Gregorian equivalent for the birth date of 510 should be 1116, not 1126. That for his death date of 597 should be 1201, not 1200, as he died in the month of Ramaḍān.

104 al-Shāwīs, "Tarjamah," 1:23.

105 al-Shāwīs, "Tarjamah," 1:21 and al-Dāwūdī, *Ṭabaqāt*, 1:272. The *nisbah*, al-Jawzī, remains a matter of discussion. It is most commonly derived from either a section of Baṣrah (where, presumably, Ibn al-Jawzī's eponym lived) or the "incomparable" walnut tree in the courtyard of his ancestor's house in Wāsiṭ. See al-Dāwūdī, *Ṭabaqāt*, 1:270 and al-Shāwīs, "Tarjamah," 1:21.

for raising him, there being apparently no eligible male to do so. It was his aunt who took him, at the age of six, to the mosque school of Abū al-Faḍl b. Nāṣir, a noted Baghdādī *ḥāfiẓ*.[106] Under his guidance Ibn al-Jawzī memorized the Qurʾān and commenced the study of *ḥadīth*. From there he went on to study with Baghdād's leading scholars. His breadth of interest and ability was remarkable. He reported that from very early childhood he was fascinated with all areas of knowledge and found it impossible to restrict his range of interest.[107] As a youth the search for knowledge became his consuming passion, one for which he was willing to sacrifice the comforts of a more leisured existence. In illustration of this stands a charming vignette of his student days. When he would go out in search of *ḥadīth*, it was his habit to carry with him a chunk of dried flat-bread. Sitting by the ʿĪsā canal and dunking his dry loaf he found "a delight in knowledge and sweetness in belief (*ladhdhat al-ʿilm wa-ḥalāwat al-īmān*) which he feared would make him sound odd if he explained it."[108]

Among his famous teachers were Abū al-Ḥasan b. Zāghūnī (d. 527/1133) and Abū Manṣūr Mawhūb b. Aḥmad al-Jawālīqī (d. 539/1144). The former held a study circle in the Jāmiʿ al-Manṣūr every Friday morning before the prayer. The latter, who was the leading Arabic philologist of his day, taught at the Niẓāmīyah *madrasah* and was *imām* to Caliph al-Muqtafī (530/1136–555/1160). Ibn al-Jawzī's intellectual formation was not limited to these direct contacts. Henri Laoust has noted the influence of the following earlier scholars as well: the Shāfiʿī Ashʿarī Abū Nuʿaym al-Iṣfahānī (d. 430/1038–39), the traditionist and jurisconsult al-Khaṭīb al-Baghdādī, and the Ḥanbalī Abū al-Wafāʾ ʿAlī b. ʿAqīl (d. 513/1119–20).[109] Allusion to his ascetic practices can also be found in the biographical material on this exegete. Yet while reference is made to both supererogatory fasting (*sarada al-ṣawm muddatan*) and to following those who practiced renunciation (*ittabaʿa al-zuhhād*), the preeminence of a life concentrated upon the religious sciences gradually asserted itself within him.[110]

While this education and spiritual formation laid the groundwork for Ibn al-Jawzī's later renown as a *ḥāfiẓ*, Ḥanbalī *faqīh*, exegete, historian, and man of letters (*adīb*), it is as a stirring preacher (*wāʿiẓ*) that he became

106 al-Shāwīs, "Tarjamah," 1:21.

107 al-Shāwīs, "Tarjamah," 1:23.

108 al-Shāwīs, "Tarjamah," 1:23.

109 H. Laoust, "Ibn al-Djawzī," 3:751. Āminah Muḥammad Naṣīr has collected biographical information on Ibn al-Jawzī's principal teachers and intellectual forebears in *Abū al-Faraj b. al-Jawzī, ārāʾuhu al-kalāmīyah wa-al-akhlāqīyah* (Cairo: Dār al-Shurūkh, 1407/1987), 43–53.

110 ʿAbd al-Raḥmān b. Aḥmad b. Rajab, *Dhayl ʿalā ṭabaqāt al-ḥanābilah*, (Cairo: Dār al-Maʿārif, n.d.), 1:403. The criticisms of certain forms of Ṣūfism that Ibn al-Jawzī made in works such as his *Talbīs Iblīs* should be read against this biographical background.

most celebrated. Testimonies to this fame echo through his biographies. His congregations were filled with the notables of Baghdād and both his sonorous recitation of the Qur'ān and his impassioned sermons would move men to tears.[111] The size claimed for these congregations strains one's credence. Some of his audiences were said to have numbered over 100,000 and it is claimed that he preached regularly to upwards of 10,000. His grandson, Shams al-Dīn Abū al-Muẓaffar Sibṭ b. al-Jawzī, who was himself a celebrated preacher, professed to have heard these figures from his grandfather's own lips. He also heard him credit the success of his exhortations with 100,000 penitents and 20,000 converts.[112]

The Andalusian traveler Abū al-Ḥusayn b. Jubayr has left a detailed and colorful account of his attendance at three of Ibn al-Jawzī's sermons. The effect he had on his listeners so impressed Ibn Jubayr that the traveler was moved to exclaim: "If we had ridden the crest of the sea and wandered the desert's emptiness only to be present in this man's audience, it would have been a good deal and a fortunate and successful effort."[113] On one memorable evening Ibn al-Jawzī was escorted to his *minbar* (pulpit) by throngs from the Bāb al-Baṣrah and the Ḥarbīyah quarters of Baghdād. The crowd, which was estimated at 300,000, lit his way with a thousand candles.[114]

His preaching and teaching were marked not only by extraordinary el-

111 al-Shāwīs, "Tarjamah," 1:25. A recent monograph on Ibn al-Jawzī's *Dhamm al-hawā* highlights his popularity as a preacher within the lively intellectual climate of twelfth-century Baghdād. Stefan Leder, *Ibn al-Jauzī und seine Kompilation wider die Leidenschaft: der Traditionalist in gelehrter Überlieferung und originärer Lehre* (Beirut: Orient-Institut der Deutschen Morgenländischen Gesellschaft; Wiesbaden: Franz Steiner, 1984).

112 al-Dāwūdī, *Ṭabaqāt*, 1:273. Al-Shāwīs ("Tarjamah," 1:24) adds the statement from Ibn al-Jawzī that "due to me two hundred of the *ahl al-dhimmah* became Muslims." On the grounds of textual interconnections, Tryggve Kronholm argues persuasively to secure the authorial claim of a manuscript attributed to Sibṭ b. al-Jawzī. "Akhbaranā jaddī: Preliminary Observations on the dependence of Sibṭ ibn al-Jauzī in his *Kitāb al-Jalīs aṣ-ṣāliḥ wal-anīs an-nāṣiḥ* on the Works of His Grandfather," *Orientalia Suecana* 33–35 (1984–86): 241–56.

113 Abū al-Ḥusayn Muḥammad b. Aḥmad b. Jubayr, *Riḥlah*, ed. by William Wright (Leiden: E.J. Brill, 1907), 222. This passage has become a favorite quote for contemporary students of Ibn al-Jawzī. See ʿAbd al-Raḥmān Ṣāliḥ ʿAbdallāh, *Ibn al-Jawzī wa-tarbiyat al-ʿaql* (Mecca: Sharikah Makkah lil-Ṭibāʿah wa-al-Nashr, 1406/1986), 14; Merlin Swartz, "The Rules of Popular Preaching in Twelfth-Century Baghdād, According to Ibn al-Jawzī," in *Prédication*, 233. J. Pedersen checks Ibn Jubayr's account with the information found in Ibn al-Jawzī's own *Kitāb al-mudhish*. "The Islamic Preacher: *wāʿiẓ, mudhakkir, qāṣṣ*," *Ignace Goldziher Memorial Volume*, ed. by Samuel Löwinger and Joseph Somogyi (Budapest: n.p., 1948), 1:240–43.

114 al-Shāwīs, "Tarjamah," 1:25. Merlin Swartz cites this as the largest total given for any of Ibn al-Jawzī's *majālis al-waʿẓ* but also notes that the competitive arena of popular preaching in Baghdād may account for some degree of exaggeration. "The Rules," 232. Swartz has published an edition and translation of Ibn al-Jawzī's monograph on popular preaching. *Kitāb al-quṣṣāṣ wa'l-mudhakkirīn* (Beirut: Dar El-Machreq, 1971).

oquence but also by a remarkable ability to extemporize. Two examples must suffice. The first concerns a question addressed to him in a period of heightened Sunnī-Shīʿī conflict. Asked to judge the superiority of Abū Bakr or ʿAlī, Ibn al-Jawzī responded: "The more excellent of the two is the one whose daughter is beneath him (*taḥtahu*)."[115] This deliberately ambiguous answer apparently satisfied both factions because they could apply it equally to ʿĀʾishah and Fāṭimah. Ibn Khallikān was particularly impressed with this reply which he thought would be "extremely good if it were to result from full reflection and close examination, let alone *ex tempore*!"[116] The second instance is Ibn al-Jawzī's quick reply to being asked whether praising God or asking His forgiveness is better: "Filthy dress is more in need of soap than of incense."[117]

As a writer, Ibn al-Jawzī ranks among the most prolific in Islamic history. In fact, the noted Damascene historian Shams al-Dīn al-Dhahabī (d. 748/1348) is reported to have stated unequivocally: "I know of no scholar who wrote as much as this man wrote."[118] His daily output is said to have averaged twenty-four pages and his range of topics matched his encyclopedic interests.[119] Most prominent are his works in history, biography, heresiography, polemic, and *tafsīr*. His strong Ḥanbalism is evident throughout and decisively influences his choice of subjects. Among those of subsequent generations who were deeply influenced by his writings, the fourteenth-century Ḥanbalī Ibn Taymīyah is certainly the most prominent.

Somewhat uncharacteristically, his biographers include details not only about Ibn al-Jawzī's appearance but also about his diet, dress, and demeanor. He is described as possessing a well-formed face, a pleasant disposition, a fine voice, a well-coordinated carriage, and a good sense of humor.[120] He is credited with being careful of his health and diet so as to keep his mind sharp. His success in this is evident from reports of his witticisms and quick retorts.[121]

Such were apparently not enough to save him from the change of fortune that marred his declining years. Ibn al-Jawzī's career had flourished under the caliphates of al-Muqtafī (530/1136–555/1160), al-Mustanjid (555/1160–566/1170), and al-Mustaḍīʾ (566/1170–575/1180). Throughout this period his fame in both *minbar* and *madrasah* steadily advanced. By 574/1178–79 he was "directing five *madrasah*s and had already written more

115 Ibn Khallikān, *Wafayāt*, 3:141.
116 Ibn Khallikān, *Wafayāt*, 3:142.
117 al-Shāwīs, "Tarjamah," 1:24.
118 al-Dāwūdī, *Ṭabaqāt*, 1:272.
119 al-Dāwūdī, *Ṭabaqāt*, 1:274.
120 al-Dāwūdī, *Ṭabaqāt*, 1:274.
121 al-Dāwūdī not only includes details of diet but also notes that Ibn al-Jawzī was reputed to have an eye for beautiful women. *Ṭabaqāt*, 1:272.

than one hundred and fifty works."[122] But with the accession of al-Nāṣir to the caliphate, shifts of power were precipitated that affected Ibn al-Jawzī. During his reign of almost half a century (575/1180–622/1225) al-Nāṣir tried to recoup for the ʿAbbāsid caliphate some of the power it had lost under Būyid and Saljūq domination. He dismissed officials who had been instrumental in promoting Ibn al-Jawzī and appointed others in their place. One of these appointees was the Shīʿī vizier Ibn al-Qaṣṣāb. Moreover, at the instigation of a nameless enemy and for an unknown reason, Ibn al-Jawzī was transported to Wāsiṭ and placed under house arrest for five years. His grandson, the above-mentioned Shams al-Dīn Abū al-Muẓaffar Ṣibt b. al-Jawzī, pleaded his grandfather's case with the Caliph's mother, who interceded and Ibn al-Jawzī was freed.[123] Within two years of his return, however, he died on 13 Ramaḍān 597/1201 and was buried, after a large funeral procession, in the cemetery of the Ḥarb Gate. It was for this most famous of twelfth-century Ḥanbalīs a fitting resting place, for Aḥmad b. Ḥanbal himself lay entombed there.[124]

Ibn al-Jawzī's *tafsīr*, *Zād al-masīr fī ʿilm al-tafsīr* (Provisions for the Journey 'into' the Science of Exegesis), runs to nine volumes in its most recent edition.[125] Although infrequently mentioned by Western scholars of the genre, it provides an excellent overview of traditional exegesis of the Qur'ān. Standing temporally between the far larger works of al-Ṭabarī and Ismāʿīl b. ʿUmar b. Kathīr, this *tafsīr* summarizes and coordinates the principal areas of exegetical debate on each verse. The approach Ibn al-Jawzī takes is a highly ordered one. In fact, the *Zād al-masīr* is a kind of shorthand *tafsīr*. So elliptical is his method that Ibn al-Jawzī's work would be very difficult to understand for one who had no acquaintance with the other principal works of traditional exegesis.

This exegete's basic procedure is to divide the verse under discussion into discrete words or phrases and then to present, in numerical form, the various interpretations that have been adduced for each. The interpretations themselves have usually been extracted from the relevant exegetical *ḥadīth*s, in which case he includes the name (e.g., Ibn ʿAbbās, Qatādah, Mujāhid) to which the *ḥadīth* is attributed. He never, however, includes the full text of the *ḥadīth* or the complete *isnād*. His *tafsīr* was surely intended for an audience so deeply versed in the subject that such full citation would have been superfluous.

122 H. Laoust, "Ibn al-Djawzī," 3:751.
123 al-Dāwūdī, *Ṭabaqāt*, 1 273–74.
124 Guy Le Strange, *Baghdad during the Abbasid Caliphate* (Oxford: Clarendon Press, 1900), 158.
125 Abū al-Faraj ʿAbd al-Raḥmān b. al-Jawzī, *Zād al-masīr fī ʿilm al-tafsīr*, 9 vols. (Beirut: al-Maktab al-Islāmī lil-Ṭibāʿah wa-al-Nashr, 1384/1964).

In introducing *Zād al-masīr fī ʿilm al-tafsīr* Ibn al-Jawzī explicitly outlines this hermeneutical procedure by contrasting his own approach with earlier products of the exegetical enterprise. He confesses that he has surveyed the field, has sampled the results of this centuries-long effort, and has found them wanting. He criticizes his exegetical predecessors on the grounds of length, arrangement, and selectivity. In themselves, these critiques offer an interesting perspective on Ibn al-Jawzī's own sense of exegetical priorities. A commentary on the Qurʾān is no mere reference work, nor overstocked compendium. A *tafsīr* should be a concise distillation of Qurʾānic understanding. But that understanding, in turn, can only be fully realized in the act of memorization. Drawing upon the ancient patterns of *masjid* and *madrasah* education, Ibn al-Jawzī finds in memorization the ultimate interiorization of all hermeneutical effort.[126]

Continuing this critique of previous interpretive efforts, Ibn al-Jawzī, by a kind of *via negativa*, outlines his conception of an adequate hermeneutics. In so doing, he places before the readers a full-scale exegetical typology. He succinctly presents the range of interpretive perspectives that had long occupied traditional *mufassirūn*. In the introductions to those longer commentaries, which Ibn al-Jawzī dismisses as "so vast as to induce despair in the would-be memorizer," each of these categories would likely have received prolonged and detailed treatment.[127] Together they constitute the component elements of that subsection of the religious sciences known as *ʿulūm al-Qurʾān*. Attention to *nāsikh* and *mansūkh* (abrogating and abrogated verses), to *asbāb al-nuzūl* (the situations that coincided with revelation), to the distinction between Meccan and Medinan revelation, to the *aḥkām* (the prescriptive implications of a verse), and to the *mutashābihāt* (uncertain or ambiguous elements) are the expected hallmarks of traditional Qurʾānic interpretation.

In his effort to consolidate and marshal such exegetical material, Ibn al-Jawzī makes no claim to originality. Rather he would wish to pride himself on successful attention to those concerns about length, arrangement, and selectivity that he found so lacking in the productions of previous *mufassirūn*. His views enter only obliquely, with a brief comment on the adequacy of a particular interpretation, or may be discerned by studying what he includes or omits of competing explanations. The fundamental aim that motivates his effort is self-expressed: "This book of ours has selected the choicest works of *tafsīr* and taken from them what is most sound, most fitting, and best preserved, and arranged it in concise form."[128] Clearly his

126 Ibn al-Jawzī, *Zād al-masīr*, 1:3.
127 Ibn al-Jawzī, *Zād al-masīr*, 1:3.
128 Ibn al-Jawzī, *Zād al-masīr*, 1:7.

goal was to sum up the "state of the art" of twelfth-century traditional exegesis, a task in which he succeeded admirably.

FAKHR AL-DĪN AL-RĀZĪ

Far to the east of Ibn al-Jawzī's Baghdād lived a man whose fame was destined to overshadow even that of the famous Ḥanbalī preacher.[129] So singular is Muḥammad b. ʿUmar Fakhr al-Dīn al-Rāzī's place in the intellectual history of Islam's twelfth century that he has been called its "renewer of religion (*mujaddid al-dīn*)."[130] Fakhr al-Dīn was born in Rayy, a city now absorbed by the urban sprawl of Tehran. His birth date is usually given as 543/1149 or 544/1150, little more than a century before the final Mongol incursions into central and western Asia.[131]

This exegete's early education was directed by his father, himself a noted preacher. In his *Taḥṣīl al-ḥaqq*, Fakhr al-Dīn cites his father's intellectual genealogy in both *ʿilm al-uṣūl* (foundational theology) and *fiqh* (jurisprudence) tracing the former back to the famed theologian Abū al-Ḥasan ʿAlī b. Ismāʿīl al-Ashʿarī (d. 324/935–36) and the latter to the Imām al-Shāfiʿī himself.[132] His further education included work in both Rayy and then

129 It is worth noting at this point how many of the classical *mufassirūn* were Persian-born, a fact that did not escape the notice of the historian and social theorist Ibn Khaldūn. After remarking that "most Qur'ān commentators" were Persians, he quotes the Prophetic *ḥadīth*: "If scholarship hung suspended at the highest parts of heaven, the Persians would (reach it and) take it." *The Muqaddimah*, 313. Daud Rahbar remarks upon the fact that the "majority of great exponents of Muslim religious sciences have been non-Arabs," because working in a language other than their own they must "tarry at each word of the text they read, and thus they enjoy a longer and a deeper contact with each and every word of the text." "Aspects of the Qur'ān Translation," *Babel: International Journal of Translation* 9 (1963): 68.

130 al-Dāwūdī, *Ṭabaqāt*, 2:214. For further consideration of this notion of periodic religious renewal see Hava Lazarus-Yafeh, "*Tajdīd al-Dīn*: A Reconsideration of Its Meaning, Roots and Influences in Islam," in *Studies in Islamic and Judaic Traditions*, ed. by William M. Brinner and Stephen D. Ricks (Atlanta: Scholars Press, 1986), 99–108. Fathalla Kholeif has discussed the authenticity of the Prophetic tradition from which this epithet was drawn and has also recorded some of the uncomplimentary statements about al-Rāzī that the biographies preserve. See *A Study on Fakhr al-Dīn al-Rāzī and His Controversies in Transoxiana* (Beirut: Dar El-Machreq, 1966), 9–13. Kholeif has reproduced the biographical information presented in this work as the first section of his more recent Arabic treatise on al-Rāzī. In the latter he has surveyed Fakhr al-Dīn's efforts in *fiqh*, *tafsīr*, *kalām*, and philosophy, appending to his discussion brief excerpts from al-Rāzī's major works. *Fakhr al-Dīn al-Rāzī* (Cairo: Dār al-Maʿārif bi-Miṣr, 1389/1969). This more recent treatise, in turn, has been reproduced (minus the brief excerpts from al-Rāzī's writings) as pp. 273–378 of Kholeif's *Falāsifat al-islām: Ibn Sīnā, al-Ghazālī, Fakhr al-Dīn al-Rāzī* (Alexandria: Dār al-Jāmiʿāt al-Miṣrīyah, 1976).

131 Jamāl al-Dīn Abū al-Ḥasan ʿAlī b. Yūsuf b. al-Qifṭī (d. 646/1248) gives only the first date of 543. *Ta'rīkh al-ḥukamā'*, ed. by Julius Lippert (1903; reprint, Baghdād: Maktabat al-Muthannā, 1967), 291.

132 Ibn Khallikān, *Wafayāt*, 4:252.

further west in the Ādharbāyjānī city of Marāgha. He went to Marāgha to follow his teacher Majd al-Dīn al-Jīlī. This latter was also the teacher of Fakhr al-Dīn's contemporary, the mystic philosopher Shihāb al-Dīn Yaḥyā al-Suhrawardī (d. 587/1191).[133] Through his studies he became conversant with the Islamic philosophical tradition as represented by, among others, al-Fārābī (d. 339/950) and Ibn Sīnā. One of his earlier works, *Sharḥ al-ishārāt*, is a commentary on Ibn Sīnāʾs *Kitāb al-ishārāt wa-al-tanbīhāt*. The results of this education were an impressive list of intellectual qualifications. Fakhr al-Dīn's biographer, Khalīl b. Aybak al-Ṣafadī, has summarized these talents: "As distinguished from others like him, he had five qualities which God gathered together for no one else. They were a masterly expressiveness in discourse, a sound intellect, a limitless store of knowledge, a comprehensive memory (*al-ḥāfiẓah al-mustawʿibah*) and ability to recall apposite instances of demonstrations and corroborating proofs (*al-dhākirah allatī tuʿayyinuhu ʿalā mā yurīdu fī taqrīr al-adillah wa-al-barāhīn*)."[134]

Fakhr al-Dīn put these gifts to wide use both intellectually and geographically. Not only was he a master of many fields of knowledge, his career as a teacher and preacher took him all over central Asia and perhaps into India as well.[135] His travels were not always those of a celebrity, however. One stage of his journeys in Transoxiana found him penniless and sick in Bukhārā, albeit eventually rescued by the charity of some local merchants.[136] At other times he was more fortunate and his rapidly growing reputation assured him large audiences and eager students. Al-Rāzī's linguistic talents served him well in such venues, allowing him to preach in either Arabic or Persian as the situation required.[137] At various points in

133 Ibn Khallikān, *Wafayāt*, 4:250; Majid Fakhry, *A History of Islamic Philosophy* (New York: Columbia University Press, 1970), 355. The Italian Arabist, Giuseppe Gabrieli, described the youthful al-Rāzī as "dotato di vivace ed acuto ingegno, di bella parola e di straordinaria energia fisica, bramoso di studio e di sapere, tanto da lamentar come perduto perfino il tempo dedicato al sonno ed al cibo." "Fakhr al-Din al-Razi," *Isis* 7 (1925): 9.

134 Khalīl b. Aybak al-Ṣafadī, *al-Wāfī bi-al-wafayāt*, ed. by Sven Dedering et al. (Damascus: Druckerei al-Hāshimīyah, 1959), 4:248. In the biographical section of a recent study of Fakhr al-Dīn's *Nihāyat al-ījāz fī dirāyat al-iʿjāz*, Māhir Mahdī Hilāl has collected the accolades of al-Rāzī's biographers, both classical and modern. *Fakhr al-Dīn al-Rāzī balāghīyan* (Baghdad: Wizārat al-Iʿlām fī al-Jumhūrīyah al-ʿIrāqīyah, 1397/1977), 57–64.

135 Ibn Khallikān praises his knowledge of *kalām* and logic and refers to him as "the Shāfiʿī *faqīh*, unique in his age and unique of his kind." *Wafayāt*, 4:248. Al-Dāwūdī characterizes him as the leading figure of his age in the rational sciences and one of the most eminent in the legal sciences, but most prominently as the *sulṭān al-mutakallimīn*. *Ṭabaqāt*, 2:214.

136 Ibn al-Qifṭī, *Taʾrīkh*, 291. Paul Kraus, on the basis of his studies of al-Rāzī's *Munāẓarāt*, has dated this period in Transoxiana to the second half of Fakhr al-Dīn's fifth decade. "The 'Controversies' of Fakhr al-Dīn Rāzī," *IC* 12 (1938): 135.

137 al-Subkī, *Ṭabaqāt*, 8:86.

his travels he is reported to have attracted upwards of three hundred students and jurisprudents (*fuqahā'*) to his study circles.[138] One who was present in his *madrasah* in Khwārazm has recorded an affecting tale that could bring to mind the medieval Christian saint, Francis of Assisi. It seems that Fakhr al-Dīn was lecturing one very cold and snowy day to a large group of notables when a pigeon fell at his feet. The bird, which had been chased by a predator, lay there incapacitated by fright and cold. To the amazement of this auditor, Fakhr al-Dīn interrupted his oration and stooped to minister to the stricken bird.[139]

His preaching and lecturing were frequently aimed at such controversial groups as the Muʿtazilīs and the Karrāmīs. As Ignaz Goldziher has noted, Khwārazm was "the primary homestead of the Muʿtazilī in the twelfth and thirteenth century."[140] His vigorous defense of Ashʿarī Sunnism aroused such hostility there that he was forced to flee.[141] After similar experiences in Transoxiana and trips as far afield as Samarqand and perhaps northern India, he finally settled in Herāt. This city, in present-day Afghanistan, was to be his primary residence for the rest of his life. There his success against the dissident Karrāmīs was evidently better than it had been against the Muʿtazilīs of Khwārazm and elsewhere: many of the former group "reverted to the Sunnī position (*ahl al-sunnah*)."[142]

In Herāt he became known as *shaykh al-islām* and reaped the full benefits of his growing prestige and political connections. At various points in his career al-Rāzī had been the recipient of noble patronage. A pithy exchange attributed to Fakhr al-Dīn and an unnamed ruler nicely captures the mutual advantage of such arrangements. To al-Rāzī's comment "We are in the shade of your sword," the ruler returned the compliment, "We are in the sun of your knowledge."[143] The Khwārazmshāh Sulṭān Muḥammad b. Takash is known to have been generous in his favor.[144] Through his influence Fakhr

138 al-Dāwūdī, *Ṭabaqāt*, 2:214.

139 Ibn Khallikān, *Wafayāt*, 4:251.

140 Ignaz Goldziher, "Aus der Theologie des Fachr al-dīn al-Rāzī," *Der Islam* 3 (1912): 222.

141 Ibn Khallikān, *Wafayāt*, 4:249.

142 Ibn Khallikān, *Wafayāt*, 4:250. Roger Arnaldez sees al-Rāzī's stance toward such groups as the Muʿtazilah and the Karrāmīyah to be less that of an opponent than that of a conciliator: "La conciliation d'al-Rāzī est peut-être moins une tentative pour accorder des doctrines, en évitant ce qui est excessif et en conservant ce qui est le plus modéré, qu'un effort pour offrir à des esprits différents un champ commun de pensée, où ils puissent tous se retrouver et évoluer à leur aise." "L'oeuvre de Fakhr al-Dīn al-Rāzī, commentateur du Coran et philosophe," *Cahiers de civilisation médiévale* 3 (1960):314.

143 Shihāb al-Dīn Abū al-Faḍl Aḥmad b. ʿAlī b. Ḥajar al-ʿAsqalānī, *Lisān al-mīzān* (Beirut: Mu'assasat al-Aʿlāmī lil-Maṭbūʿāt, 1390/1971), 4:427.

144 Ibn Khallikān, *Wafayāt*, 4:250.

al-Dīn was able to find a wealthy and influential husband for his daughter. He himself amassed considerable wealth both from his writings and from marriages that he arranged for his two sons with the daughters of a wealthy doctor from Rayy. When that gentleman died, al-Rāzī also acquired part of his wealth.[145] In Herāt, which was under the authority of the Sulṭān of Ghaznah, Ghiyāth al-Dīn, Fakhr al-Dīn was permitted to open a *madrasah* within the precincts of the palace.[146] So successful were these various sources of wealth and patronage that at his death al-Rāzī left behind "80,000 dīnār in gold pieces [alone], not counting livestock, real estate and other assets."[147]

Yet even in this more congenial environment al-Rāzī's intellectual pugnacity was not entirely stilled. A contemporary, the urbane chronicler Ibn al-Athīr, records an episode in his account of the year 595/1198–99 that indicates the extent of al-Rāzī's intemperate irascibility.[148] While the ruler of Ghaznah was encamped in the provincial city of Fīrūzkūh, a disputation was convened among various of the *fuqahā'* including both Fakhr al-Dīn and the judge (*qāḍī*), Ibn al-Qudwah. The latter was held in high regard by the Karrāmīs both for his great learning and for his personal asceticism. Debate between the two men was prolonged and heated. When Ghiyāth al-Dīn tried to intervene, al-Rāzī turned on *him*, shouting insults and abuse. The ruler's cousin and son-in-law begged him to renounce Fakhr al-Dīn and the next day Ibn al-Qudwah's cousin preached a rousing sermon in the mosque calling obliquely for al-Rāzī's expulsion from "the religion of God and the *sunnah* of his Prophet."[149] So incensed did the people become that Ghiyāth al-Dīn had to deploy troops to quell incipient civil disorder. Yet with Fakhr al-Dīn he showed a restraint that can only reflect the esteem in which the ruler held him. Making no move to avenge the insults, he simply sent al-Rāzī back to Herāt.[150]

Although al-Rāzī prospered in Herāt, controversy never entirely disappeared from his life. Even the facts about Fakhr al-Dīn's death have been a cause for some speculation. According to his biographers he died on the feast day following the fast of Ramaḍān (*'īd al-fiṭr*), 606/1210, in Herāt.[151]

145 G.C. Anawati, "Fakhr al-Dīn al-Rāzī," *EI*² 3:752.
146 Anawati, "Fakhr al-Dīn al-Rāzī," 3:752.
147 al-Dāwūdī, *Ṭabaqāt*, 2:215. If Ibn al-Qifṭī is to be believed, the sum would have been even higher had al-Rāzī not squandered some of his wealth dabbling in alchemy. *Ta'rīkh*, 292.
148 Ibn al-Athīr, *al-Kāmil*, 12:151.
149 Ibn al-Athīr, *al-Kāmil*, 12:152.
150 Ibn al-Athīr, *al-Kāmil*, 12:152.
151 Aḥmad b. al-Qāsim b. Abī 'Uṣaybi'ah, *'Uyūn al-anbā' fī ṭabaqāt al-aṭibbā'*, ed. by August Müller (1884; reprint, Farnborough: Gregg International, 1972), 2:27. In secondary sources Fakhr al-Dīn's death date is often incorrectly given as 1209, which

Some have said he was poisoned because of his attacks against the Karrāmīyah.[152] Ibn al-Qifṭī maintained that although he was ostensibly buried outside of the city, in reality his corpse was secretly interred in his house for fear that his enemies would mutilate his remains.[153] Georges Anawati has discounted such theories and concluded that al-Rāzī was, in fact, buried on the mountain of Mazdakhan near Herāt, for his tomb is still venerated there.[154]

One of the most quoted of the autobiographical fragments culled from Fakhr al-Dīn's work is a statement from his last testament, dictated to his pupil, Ibrāhīm b. Abī Bakr b. ʿAlī al-Iṣfahānī. In it he laments the time he has spent in theological and philosophical speculation: "I have diligently explored the paths of *kalām* and the ways of philosophy but have not found what quenches thirst or heals the sick; but now I see that the soundest way is the way of (the) Qur'ān read deanthropomorphically (*fī al-tanzīh*)."[155] This evidence of piety is but one aspect of a complex personality. His aggressive and arrogant style of argumentation is well-recorded in the account of disputations he held in Transoxiana (*Munāẓarāt fī bilād mā warā' al-nahr*). In a manuscript of the *Rawḍat al-afrāḥ wa-nuzhat al-arwāḥ* of Shams al-Dīn Muḥammad b. Maḥmūd al-Shahrazūrī, Fathalla Kholeif has come across a quatrain in which al-Rāzī bemoans his "changeful temper which extinguishes the light from my reason and faith."[156] That he was a man of strong feelings is attested to by accounts of his preaching that refer to his being overcome with emotion and weeping.[157] It is also clearly evident in the notes he appends to the discussions of *sūrah*s 10–13 of his *tafsīr* mourning the death of his son and begging prayers on his behalf.[158]

The *tafsīr* itself, known as either *Mafātīḥ al-ghayb* (The Keys of the Unseen – a phrase found in *sūrat al-anʿām* [6]:59) or *al-Tafsīr al-kabīr* (The

corresponds to the first part of 606 *hijrī*. The date of ʿ*īd al-fiṭr*, i.e., 1 Shawwāl, would be Monday, 29 March 1210.

152 J.H. Kramers, "al-Rāzī," in *Shorter Encyclopaedia of Islam* (Leiden: E.J. Brill, 1953), 470.

153 Ibn al-Qifṭī, *Ta'rīkh*, 291.

154 G. Anawati, "Fakhr al-Dīn al-Rāzī," 3:752.

155 al-Dāwūdī, *Ṭabaqāt*, 2:215. This statement is reminiscent of one that Thomas Aquinas is said to have made in the last year of his life. After a spiritual experience on 6 December 1273 that profoundly affected him, Thomas confessed to his companion, Reginald of Piperno: "All that I have written seems to me like straw compared to what has now been revealed to me." See James A. Weisheipl, O.P., *Friar Thomas D'Aquino: His Life, Thought and Works* (Garden City, N.Y.: Doubleday and Company, 1974), 322.

156 F. Kholeif, *A Study*, 20.

157 Ibn Khallikān, *Wafayāt*, 4:249.

158 Jacques Jomier, O.P., "Les *Mafātīḥ al-ghayb* de l'Imām Fakhr al-Dīn al-Rāzī: quelques dates, lieux, manuscrits," *MIDEO* 13 (1977): 265–68.

Great Commentary), is al-Rāzī's magnum opus.[159] It is a massive work of thirty-two volumes (in the most widely available printed edition) and has been both extravagantly praised and roundly damned.[160] It was dismissed by Taqī al-Dīn b. Taymīyah as containing "everything but *tafsīr*."[161] Abū al-Ḥasan ʿAlī al-Subkī's (d. 756/1355) rejoinder was that it contained "everything else in addition to *tafsīr*."[162] It is certainly far different from much traditional *al-tafsīr bi-al-maʾthūr*, for al-Rāzī has packed it with philosophical and theological erudition.[163] Yet he has not done so to the neglect of numerous earlier authorities with whom he remains engaged in a wide-ranging exegetical discourse.[164]

In terms of method and arrangement, the closest, near-contemporary

159 Although the title *al-Tafsīr al-kabīr* is usually ascribed to either the size and/or the renown of the work, Muḥammad Ṣāliḥ al-Zurkān says that it was applied to *Mafātīḥ al-ghayb* to distinguish it from al-Rāzī's *Asrār al-tanzīl wa-anwār al-taʾwīl*, which was known as 'the little tafsīr (*tafsīr al-Qurʾān al-ṣaghīr*)'. *Fakhr al-Dīn al-Rāzī wa-ārāʾuhu al-kalāmīyah wa-al-falsafīyah* (Beirut: Dār al-Fikr, 1383/1963), 45, note 5.

160 Muḥammad b. ʿUmar Fakhr al-Dīn al-Rāzī, *al-Tafsīr al-kabīr*, 32 vols. (Cairo: al-Maṭbaʿah al-Bahīyah al-Miṣrīyah, n.d.). Michel Lagarde has announced his intention to complete an index to this edition. "Un index en préparation pour le *Grand Commentaire* de Fakhr al-Dīn al-Rāzī," *Arabica* 33 (1986): 383–84.

161 al-Ṣafadī, *Wāfī*, 4:254.

162 al-Ṣafadī, *Wāfī*, 4:254. Citation of this pair of assessments has become a commonplace in contemporary studies on Fakhr al-Dīn al-Rāzī. ʿAbd al-ʿAzīz al-Majdūb, who deems the *tafsīr* an 'encyclopedic work (*al-ʿaml al-mawsūʿī*)' discusses these, and similar, judgments at length. *al-Imām al-ḥakīm Fakhr al-Dīn al-Rāzī min khilali tafsīrihi* (Tunis: al-Dār al-ʿArabīyah lil-Kitāb, 1400/1980), 78–81. Even Rashīd Riḍā joined the chorus of critics by blaming Fakhr al-Dīn for unnecessary digressions, a scholarly sin for which he, in turn, was cited. See Jansen, *Interpretation*, 32.

163 While there has been no systematic and comprehensive treatment of *al-Tafsīr al-kabīr*, a number of studies have appeared that address parts of it. Mohammed Arkoun, for example, draws extensively upon this *tafsīr* in his semiotic analysis of the first *sūrah*. He justifies his choice with the assertion that Fakhr al-Dīn al-Rāzī, "doué d'une étonnante puissance de synthèse et d'une rare sagacité a, en effet, recueilli dans son Commentaire l'essentiel du travail effectué durant six siècles." "Lecture de al-Fātiḥa," in his *Lectures du Coran* (Paris: Éditions Maisonneuve et Larose, 1982), 60. Reprinted from *Mélanges d'islamologie dédiés à la mémoire d'A. Abel*, ed. by P. Salmon (Leiden: E. J. Brill, 1974), 18–44. For a brief exposition of Arkoun's approach see Carmela Baffioni, "L'esegesi coranica di Mohammed Arkoun," *ISC* 3 (1984): 17–21. Giovanna Calasso, on the other hand, has studied Fakhr al-Dīn's remarks on the last *sūrah, sūrat al-nās*. "La ʿsura degli uomini' nel commento di Fakhr ad-Din ar-Razi," *Egitto e Vicino Oriente* 2 (1979): 231–52. (Both authors make careful note of al-Rāzī's response to a position attributed to Ibn Masʿūd that denies that the first *sūrah* and last two *sūrah*s are a legitimate part of the Qurʾānic text.)

164 Jacques Jomier has collected and grouped those sources to which al-Rāzī refers in his commentary on *sūrah Āl ʿImrān*. "Fakhr al-Dīn al-Rāzī et les commentaires du Coran les plus anciens," *MIDEO* 15 (1982): 145–72. A preliminary study of sources forms part of Jomier's "The Qurʾānic Commentary of Imām Fakhr al-Dīn al-Rāzī: Its Sources and Its Originality," in *Qurʾān Congress*, 99–104.

Western parallel to *al-Tafsīr al-kabīr* would be the *Summa Theologiae* of Thomas Aquinas. In a manner analogous to the structure of that work, Fakhr al-Dīn frequently divides his analysis of a particular verse into a series of "questions (*masāʾil*)." Each *masʾalah* may then be further subdivided to present a full range of possible interpretations. His biographer, al-Ṣafadī, has remarked on the originality of Fakhr al-Dīn's method: "He was the first one to devise this arrangement in his writings. He accomplished in them what no one before him had done, for he stated the question (*masʾalah*) and then proceeded to divide it and to classify further these sub-divisions. He drew conclusions on the basis of such probing and apportioning and no relevant aspect of the *masʾalah* eluded him. He defined the basic principles and determined the scope of the *masāʾil*."[165]

A frequently noted feature of al-Rāzī's commentary is its anti-Muʿtazilī stance and its strong defense of Ashʿarī Sunnism.[166] To underscore his traditionalist loyalties, al-Rāzī's biographers are fond of quoting this remark: "Whoever adheres to the elders' way of thinking will himself be the victor."[167] Some have felt that the defense was not strong enough and accused him of purposely or inadvertently spreading unorthodox views by the very fact of his thorough investigation of such positions.[168] Paul Kraus, on the

165 al-Ṣafadī, *Wāfī*, 4:249. George Makdisi would undoubtedly question this claim to originality. His own work on Ibn ʿAqīl has highlighted the fact that the sophisticated use of elements of scholastic methodology is to be found in Islamic works of at least a century earlier. See especially "The Scholastic Method in Medieval Education: An Inquiry into its Origins in Law and Theology," *Speculum* 49 (1974): 648 ff.; "Interaction between Islam and the West," in *Colloques Internationaux de la Napoule (1976): L'enseignement en islam et en occident au moyen age*, ed. by G. Makdisi, D. Sourdel, and J. Sourdel-Thomine (Paris: Librairie Orientaliste Paul Geuthner, 1977), 298–300; and *The Rise of Colleges*, 25 ff. Makdisi himself draws a connection between Fakhr al-Dīn al-Rāzī and Ibn ʿAqīl in the literary genre of *munāẓarāt*. *The Notebooks of Ibn ʿAqīl: Kitāb al-funūn, Part One* (Beirut: Dar El-Machreq, 1970), xlvii.

166 Ignaz Goldziher has questioned the extent to which al-Rāzī was influenced by Muʿtazilī thought. See "Aus der Theologie," especially pages 233 f. In a short note entitled "A Sublime Subtlety?," Michael Schub makes the surprising statement that "Rāzī himself is in large measure dependent on Zamakhsharī." *ZAL* 6 (1981): 72. Presumably he means this in terms of grammatical issues as that is what his note discusses, but a qualifying statement to that effect would have been appropriate. For corrections, see Michael G. Carter, "Remarks on M.B. Schub: 'A Sublime Subtlety?'," *ZAL* 7 (1982): 79–81.

167 ʿAlī b. Anjab b. al-Sāʿī al-Khāzin, *al-Jāmiʿ al-mukhtaṣar, Part Nine*, ed. by Muṣṭafā Jawād and Père Anastase-Marie de St. Elie (Baghdad: Imprimerie Syrienne Catholique, 1934), 307. In Ibn Ḥajar al-ʿAsqalānī's rendering of this remark, the phrase here translated as "elders' way of thinking (*madhhab al-ʿajāʾiz*)" is given as *dīn al-ʿajāʾiz*. *Lisān al-mīzān*, 4:427. Ibn Ḥajar has recorded many of the criticisms leveled against al-Rāzī's *tafsīr* but concludes this compilation with the assurance that "he wrote a will which demonstrates that his faith was as it should be." *Lisān al-mīzān*, 4:429.

168 In his discussion of this Ibn Ḥajar includes the novel suggestion that Fakhr al-Dīn

other hand, was eager to stress the extremely wide range of *al-Tafsīr al-kabīr*. He insisted that it "is not merely, as it is frequently supposed, an Ashʿarite answer to Muʿtazilite theological commentaries such as the *Kashshāf* of Zamakhsharī."[169] Rather, he feels that in it Fakhr al-Dīn, "under the pretence of having adopted the thesis that the Qur'ān contains every science, discusses the most difficult problems of his philosophy."[170] More recently Roger Arnaldez has stressed the contemporary significance of this work, finding therein surprising discoveries which are "les délices des explorateurs."[171] He cautions his readers not to relegate al-Rāzī's great work to the storerooms of antique curiosities but to study it seriously, "car elle conserve assez de force pour nourrir une réflexion philosophique chez les hommes de notre temps."[172]

An unresolved issue, with which this discussion of al-Rāzī's commentary must conclude, is that of authorship. Several of the biographers note that Fakhr al-Dīn did not complete *al-Tafsīr al-kabīr*.[173] Jacques Jomier has begun a study of this matter and unearthed some interesting information. By scrutinizing the colophons of a number of manuscripts of the work, he has found, for example, that at some times al-Rāzī wrote with incredible speed and at others he adopted a more leisurely pace.[174] He has also discovered, again by comparison of dates, that Fakhr al-Dīn did not comment on the *sūrah*s in order, starting with the first and proceeding in numerical progression. But the main thrust of his study has been an effort to discover which parts of the commentary were, perhaps, not from Fakhr al-Dīn's hand at all. (It may be that he died before completing it or that part of the manuscript was lost in the Mongol invasions.) On the basis of both paleographic research and indications within the *tafsīr* itself, Father Jomier concludes that it is reasonable to suppose that the commentary on *sūrah*s

expended so much energy in the presentation of heretical positions that he had none left (*lā baqiya ʿindahu shay'un min al-quwā*) for their refutation. *Lisān al-mīzān*, 4:428.

169 Kraus, "Controversies," 133. Almost a century ago Martin Schreiner briefly surveyed Ashʿarī elements in *al-Tafsīr al-kabīr*. "Beiträge zur Geschichte der theologischen Bewegungen im Islām," *ZDMG* 52 (1898): 506 f.

170 Kraus, "Controversies," 133.

171 Roger Arnaldez, "Trouvailles philosophiques dans le commentaire coranique de Fakhr al-Dīn al-Rāzī," *Études philosophiques et littéraires* 3 (1968): 12.

172 Arnaldez, "Trouvailles," 24. A less sanguine assessment is recorded in a wide-ranging article by John Haywood who has decided that "doubts will remain as to whether he [al-Rāzī] made any significant contribution to Islamic thought." "Fakhr al-Dīn al-Rāzī's Contribution to Ideas of Ultimate Reality and Meaning," *Ultimate Reality and Meaning* 2 (1979): 290.

173 Ibn Khallikān, *Wafayāt*, 4:249 and al-Dāwūdī, *Ṭabaqāt*, 2:216.

174 He cites the examples of *sūrah*s 12–14, which run to more than three hundred pages of printed text but were completed in twenty-three days. J. Jomier, "Les *Mafātīḥ*," 259.

29–36 was not done by al-Rāzī himself.[175] In a yet more recent study which focuses on the attribution of this section to Shams al-Dīn Aḥmad b. al-Khalīl b. Saʿādah al-Khuwayyī, the chief Qāḍī in Damascus in 637/1239–40, Father Jomier concludes: "Il semble certain que cette section provient d'une autre plume que celle de Fakhr al-Dīn; l'attribution au Qāḍī par contre n'est qu'une hypothèse, la plus plausible. La question reste ouverte."[176]

IBN KATHĪR

Less than a century separates the death of Fakhr al-Dīn al-Rāzī and the birth of the fourteenth-century Damascene historian and exegete ʿImād al-Dīn Ismāʿīl b. ʿUmar b. Kathīr. Yet it was arguably the most disruptive period in the Middle East since the Muslim conquests six centuries earlier. The source of this disruption was, of course, the Mongol incursions then sweeping across Central Asia, Iran, and Iraq. By all contemporary accounts the ferocity and destructiveness of the Mongol advance was unprecedented. The entire area from which the first six exegetes herein studied sprang was critically affected. Baghdād, the city that had welcomed al-Ṭabarī, al-Ṭūsī, and Ibn al-Jawzī and had briefly hosted al-Zamakhsharī, was sacked in 656/1258. In Syria, however, the advance was checked. On 25 Ramaḍān 658/1260 at ʿAyn Jālūt, Mamlūk forces defeated the Mongols, the latter having reached their limit of strategic and logistical possibilities.[177]

The same Mamlūk dynasty controlled the Syria into which Ibn Kathīr was born. His birth date is given as 700/1300 or 701/1301 and his birth-

175 J. Jomier, "Les *Mafātīḥ*," 276–77. In a recent article on some of the Qurʾānic Abraham narratives, Anthony H. Johns takes account of Jomier's concern about authorship but appears more willing than the latter to argue for thematic development in the *tafsīr* based on an authorial sequence that follows the order of *sūrah*s. "Al-Rāzī's Treatment of the Qurʾānic Episodes Telling of Abraham and His Guests: Qurʾānic Exegesis with a Human Face," *MIDEO* 17 (1986): 86–87 and 110.

176 Jacques Jomier, "Qui a commenté l'ensemble des sourates al-ʿankabūt à Yāsīn (29–36) dans le 'Tafsīr al-kabīr' de l'Imām Fakhr al-Dīn al-Rāzī?," *IJMES* 11 (1980): 480. As part of an article published in the previous year, Richard Gramlich also reviews a broad range of sources relevant to this issue. Doubtless because of the proximity of publication dates, Jomier was unable to refer to Gramlich's work. "Fakhr ad-Dīn ar-Rāzī's Kommentar zu Sure 18, 9–12," *Asiatische Studien/Études asiatiques* 33 (1979): 99–152.

177 Bernard Lewis calls this the "high water mark of Mongol advance" but adds that it did not signal the end of the Mongol danger, which continued to threaten Syria and Iraq for some time to come. See "ʿAyn Djālūt," *EI*² 1:787. An account of Hulagu's conquest of Baghdād attributed to a member of his court, Naṣīr al-Dīn Ṭūsī, has been analyzed by G.M. Wickens in "Nasir ad-Din Tusi on the Fall of Baghdad: A Further Study," *JSS* 7 (1962): 23–35. For a translation of the account see J.A. Boyle's "The Death of the Last ʿAbbasid Caliph: A Contemporary Muslim Account," *JSS* 6 (1961): 151–61.

place as Boṣrā. This town, which lies southeast of Damascus, was famed for its massive citadal, itself badly damaged during the Mongol invasions. Ibn Kathīr spent only his early childhood there. His father died when he was quite young and at the age of six he became a ward of his older brother, who brought him to Damascus.[178] By the early fourteenth century Damascus was among the preeminent centers of Sunnism. Its renaissance had been initiated by the Zangī *amīr*, Nūr al-Dīn Maḥmūd, in the mid-twelfth century. This leader strengthened the intellectual and religious life of the city by building numerous mosques and *madrasahs*. Under the Mamlūk dynasty Damascus was, after Cairo, the foremost city of the empire and its political fortunes were intimately linked with those of the Egyptian capital.

As a Sunnī stronghold Damascus offered the young Ibn Kathīr a wealth of educational opportunity. His teachers rank among the leading intellectuals of his era. In *fiqh* he studied under Burhān al-Dīn al-Fazārī (d. 729/1328–29), a leading Shāfiʿī jurisconsult who taught at the Bādhrāʾīyah *madrasah*. Under the *ḥāfiẓ*, Jamāl al-Dīn al-Mizzī (d. 742/1341), he furthered his acquisition of *ḥadīth* (he also married al-Mizzī's daughter).[179] Al-Mizzī, who for twenty-three years directed the Dār al-Ḥadīth known as al-Ashrafīyah, must have found an eager student in Ibn Kathīr. The latter's biographers comment on his early and impressive mastery of this subject.[180] Later his students were to praise him as having "the best memory, of those with whom we studied, for the *matns* of *ḥadīth* and being the most knowledgeable in expounding them, in ranking their transmitters and rating their soundness or faultiness."[181]

Certainly the most famous of Ibn Kathīr's teachers, and perhaps the one who influenced him most, was the Ḥanbalī theologian and jurisconsult Ibn Taymīyah. Ibn Kathīr was only twenty-eight when this great *faqīh* died; he knew him during the periods of intermittent persecution that plagued the last ten years of Ibn Taymīyah's life. One provocation for such persecution was a *fatwā* issued by Ibn Taymīyah, contrary to the prevailing Ḥanbalī teaching, on the invalidity of the single repudiation in divorce (*ṭalāq*). Ibn Kathīr is reported to have issued a supporting *fatwā* and to

178 ʿAbd al-Ḥayy b. al- ʿImād, *Shadharāt al-dhahab fī akhbār man dhahab* (Cairo: Maktabat al-Qudsī, 1350/1931), 6:231.

179 al-Dāwūdī, *Ṭabaqāt*, 1:110. Also Henri Laoust, "Ibn Kathīr, historien," *Arabica* 2 (1955): 43–44. George Makdisi presents Ibn Kathīr's account of his father-in-law's inaugural lecture upon appointment to the professorship of Dār al-Ḥadīth al-Ashrafīyah, an account that sympathetically evaluates the event's very poor attendance. *The Rise of Colleges*, 158.

180 Ibn al-ʿImād, *Shadharāt*, 6:231; al-Dāwūdī, *Ṭabaqāt*, I:110.

181 al-Dāwūdī, *Ṭabaqāt*, 1:111.

have been subjected to trial along with Ibn Taymīyah.[182] Henri Laoust, in his study of Ibn Kathīr, expresses doubts about the historicity of this and other incidents of shared persecution.[183]

Ibn Kathīr's own career developed quietly in the years following Ibn Taymīyah's death. His reputation as a scholar of *fiqh* spread to the point that "the sheets of his *fatwās* flew through the country."[184] In 746/1345 he was appointed *khaṭīb* in a new mosque founded in al-Mizzah, a suburb located three miles southwest of the citadel of Damascus.[185] Less than three years later he became a teacher of *ḥadīth* in the *madrasah* associated with the *turbah* of Umm Ṣāliḥ.[186] This was the family mausoleum established by the son of the Ayyūbid *amīr* of Damascus, al-Malik al-ʿĀdil Sayf al-Dīn. Ibn Kathīr's immediate predecessor in the position was Shams al-Dīn al-Dhahabī, noted for his works on history and *ḥadīth*, particularly evaluative biographies (*ʿilm al-rijāl*) of the transmitters.[187]

According to al-Dāwūdī, Ibn Kathīr also replaced Taqī al-Dīn al-Subkī for a short time as director of the Dār al-Ḥadīth al-Ashrafīyah after the latter's death in 756/1355.[188] This institution, which stood near the eastern gate of the citadel of Damascus, was founded by al-Malik al-Ashraf Muẓaffar al-Dīn in 630/1232. Its first director was the noted thirteenth-century traditionist Taqī al-Dīn b. al-Ṣalāh (d. 643/1245).[189] As well as an educational institution, the Ashrafīyah was a place of pilgrimage. The relic it enshrined was one of the Prophet's sandals.[190] H. Laoust questions whether, in fact, Ibn Kathīr ever occupied the chair here because he finds no mention

182 al-Dāwūdī, *Ṭabaqāt*, 1:111; C. Brockelmann, "Ibn Kathīr," *EI*[1] 3:393.

183 "Il ne semble pas cependant, contrairement à certaines affirmations, qu'il ait partagé quelques-unes des nombreuses persécutions auxquelles Ibn Taymiyya, à la suite d'acerbes polémiques, fut de nouveau en butte de 718 à 728." "Ibn Kathīr, historien," 44.

184 Ibn al-ʿImād, *Shadharāt*, 6:231.

185 Muḥammad b. Muḥammad b. Ṣaṣrā, *A Chronicle of Damascus 1389–1397*, trans. and ed. by William M. Brinner (Berkeley: University of California Press, 1963), 1:27 (39) b, note 268.

186 al-Dāwūdī, *Ṭabaqāt*, 1:111.

187 Henri Sauvaire, "Description de Damas," *JA*, 9th series, 3 (1894): 413. Al-Dhahabī's own report on Ibn Kathīr may be found in *Tadhkirat al-ḥuffāẓ* (Hyderabad: Dā'irat al-Maʿārif al-ʿUthmānīyah, 1375/1955), 4:1508.

188 al-Dāwūdī, *Ṭabaqāt*, 1:111.

189 J. Robson, "Ibn al-Ṣalāḥ," *EI*[2] 3:927. According to Robson, Ibn al-Ṣalāḥ's book on the sciences of *ḥadīth*, published under the title *ʿUlūm al-ḥadīth al-maʿrūf bi-muqaddimat Ibn al-Ṣalāḥ*, "has a claim to be considered the standard work on the sciences of Tradition."

190 Sauvaire, "Description," 3:272. The chronicle of which Sauvaire's work is a translation also places Ibn Kathīr on the list of professors for the Ashrafīyah but does not give his order in the succession. *Ibid.*, 3:273.

of it in, for example, the author's *al-Bidāyah wa-al-nihāyah*, a major source of autobiographical information.[191]

Nevertheless, the biographical information we do have confirms that by his sixth decade Ibn Kathīr had become one of the most respected preachers and lecturers in Damascus. His prestige was such that when the caliph al-Muʿtaḍid (d. 763/1361–62) came from Cairo to Damascus in 752/1351, Ibn Kathīr was granted an audience with him.[192] Such favor is also an indication of this exegete's political connections with the ruling powers of Damascus. Along with the other leading *ʿulamāʾ* of the city he was frequently consulted on both domestic and international matters. A lifetime of such loyal support was crowned by his appointment in 767/1366, at the age of sixty-seven, to a professorship in Qurʾānic *tafsīr* at *al-Jāmiʿ al-Umawī*, one of the most famous mosques in the Muslim world. For his inaugural lecture the ruling and intellectual elite of the city assembled in fitting tribute to this celebrated scholar.[193] Seven years later, in 774/1373, Ibn Kathīr died. He was buried in the cemetery of the Ṣūfīyah near his master, Ibn Taymīyah.[194]

Ibn Kathīr's life and works bear comparison with those of two earlier commentators, Ibn Jarīr al-Ṭabarī and Abū al-Faraj b. al-Jawzī. Like the latter he achieved his renown and political prominence as a preacher and teacher. Like the former, his best-known work is a history of the world. (Ibn al-Jawzī also produced a noted historical-biographical work entitled *al-Muntaẓam fī taʾrīkh al-duwal wa-al-umam*.) Ibn Kathīr's *al-Bidāyah wa-al-nihāyah* starts with the creation and ends with the last years of the author's life.[195] It is, as are the works of al-Ṭabarī and Ibn al-Jawzī, an example of the close connection that always tended to prevail in classical Islam between the historical sciences and those of *ḥadīth*.

This same focus characterizes Ibn Kathīr's *Tafsīr al-Qurʾān al-ʿaẓīm* (Interpretation of the Mighty Qurʾān). The work has been dismissed by his principal Western bio-bibliographer, Henri Laoust, as "essentially a

191 Laoust, "Ibn Kathīr, historien," 53.

192 Laoust, "Ibn Kathīr," *EI*² 3:818. In his *Arabica* article Laoust points out Ibn Kathīr's loyalty to the historical caliphate, noting that it is an issue on which he parted company with his mentor Ibn Taymīyah. Ibn Kathīr "reste un partisan du caliphat qurayshite, et il ne met jamais en doute, même aux heures de défaillance ou d'éclipse, la nécessité de sa pérennité." "Ibn Kathīr, historien," 74.

193 Laoust, "Ibn Kathīr, historien," 61–62.

194 Ibn al-ʿImād, *Shadharāt*, 6:232; al-Dāwūdī, *Ṭabaqāt*, 1:111.

195 The basis for this work was the chronicle of al-Birzalī (d. 740/1339) who preceded Ibn Kathīr as a teacher at the Ashrafīyah. See A.A. Vasiliev, *Byzance et les Arabes*, ed. and trans. by Henri Grégoire and Marius Canard (Brussels: Éditions de l'Institut de Philologie et d'Histoire Orientales et Slaves, 1950), 2, pt. 2, 247. The other sources used by Ibn Kathīr are cited by Claude Cahen, *La Syrie du Nord à l'époque des Croisades* (Paris: Librairie Orientaliste Paul Geuthner, 1940), 84.

philological work" and one whose style is "very elementary."[196] Such an assessment fails to appreciate the range of interest and erudition that this *tafsīr* exhibits. While Ibn Kathīr discusses the philological concerns that had, by this time, become standard fare for the commentators, they are not his sole, or even his chief, focus. The *tafsīr* could more appropriately be characterized as the conscious and careful application of a well-developed hermeneutical theory.

As was discussed in Chapter 1, Ibn Kathīr prefaced his *tafsīr* with an extended consideration of the basic principles of Qur'ānic commentary. The various sources from which explanatory material could be garnered and the order in which they were to be consulted was thoroughly expounded. As might be expected from an author who gained such prominence in the sciences of *ḥadīth*, the *Tafsīr al-Qur'ān al-ʿaẓīm* is solidly in the class of *al-tafsīr bi-al-ma'thūr*. In fact, according to the contemporary scholar ʿAbdallāh Maḥmūd Shiḥātah, it is "one of the soundest of *al-tafāsīr bi-al-ma'thūr* if not absolutely the soundest."[197]

In addition to his inclusion of relevant *ḥadīth*s and his judgments upon them, Ibn Kathīr's commentary is distinguished by the incorporation of significant historical material from non-Muslim sources. A good example of this may be found in his discussion of *sūrah Āl ʿImrān* (3):55, where he reviews the first three and a half centuries of Christian history, including the reign of Constantine the Great. Although Ibn Kathīr rarely states his own views explicitly, he does make reference to previous commentators and freely assesses the positions cited. The Iraqi scholar, Qāsim al-Qaysī, finds these judgments to be a good "indication of the power of his intellectual ability."[198] He remarks on Ibn Kathīr's assessment procedures by saying: "When Imām Ibn Kathīr quoted a statement from someone like Ibn Jarīr [al-Ṭabarī] or [Fakhr al-Dīn] al-Rāzī, he did not accept it on blind faith (*bi-mujarrad al-taqlīd*). Rather he formed his own opinion of it. When he thought it correct, he confirmed it. When he thought it incorrect, he rejected and criticized it."[199] His care in this was matched by the attention

196 Laoust, "Ibn Kathīr," *EI²* 3:818. The edition of the *tafsīr* used here is *Tafsīr al-Qur'ān al-ʿaẓīm*, 4 vols. (Cairo: Maṭbaʿah Muṣṭafā Muḥammad, 1356/1937).

197 *Ta'rīkh al-Qur'ān wa-al-tafsīr* (Cairo: al-Hay'ah al-Miṣrīyah al-ʿĀmmah lil-Kitāb, 1392/1972), 176. Muḥammad Ḥusayn al-Dhahabī remarks that within the category of *al-tafsīr bi-al-ma'thūr* "it is considered second only to the work of Ibn Jarīr [al-Ṭabarī]." *al-Tafsīr wa-al-mufassirūn* (Cairo: Maktabah Wahbah, 1405/1985), 1:236. An index of the *ḥadīth*s found in Ibn Kathīr's *tafsīr*, giving the *sūrah* and verse for which each was adduced, has recently been published. Yūsuf ʿAbd al-Raḥmān al-Marʿashlī, Muḥammad Salīm Ibrāhīm Samārah, and Jamāl Ḥamdī al-Dhahabī, *Fibris aḥādīth tafsīr al-Qur'ān al-ʿaẓīm* (Beirut: Dār al-Maʿrifah, 1406/1986).

198 Qāsim al-Qaysī, *Ta'rīkh al-tafsīr* (Baghdad: Maṭbūʿāt al-Majmaʿ al-ʿIlmī al-ʿIrāqī, 1385/1966), 136.

199 al-Qaysī, *Ta'rīkh*, 136. Ismāʿīl Sālim ʿAbd al-ʿĀl has charted what could be called

he paid to all aspects of exegetical procedure. While the *Tafsīr al-Qur'ān al-ʿaẓīm* contains much traditional material, it is not simply a collection uncritically accumulated. Rather it is most thoughtfully ordered and evaluated. As such it bears fitting testimony to a period in Islamic history that was conservative in the positive sense of the term – an era that sought to identify and preserve the best of its received tradition, albeit an era that, in modern times, has often been dismissed as mechanical and uninspired, repetitive and routine, if not actually verging on decadence.

KĀSHĀNĪ

The second of the Persian commentaries selected for this study follows Ibn Kathīr's Arabic *tafsīr* by almost two centuries. It is the work of the early Ṣafavid exegete, Mullā Fatḥ Allāh Kāshānī. Very little is known about this scholar. Biographical entries in the available sources amount to virtually nothing but bibliographic listings. The available information is so scanty that the editor of a recent edition of Kāshānī's *tafsīr* could do little more in his biographical sketch of the author than provide a Persian translation of the relevant section of the *Rawḍāt al-jannāt* of al-Khwānsārī.[200] This latter work describes Kāshānī as a *faqīh*, a *mutakallim* and a *mufassir*. His full name is Mullā Fatḥ Allāh b. Mullā Shukr Allāh Kāshānī, and he is remembered as one of the leading scholars to grace the reign of the Ṣafavid Shāh Tahmāsp the First.[201] As his *nisbah* indicates, he is associated with the city in central Iran that became, among other things, one of the centers of the Ṣafavid carpet industry.[202] Presumably he led there the life expected of a scholar and teacher. His interests ranged beyond Qur'ānic exegesis as is indicated by the commentary he wrote on the *Nahj al-balāghah* (Path of Eloquence), which Shīʿīs have traditionally held to be a collection of dis-

the mixed fortunes of Ibn Kathīr's *tafsīr*. He found no reference to it in such subsequent popular commentaries as Abū al-Suʿūd's (d. 982/1574) *Irshād al-ʿaql al-salīm*, Sulaymān b. ʿUmar al-ʿUjayhī's (d. 1204/1790) *al-Futūḥāt al-ilāhīyah bi-tawḍīḥ tafsīr al-Jalālayn*, and Ṭanṭāwī Jawharī's (d. 1359/1940) *al-Jawāhir fī tafsīr al-Qur'ān al-karīm*. In Maḥmūd Shihāb al-Dīn al-Ālūsī's (d. 1270/1854) *Rūḥ al-Maʿānī* Ibn Kathīr fared somewhat better, while in the *Tafsīr al-Manār* of Rashīd Riḍā he receives substantial citation. *Ibn Kathīr wa-manhajuhu*, 451–52.

200 Abū al-Ḥasan Shaʿrānī, "Tarjamah-i mu'allif," in Mullā Fatḥ Allāh Kāshānī, *Minhaj al-ṣādiqīn fī ilzām al-mukhālifīn* (Tehran: Kitābfurūshī-yi Islāmīyah, 1347 [solar]/1969), 1:44–45. The only thing that Shaʿrānī can add to the material from the *Rawḍāt* is his recollection of an old book in his family's library that contained an *ijāzah* from an ancestor who could trace his line of transmission back to Mullā Fatḥ Allāh.

201 al-Khwānsārī, *Rawḍāt*, 5:345.

202 For a panoramic view of the city of Kāshān see the etching published in Roger Savory's *Iran Under the Safavids* (Cambridge: Cambridge University Press, 1980), 142–43.

courses from the first Imām, ʿAlī b. Abī Ṭālib, and by the translation that he made of al-Ṭabarsī's *Iḥtijāj*.[203]

His exegetical works were three, two in Persian and one in Arabic. The most important is the one used in this study, entitled *Minhaj al-ṣādiqīn fī ilzām al-mukhālifīn* (Procedure of the Truth Affirmers in the [Intellectual] Coercion of Their Opponents). This is among the most comprehensive and renowned of Persian *tafsīrs*, dealing at length with points of Qur'ānic lexicography and grammar.[204] The work begins, as did that of Abū al-Futūḥ Rāzī, with an introductory discussion of such standard exegetical topics as the "canonical" readings, the categories of verses, and the various kinds of interpretation.

In its present edition the *Minhaj* runs to ten large volumes averaging about five hundred pages each.[205] What distinguishes the format of this *tafsīr* is that the Qur'ānic verses are not written out in full. In most classical *tafsīrs* the verse is printed first and the commentary is printed immediately beneath it. The commentary often repeats words or phrases from the verse in the process of explaining them. Kāshānī's *tafsīr*, however, carries only the commentary. His procedure is to cite a word or a phrase from the verse under discussion and then to offer a Persian translation. If he feels the need, he then includes explanatory material. This is frequently in the form of *ḥadīths*, particularly those that express the *sabab al-nuzūl* for the verse. On occasion, he moves from commentary into the realm of theological discourse, or he is apt to append some remarks on the moral implications of the verse.

An abridgment of this work was given the appropriate title *Khulāṣat al-minhaj* (Epitome of "The Minhaj").[206] His Arabic work of exegesis was entitled *Zubdat al-tafsīr* and was completed in 977/1569, eleven years before his death in 988/1580.[207] In addition to the traditions (*akhbār*) of the *ahl al-bayt* (the family of the Prophet), this work contains references from the works of al-Zamakhsharī, al-Bayḍāwī, and al-Ṭabarsī.[208] Doubtless as part

203 In his biographical remarks Manṣūr Pahlavān, the editor of Kāshānī's translation and commentary on the *Nahj al-balāghah*, also reproduces the relevant passages from al-Khwānsārī's *Rawḍāt al-jannāt*. Fatḥ Allāh Kāshānī, *Tanbīh al-ghāfilīn va taẕkirat al-ʿārifīn: tarjumah va sharḥ-i fārsī-yi nahj al-balāghah* (Tehran: Mīqāt, 1364–66 [solar]/1986–88).

204 al-Khwānsārī, *Rawḍāt*, 5:345.

205 Mullā Fatḥ Allāh Kāshānī, *Minhaj al-ṣādiqīn fī ilzām al-mukhālifīn* (Tehran: Kitābfurūshī-yi Islāmīyah, 1347 [solar]/1969).

206 al-Amīn, *Aʿyān al-shīʿah*, 42:261.

207 al-Khwānsārī, *Rawḍāt*, 5:346. A eulogistic chronogram written on the date of his death ends with the epithet "refuge of the *fuqahā'*."

208 al-Khwānsārī, *Rawḍāt*, 5:346.

of his exegetical endeavor, he completed a Persian translation of the Qur'ān that found wide acceptance.

A more recent biographer-bibliographer, Muḥammad Shafī'ī, who confines himself chiefly to the manuscript dispersion and the publication history of Kāshānī's various works, includes an intriguing story about this author.[209] It seems that Kāshānī suffered a heart attack and, unbeknown to his mourners, was buried while still alive. In the tomb he regained consciousness and was discovered by grave robbers when they exhumed his body. While Shafī'ī admits that this event has also been applied to al-Ṭabarsī, he includes it in his biography because of a reputed consequence. According to the report, Kāshānī wrote his *tafsīr* in fulfillment of a vow he made in the tomb when praying for deliverance.

RASHĪD RIḌĀ

The last two commentaries to be examined bring this study into the twentieth century. The first is the *Tafsīr al-Manār* (The Commentary [reprinted from the journal entitled] *The Lighthouse*) of Muḥammad Rashīd Riḍā (and also Muḥammad 'Abduh). The placement of Rashīd Riḍā's name before that of 'Abduh in ascribing authorship of the *tafsīr* contradicts most previous references to this work. From the time of Goldziher on, it has been common to attribute the work to 'Abduh and to mention Rashīd Riḍā in the role of scribe. Such is the course followed by Charles C. Adams in his pioneering study of Egyptian modernism, as well as the position taken by Joseph Schacht, who speaks of Muḥammad 'Abduh's unfinished "commentary on the Qur'ān, on which he laid great importance and of which only portions appeared in his lifetime; it was revised and completed by his disciple and friend Shaikh Muḥammad Rashīd Riḍā."[210]

Certainly the work as initially conceived was that of Muḥammad 'Abduh, not in the sense that he wrote it but inasmuch as it was based on his lectures. As the biographical accounts of both these men's lives report, Rashīd Riḍā took notes at 'Abduh's lectures and then reworked this material into publishable form. He passed this version back to 'Abduh so that the latter could make any corrections he wished.[211] Such a procedure was fol-

209 Shafī'ī, *Mufassirān*, 133.

210 Charles C. Adams, *Islam and Modernism in Egypt* (London: Oxford University Press, 1933), 111; Joseph Schacht, "Muḥammad 'Abduh," *EI*[1] 6:679. Goldziher says of the work: "Es stellt die Konzentration der durch Dschemāl al-dīn und M. 'Abduh propagierten theologischen Lehre dar." *Richtungen*, 325. More recent examples of giving first attribution to Muḥammad 'Abduh are those of G.H.A. Juynboll, *The Authenticity of the Tradition Literature: Discussions in Modern Egypt* (Leiden: E.J. Brill, 1969), 21; and J.J.G. Jansen, *Interpretation*. Chapter 2 of Jansen's book is entitled "Muḥammad Abduh's Koran Interpretation."

211 Adams, *Islam and Modernism*, 199; Muḥammad al-Ṣabbāgh, *Lamaḥāt*, 220–21.

lowed for the treatment of the first one-and-a-half *sūrah*s, which is all that was actually in print by the time of ʿAbduh's death in 1905. The al-Azhar lectures, given between 1899 and 1905, from which the printed version was drawn, had reached only as far as *sūrat al-nisā'* (4):125.[212] Yet the final printed version of the *tafsīr* runs through *sūrah Yūsuf* (12):52.[213] To speak in terms of the thirty traditional recitational divisions of the Qur'ān (*ajzā'*, *s. juz'*), Muḥammad ʿAbduh's lectures covered less than five *ajzā'* (of which only the first *juz'* received his "imprimatur"), while the section for which Rashīd Riḍā is solely responsible is almost eight *ajzā'* or two-thirds of the total published.

That Rashīd Riḍā's stated intent was to continue the work of one he looked upon as "*al-ustādh al-imām*," his intellectual and spiritual master, is undeniable. In fact he often uses this honorific to introduce Muḥammad ʿAbduh's views, particularly in the earlier portions of the commentary. However the amount of material not so attributed, as well as the overall shape of what has been published, compels agreement with Jomier's statement on the *tafsīr* that "the basis of the work rightly seems to be that of Rashīd Riḍā."[214]

212 Jacques Jomier, *Le commentaire coranique du Manār: tendances modernes de l'exégèse coranique en Égypte* (Paris: G.P. Maisonneuve, 1954), 50.

213 There is some discrepancy about this number that may be due to different editions of the work or to simple error. Jane Smith says that the commentary ends with 12:25, which is presumably an accidental transposition of the Arabic numbers. *An Historical and Semantic Study*, 187. Jansen in *Interpretation* (p. 24) states that the *tafsīr* ends with 12:107. This would be in line with what Jomier reported in *Le commentaire* (p. xvi) about its publication history in the journal *al-Manār*, i.e., that commentary covering the beginning of *juz'* thirteen up to 12:107 was published in the first three numbers of vol. 35 of the journal. Rashīd Riḍā died after the issuance of number two of this volume. However, the edition of the *tafsīr* used in this study, as well as the one listed in the bibliography of Jansen's book, does not include these additional fifty-five verses. The edition used here is *Tafsīr al-Qur'ān al-ḥakīm al-shahīr bi-tafsīr al-Manār* (Beirut: Dār al-Maʿrifah lil-Ṭibāʿah wa-al-Nashr, n.d.).

A more recent work on Rashīd Riḍā sheds some light. According to Aḥmad al-Sharabāṣī, Rashīd Riḍā completed the *tafsīr* to 12:101 before his death. At this point Shaykh Muḥammad Bahjah al-Bayṭār undertook completion of the rest of *sūrah Yūsuf*, i.e., through 12:111. The author reproduces a letter from Rashīd Riḍā's nephew to al-Bayṭār expressing hope that the latter will be able to continue beyond this point. But very shortly thereafter *al-Manār* ceased publication. In the final issues someone identified by al-Sharabāṣī only as "one of the scholars" published the *tafsīr* for a section from *sūrat al-raʿd* (13). *Rashīd Riḍā al-ṣiḥāfī al-mufassir al-shāʿir al-lughawī* (Cairo: al-Hay'ah al-ʿĀmmah li-Shu'ūn al-Maṭābiʿ al-Amīrīyah, 1977), 157–59. An abridgment of the *tafsīr*, which was begun by Rashīd Riḍā himself, carries the commentary to 12:111. Muḥammad Rashīd Riḍā and Muḥammad Aḥmad Kanʿān, *Mukhtaṣar tafsīr al-Manār*, ed. by Zuhayr al-Shāwīsh (Beirut: al-Maktab al-Islāmī, 1404/1984).

214 Jomier, *Le commentaire*, 51. He later adds (p. 52): "Bref, la rédaction doit être tenue avant tout pour l'oeuvre de Rachīd Riḍā, et l'opinion du Cheikh ʿAbdoh ne peut être

More has been written in Western languages about al-Sayyid Muḥammad Rashīd Riḍā (and Muḥammad ʿAbduh) than about any of the commentators heretofore discussed.[215] Therefore, while much of such material is tendentious, only the main outlines of his life and thought will be sketched here. Although he spent most of his adult life in Egypt, Rashīd Riḍā was not a native Egyptian. He was a Syrian, born in 1282/1865 in the seacoast village of Qalamūn, about three miles north of the present Lebanese city of Tripoli. He took his earliest education in that village and from there went on to a government *madrasah* in Tripoli.[216] He transferred from that school, at least partly to gain exemption from military service, to the national Islamic *madrasah*, also in Tripoli.[217]

The founder and principal instructor at this latter institution was Shaykh Ḥusayn al-Jisr (d. 1327/1909), who included in his curriculum, naturally still taught entirely in Arabic, the traditional religious sciences as well as logic, mathematics, and European works on the natural sciences. Additionally, there was some language study in Turkish and French.[218] While this educational breadth doubtless made him receptive to the thought of Muḥammad ʿAbduh, Rashīd Riḍā was far from being indiscriminately open to nontraditional studies. Years later he claimed, in his zeal for the sacred language of Arabic, total indifference to further Turkish and French language study.[219]

What did interest him profoundly were the writings of al-Ghazālī, particularly his *Iḥyāʾ ʿulūm al-dīn* (The Spiritual Enlivening of the Religious Sciences).[220] Imbued with their spirit, he joined the Naqshbandīyah *ṭarīqah*

déduite que des passages, à vrai dire très nombreux, que le contexte signale expressément comme étant de lui."

215 In a biography of Rashīd Riḍā, Aḥmad al-Sharabāṣī presents textual evidence of two *kunyahs*, Abū Muḥammad Shafīʿ and Abū ʿAbdallāh. His second child was, in fact, named Muḥammad Shafīʿ. *Rashīd Riḍā ṣāḥib al-Manār ʿaṣruhu wa-ḥayātuhu wa-maṣādir thaqāfatihi* (Cairo: n.p., 1369/1970), 104 and 225.

216 ʿAbd al-Mutaʿālī al-Ṣaʿīdī, *al-Mujaddidūn fī al-islām min al-qarn al-awwal ilā al-rābiʿ ʿashar* (Cairo: Maktabat al-Ādāb, n.d.), 539.

217 al-Ṣaʿīdī, *al-Mujaddidūn*, 539; Jomier, *Le commentaire*, 26.

218 Albert Hourani, *Arabic Thought in the Liberal Age, 1798–1939* (1962; corrected reprint, London: Oxford University Press, 1967), 223. In a series entitled "Les Africains," Hourani has also published a brief biography of Muḥammad ʿAbduh which is drawn against the background of his times and includes extracts from relevant writings by or about him. *Moh'ammed ʿAbduh (1849–1905) ou les voies contemporaines du réformisme musulman* (Paris: Éditions J.A., 1977).

219 Jomier, *Le commentaire*, 26.

220 This translation of al-Ghazālī's title is suggested by the remarks made about it in G. M. Wickens's "Notional Significance in Conventional Arabic 'Book' Titles: Some Unregarded Potentialities," in *The Islamic World, from Classical to Modern Times: Essays in Honor of Bernard Lewis*, ed. by C.E. Bosworth, Charles Issawi, Roger Savory, and A. L. Udovitch (Princeton: Darwin Press, 1989), 371.

(Ṣūfī order), only to become disillusioned with the antinomianism of much Ṣūfī practice.[221] According to Albert Hourani "the suspicion of Sufism thus generated was one of the factors which in later years was to draw him nearer to the teachings of Ibn Taymīyah and the practices of Wahhabism."[222] The decisive influence in his life came, however, not from such centuries-old texts but from a contemporary periodical or more properly from its authors.

The periodical, entitled *al-ʿUrwah al-wuthqā* (The Firmest Bond), was the product of a collaboration between Jamāl al-Dīn al-Afghānī (d. 1314/1897) and Muḥammad ʿAbduh. Although short-lived, the periodical was widely influential and inspired Rashīd Riḍā's emigration to Egypt in 1897.[223] This journey was to be the turning point in his life. But for brief trips, he stayed there until his death in 1935. He went for the sole purpose of working with Muḥammad ʿAbduh and became, in Albert Hourani's phrase, "ʿAbduh's liege man."[224] Theirs was a short but extremely productive affiliation, lasting the eight years from Rashīd Riḍā's arrival until ʿAbduh's death in 1905. ʿAbd al-Mutaʿālī al-Ṣaʿīdī speaks of their intellectual compatibility and notes that ʿAbduh welcomed the younger scholar not only into his lecture hall but also into his home.[225] From this association, apparently at the instigation of Rashīd Riḍā, grew that "beacon"

221 al-Ṣaʿīdī, *al-Mujaddidūn*, 539.

222 Hourani, *Arabic Thought*, 225. Rashīd Riḍā's affinity for the reformist ideology of the Wahhābīyah, an affinity that Ḥusayn Ḍanāwī deems "substantive (*mawḍūʿī*) and decisive (*ḥatmī*)," is discussed at length in his study *al-Sayyid Rashīd Riḍā fikruhu wa-niḍāluhu al-siyāsī* (Tripoli: Dār al-Inshā', 1983), 212–20.

223 On the basis of his study of ʿAbduh's contributions to *al-ʿUrwah al-wuthqā*, P.J. Vatikiotis has tried to prove that "ʿAbduh preached a liberal and humanistic Islam, free of rigid traditional formulations and invigorated by rational and historical methods of criticism." "Muḥammad ʿAbduh and the Quest for Muslim Humanism," *Arabica* 4 (1957): 71–72. Jacques Jomier sounds a more conservative note in his "La revue 'al-orwa al-wothqa' (13 mars–16 octobre 1884) et l'autorité du Coran," *MIDEO* 17 (1986): 9–36. A doctoral thesis for al-Azhar by Ḥasīb al-Sāmarrā'ī deals at length with Rashīd Riḍā's *tafsīr* precisely in the context of its relation to the thought of both Muḥammad ʿAbduh and Jamāl al-Dīn al-Afghānī. *Rashīd Riḍā al-mufassir* (Baghdad: Dār al-Risālah lil-Ṭibāʿah, 1396/1976).

224 Hourani, *Arabic Thought*, 226. Olaf H. Schumann, who declares that "mit Muḥammad ʿAbduh begann für den ägyptischen Islam eine neue Epoche," devotes a chapter of his work on Islamic Christology to ʿAbduh and "die Manâr-Schule." *Der Christus der Muslime*, 113.

225 al-Ṣaʿīdī, *al-Mujaddidūn*, 540. J.J.G. Jansen has drawn an interesting parallel between the generation of *Tafsīr al-Manār* and the exegetical writings of a prominent contemporary religious personality in Egypt, Shaykh Muḥammad Mutawallī al-Shaʿrāwī. Calling attention to the role played by Rashīd Riḍā, Jansen remarks, "It is fascinating to see how something very similar seems to be happening to Shaikh al-Shaʿrāwī. His admirer Aḥmad Zayn announces, obviously full of pride, that the Shaikh has assented to his suggestion to write a commentary on the whole Qur'ān. . . . " "Shaikh al-Shaʿrāwī's Interpretation of the Qur'ān," *UEAI 10*, 24.

of Islamic modernism, the journal *al-Manār* (The Lighthouse).[226] Its agenda was reform: social, educational, but above all, religious. This journal, which served especially in the early years as a mouthpiece for Muḥammad ʿAbduh's ideas, was the principal lifework of Rashīd Riḍā. He gave much of his adult years to it and, significantly, it ceased publication not long after his death.

It was in this periodical that the exegetical articles that were eventually to be issued separately as the twelve-volume *Tafsīr al-Manār* first saw the light of day. As was noted earlier, these articles were based on the notes Rashīd Riḍā took at ʿAbduh's lectures on exegesis. In his biography of Muḥammad ʿAbduh, Osman Amin has captured the ambience of these famous lectures in the lantern-lit mosque of al-Azhar:

> You would have seen all of them in the most profound silence, without hearing a word, a cough or a whisper. All of them with their ears straining and their eyes fastened on the Sheikh . . . . As for the manner of his delivery, he neither spoke hurriedly or read rapidly, his speech being punctuated with pauses between each sentence. His diction was pure and his eloquence rare, so that the slow writer could easily put down what he heard without having to make later corrections.[227]

The ardor with which Rashīd Riḍā promoted the ideas of Muḥammad ʿAbduh has prompted one critic to complain that he treated ʿAbduh's work itself like a religious text.[228] Others have highlighted the differences that developed between the thought of the two men, differences more of emphasis than of fundamental principle. Even before his death, Rashīd Riḍā was ranked by Charles C. Adams as "more and more on the side of the Conservatives rather than the Liberal and progressive element."[229] Whereas Muḥammad ʿAbduh had sought to balance the twin demands of Islamic values and those of modern civilization, Rashīd Riḍā laid heavy "emphasis on the unchanging nature of the central doctrines of Islam . . . and moved in the direction of a Hanbali or Wahhabi fundamentalism."[230] Put more

226 Some of the initial contacts and conversation between Muḥammad ʿAbduh and Rashīd Riḍā, particularly those concerning the development of al-Manār, are detailed by Ibrāhīm Aḥmad al-ʿAdawī in *Rashīd Riḍā al-imām al-mujāhid* (Cairo: al-Muʾassasah al-Miṣrīyah al-ʿĀmmah lil-Taʾlīf, n.d.), 129–50.

227 Osman Amin, *Muḥammad ʿAbduh*, trans. by Charles Wendel (Washington, D.C.: American Council of Learned Societies, 1953), 86. Fazlur Rahman describes Muḥammad ʿAbduh's efforts to secure academic and administrative reforms at al-Azhar. *Islam and Modernity*, 63–69.

228 Zaki Badawi, *The Reformers of Egypt–A Critique of Al-Afghani, ʿAbduh and Ridha* (Slough, Berkshire, England: The Open Press, 1976), 67.

229 Adams, *Islam and Modernism*, 185. See also H.A.R. Gibb, *Modern Trends*, 33–36.

230 Albert Hourani in the "Preface" to Jamal Mohammed Ahmed's *The Intellectual Origins of Egyptian Nationalism* (London: Oxford University Press, 1960), p. x. Mahmudul Haq feels that for "a real appreciation of the *tafsīr* a distinction must be made between

positively, Muḥammad ʿAbduh's impatience with the minutiae of conventional Islamic scholarship is contrasted with Rashīd Riḍā's willingness to enter the fray in defense of "an entire range of the traditional heritage."[231]

It may be that much of the difference between the two men can be tied to their diversity of cultural background. Whereas Muḥammad ʿAbduh, through his friends and his travels, knew a good deal about European civilization, Rashīd Riḍā's exposure to it was much more limited and not gladly accepted, even so. According to Albert Hourani "he belonged to the last generation of those who could be fully educated and yet alive in a self-sufficient Islamic world of thought."[232] If his cultural scope was more restricted than that of ʿAbduh so was his influence within Egypt and beyond. Unlike the latter, who in 1899 was appointed the Muftī of Egypt, the highest religio-legal post in the country, Rashīd Riḍā held no public office or al-Azhar lectureship. His professional concerns were focused rather on the continued propagation of those ideas of religious renewal and reform which, in particular, had first excited him in the thought of Muḥammad ʿAbduh. To this end he continued to write and publish, especially in the pages of *al-Manār*, until his death in 1354/1935.

The most lasting result of that life's work is the series of articles now separately published as *Tafsīr al-Manār*. While occasionally embroiled in controversy when first published, the *Tafsīr* is now held "to be authoritative by both progressive and conservative Egyptian Moslem theologians."[233] Its innovations range from those of format to those of substance. Unlike earlier commentaries, both manuscript and printed, the *Tafsīr al-Manār* numbered the verses of each *sūrah*, a procedure now commonplace in published *tafsīrs*.

the liberal attitude of ʿAbduh and the more puritan and fundamentalist attitude of his disciple." *Muḥammad ʿAbduh: A Study of a Modern Thinker of Egypt* (Aligarh: Institute of Islamic Studies, Aligarh Muslim University, 1970), 110.

231 Jomier, *Le commentaire*, 63. G.H.A. Juynboll discusses Rashīd Riḍā's greater interest in *ʿilm al-ḥadīth*. *Authenticity, passim*. Henri Laoust sees in the activities and writings of Rashīd Riḍā a reappropriation of the medieval notion of active religious exhortation and propagation (*daʿwah*). "Renouveau de l'apologétique missionnaire traditionnelle au xxe siècle dans l'oeuvre de Rashīd Riḍā," in *Prédication*, 271–92. Juan R. Cole argues that Rashīd Riḍā's views about such missionary activity were forged in the encounter with both his Christian and Bahā'ī counterparts. "Rashid Rida on the Baha'i Faith: A Utilitarian Theory of the Spread of Religions," *Arab Studies Quarterly* 5 (1983): 276–91.

232 Hourani, *Arabic Thought*, 235. Malcolm Kerr also noted the discrepancy of cultural interests between ʿAbduh and Rashīd Riḍā in his *Islamic Reform: The Political and Legal Theories of Muḥammad ʿAbduh and Rashīd Riḍā* (Berkeley: University of California Press, 1966), 154–55. The social and political influences upon Rashīd Riḍā's varying assessments of the Western cultural heritage are examined in Emad Eldin Shahin, "Muḥammad Rashīd Riḍā's Perspectives on the West as Reflected in *al-Manār*," *MW* 79 (1989): 113-32.

233 Jansen, *Interpretation*, 20.

On the other hand, in the text of the commentary, repetitions of the verse under discussion, or parts thereof, are overlined, not underlined. According to Jomier, Riḍā purposely continued this traditional practice of written Arabic and criticized those who aped the European system of underlining.[234]

Its substantive differences from the previous exegetical tradition involve omissions as much as additions. In line with his goal of making the Qurʾān accessible to those who had not studied the full panoply of religious sciences, the source of this *tafsīr*, Muḥammad ʿAbduh steered away from elaborate philological or syntactical analyses. In fact, he considered most such discussions to be an unnecessary obfuscation of the text. He also abstained from attempting to explain what were traditionally recognized as obscure (*mubham*) terms in the text.[235] The exegete, in Muḥammad ʿAbduh's view, "has no right, is in fact forbidden, to identify anything that is left unidentified by the Koran itself."[236] For much the same reason ʿAbduh was very sparing in his use of *asbāb al-nuzūl* material or any other sort of supplementary data. He was also unenthusiastic about exegetical attempts to find in the Qurʾān statements that anticipate the discoveries of modern science (*tafsīr ʿilmī*). Where he does associate the two, it is not to suggest that the Qurʾān contains concealed references to such discoveries but simply to indicate that the two are not incompatible.[237] Unlike most – but not all – previous commentators, he grouped the verses of a *sūrah* into mean-

234 Jomier, *Le commentaire*, 53.

235 ʿAbdallāh Maḥmūd Shiḥātah devotes a chapter of his study on Muḥammad ʿAbduh to this hermeneutical judgment. The examples culled from ʿAbduh's exegesis include such matters as the unidentified town (*al-qaryah*) mentioned in *sūrat al-baqarah* (2):58, the plague from heaven (*rijzan min al-samāʾ*) cited in *sūrat al-baqarah* (2):59, and the food (*rizq*) that Zachary found in Mary's chamber in *sūrah Āl ʿImrān* (3):37. Beyond that Shiḥātah discusses ʿAbduh's exegetical restraint in dealing with various issues of eschatology (*al-ṣirāṭ wa-al-mīzān wa-al-jannah wa-al-nār*) as well as the substantive theological issue of God's determining decree (*al-qaḍāʾ wa-al-qadar*). To highlight the positions taken by Muḥammad ʿAbduh, Shiḥātah compares them with those of his predecessors like al-Zamakhsharī, Fakhr al-Dīn al-Rāzī, al-Bayḍāwī, and Jalāl al-Dīn al-Suyūṭī. *Manhaj al-Imām Muḥammad ʿAbduh fī tafsīr al-Qurʾān al-karīm* (1960; reprint, Cairo: Maṭbaʿah Jāmiʿat al-Qāhirah, 1984), 137–60.

236 Jansen, *Interpretation*, 26. In an earlier study Jansen draws upon this hermeneutical principle of agnosticism to explain British Agent and Consul General Cromer's suspicion that ʿAbduh was an agnostic. See " 'I suspect that my friend Abdu (. . .) was in reality an agnostic,' " in *Acta Orientalia Neerlandica: Proceedings of the Congress of the Dutch Oriental Society, 1970*, ed. by P.W. Pestman (Leiden: E.J. Brill, 1971), 71–74. Jansen's defense of ʿAbduh was a response to the highly critical, revisionist study by Elie Kedourie entitled *Afghani and ʿAbduh: An Essay on Religious Unbelief and Political Activism in Modern Islam* (New York: The Humanities Press, 1966).

237 ʿAbd al-Majīd ʿAbd al-Salām al-Muḥtasib comments on Rashīd Riḍā's rejection of *tafsīr ʿilmī* in *Ittijāhāt al-tafsīr fī al-ʿaṣr al-ḥadīth* (Beirut: Dār al-Fikr, 1973), 302–03.

ingful units and sought to establish connections among the *sūrah*s themselves. In other words, the notion of context and integrity enters as a hermeneutical principle and is expressed in terms of the literary excellence (*iʿjāz*) of the Qurʾān.[238]

In his own contributions to the *Tafsīr* Rashīd Riḍā gradually reintroduced much of the traditional material that ʿAbduh had eliminated. Thus, Riḍā includes the classical philological and syntactical considerations, where relevant, and has recourse to the *asbāb al-nuzūl* material. He continues ʿAbduh's practice of discoursing on the moral implications of a passage, but such digressions become longer and more frequent.[239] One of Rashīd Riḍā's most helpful additions is the summary of principal ideas with which he concludes each *sūrah*. These amount to concise theological treatises and provide a useful introduction to the study of the *sūrah* as a whole. They also go far to secure Rashīd Riḍā's position as one of the preeminent exegetes of this century.

ṬABĀṬABĀʾĪ

Rashīd Riḍā's counterpart for twentieth-century Shīʿī commentary is undoubtedly Muḥammad Ḥusayn Ṭabāṭabāʾī, an Iranian scholar who died but a few years after the revolutionary events of 1979. Because of the efforts of one of his former students, English-speaking readers are likely to consider Ṭabāṭabāʾī among the most prominent Shīʿī scholars of the latter part of this century. Over the last two decades Seyyed Hossein Nasr has promoted and nurtured a publishing project that drew upon the authorial and editorial skills of Ṭabāṭabāʾī. In an effort to make material on Shīʿī Islam available to Western readers, Nasr persuaded Ṭabāṭabāʾī to write two works in Persian, *Shīʿah dar Islām* and *Qurʾān dar Islām*. Nasr then translated the first of these monographs and saw them both through publication in the United States and Great Britain.[240] Additionally, Ṭabāṭabāʾī made a selection of Shīʿī *ḥadīth*s and prayers that were then translated into English and published as a short anthology.[241] In the introductions to this Ṭabāṭabāʾī

238 Haq, *Muḥammad ʿAbduh*, 113–14; Adams, *Islam and Modernism*, 201–02; Goldziher, *Richtungen*, 345.

239 J.M.S. Baljon finds the "desire to give moral lessons whenever the text affords an opportunity" to be the most distinguishing feature of this commentary. *Modern Muslim Koran Interpretation, 1880–1960* (Leiden: E.J. Brill, 1961), 5.

240 ʿAllāmah Sayyid Muḥammad Ḥusayn Ṭabāṭabāʾī, *Shīʿite Islam*, ed. and trans. by Seyyed Hossein Nasr (London: George Allen and Unwin, 1975), and *The Qurʾān in Islam: Its Impact and Influence on the Life of Muslims*, trans. by Assadullah ad-Dhaakir Yate (London: Zahra, 1987). In the Foreword to the second work Nasr notes that both of these works have been very popular in their Persian editions and have been translated into other Islamic languages.

241 *A Shīʿite Anthology*, ed. and trans. by William C. Chittick (London: Muḥammadi Trust of Great Britain and Northern Ireland, 1980).

trilogy Nasr has provided some biographical information on his revered teacher.[242]

ʿAllāmah Sayyid Muḥammad Ḥusayn Ṭabāṭabāʾī was born in 1321/1903 in the northwestern Iranian city of Tabrīz. As the word "Sayyid" in his name indicates, his family claims descent from the Prophet. It is a family whose tradition of scholarship is several hundred years old. His earliest education, which included Arabic and the fundamentals of the religious sciences, was local, in his native city of Tabrīz. As a young adult, he left Iran and went to Najaf in Iraq, a city sacred to the Shīʿī as the location of ʿAlī's tomb.[243] During the nineteenth and the early twentieth centuries Najaf was under Ottoman authority and thus beyond the jurisdiction of Nāṣir al-Dīn Shāh and his successors. It served politically active *ʿulamāʾ* as a kind of battle station in exile from which to launch offensives against the perceived corruptions of the Qājārs.[244]

In Najaf, Ṭabāṭabāʾī pursued advanced studies in *uṣūl al-fiqh* and *fiqh* under Mīrzā Muḥammad Ḥusayn Nāʾīnī and Shaykh Muḥammad Ḥusayn Iṣfahānī.[245] About his competence in these areas Nasr makes the following remark: "He became such a master in this domain that had he kept completely to these fields he would have become one of the foremost *mujtahid*s or authorities on Divine Law and would have been able to wield much political and social influence."[246] However, Ṭabāṭabāʾī's interests took a philosophical turn and he began work on such major sources as the *Shifāʾ* of Ibn Sīnā and the *Asfār* of Ṣadr al-Dīn Shīrāzī (Mullā Ṣadrā, d. 1050/1642). It was in this field that Ṭabāṭabāʾī would concentrate much of his scholarly effort. Among his published works is the *Ḥāshiyah bar Asfār*, glosses on a new edition of Mullā Ṣadrā's *Asfār*.[247]

His study of Islamic philosophy did not remain solely an intellectual

242 As the principal source for the biographical information that follows see Nasr, "Preface," *Shiʿite Islam*, 22–25. See also Yann Richard, *Le Shi'isme en Iran* (Paris: Jean Maisonneuve, 1980), 105–06.

243 A short chronology of Ṭabāṭabāʾī's life dates this move to 1926. It is published in the initial, unnumbered pages of a commemorative volume issued a year after his death. The work carries eulogistic remarks from leading religio-political figures, such as Ayatollah Khomeini (d. 1409/1989), Ayatollah Montazeri, and representatives of major educational institutions, as well as articles about Ṭabāṭabāʾī's thought and works. *Yādnāmah-i mufassir-i kabīr ustād ʿAllāmah-i Ṭabāṭabāʾī* (Qum: Intishārāt-i Shafaq, 1361 [solar]/1983).

244 Dwight M. Donaldson, *The Shiʿite Religion* (London: Luzac, 1933), 63.

245 A sample syllabus for the traditional *madrasah* course of study may be found in Michael Fischer, *Iran: From Religious Dispute to Revolution* (Cambridge, Mass.: Harvard University Press, 1980), 247–49.

246 Nasr, "Preface," *Shiʿite Islam*, 22.

247 Ṭabāṭabāʾī, *Shiʿite Islam*, 239; Seyyed Hossein Nasr, "Ṣadr al-Dīn Shīrāzī (Mullā Ṣadrā)," in *A History of Muslim Philosophy*, ed. by M.M. Sharif (Wiesbaden: Otto Harrassowitz, 1966), 433, note 3.

endeavor. Under the guidance of Mīrzā ʿAlī Qāḍī, he embarked upon the time-honored spiritual exercises of the mystical quest. These evidently marked him permanently, for Nasr describes him as one whose "presence carries with it the silence of perfect contemplation and concentration even when he is speaking."[248]

In 1353/1934 Ṭabāṭabāʾī went back to Tabrīz and spent a few quiet years teaching and writing. After the Second World War he settled in the pilgrimage city of Qum, the intellectual center of Persian Shīʿism.[249] He taught chiefly in the fields of *tafsīr* and philosophical mysticism, in the latter concentrating particularly on the works of Mullā Ṣadrā. His reputation grew quickly and he soon attracted large numbers of students. Two of his books, *Uṣūl-i falsafah wa-rawish-i riʾālīsm* (The Fundamentals of Philosophy and the Procedure of Realism) and *Masāʾil-i jadīd-i falsafah* (New Philosophical Questions), became part of the standard *madrasah* curriculum.[250] The first of these is a philosophical and theological response to the theory of dialectical and other materialisms.

The philosophical foundations of Marxism-Leninism were not the only non-Islamic thought forms that drew his attention. Through his association with Henri Corbin, Ṭabāṭabāʾī became interested in the study of comparative mysticism. For a number of years Corbin, Ṭabāṭabāʾī, Nasr (who frequently served as translator for the two), and others met regularly in Tehran to study the classics of mysticism.[251] At each meeting "the sacred texts of one of the major religions, containing mystical and gnostic teachings, such as the Tao Te-Ching, the Upanishads and the Gospel of John, were discussed and compared with Sufism and Islamic gnostic doctrines in general."[252] This background in comparative religion is quite prominent in Ṭabāṭabāʾī's *tafsīr*, as will be evident in those sections of it analyzed in this study.

Ṭabāṭabāʾī, who died on 18 Muḥarram (5 November) 1403/1982, lived to be eighty years old. Almost half of those years were spent in Qum, where he gained a reputation that spread far beyond its boundaries. In a tribute that could have been penned only by an ardent disciple, he is praised as "a symbol of what is most permanent in the long tradition of Islamic schol-

248 Nasr, "Preface," *Shīʿite Islam*, 23.

249 While the chronology in *Yādnāmah* dates this move to 1947, Nasr places it earlier, in 1945. See "Foreword," *The Qurʾān in Islam*, 10. For a glimpse of Qum as a center of religious learning and a depiction of the religious and spiritual formation of a twentieth-century intellectual within that traditional milieu, see Roy Mottahedeh, *The Mantle of the Prophet: Religion and Politics in Iran* (New York: Pantheon, 1985).

250 Fischer, *Iran*, 248.

251 Nasr, "Foreword," *Qurʾān in Islam*, 10–11, and "Introduction," *Shīʿite Anthology*, 9.

252 Nasr, "Preface," *Shīʿite Islam*, 24.

arship and science," and a person whose "presence carries a fragrance which can only come from one who has tasted the fruit of Divine Knowledge."[253]

Ṭabāṭabā'ī's *al-Mīzān fī tafsīr al-Qur'ān* (The [Justly Held] Scales in the Interpretation of the Qur'ān) itself bears witness to the breadth of his scholarship. It is a large, twenty-volume work that, according to its colophon, was completed in 1392/1972.[254] Like Rashīd Riḍā, this exegete has divided the verses of a *sūrah* into internally cohesive units. Unlike most classical commentators, therefore, he does not analyze one verse at a time but seeks to exhibit the connections between various sections of a *sūrah*. The commentary on the chosen group of verses is then further subdivided.

After citing the verse(s) under discussion, Ṭabāṭabā'ī begins his Exposition (*bayān*). This usually includes such exegetical "standards" as etymological and grammatical discussions. It is also likely to contain reference to other verses in the Qur'ān that the author considers relevant.[255] In the main, however, it presents Ṭabāṭabā'ī's own thoughts and elucidations of the passage under consideration. Frequently these will develop into lengthy discourses on the moral implications to be elicited from the passage. At other times he draws attention to the mystical-philosophical ramifications that may be uncovered by one who is prepared to perceive them.[256]

What he does not usually include are references to the *ḥadīth* literature, which form so much a part of other commentaries. These he reserves for a separate section following the *bayān*. This section, entitled Discussion of Transmitted Material (*baḥth riwā'ī*), contains relevant excerpts from *ḥadīth*

253 Nasr, "Preface," *Shi'ite Islam*, 25. William Montgomery Watt in a review of Ṭabāṭabā'ī's *Shi'ite Islam* notes that, at least in that work, the author has made no "attempt to come to terms with occidental thought. The author still lives in the world of traditional Islamic theology, virtually untouched by any 'impact of the West'." *RS* 13 (1977): 378.

254 Muḥammad Ḥusayn al-Ṭabāṭabā'ī, *al-Mīzān fī tafsīr al-Qur'ān*, 20 vols. (Beirut: Mu'assasat al-A'lāmī lil-Maṭbū'āt, 1394/1974). Although written in Arabic, *al-Mīzān* has been translated into Persian as *Tarjumah-i tafsīr-i al-mīzān*, trans. by Nāṣir Makārim Shīrāzī et al. (Qum: Chāpkhānah-i Dār al-'Ilm, 1337–54/1959–78). There is a subject index to the Persian translation by Ilyās Kalāntarī, *Rāhnamā-yi mawḍū'āt-i tarjumah-i al-mīzān fī tafsīr al-Qur'ān* (Tehran: Intishārāt-i Wafā, 1361 [solar]/1983). An English translation through 3:41 has been published as *Al-Mīzān: An Exegesis of the Qur'ān*, trans. by Sayyid Saeed Akhtar Rizvi (Tehran: World Organization for Islamic Services, 1403/1983–).

255 The classical hermeneutical principle of allowing one portion of the Qur'ān to illumine another receives prominent consideration in Ṭabāṭabā'ī. For a brief discussion see Abū al-Qāsim Razzāqī, "Bā 'Allāmah Ṭabāṭabā'ī dar al-mīzān," *Yādnāmah*, 216–18. This article also includes summary reference to the noteworthy contents of each volume of *al-Mīzān*.

256 Henri Corbin, in fact, refers to this as "un commentaire philosophique." See his "La philosophie islamique depuis la mort d'Averroës jusqu'à nos jours," *Histoire de la philosophie (Encyclopédie de la Pléiade)*, ed. by Yvon Belaval (Paris: Éditions Gallimard, 1974), 3:1171.

collections and from previous commentaries, particularly those of Muḥammad b. Masʿūd al-ʿAyyāshī (d. 320/932), ʿAlī b. Ibrāhīm b. Hāshim al-Qummī (d. 328/939), and al-Ṭabarsī.[257] He frequently glosses these too with explanatory remarks.

In addition to this transmitted material Ṭabāṭabā'ī, on occasion, will add an *excursus* (or a series of them) on some issue prompted by the passage under discussion. These vary from short to quite lengthy treatises, and range broadly over such areas as the religious sciences of Qur'ān and *ḥadīth*, as well as the historical, philosophical and natural sciences.[258] An index to these treatises, with which each volume of *al-Mīzān* concludes, is the best evidence of the remarkable versatility of this exegete.

257 ʿAlī Awsī has surveyed the varied exegetical, linguistic, and historical sources upon which *al-Mīzān* draws, including a list of all the works from which Ṭabāṭabā'ī quotes *ḥadīths*. *al-Ṭabāṭabā'ī wa-manhajuhu fī tafsīrihi al-mīzān* (Tehran: al-Jumhūrīyah al-Islāmīyah fī Īrān, 1985), 59–94.

258 Tributes to the remarkable breadth of *al-Mīzān* are offered by, among others, Kalāntarī, *Rāhnamā*, 5–6, and Sayyid Jalāl al-Dīn Ashtiyānī, "Chihrahā-yi dirakhshān," *Maʿārif-i islāmī* 5 (1347 [solar]/1969): 50.

PART II

Qurʾānic commendation of Christians

3

Nazarenes of faith and action

The first clear instance of Qur'ānic approbation of Christians denies them the stature of singularity. It compliments them in a cluster, yoked with others in a common nod of approval. The verse links Christians with Jews, with a somewhat mysterious group named the Ṣābi'ūn, and yet more generally, with any who believe in God. A preliminary translation offered here is tagged with the proviso that should mentally accompany the translation of each of the verses as they occur. Any translation is, of course, an exegetical act, a choice among varying – sometimes competing – understandings of the text. To provide a translation at this introductory stage inevitably compromises, to some degree, the unfolding presentation of that range of exegetical options which have been exercised in the long history of commentary on these verses. Yet to make this discourse accessible to the non-Arabist, provisional English renderings must be given. In each instance, however, this rendering is best read as preliminary, as simply a way to begin the hermeneutical conversation. The verse with which this chapter deals is from the second *sūrah* of the Qur'ān, *sūrat al-baqarah* (2):62:

> Truly those who believe and those who are Jews, the Christians and the Ṣābi'ūn, whoever believes in God and the Last Day and does right, for them is their reward near their Lord; they will have no fear, neither will they grieve.

The interpretation of this verse, as it has developed over the many centuries of Muslim exegetical activity, may be divided into a series of overlapping questions. It should be made clear at the outset, however, that these questions do not reflect categories or subdivisions within the individual commentaries themselves. Rather they are an analytical device which this author has devised for the purpose of clarifying the lines of inquiry that emerge in the study of this exegetical tradition. It can be argued, however, that the questions are implicit in the interpretive data that the commentaries yield even if they did not constitute a conscious agenda on the part of the exegetes themselves.

THE QUR'ĀNIC TERM FOR CHRISTIANS

Not unexpectedly, issues of identification figure prominently in the exegetical concerns that surround this verse. The verse begins with four phrases: *those who believe, those who are Jews, the Christians,* and *the Ṣābi'ūn*. For each of those phrases the commentators have sought both general and specific identification. Al-Ṭabarī's opening definition of *those who believe* is short and precise: they are "the ones who accept what the Messenger of God brought them of God's truth. They believe it and acknowledge the truth of it."[1] He follows this with a word study of the three other groups mentioned in the opening phrases of this verse. While his etymological analysis of *those who are Jews* is perfunctory, that of *the Ṣābi'ūn* is prolonged and prolific. The lack of a clear referent for this word occasioned a multiplicity of theories.[2]

1 al-Ṭabarī, *Jāmiʿ al-bayān*, 2:143. In this and subsequent chapters phrases excerpted from each verse for discussion will be printed in italics and will uniformly follow the initial translation of the verse. In the present instance, for example, *those who believe* will be the consistent rendering of *alladhīna āmanū*. Wilfred Cantwell Smith has performed a valuable service in pointing out the difficulties inherent in using the common modern connotations of the word 'belief' as a translation for *īmān* and its cognates. Particularly in Chapter 3 of his book, *Faith and Belief* (Princeton: Princeton University Press, 1979), he has argued at length for substituting what he deems to be the more inclusive term 'faith'. In an earlier, related discussion Smith has noted that the words "accepte my bileve" in the *Canterbury Tales* of Chaucer actually mean "accept my loyalty; receive me as one who submits himself to you." *Belief and History* (Charlottesville: University Press of Virginia, 1977), 42. This use of the verb 'submit', the most common English rendering of the Arabic *maṣdar, islām,* provides a fortuitous example of how apposite the term 'belief' can be in the present context when taken in this broader sense. (A former student of Smith's, Jane I. Smith, has, in turn, published a dissertation that traces the exegetical treatment of the Qur'ānic use of the word *islām*. See *An Historical and Semantic Study of the Term 'Islām' as Seen in a Sequence of Qur'ān Commentaries* [Missoula, Mont.: Scholars Press, 1975].)

In a recent article Richard Frank argues that the English word 'faith', "though adequate, not to say appropriate, in some contexts, on the one hand tends to evoke a number of strictly Christian connotations that are conceptually alien to the religious semantics of Arabic '*īmān*' as used by Muslim writers and on the other, as employed in works on comparative religion, is often extremely vague and so misses the carefully drawn Muslim conception altogether." "Knowledge and *Taqlīd*: The Foundations of Religious Belief in Classical Ashʿarism," *JAOS* 109 (1989): 38 note 3. A further issue with respect to the English translation of such forms as *āmana* and *āmanū* is presented in the decision of certain commentators to equate the phrase *alladhīna āmanū* with the 'hypocrites', as will be seen in the ensuing analysis.

2 For a survey of exegetical theories on the term *ṣābi'ūn*, see my "Exegetical Identification of the Ṣābi'ūn," *MW* 72 (1982): 95–106. Two recent articles reexamine the problem of Ṣābi'ūn identity: Christopher Buck, "The Identity of the Ṣābi'ūn: An Historical Quest," *MW* 74 (1984): 172–86; and Michel Tardieu, "Ṣabiens coraniques et 'ṣabiens' de Ḥarrān," *JA* 274 (1986): 1–44. Reading a parallel mention of the Ṣābi'ūn in 5:69 in tandem with

With *the Christians,* the phrase of most interest for this study, al-Ṭabarī charts a middle course, offering a brief discussion of alternative plurals for *al-naṣārā*, the term by which Christians are designated, and advancing three explanations for the name. The first is that this lexeme, one of whose notional root meanings in Arabic could be 'to help', 'to offer assistance', was applied to this group "because of their support (*nuṣrah*) for each other and their offering mutual assistance (*tanāṣur*) among themselves."[3] The second reason for the name is that these people were associated with a place called *Nāṣirah*, with Jesus himself being called the Nazarene (*al-nāṣirī*). The third is that its etymology is Qurʾānic, being based on Jesus' question to his disciples as recorded in *sūrat al-ṣaff* (61): 14: "Who will be my helpers (*anṣār*) for God?"[4] (The word here translated as 'helpers' is yet another form of the Arabic radicals *NṢR* from which *al-naṣārā* was thought to be formed. Thus this third derivational hypothesis is really a variant on the first.) Clearly the preferred explanation in al-Ṭabarī's view is the second, as indicated by the number of *ḥadīth*s he records in support of it. In several of these *ḥadīth*s more precise identification is made and *Nāṣirah* is specifically identified as the village where Jesus used to live (i.e., Nazareth).[5]

Al-Ṭūsī's commentary on this verse closely follows the pattern set by al-Ṭabarī. He, too, begins with an etymological analysis of the verse's initial

its preceding verse allows Tardieu to assert confidently that *sūrat al-māʾidah* "les classe explicitement parmi les *ahl al-kitāb*" (p. 40). Such a reading, however, ignores the exegetical – and legal – complexities created by the Qurʾānic mention of this group.

3 al-Ṭabarī, *Jāmiʿ al-bayān*, 2:144. For a standard lexical explanation of *al-naṣārā* consult Majmaʿ al-lughah al-arabīyah's *Muʿjam alfāẓ al-Qurʾān al-karīm* (Cairo: al-Maṭbaʿah al-Thaqāfīyah, 1390/1970), 6:124. The basic etymological investigation of *al-naṣārā* is that of Josef Horovitz, *Koranische Untersuchungen* (Berlin: Walter de Gruyter, 1926), 144–46. A.S. Tritton draws upon this in his "Naṣārā," *EI*[1] 6:848–51, and Arthur Jeffery offers additional analysis in his *The Foreign Vocabulary of the Qurʾān* (Baroda: Oriental Institute, 1938), 280–81. Richard Bell notes that *al-naṣārā* had "become the usual name for Christians in Arabic, and as such was in use amongst the Arabs before Muhammad's time. . . . " *The Origin of Islam in its Christian Environment* (London: Macmillan, 1926), 149. Neither the terms *al-naṣārā* nor *al-ṣābiʾūn* are mentioned by al-Suyūṭī in his section of the *Itqān* devoted to non-Arabic terms, while *majūs* (which will appear in the parallel verse, *sūrat al-ḥajj* [22]: 17) and *al-hūd*, another Qurʾānic designation for the Jews, are included, both of them on the authority of Abū Manṣūr al-Jawālīqī. *Itqān*, 2:116–17. Rachad Hamzaoui, author of a work on the Cairo Academy of the Arabic Language, has surveyed a number of the standard classical sources on the issue of linguistic borrowing in the Qurʾān, including relevant works by al-Suyūṭī. He finds the lines of argument remarkably similar to contemporary debates about nationalistic linguistic integrity. "Idéologie et langue ou l'emprunt linguistique d'après les exégètes du Coran et les théologiens: interprétation socio-linguistique," *Atti 2 congresso internazionale di linguistica camito-semitica, 1974* (Florence: Istituto di Linguistica et di Lingue Orientale, 1978), 157–71.

4 al-Ṭabarī, *Jāmiʿ al-bayān*, 2:145.

5 al-Ṭabarī, *Jāmiʿ al-bayān*, 2:145.

phrases. When treating the term *al-naṣārā*, al-Ṭūsī spends some time listing variant forms and then enumerates the same three possible derivations for the word given by al-Ṭabarī.[6] His source authorities for supporting *ḥadīths*, namely ʿAbd al-Malik b. ʿAbd al-ʿAzīz b. Jurayj (d. 150/767), Ibn ʿAbbās, and Qatādah b. Diʿāmah (d. 117/735), also duplicate those offered by al-Ṭabarī. Yet he breaks with al-Ṭabarī in preferring the linguistic to the geographical etymology.

Identification of *the Ṣābiʾūn* fascinates al-Ṭūsī as it did his predecessor. He devotes a goodly proportion of his commentary on this verse to recounting the various theories that have been proposed to establish the identity of this group. One assertion he makes in connection with the *Ṣābiʾūn* is of particular interest to the subject of this study. That is, he refuses to consider them part of the 'people of the book *(ahl al-kitāb)*', that Qur'ānic designation which denotes receptors of previous revelations: "All the jurisprudents *(fuqahā')* authorize imposition of the *jizyah* on them; but I consider it unnecessary because they are not *ahl al-kitāb*."[7] Such a denial by

6 al-Ṭūsī, *al-Tibyān*, 1:281–82.

7 al-Ṭūsī, *al-Tibyān*, 2:283. For the *ahl al-kitāb* see the article thus titled by G. Vajda in *EI²* 1:264–66. David Künstlinger notes the correspondence between *kitāb*, in the sense of 'holy book', and its cognates in other Semitic languages. For the phrase *ahl al-kitāb* he finds no such equivalents and concludes: "Einem Terminus wie *ahlu l-kitābi* begegnet man weder in der jüdischen noch in der christlichen Literatur, er wird wohl eine Schöpfung Muḥammads sein." "'Kitāb' und 'ahlu l-kitābi' im Ḳurān," *Rocznik Orientalistyczny* 4 (1926): 246. Denise Masson provides a selection of self-referential texts from the scriptures of Judaism, Christianity, and Islam in *Monothéisme coranique et monothéisme biblique*, 2nd ed. (Paris: Desclée de Brouwer, 1976), 259–86. (First edition entitled *Le Coran et la révélation judéo-chrétienne* [Paris: Adrien Maisonneuve, 1958].)

The *jizyah* is most commonly defined as a poll tax levied on those of the *ahl al-kitāb* living under Muslim hegemony. See Claude Cahen, "Djizya," *EI²* 2:559–62. The only Qur'ānic occurrence of the term is *sūrat al-tawbah* (9):29 in the phrase *ḥattā yuʿṭū al-jizyata ʿan yadin wa-hum ṣāghirūna*. Analysis of this phrase has generated several significant studies. In chronological order, these are: Franz Rosenthal, "Some Minor Problems in the Qur'ān," *The Joshua Starr Memorial Volume: Studies in History and Philology* (New York: Conference on Jewish Relations, 1953), 67–84; Claude Cahen, "Coran IX-29: ḥattā yuʿṭū l-jizyata ʿan yadin wa-hum ṣāghirūna," *Arabica* 9 (1962): 76–79; Meïr M. Bravmann, "A propos de Qur'ān IX-29: ḥattā yuʿṭū l-jizyata [. . .] wa-hum ṣāghirūna," *Arabica* 10 (1963): 94–95 (this volume included a brief rejoinder from Cahen); and M.J. Kister, " 'ʿAn yadin' (Qur'ān, IX/29): An Attempt at Interpretation," *Arabica* 11 (1964): 272–78. All four – that from Rosenthal is the relevant extract from his longer study – have been reprinted in *Der Koran*, ed. by Rudi Paret (Darmstadt: Wissenschaftliche Buchgesellschaft, 1975), 283–303. For a related study of 9:29 see my "Fakhr al-Dīn al-Rāzī on *āyat al-jizyah* and *āyat al-sayf*," in *Conversion and Continuity: Indigenous Christian Communities in Islamic Lands, Eighth to Eighteenth Centuries*, ed. by Michael Gervers and Ramzi J. Bikhazi (Toronto: Pontifical Institute of Mediaeval Studies, 1990), 103–19. Sidney Griffiths notes the coincidence in the middle of the first ʿAbbāsid century of legal clarification of the *jizyah*, of increased Christian conversion to Islam, and of "the appearance of the earliest Christian Arabic literature, when Chrisal-Ṭūsī indicates that he has a stricter definition of the *ahl al-kitāb* than most commentators.

With al-Zamakhsharī the threefold etymological identification of *al-naṣārā* is reduced to a single terse choice. In concert with al-Ṭūsī, al-Zamakhsharī insists that the Christians are so designated because they 'helped (*naṣarū*)' the Messiah.[8] Abū al-Futūḥ Rāzī, on the other hand, completely ignores this association and refers only to those derivations that connect the word with the Qurʾānic use of the term *anṣār* and with a village called *Nāṣirah*. It is the latter to which he gives preference in stating that the word *al-naṣārā* "refers to a tribe (*qabīlah*) associated with *Naṣrat* [*sic*], the village in which Jesus lived."[9]

While Ibn al-Jawzī briefly notes the now-standard tripartite identification of the term *al-naṣārā*, he cites no authorities in textual support.[10] Nor does his near contemporary, Fakhr al-Dīn al-Rāzī, pay much attention to the etymology of this term. While he does include reference to the *ḥadīth*s of Ibn Jurayj, Ibn ʿAbbās, and Qatādah in listing the customary etymologies, his treatment is concise and derivative. It concludes with a direct quotation from that line in the *Kashshāf* in which al-Zamakhsharī expressed his own preference.[11]

Ibn Kathīr's preferred explanation of the term *al-naṣārā*, like several of his predecessors, is that taken from the notional root meaning of the word: "They are called that because of their helping each other."[12] However, he

tians within *dār al-islām* must finally have realized that their lot for the foreseeable future was to live as a subject population in an Islamic state." "The Monks of Palestine and the Growth of Christian Literature in Arabic," *MW* 78 (1988): 3.

8 al-Zamakhsharī, *al-Kashshāf*, 1:146.

9 Abū al-Futūḥ Rāzī, *Rawḥ al-jinān*, 1:209.

10 Ibn al-Jawzī, *Zād al-masīr*, 1:91.

11 Fakhr al-Dīn al-Rāzī, *al-Tafsīr al-kabīr*, 3:104. For contrastive purposes it is interesting to note the exegesis offered in a Ṣūfī commentary popularly ascribed to Fakhr al-Dīn al-Rāzī's contemporary Muḥyī al-Dīn b. al-ʿArabī. Ibn al-ʿArabī breaks the exegetical thread of conventional etymology. His commentary on this verse begins, as have those of his predecessors, with an effort to explain the four introductory phrases. He does this by paraphrasing the opening statement so that the equivalent of *those who believe* becomes "those who believe with uncritically-accepted belief (*al-īmān al-taqlīdī*)," while *those who are Jews* is equated with "those who take things literally (*al-ẓāhiriyūn*)." By contrast, then, *the Christians* (*al-naṣārā*) is paraphrased as "those who find hidden meanings (*al-bāṭiniyūn*)." The periphrastic substitution for *al-ṣābiʾūn* is more complex and figurative, and yet includes allusions to religious behavior commonly ascribed to this group, e.g., veneration of angels and of the stars. Ibn al-ʿArabī characterizes *the Ṣābiʾūn* as "those who venerate the angels of intellects (*malāʾikat al-ʿuqūl*) because of their being veiled by the intelligibles (*al-maʿqūlāt*) and the stars of the spiritual powers (*kawākib al-quwā al-nafsānīyah*), given the fact of their being veiled by those things imagined and those things fancied." Muḥyī al-Dīn b. [al-]ʿArabī, *Tafsīr al-Qurʾān al-karīm* (Beirut: Dār al-Yaqẓah al-ʿArabīyah, 1387/1968), 1:54.

12 Ibn Kathīr, *Tafsīr al-Qurʾān al-ʿaẓīm*, 1:103.

also cites the other two common explanations, that the term is derived from the Qur'ānic statement attributed to Jesus in *sūrat al-ṣaff* (61): 14 or from the area called *Nāṣirah*. Clearly Ibn Kathīr's choice places him squarely within the etymological tradition of al-Ṭūsī, al-Zamakhsharī, and Fakhr al-Dīn al-Rāzī. Kāshānī, on the other hand, equivocates. He ties the lexical explanation to the Qur'ānic reference and mentions the geographical as well. With the latter, however, he adds a qualifying remark indicating that he is not sure whether this group is named for a place or an individual.[13] Muḥammad Ḥusayn Ṭabāṭabā'ī displays no such uncertainty. In fact, his mention of this etymology for the term *al-naṣārā* indicates a closer familiarity with the Gospel narratives than that expressed by any of the other commentators: the word is associated "with a village called *Nāṣirah* in the land of Syria where Jesus and Mary lived after their return from Egypt."[14]

THE SIGNIFICANCE OF VERBAL REPETITION

While the interpretation of this verse's introductory reference to *those who believe* did not involve the commentators in extensive etymological considerations, it did raise other issues of identification for them. Al-Ṭabarī, as was noted above, makes a clear equation between belief and the acceptance of Muḥammad's message. Ibn Kathīr then specifies this further, spelling out precisely what is meant by 'believer (*mu'min*, pl. *mu'minūn*)': they are the individuals who accept Muḥammad as the 'seal' of the prophets and the messenger to mankind (*banū ādam*), attesting to the truth that he announces, doing what he commands and refraining from what he prohibits. "The community (*ummah*) of Muḥammad are called *mu'minūn* because of the extent and intensity of their belief and certitude and because they believe in all the past prophets and the hidden things to come."[15] Such univocal recognition does not go unchallenged, however. A subsidiary line of interpretation for this phrase does develop within the tradition, one that understands the reference as an allusion to the 'hypocrites (*munāfiqūn*)', those whose lips profess belief but whose hearts do not assent. Within the group of commentators under consideration, this view first appears in al-Ṭūsī but is most strongly asserted by both al-Zamakhsharī and Kāshānī.[16] In none of these exegetes, however, is the issue simply one of identification. Rather it is intertwined with semantic considerations and can only be understood within that full complex.

13 Kāshānī, *Minhaj al-ṣādiqīn*, 1:221.

14 Ṭabāṭabā'ī, *al-Mīzān*, 1:193.

15 Ibn Kathīr, *Tafsīr al-Qur'ān al-ʿaẓīm*, 1:104.

16 al-Ṭūsī, *al-Tibyān*, 1:285; al-Zamakhsharī, *al-Kashshāf*, 1:146; Kāshānī, *Minhaj al-ṣādiqīn*, 1:220. Toshihiko Izutsu provides a thoughtful semantic analysis of *nifāq* in the ninth chapter of his *Ethico-Religious Concepts in the Qur'ān* (Montreal: McGill University Press, 1966), 178–83.

To seek such understanding necessitates turning, then, to the second major question that motivates the exegetical consideration of this verse. Following the four introductory phrases that apparently indicate religious groupings is the remark *whoever believes in God and the Last Day.* What, pondered the commentators, is the relation between *those who believe* and *whoever believes*? Furthermore, what is the grammatical connection of this whole expression to the four introductory phrases? Grappling with these questions calls forth from the exegetes further refinements of religious identification and a fuller explication of the required content of belief.

As al-Ṭabarī's interest moves from etymology to syntax, he poses the central problem of the relation of *whoever believes* to the preceding *those who believe.* To begin to answer this difficulty he suggests that the sense of 'among them (*minhum*)' is implied.[17] Thus the opening phrase, *truly those who believe and those who are Jews, the Christians and the Ṣābiʾūn*, is completed by this second phrase when it is understood as 'whoever *among them* believes in God and the Last Day'. To underscore this partitive understanding of the second phrase, al-Ṭabarī repeats the tandem construction with a slight grammatical modification.[18] He then proceeds to distinguish the 'believing' of a 'believer (*muʾmin*)' from that of a Jew, Christian, or Ṣābiʾ. In the latter instances 'believing' means 'coming to believe' – turning from a previous belief in Jesus (in the Christian case) to an acceptance of Muḥammad. The believing of a 'believer' does not mean his shifting from one religion to another, that is, his 'coming to believe'. Rather it means his "standing firm in belief and *not* changing."[19] Had conversion from one belief system to another been intended, the statement would have been "they believed (*āmanū*) in Muḥammad and what he brought."[20] Therefore the belief of Jews, Christians, and Ṣābiʾūn, which does involve a conversion or change from a former belief, may be included in the meaning of this phrase if it accords with the established pattern: "Those among them who believe in Muḥammad and what he brought and in the Last Day, and who do right – and do not change or alter until death – will be recompensed for their action and rewarded in the sight of the Lord, as God has described."[21]

17 al-Ṭabarī, *Jāmiʿ al-bayān*, 2:148.

18 Al-Ṭabarī here uses *man* and the jussive form of the verb rather than the Qurʾānic *al-māḍī*. *Jāmiʿ al-bayān*, 2:148.

19 al-Ṭabarī, *Jāmiʿ al-bayān*, 2:148.

20 al-Ṭabarī, *Jāmiʿ al-bayān*, 2:148.

21 al-Ṭabarī, *Jāmiʿ al-bayān*, 2:148–49. The idea that this verse reflects an earlier stage of good relations with the Jews is stressed in the seminal study by Arent Jan Wensinck, *Muhammad and the Jews of Medina (Mohammed en de Joden te Medina)*, 2nd ed., trans. by Wolfgang H. Behn (Berlin: Adiyok, 1982), 49. Some years later Frank H. Foster spoke of this verse as "a very broad and liberal formulation" and as "the last flaring of a candle before it goes out." *A Brief Doctrinal Commentary on the Arabic Koran* (London: Sheldon Press, 1932), 50.

Al-Ṭūsī, too, is preoccupied with the relation of *whoever believes* to the preceding four categories (*those who believe, those who are Jews, the Christians,* and *the Ṣābiʾūn*). He solves the problem as al-Ṭabarī did by positing an implied 'among them (*minhum*)' so that the entire first part of the verse functions as a nominal absolute followed by a quasi-conditional.[22] Al-Ṭūsī's justification for this interpretation bears examination, for although his conclusion accords with that of al-Ṭabarī, he offers additional reasons to support it. In one case he says the phrase *whoever believes in God and the Last Day* can refer only to the Jews, Christians, and Ṣābiʾūn because it would be nonsensical to apply it also to *those who believe.* The latter are already believers, so that including them as a referent for *whoever believes* is tautological.[23] In another explanation, however, he follows al-Ṭabarī by letting *those who believe* suggest steadiness and perseverance in belief while for the Jews, Christians, and Ṣābiʾūn, *whoever believes* means the assumption of belief in the Prophet and what he brought.[24]

In characteristic fashion al-Zamakhsharī ties his semantic considerations to grammatical analysis. Following an equation of *those who believe* with the hypocrites (*munāfiqūn*), he solves the relation of the four introductory phrases to *whoever believes* thus: the four are termed "these infidels (*hāʾulāʾi al-kafarah*)," and only those individuals among them who believe with a "pure belief (*īmānan khāliṣan*)," and who truly enter the religion of Islam, will know God's reward.[25] Given this understanding, al-Zamakhsharī acknowledges two syntactical possibilities for the phrase *whoever believes.* It can be read as the subject of a nominal sentence for which *for them is their reward* is the predicate. In this view it serves as a subjective complement to the preceding phrase: "Truly those who believe and those who are Jews, the Christians and the Ṣābiʾūn, whoever believes in God . . . " However,

22 al-Ṭūsī, *al-Tibyān*, 1:283.
23 al-Ṭūsī, *al-Tibyān,* 1:283.
24 al-Ṭūsī, *al-Tibyān*, 1:284.
25 al-Zamakhsharī, *al-Kashshāf*, 1:146. On the term *kāfir* (pl. *kāfirūn, kuffār, kafarah, kifār*) see W. Björkman, "Kufr," *EI²* 4:407–09. Toshihiko Izutsu begins his semantic analysis of *īmān* (belief/faith) and *islām* with a chapter on "The Infidel (*kāfir*)." *The Concept of Belief in Islamic Theology* (1965; reprint, New York: Books for Libraries, 1980). This study complements an earlier work by the author, *The Structure of the Ethical Terms in the Koran* (Tokyo: Keio University, 1959). A revised edition was published as *Ethico-Religious Concepts in the Qurʾān* (Montreal: McGill University Press, 1966). Marilyn Waldman takes issue with Izutsu's analysis of *kufr* in her "The Development of the Concept of *Kufr* in the Qurʾān," *JAOS* 88 (1968): 442–55. Peter Antes draws specifically upon both al-Ṭabarī and Muḥammad ʿAbduh in his brief article "Relations with Unbelievers in Islamic Theology," in *We Believe in One God: The Experience of God in Christianity and Islam,* ed. by Annemarie Schimmel and Abdoldjavad Falatūri (New York: Seabury, 1979), 101–11. The denotation of *kufr* developed paradoxically within Ṣūfism, an issue addressed from several perspectives by Peter J. Awn, *Satan's Tragedy and Redemption: Iblīs in Sufi Psychology* (Leiden: E.J. Brill, 1983).

as a second possibility, *whoever believes (man āmana)* can be read as one of the accusatives following the initiatory particle *inna*. (In this case the connective *wa* must be understood between *al-ṣābiʾūn* and *man āmana*.) Then *for them is their reward* functions as a predicate for all that comes after *inna*.[26]

In his own explanation of the grammatical relation between *whoever believes* and the fourfold categorization with which this verse begins, Abū al-Futūḥ Rāzī both follows and refines his predecessors. His first explanation of the *whoever believes* clause is that it refers back either to *those who believe* or to *those who are Jews, the Christians and the Ṣābiʾūn*. In the first case, it would explain the content of belief, while in the second the implied 'among them (*minhum*)' to which previous commentators have also made reference, must be understood.[27] (Abū al-Futūḥ Rāzī carefully explains that the actual addition of *minhum* is unnecessary since the phrase implies it.) Another explanation offered for the two phrases *those who believe* and *whoever believes* is that the former does not really mean what it says. Like others before him, Abū al-Futūḥ Rāzī speculates that it may be a cryptic reference to the shallow belief of those hypocrites who with their tongues profess thoughts to which their hearts withhold assent. Unlike his predecessors, however, Abū al-Futūḥ Rāzī calls forth two Qurʾānic citations in support of this interpretation: (1) "those who say 'we believe' with their mouths but their hearts do not believe" (*sūrat al-māʾidah* [5]:41) and (2) "O you who believe, believe in God" (*sūrat al-nisāʾ* [4]:136). He clarifies his use of this second quotation by paraphrasing and expanding it: "O you who exhibit belief with your tongues, believe with your hearts."[28] Like al-Ṭabarī and al-Ṭūsī, Abū al-Futūḥ Rāzī also presents as a final possibility for the signification of *whoever believes* the notion of perseverance: it could connote all those who are steadfast and persistent in belief.[29]

True to his penchant for brevity and concision, Ibn al-Jawzī enumerates the several possibilities that have now surfaced in this particular exegetical discussion. They are offered here chiefly for their value as a recapitulation. Thus for the relation of *whoever believes* to *those who believe* Ibn al-Jawzī offers three explanations: (1) since groups of unbelievers (*kuffār*) are mentioned together with the believers, the phrase *whoever believes* refers to the former; (2) the phrase *whoever believes* means one who persists in his belief; and (3)

26 al-Zamakhsharī, *al-Kashshāf*, 1:146. Régis Blachère in his translation of the Qurʾān also offers two suggested renderings of this verse. One agrees with the first possibility offered by al-Zamakhsharī but the second rendering is as follows: "Ceux qui croient [= les Musulmans], ceux qui pratiquent le Judaïsme, les Chrétiens et les Sabéens sont ceux qui croient en Allah et au Dernier Jour et accomplissent oeuvre pie. . . ." *Le Coran*, 3:743–44.

27 Abū al-Futūḥ Rāzī, *Rawḥ al-jinān*, 1:211.

28 Abū al-Futūḥ Rāzī, *Rawḥ al-jinān*, 1:211.

29 Abū al-Futūḥ Rāzī, *Rawḥ al-jinān*, 1:211.

those who believe refers to the hypocrites confessing *islām* while *whoever believes* connotes true, heartfelt belief. As a correlative to the second explanation, Ibn al-Jawzī then understands this verse's reference to [*whoever*] *does right* as persistence in religious duties (*farā'iḍ*).[30]

With the twelfth-century commentator, Fakhr al-Dīn al-Rāzī, analysis of this combined grammatical and semantic conundrum takes on greater depth and clarity. In dealing with the phrases *those who believe* and *whoever believes*, Fakhr al-Dīn al-Rāzī immediately recognizes that the meaning of "believing" must be different in each instance. Like Abū al-Futūḥ Rāzī, he turns to the phrase in *sūrat al-nisā'* (4):136 ("O you who believe, believe . . . ") for a Qur'ānic parallel, another instance in which the same verb carries different connotations. He then cites the major explanations proffered by previous commentators but does so in a way that expands and clarifies them. The first explanation he attributes to Ibn ʿAbbās: *those who believe* refers to those who believed in Jesus before Muḥammad was sent and also kept themselves free from Jewish and Christian falsehoods (*abāṭīl*). To express this interpretation better Fakhr al-Dīn al-Rāzī paraphrases and expands the Qur'ānic statement: "Those who believed before Muḥammad was sent and those who belonged to the false/vain religion (*al-dīn al-bāṭil*) of the Jews and to the false/vain religion of the Christians – all those among them who believe, after the coming of Muḥammad, in God and in the Last Day and in Muḥammad – will have their reward near their Lord."[31]

The second explanation, which is attributed to Sufyān al-Thawrī, draws its support from the description of the hypocrites in the early verses of this *sūrah*, a description followed by mention of the Jews. The logic of this view is that since the group described before the Jews in the early part of the *sūrah* is the hypocrites (*munāfiqūn*), the phrase that precedes reference to the Jews in this verse, *those who believe,* must also refer to the hypocrites.[32] All four divisions – hypocrites, Jews, Christians, and Ṣābi'ūn – are referred to as *mubṭilūn*, a Qur'ānic term that carries such significations as 'speaking what is untrue' and 'rendering something worthless'. Of course only those among the *mubṭilūn* "who achieve true belief arrive with the believers near God."[33]

30 Ibn al-Jawzī, *Zād al-masīr*, 1:92.

31 Fakhr al-Dīn al-Rāzī, *al-Tafsīr al-kabīr*, 3:104.

32 Fakhr al-Dīn al-Rāzī, *al-Tafsīr al-kabīr*, 3:104.

33 Fakhr al-Dīn al-Rāzī, *al-Tafsīr al-kabīr*, 3:104. In each of its five Qur'ānic occurrences, *sūrat al-aʿrāf* (7):173, *sūrat al-ʿankabūt* (29):48; *sūrat al-Rūm* (30):58, *sūrat al-mu'min* (40):78, and *sūrat al-jāthiyah* (45):27, the term *mubṭilūn* concludes the verse in which it stands. In his survey of Qur'ānic pejoratives Dirk Bakker describes the *mubṭilūn* as "the pursuers of vanity" who "worship idols" but he bases this interpretation of the word on but one of its Qur'ānic occurrences. *Man in the Qur'ān* (Amsterdam: Drukkerij Holland, 1965), 112.

The last opinion that Fakhr al-Dīn al-Rāzī presents is attributed generally to the theologians (*mutakallimūn*), who distinguish between the referents of the two phrases on temporal grounds. Thus *those who believe* means those who believed in Muḥammad in the past. Then *whoever believes* points to the future and includes past believers who abide in their faith and continue it in the future.[34]

As has already been noted, Kāshānī's initial identification of *those who believe* with "those who merely speak a confession of belief without believing in their hearts" is strong and immediate.[35] *Whoever believes*, according to this commentator, refers to all those among the four previously mentioned groups – the hypocrites, Jews, Christians, and Ṣābiʾūn – "who believe with complete sincerity in God and in His negative and immutable attributes (*ṣifāt-i salbīyah va s̱ubūtīyah*)."[36] The implication of conversion is unmistakable in such an understanding. Kāshānī then makes an interesting distinction regarding the phrase *those who believe* (*alladhīna āmanū*) when introduced by the conjunction "and (*wa*)." This is of frequent occurrence in the Qurʾān, and, in fact, next occurs some twenty verses after the passage under discussion, in *sūrat al-baqarah* (2):82. He understands this phrase, *wa-alladhīna āmanū*, to mean "those who are devout adherents of the religion of Islam, believing in Muḥammad, and those among the Jews, Christians and Ṣābiʾūn who live in accordance with the Exalted One and the requirements of His law."[37]

After a discussion of the concluding phrases of this verse, Kāshānī again takes up the perplexities of the two phrases *those who believe* and *whoever believes*. He first sketches the grammatical basis whereby the phrase beginning *for them is their reward* serves as the predicate for *whoever believes*. In turn this latter phrase, which should be understood with the suppressed pronominal partitive 'among them', serves as a specification of the fourfold introductory statement. While this grammatical analysis is not original with Kāshānī it is particularly well-ordered and expressed in his commentary. He also probes further, questioning whether the particle *fa* can introduce the apodosis of a statement commencing with *inna*. Demurring grammarians are silenced by the proof of Qurʾānic usage in *sūrat al-burūj* (85):10.[38]

The two twentieth-century commentaries, those of Rashīd Riḍā and Ṭa-

34 Fakhr al-Dīn al-Rāzī, *al-Tafsīr al-kabīr*, 3:104–05.

35 Kāshānī, *Minhaj al-ṣādiqīn*, 1:220.

36 Kāshānī, *Minhaj al-ṣādiqīn*, 1:221.

37 Kāshānī, *Minhaj al-ṣādiqīn*, 1:221.

38 Kāshānī, *Minhaj al-ṣādiqīn*, 1:221. The authors of a dictionary of Qurʾānic particles and pronouns note the anomaly in *sūrat al-burūj* (85):10 but not in 2:62. Ismāʿīl Aḥmad ʿAmāyrah and ʿAbd al-Ḥamīd Muṣṭafā al-Sayyid, *Muʿjam al-adawāt wa-al-ḍamāʾir fī al-Qurʾān al-karīm* (Beirut: Muʾassasat al-Risālah, 1407/1986), 125 and 156–57.

bāṭabāʾī, pay scant attention to the developed discussion of this semantic and grammatical issue. Rashīd Riḍā gives a temporal cast to the identification of *those who believe*, allowing it to refer to both those Muslims who followed Muḥammad during his lifetime and all those who will follow him until the Day of Resurrection.[39] *Whoever believes* functions not as a repetition of this but only as a specification of the three other groups mentioned, that is, the Jews, the Christians, and the Ṣābiʾūn. Within these latter categories it denotes those who believe in God with a sound belief (*īmānan ṣaḥīḥan*). Rashīd Riḍā then uses the occasion of commenting upon [*whoever*] *does right* to offer a passing compliment to the *ahl al-kitāb*. After describing the benefits to be derived from 'good works' he remarks that "doing good is not unknown in the customs of these peoples; their scriptures have made it clear."[40]

With Ṭabāṭabāʾī the interpretation of this syntactical issue takes a decidedly theological turn. The major point this exegete finds in the entire verse is that group identification is not decisive in God's eyes. For Ṭabāṭabāʾī *those who believe* means those openly characterized as 'believers'. No name, be it that of "the believers, Jews, Christians or Ṣābiʾūn, makes it incumbent upon God to grant reward or protection from punishment."[41] The name holds no guarantee of salvation. What does count is true belief in God and the Last Day and right action. Thus *whoever believes* is sufficient; there is no need for the partitive particularization of 'among them', trying to tie this second phrase into *those who believe* and the other group designations. None of these names is of any use to the one so identified. As Ṭabāṭabāʾī descriptively explains: "Bliss (*saʿādah*) and favor (*karāmah*) rotate on the axis of humble veneration (*ʿubūdah*)."[42] No one, not even the prophets, is exempt from this dual imperative of true belief and right action. Ṭabāṭabāʾī refers to *sūrat al-anʿām* (6):88 in confirmation of this: "God said about His prophets, after describing them with superlatives: 'But if they had associated [other gods with God], then what they did would have availed them nothing.' "[43] As further proof of the irrevocability of this twofold demand, the exegete cites *sūrat al-fatḥ* (48):29, a Qurʾānic paean to the believers. Once more professions of praise are not allowed to overshadow the central mandate, as Ṭabāṭabāʾī points out by quoting the verse's concluding phrase: "God has promised those of them who believe and do good, forgiveness and a great reward."[44] These passages from the Qurʾān

39 Rashīd Riḍā, *Tafsīr al-Manār*, 1:335.
40 Rashīd Riḍā, *Tafsīr al-Manār*, 1:335.
41 Ṭabāṭabāʾī, *al-Mīzān*, 1:193.
42 Ṭabāṭabāʾī, *al-Mīzān*, 1:193.
43 Ṭabāṭabāʾī, *al-Mīzān*, 1:193.
44 Ṭabāṭabāʾī, *al-Mīzān*, 1:193.

attest to and provide additional support for Ṭabāṭabāʾī's basic interpretation of this verse. He sums up the discussion himself most aptly in his concluding phrase: "True worth lies in the reality not in the outward display."[45]

NARRATIVE CIRCUMSCRIPTION

Building upon these efforts of identification and grammatical analysis, the commentators broached matters of historical consideration. What prompted, they wonder, this reference to 'Christians', 'believers', and others? Was there an incident in the nascent life of the community for which this verse provides illumination? Or to use the phrase that became a technical designation in the developed Qurʾānic sciences (*ʿulūm al-Qurʾān*), what was the 'occasion of revelation (*sabab al-nuzūl*)' of this verse?[46]

Al-Ṭabarī opens his discussion of the issue by stating that he wishes to give an account of those who maintain that the verse refers to those of the *ahl al-kitāb* who "lived into the time of (*adrakū*)" Muḥammad. The account consists of exegetical *ḥadīth*s from Ismāʿīl b. ʿAbd al-Raḥmān al-Suddī (d. 128/745) and Mujāhid b. Jabr dealing with an early convert named Salmān al-Fārisī.[47] Al-Suddī's brief summation of the history of Salmān al-Fārisī goes as follows: Salmān was a young nobleman from Jundaysābūr who, in the company of the king's son, came upon a man weeping as he read from a book. Questioned by the two youths, the man explained that his book was one sent from God in which might be found certain commands and prohibitions – the Gospel revealed to Jesus. As they listened the young men's hearts opened to the truth of what they heard, so they concurred with it and "submitted to God (*aslamā*)."[48] Upon his return, the king's son fell into dispute with his father, refusing to eat the sacrificial animals on the grounds that they were unlawful and calling his countrymen infidels (*kuffār*). The king, then, confronted the preacher and threatened him with banishment.

45 *al-karāmah bi-al-ḥaqīqah dūna al-ẓāhir*, Ṭabāṭabāʾī, *al-Mīzān*, 1:193.

46 The most noted collection in this category is that of ʿAlī b. Aḥmad al-Wāḥidī (d. 468/1075), *Asbāb al-nuzūl* (Beirut: Dār wa-Maktabat al-Hilāl, 1983). Andrew Rippin has argued for the fundamentally haggadic rather than halakic (to use John Wansbrough's categories) role of such exegetical material. "The Function of *asbāb al-nuzūl* in Qurʾānic Exegesis," *BSOAS* 51 (1988): 1–20. See also his earlier study, "The Exegetical Genre *asbāb al-nuzūl*: A Bibliographical and Terminological Study," *BSOAS* 48 (1985):1–15.

47 al-Ṭabarī, *Jāmiʿ al-bayān*, 2:150–54. For further on Salmān al-Fārisī see the article so titled by G. Levi Della Vida, *EI*[1] 7:116–17. Josef Horovitz examines the historical background of this figure in his article, "Salmān al-Fārisī," *Der Islam* 12 (1922):178–83.

48 A sense of Islam as the primordial and perennial religion is nicely conveyed in the use of the term *aslama* to denote conversion to Christianity, a Christianity that is of course understood as prefiguring the final divine revelation.

Salmān eventually parted from the king's son and joined a community of monks (*ruhbān*), distinguishing himself by the severity of his ascetic practices. When he accompanied the community's leader to Jerusalem, he was offered the chance to study with some learned men and grew sad as he came to realize that prophetic marvels were events of the past. To console him, the leader related that a prophet was soon to arise in the land of the Arabs, wearing the sign of prophecy, a prophet who would "eat gifts but not charitable offerings."[49]

Returning from Jerusalem Salmān was captured and sold into slavery. While tending sheep for his owner he heard that a prophet had arrived in Medina. Salmān rushed to that city where he encountered the Prophet and recognized him by the signs his former leader had revealed to him. When Salmān described to the Prophet the prayerful community in which he used to live, the Prophet responded by saying: "They are among the people destined for Hell (*ahl al-nār*)."[50] In distress Salmān declared: "Had they known about you, they would have believed in you and followed you."

The *ḥadīth* concludes with the customary phrase, "So God sent down this verse," implying that it was revealed to ease Salmān's mind by specifying the necessary criteria of belief.[51] The second *ḥadīth* that al-Ṭabarī includes, that from Mujāhid, also connects the circumstances of revelation (*asbāb al-nuzūl*) with Salmān al-Fārisī. His dismay at being told of the certain perdition of his former companions called forth this divine clarification. This second *ḥadīth* closes with an explanation by the Prophet: "Whoever dies in the religion of Jesus and dies in submission to God (*islām*) before hearing me will be fine, but whoever hears me today and does not believe in me is already doomed."[52]

Al-Ṭūsī also makes brief reference to this verse's connection with Salmān

49 al-Ṭabarī, *Jāmiʿ al-bayān*, 2:153. In his study of this *ḥadīth* Louis Massignon notes the distinction thereby conveyed between alms properly belonging to the community (*ṣadaqah*) and private offerings (*hadīyah*). "Salman Pak et les prémices spirituelles de l'islam iranien," in his *Opera Minora*, ed. by Y. Moubarac (Paris: Presses Universitaires de France, 1969), 1:451. Reprinted from *Société d'études iraniennes* 7 (1934).

50 al-Ṭabarī, *Jāmiʿ al-bayān*, 2:154. Khalil Samir has drawn attention to the four geographical loci of the Salmān narrative, i.e., Jundaysābūr, Mosūl, Jerusalem, and Medina, noting the significant events connected with each. "Le commentaire de Ṭabarī sur Coran 2/62 et la question du salut des non-musulmans," *Annali: Istituto orientale di Napoli* 40/n.s. 30 (1980): 577–80. For an English rendering of this *ḥadīth* from al-Suddī see *The Commentary on the Qur'ān*, trans. by J. Cooper, 360–63.

51 al-Ṭabarī, *Jāmiʿ al-bayān* 2:154. In an interesting study of those individuals who are thought to be an 'occasion' for Qur'ānic revelation, ʿAbd al-Raḥmān ʿUmayrah has devoted a chapter to Salmān al-Fārisī. See *Rijāl anzala Allāh fīhim Qur'ānan* (Riyadh: Dār al-Liwā' lil-Nashr wa-al-Tawzīʿ, 1397/1977), 2:13–33.

52 al-Ṭabarī, *Jāmiʿ al-bayān*, 2:155.

al-Fārisī and his Christian companions "who had already told him that he [the Prophet] would be coming and that they would believe in him if they came upon him."[53] Ibn al-Jawzī, on the other hand, while including a very brief mention of Salmān al-Fārisī, produces his usual systematic survey of possible historical referents. The 'believers' with whom this verse is concerned may be: (1) according to Ibn ʿAbbās, a group who believed in Jesus before Muḥammad was sent; (2) in the opinion of al-Suddī, those who believed in Moses and lived in accord with the Mosaic law until the coming of Jesus, after which they believed in Jesus and followed his law until the time of Muḥammad; (3) for Sufyān al-Thawrī, the hypocrites; and (4) according to others, the ones who were searching for Islam, like Quss b. Sāʿidah, Baḥīrā, Waraqah b. Nawfal and Salmān [al-Fārisī]. Finally (5), some have thought that they are the believers within the community (*ummah*) of Islam, that is, all who call themselves Muslims.[54] Fakhr al-Dīn al-Rāzī, in turn, amplifies the fourth category created by Ibn al-Jawzī by expanding the list of names. The members of this group whom he specifically mentions are: Quass b. Sāʿidah, Baḥīrā the Monk, Ḥabīb al-Najjār, Zayd b. ʿAmr b. Nufayl, Waraqah b. Nawfal, Salmān al-Fārisī, Abū Dharr al-Ghifārī, and the delegation sent by the Najāshī.[55]

53 al-Ṭūsī, *al-Tibyān*, 1:284.

54 Ibn al-Jawzī, *Zād al-masīr*, 1:91.

55 Fakhr al-Dīn al-Rāzī, *al-Tafsīr al-kabīr*, 3:104. The reference to "the delegation sent by al-Najāshī" anticipates a *sabab al-nuzūl* that will figure prominently in the Qurʾānic verses to be discussed in Chapters 5 and 7. In his article entitled "Ḳuss b. Sāʿida" Charles Pellat allows for the fact that this individual may have had some connection with the Christians of Najrān but denies that he was the bishop of that town. EI^2 5:528. J. Spencer Trimingham refers unequivocally to "Quss ibn Sāʿida, Bishop of the ʿIrāqī Najrān. . . ." *Christianity Among the Arabs in Pre-Islamic Times* (London: Longman, 1979), 177–78. Each of these authors speaks of him as a semilegendary figure, renowned for his eloquence.

In Islamic tradition, Baḥīrā is remembered as the Syrian monk who foretold Muḥammad's call to prophethood. See A. Abel, "Baḥīrā," EI^2 1:922–23. Among the standard accounts of Muḥammad's meeting with Baḥīrā is Muḥammad b. Isḥāq's (d. 150/767) life of the Prophet in the recension of Abū Muḥammad ʿAbd al-Malik b. Hishām (d. 218/833). *Sīrah rasūl Allāh*, ed. by Ferdinand Wüstenfeld (1858; reprint, Frankfurt-am-Main: Minerva, 1961), 1:115–17. For an English translation see A. Guillaume, *The Life of Muhammad* (London: Oxford University Press, 1955), 79–81. Trimingham notes that Baḥīrā is not a proper name but is derived from the Syriac title of "Reverend," a fact to which he also found attestation in the work of the tenth-century historian and geographer Abū al-Ḥasan ʿAlī b. al-Ḥusayn al-Masʿūdī (d. 345/956). *Christianity Among the Arabs*, 258–59.

For Ḥabīb "the Carpenter" see G. Vajda, "Ḥabīb al-Nadjdjār," EI^2 3:12–13. Zayd b. ʿAmr b. Nufayl was a Meccan Qurayshī, a religious seeker whom some accounts remember as predicting Muḥammad's prophethood. V. Vacca, "Zaid B. ʿAmr B. Nufail," EI^1 8:1194. Waraqah b. Nawfal was the Christian cousin of Muḥammad's first

Like some of his predecessors, Ibn Kathīr attributes this revelation to the dismay felt by Salmān al-Fārisī upon hearing from Muḥammad that his former coreligionists are consigned to the Fire. Ibn Kathīr's account of the *ḥadīth* from al-Suddī is somewhat different, however, which gives rise to an interesting point. According to this account, after Salmān al-Fārisī has told the Prophet that his Christian friends "prayed and fasted and believed in you and attested to the fact that you would be sent as a prophet," Muḥammad responded by saying not (as al-Ṭabarī reported) "they are among the people of the Fire" but "among them are the people of the Fire." (In the Arabic this entails a transposition of *min* and *hum*).[56] While this could be attributed to scribal error in the manuscript tradition of the text, it may reflect a slight refinement in Ibn Kathīr's understanding of this *ḥadīth*, for in his version, unlike al-Ṭabarī's, not all Salmān's former associates were condemned to Hell.

With Kāshānī, one encounters a listing of historical possibilities reminiscent of that given by Ibn al-Jawzī but also including some of the names mentioned by Fakhr al-Dīn al-Rāzī. Here the reshaping of now-familiar material is interesting for both additions and omissions as well as for the reordering of relevant categories. Kāshānī first notes that this phrase could refer to "those who believed in Jesus but had not become Jews, Christians or Ṣābiʾūn, and were waiting for the emergence of the Seal of the Prophets; when he was sent they believed in him."[57] Another view suggested is that they were men seeking religion (*ṭullāb-i dīn*). Among their number were Ḥabīb al-Najjār, Zayd b. ʿAmr b. Nufayl, Waraqah b. Nawfal, Abū Dharr al-Ghifārī, Salmān al-Fārisī, Baḥīrā the Monk, and the delegation from the Najāshī. Their distinguishing mark was their prelusive belief in the Prophet; "some achieved the honor of following him and some carried this desire to the dust."[58] As a third possibility, Kāshānī reports the speculation that these are believers of past generations (*umam-i māżī*) or this generation (*īn ummat*).[59] On the authority of al-Suddī, a fourth and final proposal is advanced: the reference is to Salmān al-Fārisī and the group of Christians who gave him advance notice of Muḥammad's prophetic mission.[60]

To solve the problem of plurality, Kāshānī ties issues of history to those

wife, Khadījah, and is remembered for his support and encouragement of the Prophet in the early years of his mission. V. Vacca, "Waraḳa," *EI*[1] 8:1121–22. Abū Dharr al-Ghifārī was an early convert and Companion who "was noted for humility and asceticism, in which respect he is said to have resembled Jesus." J. Robson, "Abū Dharr," *EI*[2] 1:114.

56 Ibn Kathīr, *Tafsīr al-Qurʾān al-ʿaẓīm,* 1:103.
57 Kāshānī, *Minhaj al-ṣādiqīn,* 1:221–22.
58 Kāshānī, *Minhaj al-ṣādiqīn,* 1:222.
59 Kāshānī, *Minhaj al-ṣādiqīn,* 1:222.
60 Kāshānī, *Minhaj al-ṣādiqīn,* 1:222.

of grammar. He links these multiple possibilities for the "occasion of revelation" to the grammatical dilemma discussed above. His analysis moves backward from the range covered by *whoever believes* and terminates in a dual possibility. If, he reasons, the phrase *whoever believes* refers to all four of the verse's introductory categories, then *those who believe*, the first category, are either the hypocrites or those whose belief is firm and constant. If only the latter three categories are intended, then *those who believe* are the people whose faith is pure (*ahl-i ikhlāṣ*).[61]

CONTEXT AS INTERPRETATION

In addition to an interest in ascertaining any historical circumstances that may have prompted the revelation of this verse, some of the exegetes have sought illumination in the verse's very placement within the Qurʾān or in other, complementary Qurʾānic revelations, or in both. While such a concern with contextuality is not shared by a majority of the commentators, it does play an important role in the considerations of some of them. It also represents acceptance of that hermeneutical perspective which views the Qurʾān as a self-reflective text.

Fakhr al-Dīn al-Rāzī makes a particularly important contribution to the exegetical use of Qurʾānic contextuality. Very early in his commentary on this verse he discusses its relation to what immediately precedes it. The connection between them is grounded in the general hermeneutical observation that when God issues a promise or threat, He follows with its opposite, so that the statement is completed.[62] In this instance, the preceding verse describes the punishment due the unbelievers (*kafarah*) among the *ahl al-kitāb*. It is appropriately balanced, then, by a promise of great reward to the believers which proves that "God repays the one who does good by doing good to him and the one who does evil by doing evil to him."[63] Fakhr al-Dīn al-Rāzī then correlates this with a statement in *sūrat al-najm* (53):31: "He rewards those who do evil on the basis of what they do and He rewards those who do good with what is good."

Additionally, Fakhr al-Dīn al-Rāzī is the only one of the commentators to make explicit reference to the two Qurʾānic parallels to this verse, *sūrat*

61 Kāshānī, *Minhaj al-ṣādiqīn,* 1:222. The phrase *ahl-i ikhlāṣ* may echo al-Zamakhsharī's reference to *īmānun khāliṣun*. This latter recalls the reference to *al-dīn al-khāliṣ* in *sūrat al-zumar* (39):3. Kāshānī's expression more closely resembles the Qurʾānic use of the fourth form of the verb in *sūrat al-nisāʾ* (4):146, i.e., *wa-akhlaṣū dīnahum lillāh*. Among the most frequently recited portions of the Qurʾān is *sūrat al-ikhlāṣ* (112), a strong adjuration to the profession of God's oneness (*tawḥīd*); in fact, the *sūrah* is also known as *sūrat al-tawḥīd*.

62 Fakhr al-Dīn al-Rāzī, *al-Tafsīr al-kabīr,* 3:104.

63 Fakhr al-Dīn al-Rāzī, *al-Tafsīr al-kabīr,* 3:104.

al-māʾidah (5):69 and *sūrat al-ḥajj* (22):17. (These will be discussed in more detail at the end of this chapter.) Both these passages open with listings similar to those in 2:62, yet the relative placement of terms differs. In both instances, for example, the placement of *al-ṣābiʾūn* and *al-naṣārā* is reversed. While Fakhr al-Dīn al-Rāzī notes this fact he offers no substantive explanation for it. His answer is the ultimate exegetical refuge: "When the Speaker (*al-mutakallim*) is the Wisest of judges, these variations of wise pronouncements (*ḥikam*) and pregnant statements (*fawāʾid*) are inevitable. If we understand these reasons, then we have attained perfection. But if we cannot, we should attribute the inadequacy to our [own] intellects not to the words of the all-Wise; God is all-Knowing."[64]

Building upon the insights of Fakhr al-Dīn al-Rāzī, Ibn Kathīr detects in the placement of this verse an antiphonal arrangement. Immediately preceding it are described the actions of those liable to the wrath of God. Therefore, in this verse, it is to the one who does better than his ancestors in obeying God's laws and following His commands that reward is promised. Moreover, "such is the case for all time; to whoever follows the Messenger, the *ummī* Prophet, will everlasting happiness be granted."[65]

Muḥammad ʿAbduh also understands this verse as a promise of exemption (*istithnāʾ*) from the castigation of the Banū Isrāʾīl announced in the previous verse. So strong is that denunciation that were it not tempered by this verse, "every Jew on the face of the earth would rightly abandon hope."[66] Yet Muḥammad ʿAbduh is immediately faced with the task of explaining why the 'exemption' applies to the Christians and Ṣābiʾūn in addition to the Jews when the denunciation was addressed only to the latter. He does this by enlarging the scope of divine castigation. Not only the Jews but all those who have deviated from God's law are liable to His judgment: "There will come down on all who sin as they did what the wrath of God visited upon them."[67] Thus the phrase *truly those who believe*

64 Fakhr al-Dīn al-Rāzī, *al-Tafsīr al-kabīr,* 3:106.

65 Ibn Kathīr, *Tafsīr al-Qurʾān al-ʿaẓīm*, 1:103. The traditional Muslim understanding of the term *ummī*, as an adjective applied to Muḥammad, is 'illiterate'. Drawing upon the etymological analyses of Josef Horovitz (*Koranische Untersuchungen*, 51–53) Rudi Paret translates the word (and its Qurʾānic cognates) as 'heathen', noting the likelihood "that *ummī* or *ummīyūn* is a word coined by the *ahl al-kitāb* (probably the Jews especially) to describe the heathen." "Ummī," *EI*[1] 4:1016. Régis Blachère, who is in essential agreement with Paret, refines the signification to mean those who have received no prior revelation. Accepting a probable Hebrew etymology for the word, Blachère remarks that "*nabi ummi* ne signifie donc pas 'Prophète ignorant', 'illettré', mais 'Prophète des Gentiles'." *Introduction au Coran*, 2nd ed. (Paris: Éditions Besson et Chantemerle, 1959), 8. W. Montgomery Watt summarizes the discussion by remarking that "there is no argument here for Muḥammad being completely unlettered, but at most for his being ignorant of the Jewish and Christian scriptures." *Bell's Introduction*, 34.

66 Rashīd Riḍā, *Tafsīr al-Manār*, 1:334.

67 Rashīd Riḍā, *Tafsīr al-Manār*, 1:334.

introduces a dispensation potentially applicable to all who follow the guidance of a previous prophet and submit themselves to a prior revelation. God's punishments will not be directed at the Jews in particular but will be applied indiscriminately to all who transgress His law. By the same token, Muḥammad ʿAbduh, prefiguring Ṭabāṭabāʾī's remarks, makes clear that social rank or worldly prosperity are no guarantee of divine approval – nor are religious profession or creedal affiliation.[68] What really counts is sincere profession of belief in God (*ṣidq al-īmān billāh*), which Muḥammad ʿAbduh then describes at length and with poetic sensitivity.

THEOLOGICAL CONSIDERATIONS

These thoughts of Muḥammad ʿAbduh provide a fitting introduction to consideration of the two principal theological issues to which this verse has given rise. Al-Ṭabarī proposes the first of these, initiating an exegetical conversation that will receive its most thoughtful contribution centuries later in the *Tafsīr al-Manār*. In discussing al-Suddī's narrative about Salmān al-Fārisī, al-Ṭabarī amplifies the *ḥadīth*'s message by explaining the various stages of revelation throughout history. He begins with the Jews, whose duty it was to follow the Torah and the 'practice (*sunnah*)' of Moses. This obligation prevailed, however, only during the period following God's revelation to Moses until His revelation to Jesus. After this new divine disclosure, the Jews are under the obligation to follow the Gospel (*injīl*) and the laws of Jesus. Whoever does not is doomed to perish (*hālik*). Similarly is Christian observance related to the inauguration of the Islamic era. Belief in Jesus and what was revealed to him is only acceptable until the coming of Muḥammad. Then "whoever does not follow Muḥammad and renounce his adherence to the *sunnah* of Jesus and the *injīl* is damned."[69]

Ibn Kathīr follows al-Ṭabarī in postulating a theory of salvific stages. He claims that the Jews acted rightly in their adherence to the Torah and the *sunnah* of Moses, but only until the advent of Jesus. Once Jesus had come, those of the Jews who did not leave the Mosaic law and adhere to the Gospel and law of Jesus, were liable to eternal damnation. It is the same with the coming of Muḥammad. Echoing al-Ṭabarī, Ibn Kathīr, too, insists that while Christianity was an acceptable belief before the time of Muḥammad, those who do not then renounce it in favor of Islam will be damned.[70]

68 Rashīd Riḍā, *Tafsīr al-Manār*, 1:334.

69 al-Ṭabarī, *Jāmiʿ al-bayān*, 2:154. The Prophetic explanation for the *ḥadīth* reported on the authority of Mujāhid, which was cited above, clearly repeats this notion of salvific stages. For an account of the transmission history that connects Mujāhid's work with al-Ṭabarī's *tafsīr*, see Leemhuis, "MS. 1075 Tafsīr."

70 Ibn Kathīr, *Tafsīr al-Qurʾān al-ʿaẓīm*, 1:103.

In the *Tafsīr al-Manār* Rashīd Riḍā enters this theological conversation with an extended consideration of the prophetic void between Jesus and Muḥammad, remarking that this was a point that Muḥammad ʿAbduh raised when interpreting this passage. The professed reason for this *excursus* is to ask about the spiritual status of those people born in the time period between Jesus and Muḥammad. As the Qur'ān mentions the arrival of no prophet between these two, those born in this time period came to be termed the 'people of the interval (*ahl al-fatrah*)'.[71] Rashīd Riḍā suggests that the major disagreement about this group lies between those for whom belief is dependent upon exposure to a revealed message (*daʿwah*) and those who maintain that true belief may also be attained by the human intellect alone. This latter position, which is not held by the majority, Rashīd Riḍā attributes to the Muʿtazilah and some of the Ḥanafīyah.[72] The issue can be reduced to one of responsibility. To what extent must the people of this interval – particularly the Jews, Christians, and Ṣābi'ūn with whom this verse has been concerned – be held accountable for the degree and accuracy of their belief?

Rashīd Riḍā immediately eliminates the Jews from the terms of this discussion. While maintaining that their revelation had suffered from neglect and alteration (*taḥrīf*), he insists that "the substance of their religion (*jawhar dīnihim*) has remained recognizable, not distorted to the extent that guidance from its precepts is completely blocked."[73] As Qur'ānic support for this assertion Rashīd Riḍā quotes *sūrat al-mā'idah* (5):43: "They have access to the Torah in which is the judgment of God." This connection of the divine with the book of Jewish revelation is enough to warrant Jewish exclusion from the 'people of the interval'.

Christians – here termed the "adherents of the Messiah (*masīḥīyūn*)" – are also eliminated from this category for much the same reason. They have had the benefit of exposure to both the Jewish revelation and the testamentary injunctions of the Messiah (*waṣāyāt al-masīḥ*); moreover the "living

71 Charles Pellat attributes to Abū Muḥammad ʿAbdallāh b. Qutaybah (d. 276/889) the first enumeration of those individuals whom Muslim sources have characterized as the prominent religious seekers of this interval. The list he reproduces includes several of the names recorded by Ibn al-Jawzī, Fakhr al-Dīn al-Rāzī, and Kāshānī. "Fatra," *EI*² 2:865.

72 Rashīd Riḍā, *Tafsīr al-Manār*, 1:337. The Muʿtazilah were an important early theological school who developed Islamic thought along lines of rationalist argumentation. An accessible overview, and one that notes their connection with the Ḥanafīyah, is that by Josef van Ess, "Muʿtazilah," in *The Encyclopedia of Religion*, ed. by Mircea Eliade et al. (New York: Macmillan, 1987), 10:220–29. The Ḥanafīyah, who take their name from Abū Ḥanīfah (d. 150/767), are one of the four principal schools of law in Sunnī Islam. See J. Schacht and W. Heffening, "Ḥanafiyya," *EI*² 3:162–64.

73 Rashīd Riḍā, *Tafsīr al-Manār*, 1:337.

spirit of the summons (*rūḥ al-daʿwah*)" is to be found among them.[74] Rashīd Riḍā then looks at the case of the Ṣābiʾūn, first from the perspective of viewing this group as a possible Christian heresy. He uses this vantage point to issue a strong denunciation of the Christians. The Ṣābiʾūn receive commendation from him because, despite their religious confusion and their vulnerability to heresies such as star worshiping, "they were nearer to the spirit of Christianity (*al-masīḥīyah*) than the Christians because they practiced asceticism (*al-zuhd*) and self-abasement (*al-tawāḍuʿ*), two things which pour forth from every statement reported as coming from the Messiah."[75] Rashīd Riḍā then continues with a castigation of the Christians, denouncing them for becoming "the worst people on earth, arrogant, greedy and manipulative of the world's destinies."[76]

When this commentator considers the Ṣābiʾūn from another viewpoint, taking them as adherents of a quite independent religious tradition, he likens them to the Arab 'original monotheists (*ḥunafāʾ*)', noting, however, that the former had variant customs and laws. If they are to be classified with the *ḥunafāʾ*, then they must be judged by the appropriate standards. Otherwise "they, like the Jews and Christians, are responsible for acting upon their religion, after they have understood its obligations, until such time as another 'guidance (*hudan*)' reaches them."[77]

Clearly, the decisive element is access to a prior revelation. The Jews and Christians were given this advantage and therefore must be judged by more stringent standards than those by which such groups as the 'people of the interval' (of whom the Ṣābiʾūn may form a part) are to be evaluated. Rashīd Riḍā wants to make very clear the exact limit of human responsibility in relation to God's purpose. The basics are belief in God and the Last Day. Anyone who has been exposed to this message is bound to believe it whether or not he has had the benefit of a prophetic revelation. Quoting a Muʿtazilī

74 Rashīd Riḍā, *Tafsīr al-Manār*, 1:337.
75 Rashīd Riḍā, *Tafsīr al-Manār*, 1:337–38.
76 Rashīd Riḍā, *Tafsīr al-Manār*, 1:338.
77 Rashīd Riḍā, *Tafsīr al-Manār*, 1:338. Textually, the first of the twelve Qurʾānic mentions of the term *ḥanīf* (pl. *ḥunāfāʾ*) occurs in *sūrat al-baqarah* (2):135, as an epithet applied to Abraham. *Sūrah Āl ʿImrān* (3):67 states: "Abraham was not a Jew nor a Christian; rather was he a *ḥanīf*, a *muslim* and not one of the infidels (*al-mushrikūn*)." Analyses of this word's etymology and meaning abound. For a brief survey see W. Montgomery Watt's note on this in his *Bell's Introduction*, 16. A more extended consideration is his entry "Ḥanīf," EI^2 3:165–66. On the basis of etymological considerations that diverge from those offered by Watt, Geo Widengren connects Abraham as a *ḥanīf* with the *Ṣābiʾūn*. *Muhammad, the Apostle of God, and his Ascension* (Uppsala: A.-B. Lundequistska, 1955), 134. For further consideration of this see Ary A. Roest Crollius, S.J., *Thus Were They Hearing: The Word in the Experience of Revelation in Qurʾān and Hindu Scriptures* (Rome: Università Gregoriana, 1974), 123–33. Mention of those *ḥunafāʾ* who became Christian is made by Trimingham, *Christianity Among the Arabs*, 261–64.

view Rashīd Riḍā states: "Messengers come only to confirm what the intellect comprehends, clarifying and elucidating matters of vital significance, such as what the Hereafter will be like and the ways of worship most pleasing to God."[78]

The next step in this analysis is an examination of three categories established by the medieval master, Abū Ḥāmid Muḥammad al-Ghazālī (d. 505/1111), in the matter of prophetic revelation. The first group are those with no knowledge. The example Rashīd Riḍā uses is that of the people living on the American continent in the period between Jesus and Muḥammad. These, he says, are definitely 'saved (*nājūn*)' as long as some other genuine prophetic message has not reached them.[79] The second group includes those who have received an authentic message but are too negligent or obdurate to accept it. Such people are certainly to be held accountable (*mu'ākhadhūn*). The most troublesome group is the third; these are the ones whom the message has reached but not in its proper form, because of deficiencies on the part of the messenger. They should most properly be classed as a subset of the first group.[80]

Rashīd Riḍā then develops Muḥammad ʿAbduh's thought by delineating further refinements in this scheme. The third category becomes an intermediary between the first two described, and comprises those who have heard of Muḥammad but in a distorted way. Rather than a true description and characterization they are told from childhood "that a cheating liar whose name is Muḥammad has claimed to be a prophet."[81] Such misrepresentation is tantamount to ignorance so no blame can justly be ascribed to this group.

This whole discussion of the 'people of the interval' culminates in an expanded exegesis of the verse and one that more clearly specifies the referents of *those who believe* and *whoever believes*. Rashīd Riḍā dubs the latter "the people of divine religions (*ahl al-adyān al-ilāhīyah*)" and describes them as those whom an accurate and complete prophetic message (*daʿwah*) has reached. As a result of this, "they believed in God and the Last Day in the right way, as explained by their prophet, and they did good works."[82] These are the ones who are saved and rewarded in God's eyes. If they have perverted their belief or failed to accompany it with good deeds, then they are culpable and liable to divine chastisement.[83]

78 Rashīd Riḍā, *Tafsīr al-Manār*, 1:338. Olaf Schumann notes that such an adjudication of the relation between reason and revelation naturally aroused the suspicion of the "Hüter der Rechtgläubigkeit" at al-Azhar. *Der Christus der Muslime*, 118.

79 Rashīd Riḍā, *Tafsīr al-Manār*, 1:338.

80 Rashīd Riḍā, *Tafsīr al-Manār*, 1:339.

81 Rashīd Riḍā, *Tafsīr al-Manār*, 1:339.

82 Rashīd Riḍā, *Tafsīr al-Manār*, 1:339.

83 Rashīd Riḍā, *Tafsīr al-Manār*, 1:339.

Those to whom the other categories apply, that is, those who never received a message or received it in a distorted or corrupted form, fall beyond the scope of this verse. By charting the logical consequences of their possible inclusion, Rashīd Riḍā realizes the absurdity of such a position. For if those deprived of an authentic representation of revelation are guaranteed the same eternal bliss that is promised to true followers of Muḥammad, then it is only by the reception of divine revelation that an individual's soul is put in jeopardy.[84] Faced with this dilemma, Rashīd Riḍā settles for a reasonable compromise: "God will hold those to whom no notice of revelation has been granted accountable on the basis of their thoughts and beliefs about truth and goodness and their opposites."[85]

While the divine initiative of revelation and the stages of that revelatory process were an important theological issue for the commentators on this verse, the human faith response to revelation was of equal concern. Much of the exegetical cogitation provoked by this verse builds to a climactic consideration of the essence and content of faith. Al-Ṭūsī's analysis of this begins with that position which finds in this verse a reference to the hypocrites (*munāfiqūn*), be they Jew, Christian, or Ṣābiʾūn, who finally pay reluctant lip service to belief. Some of his predecessors had evidently proposed the novel view that on the basis of this verse, the hypocrites could expect the same divine reward as those whose acceptance of Islam was early and eager. The verse, then, was seen by these to refute the notion that those who came to belief late and grudgingly will have a lesser reward and recompense.[86] While al-Ṭūsī evidently feels obliged to include this interpretation he makes it quite clear that he feels little sympathy for it.

As part of his focus on faith al-Ṭūsī also has decided to counter the interpretation of another group, the Murjiʾah. This was one of the early sects of Islam who differed with another, the Khawārij, on the question of whether a Muslim ceases to be such if he commits a grave sin, a belief to which the latter group adhered.[87] By contrast, the Murjiʾah stressed the

84 Rashīd Riḍā, *Tafsīr al-Manār,* 1:339.

85 Rashīd Riḍā, *Tafsīr al-Manār,* 1:339.

86 al-Ṭūsī, *al-Tibyān*, 1:285.

87 For a description of the Khawārij and the Murjiʾah in a classical Muslim heresiography, see Muḥammad b. ʿAbd al-Karīm al-Shahrastānī (d. 548/1153), *al-Milal wa-al-niḥal*, ed. by Muḥammad Sayyid Kīlānī (Beirut: Dār al-Maʿrifah, 1402/1982), 1:114–47. Recent translations of this include A.K. Kazi and J.G. Flynn, trans., *Muslim Sects and Divisions: The Section on Muslim Sects in Kitāb al-Milal wa'l-Niḥal* (London: Routledge and Kegan Paul, 1984); J.C. Vadet, trans., *Les dissidences de l'Islam* (Paris: Librairie Orientaliste Paul Geuthner, 1984); and Daniel Gimaret and Guy Monnot, trans., *Livre des religions et des sectes* (Paris: Peeters/UNESCO, 1986). Possible Qurʾānic etymologies for the appellation *murjiʾah* are traced by Joseph Givony, " 'Wa ʾākharūna murjawna liʾamri ʾllāhi': An Inquiry into the Alleged Qurʾānic Origin of the Idea of Irjāʾ," *WO*

importance of 'faith (*īmān*)' far more than 'good works.' Al-Ṭūsī reports that "the Murji'ah have deduced, on the basis of this verse, that *īmān* does not involve doing good (*al-ʿamal al-ṣāliḥ*)."[88] Their argument is a quasi-grammatical one, based on the relative weight of elements in a series, maintaining that those mentioned first are of greater importance. Thus, the fact that God placed *whoever believes* well before [*whoever*] *does right* is proof of the former's primacy. Al-Ṭūsī counters by saying that God is not laying stress by placement within the sentence. He responds in two ways to the further objection that confessing of faith is an action and so should be counted as a 'good work': (1) the concept of action must involve the limbs, not merely one's inner disposition, and (2) profession of faith is an action only in the metaphorical sense, so that as an example it is not pertinent to the debate.[89]

The next significant contribution to this theological conversation is that of Fakhr al-Dīn al-Rāzī. Building upon his characterization of this verse's four introductory categories as *mubṭilūn*, those who speak falsely or vainly, this exegete shifts terminology to provide another explanatory perspective. To his previous list of epithets, he adds another, "those possessed of error (*arbāb al-ḍalāl*)." "When these people move out of a state of error and believe in the true religion, then indeed God will accept their faith and their compliance and will certainly not keep them from His presence."[90] For Fakhr al-Dīn al-Rāzī the phrase 'faith in God' necessarily entails belief in Muḥammad because God has made this incumbent upon mankind. In the same way belief in the Last Day involves adherence to all the other religious precepts. Such terms, then, function as a kind of shorthand: "These two phrases are really a summation of everything which has to do with religious duties in the state of imposed obligation (*taklīf*), and in the Hereafter with respect to reward and punishment."[91]

Kāshānī emphasizes not so much the content of faith as the consequences of its careful cultivation. To these he finds attestation in the concluding phrases of this verse: *they will have no fear, neither will they grieve*. He has woven a brief but consoling statement on the theme of the absence of fear and sorrow in the hearts of the righteous. Not upon them will be visited the worries about a life wasted and opportunities missed. Nor need they

12 (1981): 73–80. For a recent historical study, see Wilferd Madelung, "The Early Murji'a in Khurāsān and Transoxania and the Spread of Ḥanafism," *Der Islam* 59 (1982): 32–39.

88 al-Ṭūsī, *al-Tibyān*, 1:285. An exposition of the Murji'ī and Muʿtazilī positions on this, including the views of al-Ṭūsī's teacher, al-Sharīf al-Murtaḍā, is presented in Izutsu's *The Concept of Belief*, 159–66.

89 al-Ṭūsī, *al-Tibyān*, 1:285.

90 Fakhr al-Dīn al-Rāzī, *al-Tafsīr al-kabīr*, 3:105.

91 Fakhr al-Dīn al-Rāzī, *al-Tafsīr al-kabīr*, 3:105.

fear the effects of sins unforgiven. It is not punishment that they will face but reward.[92]

As an interesting addendum to his thoughts, Kāshānī closes his commentary on this verse with the explanation for an omission. He responds to the unspoken query: Why is there no mention of the need for renunciation of sins to accompany the injunctions for belief in God and the performance of good deeds? He answers that such renunciation is a necessary result of 'doing good'. The appropriate parallel is not 'doing good' and 'renouncing evil' but rather the verse's own juxtaposition of faith and good works, two things "whose connection is like the necessary connection of opposites."[93] Thus, as the verse indicates, these constitute the basic twofold injunction, with 'renunciation of sin' properly understood as a subset of right action.

With Rashīd Riḍā, too, the discussion centers upon the concluding promises of this verse. He echoes Muḥammad ʿAbduh's earlier statements about the equitable nature of divine reward and chastisement. The phrase *for them is their reward* applies to all "who have faith in God and do good" regardless of formal religious affiliation, for God does not favor one group while ill-treating another. For all the righteous, God has promised a reward – a reward made known to them "by the tongue of their prophet" – so that they need fear no punishment on the day when the infidels (*kuffār*) and the iniquitous (*fujjār*) will fear what confronts them.[94] Rashīd Riḍā points out that this reassurance of the virtuous is a repetition of God's promise earlier in this *sūrah*: "Those who follow My guidance will have no fear, neither will they grieve" (*sūrat al-baqarah* [2]:38). It also anticipates a similar promise in *sūrat al-nisāʾ* (4):123–24, which again pledges that the good deeds of believers will be rewarded and the evil punished.

The interpretation takes a decidedly new turn, however, in the force with which Rashīd Riḍā insists on an extended understanding of this verse. He brooks no equivocation about the signification of *whoever believes*: it includes those who believe in God and the Last Day but does *not* stipulate belief in the prophet Muḥammad. All peoples who believe in a prophet and in the revelation particular to them are potentially recipients of divine reward. Its attainment lies not in religious sectarian allegiances (*al-jinsīyāt al-dīnīyah*) but in true belief and right action. Muslim, Jewish, or Christian aspirations to religious preeminence are of no interest to God. They are not the basis upon which His judgments are made.[95]

92 Kāshānī, *Minhaj al-ṣādiqīn*, 1:221.
93 Kāshānī, *Minhaj al-ṣādiqīn*, 1:222.
94 Rashīd Riḍā, *Tafsīr al-Manār*, 1:336.
95 Rashīd Riḍā, *Tafsīr al-Manār*, 1:336. Mohamed Talbi has taken note of Muḥammad ʿAbduh's teaching on this point and its continuation by Rashīd Riḍā. From such perspectives he deems it possible for Islam "to elaborate a theology which would allow for

Rashīd Riḍā is clearly concerned with the issue of interreligious rivalry. He makes reference again to *sūrat al-nisā'* (4):123–24, a complementary verse to the phrase under discussion, by quoting a *ḥadīth* that describes the revelatory occasion. It gives an account of the wrangling of Jews, Christians, and Muslims, each asserting claims to ultimate superiority, and provides the perfect context for divine clarification.[96] Rashīd Riḍā proceeds to sketch some of the implications of an excessive concern with sectarian allegiance. He feels that God's reproach is addressed to an imbalance, namely the imbalance that develops when an individual's interest in being identified with a religion outweighs the fervor with which he practices. Such an emphasis on mere externals, with its corresponding lack of true interior understanding and devotion, has, for Rashīd Riḍā, more than personal consequences.[97] It was a critical factor in determining the reception of Muḥammad's message. Had the people to whom the Prophet addressed himself been religiously balanced, he argues, they would all have seen the truth of his message and accepted it. It was their concern with partisan identification to the exclusion of the truth that blinded them.[98]

THE QUESTION OF ABROGATION

The final question that the exegetical tradition has raised about this verse is a legal one. Its background is one of the primary hermeneutical themes in Qur'ānic studies, that of abrogation. Briefly, this category of the Qur'ānic sciences (*ʿulūm al-Qur'ān*) is concerned with those scriptural instances in which one part of the revelation may be said to cancel or supersede another part. Al-Ṭabarī uses a *ḥadīth* attributed to Ibn ʿAbbās to raise the question of abrogation. In the *ḥadīth* Ibn ʿAbbās states that after the verse under present consideration, God sent down *sūrah Āl ʿImrān* (3):85: "Should anyone desire a religion other than Islam, it will not be accepted and in the Hereafter he will be among the lost." Al-Ṭabarī comments that Ibn ʿAbbās is suggesting in this *ḥadīth* a change in the divine attitude toward former religions. Whereas God had originally promised those who acted rightly – whether Jews, Christians, or Ṣābi'ūn – paradise in the Hereafter, He abrogated that promise by the revelation of 3:85.[99]

a certain degree of plurality in the ways of salvation. . . . " "Islam and Dialogue: Some Reflections on a Current Topic," in *Christianity and Islam: The Struggling Dialogue*, ed. by Richard W. Rousseau, S.J. (Montrose, Pa.: Ridge Row Press, 1985), 63. Abdulaziz Sachedina also uses 2:62 to argue that "consistent with its rejection of exclusivism and election, the Qur'ān acknowledges the existence of righteous people in other communities who can expect to be saved." "Jews, Christians and Muslims According to the Qur'ān," *The Greek Orthodox Theological Review* 31 (1986): 120.

96 Rashīd Riḍā, *Tafsīr al-Manār*, 1:336.

97 Rashīd Riḍā, *Tafsīr al-Manār*, 1:337.

98 Rashīd Riḍā, *Tafsīr al-Manār*, 1:337.

99 al-Ṭabarī, *Jāmiʿ al-bayān*, 2:155. Abdelmajid Charfi concludes that al-Ṭabarī does not

Al-Ṭabarī concludes his discussion of this verse by rejecting the opinion attributed to Ibn ʿAbbās and restating his original position. Not only does he find it more congruent with the obvious sense of the text but also better suited to his concept of divine justice: God, al-Ṭabarī declares, would not single out some of His creatures to the exclusion of others when rewarding those who had lived in faith and acted rightly.[100]

Al-Ṭūsī is even more forceful than al-Ṭabarī in rejecting Ibn ʿAbbās's theory that this verse is abrogated by *sūrah Āl ʿImrān* (3):85. His reason is the technical one that a statement that confirms a promise cannot be abrogated.[101] In other words, once God has promised something, He will not subsequently withdraw His promise.

Ibn al-Jawzī poses the question somewhat differently. In a separate, concluding section he asks: Is this verse firmly established (*muḥkam*) or abrogated (*mansūkh*)? In so doing, he is combining exegetical categories drawn from two key verses in the Qurʾān, *sūrah Āl ʿImrān* (3):7 and *sūrat al-baqarah* (2):106.[102] In response to the query, this commentator quotes the early authorities Mujāhid and al-Ḍaḥḥāk b. Muzāḥim (d. 105/723) as maintaining that the verse is firmly established (*muḥkam*). Ibn al-Jawzī then implies that such is the standard opinion by noting that only a group among the commentators (*jamāʿah min al-mufassirīn*) opt for abrogation of this verse on the basis of *sūrah Āl ʿImrān* (3):85. As with many of his other explicative enumerations, Ibn al-Jawzī does not reveal his own position on this.[103]

While Ibn Kathīr does not actually use the term 'abrogation' in his analysis of this verse, he does include the *ḥadīth* reported from Ibn ʿAbbās

"touch upon the problem of deliverance (*najāt*), or salvation (*khalāṣ*)" because Charfi found no reference to it in al-Ṭabarī's commentary on 3:85. Although Charfi notes a possible connection with 5:69, he makes no mention of 2:62 in this regard. "Christianity," 143.

100 al-Ṭabarī, *Jāmiʿ al-bayān*, 2:155–56. Khalil Samir states that according to al-Ṭabarī the non-Muslim "n'a pas besoin de devenir Musulman pour être sauvé. Il lui suffit de croire en son coeur à l'authenticité de la mission de Muḥammad, tout en demeurant dans sa religion." "Le commentaire," 586. Unfortunately he does not proceed to spell out what belief in the "authenticity" of Muḥammad's mission while remaining in one's religion entails.

101 al-Ṭūsī, *al-Tibyān*, 1:284.

102 For a discussion of the classical Islamic understanding of abrogation see John Burton's "Introductory Essay" in his edition of *Abū ʿUbaid al-Qāsim b. Sallām's K. al-nāsikh wa-l-mansūkh* (Cambridge: E.J.W. Gibb Memorial Trust, 1987), 1–45; and David Powers, "The Exegetical Genre *nāsikh al-Qurʾān wa-mansūkhuhu*," in *Approaches*, 117–38. Earlier work by Burton on this topic includes an article on the so-called 'Satanic verses', "Those Are the High-flying Cranes," *JSS* 15 (1970): 246–65, as well as "The Interpretation of Q. 87,6–7 and the Theories of *Naskh*," *Der Islam* 62 (1985): 5–19. For the category of *muḥkam* as developed from 3:7 see my "Quranic Hermeneutics," 44–62.

103 Ibn al-Jawzī, *Zād al-masīr*, 1:92.

which states that after this verse was revealed, *sūrah Āl ʿImrān* (3):85 was sent down. Clearly he finds this position compatible with his own notion of salvific stages. Thus, after Muḥammad had been sent, nothing that was not in accord with his *sharīʿah* was acceptable to God. But before Muḥammad's appearance, "everyone who followed the messenger in his own era, lived a rightly guided life on the way to salvation (*najāh*)."[104]

QURʾĀNIC PARALLELS

Before concluding the consideration of this verse, it is important to mention two other verses in the Qurʾān that closely resemble the one just discussed. These are *sūrat al-māʾidah* (5):69 and *sūrat al-ḥajj* (22):17. For the most part the exegetical treatment of these two is concise; several of the commentators do little more than refer the reader to the full discussion in *sūrat al-baqarah* (2):62. However, as some interesting differences emerge in the treatment of these two verses, each will be briefly presented in turn.

The first Qurʾānic parallel is *sūrat al-māʾidah* (5):69:

> Truly those who believe and those who are Jews, and the Ṣābiʾūn and the Christians, whoever believes in God and the Last Day and does right, they will have no fear, neither will they grieve.

Because this verse replicates *sūrat al-baqarah* (2):62 in the use of *those who believe* and *whoever believes* most of the commentators repeat the various interpretations of these phrases that have already been discussed. The only notable exceptions are the two commentaries written in Persian, those of Abū al-Futūḥ Rāzī and Mullā Fatḥ Allāh Kāshānī. Both condense the more lengthy treatment of this problem, offered in their commentaries on 2:62, to one signification. For Abū al-Futūḥ Rāzī the phrase *those who believe* refers to the genuine (or fundamental/original) believers.[105] For Kāshānī, on the

104 Ibn Kathīr, *Tafsīr al-Qurʾān al-ʿaẓīm*, 1:103. This verse figures in the twelfth-century Christian polemic by Paul of Antioch (d. 575/1180), the Melkite bishop of Sidon, to which a response was given by Ibn Kathīr's teacher, Ibn Taymīyah. Paul's *Risālah ilā aḥad al-muslimīn* (Letter to a Muslim) quotes 2:62 with the argument that "by this statement the Muslims have put themselves and other peoples on an equal footing." Khoury, *Paul d'Antioche*, 67 of the Arabic text. Ibn Taymīyah's rejoinder in *al-Jawāb al-ṣaḥīḥ li-man baddala dīn al-Masīḥ* extrapolates from Christian self-understanding as the abrogation of Judaism: "Thus if there is praise in this verse for the religion which the Christians possess after the sending of Muhammad, there is praise in it as well for the religion of the Jews, and this is false to them as well as to the Muslims. Conversely, if there is no praise in it for the Jews after the abrogation and corruption of their religion, in the same way there is no praise in it for Christians after the corruption and abrogation of theirs." Michel, *A Muslim Theologian's Response*, 246. Muzammil H. Siddiqi has surveyed some of the principal issues in this exchange in "Muslim and Byzantine Christian Relations: Letter of Paul of Antioch and Ibn Taymīyah's Response," *The Greek Orthodox Theological Review* 31 (1986): 33–45.

105 *muʾminān kih dar aṣl muʾmin būdand*. Abū al-Futūḥ Rāzī, *Rawḥ al-jinān*, 2:294.

contrary, the same phrase is a reference to "those who believe with the tongue," that is, the hypocrites.[106]

As might be expected, given the repetitive nature of this verse, none of the exegetes comments at length on the term 'Christians (*al-naṣārā*)'. Al-Ṭūsī, whose analysis of the term in his commentary on 2:62 was essentially etymological, paraphrases *al-naṣārā* as "those who confess the Messiah (*yuqirrūna bi-al-masīḥ*)."[107] For Abū al-Futūḥ Rāzī, as well, there is a shift from the etymological considerations of 2:62 to a definition of *al-naṣārā* as "those who are in the religious community (*millah*) of Jesus."[108] Ibn Kathīr's explanation of *al-naṣārā* is linked to, but different from, his treatment of the term in 2:62. In the latter he postulated a theory of salvific stages whereby the Gospel is understood to supplant the Torah, and the revelation to Muḥammad to complete all prior divine disclosures. In keeping with this stress on scriptures, Ibn Kathīr restates the designations of *sūrat al-mā'idah* (5):69, *those who are Jews* and *the Christians*, as "custodians of the Torah (*ḥamalat al-tawrāt*)" and as "custodians of the Gospel (*ḥamalat al-injīl*)."[109]

He also takes this opportunity to reaffirm his position on the present acceptability of either of these antecedent revelations. In both his exegesis of 2:62 and of the present verse Ibn Kathīr states very explicitly that the divine reward promised in the former verse and implied in the latter is for Muslims alone. Lest one assume that believing in God and the Last Day and doing good works is sufficient to merit such recompense, Ibn Kathīr insists: "Such is not the case, unless there is conformity to the Muḥammadan law (*al-sharī'ah al-muḥammadīyah*), after the sending of its bearer (*ṣāḥib*), who was sent to all creatures, humans and *jinn* (*al-thaqalān*)."[110]

Quite a different interpretation is advocated by Ṭabāṭabā'ī, who has found a more inclusive meaning in the exegesis of 5:69. The penultimate sentence of his commentary on this verse is an apt summation of his view. He explains that "at the Gate of Bliss no importance will be attached to names and titles, e.g., whether a group is called *the believers* or a faction *those who are Jews* or a party *Ṣābi'ūn* or others *the Christians*. The only important thing is belief in God and the Last Day and doing good."[111]

106 Kāshānī, *Minhaj al-ṣādiqīn*, 3:283.
107 al-Ṭūsī, *al-Tibyān*, 3:592.
108 Abū al-Futūḥ Rāzī, *Rawḥ al-jinān*, 2:294.
109 Ibn Kathīr, *Tafsīr al-Qur'ān al-'aẓīm*, 2:80.
110 Ibn Kathīr, *Tafsīr al-Qur'ān al-'aẓīm*, 2:80.
111 Ṭabāṭabā'ī, *al-Mīzān*, 6:67. Fazlur Rahman echoes these sentiments. Referring to 2:62 and 5:69, he asserts that "in both these verses, the vast majority of Muslim commentators exercise themselves fruitlessly to avoid having to admit the obvious meaning: that those – from any section of mankind – who believe in God and the Last Day and do good deeds are saved." *Major Themes of the Qur'ān* (Minneapolis: Bibliotheca Islamica, 1980), 166.

But such concerns are tangential to the chief exegetical problem raised by this verse. All of the commentators herein discussed feel compelled to address the grammatical anomaly created by the presence of the word *al-ṣābiʾūn* in the nominative instead of the accusative after the particle *inna*. Al-Zamakhsharī departs from his characteristic brevity to discuss this matter at length, as might be expected from one of the most eminent grammarians of Arabic.[112] However, by far the most extensive treatment is that offered by Fakhr al-Dīn al-Rāzī.[113] In a very systematic fashion he presents the positions of such classical grammarians as al-Khalīl b. Aḥmad (d. 175/791), Abū Bishr ʿAmr b. ʿUthmān Sībawayh (d. 177/793), Abū Zakarīyāʾ Yaḥyā b. Ziyād al-Farrāʾ (d. 207/822), and al-Zamakhsharī, carefully evaluating the merits of each. What distinguishes his analysis, though, is the ontological perspective within which he places this entire argument.[114]

In addition to the grammatical concern about the nominative form of the term *al-ṣābiʾūn*, importance has been attached to the placement of the word. As a close comparison of 2:62 and 5:69 indicates, the mention of *al-ṣābiʾūn* and *al-naṣārā* is reversed in the two. In the latter verse the Christians are the last-mentioned group. Rashīd Riḍā proposed the theory that this placement is representative of Christian proximity to full divine acceptability. The criterion of such acceptability is, of course, manifest by *whoever believes in God and the Last Day*. The fact that the term *al-naṣārā* is placed immediately before this phrase is, for Rashīd Riḍā, significant. It means that the Christians come nearest, of the non-Muslim groups mentioned, to meeting that criterion.[115] Furthermore, this exegete suggests, the four designated groups have been cited in order of ascending acceptability. Thus, the lowest rank is that of *those who believe* – understood as

112 al-Zamakhsharī, *al-Kashshāf*, 1:660–62. One solution which al-Zamakhsharī offers is to see the verse as an instance of hyperbaton (*taqdīm wa-taʾkhīr*). The reconstruction (*taqdīr*) that he proposes is to understand the verse as follows: "Those who believe and the Jews and the Christians, their situation is thus and so and the *Ṣābiʾūn* likewise." John Wansbrough, in his work on Abū ʿUbaydah (d. 209/824), finds a functional similarity between what al-Zamakhsharī and other, later grammarian-commentators call *taqdīr* and what the earlier Abū ʿUbaydah calls *majāz*. "Majāz al-Qurʾān: Periphrastic Exegesis," *BSOAS* 33 (1970): 247–66. Ella Almagor takes issue with Wansbrough's conclusion in "The Early Meaning of *majāz* and the Nature of Abū ʿUbayda's Exegesis," in *Studia Orientalia Memoriae D.H. Baneth Dedicata*, ed. by J. Blau et al. (Jerusalem: Magnes Press, 1979), 307–26. John Burton has defined *taqdīr* succinctly as "interpolation" or an "appeal to words not in the Qurʾān text, but allegedly 'understood.' " "*Mutʿa, tamattuʿ* and *istimtāʿ*—a Confusion of *tafsīr*s," *UEAI 10*, 4–5.

113 Fakhr al-Dīn al-Rāzī, *al-Tafsīr al-kabīr*, 12:54–55.

114 Fakhr al-Dīn al-Rāzī, *al-Tafsīr al-kabīr*, 12:53. John Burton offers an extended analysis of this inflectional anomaly in "Linguistic Errors in the Qurʾān," *JSS* 33 (1988): 188–96.

115 Rashīd Riḍā, *Tafsīr al-Manār*, 6:479.

applying to the hypocrites – with *those who are Jews, al-ṣābiʾūn*, and *al-naṣārā* presented as ever closer approximations to the divine imperative.[116]

A second Qurʾānic parallel to 2:62 may be found in *sūrat al-ḥajj* (22):17:

> Truly those who believe and those who are Jews, the Ṣābiʾūn, the Christians, the Zoroastrians (*al-majūs*) and those who associate (*alladhīna ashrakū*), surely God will decide among them on the Day of Resurrection. Truly God is a witness to everything.

God's activity on the Day of Judgment is the aspect of this verse that the commentators find of prime importance. Virtually no attention is paid to repeating identifications of the terms that this verse shares with 2:62 and 5:69, namely, *those who believe, those who are Jews, the Ṣābiʾūn*, and *the Christians*. For the two new categories, *the Zoroastrians* and *those who associate*, Abū al-Futūḥ Rāzī is content to supply a Persian translation for the former (*gabrakān*) and a gloss for the latter as those who "associate partners with God in worship."[117] Kāshānī repeats this with the addition that *those who associate* means "idol worshipers (*ʿabadah-i aṣnām*)."[118]

The most persistent element in the exegesis of this verse is the use of a *ḥadīth* (with variants) that highlights the dividing judgment of the Last Day. The first mention of this is found in al-Ṭabarī. After indicating that the decisive factor in the divine judgment will be belief in God and His Messenger, this exegete states: "The religions (*al-adyān*) are six, five for Satan and one for al-Raḥmān (the Merciful)."[119] Fakhr al-Dīn al-Rāzī repeats this with a further clarification: "The religions are six, one for God, which is Islam, and five for Satan."[120] Although neither of these commentators explicitly draws the connection, it is clear that the *ḥadīth* nicely fits the enumeration of religions in this verse. As long as *those who believe* is taken to mean Islam, the other five categories (*those who are Jews, the Ṣābiʾūn, the Christians, the Zoroastrians* and *those who associate*) may be consigned to Satan. The fit is far less neat for the variant of this *ḥadīth* recorded by al-Zamakhsharī, Abū al-Futūḥ Rāzī, and Kāshānī.[121] In this version

116 Rashīd Riḍā, *Tafsīr al-Manār*, 6:479. This variation of listing prompted Michel Tardieu to remark upon its possible significance with respect to the Ṣābiʾūn. Bearing the chronology of revelation in mind, he suggests that their final position in the list of 2:62 seems "comme si déjà la route de la Mekke à Médine estompait leur silhouette de la carte religieuse de l'Arabie." "Ṣābiens coraniques," 40.

117 Abū al-Futūḥ Rāzī, *Rawḥ al-jinān*, 8:82.

118 Kāshānī, *Minhaj al-ṣādiqīn*, 6:114.

119 al-Ṭabarī, *Jāmiʿ al-bayān* (1984 edition), 17:89.

120 Fakhr al-Dīn al-Rāzī, *al-Tafsīr al-kabīr*, 23:18.

121 al-Zamakhsharī, *al-Kashshāf* 3:148; Abū al-Futūḥ Rāzī, *Rawḥ al-jinān*, 8:82; Kāshānī, *Minhaj al-ṣādiqīn*, 6:145. In discussing these three verses (2:62, 5:69, and 22:17) Josef Horovitz notes that with the inclusion of the *Majūs* and the *mushrikūn* in 22:17 no further mention is made of eternal reward. *Koranische Untersuchungen*, 43.

the total number of religions is reduced from six to five, with the correlative sum of four for Satan and one for God. This reduction means, of course, that one of the six groups listed in this verse is no longer accounted for. The exegetical answer, in each case, has been to subsume *al-ṣābiʾūn* under some other category. Al-Zamakhsharī states that "the Ṣābiʾūn are together with the Christians because they are a species (*nawʿ*) of them."[122] Neither Abū al-Futūḥ Rāzī nor Kāshānī is willing to be so specific. The latter's lack of precision is explained thus: "Including the Ṣābiʾūn with those other four groups is not strange because they belong either to the religion of the Jews or the Christians or the Zoroastrians (*al-majūs*) or the idolaters (*al-mushrikūn*) or vice versa [i.e., each of the four could be equated with the Ṣābiʾūn]."[123]

A discussion of this verse should not close without acknowledging the special contributions of Fakhr al-Dīn al-Rāzī and Ṭabāṭabāʾī. Both have chosen to use this verse as the basis for a brief *excursus* on religious pluralism. Fakhr al-Dīn begins by dividing the fundamental disagreements that produce religious diversity into three categories. The first group are those who agree on the question of prophethood but disagree about such philosophical issues as human free will and the nature of the divine attributes. The second group is the reverse of this. There is philosophical agreement but contention over the nature of prophecy. The final category is that characterized by disagreement over the concept of divinity. Included in this group are "the Sophists who suspend judgment about truths, the materialists (*al-dahrīyah*) who do not acknowledge the existence of that which acts upon the world, and the philosophers who attest to that which acts by necessity not free choice."[124]

Having sketched this typology, al-Rāzī then seeks to relate it to various religious groupings, particularly those mentioned in this verse. He first notes that the most fundamental source of disagreement is that about the godhead itself. Possessors of such deviant views are careful not to parade them: "They are not to be found in the world making a show of their beliefs and their doctrines, but rather are covert."[125] It is on the matter of prophecy that the divisions represented in this verse rest. At issue is the authenticity

122 al-Zamakhsharī, *al-Kashshāf*, 3:148.

123 Kāshānī, *Minhaj al-ṣādiqīn*, 6:145. This commentator, as well as the other two Shīʿī exegetes, al-Ṭūsī and Abū al-Futūḥ Rāzī, depict the judgment graphically. The faces of the truthful will be whitened while those of the false will be blackened. Al-Ṭūsī, *al-Tibyān*, 7:301; Abū al-Futūḥ Rāzī, *Rawḥ al-jinān*, 8:82; Kāshānī, *Minhaj al-ṣādiqīn*, 6:144.

124 Fakhr al-Dīn al-Rāzī, *al-Tafsīr al-kabīr*, 23:18. A French translation of the relevant section of Fakhr al-Dīn al-Rāzī's commentary on 22:17 may be found in Guy Monnot, "Le panorama religieux de Fakhr al-Dīn al-Rāzī," *RHR* 203 (1986): 274–77.

125 Fakhr al-Dīn al-Rāzī, *al-Tafsīr al-kabīr*, 23:18.

of particular prophets. According to Fakhr al-Dīn al-Rāzī, some religions revere a valid prophet while others do not: "The followers of [true] prophets are Muslims, Jews and Christians and another group, between the Jews and Christians, the Ṣābiʾūn. The followers of one who only calls himself a prophet (*al-mutanabbī*) are the Majūs."[126] The final group, the *mushrikūn*, are credited with an absolute denial of prophecy and dismissed as the "worshipers of images and idols (*ʿabadat al-aṣnām wa-al-awthān*)."[127] Interestingly, this last group is not included in the third of this exegete's original three categories, those who question the nature of the godhead. Apparently, these latter individuals possess a degree of philosophical sophistication lacking in the *mushrikūn*. Fakhr al-Dīn al-Rāzī ends this discussion by going beyond the limits of this verse to include one other group in his taxonomy. This is the Hindu Brahmins (*al-barāhimah*) who are to be classed with the *mushrikūn*, "regardless of what sort they are."[128]

Ṭabāṭabāʾī does not repeat al-Rāzī's system of classification when dealing with the religions mentioned in this verse. Rather he discusses each group in terms of the scripture for which it makes particular claims. For this commentator *those who believe* means "those who believe in Muḥammad and whose book is the Qurʾān."[129] After identifying *those who are Jews* as the believers in Moses whose book is the Torah, Ṭabāṭabāʾī adds some historical notes about that scripture: "Nebuchadnezzar (*Bukht-i Naṣar*), the king of Babylon, burned it when he took possession of them in the middle of the seventh century before the Messiah. For a while they were without it. Then ʿIzrāʾ, the priest (*al-kāhin*), wrote it anew in the beginning of the sixth century before the Messiah at the time when Cyrus, the king of Persia, conquered Babylon and freed the Banū Isrāʾīl from captivity and they returned to the Holy Land (*al-arḍ al muqaddasah*)."[130] The Ṣābiʾūn are cited as a group midway between the Jews and the Majūs who have "a book which they attribute to Yaḥyā b. Zakarīyā, the prophet [i.e., John the Baptist]."[131]

When he comes to the term *al-naṣārā*, this commentator distinguishes

126 Fakhr al-Dīn al-Rāzī, *al-Tafsīr al-kabīr*, 23:18.

127 Fakhr al-Dīn al-Rāzī, *al-Tafsīr al-kabīr*, 23:18.

128 Fakhr al-Dīn al-Rāzī, *al-Tafsīr al-kabīr*, 23:18. In a Persian work entitled *Jāmiʿ al-ʿulūm*, al-Rāzī has classed the Brahmins (*al-barāhimah*) not as *mushrikūn* but as those who find the idea of divinely sent prophets inconceivable. They reason that since God has given reason (*ʿaql*) to human beings by which they can tell right from wrong, prophets who convey such information are superfluous. For a translation of the relevant section of the *Jāmiʿ al-ʿulūm* see Guy Monnot, "L'histoire des religions en Islam, Ibn al-Kalbī et Rāzī," *RHR* 187 (1975): 30–33.

129 Ṭabāṭabāʾī, *al-Mīzān*, 14:358.

130 Ṭabāṭabāʾī, *al-Mīzān*, 14:358.

131 Ṭabāṭabāʾī, *al-Mīzān*, 14:358.

himself from his predecessors by recognizing the composite nature of Christian scripture. He is the first to use the word *injīl* in the plural, which he does when he mentions "the four Gospels (*al-anājīl*) of Luke, Mark, Matthew and John [his order]."[132] He also acknowledges the importance to Christians of "writings from the ancient epoch which the Church (*al-kanīsah*) venerates and esteems."[133] While Ṭabāṭabāʾī refers to the fact that the Qurʾān speaks of the Christian scripture in the singular as *al-injīl*, he makes no attempt to harmonize this with his previous statement.

His treatment of *al-majūs* specifically mentions Zarathushtra and the *Avesta*, and then adds some other details about the community's history and present status. Within the class of *those who associate* this exegete includes Brahmins and Buddhists as well as those, "like the [pre-Islamic] Arabs of the Ḥijāz," who worshiped idols "without developing a theoretical foundation."[134]

CONCLUSION

The various issues that emerge from the centuries-long exegetical analysis of 2:62 and its parallels constitute a considerable refinement of the uncritical understanding of the texts themselves. As the first textual mention of the Qurʾānic term for Christians (*al-naṣārā*), 2:62 naturally invited the sort of etymological speculation that engaged the exegetes' attention. Two major theories gained ascendancy, one of which took the term *al-naṣārā* as a geographical designation. The other, drawing upon either Arabic philology or a Qurʾānic statement attributed to Jesus, preferred to ground the etymology of *al-naṣārā* in the triliteral Arabic root, which carries connotations of 'helping' and 'rendering assistance'. While the momentum of the Arabic lexical sciences to subsume terms under appropriate verbal stems is certainly a factor, the consequence nevertheless reinforces a positive attitude toward Christians. If the etymological preference of al-Ṭūsī, al-Zamakhsharī, Fakhr al-Dīn al-Rāzī, and Ibn Kathīr is respected, then in the very way they are named in the Qurʾān, Christians are complimented. Notions of communal care and assistance permeate the designation they are accorded.

The attempt to clarify the relation between the two similar phrases *those who believe* and *whoever believes* begins the process of delimitation that characterizes this verse and others to be discussed. The exegetical insertion of an implied partitive, 'among them', immediately signals that not all Chris-

132 Ṭabāṭabāʾī, *al-Mīzān*, 14:358. For *injīl* see Chapter 6, note 1.

133 Ṭabāṭabāʾī, *al-Mīzān*, 14:358.

134 Ṭabāṭabāʾī, *al-Mīzān*, 14:359. Jacques Waardenburg has collected examples of contemporary Muslim attention to other religions in "Twentieth-century Muslim Writings on Other Religions: A Proposed Typology," in *UEAI 10*, 107–15.

tians meet the divine criteria of belief and action. At no point are the commentators presented herein content to allow the second phrase untrammeled inclusivity. Each in turn specifies the necessary boundaries that the verse must be assumed to erect. Often these entail prelusive religious purity, adherence to a pristine revelation that permits easeful acceptance of God's final prophet.

Such elements find narrative expression in the story of Salmān al-Fārisī, which several of the commentators recount. Its concluding note of divine reassurance, prompted by a Prophetic denunciation, climaxes a finely detailed conversion story. This verse's overwhelming identification with the Christians is discursively supported as Salmān finds truth and meaning first in the Gospel of Jesus and then in the promised Prophet. But this scenario circumscribes. Salmān does not remain a Christian but moves expectantly toward the final divine disclosure. Both the narrative of Salmān itself and the lists of converts or religious seekers provided by Ibn al-Jawzī, Fakhr al-Dīn al-Rāzī, and Kāshānī serve to restrict the range of applicability that may be drawn from this verse. Praise is reserved for Christians who acknowledge the primacy of Muḥammad or who are poised in anticipation, awaiting his advent.

Even the broader contextual considerations cannot override this circumscription. Be it termed a balance to prior censure (Fakhr al-Dīn al-Rāzī), an antiphonal response (Ibn Kathīr), or an exemption (Muḥammad ʿAbduh), the verse cannot be permitted to congratulate all those who would call themselves Christian. Theological judgments developed within the scope of the verse underscore this move to delimit. Both al-Ṭabarī and Ibn Kathīr explicitly link the explanation of 2:62 to the classical Muslim understanding of salvation history. Christianity is simply a stage from which those whose allegiance has been neither corrupted nor distorted can pass into a more adequate response to divine guidance. Where the prophetic sequence is interrupted, for those generations who do not form part of the revelatory progression from Judaism through Christianity to Islam, Rashīd Riḍā would suggest that a kind of natural theology operates. It is from this perspective of those not fortunate enough to be vouchsafed a revelation that he makes some of his most trenchant criticisms of Christians.

Evolving within the exegetical tradition on this verse is a line of argumentation that seeks to push the definition of faith, of the belief herein mandated, beyond the Qurʾānic textual statement itself. Fakhr al-Dīn al-Rāzī issues a particularly strong statement of the position that belief in God and the Last Day implies acceptance of Muḥammad. All other religions have been superseded, their salvific efficacy rendered null and void. Ibn Kathīr's ratification of the view that 2:62 is abrogated by 3:85, "Should anyone desire a religion other than Islam, it will not be accepted," simply makes explicit and gives a quasi-legal penumbra to the already-established exegetical trajectory.

Yet that is not the only trajectory. Even within the early stratum of classical exegesis, both Sunnī and Shī'ī, there is a manifest unwillingness to thus restrict the applicability of this divine promise. Both al-Ṭabarī and al-Ṭūsī reject the notion of abrogation, allowing the possibility of Christian praiseworthiness to remain. That possibility, in turn, is developed obliquely in the mystical taxonomy credited to Ibn al-'Arabī and far more directly in the interpretive turn taken by both Rashīd Riḍā and Ṭabāṭabā'ī.

These two twentieth-century commentators represent a new thrust in the explication of this verse. Both develop the argument that religious self-designation is of quite secondary importance. Names do not count. Not formal religious affiliation but the adjuration to belief and right action is primary. Rashīd Riḍā, in fact, explicitly rejects the idea that this verse implicitly stipulates belief in Muḥammad. The ecumenical thrust of his remarks is unmistakable. Even more is that the case with Ṭabāṭabā'ī, who firmly excludes any notion that claims to religious priority can flow from something other than authentic belief faithfully expressed.

Such views do not mask an ignorance of particular religious traditions among the exegetes. In dealing with 22:17, a verse whose sixfold classificatory scheme prompted a miniature heresiography from several of the commentators, Fakhr al-Dīn al-Rāzī reveals a sophisticated awareness of diverse traditions. In an even more factual manner, Ṭabāṭabā'ī derives his own typology from this verse, indicating full awareness of the variety of faith commitments, yet allowing none to claim an automatic preeminence. Such consistency, however, is not without an occasional crack. Although insistent that names are irrelevant when treating 2:62, Rashīd Riḍā actually builds an argument upon the semantic placement of a name in 5:69. The proximity of *al-naṣārā* in this verse to the phrase *whoever believes in God and the Last Day* works to the Christians' advantage, edging them close to fulfilling the divine requirements.

4

Followers of the Qur'ānic Jesus

Consideration of the Christians is refracted through a Christological prism in the next verse to be discussed. Allusion to the 'followers' is understandable only in relation to the clearly articulated name of ʿĪsā (Jesus). In fact, the opening clauses of *sūrah Āl ʿImrān* (3):55 are cast in the form of divine direct address to Jesus:

When God said, "O Jesus, I am the One who will take you and raise you to Me and cleanse you of those who disbelieve and place those who follow you over those who disbelieve until the Day of Resurrection. Then to Me is your return. I shall judge between you in that about which you disagree."

Much of the exegetical effort expended on this verse concentrates upon God's statements to Jesus. As it unfolds, the explication of this verse section provides a fuller portrait of the Qur'ānic Jesus, in itself an indispensable propaedeutic to understanding the clauses that refer to his 'followers'.

SŪRAH ĀL ʿIMRĀN (3):54 AS PRELUDE

The first word of this verse, the Arabic particle *idh* (here translated *when*) provokes an immediate concern for contextuality among several of the commentators. Al-Ṭabarī initiates this aspect of the exegetical investigation by pondering what connection this verse might have to the verses preceding it. The verse just before this one ends with the words "They [the Jews] plotted and God plotted but God is the best of plotters" (3:54). By taking this following verse as an instance of God's plotting, al-Ṭabarī can make the connection of signification thus: "God plotted against them *when* God said to Jesus. . . ."[1]

While al-Ṭūsī, too, pays attention to the question of contextuality, it is

1 al-Ṭabarī, *Jāmiʿ al-bayān*, 6:455. Although he does not focus specifically on the Arabic verb here translated as 'plotted (*makara*)', Helmer Ringgren presents a study of terminology, drawn from both Qur'ānic and extra-Qur'ānic sources, used to denote God's purposive activity. *Studies in Arabian Fatalism* (Uppsala: A.-B. Lundequistske Bokhandeln, 1955).

with al-Zamakhsharī that the connection to the preceding verse is made much more explicit.[2] Building upon the concluding phrases of 3:54, al-Zamakhsharī concurs with the view that finds in the verse under discussion an instance of God's superior cunning.[3] In the face of those attempting to destroy Jesus, God protects him until his appointed hour. The commentator paraphrases the opening section of this verse thus: "I am the One who protects you lest the unbelievers kill you, and the One who holds you back [from death] until the time I have written for you."[4]

Fakhr al-Dīn al-Rāzī concurs in the perception of this verse as an instance of the divine contrivance alluded to in 3:54, noting that the implied textual reconstruction (*al-taqdīr*) could be made by expanding the sense of the introductory phrase to read "such was the case when God said. . . . "[5] Kāshānī preserves this same exegetical tradition when he, too, advances the possibility that there is a linking phrase between these two verses which must be understood by implication. His paraphrase of some of the initial phrases of 3:55 makes this connection explicit and anticipates a subsequent exegetical consideration: "I am your protector from the Jews killing you until your soul is overtaken by a natural death at the appointed time."[6]

The two modern commentators whose works form a part of this study continue the hermeneutical inquiry with little modification or redirection. When Rashīd Riḍā comments upon the contextuality of this verse he observes that, as a whole, the verse can be conceived as an instance of divine intervention. God pays specific attention to Jesus in order to foil Jewish plots against him.[7] For Ṭabāṭabā'ī the placement of this verse signifies yet another instance of divine wrath against the Jews and the intensification of divine punishment against the Jewish community.[8]

TAKEN IN SLEEP OR DEATH

While the matter of contextuality afforded, for some of the commentators, an apt hermeneutical entrée, the most pressing and persistent concerns

2 al-Ṭūsī, *al-Tibyān*, 2:477.

3 al-Zamakhsharī, *al-Kashshāf*, 1:366. ʿAlī Ḥaydar explains the grammatical necessity by which the adverb of time, *idh*, requires a verbal antecedent in his *Iʿrāb sūrah Āl ʿImrān* (Damascus: Manshūrāt Dār al-Ḥikmah, 1392/1973), 99.

4 al-Zamakhsharī, *al-Kashshāf*, 1:366.

5 Fakhr al-Dīn al-Rāzī, *al-Tafsīr al-kabīr*, 8:71.

6 Kāshānī, *Minhaj al-ṣādiqīn*, 2:238.

7 Rashīd Riḍā, *Tafsīr al-Manār*, 3:316. In his careful study of the Qur'ānic depiction of Jesus, Heikki Räisänen continues this stress on contextuality with a forthright declaration: "Für die koranische Theologie sind die 'historischen' Einzelheiten nicht wichtig; die Hauptsache ist, dass Gott für seinen Gesandten wider die Gegner 'Ränke schmiedete' (3:47 [3:55]) und ihre Pläne annullierte." *Das Koranische Jesusbild*, 73.

8 Ṭabāṭabā'ī, *al-Mīzān*, 3:210.

expressed about this verse are philological. The divine address to Jesus consists of a series of promises. To determine the precise signification of each poses the primary exegetical challenge.

The first of these is the phrase *innī mutawaffīka*, whose key element is a fifth form active participle of the Arabic root *WFY*. (Because the entire argument in this part of the commentaries on 3:55 hinges on the exact meaning of words, there is no way to avoid the use of transliterated Qurʾānic terms. Any attempt at translation of terms would make the exegetical discourse appear tautologous or meaningless. Every effort will be made, however, to keep the lines of discussion as clear as possible for the non-Arabist.) Among the classical commentators the significant participants in this discourse are the Sunnī exegetes al-Ṭabarī and Fakhr al-Dīn al-Rāzī and the Shīʿī commentators Abū al-Futūḥ Rāzī and Kāshānī.

Al-Ṭabarī establishes these principal lines of inquiry by sorting out the various possible meanings of this phrase. Following his usual procedure, he systematically examines all likely referents and their support before offering his own determination. In the present instance, the first meaning proposed for the above verbal root is sleep or, more precisely, being taken by God in sleep. One of the *ḥadīth*s offered in support of this quotes the Prophet as saying: "Jesus did not die and he will return to you before the Day of Judgment."[9] Al-Ṭabarī then discusses the judgments of those who hold *wafāʾ* (the *maṣdar* or verbal noun of the root *WFY*) to be a synonym of *qabḍ*, a word that can be used to connote the collection of a debt. The phrase *innī mutawaffīka wa-rāfiʿuka ilayya* would thus mean: "I am the One who collected you (*qābiḍuka*) from the earth and raised you from among the idolaters and those who disbelieve in you."[10] A long biographical sketch of Jesus, presented on the authority of Kaʿb al-Aḥbār (d. 32/652–53), states that Jesus did not die and offers the reasons for this revelation (*asbāb al-nuzūl*).[11] Jesus, noting the few adherents and many detractors surrounding

9 al-Ṭabarī, *Jāmiʿ al-bayān*, 6:455. The Prophet's statement is quoted on the authority of al-Ḥasan al-Baṣrī. The Qurʾānic denial of Jesus' death by crucifixion and assertion that God "raised him (*rafaʿahu*)" is in *sūrat al-nisāʾ* (4):157–58. Related passages are *sūrat al-māʾidah* (5):117 and *sūrah Maryam* (19):31–33. Foundational studies on these verses from a Christian perspective have been summarized by Josef Henninger, S.V.D., *Spuren christlicher Glaubenswahrheiten im Koran* (Schöneck: Administration der neuen Zeitschrift für Missionswissenschaft, 1951), 25–29. Giuseppe Rizzardi groups the verses into those with a polemical, anti-Jewish thrust and those with an apologetic focus, finding in the former a stress on the exaltation of Jesus that is absent in the latter. *Il Problema della cristologia coranica* (Milan: Istituto Propaganda Libraria, 1982), 141–43.

10 al-Ṭabarī, *Jāmiʿ al-bayān*, 6:455–56.

11 Kaʿb al-Aḥbār was a Yemenite Jew who became a Muslim and proved to be a major source for the variety of *ḥadīth* known as *isrāʾīlīyāt*. For a summary of information on this figure see M. Schmitz, "Kaʿb al-Aḥbār," *EI*[2] 4:316–17. Moshe Perlmann has offered two accounts of Kaʿb's conversion to Islam (which reportedly occurred when he was a

him, complained to God. To console him, God revealed his future: he would be raised living to heaven and then sent back to earth to conquer the Antichrist (*al-dajjāl*). After living another twenty-four years he would then die a natural death.[12] It was further noted by Kaʿb al-Aḥbār that this confirms Muḥammad's rhetorical question: "How can a people of which I am the beginning and Jesus is the end perish?"[13]

Another, more curious, proof for this interpretation of the term *wafā'* is offered on the basis of the age attained by Jesus, as expressed in the Qur'ān. Verse 46 of *sūrah Āl ʿImrān* (3) states: "He will speak to the people in the cradle and as a middle-aged man (*kahlan*)." Thus, since God raised Jesus to Himself before his full maturity, He must have raised him while still alive, in order to fulfill the testimony of the just-quoted verse that Jesus lived to be middle-aged.[14]

According to other sources which the commentator quotes, the meaning intended by the term is 'death'. Jesus did die – the hour is a matter of some dispute – and was then revivified by God.[15] This enumeration of likely meanings then concludes with a last possibility; the question is less one of word meaning than of word placement. If the initial statements of this verse were transposed, with the phrases *I will raise you (rāfiʿuka)* and

very old man): "A Legendary Story of Kaʿb al-Aḥbār's Conversion to Islam," in *The Joshua Starr Memorial Volume* (New York: Conference on Jewish Relations, 1953), 85–99; and "Another Kaʿb al-Aḥbār Story," *The Jewish Quarterly Review* 45 (1954):48–51. More recently David Halperin and Gordon Newby have published an article about a cosmological prediction attributed to Kaʿb in al-Ṭabarī's *Ta'rīkh al-rusul wa-al-mulūk*. On the basis of their source analysis of this text they conclude that the Judaism with which Kaʿb was associated "is not rabbinic Judaism but some more archaic form akin, if not identical, to that which produced the Enoch literature." "Two Castrated Bulls: A Study in the Haggadah of Kaʿb al-Aḥbār," *JAOS* 102 (1982): 638. In 1976 Isrā'īl Abū Dhu'ayb published a monograph entitled *Kaʿb al-Aḥbār* (Jerusalem: Maṭbaʿat al-Sharq al-Taʿāwunīyah, 1976), which discusses the life and conversion of Kaʿb and his contribution to the development of popular narratives, particularly *qiṣaṣ al-anbiyā'*.

12 al-Ṭabarī, *Jāmiʿ al-bayān*, 6:456. In his broad-ranging *Encyclopedia of Islam* entry on ʿĪsā, Georges Anawati points out, as have others, the narrative consistency in the Qur'ānic denial of Jesus' death by crucifixion. The frequent Qur'ānic allusions to the rejection suffered by former prophets – what Kenneth Cragg calls "the occupational hazard of being a prophet" (*Jesus and the Muslim: An Exploration* [London: George Allen and Unwin, 1985], 167) – function as reassurance for Muḥammad precisely because these prophet narratives conclude with the eventual triumph of right over the forces arrayed against it. "ʿĪsā," *EI*² 4:84.

13 al-Ṭabarī, *Jāmiʿ al-bayān*, 6:457. It is worth recalling that according to traditional sources the reality of Muḥammad's death was questioned. The *Sīrah* of Ibn Isḥāq records the doubt raised by ʿUmar and Abū Bakr's rebuttal of it. *Sīrah rasūl Allāh*, 1:1012–13; Guillaume, *Life*, 682–83. In the introduction to his major heresiographical work al-Shahrastānī refers to this as an instance of the differences that arose among Muḥammad's Companions without serious doctrinal consequences. *al-Milal wa-al-niḥal*, 1:23.

14 al-Ṭabarī, *Jāmiʿ al-bayān*, 6:457.

15 al-Ṭabarī, *Jāmiʿ al-bayān*, 6:457–58.

I will cleanse you (*muṭahhiruka*) preceding *mutawaffīka*, then the sequence of events would be clarified. Al-Ṭabarī explains it thus: "This is an instance in which what is mentioned first happens last and what happens last is mentioned first."[16] Such is, of course, not an uncommon exegetical solution.

Having presented the range of meanings offered for the term *mutawaffīka* al-Ṭabarī chooses the second, that which holds it to be a synonym of *qābiḍuka* (i.e., I am the One who 'grasps' you or 'collects' you), as the most appropriate. He finds strong support for his choice in a multiplicity of *ḥadīth*s from the Prophet. He himself summarizes the *ḥadīth*s he reports in the following way: "ʿĪsā b. Maryam will be sent down and will kill the Antichrist. Then he will remain on earth for a certain period, concerning the extent of which accounts disagree. He will then die and the Muslims will pray over him and bury him."[17] What is noteworthy in this summary is that Jesus does not die until the end of his second coming. Therefore to interpret the use of the root *WFY* in this verse as a reference to death would be meaningless.[18]

Al-Ṭabarī feels that this point must be made clearly and forcefully: Jesus did not die twice. The Qur'ān itself has sketched the life plan of every human being: "God is the One who creates you, gives you sustenance, causes you to die and gives you life again" (*sūrat al-Rūm* [30]:40). The historical motive for this statement is, according to al-Ṭabarī, the assertions

16 al-Ṭabarī, *Jāmiʿ al-bayān*, 6:458. In discussing the issue of hyperbaton or transposition (*al-taqdīm wa-al-ta'khīr*) in relation to this verse, Roger Arnaldez offers the homely example of one who says to a friend: "Je t'invite à venir passer l'été prochain à la campagne et je vais préparer la maison pour te recevoir." *Jésus*, 190.

17 al-Ṭabarī, *Jāmiʿ al-bayān*, 6:458.

18 It is worth noting that the fifth form passive of *WFY* only comes to mean 'die' by extension. The original sense seems to be 'take' or 'seize', which is then broadened to cover the idea of God's taking the soul unto Himself. Fundamental to the exegetical examination of *tawaffā* are the several Qur'ānic uses of this verb, particularly that in *sūrat al-zumar* (39):42: "God takes (*yatawaffā*) souls at the time of their death. Those who do not die, [He takes] in their sleep. He holds fast to those for whom He has decreed death but sends back the others for a designated term." Henri Michaud concludes his own word study of the Qur'ānic use of *tawaffā* with the judgment that "*tawaffā* signifie le retour à Allah pour la rétribution dernière." *Jésus*, 61. For an exposition of the Qur'ānic connection between sleep and death, see Ringgren, *Arabian Fatalism*, 92–95; Thomas O'Shaughnessy, S.J., *Muhammad's Thoughts on Death: A Thematic Study of the Qur'anic Data* (Leiden: E.J. Brill, 1969), 39–41; and Jane Idleman Smith and Yvonne Yazbeck Haddad, *The Islamic Understanding of Death and Resurrection* (Albany: State University of New York Press, 1981), 48–49. Alford Welch has collated the various Qur'ānic uses of *tawaffā* with particular attention to the expressed or unexpressed subject of each mention. "Death and Dying in the Qur'ān," in *Religious Encounters with Death: Insights from the History and Anthropology of Religions*, ed. by Frank E. Reynolds and Earle H. Waugh (University Park, Pa.: Pennsylvania State University Press, 1977), 183–99. A recent treatment is A.H. Mathias Zahniser, "The Forms of Tawaffā in the Qur'ān: A Contribution to Christian-Muslim Dialogue," *MW* 79 (1989): 14–24.

of the delegation from Najrān and of various Jewish groups that Jesus had died on the cross. The *ḥadīth* from ʿAbdallāh b. al-Zubayr (d. 73/692) that he uses to explain this describes the debate Muḥammad had with the Christians from Najrān, particularly over the question of Jesus' reappearance after the crucifixion.[19]

Both al-Ṭūsī[20] and al-Zamakhsharī[21] replicate much of this etymological and grammatical analysis with some variation of emphasis and explanatory hypotheses. Abū al-Futūḥ Rāzī, too, engages the same set of semantic issues, relying extensively on intra-Qur'ānic modes of exposition.[22] He is

19 al-Ṭabarī, *Jāmiʿ al-bayān*, 6:461. See A. Moberg, "Nadjrān," *EI*[1] 6:823–25. Drawing upon Régis Blachère's hypothesis about Qur'ānic chronology, Thomas O. Shaughnessy suspects that this verse and *sūrat al-mā'idah* (5):117 "may originally have been part of a single discourse addressed to the Christian deputation from Najrān in 631." *Muhammad's Thoughts on Death*, 41. The Christians of Najrān figure prominently in the interpretation of at least two other Qur'ānic verses. *Sūrat al-burūj* (85):4–10 is frequently understood as a reference to the early sixth-century persecution that this group suffered. For a study of the manuscript sources from which the history of this episode is developed, see Irfan Shahīd's *The Martyrs of Najrān: New Documents* (Brussels: Société des Bollandistes, 1971). In the *sūrah* under discussion, verses 59–61 are commonly interpreted as a reference to the *mubāhalah* to which Muḥammad summoned the Christian delegation from Najrān. Louis Massignon defined the term *mubāhalah* as "un rite spécial de malédiction conditionnelle réciproque" in an article devoted to the discussion of its Qur'ānic origin and subsequent legal and theological development. "La Mubahala de Médine et l'hyperdulie de Fatima," in *Opera Minora*, ed. by Y. Moubarac (Beirut: Dar al-Maareef, 1973), 1:550. Reprinted from *Annuaire de l'École des Hautes Études*, 1943. Sharif al-Hasan comments on both of these Qur'ānic loci in his "A Fresh Look at Ancient Christians of Najrān and Present Religious Dialogues," *IS* 16 (1977):367–75.

20 al-Ṭūsī, *al-Tibyān*, 2:478. When dealing with the possible meanings of *mutawaffīka*, al-Ṭūsī condenses al-Ṭabarī's analysis into three succinct alternatives. The term may mean the One who takes you, while still living, from earth to heaven; it may mean the One who receives you while sleeping; or it may be an instance of transposition of significance (*al-taqdīm wa-al-ta'khīr*). The last alternative involves, of course, the relation of *mutawaffīka* and *rāfiʿuka* ("I will raise you"), the phrase immediately following it in the verse.

21 al-Zamakhsharī, *al-Kashshāf*, 1:366–67. There is a threefold range of signification offered by al-Zamakhsharī as well, but its constituent elements, while overlapping, do not precisely match those tendered by either al-Ṭabarī or al-Ṭūsī. For the term *mutawaffīka* al-Zamakhsharī gives the following connotations: (1) It is a synonym of *qābiḍuka*, in the sense of one who 'collects' something. The example that al-Zamakhsharī draws upon is the collection of a debt. (2) It means *mumītuka*, i.e., "the One who causes your death," after sending you down from heaven and now raising you. (3) It must be understood in light of the statement in *sūrat al-zumar* (39):42. Al-Zamakhsharī quotes only the second half of this latter verse's opening phrase: "God takes (*yatawaffā*) souls at the time of their death and those who do not die, in their sleep." He elaborates on this by explaining that when death occurs during sleep, there is no fear; the individual awakes to find himself in heaven, safe and near God.

22 Abū al-Futūḥ Rāzī, *Rawḥ al-jinān*, 3:55–56. When Abū al-Futūḥ Rāzī sets forth *qabḍ* as a synonym for *wafā'*, he emphasizes that this means taking Jesus while he is still alive by contrasting it with two Persian expressions for death, *qabż-i rūh* and *jān*

particularly concerned with the problem of transposition of meaning. Does the sequence of events in the life of Jesus match the sequence of Qur'ānic phrases? Abū al-Futūḥ Rāzī suggests that this dilemma is shared with *sūrah Ṭā' Hā'* (20):129 and paraphrases the present verse to suggest the following order of events: "I will raise you to Me and cleanse you from those who disbelieve and cause you to die after sending you down from heaven."[23]

The commentator elaborates upon this sequence by quoting a long Prophetic *ḥadīth* both in Arabic and in Persian translation – as is his usual procedure when citing *ḥadīth*s. His translation, in this instance, is far from a mere mechanical rendering. Rather it is an interpretation of the Arabic original that even contradicts, at one point, the wording of that original. Transmitted on the authority of Abū Hurayrah (d. 58/678), the *ḥadīth* begins: "The prophets are brothers from different mothers but their religion is one; I am superior to ʿĪsā b. Maryam because there is no prophet between him and me. He will come down from heaven for my community and be my caliph over them (*khalīfatī ʿalayhim*)."[24] It is this last phrase that Abū al-Futūḥ Rāzī finds troublesome. He interrupts his translation to comment (in Persian) "but he [Jesus] cannot be the caliph for the Messenger because his law has been abrogated and he did not know our law. Inevitably he must return with someone [i.e., the *Mahdī*] – and [attended by] the return of the whole community – who knows the law (*sharʿ*) of Muḥammad and considers it proper that Jesus, son of Mary, follow him [the 'someone'] and accept him. Surely there was an error (*khalal*) on the part of the narrator

bardāshtan. He finds further support for this view in *sūrat al-mā'idah* (5):117, where he reads another use of the fifth form of *WFY*, *tawaffaytanī*, as equivalent to the Arabic phrase *qabaḍtanī ilā al-samā' ḥayyan* (you took me alive to heaven). Abū al-Futūḥ Rāzī is careful to point out that with this understanding of *mutawaffīka*, the following phrase, "I will raise you to me (*rāfiʿuka ilayya*)," becomes a repetition. This commentator continues to use the hermeneutical device of adducing supportive Qur'ānic citations when he mentions the approach of those who consider the fifth form of *WFY* to mean 'sleep'. The resultant scenario, exemplified by reference to *sūrat al-anʿām* (6):60 and *sūrat al-zumar* (39):42, is one in which God first puts Jesus to sleep and then, when he is asleep, carries him to heaven. However, the exegete's full approval is reserved for the third option, that which takes *mutawaffīka* to be a synonym of the Persian phrase "I am the one who causes you to die (*man tūrā bimīrānam*)." Again Qur'ānic proof is brought in support. The two instances cited are *sūrat al-sajdah* (32):11: "Say, 'the angel of death will cause you to die' (*qul yatawaffākum malaku al-mawti*)" and *sūrah Yūnus* (10):46: "And whether We show you some of that with which We promised them or We cause you to die (*wa-immā nuriyannaka baʿḍa alladhī naʿiduhum aw natawaffayannaka*)." The period of time between Jesus' death and revivification, whether three hours or seven hours, is also discussed.

23 Abū al-Futūḥ Rāzī, *Rawḥ al-jinān*, 3:56. *innī rāfiʿuka ilayya wa-muṭahhiruka min al-ladhīna kafarū wa-mutawaffīka baʿda inzālika min al-samā'*.

24 Abū al-Futūḥ Rāzī, *Rawḥ al-jinān*, 3:57.

and the *ḥadīth* should read as follows: 'He will be sent down to my community together with a caliph who is from my line (*min waladī*).'"[25]

The original *ḥadīth* then continues with a physical description of Jesus and an account of what will happen when he returns to earth. In the concluding statement occurs the phrase "then he will die and the Muslims will pray for him (*thumma yatawaffā wa-yuṣallī al-muslimūn ʿalayhi*)."[26] Abū al-Futūḥ Rāzī once again interrupts his accompanying translation to explain and expand on this, remarking that "in the traditions (*akhbār*) of the Shīʿīs (*ahl al-bayt*) it seems that the *Mahdī* prays for him and surely it is better to pray for Jesus than for any mortal man."[27] In fact, for this commentator the chief importance of this lengthy *ḥadīth* is the light it throws upon events surrounding the *Mahdī*'s return. To counter assertions that there is no Qur'ānic record of Jesus' return and involvement in such events, he refers, as did al-Ṭabarī, to *sūrah Āl ʿImrān* (3):46 which contains the phrase "he [Jesus] will speak to the people in the cradle and as a middle-aged man (*kahlan*)." Abū al-Futūḥ Rāzī's reasoning, like that of al-Ṭabarī, is that since he had not reached full maturity when he was carried to heaven, he could only achieve this state after returning to earth.[28]

Ibn al-Jawzī contributes additional detail to the etymological considerations and clarifies further those matters of chronological versus textual sequence that had preoccupied Abū al-Futūḥ Rāzī.[29] Accepting a variation

25 Abū al-Futūḥ Rāzī, *Rawḥ al-jinān*, 3:57. On the connection of Jesus with the *Mahdī* see Hava Lazarus-Yafeh, "Is There a Concept of Redemption in Islam?," in her *Some Religious Aspects of Islam* (Leiden: E.J. Brill, 1981), 48–57. This is reprinted from R.I.Z. Werblowsky and C.J. Bleeker, *Types of Redemption* (Leiden: E.J. Brill, 1970), 168–80.

26 Abū al-Futūḥ Rāzī, *Rawḥ al-jinān*, 3:57. In his entry on the Prophet's tomb, Thomas Hughes presents a plan of the enclosure that indicates a space reserved for the tomb of Jesus "whom Muslims say will again visit the earth, and die and be buried at al-Madīnah." "Ḥujrah," in *Dictionary of Islam* (1885; reprint, New Delhi: Cosmo, 1977), 183. The *Qiṣaṣ al-anbiyāʾ*, which circulated under the name of *al-Kisāʾī*, contains a reference to this burial place. Thackston, *Tales*, 335. Gordon Newby's translation of the reconstructed text of Ibn Isḥāq's *Kitāb al-mubtadaʾ* offers an account of the discovery of Jesus' tomb near Medina. *The Making of the Last Prophet* (Columbia, S.C.: University of South Carolina Press, 1989), 210–11.

27 Abū al-Futūḥ Rāzī, *Rawḥ al-jinān*, 3:58.

28 Abū al-Futūḥ Rāzī, *Rawḥ al-jinān*, 3:58.

29 Ibn al-Jawzī, *Zād al-masīr*, 1:396–97. Ibn al-Jawzī offers two alternatives for the meaning of the term *wafāʾ*. The first is 'lifting up to heaven (*al-rafʿ ilā al-samāʾ*)'. To be thus understood the phrase may be taken on its own, without reference to what precedes or follows it. He then repeats al-Ṭabarī's synonym as further clarification: *qābiḍuka min al-arḍ*. Jesus is 'grabbed' from earth so as to foil Jewish designs upon him. Support for this position Ibn al-Jawzī finds in *sūrat al-māʾidah* (5):117: "When You took me (*tawaffaytanī*), You were vigilant against them." He understands this 'taking' to be a lifting up to heaven and then remarks "they made the substitution (*baddalū*) after his

of the latter's restatement of the verse (i.e., "I raised you to Me and purified you from those who disbelieve and I caused you to die after that"), Ibn al-Jawzī pauses to stress the point that Jesus' being raised up to heaven does not preclude his dying at some future date.[30] He concludes his remarks by relating a tradition that specifies the circumstances of Jesus' raising: at age thirty-three he was raised from Jerusalem on the night of destiny (*laylat al-qadr*) during Ramaḍān; some say his mother, Mary, lived for six years after that while others say she died before he was raised.[31]

When Fakhr al-Dīn al-Rāzī turns his attention to the possible meanings of *mutawaffīka* his performance is nothing short of an exegetical *tour de force*. He first divides his analysis on the issue of whether to follow the given word order or to assume a transposition of terms. If the present sequence is not disregarded, Fakhr al-Dīn al-Rāzī offers nine points of discussion. The first suggests as a synonym for *mutawaffīka* the phrase 'the one who brings your appointed span to completion (*mutammimu ʿumrika*)'. The original statement is then rephrased and expanded as follows: "When I do cause you to die, I will raise you to My heaven and My angels will draw you near."[32] This expanded version closes with a repetition and intensification of the divine promise of protection: "I will protect you from their even having the ability to kill you."[33]

The next synonym offered for this term is the fourth-form active participle *mumītuka*, 'the one who brings about your death', which had earlier been suggested by al-Zamakhsharī. Again the intended sense is that not only were the Jews frustrated in their efforts to kill Jesus but these same attempts were the occasion of further divine benefit to Jesus, his being raised to heaven. An additional specification is provided on the disputed questions of how long he was dead before revivification, and whether the latter oc-

being lifted up, not after his death." This is a reference to the belief that Jesus did not die on the cross; rather a substitute died in his place.

30 Ibn al-Jawzī, *Zād al-masīr*, 1:397.

31 Ibn al-Jawzī, *Zād al-masīr*, 1:397. Building upon the preliminary investigation pursued by Régis Blachère and Denise Masson, among others, J. Peters draws a suggestive parallel between the developed Qurʾānic reference to *laylat al-qadr* in *sūrat al-qadr* (97):1–3 and the Annunciation narrative in the Gospel of Luke. "In the Fullness of Time: An Exegetical Analysis of *sūra* 97 of the Qurʾān," in *Von Kanaan bis Kerala: Festschrift für Prof. Mag. Dr. Dr. J.P.M. van der Ploeg O.P. zur Vollendung des siebzigsten Lebensjahres am 4. Juli 1979*, ed. by W.C. Delsman et al. (Kevelaer: Butzon und Bercker, 1982), 389–409. Peters makes critical use of the relevant hypotheses advanced by Gunter Lüling in *Über den Ur-Qurʾān: Ansätze zur Rekonstruktion vorislamischer christlicher Strophenlieder im Qurʾān* (Erlangen: H. Lüling, 1974) and by K. Wagtendonk in *Fasting in the Qurʾān* (Leiden: E.J. Brill, 1968).

32 Fakhr al-Dīn al-Rāzī, *al-Tafsīr al-kabīr*, 8:71.

33 Fakhr al-Dīn al-Rāzī, *al-Tafsīr al-kabīr*, 8:71.

curred before or after he was raised to heaven. The view that Jesus died at the time of his being raised is supported by reference to *sūrat al-zumar* (39):42, a Qurʾānic proof-text cited previously by both al-Zamakhsharī and Abū al-Futūḥ Rāzī.[34]

Deeming the *wa* (and) that connects *mutawaffīka* and *rāfiʿuka* to be one of sequential arrangement presents a fourth perspective. This would mean that the first action was prior in time to the second. Fakhr al-Dīn al-Rāzī is unwilling to concede this point, preferring the view that while "the verse certainly indicates that God did these things to him, the 'how' and the 'when' depend on demonstrative proof (*al-dalīl*)."[35] The exegete continues his argument by explaining that there is independent attestation to the fact that Jesus lived, and offers as compelling evidence against this particular grammatical argument a *ḥadīth* from the Prophet. This *ḥadīth* implicitly contradicts the time sequence supported by this fourth perspective. It states that Jesus "will be sent down and will then kill the antichrist (*al-dajjāl*). It is only after this that God will receive him/cause him to die (*yatawaffāhu*)."[36] Thus the action mentioned first in the Qurʾānic phrase is mentioned last in the *ḥadīth*. Even more obviously, in order for Jesus to be 'sent down' he must first have been 'raised up'.

The fifth interpretation proposed by Fakhr al-Dīn al-Rāzī presents a more metaphorical understanding of *mutawaffīka* – and one couched in decidedly Ṣūfī terminology – as the one who receives you from your ardent desires (*shahawātika*) and the passions of your soul (*ḥuẓūẓa nafsika*). These two terms are to be understood in a negative sense as impediments to spiritual development. By removing them from the individual, God is freeing him from an onerous burden on the spirit. The additional phrase *wa-rāfiʿuka ilayya* is then explained as representing the next stage requisite to union with God: only 'one who passes away (*fānī*)' is capable of attaining knowledge (*maʿrifah*) of God. As applied to Jesus, this means that "when he was raised to heaven, his condition/state became like that of the angels, in the sense that it brought the cessation of cupidity, anger, and various objectional dispositions."[37]

The sixth vantage point from which Fakhr al-Dīn al-Rāzī surveys this phrase necessitates positing divine foreknowledge of future exegetical dispute. In this instance, then, the term *tawaffā* must mean to "receive something in its completeness" because "God knew that some people would come to hold the view that what was raised was [Jesus'] spirit not his

34 Fakhr al-Dīn al-Rāzī, *al-Tafsīr al-kabīr,* 8:71.
35 Fakhr al-Dīn al-Rāzī, *al-Tafsīr al-kabīr,* 8:72.
36 Fakhr al-Dīn al-Rāzī, *al-Tafsīr al-kabīr,* 8:72.
37 Fakhr al-Dīn al-Rāzī, *al-Tafsīr al-kabīr,* 8:72.

body."[38] Therefore this statement was revealed to prove that Jesus was taken to heaven as an entity, both body and spirit. The soundness of this interpretation is reinforced for the commentator by its consonance with *sūrat al-nisāʾ* (4): 113: "They do not harm you in any way."

Another way in which *innī mutawaffīka* may be understood is 'I made you to appear as one who has died (*ajʿaluka ka-al-mutawaffā*)'. This view of the matter neatly circumvents the problem by drawing upon the distinction between divine and human knowledge: Jesus may have appeared dead to those whom he left behind on earth, but God knew that he was raised alive to heaven. Fakhr al-Dīn al-Rāzī underscores the validity of this understanding with a linguistic argument: "Applying the name of something to what resembles it in most of its characteristics and particularities is perfectly acceptable."[39]

It is not until near the end of this survey of exegetical comments on *mutawaffīka* that Fakhr al-Dīn al-Rāzī mentions the synonym preferred by al-Ṭabarī, al-Zamakhsharī, and Abū al-Futūḥ Rāzī: *qabḍ*. Among its various meanings, this word can be used in the sense of 'collecting' something, particularly a debt. A parallel term mentioned by Fakhr al-Dīn al-Rāzī is *salāmah*, which can connote handing something over intact, in its entirety. As well as presenting these two synonyms, he specifies the interrelated meanings of the various forms of *WFY*, which can mean both 'to pay in full' and 'to collect in full', thus carrying the sense of both the synonyms discussed. By extension, then, Fakr al-Dīn al-Rāzī maintains that the fifth form of *WFY* points both to Jesus' "departing from the earth and his being raised to heaven."[40] To the potential objection that this position makes the verse's following phrase, *I am the One who will raise you to Me* (*rāfiʿuka ilayya*), nothing more than a repetition of what is already understood, Fakhr al-Dīn al-Rāzī has a prompt rebuttal. It is not, he says, duplication but particularization. In other words, since the fifth form of *WFY* can be var-

38 Fakhr al-Dīn al-Rāzī, *al-Tafsīr al-kabīr,* 8:72. The postmortem relation of body and spirit has long been a matter of dispute in Islamic thought. A foundational study is that of Duncan B. Macdonald which explores the relation of *nafs* and *rūḥ* as expressed in a broad range of classical *kalām* and Ṣūfī texts. "The Development of the Idea of Spirit in Islam," *MW* 22 (1932): 25–42 and 153–68. Reprinted from *Acta Orientalia* 9 (1931): 307–51. For further consideration of this see Ragnar Eklund, *Life Between Death and Resurrection According to Islam* (Uppsala: Almqvist and Wiksells, 1941), 12–19. The issue also figures prominently in the various understandings of Muḥammad's night journey and heavenly ascent (*isrāʾ* and *miʿrāj*). For a recent presentation of this with an annotated bibliography of scholarship in Western languages see Gerhard Böwering, "Miʿrāj," in *The Encyclopedia of Religion*, edited by Mircea Eliade et al. (New York: Macmillan, 1987), 9:552–56.

39 Fakhr al-Dīn al-Rāzī, *al-Tafsīr al-kabīr,* 8:72.

40 Fakhr al-Dīn al-Rāzī, *al-Tafsīr al-kabīr,* 8:72.

iously understood, the addition of *rāfiᶜ* is needed for further specification and refinement.

The last in this long list of interpretive possibilities takes quite a different turn. It hinges not on the consideration of the possible connotations of the two main terms but on the elucidation of a suppressed term. The term to be inserted is 'deed/action (*ᶜamal*)' (i.e., *mutawaffīka* should be understood as *mutawaffī ᶜamalika* and *rāfiᶜuka ilayya* should be understood as *rāfiᶜu ᶜamalika ilayya*.) It is not a question of Jesus being brought bodily before God but of his good deeds and praiseworthy actions being raised to divine attention and acceptance. This opening phrase of 3:55 is then to be understood as God's announcement to Jesus that his obedience and right doing are deemed acceptable. Fakhr al-Dīn al-Rāzī amplifies this further by saying that Jesus is being informed that the very struggles and difficulties involved in observing his religious duty in the face of strong opposition will not go unrecorded when his eternal reward is calculated.[41]

One question left untouched by Fakhr al-Dīn al-Rāzī is precisely the point brought forward by Ibn Kathīr. This commentator concentrates on the query of whether the fifth form of *WFY* is being used to mean actual death or the figurative death of sleep. It is the latter that he supports both with Qur'ānic quotations and selected *ḥadīth*s. Ibn Kathīr does make note of the Christian claim that "God caused him [Jesus] to be dead for three days, then revived him and raised him."[42] But he uses *sūrat al-nisā'* (4):156–59 which refutes Jewish claims of having killed Jesus, as his principal support for understanding the fifth form of *WFY* as sleep. Among the *ḥadīth*s quoted is one in which the Prophet states "truly Jesus did not die but will return to you on the Day of Resurrection."[43]

The Persian Shīᶜī, Kāshānī, returns the line of discussion to that elaborated by his predecessor, Abū al-Futūḥ Rāzī. He, too, makes an interesting contribution to the question of whether the *wa* (and) that connects the first two phrases of this verse should be considered sequential or not. While previous exegetes have alluded to the latter possibility, Kāshānī supports

41 Fakhr al-Dīn al-Rāzī, *al-Tafsīr al-kabīr*, 8:72. In the interpretation of 3:55 Kenneth Cragg strikes a similar note which he has decided is "probably the most appropriate." According to Cragg this verse "can well be read as the Qur'ān's clue to the inner experience of Jesus within that gathering sense of threat and rejection accompanying his ministry amid the vested interests and passions which he challenged. In his consciousness it must have seemed like an anticipation of death – death casting its shadow over his faithful course in God's name." *Jesus and the Muslim*, 168–69. Fakhr al-Dīn al-Rāzī returns to the theological issue of Jesus' death at the end of his commentary on this verse. His discussion centers on the controversy occasioned by *sūrat al-nisā'* (4):157 and takes the characteristic form of possible *objectiones* and their rebuttal. See *al-Tafsīr al-kabīr*, 8:74–76.

42 Ibn Kathīr, *Tafsīr al-Qur'ān al-ᶜaẓīm*, 1:366.

43 Ibn Kathīr, *Tafsīr al-Qur'ān al-ᶜaẓīm*, 1:366.

it with a novel Qurʾānic argument. In *sūrat al-qamar* (54):16 is the statement: "How [terrible] were My punishments (*ʿadhābī*) and My warnings (*nudhūrī*)." But, says Kāshānī, based on the promise contained in *sūrat al-isrāʾ* (17):15, "We are not Punishers until We have sent a messenger," warning must come before punishment. Therefore 54:16 is a clear Qurʾānic instance of the nonsequential usage of *wa* and, by implication, the possibility of this in 3:55 is readily apparent. In light of such considerations, the commentator summarizes his own interpretation of these opening phrases as follows: "I am the One who raised you to heaven and took your spirit after having sent you down from heaven to earth."[44]

A lengthy portion of what follows in Kāshānī's commentary on this verse reviews the eschatological material that deals with Jesus' role at the time of the return of the *Mahdī*. Reference is also made to *sūrah Āl ʿImrān* (3):46: "He [Jesus] will speak to the people in the cradle and as a middle-aged man," in a way that parallels Abū al-Futūḥ Rāzī's use of it.[45] Kāshānī also quotes the long *ḥadīth*, found in the *Rawḥ al-jinān*, describing Jesus and his eschatological function. However the Arabic text of the *ḥadīth*, on the authority of Ibn ʿAbbās, from which Kāshānī makes his translation, differs from that presented by Abū al-Futūḥ Rāzī in the crucial description of Muḥammad's *khalīfah*.[46] This obviates the need Abū al-Futūḥ Rāzī felt to emend the text when translating it into Persian.

While Rashīd Riḍā tenders the expected lexical explanations, his interest is quickly drawn to a discussion of the exegetical tradition that finds in the verse proof of Jesus' bodily sublevation. To do so he draws upon the teaching of Muḥammad ʿAbduh. This latter cites the paraphrase of the majority of commentators as: "I rescued you from those aggressors so that they could not kill you. Rather I caused you to die a natural death (*umītuka ḥatfa anfika*) and then raised you to Me."[47] Yet he acknowledges that there are substantial numbers who understand it differently. Among them, of course, would stand most of his exegetical predecessors.

This second group, whose opinion Rashīd Riḍā is most anxious to counter, believes that Jesus was raised to heaven alive in body and spirit. At the end of time he will be sent down from heaven to judge the people on earth. It is only after this judgment that God will cause him to die.

44 Kāshānī, *Minhaj al-ṣādiqīn*, 2:239.

45 Kāshānī, *Minhaj al-ṣādiqīn*, 2:240.

46 Here the text reads *wa-annahu nāzilun ʿalā ummatī maʿa khalīfatin min waladī* (Kāshānī, *Minhaj al-ṣādiqīn*, 2:240), whereas in Abū al-Futūḥ Rāzī's commentary it reads *wa-annahu nāzilun ʿalā ummatī wa-khalīfatī ʿalay him* (Abū al-Futūḥ Rāzī, *Rawḥ al-jinān*, 3:57). As a concluding remark Kāshānī reiterates his interpretive paraphrase of this opening section, first in Arabic and then in Persian, using his preferred synonym for *mutawaffīka*, *qābiḍuka*. Kāshānī, *Minhaj al-ṣādiqīn*, 2:240.

47 Rashīd Riḍā, *Tafsīr al-Manār*, 3:316.

Muḥammad ʿAbduh mentions the extensive discussion that exists in Islamic scholarly literature about Jesus' life on earth when he returns to it from heaven.[48] He also realizes that the key to this interpretation lies in the *wa* (and) that links the first two phrases of this verse. The exegetical argument expressed by such as Abū al-Futūḥ Rāzī and Kāshānī that *wa* does not necessitate temporal sequence brings this retort: "It has escaped them that contrasting the order of the citation to the order of actual events (*al-tartīb fī al-wujūd*) has no place in serious discussion except as a joke. There is, however, no joke involved in giving the fifth form of *WFY* [in the first phrase] precedence over *RF*ʿ [the verbal root in the second phrase] because 'raising (*raf*ʿ)' is more important for the positive news it brings of salvation (*najāt*) and elevated spiritual rank (*rifʿat al-makānah*)."[49]

The alternative, and in both Muḥammad ʿAbduh's and Rashīd Riḍā's eyes the preferable, view is that *al-tawaffī* means 'causing to die' in the usual sense of death induced by ordinary means (*al-imātah al-ʿādīyah*) and that the 'raising' comes after it, a 'raising' of the soul not the body. If challenged to explain why the personal pronoun "you" should apply only to the soul, Muḥammad ʿAbduh maintains he would respond that such usage is quite commonplace. One often speaks of an individual, meaning only his soul, "because the soul (*al-rūḥ*) is the true essence of man while the body is like a borrowed garment. It increases and decreases and changes. But the human being is human because his soul persists."[50] Muḥammad ʿAbduh's explanation for the existence of *ḥadīth*s that support a belief in Jesus' *bodily* resurrection, and eventual return to earth as judge, follows similar lines.

Such beliefs are to be understood, according to Muḥammad ʿAbduh, as revealing the triumph of Jesus' spirit (*ghalabah rūḥihi*) and the underlying meaning of his being sent as an apostle to humanity.[51] The basic thrust of Jesus' message must be seen as a movement beyond the externals of the law to its more basic intention, beyond the superficialities to the essential core. Muḥammad ʿAbduh pits Jesus' message against Jewish intractability in the following passage:

48 Rashīd Riḍā, *Tafsīr al-Manār*, 3:316.

49 Rashīd Riḍā, *Tafsīr al-Manār*, 3:316–17. The lively controversy occasioned by questions of *wa* as conjunctive or sequential is noted by Bernard Weiss in his discussion of Sayf al-Dīn al-Āmidī's (d. 631/1233) *Iḥkām fī uṣūl al-aḥkām*, including relevant verses in support of the sequential position from *sūrat al-baqarah* (2) and *sūrat al-ḥajj* (22). "Language and Law: The Linguistic Premises of Islamic Legal Science," in *Quest*, 20.

50 Rashīd Riḍā, *Tafsīr al-Manār*, 3:317.

51 Rashīd Riḍā, *Tafsīr al-Manār*, 3:317. In the exegesis of a related verse, *sūrat al-nisā'*, (4):157, may be found another instance in which *Tafsīr al-Manār* takes "the traditions regarding the ascension of Jesus and his return at the end of time metaphorically and with caution." Mahmoud Ayoub, "Towards an Islamic Christology, II: The Death of Jesus, Reality or Delusion," *MW* 70 (1980): 113.

The Messiah did not bring a new law to the Jews: he brought them something which would prize them from their inflexibility over the external signification of the words (*ẓawāhir alfāẓ*) of the Mosaic law and set them to understanding it clearly in its real meaning. He instructed them to observe this true essence and to do whatever would draw them to the world of the spiritual by paying great heed to the complete fulfillment of religious obligations. That is to say, since those connected with the last manifestation of the *sharīʿah* had become frozen in the external significations of its words – or more precisely, not the words of the *sharīʿah* but the words of those who wrote about it, which were an expression of their own opinions and understandings – there was no way out for them but Jesus' reformation, which clarified for them the underlying reasons of the *sharīʿah*, the spirit of religion and its true practice. All that is contained in the Qur'ān, from which they hide by uncritical religious adherence (*taqlīd*), which is the very bane of truth and the enemy of religion in every era. The era of Jesus, according to this explanation, was the time when people received the spirit of religion and Islamic law so as to restore the core meanings without being shackled by traditional practices (*rusūm*) and literalisms (*ẓawāhir*).[52]

As the most recent commentary to be considered, Ṭabāṭabā'ī's treatment of the opening phrases of this verse brings no major surprises but does provide a fuller perspective on the standard etymologies, thus bringing the discussion full circle back to the initiatory concerns expressed by al-Ṭabarī. He spells out more explicitly than have previous commentators why the fifth form of *WFY* has come to mean death: "*al-tawaffī* is taking something in its entirety. It therefore refers to death because God takes, at the time of death, the soul of man from his body."[53] Yet he distinguishes between this general lexical statement and the connotation that the term carries in its various Qur'ānic (and common) usages. Based on a comparison of citations, Ṭabāṭabā'ī feels it would appear that the fifth form of *WFY* more often carries the sense of 'receiving' and 'sustaining'. The idea here is that death is not an extinction or cessation, as might be ignorantly supposed, because the human soul persists. God "receives" it at the time of death or "takes it into His safekeeping until the time when He sends for it to be raised to Him."[54] As further indication of his position, Ṭabāṭabā'ī contrasts the Qur'ānic instances of the most common word for death, *al-mawt*, with those of the fifth form of *WFY* but in his commentary on this verse chooses not to discuss the question of whether Jesus actually died on the cross.

RAISED AND PURIFIED

Two other terms have demanded clarification within the exegetical tradition on this verse. They are those that constitute the principal elements of the

52 Rashīd Riḍā, *Tafsīr al-Manār*, 3:317.
53 Ṭabāṭabā'ī, *al-Mīzān*, 3:206.
54 Ṭabāṭabā'ī, *al-Mīzān*, 3:206.

second and third phrases of this verse. Reference to the former of these, that most frequently associated with the idea of 'raising', has already been made in dealing with the initial phrase *innī mutawaffīka*. It will now be treated more systematically. Neither the second nor the third phrase, however, has occasioned the sort of linguistic and theological controversy to which the first gave rise. They may thus be discussed in tandem and in more succinct fashion.

While al-Ṭabarī weaves together his treatment of the first and second phrases of this verse, he offers a separate analysis of the third. His attention is caught by that phrase's reference to 'unbelievers'. In dealing with the statement *I am the One who will cleanse you of those who disbelieve* al-Ṭabarī lists various explanations of who such unbelievers are. The first is "those among the Jews and adherents of other creeds who reject the truth that was brought to them."[55] The second is those who "resolved against you (i.e., Jesus) what they resolved"; while the third is "the Jews, Christians, and Majūs and whoever of his people (*qawmihi*) are unbelievers."[56] All three are very general identifications with no historical particularization indicated.

Al-Ṭūsī presents a separate consideration of both the second and third phrases of this verse, proposing two levels of signification for each. The first explanation of the phrase *I will raise you to Me* (*rāfiʿuka*) involves God's lifting Jesus up to heaven as a way of exalting and glorifying him, while the second has a much more pedestrian significance. It means God's commending Jesus to His favor. To explain such a usage the commentator offers the examples of a person being presented (*rufiʿa*) to the *sulṭān* and a document being offered (*rufiʿa*) to the government office (*dīwān*).[57] Obviously the issue of the term's relation to the first phrase of this verse is not pertinent to such an explanation, for what is intended is clearly a metaphorical usage. Al-Ṭūsī cites *sūrat al-ṣāffāt* (37):99 as a similar instance. Here the prophet Abraham is reported to say: "I will go to my Lord (*dhāhibun ilā rabbī*)," meaning from Iraq to Syria, the place to which the Lord had ordered him to proceed.[58]

The phrase *I will cleanse you of those who disbelieve* is also offered with two connotations, one literal and one metaphorical. It can mean that God purified Jesus by removing him from the midst of squalor occasioned by his mere proximity to certain groups. Or the intention could be purification in the sense of "from the disbelief which they would act upon by plotting

55 al-Ṭabarī, *Jāmiʿ al-bayān*, 6:461.
56 al-Ṭabarī, *Jāmiʿ al-bayān*, 6:461–62.
57 al-Ṭūsī, *al-Tibyān*, 2:478.
58 al-Ṭūsī, *al-Tibyān*, 2:478.

his death."[59] The first response carries indications of physical purification while the second is concerned with the maintenance of moral and intellectual purity.

Spatial concerns figure prominently in the glosses that al-Zamakhsharī gives to the two phrases under discussion. God's 'raising' of Jesus is "to My heaven and the abode of My angels" while his purification is from "the evil of proximity" to those who disbelieve and "the wickedness of associating with them."[60] Such spatial imagery becomes even more prominent in Abū al-Futūḥ Rāzī's commentary. This exegete's treatment of *I will raise you to Me* takes the form of adducing two attractive *ḥadīth*s, the first vividly descriptive: "Jesus was standing on Mt. Sinai wearing a garment of goat hair. A strong wind came up, Jesus ran and while running the wind caught him and carried him to heaven."[61] (To clarify further, Abū al-Futūḥ Rāzī adds the statement that "Moses only wore woolen garments and Jesus only wore hair garments, the wool being sheep fleece and the hair, goat hair.") The second *ḥadīth* is more strictly exegetical:

> God's servant ʿUmar [the second Caliph] said:
> "I saw the Messenger walking about and in the midst of his stroll, he smiled. He was asked, 'O Messenger of God why did you smile?' He replied, 'While walking I saw ʿĪsā b. Maryam and there were two angels with him. They were explaining the meaning of that [i.e., *I will raise you to Me*] as "I will be the One who raises you into the ranks of paradise (*rāfiʿuka fī darajāt al-jannah*)." ' "[62]

While Ibn al-Jawzī adds nothing substantial to this aspect of the commentary, Fakhr al-Dīn al-Rāzī gives it careful theological attention. When he tackles the second instance of Jesus' exaltation in the verse, the phrase *I will raise you to Me,* his immediate concern is the problem of divine location. He firmly refutes the attribution of a physical position (*makān*) to God, insisting that any such reference must be understood metaphorically. To illustrate this, he offers a number of examples. The first, of course, applies to the phrase under discussion. The 'raising' could be understood in terms of honoring or extolling so that the implied 'place' would be the "source of My [i.e., God's] favor (*maḥall karāmatī*)." Other metaphorical uses of spatial terminology mentioned are the facts that "pilgrims to Mecca

59 al-Ṭūsī, *al-Tibyān*, 2:478. While maintaining that "another interpretation is possible and preferable," Fred Leemhuis suggests that the *min* in *muṭahhiruka min alladhīna kafarū* could be that of comparison, i.e., "I will make you purer than those who do not believe." *The D and H Stems in Koranic Arabic* (Leiden: E.J. Brill, 1977), 81.

60 al-Zamakhsharī, *al-Kashshāf*, 1:366.

61 Abū al-Futūḥ Rāzī, *Rawḥ al-jinān*, 3:58. Although claiming 3:55 to be "the passage which denotes this event," J.M.S. Baljon states that among modern Islamic exegetes "an Ascension of Christ is usually not admitted." *Modern Muslim*, 70.

62 Abū al-Futūḥ Rāzī, *Rawḥ al-jinān*, 3:59.

are sometimes called 'visitors to God (*zuwwār Allāh*)' " and "those living near a mosque are called 'God's neighbors (*jīrān Allāh*)'."[63]

Fakhr al-Dīn al-Rāzī next suggests that this verbal form could mean not so much 'honoring' as removal to a place where only God has jurisdiction. Necessarily this would not be anywhere on earth "because on earth humanity has already assumed responsibility for the various areas of government."[64] Yet another proposal takes quite a different line of argument. Jesus was not raised to where God is in order to increase the level of God's own pleasure, but rather to offer Jesus the reward of rest and repose. The prime result of 'raising' is reward (*thawāb*) and recompense (*mujāzāt*), whether they take the form of 'honor' or of 'repose'.[65] In any event, Fakhr al-Dīn al-Rāzī insists, the phrase has nothing to do with ascribing a particular location to God.

Although this commentator offers no extensive analysis of this verse's third phrase, he does note that it is but another facet of the special honor accorded to Jesus. In fact, he summarizes his entire examination of these three introductory phrases very succinctly: "All this bespeaks the considerable extent of his [Jesus'] exaltation and glorification in God's eyes."[66]

For Ibn Kathīr purification is itself the reason for 'raising', that is, God raised Jesus to Himself in order to purify him from the contamination of unbelievers.[67] Inasmuch as both he and Kāshānī have followed al-Ṭabarī's lead in treating the first two phrases of this verse in tandem, their attention to the third is necessarily a separate focus. For Kāshānī an interpretation of *I will cleanse you of those who disbelieve* takes the form of an expanded restatement, which closely follows al-Ṭūsī's interpretations.[68]

Rashīd Riḍā employs the time-honored hermeneutical technique of intra-Qur'ānic cross-references to explain the significance of God's 'raising' Jesus. Citing *sūrah Maryam* (19):57 he signals the divine attention paid the prophet Idrīs: "We raised him (*rafaʿnāhu*) to a high place." Added to this are mention of *sūrah Āl ʿImrān* (3):169 and *sūrat al-qamar* (54):55–56, both

63 Fakhr al-Dīn al-Rāzī, *al-Tafsīr al-kabīr*, 8:73.
64 Fakhr al-Dīn al-Rāzī, *al-Tafsīr al-kabīr*, 8:73.
65 Fakhr al-Dīn al-Rāzī, *al-Tafsīr al-kabīr*, 8:73.
66 Fakhr al-Dīn al-Rāzī, *al-Tafsīr al-kabīr*, 8:73. Although speaking from a very different perspective, Johan Bouman's brief remarks on this verse include attention to how aptly it reinforces the full Qur'ānic depiction of Jesus, stressing his exalted rank as prophet on several grounds. *Das Wort vom Kreuz und das Bekenntnis zu Allah: Die Grundlehren des Korans als nachbiblische Religion* (Frankfurt-am-Main: Otto Lembeck, 1980), 237.
67 Ibn Kathīr, *Tafsīr al-Qur'ān al-ʿaẓīm*, 1:366.
68 Kāshānī, *Minhaj al-ṣādiqīn*, 2:240. It can mean 'I will cleanse you from physical encounter with pollution (*mulāqāt-i najāsat bi-badan*)' of *those who disbelieve* or 'I will purify you of their malicious intent (*khubs-i qaṣd-i īshān*) and free you from their chicanery towards you (*makr-i īshān nisbat bi-tū*)'.

of which make reference to heavenly placement near God.[69] With respect to the phrase *I will cleanse you of those who disbelieve*, however, Rashīd Riḍā contents himself with the straightforward sense of God's "rescuing him [Jesus] from their annoying or ridiculing him and intending him evil."[70]

Ṭabāṭabā'ī, on the other hand, reasserts with singular force the attitude earlier expressed by Fakhr al-Dīn al-Rāzī. Like that twelfth-century commentator Ṭabāṭabā'ī strongly denies that 'raising (*raf*ᶜ)' has anything to do with 'place'. In like manner he maintains that the divine 'purification (*ṭahārah*)' of Jesus has nothing to do with the removal of 'dirtiness'.[71] The very fact that God particularized the notion of 'raising' by adding *to Me* proves that the term must be understood in a spiritual, not physical, sense because God should not be comprehended in corporeal and material terms.[72] The sense conveyed, then, must be that of the degree of spiritual exaltation. Like Rashīd Riḍā this exegete draws upon *sūrah Maryam* (19):57 and *sūrah Āl ᶜImrān* (3):169 for further Qur'ānic support.

This same spiritual interpretation then carries over to the phrase about purification, which must, therefore, be understood to lack any connection with external, bodily cleansing. It means for Ṭabāṭabā'ī "keeping him [Jesus] far from the unbelievers and safeguarding him from their opposition and from accidental involvement with their groups, contact with whom defiles with the filth of unbelief (*kufr*) and willful evasion of the truth (*juḥūd*)."[73]

THE TRIUMPH OF JESUS' FOLLOWERS

These extensive Christological concerns reach their fulfillment and clearest focus in the fourth divine pledge to Jesus that this verse recounts. But here the scene shifts or, more precisely, the cast of characters is enlarged. For no longer is Jesus alone the beneficiary of God's largesse. Rather the promise

69 Rashīd Riḍā, *Tafsīr al-Manār*, 3:316.

70 Rashīd Riḍā, *Tafsīr al-Manār*, 3:316. Kenneth Cragg draws attention to this use of 'cleansing' "in the sense of 'vindication' " in his discussion of the work of the Egyptian surgeon and writer Muḥammad Kāmil Ḥusayn (d. 1977), author of *Qaryah ẓālimah* (City of Wrong), a remarkable narrative on the crucifixion of Jesus. *The Pen and the Faith*, 133–35. Hélène Expert-Bezancon includes a bibliography of Ḥusayn's works, with attention to translations into Western languages, in her anthology of textual extracts, "Regard d'un humaniste égyptien, le Dr. Kāmil Ḥusayn sur les religions non-musulmans," *Islamo* 14 (1988): 17–49.

71 Ṭabāṭabā'ī, *al-Mīzān*, 3:207.

72 Yet Ṭabāṭabā'ī includes a *ḥadīth* from the sixth Imām, Muḥammad al-Bāqir (d. 117/735), as recorded in the *tafsīr* of al-Qummī, which recounts the ascension of Jesus "from the corner of the house while his disciples watched." Before ascending, Jesus told them that God had revealed to him that "He would raise me to Him (*rāfiᶜī ilayhi*) now and cleanse me from the Jews (*muṭahhirī min al-yahūd*)." *al-Mīzān*, 3:218.

73 Ṭabāṭabā'ī, *al-Mīzān*, 3:208.

expands to include his 'followers': *I will place those who follow you over those who disbelieve until the Day of Resurrection.* Just who are the 'followers' and precisely what is intended by both the verb 'to place' and the preposition 'over' have fascinated those generations of exegetes who have applied themselves to this verse.

Al-Ṭabarī's chief concern is to sort out the two groups, *those who follow you* and *those who disbelieve*, to whom this citation could refer. He first lists the interpretations that equate the 'followers' with the 'believers (*muʾminūn*)'. An example of this series of *ḥadīth*s is one transmitted from al-Ḥasan al-Baṣrī (d. 110/728) which states: "The Muslims are the ones who are 'over them (*fawqahum*)'; they are placed higher than those who deny Islam until the Day of Resurrection."[74] The only break in this pattern of identification is the *ḥadīth* from al-Suddī which, like the others, names the believers as the followers of Jesus but then adds as an afterthought, "it is said they [the 'followers'] are the *Rūm*," a generic designation for the people of Byzantium or the Hellenistic Christian world.[75]

Another interpretation of this which al-Ṭabarī cites and documents is one that pits the Christians against the Jews. In this view the term *those who disbelieve (alladhīna kafarū)* in both this phrase and the preceding one means the Jews of the Banū Isrāʾīl. The importance of this qualification rests in the fact that in the *ḥadīth* the commentator quotes, the believers among the Banū Isrāʾīl are identified as Christians while the nonbelievers are called Jews. Thus the *ḥadīth* from Ibn Zayd concludes with the assertion that "the Christians are over the Jews until the Day of Resurrection; and there is no community of Christians in the East or West that is not superior to (*fawqa*) the Jews: in all countries they [the Jews] are the ones despised (*mustadhallūn*)."[76]

In adopting the two interpretive possibilities proffered by al-Ṭabarī, al-Ṭūsī recasts them with additional explanatory material. The relation of the preposition 'over' to the group designations is the pivot of his analysis. If, as he first suggests, the superiority (*fawq*) is that expressed in convincing

74 al-Ṭabarī, *Jāmiʿ al-bayān*, 6:463. See Michaud, who ignores this line of exegetical tradition. *Jésus*, 61.

75 al-Ṭabarī, *Jāmiʿ al-bayān*, 6:463.

76 al-Ṭabarī, *Jāmiʿ al-bayān*, 6:463. In underscoring this interpretation Rudi Paret draws attention to *sūrat al-ṣaff* (61):14 which concludes: "Then a portion of the Banū Isrāʾīl believed and a portion disbelieved. We supported those who believed against their enemies and they became the victorious." *Der Koran: Kommentar und Konkordanz*, 2nd ed. (1971; reprint, Stuttgart: W. Kohlhammer, 1980), 70. An earlier form of Paret's methodology in this work may be found in his *Grenzen der Koranforschung* (Stuttgart: W. Kohlhammer, 1950). Drawing upon related Qurʾānic passages, John Bowman has suggested the identification of Banū Isrāʾīl with the Samaritans. "Banū Isrāʾīl in the Qurʾān," *IS* 2 (1963): 447–55.

evidence (*ḥujjah*) and conclusive argumentation (*burhān*), then clearly the 'followers' are the true believers (*ahl al-īmān*). The 'unbelievers' are "those who call him [Jesus] a liar or tell lies against him."[77]

However if the *fawq* is political and military rather than spiritual and intellectual, the identification of *those who follow you* and *those who disbelieve* is of a different nature. Quoting the same *ḥadīth* from Ibn Zayd on the notion of Christian hegemony, al-Ṭūsī adds the remark that the Jews have lost all worldly power while the Christians have maintained political dominance in Byzantium (*bilād al-Rūm*) and elsewhere. He then goes on to mention the view of the noted Muʿtazilī, Abū ʿAlī Muḥammad b. ʿAbd al-Wahhāb al-Jubbāʾī (d. 303/915–16), that this Qurʾānic statement functions as a proof and prediction of Jewish subjugation until the end of time.[78] Yet al-Ṭūsī concludes his presentation of this second interpretation by discounting it. For him the first meaning is far more persuasive and trustworthy.

Al-Zamakhsharī, too, opts for the connotation of superiority in terms of intellectual argumentation and only secondarily with respect to military supremacy. The 'followers', according to al-Zamakhsharī, are "the Muslims, because they were his [Jesus'] followers in the original sense of *islām* even if the laws were different, as opposed to those of the Jews and Christians who called him a liar and told lies about him."[79] While Abū al-Futūḥ Rāzī adopts the now-standard polarity of superiority in either religiously convincing evidence (*ḥujjah*) or political domination, he first notes that the entire phrase may be viewed as proof of the divine promise to 'cleanse' or to 'purify' Jesus. As a curious historical observation, Abū al-Futūḥ Rāzī sees Christian superiority manifest in the fact that "the Greeks (*Rūmīyān*), who are Christian, have a king but the Jews, who continue to be vanquished, conquered and debased, do not."[80] It is, however, the first interpretation that Abū al-Futūḥ Rāzī prefers because "it includes exhortation to the truth and in the religion of truth."[81]

In his usual fashion, Ibn al-Jawzī summarizes the developed exegetical tradition, thereby giving it clearer resolution and circumscription. Thus as the first signification of *those who follow you*, that commonly associated with al-Ḥasan al-Baṣrī, Qatādah, al-Rabīʿ, and [here] Ibn al-Sāʾib al-Kalbī (d. 146/763–64), Ibn al-Jawzī forthrightly states: "They are the Muslims of the community (*ummah*) of Muḥammad, for they have acknowledged the authenticity of his [Jesus'] prophethood and that he is the spirit of God

77 al-Ṭūsī, *al-Tibyān*, 2:478.
78 al-Ṭūsī, *al-Tibyān*, 2:478.
79 al-Zamakhsharī, *al-Kashshāf*, 1:367.
80 Abū al-Futūḥ Rāzī, *Rawḥ al-jinān*, 3:59.
81 Abū al-Futūḥ Rāzī, *Rawḥ al-jinān*, 3:59.

(*rūḥ Allāh*) and His word (*kalimah*)."[82] As the second possible meaning Ibn al-Jawzī cites Ibn Zayd's familiar explanation of the phrase: *those who follow you* are the Christians, who are superior to the Jews, "a disparaged and subjugated people."[83]

Fakhr al-Dīn al-Rāzī defines "those who follow the Messiah" as "those who believe that he is the servant of God (*ʿabd Allāh*) and His messenger (*rasūl*); after [the advent of] Islam, this means the Muslims."[84] As to the relation of that group known as Christians (*al-naṣārā*) to the "followers of the Messiah," he could scarcely be clearer or more condemnatory: "Even though the Christians make an outward show of agreement about him [Jesus] among themselves, they, in fact, are in violent disagreement since an uncontaminated mind will confirm that Jesus would not be satisfied with anything these ignorant people have to say."[85]

Yet when it comes to the second main issue Fakhr al-Dīn al-Rāzī appears to forsake his own definition and to fall back on equating *those who follow you* with *al-naṣārā*. The question here is the particular meaning of *fawqa*: in what sense are those who follow Jesus 'over' those who do not believe? The exegete's answer begins with identifying *those who disbelieve* as the Jews. He next defines *fawqa* as political superiority and domination, regarding this whole phrase as "an announcement about the debasement (*dhull*) of the Jews."[86] Among the instruments of this derogation are the Christians: "We see that the empire (*dawlah*) of the Christians on earth is greater and more powerful than that of the Jews. In no region on earth do we see a Jewish kingdom, nor any country filled with Jews. Rather their status is always one of humiliation and poverty, whereas the Christian situation is quite the opposite."[87] As these passages indicate, the fact that Fakhr al-Dīn al-Rāzī is, at least to some extent, equating *those who follow you* with the Christians is inescapable.

This commentator also mentions the metaphorical understanding of *fawqa* as not political superiority but superiority in convincing evidence (*ḥujjah*) and demonstrative proof (*dalīl*). Fakhr al-Dīn al-Rāzī feels that

82 Ibn al-Jawzī, *Zād al-masīr*, 1:397. Although Ibn al-Jawzī does not specify his pronominal referents, his mention of "the spirit of God and His word" is likely an allusion to *sūrat al-nisāʾ* (4):171, where Jesus is so designated.

83 Ibn al-Jawzī, *Zād al-masīr*, 1:397.

84 Fakhr al-Dīn al-Rāzī, *al-Tafsīr al-kabīr*, 8:73.

85 Fakhr al-Dīn al-Rāzī, *al-Tafsīr al-kabīr*, 8:73–74. While respecting the theological perspective of this remark, Jacques Jomier excuses Fakhr al-Dīn al-Rāzī's use of such epithets as "ignorant" on the grounds that "elles appartiennent au vocabulaire de l'époque." "Unité de Dieu, Chrétiens et Coran selon Fakhr al-Dīn al-Rāzī," *Islamo* 6 (1980): 149–50.

86 Fakhr al-Dīn al-Rāzī, *al-Tafsīr al-kabīr*, 8:73.

87 Fakhr al-Dīn al-Rāzī, *al-Tafsīr al-kabīr*, 8:74.

such an understanding correlates well with those views of Jesus' 'raising' that held it to be a reference to honoring and glorifying rather than a physical 'raising up'. "Similarly, the 'overness (*fawqīyah*)' in this verse is not of place but of degree (*darajah*) and exalted rank (*rifʿah*)."[88]

The commentary of Ibn Kathīr on this phrase constitutes the most notable deviation from the previous exegetical tradition. His departure takes the form of an historical *excursus*, which seeks to explain both Christian internal contradictions and temporary sovereignty, and of an apologetic that justifies eventual Islamic supremacy. Because of its inherent interest and because a paraphrase might well distort its emphases, this passage of Ibn Kathīr is here reproduced in its entirety.

> It so happened that when God raised the Messiah to heaven, his followers afterwards became divided into factions. There were those among them who believed in what God had revealed to him on account of his being the servant of God, His messenger, and the son of his community. But among them there were those who made exaggerated claims for him and made him out to be the son of God. Others said "he is God," while yet others said "he is the third of three." God has passed final judgment on their contentions in the Qurʾān, refuting every faction. Yet they persisted in that kind of thing for nearly three hundred years.
>
> Then there arose for them a Greek king called Constantine and he entered the Christian religion. Some say this was a stratagem on his part to ruin it since he was a 'philosopher'; others say he did it out of ignorance. However he did change and pervert the religion of the Messiah, both adding to it and subtracting from it. He superimposed upon it the legal code and 'the great creed (*al-amānah al-kubrā*)' which was a perfidious betrayal.[89] In his time the eating of pork was legalized. People prayed facing East and built churches (*kanāʾis*), shrines (*maʿābid*) and cloisters (*ṣawāmiʿ*). Constantine extended the Christians' period of fasting by ten days to expiate a sin he had committed – or so they say. The religion of the Messiah thus became the religion of Constantine to the point that he built for Christian use churches, shrines, and cloisters in excess of 12,000. He also built the city named for him and there followed from him a royal succession.
>
> In this whole period these Christian successors have been subjugators of the Jews, whom the hand of God is against. The reason for this is that Christianity is closer to the truth than the Jews, even if the whole lot are infidels – may God curse them.
>
> When God sent Muḥammad, whoever believed in him would also believe in

88 Fakhr al-Dīn al-Rāzī, *al-Tafsīr al-kabīr*, 8:74. Ṣūfī references to Jesus are highlighted in David Pinault's bibliographical prelude to a discussion of Christ imagery in contemporary fiction. "Images of Christ in Arabic Literature," *WI* 17 (1987): 103–25.

89 On the basis of its use by Ibn Khaldūn, R. Dozy defines *al-amānah* as "le symbole de Nicée," i.e., the Nicene Creed. *Supplément aux dictionnaires Arabes* (1881; reprint, Beirut: Librairie du Liban, 1968), 1:39. Earlier sources for the Muslim view of Constantine are presented in M.S. Stern, "ʿAbd al-Jabbār's Account of How Christ's Religion was Falsified by the Adoption of Roman Customs," *Journal of Theological Studies* 19 (1968): 129–76. Reprinted in S.M. Stern, *History and Culture of the Medieval Muslim World* (London: Variorum, 1984).

God, His angels, His books, and His messengers, as accurately conceived. Thus they became followers of every prophet on the face of the earth. Since they gave full assent to the Messenger, the *ummī*[90] Arabic Prophet, the seal of the messengers, master (*sayyid*) of the sons of Adam without exception, who has called them to belief in the whole truth, then they were more entitled to each prophet than his own people who claim to follow his creed (*millah*) and his path (*ṭarīqah*) despite having perverted (*ḥarrafū*) and changed (*baddalū*) it.[91]

On this account God opened the eastern and western regions of the earth for the Companions of Muḥammad. They took possession of entire kingdoms and whole empires fell subject to them. They defeated the Persian king (*kasarū kisrā*) and reined in the Roman emperor (*qaṣarū qayṣar*), stripping both of their hoarded treasures and disbursing these as God wished. Their Prophet announced all this to them on the authority of the Lord who said: "God has promised those of you who believe and do good works that God will make them vicars on earth as He did for those who came before them. He will firmly establish for them their religion which He approved for them. He will exchange their former fear for security. They will worship Me and not associate anything with Me, etc." (*sūrat al-nūr* [24]:55.)

So it is that since they were the real 'believers in the Messiah' they plundered the Christians in the land of Syria and forced them back to *Rūm* so they had to take refuge in Constantinople. Islam and its people will continue to dominate them until the Day of Resurrection. The Confirmer of the Truth [Muḥammad] has informed his community that the last of them will one day conquer Constantinople, apportioning its opulence as booty and slaughtering the Byzantines in a massacre the like of which has never been seen nor ever will be seen.[92]

While Kāshānī bluntly identifies *those who disbelieve* as the Jews, his gloss of *those who follow you* is considerably less clear. He restates the phrase as 'the believers of your community (*mu'minān-i ummat-i tū*)' without clarifying the content of that belief. He does, however, spell out the two standard interpretations of *fawqa* more precisely than do most of the commentators: "This 'superiority' lies in the fact that the Christians have vanquished the Jews with convincing evidence and conclusive argumentation (*ḥujjat va burhān*) in proving the prophetic mission of Jesus or they have been victorious by the sword in supporting the Christian emperors (*muʿāwanat-i qayāṣirah*)."[93] Kāshānī goes on to insist that so secure is this superiority that the Jews will never conquer those who believe in Jesus, whether Christian or Muslim, but will always be dominated by and subjugated to them *until the Day of Resurrection* (*ilā yawm al-qiyāmah*).

With the modern commentaries of Rashīd Riḍā and Ṭabāṭabā'ī, inter-

90 See Chapter 3, note 65.

91 The charge of perversion/falsification (*taḥrīf*) and change/modification (*tabdīl*) could well reflect the influence of Ibn Kathīr's teacher, Ibn Taymīyah. The latter devoted a section of his *al-Jawāb al-ṣaḥīḥ li-man baddala dīn al-masīḥ* to this issue. Michel, *A Muslim Theologian's Response*, 210–40.

92 Ibn Kathīr, *Tafsīr al-Qur'ān al-ʿaẓīm*, 1:366–67.

93 Kāshānī, *Minhaj al-ṣādiqīn*, 2:240.

pretation of this phrase takes a new turn. The former first defines the 'followers' of Jesus in a general sense as those who accepted the guidance he brought. When raising the exegetical commonplace of whether the followers are 'over (*fawqa*)' the nonbelievers in a spiritual/moral or temporal sense, Rashīd Riḍā responds from a historical perspective. At the time when Jesus lived, he rightly points out, there was no question of his followers winning political supremacy. Rather they were dominated by the Jews. Therefore *fawqa* must refer to moral excellence and spiritual superiority. That being the case, the explanation of *until the Day of Resurrection* is straightforward, since moral and spiritual superiority cannot be revoked from outside.[94] It is on this basis that the divine judgment, foretold in the last phrase of this verse (*I shall judge between you in that about which you disagree*), will be made.

When Ṭabāṭabā'ī addresses the phrase *I will place those who follow you over those who disbelieve* he makes use of a nice rhetorical ploy. He first presents the well-argued exposition of a standard interpretation and then counters it with his own conviction. That first presentation begins with a cautionary note on the identification of *those who disbelieve*: "God denoted them only as 'those who do not believe'; without saying whether they were the Banū Isrā'īl or the Jews, who claim for themselves the law of Moses, or others."[95] The 'followers', on the other hand, are usually identified more specifically. Following Jesus, Ṭabāṭabā'ī relates, means "following the truth" and "following the will of God." Those who do so, and who may thus be included in the category of *those who follow you* are "those among the Christians who remained upright (*al-mustaqīmūn*) before the advent of Islam and its abrogation of the religion of Jesus, and [also] the Muslims after the appearance of Islam because they are truly his [Jesus'] followers."[96]

Bearing this specification of the two groups in mind, it follows that the meaning of *over (fawqa)* is best explained in eristic terms. It is a matter of the 'case' or argument of *those who follow you* being superior to that of the unbelievers. Ṭabāṭabā'ī, as have others before him, uses the term *ḥujjah*, whose ordinary meaning is 'proof', in his paraphrase of the passage under consideration: "The *ḥujjah* (convincing evidence) of your followers among the Christians and Muslims will be superior to the *ḥujjah* of those among the Jews who disbelieve in you, until the Day of Resurrection."[97] It is worth noting that the exegete mentions the Christians along with the Muslims in this paraphrase, without reference to the chronological distinction between those who may be identified as 'followers' before and after Islam.

94 Rashīd Riḍā, *Tafsīr al-Manār*, 3:318.
95 Ṭabāṭabā'ī, *al-Mīzān*, 3:208.
96 Ṭabāṭabā'ī, *al-Mīzān*, 3:208.
97 Ṭabāṭabā'ī, *al-Mīzān*, 3:208.

Perhaps this is a clue, considered or inadvertent, to Ṭabāṭabāʾī's own understanding of this passage.

From having thus carefully presented this standard interpretation, which he labels the common exegetical view, this commentator proceeds to take exception to it, questioning its logicality and proposing an alternative view. His rebuttal begins with the remark that this series of divine promises to Jesus is a statement about the future, susceptible of realization only at a later time. The phrase beginning *I will place those who follow you* is "a promise of beauty and great hope which can only be a future condition."[98] But the foregoing commentary ignores this future-oriented sense of the verse. For example, says Ṭabāṭabāʾī, to speak of the *ḥujjah* of the followers of Jesus as if it were something other than that of Jesus himself is nonsensical. The incisiveness of Jesus' claims and their ability to counter the doubt and hostility of the unbelievers were all in evidence during his lifetime, "so what does it mean to promise that the *ḥujjah* of his followers will be superior to the *ḥujjah* of those who oppose him?"[99] Certainly his followers can add nothing to the truth of Jesus' message. Moreover, the very fact of the time specification *until the Day of Resurrection* works against this interpretation. The superior truth-value of Jesus' claims over those of his opponents is not time-conditioned.

In the tradition of all good dialecticians, Ṭabāṭabāʾī then sets down a possible query in support of this standard interpretation: perhaps the superiority of the followers' *ḥujjah* lies in the greater acceptance it found in the period after Jesus? If the preaching of Jesus' message won a greater following in subsequent generations, then *fawqa* could refer to sovereign power and numerical superiority.[100] The exegete then counters this claim in two ways. First, the future cast of this verse militates against the assertion of sovereign power. Second, if the 'followers' of Jesus are equated with 'the people of truth (*ahl al-ḥaqq*)' and their opposition, the 'unbelievers', are identified as the 'people of error (*ahl al-bāṭil*)', it is simply untrue to say that the former are numerically superior to the latter. "The *ahl al-bāṭil* continue to grow and their aggregate has increased over the *ahl al-ḥaqq* from the time of Jesus to this very day; the disparity has grown over the course of twenty centuries."[101]

What, according to Ṭabāṭabāʾī, may be rightly said about this verse is that the phrases *those who follow you* and *those who disbelieve* do not admit of easy specification. However, given the Qurʾānic precedent of disparaging a group on the basis of its ancestors' behavior, subsequently sanctioned by

98 Ṭabāṭabāʾī, *al-Mīzān*, 3:208.
99 Ṭabāṭabāʾī, *al-Mīzān*, 3:209.
100 Ṭabāṭabāʾī, *al-Mīzān*, 3:209.
101 Ṭabāṭabāʾī, *al-Mīzān*, 3:209.

the majority, it is reasonable to identify *those who disbelieve* as the Jews. By the same token, *those who follow you* must mean the Christians, "whose believing in Jesus and following of him was a satisfactory belief and a true following, even if God was not satisfied with their following him after the appearance of Islam."[102] On the basis of these identifications the whole point of the passage becomes, of course, Christian superiority over the Jews.

CULMINATING CONCERNS

Two further issues preoccupy the exegetical tradition on 3:55. Neither, however, has rated the sort of extended attention paid to the foregoing matters. Yet brief mention of them will justly round out the treatment of this verse and testify to the exquisite detail that marks the Muslim hermeneutical endeavor. The issues arise in the concluding sentences of this verse: *Then to Me is your return. I shall judge between you in that about which you disagree.*

The first sentence presents a grammatical problem. Up to this point, the verse has been in the form of a divine address to Jesus. But this last section, as indicated by the change from a singular to a plural pronominal form, is spoken not to Jesus but to his 'followers' and to *those who disbelieve*. As explanation, al-Ṭabarī paraphrases this section: "Then to me is the return of the two factions (*farīqayn*), those who follow you and those who do not believe in you."[103] He notes a similar instance in *sūrah Yūnus* (10):22, in which the change is not from singular to plural but from second to third person.

While allusion to this matter is made by subsequent commentators, such as Kāshānī, there is little expansion upon the basic observation.[104] Al-Ṭūsī, for example, notes the grammatical change and also acknowledges that these concluding sentences operate as another sort of turning point: they direct attention away from the world and toward the Hereafter.[105] Fakhr al-Dīn al-Rāzī treats this section of the verse as the final, summative declaration of Jesus' divine commendation. The sentence *then to Me is your return* should

102 Ṭabāṭabā'ī, *al-Mīzān*, 3:210. As an addendum – and as yet further evidence of his interest in hermeneutical contextuality – Ṭabāṭabā'ī remarks that while it is not utterly inconsistent to broaden the signification of *those who follow you (alladhīna ittabaʿūka)* to mean 'people of truth' (both Muslim and Christian), it makes the reading of a subsequent verse rather awkward. The verse in question is 3:57: "As for those who believe and do good works (*wa-ammā alladhīna āmanū wa-ʿamilū al-ṣāliḥāt*), He will give them their full recompense." The exegete questions why, if the signification of the two *alladhīna* phrases is coextensive, the former was not repeated in this closely-following verse.

103 al-Ṭabarī, *Jāmiʿ al-bayān*, 6:464.

104 Kāshānī, *Minhaj al-ṣādiqīn*, 2:241.

105 al-Ṭūsī, *al-Tibyān*, 2:479.

be understood as a recapitulation of the whole sequence of honorific announcements that preceded it.[106] More persistent, however, is the attention paid by commentators to the divine adjudication that the final sentence of this verse announces.

For al-Zamakhsharī this announcement can only be understood within the larger context of the verses that follow. Therein is spelled out the results of God's judgment, chastisement for the unbelievers and great reward for the believers – a promise that al-Zamakhsharī feels needs no further comment.[107] Abū al-Futūḥ Rāzī, on the other hand, emphasizes not the results of judgment in punishment or reward but its subject and focus in Jesus. All the contrary Christologies, he says, be they those that see Jesus as God or the son of God or those that view him as God's servant, will be finally adjudicated.[108] Ibn al-Jawzī echoes this emphasis, finding in the verse's concluding sentence yet an additional indication of the Jewish-Christian controversy highlighted in the preceding pages.[109] For Fakhr al-Dīn al-Rāzī this focus is further specified as a distinction "between those who believe in him [Jesus] and those who reject his status as messenger."[110]

Kāshānī reiterates the interpretation of the concluding sentence as the definitive adjudication of interreligious truth claims but does so more inclusively. That is to say, the disputed matters among Jews, Christians, and Muslims will be divinely arbitrated.[111] Ṭabāṭabā'ī takes this a step further in his remark that these concluding sentences are addressed to all parties represented in this verse, a position that encompasses most of the previous exegetical stances. The verse itself, he adds, completes an entire Qur'ānic section on "Jesus and the information about him from the time of his annunciation to the end of his command and his prophethood."[112]

106 Fakhr al-Dīn al-Rāzī, *al-Tafsīr al-kabīr*, 8:74.
107 al-Zamakhsharī, *al-Kashshāf*, 1:367.
108 Abū al-Futūḥ Rāzī, *Rawḥ al-jinān*, 3:59.
109 Ibn al-Jawzī, *Zād al-masīr*, 1:397.
110 Fakhr al-Dīn al-Rāzī, *al-Tafsīr al-kabīr*, 8:74. With (pseudo) Ibn al-ʿArabī an interpretation more consistent with his mystical hermeneutic is presented. The judgment that God will deliver *in that about which you disagree* is seen in the light of his postulated spiritual stages. All such "contending and contesting (*al-tajādhub wa-al-tanāzuʿ*)" can only be an aspect of existence "before [the station of] *al-waḥdah*." All such disagreements will be effaced by the God who could vow: 'I will settle each in his place and give him that of which, in My view, he is worthy'. Ibn al-ʿArabī, *Tafsīr al-Qur'ān al-karīm*, 1:190.
111 Kāshānī, *Minhaj al-ṣādiqīn*, 2:241. For a review of Jewish, Christian, and Muslim ideas of divine judgment see Tor Andrae, *Les Origines de l'Islam et le Christianisme,* trans. by Jules Roche (Paris: Adrien-Maisonneuve, 1955), 91–100. Originally published as "Der Ursprung des Islams und das Christentum," *Kyrkohistorisk Arsskrift* 23 (1923): 149–206; 24 (1924): 213–92; 25 (1925): 45–112.
112 Ṭabāṭabā'ī, *al-Mīzān*, 3:210.

CONCLUSION

Such contextual sensitivity was apparent in that initial inquiry which several of the commentators made of this verse. Linkage with the immediately preceding verse established 3:55 as a particular instance of God's activity. For the classical trio, al-Ṭabarī, al-Zamakhsharī, and Fakhr al-Dīn al-Rāzī, the divine deed could be termed contrivance. The modern commentators, Rashīd Riḍā and Ṭabāṭabāʾī, speak instead of intervention and even of the expression of divine wrath. By whatever designation, the Muslim exegetes have understood this verse both to begin and to conclude with a reference to God's action. For the concluding action, that of divine judgment, the reference is textually explicit while the understanding of that cited initially depends upon a hermeneutical attentiveness to placement and sequence.

This first set of interpretive brackets encloses yet another pair. The verse itself begins and ends with – to borrow a word from the Christian theological tradition – a Christological focus. Cast initially in the form of a series of divine promises to Jesus, the audience addressed broadens to include both his followers and rejectors, those whose competing claims provide the provocation for God's final pledge. The figure of Jesus, then, and the statements that may properly be made about him supply the textual ambience in which reference to his followers is made. The varied proportions of interpretive interest expended on both are worth noting, just as attention to the portrait of the Qurʾānic Jesus that begins to emerge here is indispensable to a determination of those whom this exegetical tradition would deem to be his followers.

The notion of divine protection predominates in the promissory statements addressed to Jesus. In itself this subtly reinforces the Qurʾānic disavowal of Christian belief in the divinity of Jesus. Several scenarios thread themselves through the sometimes convoluted treatment of the phrase here translated as *I am the One who will take you*. All place the initiative and the power of performance with God. In one sequence Jesus is apparently taken by God in sleep; in another he is awake. (Using the synonym 'collect (*qabḍ*)' obviates the need to specify this.) Alternatively, God allows Jesus to die and then takes and revives him. With some of the commentators rearrangement of the Qurʾānic phrases reflects a revised chronology, one that places the death at the closure of a second coming. This is especially noteworthy in the Shīʿī commentaries of Abū al-Futūḥ Rāzī and Kāshānī, which relate this event to the advent of the anticipated *Mahdī*. Yet at no point in the exegesis of this phrase is there any attempt to deal in historical specifics. Even Muḥammad ʿAbduh's insistence upon the earthly death of Jesus is not accompanied by any extra-Qurʾānic historical reference. The life of Jesus unfolds only against the Qurʾānic backdrop. The unusually large number of intra-Qurʾānic explications brought forward in the discussion of this phrase underscore these scriptural parameters.

The two subsequent pledges that God makes to Jesus, *I will raise you to Me and cleanse you of those who disbelieve*, arouse sustained interest among the commentators. The Muʿtazilī rejection of spatial attribution to God prompts al-Zamakhsharī's glosses, which are subsequently echoed in the remarks of Fakhr al-Dīn al-Rāzī. The latter, in fact, introduced a metaphorical reading into his ninefold interpretation of *I am the One who will take you* by viewing it as a kind of spiritual purgation. Having divested Jesus' soul of any possible impediments, God can now exalt and honor him. In similar fashion, the promise to cleanse moves quickly from a physical to an intellectual and/or moral signification. Again, however, it should be pointed out that historical considerations are entirely absent. There is no attempt to create a historical context for these promises to Jesus, to sketch a scenario of the incident or moment in his life that might have prompted them. In other words, there is no Christological analogue to the occasions of revelation (*asbāb al-nuzūl*) noted in the biography of the Prophet.

Taken together, the exegetical discussion of these first three phrases affords a striking example of the contrapuntal complexity of Qurʾānic *tafsīr*. Each of the commentators picks up a tone within the spectrum of expressed possibilities, allowing that to be the keynote, the point of harmonic balance upon which the argument must rest. In turn, that discussion expresses and encapsulates an understanding of Jesus that creates the perspective within which all talk of his 'followers' must be comprehended. Only thus will the dynamics underlying the repeated identification of the 'followers' of Jesus with the 'believers'/Muslims be laid bare. Beginning with al-Ṭabarī there is a consistent attempt to define the followers of Jesus not as Christians but as Muslims. Al-Ṭabarī uses the term *muʾminūn* (believers), which for him is coextensive with the idea of 'adherent of the true religion', that is, Islam. Al-Zamakhsharī, Ibn al-Jawzī, and Fakhr al-Dīn al-Rāzī, on the other hand, make straightforward reference to the *muslimūn*, whether the term be understood as adherents of the primordial revelation before the time of Muḥammad or after. The logic of such identification becomes apparent when it is remembered that the "true" followers are necessarily those whose dogmatic assertions about Jesus accord with God's final and full revelation, the Qurʾān. Those who make pronouncements about Jesus that run counter to this scripture obviously forfeit any claim to authenticity.

Such is the underlying argumentation that supports the persistent equation of doctrinal purity (as defined by the Qurʾān) with "true" follower. With few exceptions, when the notion of 'overness', of superiority, is understood in theological terms, then it is the Muslims who are deemed to have an undefiled comprehension of Jesus' nature and mission and thus will rank *over those who disbelieve* as expressed by their false claims about his life, death, and divinity.

What makes the exegetical tradition on this verse unusual, however, is that the matter does not end there. Rather the discussion proceeds to record another hermeneutical possibility, one that allows the commentators to take brief cognizance of the course of history and political change in the Middle East and beyond by shifting the connotation of *over (fawqa)* from the realm of revelation and reason to that of the changing fortunes of peoples and nations. Within this latter sphere Christian political dominance is asserted as a historically undeniable fact. Yet very little detail is marshaled to support the assertion. The earlier exegetes refer generally to Byzantine hegemony but without distinguishing among its periods of prominence and decline. The only moment of historical precision in the classical tradition belongs to Ibn Kathīr, whose fame rests as much on his historical writings as on his exegetical works. That very specificity allows him to discount claims of unrestricted Christian superiority. Writing in the post-Crusades era, Ibn Kathīr charts the rise of Christian fortunes (and the decline of Jewish) in the first centuries of Christian existence but then immediately applauds the post-Prophetic triumph of Islam and assures his readers that it will endure to the end of time.

Among the modern commentators, Rashīd Riḍā builds an argument against this line of interpretation on historical grounds. Restricting himself to the period of Jesus' life, he recognizes the overriding Jewish influence within that time-frame and thus dismisses any thought that the signification of this phrase compliments Christian political superiority.

It is important to note that where such compliments are proffered, it is always at the expense of the Jews. Over and over again is the point made in the commentary on these verses that in all times and places the Jews have been a subjugated people. Fakhr al-Dīn al-Rāzī regards this phrase principally as "an announcement about the debasement of the Jews." Whatever praise is cautiously meted out to the Christians is produced with a concomitant denigration of the Jews. Moreover, the praise-provoking situation is temporary, awaiting the final divine adjudication with which this verse concludes.

5

Steadfast and submissive

Another shift of philological taxonomy occurs in this, the third verse that presents itself for consideration. While *sūrat at-baqarah* (2):62 made unequivocal reference to *the Christians*, the allusion was somewhat less direct in *sūrah Āl ʿImrān* (3):55 with its mention of *those who follow* Jesus. In the verse to be discussed now the classificatory phrase is yet more amorphous and partitive. A critical phrase is *people of the book (ahl al-kitāb)*, a designation whose range of signification is not constant within either the domain of Qurʾānic *tafsīr* or the Islamic religious sciences generally. Identification in this context with those known as Christians is less a function of direct verbal apprehension than of recourse to the exegetical tradition on the verse. The verse itself is the penultimate entry in the same *sūrah* from which the one treated in the previous chapter was drawn. A possible translation of *sūrah Āl ʿImrān* (3): 199 would be:

> Truly among the people of the book are those who believe in God and what was sent down to you and what was sent down to them, submissive before God. They do not sell the verses of God for a small price. For them is their reward near their Lord. Surely God is quick to reckon.

OPTING FOR INCLUSIVITY

Muslim commentators have discerned a multiplicity of issues within these few brief lines, but the preeminent consideration has clearly been that of ascertaining what circumstances occasioned this revelation, a hermeneutical procedure called *sabab al-nuzūl*. Once again al-Ṭabarī charts the course along which many of the later commentators travel. He mentions three possible referents for the phrase *truly among the people of the book are those who believe in God and what was sent down to you and what was sent down to them, submissive before God.* The first of these is the Najāshī, the Arabic designation for the king of Abyssinia (the Negus), whose name is here given as Aṣḥamah. (Many references to the Najāshī may be found in the *ḥadīth* and the *sīrah*, and he will figure prominently in the exegetical discussion of some of the verses to follow.) From the several *ḥadīth*s that al-Ṭabarī presents in support of this position, the following composite scenario may be drawn: when the news of the Najāshī's death reached Muḥammad, he urged his companions to "pray for your brother who has died in another country."[1] He then led the group in prayer to the extent of reciting four components of the standard ritual. Discontented mutterings greeted this action, some credited to the whole group whom the Prophet had addressed and others attributed specifically to the hypocrites among them. The more general grumbling was expressed as consternation at the idea of "praying for a man who is not a Muslim."[2] The dissatisfaction attributed to the hypocrites (*ahl al-nifāq*) took both a mild and strong form. The more gentle version, which appears in a *ḥadīth* on the authority of Qatādah, was phrased as a question: "Is he praying for a dead man who is not even among the people of his religion?"[3] Put more harshly, in a *ḥadīth* attributed to Jābir b. ʿAbdallāh (d. 78/697), the tone is not questioning but exclamatory: "Look at this – he is praying for a foreign Christian infidel/barbarian (*ʿilj naṣrānī*) whom he has never seen!"[4] It was precisely because of such defamatory discontent that this verse was revealed.

Another *ḥadīth* from Qatādah cited by al-Ṭabarī adds an additional point of clarification that ties this verse to *sūrat al-baqarah* (2):115. The unexpressed background to this connection would appear to be the objections that the Najāshī did not pray toward the *qiblah*, the Muslim prayer orientation toward Mecca. To those who would insist that such is a prerequisite for the kind of posthumous recognition that Muḥammad accorded to the Najāshī, the verse from *sūrat al-baqarah* is offered in response: "To God belong the East and the West; wherever you turn, there is the face of God."[5]

The second referent proposed by al-Ṭabarī is the early Jewish convert to Islam, ʿAbdallāh b. Salām (d. 43/663–64), and his associates.[6] While the *ḥadīth* from Ibn Jurayj mentions ʿAbdallāh by name, that from ʿAbdallāh

1 al-Ṭabarī, *Jāmiʿ al-bayān*, 7:497. Muḥammad's prayers at the time of the Abyssinian king's death are mentioned by A. J. Wensinck in "al-Nadjāshī," *EI*[1] 3:818. Martin Lings's recent biography of the Prophet offers a brief narration of this scene. *Muḥammad: His Life Based on the Earliest Sources* (London: George Allen and Unwin, 1983), 316. Wim Raven has collected a significant number of texts relevant to the Najāshī episodes in "Some Early Islamic Texts on the Negus of Abyssinia," *JSS* 33 (1988): 197–218.

2 al-Ṭabarī, *Jāmiʿ al-bayān*, 7:497.

3 al-Ṭabarī, *Jāmiʿ al-bayān*, 7:498.

4 al-Ṭabarī, *Jāmiʿ al-bayān*, 7:497. A *ḥadīth* on the authority of Sufyān b. ʿUyaynah offers an Arabic gloss of the Najāshī's name, Aṣḥmah, as ʿAṭīyah (which means 'gift').

5 al-Ṭabarī, *Jāmiʿ al-bayān*, 7: 497.

6 See J. Horovitz, "ʿAbd Allāh b. Salām," *EI*[2] 1:52. For medieval attention to this figure as well as Kaʿb al-Aḥbār consult Allan Harris Cutler and Helen Elmquist Cutler, *The Jew As Ally of the Muslim: Medieval Roots of Anti-Semitism* (Notre Dame, Ind.: University of Notre Dame Press, 1986), 71–73.

b. Wahb (d. 198/813) simply refers generally to "the Jews."[7] The third explanation, supported by a *ḥadīth* from Mujāhid, is that which sees the source of this phrase as the converts to Islam (*maslamah*) from the *ahl al-kitāb*. Unlike subsequent commentators, this exegete offers no particular explanation for the term *maslamah* other than Mujāhid's statement that they are drawn from the Christians and Jews.[8]

Al-Ṭabarī does, however, hold this to be the soundest explanation for the source of this revelation. When God speaks of the *ahl al-kitāb*, al-Ṭabarī insists, he means the *ahl al-kitāb* as a whole. "He did not specify the Christians to the exclusion of the Jews or vice versa. He announced only that among the *ahl al-kitāb* are those who believe in God and both groups, Jews and Christians, are among the *ahl al-kitāb*."[9]

This commentator responds to hypothetical questions about the association of this verse with the Najāshī by a combination of *ḥadīth* criticism and deductive reasoning. He questions the soundness of at least one of the *ḥadīth*s recorded in support of this view but bases his strongest argument on the inclusive nature of divine revelation. Thus he maintains that even if the Najāshī were specifically intended by this verse, the words actually used are more comprehensive in their connotation. Those signified are described as "following the Messenger of God and attesting to the truth of what he brought them from God after their prior adherence to what God had enjoined upon them in the two books, the Torah and the Gospel."[10] Such a description may apply to the Najāshī and his associates but also to others in no way connected with that group.

7 al-Ṭabarī, *Jāmiʿ al-bayān*, 7:498–9.

8 al-Ṭabarī, *Jāmiʿ al-bayān*, 7:499. The editors of this edition of *Jāmiʿ al-bayān* have voweled the term as *muslimah*. Lane, on the authority of Abū al-Ḥasan ʿAlī b. Sīdah's (d. 458/1066) *Kitāb al-muḥkam wa-al-muḥīt al-aʿẓam*, quotes the term as a singular in the expression *kāna kāfiran thumma huwa al-yawma maslamatun*. Edward William Lane, *Arabic-English Lexicon* (1872; reprint, New York: Frederick Ungar, 1956), 4:1416. Dozy defines the term (unvoweled) as "les nouveaux musulmans" and further offers the word *al-musālimah* with the same definition expanded to include the phrase "les chrétiens ou les juifs qui ont embrassé l'islamisme." R. Dozy, *Supplément aux dictionnaires arabes* (1881; reprint, Beirut: Librairie du Liban, 1968), 1:679. Ibn Manẓūr vowels the word as *maslamah*. Muḥammad b. Mukarram b. Manẓūr, *Lisān al-ʿarab* (Beirut: Dār Ṣādir, 1375/1957), 12:300.

9 al-Ṭabarī, *Jāmiʿ al-bayān*, 7:499.

10 al-Ṭabarī, *Jāmiʿ al-bayān*, 7:499–500. For a contemporary repetition of this interpretation drawn from al-Tujībī's abridgement of *Jāmiʿ al-bayān*, see the pamphlet by Ahmad von Denffer, *Christians in the Qurʿān and Sunna: An Assessment from the Sources to Help Define Our Relationship* (Leicester: The Islamic Foundation, 1399/1979), 13–14. Summarizing al-Ṭabarī's views on a parallel use of the Najāshī traditions in *sūrat al-baqarah* (2):115, Pierre Godé concludes that "Judaïsme, Christianisme et Islâm (dans son sens spécifique) sont autant de formes particulières de l'Islâm (dans son sens absolu), bien que ce soit la tradition islamique qui affirme le plus explicitement cette universalité." *Commentaire du Coran*, 2:41.

Al-Ṭūsī and al-Zamakhsharī duplicate al-Ṭabarī's threefold identification of those intended in this verse. Al-Ṭūsī begins his survey with the Najāshī and sketches substantially the same scenario as a possible occasion for this revelation. The only original note is his inclusion of a *ḥadīth* from Qatādah in which the hypocrites' exclamation is phrased thus: "Are we to pray for a foreign infidel/barbarian (*ᶜilj*) from Najrān?"[11] No explanation is made for the Najāshī's sudden shift of locale from Abyssinia to southern Arabia (although associations between these areas were not uncommon).

In agreement with al-Ṭabarī, then, he continues with a second and third possibility: the verse "was sent down about a group of Jews at the time when they became Muslims, among whom were ᶜAbdallāh b. Salām and those with him." Or "it was sent down about any of the *ahl al-kitāb* who became Muslim, whether Jew or Christian."[12] He, too, prefers the third alternative because its lack of specificity permits it to refer to the Najāshī and ᶜAbdallāh b. Salām as well as others.

Al-Zamakhsharī, on the other hand, combines these second and third options by saying that is was "sent down about ᶜAbdallāh b. Salām and other *maslamah* of the *ahl al-kitāb*"[13] It is worth noting that al-Zamakhsharī makes no explicit connection between ᶜAbdallāh b. Salām and the Jews. His most significant departure from his predecessors is another possibility that he includes: the verse was revealed "about forty people from Najrān, thirty-three Abyssinians, and eighty from Byzantium (*Rūm*)."[14] Although al-Zamakhsharī does not explicitly state a preference for any of these three opinions, he does spend much more time detailing the circumstances of Muḥammad's prayer for the dead Najāshī than he does on the other two.

The details that he presents are, in turn, repeated by Abū al-Futūḥ Rāzī. These accounts add that it was Gabriel who announced the Najāshī's death to the Messenger, prompting Muḥammad to call his followers to prayer for this Abyssinian Christian. In Abū al-Futūḥ Rāzī's commentary the narrative then continues: "The Messenger went into the cemetery of Baqīᶜ [at the southern edge of Medina] with his companions. God lifted the veil (*ḥijāb bardāsht*) so that the Messenger saw his [the Najāshī's] corpse (*jināz*). He prayed for him and asked God's forgiveness for him."[15] The account concludes with the hypocrites' exclamation to which this verse is seen as a response.

This commentator's next suggestion again repeats one first mentioned by al-Zamakhsharī but with some numerical variation. The forty people of

11 al-Ṭūsī, *al-Tibyān*, 3:93.
12 al-Ṭūsī, *al-Tibyān*, 3:93.
13 al-Zamakhsharī, *al-Kashshāf*, 1:458.
14 al-Zamakhsharī, *al-Kashshāf*, 1:458.
15 Abū al-Futūḥ Rāzī, *Rawḥ al-jinān*, 3:299.

Najrān are identified as from the Banū al-Ḥārith b. Kaʿb.[16] Those from Abyssinia are thirty-two rather than thirty-three and the Byzantine contingent is noted as eight rather than al-Zamakhsharī's eighty. The distinguishing characteristic of this whole group is that "they belonged to the religion of Jesus but believed in Muḥammad."[17] Abū al-Futūḥ Rāzī's two final suggestions duplicate material found in the earlier commentators. Mention is made of ʿAbdallāh b. Salām and his associates although, again in concert with al-Zamakhsharī, without naming them as Jews. The concluding possibility is that the verse refers to all believers from the *ahl al-kitāb*.[18]

Ibn al-Jawzī presents, in more abbreviated form, the four suggestions that Abū al-Futūḥ Rāzī offered for the *sabab al-nuzūl* of this verse. He differs from the latter in but one minor detail. His list of converted Christians includes thirty from Abyssinia – not thirty-two or al-Zamakhsharī's thirty-three. This *ḥadīth* and its variants, both here and in the commentary of Abū al-Futūḥ Rāzī, is credited to ʿAṭāʾ b. Abī Rabāḥ (d. 114/732).[19]

As prelude to his choice among competing *asbāb al-nuzūl*, Fakhr al-Dīn al-Rāzī moves beyond a mere listing of possibilities and sets this verse into the context developed by those preceding it. Inasmuch as God revealed that Hell was to be the abode of the unbelievers and Paradise the promised goal of the believers, He then "explained that whoever among the former comes to believe is included in the description of those who are dealt with mercifully."[20] He next lists the now familiar options cited as occasions for the revelation of this verse, mentions their expected attributions, and ends with the most inclusive, that "it was sent down about all the believers of the *ahl al-kitāb*."[21] His preference for this view is expressed in somewhat different terms from those of former exegetes. He favors this more inclusive interpretation because it supports his understanding of the placement of this verse as just discussed.

Ibn Kathīr makes a marked departure from the now-established exegetical pattern. His remarks are noteworthy both for the broader perspective he brings to the discussion and for the historical and sociological judgments that he includes therein. Commencing with a rewording of the opening phrases of this verse, he immediately opts for the most inclusive understanding of those to whom this revelation is directed. Those intended, he

16 A tribe of the Yemen group usually called Balḥārith. See J. Schleifer, "Banu'l-Ḥārith b. Kaʿb," *EI*[1] 3:268–69. Unrevised reprint in *EI*[2] 3:223.

17 Abū al-Futūḥ Rāzī, *Rawḥ al-jinān*, 3:299.

18 Abū al-Futūḥ Rāzī, *Rawḥ al-jinān*, 3:299.

19 Ibn al-Jawzī, *Zād al-masīr*, 2:533; Abū al-Futūḥ Rāzī, *Rawḥ al-jinān*, 3:299. Al-Zamakhsharī does not give an attribution for this *ḥadīth*.

20 Fakhr al-Dīn al-Rāzī, *al-Tafsīr al-kabīr*, 11:154.

21 Fakhr al-Dīn al-Rāzī, *al-Tafsīr al-kabīr*, 11:154.

says "are the best (*khīrah*) of the *ahl al-kitāb*; these characteristics are the same whether they be Jews or Christians."[22] To support this decision, Ibn Kathīr repeats five Qur'ānic passages that speak with approval of members of the *ahl al-kitāb*. The five he has chosen are, in the order in which he cites them, *sūrat al-qaṣaṣ* (28):52–54, *sūrat al-baqarah* (2):121, *sūrat al-aʿrāf* (7):159, *sūrah Āl ʿImrān* (3):112, and *sūrat al-isrā'* (17):107–09.[23]

The spiritual qualities that these verses and the verse under discussion commend are not widely visible among the *ahl al-kitāb*, according to this commentator. Their relative availability differs, however, between Jews and Christians. "These qualities," Ibn Kathīr maintains, "are to be found among the Jews but only a few, such as ʿAbdallāh b. Salām and his like among the learned men (*aḥbār*) of the Jews who believed. In all, they do not amount to ten souls."[24] The situation with the Christians is clearly different: "Among them are the rightly-guided and those obedient to the truth."[25] As further proof of this disparity Ibn Kathīr cites *sūrat al-mā'idah* (5):82–85, a revelation that both praises the Christians and denigrates the Jews and that includes a promise of divine reward for the former.[26]

In like manner, Ibn Kathīr points out, this verse includes the phrase "for them is their reward near their Lord." This exegete then has recourse to the story of the Prophet's prayer for the Najāshī as an instance of calling blessings upon a Christian. Ibn Kathīr records a considerable number of *ḥadīth*s recounting this episode, among the most interesting of which is one credited to Muḥammad's wife, ʿĀ'ishah (d. 59/678). In it she makes reference both to Muḥammad's spiritual powers and to the signal honor accorded the Najāshī: "When the Najāshī died we were told that he [Muḥammad] continued to see a light over his tomb."[27]

As further proof of the Najāshī's particular suitability for such divine commendation, Ibn Kathīr relates an interchange on the authority of al-Zubayr al-ʿAwwām (d. 36/656) that took place between the Abyssinian king and the Muslims who had emigrated from the Arabian peninsula, seeking asylum with him. When requested by the Muslim delegation to expel those of Muḥammad's opponents who were attempting to turn the sovereign's mind against the emigrants, the Najāshī concurred, agreeing that "an injury in aid of God is better than a remedy in aid of people."[28] This commentator concludes his treatment of this section of the verse by

22 Ibn Kathīr, *Tafsīr al-Qur'ān al-ʿaẓīm*, 1:443.
23 Ibn Kathīr, *Tafsīr al-Qur'ān al-ʿaẓīm*, 1:443.
24 Ibn Kathīr, *Tafsīr al-Qur'ān al-ʿaẓīm*, 1:443.
25 Ibn Kathīr, *Tafsīr al-Qur'ān al-ʿaẓīm*, 1:443.
26 This verse will be the subject of Chapter 7.
27 Ibn Kathīr, *Tafsīr al-Qur'ān al-ʿaẓīm*, 1:443.
28 Ibn Kathīr, *Tafsīr al-Qur'ān al-ʿaẓīm*, 1:443.

citing the *ḥadīth* from Mujāhid that states that the phrase refers to the *maslamah* of the *ahl al-kitāb*.[29] By reference to yet another early authority, this time al-Ḥasan al-Baṣrī, he explains the term as meaning "those who belonged to the *ahl al-kitāb* before Muḥammad but then followed him and professed *islām*."[30]

Kāshānī, who treats this as two verses, 3:198 and 3:199, commences with a combination of Persian translation and paraphrase. In discussing the possible referents of this verse he offers a surprise: he is the only one of the commentators who does not mention the Najāshī in connection with it. He does, however, include the other three possibilities, beginning with the numerical list of converts from Najrān, Abyssinia, and Rūm, as recounted from ʿAṭāʾ b. Abī Rabāḥ, and including alternative interpretations suggested by Mujāhid and Ibn Jurayj.[31] Doubtless his most original contribution is the decision to phrase this issue (i.e., that of those intended by the verse) in scriptural terms. The distinguishing characteristic of the individuals specified is that they "believe in God and in the Qurʾān, Torah, and Gospel."[32]

Rashīd Riḍā, too, devotes a considerable portion of his commentary on this verse to detailing the various theories about the occasion of this revelation. He refers to the standard explanations transmitted on the authority of such as Qatādah, Jābir b. ʿAbdallāh, al-Zubayr, Ibn Jurayj, and Mujāhid and cites such additional textual references as the commentaries of al-Ṭabarī and Fakhr al-Dīn al-Rāzī as well as the *Lubāb al-nuqūl [fī asbāb al-nuzūl]* of al-Suyūṭī.[33] One *ḥadīth* that Rashīd Riḍā records on the authority of Anas b. Mālik (d. 91–93/709–11) refers to the Najāshī with the epithet "Abyssinian slave/servant (*ʿabd ḥabashī*)."[34]

Like many of his predecessors, this commentator sought to include as referent not only the Najāshī and his companions but any other Christians or Jews to whom the descriptives of this verse would apply. He goes beyond even this, however, with his mention of the Zoroastrians (*al-majūs*). These, too, are to be counted among the *ahl al-kitāb*. Yet for Rashīd Riḍā this inclusion remains largely theoretical. "We do not know," he remarks, "of a single one of them who became a Muslim in the period of the Qurʾān's revelation (*ʿahd al-tanzīl*) except Salmān al-Fārisī. Even he became a Christian before becoming a Muslim."[35]

29 The word is unvoweled in this edition of Ibn Kathīr's *Tafsīr al-Qurʾān al-ʿaẓīm*.
30 Ibn Kathīr, *Tafsīr al-Qurʾān al-ʿaẓīm*, 1:443.
31 Kāshānī, *Minhaj al-ṣādiqīn*, 2:420. Like Abū al-Futūḥ Rāzī he lists the number from Byzantium (*Rūm*) as eight rather than al-Zamakhsharī's eighty.
32 Kāshānī, *Minhaj al-ṣādiqīn*, 2:421.
33 Rashīd Riḍā, *Tafsīr al-Manār*, 4:315–16.
34 Rashīd Riḍā, *Tafsīr al-Manār*, 4:315.
35 Rashīd Riḍā, *Tafsīr al-Manār*, 4:315–16. For Salmān al-Fārisī see Chapter 3.

Rashīd Riḍā's next step in this discussion is to consult Fakhr al-Dīn al-Rāzī's commentary. He quotes verbatim the entire section in which Fakhr al-Dīn al-Rāzī details four possible explanations for the occasion of this revelation, concluding with the statement from *al-Tafsīr al-kabīr* that supports the most comprehensive understanding. It provides strong textual reinforcement for Rashīd Riḍā's own inclusive exegesis.[36]

Although Ṭabāṭabāʾī, too, feels an obligation to cite the episode of Muḥammad's prayer for the Najāshī, he gives it minimal attention. In fact, his most noteworthy contribution to the whole discourse on this hermeneutical category known as "occasion of revelation" is to clarify and delimit its scope and validity. At the conclusion of his list of standard *ḥadīth*s for the several verses under his consideration, Ṭabāṭabāʾī remarks: "All of these are reports that make the verses coincident with certain narrative accounts but they are not actually reasons/occasions for the revelation (*laysat bi-asbāb lil-nuzūl ḥaqīqatan*)."[37]

INTERPRETIVE GLOSSING

Issues of specification and identification follow quickly upon the exegetical interest in *asbāb al-nuzūl*. Terms and phrases within this verse elicit clarification from a number of the commentators, although they do not receive the near-universal attention paid to the first hermeneutical category. Such periphrastic treatment of verse elements occupies several of the commentators, beginning with al-Ṭabarī. While much of this exegete's paraphrase repeats meanings he made explicit in dealing with the *sabab al-nuzūl*, his amplification shows a slight move toward greater scriptural specificity. In glossing the term *people of the book* he mentions only the Torah and Gospel but his identification of *what was sent down to them* adds to these two texts a reference to the Psalms (*al-zabūr*).[38] Al-Ṭūsī repeats verbatim elements of al-Ṭabarī's periphrasis but with occasional expansion. For example, both designate "the one who believes in God" as "one who acknowledges His unicity (*yuqirru bi-waḥdānīyatihi*)," with al-Ṭūsī adding the largely redundant gloss of "one who confesses belief in God (*yuṣaddiqu billāh*)."[39] Al-Ṭūsī does not, however, follow his predecessors' scriptural specificity about *what was sent down to them*, preferring to let the phrase mean any kind of writings (*kutub*) received by the *ahl al-kitāb*.

36 Rashīd Riḍā, *Tafsīr al-Manār,* 4:316. See Fakhr al-Dīn al-Rāzī, *al-Tafsīr al-kabīr*, 9:154.
37 Ṭabāṭabāʾī, *al-Mīzān*, 4:91.
38 al-Ṭabarī, *Jāmiʿ al-bayān*, 7:500. In an analysis of the second and fourth forms of *NZL*, Fred Leemhuis notes that the latter is most often used "when the object of sending down is a scripture." The fact that this is the "logically expected object" is underscored by the forty-five instances in which the object of the active or passive fourth form is named no "more explicitly than by a simple *mā*." *The D and H Stems*, 34.
39 al-Ṭūsī, *al-Tibyān*, 3:94; al-Ṭabarī, *Jāmiʿ al-bayān*, 7:500.

Al-Zamakhsharī manifests a propensity for conciseness in his gloss of *what was sent down to you* and its coordinate phrase *what was sent down to them*. While he explicitly identifies the former as the Qur'ān, the latter is referred to somewhat ambiguously as "the two books (*al-kitābayn*)," a phrase that should presumably be taken to refer to the Torah and the Gospel.[40] The ambiguity increases when Ibn al-Jawzī makes reference simply to "their book," using a singular form with no further specification.[41]

SCRIPTURAL DISTORTION AS SPIRITUAL PERVERSION

Scriptural concerns intensify when the commentators turn their attention to the declaration that *they do not sell the verses of God for a small price*. Al-Ṭabarī understands the statement quasi-metaphorically and as comprising several areas of concern. The issue is not one of commercial dealings involving Jewish, Christian, or Muslim scriptures. Rather it is a matter of Muslim charges that the Jews and Christians have changed or distorted their divine revelations. The Jews and Christians are accused of changing (*yuḥarrifūna*) the description (*naʿt*) of Muḥammad that God had revealed to them in their own scriptures. They are also reproached for altering (*yubaddilūna*) God's statutes (*aḥkām*) and His authoritative proofs (*ḥujaj*).[42] The results of such scriptural tampering include vulnerability to worldly contamination (*ʿaraḍ min al-dunyā*) and an overweening desire to rule over the ignorant (*ibtighā' al-riyāsah ʿalā al-jahūl*).[43] To none of these accusations

40 al-Zamakhsharī, *al-Kashshāf*, 1:458.

41 Ibn al-Jawzī, *Zād al-masīr*, 2:533.

42 al-Ṭabarī, *Jāmiʿ al-bayān*, 7:500. The charge of scriptural alteration (*taḥrīf*) is a major feature of the Muslim-Christian polemic. John Wansbrough has judged it the theme "destined to bear the major burden of Muslim external polemic." *The Sectarian Milieu: Content and Composition of Islamic Salvation History* (Oxford: Oxford University Press, 1978), 41. An early foundational study of the topic is Ignazio Di Matteo, "Il 'taḥrīf' od alterazione della Bibbia secondo i musulmani," *Bessarione* 26 (1922): 64–111 and 223–60. A very abbreviated translation of this was done by M. H. Ananikian for *MW* 14 (1924): 61–84. This accusation has been the basis of a substantial literature, the main lines of which may be divided into two subcategories. The first of these contains charges that the texts themselves of pre-Qur'ānic scriptures have been falsified (*taḥrīf al-naṣṣ*). The second category would be that group of writings that identify falsification not in the text but in its interpretation (*taḥrīf al-maʿānī*). The best recent discussion is an article by Jean-Marie Gaudeul and Robert Caspar based chiefly on relevant texts from the commentary of Fakhr al-Dīn al-Rāzī, the *Tafsīr al-Manār*, and works by Abū Muḥammad ʿAlī b. Ḥazm (d. 456/1063), ʿAbd al-Malik b. ʿAbdallāh al-Juwaynī (d. 478/1085), and Ibn Khaldūn. "Textes de la tradition musulmane concernant le *taḥrīf* (falsification) des écritures," *Islamo* 6 (1980): 61–104. Al-Juwaynī's principal text on this issue, *al-Shifā' al-jalīl fī al-tabdīl*, has been edited and translated by Michel Allard in his *Textes apologétiques de Juwainī* (Beirut: Dar El-Machreq, 1968). His introduction surveys the major treatises on this topic preceding that of al-Juwaynī.

43 al-Ṭabarī, *Jāmiʿ al-bayān*, 7:500.

are those intended by this verse liable. They, by contrast to those just specified, "yield to the truth and do what God commanded them in His revelation, refraining from what He prohibited: they prefer the command of God to their own selfish desire."[44]

In commenting on the statement *they do not sell the verses of God for a small price*, al-Ṭūsī repeats sentences from al-Ṭabarī word for word. He does, however, expand upon his predecessor's treatment by relating this charge of scriptural alteration to two other Qurʾānic allegations. He compares those who suppress Muḥammad's description and ignore God's commands to "those who buy error for guidance" (*sūrat al-baqarah* [2]:16) and to "those who buy the life of the world for the Hereafter" (*sūrat al-baqarah* [2]:86). Al-Ṭūsī's hermeneutical use of such intra-Qurʾānic parallelism evidently focuses upon the commercial metaphor that the three verses share.[45]

Al-Zamakhsharī chooses not to explain the charge of scriptural alteration, from which those of the *ahl al-kitāb* addressed in this verse are exonerated, but simply to lay it on "those of their learned men (*aḥbār*) and distinguished leaders (*kibār*) who do not become Muslims."[46] With Abū al-Futūḥ Rāzī it is the motivation of those thus charged, namely, "greed for the vanities of the world (*ṭamaʿ-i ḥuṭām-i dunyā*)" that is stressed. As further explication, he, too, draws upon a Qurʾānic parallel: "They sell the promise of God and their faith for a low price" (*sūrah Āl ʿImrān* [3]:76).[47]

Unlike previous commentators Ibn al-Jawzī applies the charge of selling *the verses of God for a small price* only to the Jews. He insists that this is something that "the leaders of the Jews did (*faʿala ruʾasāʾ al-yahūd*)." The results of such behavior are noted in a phrase taken directly from the longer identical passages in both al-Ṭabarī and al-Ṭūsī: vulnerability to worldly contamination (*ʿaraḍ min al-dunyā*).[48]

44 al-Ṭabarī, *Jāmiʿ al-bayān*, 7:500.

45 al-Ṭūsī, *al-Tibyān*, 3:94. See al-Ṭabarī, *Jāmiʿ al-bayān*, 7:500. In dealing with this Charles Torrey states unequivocally that in the Qurʾān the eighth form of *SHRY* always means 'to buy.' He then glosses a phrase similar to the one under discussion which occurs in *sūrat al-baqarah* (2):41 (*lā-tashtarū bi-āyātī thamanan qalīlan*) as "do not make the *bad bargain* [Torrey's italics] of misusing our revelations, or withholding them for your own purposes!" The sense conveyed hardly seems to be that of 'buying' nor is that the common exegetical understanding of the verse. Torrey completes his *excursus* on this phrase with the egregious argument that "to be called *kāfir*, or promised the most blood-curdling tortures in *jahannam* would give no unbeliever much concern, but to be charged with making a *foolish bargain* [Torrey's italics] – that was a reproach that every Arab could feel!" *The Commercial-Theological Terms in the Koran* (Leiden: E. J. Brill, 1892), 36–37. T. Sabbagh has chosen the more neutral term of 'to barter (troquer)' to convey the sense of *yashtarūna* in this verse. *La Métaphore dans le Coran* (Paris: Adrien-Maisonneuve, 1943), 214.

46 al-Zamakhsharī, *al-Kashshāf*, 1:458.

47 Abū al-Futūḥ Rāzī, *Rawḥ al-jinān*, 3:299.

48 Ibn al-Jawzī, *Zād al-masīr*, 2:533. The *tafsīr* often attributed to Ibn al-ʿArabī provides

Kāshānī is more explicit than others about the sources of such textual corruptions, attributing them to bribe-takers (*rishvah-khvār*) among the religious leaders (*aḥbār*).[49] Muḥammad ʿAbduh, in turn, does far more than provide a simple gloss or historical identification for this phrase. Rather he ties it to those words that describe its opposite, the proper response to divine revelation. Against the accusation addressed to those who *sell the verses of God for a small price* may be placed the praise of those who are *submissive before God* (*khāshiʿīna lillāh*). It is this religious sensitivity around which Rashīd Riḍā weaves the threads of his interpretation.

A POSTURE PRESCRIBED

Commentators prior to Rashīd Riḍā have done little more than gloss the phrase *submissive before God*. Al-Ṭabarī, for example, provides the brief expansion: "Those who submit (*khāḍiʿūn*) to God in obedience, resigning themselves (*mustakīnūn*) to Him in obedience as a people humbled (*mutadhallilūn*)."[50] Al-Ṭūsī expands this somewhat by defining one who is submissive as "one who feels fearful self-abasement (*al-mutadhallil al-khāʾif*)."[51] In the *Tafsīr al-Manār*, however, this phrase assumes central importance.

Rashīd Riḍā here presents the teaching of Muḥammad ʿAbduh as the latter develops his thoughts on this statement. According to Muḥammad ʿAbduh "this submissiveness (*khushūʿ*) is the very spirit of religion (*rūḥ al-dīn*); it is the force which drives people to belief in the new prophet (*al-nabī al-jadīd*)."[52] A sure sign of the presence of this religious attribute is that *they do not sell the verses of God for a small price*. For him the word 'price (*thaman*)' connotes not only money or possessions (*māl*) but also rank or dignity (*jāh*). Functioning as a psychologist of religion he astutely notes that these latter considerations form no small obstacle to the acceptance of a more recent revelation. The binding force of custom is a powerful hindrance to religious change. "How very difficult it is," observes Muḥammad ʿAbduh, "for man to renounce that to which he is habituated."[53] The real laudability of this group of the *ahl al-kitāb* lies in their willingness to hold

an interesting counterpoint to this exegetical theme. The word *āyāt* (here translated as *verses*), which other exegetes have understood in terms of antecedent scriptures, for Ibn al-ʿArabī refers very generally to the revelation of God's attributes. The contextual issue is thus not that of bartering scripture or altering divinely revealed commands and prohibitions. It is rather that of insufficiently valuing this revealed knowledge of God's attributes, of treating it as worth only what other things are worth. Ibn al-ʿArabī, *Tafsīr al-Qurʾān al-karīm*, 1:245.

49 Kāshānī, *Minhaj al-ṣādiqīn*, 2:420.
50 al-Ṭabarī, *Jāmiʿ al-bayān*, 7:500.
51 al-Ṭūsī, *al-Tibyān*, 3:94.
52 Rashīd Riḍā, *Tafsīr al-Manār*, 4:316.
53 Rashīd Riḍā, *Tafsīr al-Manār*, 4:316.

steadfastly to the truth wherever it presents itself, be that in their traditional religion or in a new one.

Lest anyone assume that large numbers of Christians and Jews were eligible for such approbation, Muḥammad ʿAbduh stresses the infrequency of this fidelity to the truth among them. Even the Qurʾānic formulation in its emphatic wording attests to this. In fact, says Muḥammad ʿAbduh, since they are misled by their scriptures (*ghurūruhum bi-kitābihim*) and suffer from the delusion that they are religiously self-sufficient, without need for recourse to anything else (*tawahhumuhum al-istighnāʾ bi-mā ʿindahum ʿan ghayrihi*), "they are the people farthest from belief."[54] So convinced is he of the general inadequacy of the *ahl al-kitāb*, he finds any evidence of divine acceptability a source of amazement: "It is indeed a marvel if, given that opposition to and disdainful treatment of the Prophet, the disavowal of his prophetic claim and the relentless efforts to destroy him (*tashaddud fī īdāʾihi*), some of them believed with a true, perfect faith."[55]

Those few who did become believers were not from the ordinary ranks of adherents. They were of "the elite – learned and distinguished men endowed with discrimination."[56] Having said this, Muḥammad ʿAbduh feels compelled to differentiate between the scholars of that epoch and those of his own time, few of whom would apparently qualify in his eyes as men of discrimination. Look, he asks his listener, at how "our clever savants in this era (*ʿulamāʾunā al-adhkiyāʾ fī hādhā al-ʿaṣr*)" perform. "Rarely do they fail to agree with a religious conviction or view; they proceed in accordance with it and accept it on the authority of their spiritual mentors (*mashāyikhuhum*) and recite it in their books even if it is a falsehood and an evident error."[57]

A PENULTIMATE SUMMARIZATION

In the preceding remarks of Muḥammad ʿAbduh and in the entire exegetical tradition on this verse repeated reference has been made to the *ahl al-kitāb*, the category with which the verse itself begins. Issues of identification and historical specification have been developed, concurrent with the hermeneutical pattern of periphrastic glossing. Yet treatment of this category has been, in the main, fragmentary. Continual allusion is made but systematic development is lacking. An exception to this within the exegetical chronology did develop, however. It begins in the *al-Tafsīr al-kabīr* of Fakhr al-Dīn al-Rāzī and comes to full fruition in Rashīd Riḍā's *Tafsīr al-Manār*.

54 Rashīd Riḍā, *Tafsīr al-Manār*, 4:316.
55 Rashīd Riḍā, *Tafsīr al-Manār*, 4:316.
56 Rashīd Riḍā, *Tafsīr al-Manār*, 4:316.
57 Rashīd Riḍā, *Tafsīr al-Manār*, 4:316.

Fakhr al-Dīn al-Rāzī's treatment of this verse's individual phrases is more systematic than that of his predecessors. Rather than simply paraphrasing each individual statement, he groups them under the rubric of what might be termed "divine descriptives." This hermeneutical taxonomy focuses upon that category which is central to the analysis of this verse, *the people of the book*. Although, as just noted, there has been frequent use of this phrase in the verse's earlier exegetical tradition, Fakhr al-Dīn al-Rāzī brings it forward as the fulcrum upon which to balance his entire interpretive exercise. God, he maintains, was distinguishing this faithful group from others of the *ahl al-kitāb* in five distinct ways: "(1) believers in God, (2) believers in what God sent down to Muḥammad, (3) believers in what was sent down to the prophets who came before Muḥammad, (4) their being submissive (*khāshiʿūn*) before God, and (5) that they do not sell the verses of God for a low price as did those among them of the *ahl al-kitāb* who concealed the matter of the messenger (*amr al-rasūl*) and of the authenticity of his claim to prophecy (*ṣiḥḥah nubūwatihi*)."[58]

Full development of Fakhr al-Dīn al-Rāzī's systematization awaits the attention of Rashīd Riḍā in the *Tafsīr al-Manār*. Whereas Fakhr al-Dīn al-Rāzī had simply listed the five descriptives that this verse applied to the faithful group from the *ahl al-kitāb*, Rashīd Riḍā provides considerable explanatory material. The first attribute is, of course, belief in God, which Rashīd Riḍā discusses by a kind of *via negativa*. Authentic belief is that in which "there is no contamination by the evil insinuations (*nazaghāt*) of associating anything with God (*shirk*), and no withholding of the submission which provokes action (*al-idhʿān al-bāʿith ʿalā al-ʿamal*)."[59] As additional negative examples, this commentator quotes two Qur'ānic passages: (1) "Among people there are some who say 'We believe in God and the Last Day' but they do not believe" (*sūrat al-baqarah* [2]:8) and (2) "Most

58 Fakhr al-Dīn al-Rāzī, *al-Tafsīr al-kabīr*, 11:154. Attention to the *ahl al-kitāb* as a hermeneutical category characterizes (pseudo) Ibn al-ʿArabī's treatment of this verse as well. For this exegete the *ahl al-kitāb* are not those who share a particular religious affiliation, be it Jewish or Christian. Rather, they are to be defined negatively as "those who are veiled from the oneness of God." Furthermore they are those whose spiritual attainments are ephemeral, lacking both constancy and consistency. Yet among the *ahl al-kitāb* are *those who believe in God*. Ibn al-ʿArabī is unequivocal in his specification of this subgroup. They are those who are utterly convinced of God's essential oneness (*al-tawḥīd al-dhātī*). Knowledge of this oneness and the rectitude (*istiqāmah*) that flows from the realization of it are the result of *what was sent down to you*. The coordinate phrase, *what was sent down to them*, is interpreted in the most inclusive way possible. Understood as knowledge of cosmology and eschatology (*al-mabda' wa-al-maʿād*) it encompasses the whole of revelation and of life as lived in accordance with it. As such it is the plenitude of which *al-tawḥīd* and *al-istiqāmah* are the essential poles. Ibn al-ʿArabī, *Tafsīr al-Qur'ān al-karīm*, 1:245.

59 Rashīd Riḍā, *Tafsīr al-Manār*, 4:317.

of them believe in God only by associating [others with Him]" (*sūrah Yūsuf* [12]:106).

The second characteristic, belief in *what was sent down to you*, refers to "God's revelation to Muḥammad." To it must be given priority over all previous revelation "because it is the basis for action (*al-ʿumdah alladhī ʿalayhi al-ʿamal*)."[60] It is not subject to change but remains with absolute certainty (*thubūt bi-al-yaqīn*). This changelessness stands in stark contrast to the scriptures intended by the third descriptive, *what was sent down to them*. These are identified by Rashīd Riḍā in the general sense of "what God revealed to their [the *ahl al-kitāb*'s] prophets."[61] Such scriptures may not be characterized as invulnerable to change for they are subject to partial oblivion through the forgetfulness of their adherents. They are also endangered by the alterations and omissions that can occur in the processes of translation and transmission. What is commended by this Qurʾānic verse is a kind of generalized acceptance of these scriptures, but under the overriding guidance of the Qurʾān on points of detail or discrepancy. "The Qurʾān is the basis," Rashīd Riḍā insists, "so no one can be credited with belief (*īmān*) who knows it [the Qurʾān] and yet disagrees with it by preferring his own scriptures."[62]

To praise certain of the *ahl al-kitāb* as being *submissive* is to commend them for the sincerity of their belief. "Submission (*khushūʿ*) is the fruit of true belief, which seeks to actualize the exigencies of faith; it is a mark of fear of God (*khashyat Allāh*) in the heart which floods the limbs and senses."[63] The presence of this affective quality in the religious personality authenticates the bearer's attestations of belief. One who can be termed submissive would not then *sell the verses of God for a small price*, which is the fifth and final distinguishing characteristic marked by this Qurʾānic verse. The notion of 'buying' and 'selling' additionally connotes preferring worldly pleasures to spiritual ones. Those most susceptible to this temptation, according to Rashīd Riḍā, are people who accept belief uncritically, "through ethnic identification with the learned men of their religious community (*ʿulamāʾ millatihim*)."[64]

A PROMISE OF RECKONING AND REWARD

The systematization afforded by both Fakhr al-Dīn al-Rāzī's and Rashīd Riḍā's categorization of this verse's fivefold description of the *ahl al-kitāb* finds its climax in the divine promise that *for them is their reward near their*

60 Rashīd Riḍā, *Tafsīr al-Manār*, 4:317.
61 Rashīd Riḍā, *Tafsīr al-Manār*, 4:317.
62 Rashīd Riḍā, *Tafsīr al-Manār*, 4:317.
63 Rashīd Riḍā, *Tafsīr al-Manār*, 4:317.
64 Rashīd Riḍā, *Tafsīr al-Manār*, 4:317.

Lord. To this penultimate pledge is appended the reassuring comment that *surely God is quick to reckon*. Together these statements draw the verse to conclusion upon eschatological concerns. For al-Ṭabarī such eternal reward is understood simply as compensation for good deeds and obedience. The final phrase of the verse is, for him, a reference to divine omniscience, a sense that is later reiterated by Fakhr al-Dīn al-Rāzī. "None of their deeds are concealed from Him, either before or after they are performed, so He does not need to count their number."[65] God's computation is instantaneous; it is not slowed down by counting (*iḥṣāʾ*). Al-Ṭūsī puts this last point in a particularly felicitous way: "God is described as 'quick' because He does not postpone the reward of the one so entitled on account of protracted calculation."[66]

Of more importance, however, is the explanation that al-Ṭūsī offers for the inclusion of this phrase promising a divine reward. For those addressed not only is this a confirmation that their good deeds will be recompensed, it is an assurance to them that the unbelief of their former coreligionists will not affect their status as Muslims.[67] He thereby introduces a consideration that will be developed more prominently by such later commentators as Fakhr al-Dīn al-Rāzī and Ṭabāṭabāʾī.

Al-Zamakhsharī raises an interesting notion when discussing the recompense promised to those whom this verse praises. He first equates the relevant phrase with two subsequent Qurʾānic statements: (1) "those will be given their reward twice" (*sūrat al-qaṣaṣ* [28]:54) and (2) "He will give you two guarantees of His mercy" (*sūrat al-ḥadīd* [57]:28).[68] Then this exegete proposes a possible two-stage sequence of revelation whereby this verse promises only proximity to the Lord. It is not until later revelations that the amount of recompense is clarified.[69]

Ibn Kathīr ties explanation of the verse's penultimate phrase directly to the connotation of *maslamah*, which, as previously noted, he defined as "those who belonged to the *ahl al-kitāb* before Muḥammad but then followed him and professed *islām*."[70] Like al-Zamakhsharī, Ibn Kathīr connects this divine pledge to certain Qurʾānic statements that promise a twofold reward. Unlike his predecessor, however, he offers a reason for this

65 al-Ṭabarī, *Jāmiʿ al-bayān*, 7:501; Fakhr al-Dīn al-Rāzī, *al-Tafsīr al-kabīr* 11:154. The idea of 'reckoning' is the second of the two commercial notions that this verse entails. Charles Torrey finds the idea of *ḥisāb* characteristic of the earliest *sūrah*s but also identifies *sarīʿu al-ḥisābi* as a "convenient verse ending" or "stock expression." *The Commercial-Theological Terms*, 9 and 12.

66 al-Ṭūsī, *al-Tibyān*, 3:94.

67 al-Ṭūsī, *al-Tibyān*, 3:93–94.

68 The first of these Qurʾānic citations will be discussed in Chapter 8.

69 al-Zamakhsharī, *al-Kashshāf*, 1:458.

70 Ibn Kathīr, *Tafsīr al-Qurʾān al-ʿaẓīm*, 1:443.

connection: "God promised them a twofold reward because of the belief to which they adhered before the time of Muḥammad and because they followed him." He also quotes a saying of the Prophet, cited on the authority of Abū Mūsā al-Ashʿarī (d. 42/662), which proclaims that among those who will be given their reward twice is "any man of the *ahl al-kitāb* who believes in his own prophet and believes in me."[71]

The phrase *for them is their reward near their Lord* begins a new verse, according to Kāshānī's *Minhaj al-ṣādiqīn*. He, too, connects this with the Qurʾānic declaration in *sūrat al-qaṣaṣ* (28):54 that promises a twofold reward. The sense of divine dispatch in calculation is reiterated as an assurance that there will be no postponement of the avowed recompense. Kāshānī depicts the scene on Judgment Day as follows: "God gathers all creation and in one instance He speaks to every individual with a word particular to each."[72]

In a comment reminiscent of Fakhr al-Dīn al-Rāzī's use of context as a hermeneutical device, this exegete remarks upon the importance for the *ahl al-kitāb* of this divinely specified promise. Given the Qurʾānic denigration of unbelievers, one instance of which immediately precedes this verse, it was important that reassurance be offered to those of the *ahl al-kitāb* who became believers. Lest they fear contamination from their former coreligionists, Kāshānī – echoing al-Ṭūsī – promises them that "the disbelief of some who are close to them or of their companions does them no harm (*żarar bi-īshān nakhvāhad rasānīd*)."[73]

For Rashīd Riḍā, as well, contextual considerations loom large in gauging the significance of this verse's penultimate phrase. God included this verse, explains Rashīd Riḍā, as an exception to the foregoing generalization about the *ahl al-kitāb*. Those previous verses, which note the apparent worldly success of some unbelievers, also promise that the enjoyment of such success will be brief. Hell will be their destination. Thus Muslims are urged to avoid any trace of envy: "That [i.e., Hell] is the punishment for those whose enjoyments you hold in such high regard, those [that is] who persist in their disbelief."[74] In presenting the teaching of Muḥammad ʿAbduh, Rashīd Riḍā underlines the contrast between this verse and those preceding it which condemn the unbelievers. As an exception to this denunciation, Muḥammad ʿAbduh notes, God "mentioned a group of the *ahl al-kitāb* who are guided by this Qurʾān (*yahtadūna bi-hādhā al-Qurʾān*) and who were guided, even before the revelation of the Qurʾān, by what they possessed in the way of prophetic guidance."[75]

71 Ibn Kathīr, *Tafsīr al-Qurʾān al-ʿaẓīm*, 1:444.
72 Kāshānī, *Minhaj al-ṣādiqīn*, 2:421.
73 Kāshānī, *Minhaj al-ṣādiqīn*, 2:421.
74 Rashīd Riḍā, *Tafsīr al-Manār*, 4:315.
75 Rashīd Riḍā, *Tafsīr al-Manār*, 4:316.

Later in his commentary Rashīd Riḍā returns to the theme of apparent inequity in the earthly bounty that God permits. He finds in this verse divine approbation for any shortage of material good that the Muslims might suffer, in contrast to the apparent abundance enjoyed by some of the unbelievers. It is as if the Lord were saying: "Look at the condition of the leading men among the *ahl al-kitāb*, how unconcerned they are with worldly goods (*al-matāʿ al-dunyawī*). Rather do they prefer godly affairs. In this lies part of their likeness and similarity to the Muslims."[76] This exegete can, of course, draw such an implication from the present verse because of his prior emphasis on the importance of context for understanding it.

Yet Rashīd Riḍā boldly underscores the partitive nature of this verse's complimentary descriptives of the *ahl al-kitāb*. In fact, he uses the reference to a promised reward as an opportunity for castigation of those of this group to whom the fivefold characterization does not apply. These are the "self-deluded (*al-maghrūrūn bi-anfusihim*)" whose predecessors knowingly concealed the truth of Muḥammad's claim to prophecy.[77] For them there is no reward, only consignment to the Fire. Rashīd Riḍā underscores his accusation in ways reminiscent of his discussion in Chapter 3 of the 'people of the interval (*ahl al-fatrah*)', those people born between the time of Jesus and Muḥammad, which formed part of his commentary on *sūrat al-baqarah* (2):62. "Everyone reached by the call (*daʿwah*) of Muḥammad and to whom its truth is evident, as it is to them, but who rejects and resists, as they reject and resist, gains no positive credit for his belief in former prophets and their books. His belief in God is not an authentic belief, one linked to fear of God and submission (*khushūʿ*)."[78] In fact, he makes direct reference to the discussion on 2:62 by explaining that some of the factors considered there are not present in this instance. This verse, he emphasizes, does not refer (even by contrast) to those whom the call of the Prophet did not reach or to whom it came in a distorted form.[79]

His commentary on the verse's final phrase is noteworthy chiefly for the analogy drawn on the procedure of divine judgment. "God is *quick to reckon* because the effects of each individual's action are imprinted on his soul just like the series of images – and here Rashīd Riḍā uses a newly topical simile – that compose a motion picture.[80]

76 Rashīd Riḍā, *Tafsīr al-Manār*, 4:316–17.
77 Rashīd Riḍā, *Tafsīr al-Manār*, 4:318.
78 Rashīd Riḍā, *Tafsīr al-Manār*, 4:318.
79 Rashīd Riḍā, *Tafsīr al-Manār*, 4:318.
80 Rashīd Riḍā, *Tafsīr al-Manār*, 4:318. Although such references to modern technology are not uncommon in the *Tafsīr al-Manār*, they are not, in general, aspects of what has been called *al-tafsīr al-ʿilmī*. This latter is a conscious attempt to find every aspect of human knowledge and endeavor in the Qur'ān. J.J.G. Jansen has characterized its

Ṭabāṭabāʾī resumes a theme played earlier by al-Ṭūsī and Kāshānī when he repeats the reassurance that those of the *ahl al-kitāb* who acknowledge *all* the prophets will share with Muslims the bliss of the Hereafter. For Ṭabāṭabāʾī "the issue turns on the axis of belief in God and His messengers."[81] Therefore those of the *ahl al-kitāb* who satisfy the spiritual requirements are deemed eligible.

CONCLUSION

The entire exegetical tradition on this verse repeatedly attests to its central focus as a Qurʾānic 'conversion' verse. As constituent members of that category known as *the people of the book*, Christians are here the subject of divine praise only insofar as they accept the prophethood of Muḥammad and the revelation entrusted to him. Such Christians who thereby convert to Islam are those herein praised. Virtually all of the concern with historical specificity that the exegetes display supports this understanding. Conversion scenarios such as that featuring the Abyssinian ruler as well as lists of early converts from Judaism, Christianity, and even Zoroastrianism predominate from one generation of exegetes to the next. Yet the persons mentioned by name and the varying enumerations associated with such diverse locales as the Christian settlement of Najrān in the Arabian peninsula, the Coptic kingdom of Abyssinia, and the territories under Byzantine hegemony are ultimately unimportant. They function simply as symbolic synopses of the centuries-long process of conversion and acculturation under changing Muslim dynasties. Figures such as the Najāshī, ʿAbdallāh b. Salām, and Salmān al-Fārisī are largely lost to history in their individual particularity but stand as religio-ethnic representatives of the earliest Muslim converts from Christianity, Judaism, and Zoroastrianism.

Although the names and numbers are repeated, there is little attempt at historical circumscription. Virtually all of the commentators explicitly opt for the most inclusive understanding of those divinely intended by this verse. The largely representative nature of the individuals and groups actually cited is reinforced by the repeated insistence that *any* who meet the stated criteria are eligible for the promised reward. The term *maslamah*,

advocates as those who believe that the "Koran, as we know it, contains everything that can be known, and that all sciences, skills and techniques have their roots in the Koran. Given sufficient insight, as many supporters of scientific exegesis maintain, one might be able to deduce from the text of the Koran the laws and techniques brought to light by man's scientific efforts." *Interpretation*, 35–36. A repudiation of *al-tafsīr al-ʿilmī* by Muḥammad Kāmil Ḥusayn has been extracted from his *Mutanawwiʿāt* and translated by R.P. Pierre Noury as "Le commentaire 'scientifique' du Coran: une innovation absurde," *MIDEO* 16 (1983): 293–300.

81 Ṭabāṭabāʾī, *al-Mīzān*, 4:89.

used here to connote those who convert to Islam, stands as a primary linguistic locus for this exegetical judgment.

Within this nearly unanimous chorus there is, of course, some variation. Fakhr al-Dīn al-Rāzī relies upon a contextual argument to undergird his agreement with the option for inclusivity. Ibn Kathīr puts the most decidedly pro-Christian spin on the verse's trajectory of denotation. While maintaining that but a fraction of the *ahl al-kitāb* are candidates for this divine praise, he posits a considerable disparity between the eligible numbers of Jews and of Christians, once again praising the latter at the expense of the former.

An interesting concentration on scriptural categories characterizes this verse. Kāshānī even uses a threefold revelatory schema – the Qurʾān, Torah, and Gospel – as the primary identifying feature of those intended. But such explicit equation of a *people* and their *book* is not consistent in the exegetical tradition on this verse. Both al-Zamakhsharī and Ibn al-Jawzī express varying degrees of ambiguity, with the latter's use of a singular form indicating but slight concern with such particulars.

Scriptural concerns reach special prominence in the elliptical remark *they do not sell the verses of God for a small price*. The general exegetical understanding of this phrase recapitulates and refines the perennial Muslim charge that previous revelations, especially the Torah and Gospel, have been the subject of deliberate or inadvertent alteration. Both al-Ṭabarī and al-Ṭūsī briefly spell out the specifics of this accusation, asserting that it affects the prophetic, doctrinal, and legal authenticity of antecedent scriptures. Others of these exegetes have fastened upon aspects as various as the spiritual perversion that would prompt such behavior or the classes of religious functionaries most liable to the charge. Ibn al-Jawzī restricts the accusation to Jewish authorities, thereby implicitly exonerating Christians and others from such reproach. Kāshānī later combined these perspectives with the succinct explanation that scriptural tampering was done by bribe-taking religious leaders. By contrast, the requisite and divinely rewarded spiritual posture is one of submission. Muḥammad ʿAbduh's psychological insights delineate the difficulties attendant upon the cultivation of such an attitude. Restriction to a religious elite is insured by the rigor prescribed in his interpretation.

Fakhr al-Dīn al-Rāzī summarizes the exegetical agenda to this point as a fivefold description of the *ahl al-kitāb*, a taxonomy developed and elaborated by Rashīd Riḍā. That summarization, in turn, opens the way for analysis of the concluding Qurʾānic pledge. Like many verses this one caps a series of divine descriptives with a divine promise. The patterning is one of preliminary characterization and delimitation followed by a fulfillment prediction. While general reference to future joys is a feature of the exegetical consideration of this verse's concluding phrases, context functions to shape the more particular concerns. The stress on conversion is underscored by al-Ṭūsī's and Kāshānī's reassurance that God will not hold the unbelief of former coreligionists against those of the *ahl al-kitāb* who become Muslims. This refrain will be sounded again in the discussion of 28: 52–55 in Chapter 8. Verse 28:54's mention of a twofold reward may be an unexpressed intra-Qurʾānic locus for al-Zamakhsharī's, Ibn Kathīr's, and Kāshānī's sense of this verse as the promise of a twofold reward. Ibn Kathīr even anticipates the standard interpretation of this in 28:52–55, one that finds justification for the double recompense in the two stages of belief that converts experience. Finally, context operates on a somewhat larger scale with those commentators who look beyond the confines of the verse itself and see the pledge therein contained as a contrast to prior divine denunciation. One such hermeneutical visionary, Rashīd Riḍā, cannot, however, restrain himself from indulging in some denunciation of his own. Intent upon emphasizing how few Christians (or others) are eligible for this verse's complimentary descriptives of the *ahl al-kitāb*, he harshly condemns the majority, leaving them the sole prospect of torment in the Fire.

6

The promised bounty of piety

The fourth Qur'ānic text to be considered is associated with the Christians not by direct name, that is, by use of the term *al-naṣārā*, or by reference to the person of Jesus, or by general inclusion within the *ahl al-kitāb,* but rather by designation of a specific scripture, the Gospel (*injīl*). Like the preceding verse, this one climaxes in a divine promise, a promise phrased in pungent, physical language. But unlike previous passages, this verse carries a striking grammatical structure. It is formed as a hypothetical sentence or, more precisely, as a conditional contrary to fact. As such it has posed particular problems for the exegetical tradition where the need for identification and specification is enhanced by the implied negativity. The pertinent text is from *sūrat al-mā'idah* (5):66:

If they had adhered to the Torah and the Gospel and what was sent down to them from their Lord, they would have eaten from above them and from beneath their feet. Among them is a balanced people but many of them are evildoers.

A SCRIPTURAL CONUNDRUM

An initial concern for virtually all of the commentators is the precise significance of the first verb in this verse. In his paraphrase of the opening lines al-Ṭabarī suggests a synonym that would permit the translation "if they had acted in accordance with (*ᶜamilū bi*) the Torah and the Gospel."[1]

1 al-Ṭabarī, *Jāmiᶜ al-bayān,* 10:462. The Qur'ānic terms here translated as Torah and Gospel are *tawrāt* and *injīl*. The former is used, according to Arthur Jeffery, as "a general term for the Jewish scriptures" and is a direct borrowing from the Hebrew. *Foreign Vocabulary*, 96. Abū al-Qāsim al-Ḥusayn al-Rāghib al-Iṣfahānī (d. 502/1108) explains *tawrāt* as a derivative of *WRY*. *Muᶜjam mufradāt alfāẓ al-Qur'ān* (Beirut: Dār al-Kitāb al-ᶜArabī, 1392/1972), 73. Jeffery finds the route of derivation for the second term, *injīl*, more problematic. While he does not question that it is ultimately derived from the Greek *evangēlion*, the possible intermediaries that he surveys include Syriac, Hebrew, Ethiopic, and Sabaean. See *Foreign Vocabulary*, 71–72. It should be noted that the term is always found in the singular in both the Qur'ān and among the classical commentators. Neither source evinces any awareness that the Christian scriptures are a collection of

Yet he is aware of the objection that could immediately be made against such an exhortation. His hypothetical questioner phrases the query thus: "How can they adhere to the Torah and Gospel and what was sent down to Muḥammad, given the fact that these books disagree with each other and some abrogate others?"[2]

This exegete next responds by acknowledging that contradictions and discrepancies exist in some parts of these earlier scriptures but denies their complete invalidity. Rather he maintains that there is present in these writings an authentic witness to the messengers of God and to the divine origination of these scriptures. With this in mind, al-Ṭabarī can amplify his explanation of the verse's initial statement to mean "their acknowledging the truth of what is in these [writings] and acting in accordance with what they are agreed on (*al-ʿamal bi-mā hiya muttafiqatun fīhi*) in each instance of such within the allotted time ordained for the act."[3]

Al-Ṭūsī's understanding of the conditional *if they had adhered to the Torah and the Gospel* emphasizes knowledge rather than behavior. Had they known these scriptures as originally revealed before the contamination of any de-

books. Such awareness, however, was not completely absent among Muslim writers of the early classical period. R.G. Khoury has published a preliminary survey of biblical citations that appear in the first two Islamic centuries, with special attention to Wahb b. Munabbih (d. 110/728 or 114/732), an early scholar of *isrāʾīlīyāt*. Khoury has noted the frequent occurrence of a particular methodology in these early Arabic citations of the Bible: "Le parallélisme initial, souvent minime, aboutit à une paraphrase rappelant de moins en moins un contenu biblique et terminant dans une ambiance tout à fait coranique et islamique." "Quelques réflexions sur les citations de la Bible dans les premières générations islamiques du premier et du deuxième siècles de l'Hégire," *BEO* 29 (1977): 277. Subsequent references have been culled from the works of such authors as Ibn Qutaybah, al-Masʿūdī, Ibn Ḥazm, and al-Ghazālī. For pertinent information see G. Lecomte, "Les citations de l'Ancien et du Nouveau Testament dans l'oeuvre d'Ibn Quytaba," *Arabica* 5 (1958): 34–46; Ahmad M. H. Shboul, *Al-Masʿūdī and His World* (London: Ithaca Press, 1979) 290–93; Ignazio Di Matteo, "Le pretese contraddizioni della S. Scrittura secondo Ibn Hazm," *Bessarione* 27 (1923): 77–127. J. Sadan has identified several manuscript sources of a kind of *tawrāt* presented in the style of the Qurʾān. "Some Literary Problems Concerning Judaism and Jewry in Medieval Arabic Sources," in *Studies in Islamic History and Civilization in Honour of Professor David Ayalon*, ed. by M. Sharon (Jerusalem, Cana/ Leiden: E. J. Brill, 1986), 370–94. A recent note by David Wasserstein even traces the possible reference to a tractate of the Mishnah in a tenth-century Muslim document. "An Arabic Version of *Abot* 1:3 from Umayyad Spain," *Arabica* 34 (1987): 370–74.

2 al-Ṭabarī, *Jāmiʿ al-bayān*, 10:462. Muslim authors have addressed the issue of abrogation among the *ahl al-kitāb*. One example of this is Gérard Tropeau's presentation of a brief section from Ibn Taymīyah's *Iqtiḍāʾ al-ṣirāt al-mustaqīm wa-mujānabat aṣḥāb al-jaḥīm*. In these remarks Ibn Taymīyah criticizes the Jews for refusing to acknowledge the very possibility of scriptural abrogation and castigates the Christians for allowing their priests and monks to engage in it indiscriminately. "Les fêtes des Chrétiens vues par un juriste musulman," in *Mélanges offerts à Jean Dauvillier* (Toulouse: Centre d'Histoire Juridique Méridionale, 1979), 797.

3 al-Ṭabarī, *Jāmiʿ al-bayān*, 10:462–63.

liberate or inadvertent substitutions or alterations, they would have received the rewards promised in the apodosis of this conditional statement.[4] Al-Ṭūsī also includes a much more concrete interpretation of the verse, based on the fundamental sense of the verb at issue (*aqāmū*) as 'to set up' or 'to set straight.' From this perspective, the exegete comments, the phrase could mean that they actually "set the two [books] before their eyes lest they make any error concerning the divine ordinances (*ḥudūd*) in them."[5]

Al-Zamakhsharī's preliminary paraphrase of the opening statement of this verse repeats material found in earlier commentators. He, too, understands "adherence to the Torah and Gospel" in a primarily legal sense as perseverance "in the statutes (*aḥkām*) and restrictive ordinances (*ḥudūd*) of the two and what they contain by way of description (*naᶜt*) of the Messenger of God."[6] Abū al-Futūḥ Rāzī and Ibn al-Jawzī, as well, follow this exegetical tradition, understanding the relevant verb in terms of orthopraxis, or behavior according to the laws revealed therein.[7]

A far more expanded treatment of this issue may be found in *al-Tafsīr al-kabīr* of Fakhr al-Dīn al-Rāzī. In his usual systematic way, Fakhr al-Dīn al-Rāzī lists three possible clarifications for the initial phrase, the first of which he finds the most satisfactory. This understanding, which apparently builds upon that of al-Zamakhsharī, stresses not only active participation and intellectual assent but includes in the latter category consent "to the convincing proofs for the sending (*baᶜth*) of Muḥammad."[8] The second explanation returns to the notion of physical performance of religious requirements, while the third repeats the most literal interpretation, that which sees the connotation as one of actually keeping the books in sight as an aid to correct practice.

In his restatement of the opening section of this verse Ibn Kathīr follows Fakhr al-Dīn al-Rāzī's lead in emphasizing both the injunction to recommended (*mandūb*) action and to obligatory belief. Ibn Kathīr, too, stresses that the Torah and Gospel attest to the truth of Muḥammad. He

4 al-Ṭūsī, *al-Tibyān*, 3:585. Al-Ṭūsī is here making reference to the polemical charge of *taḥrīf*. Two of the four Qur'ānic instances of the second form of *ḤRF* occur in the *sūrah* under discussion, *sūrat al-mā'idah* (5):13 and 41.

5 al-Ṭūsī, *al-Tibyān*, 3:585. As the first signification of *aqāma* John Penrice offers the phrase "to cause to stand upright." *A Dictionary and Glossary of the Kor-ân* (1873; reprint, London: Curzon Press, 1971), 122. Although within Islamic law the term *ḥudūd* carries the technical signification of mandated punishments, such a restricted connotation seems inappropriate here.

6 al-Zamakhsharī, *al-Kashshāf*, 1:658.

7 Abū al-Futūḥ Rāzī, *Rawḥ al-jinān*, 4:273; Ibn al-Jawzī, *Zād al-masīr*, 2:395. The most frequent use of the verb *aqāma/aqāmū* in the Qur'ān occurs in conjunction with the term for ritual prayer, *al-ṣalāt*, and refers to steadfast performance of the mandated daily liturgy.

8 Fakhr al-Dīn al-Rāzī, *al-Tafsīr al-kabīr*, 12:46.

then adds, apparently in response to objections that these prophetic passages in the two scriptures are ambiguous, that "the order to follow him [Muḥammad] is an imperative about which there is no doubt whatsoever."[9] Following al-Ṭabarī, Ibn Kathīr also alludes to the accusation that these two scriptures have been altered by those who possess them either inadvertently or deliberately.

In the paraphrase with which Rashīd Riḍā begins his treatment of this verse there is repetition of some of the now-familiar material as well as specification of matters about which previous commentators made only general remarks. References by al-Zamakhsharī and Fakhr al-Dīn al-Rāzī to statements in earlier scriptures that foretold the coming of Muḥammad are here particularized. Rashīd Riḍā expands the verse's opening phrase thus: "if they had adhered to what is in the Torah and the Gospel . . . announcing the good news of the Prophet who would come from the tribes of their brother Ismāᶜīl, as Moses said, and the Paraclete (*al-bāraqlīṭ*), the spirit of truth who would teach them everything, as Jesus said."[10] Further amplification of the conditional's protasis adds the stipulation: if "after that they had adhered to *what was sent down to them from their Lord* on the tongue of this Prophet whom their books announced . . . and had not made distinctions among the messengers of God and His books." He then proceeds to paraphrase the apodosis with the concluding declaration that "they would

9 Ibn Kathīr, *Tafsīr al-Qurʾān al-ᶜaẓīm*, 2:76.

10 Rashīd Riḍā, *Tafsīr al-Manār*, 6:460. Behind this mention of the term *al-bāraqlīṭ* lies the Muslim declaration that Muḥammad's coming had been foretold in previous scriptures. The major New Testament citations offered in evidence of this are several passages from the Gospel of John in which the coming of the *paraklētos* is foretold. The Qurʾānic promise in *sūrat al-ṣaff* (61):6 of a *rasūl* to follow Jesus "whose name is Aḥmad (*ismuhu aḥmad*)" was tied to these passages in John. The word *aḥmad* was thought by Muslims to be an Arabic translation of the Greek term *paraklētos*. An early mention of this may be found in the *Sīrah* of Ibn Isḥāq where, after rendering John 15:23, he adds the gloss: "*al-manḥamannā* in Syriac is Muḥammad [another form of *ḤMD*, as is Aḥmad] and in Greek it is *al-baraqlītis*." Ibn Isḥāq, *Sīrah*, 1:150. Alfred Guillaume has reproduced this passage from Wüstenfeld's edition but changed the vocalizations to *al-munaḥamannā* and *al-baraqlītus*. "The Version of the Gospel Used in Medina Circa 700 A.D.," *al-Andalus* 15 (1950): 291. In Guillaume's own translation of the *Sīrah* the vocalization is *Munaḥḥemana*. *Life*, 104. The confusion is evidently a lexical one whereby *paraklētos* (comforter/protector) is confused with *periklutos* (illustrious), which is then equated with *aḥmad* (highly praised). The principal Western studies of this issue are three that were published over a twenty-five-year period in *The Muslim World*: (1) L. Bevan Jones, "The Paraclete or Mohammed," *MW* 10 (1920): 112–25; (2) A. Guthrie and E.F. Bishop, "The Paraclete, Almunhamanna and Aḥmad," *MW* 41 (1951): 251–56; and (3) W. Montgomery Watt, "His Name is Aḥmad," *MW* 43 (1953): 110–17. Watt has also summarized his views on this problem in an article entitled "The Early Development of the Muslim Attitude to the Bible," *Transactions of the Glasgow University Oriental Society* 16 (1955–56): 50–62.

have enjoyed what God promised this Prophet and his *ummah* in the way of material abundance (*sa'at al-milk*)."[11]

PRECURSORY AND CONCLUSIVE REVELATION

Rashīd Riḍā's restatement serves as a fitting introduction to a second issue that commentators on this verse have sought to clarify. While the verse makes specific mention of the Torah and Gospel, it appends to these an ambiguous reference to *what was sent down to them from their Lord*. One exegetical trend has been to understand this as a circumlocutory citation of the Qur'ān. Al-Ṭabarī, for example, offers the unequivocal explanation of this phrase as "that which was sent down to them as the Proof (*al-furqān*) that Muḥammad brought them."[12] Al-Ṭūsī duplicates the use of this particular epithet but presents a second interpretive option as well. The second view, whose attribution is not given, claims a very broad referent area for this phrase. It could mean "everything that God refers to in the matters pertaining to religion."[13] This would include, of course, the Qur'ān, the Torah, the Gospel, and possibly other sacred writings.

For al-Zamakhsharī the relevant phrase means the rest of the books of God (*sā'ir kutub Allāh*) because "the faithful are obligated to believe in all of these books as if they had been sent down on them."[14] He makes no mention of the charge of scriptural alteration that is usually laid against these writings and mentions, only as an afterthought, that some say this phrase refers to the Qur'ān.

Abū al-Futūḥ Rāzī cites no other meaning for the phrase than the Qur'ān, that is, he makes no mention of other antecedent revelations either named or unnamed. However, with the inclusion of the Qur'ān, the connotation of "adherence" in the verse's initial phrase shifts. It now must include orthodoxy as well as orthopraxis. One must both "acknowledge

11 Rashīd Riḍā, *Tafsīr al-Manār,* 6:460.

12 al-Ṭabarī, *Jāmi' al-bayān*, 10:462. *Al-furqān*, one of the epithets by which the Qur'ān is sometimes known, has occasioned considerable discussion, both etymological and exegetical. See especially Wilhelm Rudolph, *Die Abhängigkeit des Korans von Judentum und Christentum* (Stuttgart: W. Kohlhammer, 1922), 39; J. Horovitz, *Koranische Untersuchungen*, 76–77; Richard Bell, *Introduction to the Qur'ān* (Edinburgh: The University Press, 1953), 136–38; and R. Paret, "Furḳān," *EI*² 2: 949–50. Jansen compares Muḥammad 'Abduh's treatment of this term with that of his classical predecessors in *Interpretation*, 21–23. After surveying and summarizing various expositions of the term, Frederick Denny comments that *furqān* "is one of those rich, distinctly Quranic (regardless of other possible Semitic antecedents and parallels), poly-interpretable terms (like *ḥanīf, ummah, īmān, islām, hudan*) which lead into the very heart of the Message, and radiate meaning and power in all directions." "The Problem of Salvation in the Quran: Key Terms and Concepts," in *Quest*, 203.

13 al-Ṭūsī, *al-Tibyān,* 3:585.

14 al-Zamakhsharī, *al-Kashshāf*, 1:658.

belief in the Qurʾān and apply its laws."[15] For Ibn al-Jawzī the phrase in question must be understood sequentially, first as "the books of the prophets of the 'Children of Israel (*Banū Isrāʾīl*)' " and then as the Qurʾān.[16] For this second identification Ibn al-Jawzī provides an interesting justification. As if to forestall any queries about the wording of this phrase, he remarks that when the Qurʾān was preached to them, that is, to those obligated by the demands of the Torah and the Gospel, "it was a 'sending down' to them."[17]

Fakhr al-Dīn al-Rāzī expresses this same twofold interpretation but without the sequential overlay. For him *what was sent down to them* may mean the Qurʾān or it may refer to "the books of the rest of the prophets."[18] Of the latter he mentions in particular the books of Isaiah, Habakkuk, and Daniel "because these books are filled with announcements of Muḥammad's coming."[19] Such an explanation is, of course, consistent with Fakhr al-Dīn al-Rāzī's emphasis upon mandated attention to scriptural attestations of the Prophet's coming, an emphasis that characterized the commentaries of al-Zamakhsharī and Rashīd Riḍā as well.

Ibn Kathīr reverses the pattern of finding multiple referents for the relevant phrase, returning to the univocal gloss of al-Ṭabarī and Abū al-Futūḥ Rāzī, that is, the Qurʾān.[20] Kāshānī, on the other hand, picks up a paraphrase from al-Zamakhsharī when he cites the signification of *what was sent down to them* as either "the Qurʾān or the rest of the heavenly books

15 Abū al-Futūḥ Rāzī, *Rawḥ al-jinān*, 4:273.

16 Ibn al-Jawzī, *Zād al-masīr*, 2:395.

17 Ibn al-Jawzī, *Zād al-masīr*, 2:395.

18 Fakhr al-Dīn al-Rāzī, *al-Tafsīr al-kabīr*, 12:47. Ibn al-ʿArabī enlarges the range of exegetical consideration beyond the appended phrase *what was sent down to them* by discussing all three scriptural categories. In a manner analogous to his treatment of the terms *those who are Jews* (*alladhīna hādū*) and *the Christians* (*al-naṣārā*) in the commentary on *sūrat al-baqarah* (2):62, he distinguishes between the respective scriptures of the two groups. Just as those designated by the phrase *those who are Jews* are "those who take things literally," so, too, their scripture, the Torah, presents a knowledge of externals and the duties inherent in daily life. In like manner the explanation of *the Christians* as "those who find hidden meanings" is linked to a characterization of the Gospel as a book concerned with an inner meaning and the duties entailed in a knowledge of the divine attributes. Ibn al-ʿArabī also draws on his exegesis of *sūrah Āl ʿImrān* (3):199 in which he referred to the scriptures of the *ahl al-kitāb* – that verse, too, contains the phrase *what was sent down to them* – as "knowledge of cosmology and eschatology (*al-mabdaʾ wa-al-maʿād*)." In his commentary on the verse under discussion, Ibn al-ʿArabī repeats this reference as a comprehensive description of both the Torah and the Gospel. Ibn al-ʿArabī, *Tafsīr al-Qurʾān al-karīm*, 1:54, 245, and 336.

19 Fakhr al-Dīn al-Rāzī, *al-Tafsīr al-kabīr*, 12:47. While Daniel is given correctly as *Dānyāl*, the names of the other two books are misprinted. The Book of Isaiah is given as *Shaʿyāʾ rather than Ashaʿyā* and *Ḥabaqqūq* is written as *Ḥayaqqūq*, i.e., a *yāʾ* is substituted for a *bāʾ*.

20 Ibn Kathīr, *Tafsīr al-Qurʾān al-ʿaẓīm*, 2:76.

(*sāyir-i kutub-i samāwī*), in which they are bound to believe just as they were bound to believe in the Torah."[21]

Rashīd Riḍā repeats the notion of multiple signification but adds further specifications and perspectives. The proper connotation for the phrase under discussion is all pre-Qur'ānic divine revelation in addition to the Torah and Gospel. This commentator mentions as examples the Psalms of David (*zabūr Dāwūd*), the Wisdom of Solomon (*ḥikam Sulaymān*), and, following Fakhr al-Dīn al-Rāzī, the books of Daniel and Isaiah (*kutub Dānyāl wa-Ashaʿyā*).[22] Ṭabāṭabā'ī, in turn, distinguishes immediately between the Torah and Gospel, as divinely revealed to Moses and Jesus respectively, and the corrupted texts bearing these titles that are now in circulation. The connection between these two scriptures and the phrase *what was sent down to them* provokes him to an interesting digression on the notion of scriptural abrogation.

The obvious meaning for the phrase, insists Ṭabāṭabā'ī, is the other prophetic books to be found among the Christians and Jews such as the *mazāmīr* (Psalms) of David, "which the Qur'ān calls *al-zabūr*."[23] To say, as some other commentators have, that this phrase may imply the Qur'ān finds no favor with this exegete. To him, such an assertion would be tantamount to denying the fact that "the Qur'ān replaces the laws of the Torah and Gospel with its own ordinances."[24] Furthermore, it makes no sense to wish that *they had adhered to* these two earlier scriptures as well as to the Qur'ān which abrogates them. To those who might argue that acting in accordance with the Qur'ān is equivalent to acting in accord with the Torah and Gospel, since the religion of God is one, Ṭabāṭabā'ī has a quick rebuttal. Such an assertion, he contends, is equivalent to saying that "acting according to the arrogating ordinances in Islam is acting according to the whole of Islam contained in both the abrogating and the abrogated together."[25]

The issue, then – though not explicitly stated as such by Ṭabāṭabā'ī – is a historical one. "Adherence to the Torah and Gospel is valid only when their two codes are not abrogated by another religious law (*sharīʿah*)."[26]

21 Kāshānī, *Minhaj al-ṣādiqīn*, 3:272. In al-Zamakhsharī's *al-Kashshāf* the phrase reads "the rest of the books of *God* (*sā'ir kutub Allāh*)."

22 Rashīd Riḍā, *Tafsīr al-Manār*, 6:460. As a Qur'ānic singular the term *zabūr* is associated solely with David. For further to this see J. Horovitz, "Zabūr," *EI*[1] 8: 1184–85, and Heinrich Speyer, *Die biblischen Erzählungen im Qoran* (1931; reprint, Hildesheim: Georg Olms, 1961), 381. J. Sadan offers a typology of *zabūr* texts in his "Some Literary Problems," 396–97.

23 Ṭabāṭabā'ī, *al-Mīzān*, 6:37.

24 Ṭabāṭabā'ī, *al-Mīzān*, 6:37.

25 Ṭabāṭabā'ī, *al-Mīzān*, 6:37.

26 Ṭabāṭabā'ī, *al-Mīzān*, 6:37–38. Fazlur Rahman allows for a more inclusive and synchronic understanding with his assertion that "man's moral maturity is condi-

Such is, of course, not the case after the revelation of the Qurʾān. As if in response to a query about the relation of the Gospel to the Torah in this matter of scriptural abrogation, Ṭabāṭabāʾī notes that "the Gospel abrogates the *sharīʿah* of the Torah only in insignificant [or few] matters (*umūr yasīrah*)."[27] He concludes this analysis of the phrase *what was sent down to them* by reaffirming that although it contains the promise of *some* revelation, it gives no indication that what is intended is the Qurʾān.

A BANQUET FOR THE FLESH OR SPIRIT

Having teased out the possible significations of the protasis of this conditional sentence, the commentators proceed, virtually in unison, to a consideration of its apodosis.[28] The structure of exegetical discourse on this verse is unusually straightforward, progressing methodically from one section to the next with very little interruption of that pattern. The resolution of the conditional raises, however, certain semantic concerns for the commentators. Put simply, is the phrase *they would have eaten from above them and from beneath their feet* to be understood literally or metaphorically?

Al-Ṭabarī favors the more literal understanding. For him the promise means that "God would have sent down on them rain from the sky and the earth would cause grains (*ḥabb*) and plants (*nabāt*) to grow up for them and fruits (*thimār*) to burst forth."[29] Among the *ḥadīth*s from Ibn ʿAbbās, Qatādah, al-Suddī, Mujāhid, and Ibn Jurayj that al-Ṭabarī quotes in support of this explanation, only one fails to coincide with his paraphrase. This one, which is attributed to Ibn ʿAbbās, could imply some sort of divinely generated nourishment. The pertinent phrase is restated as "they would eat from the sustenance (*al-rizq*) which is sent down from the heavens (*al-samāʾ*)."[30]

This commentator also feels obliged to include a much less literal understanding of this verse, one that will be found frequently among later exegetes. In this inclusion the Qurʾānic phrase under discussion is taken in the general sense of 'being amply provided for (*al-tawsiʿah*).' What must

tional upon his constantly seeking guidance from the Divine Books, especially the Qurʾān . . . ." *Major Themes,* 81.

27 Ṭabāṭabāʾī, *al-Mīzān*, 6:38.

28 Gotthelf Bergsträsser examines various forms of the Qurʾānic use of the *law-lā* construction in *Verneinungs und Fragepartikeln und Verwandtes im Ḳurʾān* (Leipzig: J.C. Hinrichs, 1914), 81. For a complete list of occurrences see ʿAmāyrah, *Muʿjam al-adawāt wa-al-ḍamāʾir*.

29 al-Ṭabarī, *Jāmiʿ al-bayān*, 10:463. Rudi Paret, while acknowledging that the commentators generally understand this phrase as a reference "to the material blessings of this life," feels that it is better explained as an allusion to "the reward in Paradise." *Kommentar und Konkordanz*, 126.

30 al-Ṭabarī, *Jāmiʿ al-bayān*, 10:464.

surely be a proverbial saying is then quoted in explanation of this more general meaning: "He is in good shape (*fī khayr*) from his crown to his feet."[31] Al-Ṭabarī remains, however, adamant in his rejection of this view and refers in strong terms to "its corruptness (*fasād*)."[32]

While al-Ṭūsī's first response to the phrase *they would have eaten from above them and from beneath their feet* agrees with al-Ṭabarī, he does not refuse to accept alternative explanations. Thus he first understands the initial clause to mean that the heavens would send forth abundant rain. In like manner the addition of *from beneath their feet* means "the goods and blessings of the earth." Then al-Ṭūsī moves on to another possibility, one that treats the prepositional phrase *from above them* in a more prosaic way. What is given *from above*, he says, could be the fruits of the date palm (*al-nakhl*) and of various other trees (*al-ashjār*); what is promised *from beneath* is a sown crop (*al-zarʿ*).[33]

Al-Ṭūsī, however, rests unsatisfied with these two explanations. He prefers to consider this whole conditional statement as an expression of regret for the opportunities lost as a result of stubborn persistence in unbelief. He paraphrases the Qurʾānic statement as follows: "If they had believed they would have held on to their homelands, their goods, and their crops and would not have been driven from their communities."[34] The exegete does not identify these victims of their own obstinacy but implies that they are the Jews, an implication founded on his charge that the hardships experienced are the consequence of saying "the hand of God is shackled" – a blasphemy attributed to the Jews in *sūrat al-māʾidah* (5):64.[35]

Although this exegete mentions the more metaphorical reading of the full phrase to which al-Ṭabarī took such grave exception, he is careful to record the latter's rejection of it. Al-Ṭūsī himself evidently feels no need to rely on the more inclusive interpretation connoted by the idea of "being amply provided for" because he sees no incongruity in the idea of God feeding the pious. "God," he maintains, "made piety (*al-tuqā*) one of the causes of sustenance (*al-rizq*)."[36] As proof of this he quotes the following Qurʾānic verses:

Whoever is devoted to God, He makes a way out for him and gives him sustenance from where he does not anticipate (*sūrat al-ṭalāq* [65]:2–3).

31 al-Ṭabarī, *Jāmiʿ al-bayān*, 10:464. Although al-Ṭabarī gives no source for this interpretation, Ibn al-Jawzī later cites it on the authority of the grammarians al-Farrāʾ and Ibrāhīm b. al-Sarī al-Zajjāj (d. 311/923). Ibn al-Jawzī, *Zād al-masīr*, 2:395.

32 al-Ṭabarī, *Jāmiʿ al-bayān*, 10:464.

33 al-Ṭūsī, *al-Tibyān*, 3:585. For a recent overview of grain production and use in seventh-century Arabia see David Waines, "Cereals, Bread and Society: An Essay on the Staff of Life in Medieval Iraq," *JESHO* 30 (1987): 263–64.

34 al-Ṭūsī, *al-Tibyān*, 3:585.

35 For al-Ṭūsī's exegesis of this earlier verse, see *al-Tibyān*, 3:579–83.

36 al-Ṭūsī, *al-Tibyān*, 3:586.

If the people of the towns had believed and been pious, We would surely have opened for them blessings from the heavens and the earth (*sūrat al-aʿrāf* [7]:96).

So I said "Beg forgiveness of your Lord: surely He is forgiving. He will send down the heavens on you as abundant rain" (*sūrah Nūḥ* [71]:10–11).

If they had stayed straight on the way, We would have given them abundant water to drink (*sūrat al-jinn* [72]:16).

Before considering the Qurʾānic apodosis for this conditional clause, al-Zamakhsharī offers his own conclusion: if they had persevered in their adherence to the above-mentioned scriptures, "then God would have sustained them generously, but instead they suffered from death."[37] No context for that last remark is provided, so it is impossible to tell what peoples and circumstances this exegete had in mind. Furthermore his subsequent treatment of the Qurʾānic conclusion is mixed. True to his Muʿtazilī leanings he first takes the statement as a metaphorical expression of a notion mentioned by both al-Ṭabarī and al-Ṭūsī, the state of being amply provided for (*al-tawsiʿah*). Yet he immediately follows this with three variations of a quite literal interpretation, proceeding from the general to the particular. First the phrase is explained as the bestowal of blessings from earth and sky; next it is read as referring to fruit-bearing trees (*al-ashjār al-muthmirah*) and crop-producing fields (*al-zurūʿ al-mughillah*).[38] Finally the statement is graphically represented as meaning that "ripe gardens will furnish them with fruit. They will harvest what hangs from the tips of trees and glean what falls to the earth *beneath their feet*."[39]

Although Abū al-Futūḥ Rāzī begins his discussion of *they would have eaten from above them and from beneath their feet* with the now-familiar notions of falling rain and sprouting plants, his fullest explanation involves taking the two prepositional phrases as an explicit trope (*majāz*).[40] From this per-

37 al-Zamakhsharī, *al-Kashshāf*, 1:658. W. Montgomery Watt has collected a number of Qurʾānic references to ecological calamities specific to the Arabian peninsula. "The Arabian Background of the Qurʾān," in *Sources for the History of Arabia: Proceedings of the First International Symposium on Studies in the History of Arabia, 1977* (Riyadh: University of Riyadh Press, 1979), 8.

38 al-Zamakhsharī, *al-Kashshāf*, 1:658. Both of these explanations draw upon *ḥadīth*s first encountered in al-Ṭabarī but used without attribution by al-Zamakhsharī.

39 al-Zamakhsharī, *al-Kashshāf*, 1:658.

40 Abū al-Futūḥ Rāzī, *Rawḥ al-jinān*, 4:273. Ibn al-ʿArabī offers a considerably more abstract understanding than that of Abū al-Futūḥ Rāzī. The nourishment is that provided on the levels of cognition which Ibn al-ʿArabī's epistemology posits. Therefore, *they would have eaten from above them* means, for this exegete, partaking of "divine intellections (*al-ʿulūm al-ilāhīyah*), assured, rational truths (*al-ḥaqāʾiq al-ʿaqlīyah al-yaqīnīyah*), and authentic information (*al-maʿārif al-ḥaqqānīyah*)." All of this would guide the recipients to knowledge of God, of His sovereignty and of His omnipotence. The nourishment that would be received *from beneath their feet* is that of another epistemological order. It is natural knowledge, acquired through sense cognition of the material

spective, one that echoes al-Ṭūsī, the entire conditional sentence can be expressed as follows: "If they had believed, such would have been their situation that they would not have had to leave their houses and dwellings; they would have stayed in their houses and sustenance would have come to them from all four quarters."[41]

As additional support for this view Abū al-Futūḥ Rāzī cites the Qur'ānic parallel "its sustenance came in abundance from every place" (*sūrat al-naḥl* [16]:112). The whole purpose of the revelation under discussion, according to Abū al-Futūḥ Rāzī, is to incite a sense of sorrow and regret among those who lacked the requisite faith and good deeds. To emphasize this further he quotes three of the four passages already brought forward by al-Ṭūsī: *sūrat al-aʿrāf* (7):96, *sūrat al-ṭalāq* (65):2–3, and *sūrat al-jinn* (72): 16.[42] Ibn al-Jawzī then repeats the reference to the first two of these Qur'ānic parallels to support his assertion that piety (*al-taqwā*) provokes divine generosity.[43]

The most novel departure that Fakhr al-Dīn al-Rāzī makes in his treatment of this verse is to pose a contextual claim, to view the verse as the second part of a pair of divine explanations: "Insofar as God explained in the first verse [5:65] that if they had believed, they would have obtained happiness in the Hereafter, He explained in this verse that if they had believed they would have obtained happiness in the world and procured its pleasures and goods."[44] Fakhr al-Dīn al-Rāzī then begins his discussion of the earthly recompense promised in *they would have eaten from above them and from beneath their feet* by noting the circumstances that provoked it. The Jews, he maintains, brought a variety of afflictions, including drought, on themselves for their persistence in calling Muḥammad a liar. They even dared to blaspheme the Almighty by saying, as recorded in a near proceeding verse, "the hand of God is shackled" (*sūrat al-mā'idah* [5]:64). Therefore God explained in this verse that had they abandoned such be-

world. Through this the recipients would be guided to a knowledge "of God by His name, both the outward (*al-ẓāhir*) and the inner (*al-bāṭin*)." In fact, by such a means would they come to a realization of all the divine names (*al-asmā'*) and attributes (*al-ṣifāt*), what one might call the creative manifestations of the divine oneness. Ibn al-ʿArabī, *Tafsīr al-Qur'ān al-karīm*, 1:336. Ignaz Goldziher has presented part of Ibn al-ʿArabī's commentary on this verse as a prime example of Ṣūfī *tafsīr*. His translation of the concluding remark on *la-akalū min fawqihim wa-min taḥti arjulihim* is as follows: "So würden sie demnach Gott erkennen mit seinen äusserlichen und innerlichen Namen, ja mit allen seinen Namen und Attributen und dadurch die Stufe beider Arten des Einheitsbekenntnisses (nämlich des äusserlichen und des mystischen) erreichen." *Die Richtungen*, 231.

41 Abū al-Futūḥ Rāzī, *Rawḥ al-jinān*, 4:273.

42 Abū al-Futūḥ Rāzī, *Rawḥ al-jinān*, 4:273.

43 Ibn al-Jawzī, *Zād al-masīr*, 2:395.

44 Fakhr al-Dīn al-Rāzī, *al-Tafsīr al-kabīr*, 12:46.

havior, their misfortunes would have been reversed and fertility (*khiṣb*) and abundance (*saʿah*) would have been their lot.[45] Fakhr al-Dīn al-Rāzī then proceeds to catalogue the principal interpretations of this phrase.

He begins where most others have ended, with the more metaphorical explanation. The issue, Fakhr al-Dīn al-Rāzī insists, is not one of precise location – it is not a matter of an actual "above" or "below" – but of general abundance: "The meaning of the Qurʾānic statement is food in continuous, large quantities."[46] From there Fakhr al-Dīn al-Rāzī cites both the proverbial expression noted by al-Ṭabarī and Ibn al-Jawzī as well as the parallel from *sūrat al-aʿrāf* (7):96 before concluding with an unacknowledged verbatim quotation from al-Zamakhsharī: "Ripe gardens will furnish them with fruit. They will harvest what hangs from the tips of trees and glean what falls to the earth *beneath their feet*."[47]

In conclusion, he returns to the subject of the possible Jewish provocation of this revelation. This time, however, he is more specific, naming two Jewish tribes, the Banū Qurayẓah and the Banū al-Naḍīr. Without giving any background information, Fakhr al-Dīn al-Rāzī wonders whether this verse is an allusion to what happened to these two groups in terms of "their date palms being cut down, their crops spoiled, and their own forced eviction from their native territories."[48] (According to traditional historians, what Fakhr al-Dīn al-Rāzī has described is, in fact, the fate actually suffered only by the Banū al-Naḍīr; the Banū Qurayẓah, on the other hand, were subject to far harsher repercussions for their treachery. On the advice of an arbitrator, Muḥammad ordered the men of this tribe to be executed and the women and children sold into slavery.)[49]

Ibn Kathīr includes in his *Tafsīr al-Qurʾān al-ʿaẓīm* the commonly as-

45 Fakhr al-Dīn al-Rāzī, *al-Tafsīr al-kabīr*, 12:47. Although *khiṣb* is not itself a Qurʾānic term, this promise of fertility and abundance echoes the frequent Qurʾānic mention of wealth (*māl, amwāl*) and sons (*banūn, awlād*), e.g., *sūrah Āl ʿImrān* (3):24, *sūrat al-tawbah* (9):69, *sūrah Banī Isrāʾīl* (17):6, and *sūrat al-kahf* (18):46.

46 Fakhr al-Dīn al-Rāzī, *al-Tafsīr al-kabīr*, 12:47.

47 Fakhr al-Dīn al-Rāzī, *al-Tafsīr al-kabīr*, 12:47. Al-Rāzī's dependence upon al-Zamakhsharī has been frequently noted but never thoroughly investigated. A.H. Johns has collected some examples in his article "Solomon and the Queen of Sheba: Fakhr al-Dīn al-Rāzī's Treatment of the Qurʾānic Telling of the Story," *Abr-Nahrain* 24 (1986): 82 note 35.

48 Fakhr al-Dīn al-Rāzī, *al-Tafsīr al-kabīr*, 12:47.

49 A narrative description of these events may be found in Lings's *Muḥammad*, Chapters 57 and 59. W. Montgomery Watt has made a detailed study of the various accounts of the punishment of the Banū Qurayẓah. "The Condemnation of the Jews of Banū Qurayẓah: A Study in the Sources of the *Sīrah*," *MW* 42 (1952): 160–71. The most recent and comprehensive study is that by M. J. Kister, "The Massacre of the Banū Qurayẓa: A Re-examination of a Tradition," *JSAI* 8 (1986): 61–96. For a critical assessment of recent scholarship on this event see Gordon Newby, *A History of the Jews of Arabia* (Columbia, S.C.: University of South Carolina Press, 1988), 90–93.

cribed meanings for the verse section under discussion, citing Qurʾānic parallels, relevant *ḥadīth*s on the authority of Ibn ʿAbbās, Mujāhid, Saʿīd b. Jubayr (d. 95/714), Qatādah, and al-Suddī as well as the familiar proverbial expression, here attributed to Ibn Jurayj. What is new with him is the incorporation of a notion that echoes the prelapsarian period depicted in Genesis: "Some say the meaning of *they would have eaten from above them and from beneath their feet* is without labor (*kadd*), fatigue (*taʿab*), drudgery (*shaqāʾ*), or pains (*ʿanāʾ*)."[50] He also mentions the most metaphorical interpretation but, like al-Ṭabarī, immediately denies it any validity.

Ibn Kathīr's most notable contribution to the exegetical development of this verse is his inclusion of a Prophetic *ḥadīth* from a variety of sources, including Ibn Ḥanbal and Wakīʿ b. Jarrāḥ (d. 129/746), which gives the background or "occasion" for this revelation (*sabab al-nuzūl*). A composite account opens with Muḥammad's lament for the possible loss of religious knowledge. Ziyād b. Labīd, one of the Medinan 'helpers (*anṣār*)', countered with the objection that such a thing could never happen. How could it, he exclaims, since "we recite the Qurʾān and we recite it to our sons and our sons will recite it to their sons until the Day of Resurrection?" Muḥammad retorted: "May you be bereaved of your mother, O Ibn Labīd! Surely you are one of the most intelligent men in Medina! Did not those Jews and Christians recite the Torah and Gospel? Yet they profited not at all from what is in the two!"[51] Muḥammad then began the recitation of this verse: *If they had adhered to the Torah and the Gospel*, and so on.

While the sixteenth-century commentator, Kāshānī, adds nothing to the established lines of interpretation on this phrase, the twentieth-century exegetes, Rashīd Riḍā and Ṭabāṭabāʾī, move this apodosis far beyond such conventional understandings. In the view of Rashīd Riḍā, had those addressed by earlier revelation been faithful to it, two consequences would have followed, one material and the other spiritual. They would have escaped the tyranny (*al-ṭughyān*) and the corruption (*al-fasād*) to which historians attest. More importantly, "they would not have opposed the foretold Prophet with such obstinacy."[52] Then, in a sweeping denunciation, Rashīd Riḍā characterizes the religion of the group intended by this Qurʾānic verse as manifesting but a wished-for sense of security, innovations (*bidaʿ*), and inherited postures of uncritical acceptance. Its adherents swing between the extremes of exaggeration and shortcoming (*ghulūw wa-taqṣīr*) and of excess and negligence (*ifrāṭ wa-tafrīṭ*).[53]

50 Ibn Kathīr, *Tafsīr al-Qurʾān al-ʿaẓīm*, 2:76.
51 Ibn Kathīr, *Tafsīr al-Qurʾān al-ʿaẓīm*, 2:76.
52 Rashīd Riḍā, *Tafsīr al-Manār*, 6:460.
53 Rashīd Riḍā, *Tafsīr al-Manār*, 6:460.

In addition to noting some of the standard Qurʾānic parallels, Rashīd Riḍā draws upon two versions of the *ḥadīth* introduced by Ibn Kathīr to stress a point emphasized by many previous commentators, the importance of acting upon the precepts of divine revelation. He examines more closely than did Ibn Kathīr the authenticity of this particular tradition, yet affirms that despite its possible inadequacies, the message it conveys is significant.[54] Moreover, Rashīd Riḍā adduces a further historical consideration. He maintains that in the era of Qurʾānic revelation, the *ahl al-kitāb* had wandered far from the authentic guidance of their religion, their nominal adherence to it being largely the result of intense racial solidarity (*shiddah ʿaṣabīyatihim al-jinsīyah*). This same sociological phenomenon Rashīd Riḍā sees operative among his contemporary coreligionists, while admitting that in many cases racial solidarity has been transmuted into linguistic or nationalistic commonality.[55]

Ignoring the colorful interpretations proposed by some previous commentators, Muḥammad Ḥusayn Ṭabāṭabāʾī views this phrase as a metonymy (*kināyah*) expressing the material blessings that would have redounded to those faithful to divine revelation. As such it provides yet another indication of the connection between human behavior and the right order of the universe (*al-niẓām al-kawnī*).[56] Ṭabāṭabāʾī's understanding of this correspondence is expressed as a conditional: if humankind were good, "then the order of the world would be good insofar as the things necessary for happy human life would be freely available, afflictions would be surmountable and blessings would be abundant."[57]

To conclude his analysis of this phrase, Ṭabāṭabāʾī draws the reader's attention to several other Qurʾānic verses that indirectly reinforce the interrelation just described. Among them are such as: "Corruption has become manifest on land and sea because of what the hands of men have gained . . . ." (*sūrat al-Rūm* [30]:41) and "whatever disaster afflicts you is because of what your hands have gained . . . ." (*sūrat al-shūrā* [42]:30). These, too, he feels can be interpreted in the same spirit with which he reads the phrase under consideration.

54 Rashīd Riḍā cites al-Suyūṭī's *al-Durr al-manthūr* as his textual source. *Tafsīr al-Manār*, 6:462.

55 Rashīd Riḍā, *Tafsīr al-Manār*, 6:462. Analysis of the emergent ideology of nationalism in the nineteenth- and twentieth-century Muslim world has generated a substantial bibliography. A good entrée is provided by William Cleveland's study of Rashīd Riḍā's contemporary and friend, Shakib Arslan (d. 1946). *Islam Against the West: Shakib Arslan and the Campaign for Islamic Nationalism* (Austin: University of Texas Press, 1985).

56 Ṭabāṭabāʾī, *al-Mīzān*, 6:38.

57 Ṭabāṭabāʾī, *al-Mīzān*, 6:38.

THE PRAISEWORTHY FEW

As this verse draws to its conclusion, the general condemnation conveyed by the conditional clause and its resolution is tempered. A penultimate exemption interrupts the tone of censure. Not all must fall liable to this verse's judgment, for *among them is a balanced people (minhum ummatun muqtaṣidatun).* Yet a swift rejoinder mutes the approbation. While there may be some who deserve the divine compliment, *many of them are evildoers.*

Al-Ṭabarī understands this phrase in specifically Christian terms. What is *balanced* about this community is their "opinion about Jesus, son of Mary, [their] speaking the truth about him, that he is the messenger of God and His word which was cast into Mary and a spirit from Him, neither exaggerating – saying that he is the son of God (May God be exalted over such speech) nor diminishing – saying that he is not lawfully born."[58] This statement encapsulates, in shorthand form, the principal aspects of Muslim-Christian theological controversy about Jesus.

The early authorities whom al-Ṭabarī cites offer explanatory substitutions for the phrase *a balanced people.* Al-Suddī uses the adjective "believing" while Mujāhid presents a phrase that was also associated with his name in the exegesis of *sūrah Āl ʿImrān* (3):199: the *maslamah* of the *ahl al-kitāb.* Qatādah and Ibn Zayd, on the other hand, define this group more generally as those who live "in accord with God's book and His command" or those "obedient to God." Perhaps the most interesting *ḥadīth*, however, is that on the authority of al-Rabīʿ b. Anas. He reiterates al-Ṭabarī's concerns about doctrinal exaggeration by defining this group in terms of religious balance: "They are those who neither ignore matters of religion nor exceed the proper bounds in them."[59]

Those who share such theological balance are but a part of the *ahl al-kitāb*, and not a very large part at that, as the concluding phrase of this verse makes clear. In fact, an interpretation offered on the authority of Qatādah makes this explicit by using the superlative form "most of the people (*akthar al-qawm*)" to gloss this final statement.[60] With the words *many of them are evildoers* al-Ṭabarī broadens his range beyond exclusively Christian considerations to catalogue the offenses of both Christians and Jews. His charges against the *ahl al-kitāb* are four (although he makes no claim to an exhaustive list): (1) they do not believe in God, (2) the Christians lie about Muḥammad, (3) the Christians claim that the Messiah is the son of God, and (4) the Jews lie about both Jesus and Muḥammad.[61]

58 al-Ṭabarī, *Jāmiʿ al-bayān*, 10:465.
59 al-Ṭabarī, *Jāmiʿ al-bayān*, 10:466.
60 al-Ṭabarī, *Jāmiʿ al-bayān*, 10:466.
61 al-Ṭabarī, *Jāmiʿ al-bayān*, 10:465.

It is for these reasons, says al-Ṭabarī, that they are appropriate candidates for this divine rebuke.

The notion of balance is repeated by al-Ṭūsī who expands *among them is a balanced people* to mean "among these unbelievers is a people moderate in behavior (*qawmun muʿtadilun fī al-ʿamal*) with neither exaggeration (*ghulūw*) nor shortcoming (*taqṣīr*)."[62] Quoting a source identified only as Abū ʿAlī, al-Ṭūsī then equates such religious moderation with becoming a Muslim and following the Prophet.[63] While this commentator ventures the possibility that "it means those who affirmed that the Messiah is the servant of God and claim for him neither divinity nor sonship," his real contribution is to offer more specific referents.[64] The first designated identification is the Najāshī and his associates. Then, on the authority of al-Zajjāj, he equates this *balanced people* with a people whose opposition to the Prophet was mild or, at least, less aggressive than that of other groups. Having cited this possibility, al-Ṭūsī quickly discards it and states unequivocally that the identification with the Najāshī is to be preferred on the grounds that "God would not permit an aggressor [of any sort] to be called 'balanced (*muqtaṣid*).' "[65] He repeats this stress on the necessary acceptance of Muḥammad by summarily describing the "evil deeds" of the verse's final phrase as obstinate persistence in disbelief and rejection of the Prophet. He, too, elevates the idea of "many" to that of "most": "Most of these Jews and Christians perform evil deeds."[66]

Al-Zamakhsharī evidently does not share al-Ṭūsī's qualms about identifying the *balanced people* as a group whose opposition to the Prophet is inconsequential. He rephrases the expression as "the believing group (*al-ṭāʾifah al-muʾminah*)" and specifies its members as "ʿAbdallāh b. Salām and his associates and forty-eight Christians."[67] This commentator characterizes

62 al-Ṭūsī, *al-Tibyān*, 3:586.

63 al-Ṭūsī, *al-Tibyān*, 3:586. A likely identification would be ʿAbd al-Wahhāb al-Jubbāʾī, the renowned Baṣrah Muʿtazilī to whom several works on the Qurʾān are credited. See Brockelmann, *GAL*, S1: 342; L. Gardet, "al-Djubbāʾī," *EI*² 2: 569–70; and Daniel Gimaret, "Matériaux pour une bibliographie de Jubbāʾī," *JA* 257 (1976): 277–332. Al-Jubbāʾī's subsequent influence is explored in Richard Martin, "The Role of the Basrah Muʿtazilah in Formulating the Doctrine of the Apologetic Miracle," *JNES* 39 (1980): 175–89; and Rosalind Gwynne, "Al-Jubbāʾī, al-Ashʿarī and the Three Brothers: The Uses of Fiction," *MW* 75 (1985): 132–61. Another possible identification is Abū ʿAlī al-Ḥasan b. ʿAlī al-Fārisī, a noted grammarian who died in Baghdād in 377/987. He was a student of al-Zajjāj, among others, and wrote a commentary on al-Zajjāj's *Maʿānī al-Qurʾān*. C. Rabin, "al-Fārisī," *EI*² 2: 802–03.

64 al-Ṭūsī, *al-Tibyān*, 3:586.

65 al-Ṭūsī, *al-Tibyān*, 3:586. To his commentary on this verse al-Ṭūsī appends a brief etymological *excursus* on the term *muqtaṣid*, defining the *maṣdar, iqtiṣād* as "evenness (*istiwāʾ*) in action leading to a goal."

66 al-Ṭūsī, *al-Tibyān*, 3:586–87.

67 al-Zamakhsharī, *al-Kashshāf*, 1:658.

the final phrase of the verse as an exclamation that draws attention to the perversity of the unbelievers. He cites but one identification theory for the statement: the evildoers are "Kaᶜb b. al-Ashraf and his associates, and the Byzantines (*al-Rūm*)."[68]

His Shīᶜī predecessor, al-Ṭūsī, is clearly the source for much of what Abū al-Futūḥ Rāzī notes about this phrase. For the adjective 'balanced (*muqtaṣidah*)' he, too, stresses the root etymological sense of undeviating moderation. The notion that those intended are a group of the *ahl al-kitāb* who believed in the Prophet is credited to the same Abū ᶜAlī. But here, Abū al-Futūḥ Rāzī adds a cautionary remark drawn from a contextual awareness: he questions how a people who have been castigated in the preceding verses can now be identified as those found praiseworthy in this one.[69]

He then notes that some have attributed the revelation of this verse to the circumstances surrounding the Najāshī and his people while others have maintained that it refers to "a people who neither dispute with the Prophet nor show open enmity to him (*bā rasūl mubāḥasah va iẓhār-i ᶜadāvat nakardand*)."[70] The final view offered, and the one that this commentator finds most satisfactory, is that attributed to Mujāhid: those intended are the "newly-converted (*musalmānān*)" of the *ahl al-kitāb*.[71] Abū al-Futūḥ Rāzī's interest in the final phrase of this verse fastened upon the distinction thereby drawn. What God wishes to remind us of, he notes, is that not all of those described in the verse are liable to the same judgment: "Some of them are good but many are bad."[72]

Ibn al-Jawzī does not expand the discussion on *a balanced people* and, in fact, passes over the verse's concluding phrase without any comment. Such is not the case with Fakhr al-Dīn al-Rāzī. After explaining the particular sense of the term *muqtaṣidah*, this commentator proposes two possibilities for the phrase that contains it. Interestingly enough, they are direct contradictions of each other. He first suggests that it means the "believers" within the *ahl al-kitāb*. Following the line of al-Zamakhsharī he proposes

68 al-Zamakhsharī, *al-Kashshāf*, 1:658. Kaᶜb b. al-Ashraf, whose mother belonged to the Jewish clan of Banū al-Naḍīr, was an opponent of Muḥammad's in Medina. His efforts in Mecca to arouse hostility against the Muslims among the Quraysh resulted in his murder by a group loyal to the Prophet. See W. Montgomery Watt's "Kaᶜb b. al-Ashraf," *EI*^{2} 4:315 and Ibn Isḥāq's *Sīrah*, 1:548–53 (Guillaume, *Life*, 364–69). A. J. Wensinck has critically analyzed the relevant sources in *Muhammad and the Jews of Medina*, 111–12.

69 Abū al-Futūḥ Rāzī, *Rawḥ al-jinān*, 4:273.

70 Abū al-Futūḥ Rāzī, *Rawḥ al-jinān*, 4:274.

71 Abū al-Futūḥ Rāzī, *Rawḥ al-jinān*, 4:274. The Arabic word usually found associated with this statement by Mujāhid is *maslamah*.

72 Abū al-Futūḥ Rāzī, *Rawḥ al-jinān*, 4:274.

ᶜAbdallāh b. Salām among the Jews as referent and (in concert with the Shīᶜī commentators, al-Ṭūsī and Abū al-Futūḥ Rāzī) the Najāshī among the Christians. Joining etymology and identification he characterizes both as proceeding on the right course (*ᶜalā al-qaṣd*) and along the straight path (*ᶜalā al-manhaj al-mustaqīm*) of their religion. They are liable to neither the extremes of excess (*al-ifrāṭ*) nor those of neglect (*al-tafrīṭ*).[73]

Fakhr al-Dīn al-Rāzī's second suggestion is that the reference is to the "unbelievers (*kuffār*)" of the *ahl al-kitāb* who are "just (*ᶜudūl*) within their own religion. They possess neither relentless obstinacy (*ᶜinād shadīd*) nor total ruthlessness (*ghilẓah kāmilah*)."[74] While this echoes a possibility mentioned by both al-Ṭūsī and al-Zamakhsharī, Fakhr al-Dīn al-Rāzī specifies the referent no further and gives no names of representative members of this category. His only elaboration is a Qurʾānic citation by which he seeks to describe further those just designated: "Among the *ahl al-kitāb* is one who, if you entrust him with great wealth, will give it back to you" (*sūrah Āl ᶜImrān* [3]:74).

Fakhr al-Dīn al-Rāzī's most notable contribution to the exegesis of this verse's concluding phrase is the specificities that he includes. The point of *but many of them are evildoers* is that "among them are boorish people (*ajlāf*), blameworthy and detestable, on whom reasoned demonstration (*al-dalīl*) leaves no trace and on whom teaching (*al-qawl*) has no useful effect."[75]

73 Fakhr al-Dīn al-Rāzī, *al-Tafsīr al-kabīr*, 12:47.

74 Fakhr al-Dīn al-Rāzī, *al-Tafsīr al-kabīr*, 12:47.

75 Fakhr al-Dīn al-Rāzī, *al-Tafsīr al-kabīr*, 12:47–48. This emphasis on intellectual receptivity is carried even further by Ibn al-ᶜArabī. His thoughts constitute a parenthetical insertion in the general exegetical pattern on the concluding phrases of this verse. Consonant with his understanding of the verse's earlier phrases, Ibn al-ᶜArabī distinguishes the *balanced people* and differentiates them from the evil majority by their level of cognition. They are "the ones who attain to the *tawḥīd* of names and attributes." For Ibn al-ᶜArabī this is a distinct level of spiritual development. Antecedent to it – as his explanation of the concluding phrase makes clear – is the stage of "one who attains to the *tawḥīd* of actions (*al-afᶜāl*)." Knowledge of God, then, begins on the plane of natural creation and history, which are the effects of God's creative activity in the world. Recognition of these divine actions leads to acknowledgment of the divine attributes from which they proceed. This is the level reached by one "who attains to the *tawḥīd* of the names and attributes" and the reward promised to "those who would eat from beneath their feet." Beyond stretches the final stage of cognition and spiritual development, that of "those who eat from above them." This is the point at which the religious seeker, nourished by divine intellections and assured truths, is propelled to a realization of the divine essence in all of its sovereignty and omnipotence. Ibn al-ᶜArabī, *Tafsīr al-Qurᶜān al-karīm*, 1:336.

In his commentary on *sūrat al-māʾidah* (5):70 Ibn al-ʾArabī relates this hierarchy of spiritual realizations to the three major prophets, Moses, Jesus, and Muḥammad. Moses was sent "to raise the veil of deeds (*ḥijāb al-afᶜāl*)" so that the divine actions would be disclosed. God then sent Jesus to raise the "veil of attributes (*ḥijāb al-ṣifāt*)" so that a more profound knowledge of the divine would be accessible. But it was not until the

A hierarchy figures in Ibn Kathīr's exegesis of these final phrases as well. He cites corresponding Qur'ānic verses as further specification of those described as *a balanced people*. The first, *sūrat al-aʿrāf* (7):159, refers particularly to the Jews: "Among the people of Moses is a community (*ummah*) who guide by the truth and who justly act upon it." The followers of Jesus are intended in *sūrat al-ḥadīd* (57):27, from which this edition of *Tafsīr al-Qur'ān al-ʿaẓīm* quotes the phrase "so we gave those of them who believed their reward."[76] But Ibn Kathīr builds his central argument around a verse, *sūrat al-malā'ikah* (35):32, that holds another Qur'ānic use of the term *muqtaṣid*.

The verse is interesting not only for its lexical parallel but because it postulates three ascending categories of "those to whom We bequeathed the book." While the middle position is occupied by the individual who is *muqtaṣid*, such a one is outranked by the person "who excels in good deeds." Reading the use of *muqtaṣid* in 5:66 and 35:32 together clearly mutes the complimentary force of the former. The divine praise here translated as *balanced* does not hold top position in Ibn Kathīr's spiritual hierarchy. Where other commentators have chosen to read this as a mark of religious maturity, by intra-Qur'ānic exegesis Ibn Kathīr has decided to see it as but an intermediary step on the road to a fully developed spiritual sensitivity.

Analogous religious grouping figures in the *ḥadīth* from Anas b. Mālik with which this commentator expands his explanation. The *ḥadīth* describes the relation between wayward Jewish and Christian groups and those who remain faithful to divine revelation: "The Messenger of God said: 'The community of Moses is split into seventy-one sects (*millah*), seventy of them are in the Fire and one in the Garden. The people of Jesus are split into seventy-two sects; one is in the Garden and seventy-one in the Fire. My community completely supersedes both: one is in the Garden and seventy-two in the Fire.' "[77] The notion of one enduring divine revelation of which

sending of Muḥammad that humankind was summoned to affirm the oneness of the divine essence (*tawḥīd al-dhāt*) which is absolute unity. Ibn al-ʿArabī further notes that at each level those addressed by the new revelation must be jarred from their sense of spiritual complacency. *Tafsīr al-Qur'ān al-karīm*, 1:336–37.

76 Ibn Kathīr, *Tafsīr al-Qur'ān al-ʿaẓīm*, 2:76. *Sūrat al-ḥadīd* (57):27 will be the subject of Chapter 9.

77 Ibn Kathīr, *Tafsīr al-Qur'ān al-ʿaẓīm*, 2:77. The connection of this *ḥadīth* with the verse under discussion is made by Ibn Kathīr on the authority of the Prophet's son-in-law, ʿAlī b. Abī Ṭālib, as transmitted by Yaʿqūb b. Zayd al-Ḥaḍramī (d. 205/821). Ignaz Goldziher contends that this *ḥadīth* and its variants, which became the structural basis for Muslim heresiographical literature, are based on the mistaken understanding of an earlier reference to the multiple doctrines and precepts that together constitute the religion of Islam. "Le dénombrement des sectes mohamétanes," *Gesammelte Schriften*,

Islam is but the last and final manifestation could scarcely be more graphically portrayed.

In discussing the phrase *among them is a balanced people* Kāshānī first announces that *them* means "the Jews" and presents the usual explanation for the adjective. He stipulates precisely what is required to negotiate the narrow path between religious exaggeration and neglect: belief in the Prophet. Then, however, he contradicts his first claim by proposing that the Najāshī and his companions may have been the occasion for this revelation. He makes no effort to explain the contradiction, but simply closes his discussion of this phrase by citing another now-familiar exegetical possibility, that the *balanced people* are those of only moderate hostility to Muḥammad.

While the concluding phrase affords Kāshānī the opportunity for further castigation of those who deny Muḥammad's claim to prophecy, he stresses the contextual sense of the remark. Following upon a promise of blessings that would have been theirs, this statement is more an expression of regret than a rebuke. Those who cannot be reckoned among the *balanced people* are urged to lament their very real losses and repent of such blasphemies as saying that "the hand of God is shackled" (5:64). To accentuate further the promise that piety is divinely rewarded, Kāshānī, like al-Ṭūsī and Abū al-Futūḥ Rāzī, draws upon such Qur'ānic parallels as *sūrat al-jinn* (72):16 and *sūrat al-ṭalāq* (65):2–3.

Rashīd Riḍā repeats a number of these emphases but from a decidedly new and broader perspective. The term *balanced people* refers to what he perceives to be a key entity in a religion's development and preservation. Using the same adjectival synonym offered by al-Ṭūsī (*muʿtadil*), Rashīd Riḍā suggests that those who have exhibited such religious moderation are the Muslim converts from the *ahl al-kitāb*. Having succumbed to neither religious excess nor negligence they can be properly receptive to the teaching of the Prophet. By staying on the straight path and not withdrawing from communal life, this group acts as a kind of leaven in the community. Their presence tips the balance of piety and sinfulness in favor of the former. Without them a religious association would cease to exist. "For how," asks Rashīd Riḍā rhetorically, "do communities perish except by the great number of those who do evil things and the paucity of those who do good?"[78]

ed. by Joseph Desomogyi (Hidlesheim: Georg Olms, 1968), 2:406–14. Arthur Jeffery cites several Talmudic sources for the predictive use of the number seventy. In a note to this he records the biblical basis: "From a calculation of the progeny of Noah as detailed in Genesis X it was held that there were seventy-two (or seventy) different nations and consequently seventy-two (or seventy) languages." *The Qur'ān as Scripture*, 42.

78 Rashīd Riḍā, *Tafsīr al-Manār*, 6:461.

Not only are the *balanced people* praised for their receptivity to the Prophet's teaching, they are also acknowledged for their role in Islamic intellectual development: "They were, together with their Arab brothers, among the renewers of monotheistic affirmation (*al-tawḥīd*), moral excellence (*al-faḍāʾil*) and ethical decency (*al-ādāb*), and among the vivifiers of the various areas of knowledge (*al-ʿulūm*), the scientific disciplines (*al-funūn*), and civilization (*al-ʿumrān*)."[79] Rashīd Riḍā then directs a question to the Muslims of his time, asking if they are now behaving as a *balanced people*. Are they acting in accordance with the Qurʾān or have they abandoned themselves to sinful behavior? Are they liable to the charges of "religious pride (*al-ghurūr bi-dīnihim*) despite non-adherence to its book [the Qurʾān] while boasting about the superior qualities of their Prophet yet neglecting his *sunnah* and *ādāb*?"[80]

Rashīd Riḍā concludes his exegesis of this verse by observing what a compelling proof is therein exhibited for the divine origin of the Qurʾān. In no book of human authorship, he insists, would one find such witness to the virtues of an adversary as in this verse's praise of some of the *ahl al-kitāb*. "Man, however virtuous and upright he is, simply does not see the virtue hidden in adversaries who are hostile and belligerent to him, nor does he testify to it."[81] In fact, continues Rashīd Riḍā, if he does see any merit in his enemy he discounts it as but hypocrisy and deception. To reinforce this observation Rashīd Riḍā draws upon a remark made to Muḥammad ʿAbduh by an unnamed Swiss woman of "great intellect, learning and age."[82] She is reported to have said to him: "Before I knew you, I did not think there was holiness to be found in other than Christians (*al-masīḥīyūn*)."[83] Describing her as a woman well-versed in psychology (*al-ʿilm bi-akhlāq al-bashar*) and the author of several books on child development, this exegete then notes the contrast she presents to one such as Muḥammad. If she, despite her obvious education and the cultural advantage of living in the historically aware twentieth century, could make such a statement, then how does anyone "think that an unlettered man in the Ḥijāz could be guided to this truth about these people [the *ahl al-kitāb*] thirteen centuries ago, without the revelation of God?"[84]

79 Rashīd Riḍā, *Tafsīr al-Manār*, 6:461.
80 Rashīd Riḍā, *Tafsīr al-Manār*, 6:461.
81 Rashīd Riḍā, *Tafsīr al-Manār*, 6:462.
82 Rashīd Riḍā, *Tafsīr al-Manār*, 6:463. Rashīd Riḍā's reference here supports the suggestion that Western influence on modern Qurʾānic *tafsīr*s "seems mainly to come from indirect sources. It is almost impossible to trace back the exact source of the knowledge of Western ideas, and this has caused some observers to think that these sources might sometimes have been oral." Jansen, *Interpretation*, 7.
83 Rashīd Riḍā, *Tafsīr al-Manār*, 6:463.
84 Rashīd Riḍā, *Tafsīr al-Manār*, 6:463.

The final section of this verse is for Ṭabāṭabāʾī, too, a particularly apt example of divine fair-mindedness. Despite the fact that hostile disbelief is the prevalent response of those addressed in this verse, there exists a "straight-acting people (*ummah muᶜtadilah*) who cannot be so described."[85] God, from whom no truth – however slight – can escape, has seen fit to include mention of this group as a matter of divine justice. To prove just how exceptional the mention of the *balanced people* is, Ṭabāṭabāʾī notes several Qurʾānic condemnations of the unbelievers that contain no such qualification. Those included are *sūrat al-māʾidah* (5):59, 62, and 64, verses that closely precede the one under discussion.

While Ṭabāṭabāʾī repeats Ibn Kathīr's use of relevant *ḥadīth*s from Anas b. Mālik and Yaᶜqūb b. Zayd, he prefaces these with one from Abū al-Ṣahbāʾ al-Kubrā, taken from the *tafsīr* of al-ᶜAyyāshī, which recounts an incident from the life of ᶜAlī b. Abī Ṭālib. In this episode ᶜAlī confronts an unnamed Christian bishop, and after a prolonged adjuration, asks him truthfully to state the extent to which "the Banū Isrāʾīl became divided after the death of Jesus."[86] When the bishop responds that there was no division of any kind, ᶜAlī rebukes him for lying and insists that, in fact, the Banū Isrāʾīl had divided into seventy-two groups, "all of them in the Fire but one." That protected remnant is, of course, the *balanced people.*

CONCLUSION

In its initial concerns, this verse presents another facet of the Muslim preoccupation with pre-Qurʾānic revelation. Rather than the denunciation of Christian and Jewish scriptural distortion recorded in the previous chapter, here can be found attestation to the at-least partial truth and value that the Torah and Gospel may contain. While mention is made of the discrepancy between these scriptures as originally revealed and their later deliberate or inadvertent alteration, the exegetical tradition on this verse indirectly acknowledges the partial veracity of such earlier disclosures. A commendable orthopraxis can be distilled from their contents. Exegetical testimony to this possibility is mandated by the syntax of this verse. Cast as a conditional sentence, the logic of divine promise contained herein demands that the protasis be at least theoretically capable of fulfillment. The penultimate reference to a *balanced people* reinforces the hermeneutical need to construe some aspects of antecedent revelation as authentic.

The chronological sequence of commentaries here discussed bears witness to a further refinement within that general notion of authenticity. The understanding of what may be salvaged from the scriptures of the Christians

85 Ṭabāṭabāʾī, *al-Mīzān*, 6:39.
86 Ṭabāṭabāʾī, *al-Mīzān*, 6:41.

and Jews shifts somewhat. An earlier exegetical sense that such scriptures contained ethical norms worthy of adherence, that a form of religious orthopraxis could be extracted from their contents, is modified and given a more precise specification. What comes to the fore in later commentaries is a stress upon the prefiguring description of Muḥammad that these earlier Christian and Jewish scriptures are thought to contain. As the Muslim-Christian theological polemic develops, the Muslim charge of scriptural alteration or corruption had to be balanced against the assertion that there had indeed been sufficient intimation of the Prophet's advent in the revelation that preceded the Qurʾān. The exegetical history of this verse reflects that developing apologetic agenda. As the divinely desired protasis, general orthopraxis gives way to the cultivation of a spiritual susceptibility, one that would render certain Christians sufficiently clear-minded and pure-hearted to recognize the prophetic foretelling.

That same tension touches the exegetical effort to identify *what was sent down to them from their Lord*. Two possibilities weave their way through the tradition on this verse. Commentators such as al-Zamakhsharī, Fakhr al-Dīn al-Rāzī, Kāshānī, and Rashīd Riḍā have taken this phrase to connote supplementary Jewish and Christian revelation. In some cases the attribution is vague and unspecified. Others, for example Fakhr al-Dīn al-Rāzī and Rashīd Riḍā, display a more knowledgeable awareness of such scriptures, citing by name the books of Isaiah, Habakkuk, Daniel, the Wisdom of Solomon, and the Psalms.

The second option exercised by the commentators on this verse treats the phrase as a circumlocution for the Qurʾān. Such an identification furnishes additional support for those who seek in the initial clause of the conditional a sufficient resource for religious orthopraxis. Ibn al-Jawzī draws upon the chronology of revelation to justify such an identification. As the Torah preceded the Gospel, so, too, are both of them succeeded by *what was sent down to them from their Lord*. He even adds the further observation that allows subsequent secondary propagation of the Qurʾānic message to Christians and Jews to stand as equivalent to its primary 'sending down.' The implicit argument that supports this second option is the universal thrust of this "seal" of prophetic revelation. In the minds of a number of the commentators the Qurʾān can quite justifiably be the correct denotation of this clause because its message was intended for all, including Christians and Jews.

Had these peoples been properly receptive to that message, had they been faithful to the authentic stream of revelation as expressed in their pristine scriptures and concluded with the Qurʾān, theirs would have been a divinely vouchsafed bounty and banquet. The Qurʾānic expression of this pledge drew forth from the exegetes lyrical declarations of God's goodness.

Explaining the apodosis of this conditional allows the commentators to sound a constant undertone of gratitude for continuing divine sustenance. Images abound of life-supporting rains, of crops that sprout profusely from the earth, of heavy-laden fruit trees whose branches droop with the weight of ripe largesse. Qurʾānic parallels detailing God's constant nourishment of His creation are frequently adduced. Contrasted with this litany of thanks are themes of exile and loss. The explicit patterning of description and promise that constitutes the conditional sentence of this verse develops as a denunciation of those whose wayward obstinacy provokes their rejection of the final Prophet. Specific incidents in the life of the nascent Muslim community are cited, incidents in which the response to rejection was retaliation and expulsion. Material abundance disappears; the spiritual consequences are yet more severe. Just as piety prompts divine generosity so does impiety incite divine rebuke, a fact that Fakhr al-Dīn al-Rāzī finds clarified by considering the larger context of this verse.

Though many stand liable, corrupted, in the eyes of Rashīd Riḍā, by the pervasive effects of unthinking religio-ethnic solidarity, some few survive unscathed. These are *a balanced people*, whose doctrinal and behavioral moderation distinguishes their 'adherence' to the Torah and Gospel. Some exegetes sketch the lineaments of such theological moderation while others have chosen, more controversially, to gauge it in political terms. Representative Christians and Jews, such as the Najāshī and ʿAbdallāh b. Salām, are presented as exemplars of the praiseworthy religious posture. More generally, all Christian and Jewish converts to Islam, the *maslamah*, by the very nature of their religious aptitude and prescience exhibit the doctrinal and behavioral balance here commended.

Yet they are few. The verse closes in a minor key. The absence of such praiseworthy theological balance is widespread. Fakhr al-Dīn al-Rāzī has chosen to couch this final condemnation in terms of intellectual deprivation or depravity. Most are thereby indicted. Although Rashīd Riḍā and Ṭabāṭabāʾī find remarkable the inclusion of any positive reference to non-Muslims, their amazement itself bespeaks the very limited range of applicability. While the verse speaks of *many* who are *evildoers*, the exegetical tradition overwhelmingly understands this as 'most'. The oft-quoted *ḥadīth* that sees one group as saved and the other seventy (or seventy-one or seventy-two) consigned to the Fire represents a vivid numerical rendering of this comprehension.

7

The praiseworthy amity of Christians

The most striking example of Qur'ānic praise of Christians occurs in *sūrat al-mā'idah* (5):82–83. These verses figure prominently in virtually all attempts to base Muslim-Christian rapprochement upon specific Qur'ānic texts. The passage itself constitutes an exegetical challenge of considerable proportions. Within the verses one finds a configuration of seven categories: the Jews, the idolaters (*mushrikūn*), 'those who believe', the Christians, priests and monks (*qissīsūn wa-ruhbān*), those who hear what was sent down upon Muḥammad and weep, and, finally, those who bear witness (*shāhidūn*). Obviously, issues of identification will occupy a considerable portion of the exegetical effort expended on this pericope, as will the desire to ascertain the circumstances surrounding this revelation (*asbāb al-nuzūl*). One possible translation of *sūrat al-mā'idah* (5):82–83 is as follows:

> You will find the people most intensely hostile to the believers are the Jews and the idolaters. You will surely find those closest in friendship to those who believe to be those who say "We are Christians." That is because among them are priests and monks and because they are not arrogant. (82)
>
> When they heard what was sent down to the Messenger their eyes overflowed with tears because of what they recognized as the truth. They say, "Our Lord, we believe, so write us with those who testify (*shāhidūn*)." (83)

THOSE PERSONS WHO ELICIT PRAISE

Al-Ṭabarī begins his discussion of 5:82 with a rapid survey of the principal groups mentioned. He then proceeds to evaluate the various views proposed about the occasion for this revelation. The first of two competing theories advanced is one that associates the verse with the contact made between Muḥammad and the Abyssinian king, the Najāshī.[1] Different scenarios for this are sketched, but the first one presented by al-Ṭabarī on the authority

1 This episode is recounted in Ibn Isḥāq, *Sīrah*, 1:208–21 (Guillaume, *Life*, 146–53). A narrative summary is offered in Mehmet Aydin, "Rapporti islamo-cristiani all'epoca di Muhammad," *ISC* 5 (1986): 12–15.

of Saᶜīd b. Jubayr runs as follows: the Najāshī sent a delegation of his Christian subjects to the Prophet who recited from the Qurʾān for them. As they listened, they were overcome and immediately declared themselves Muslims. Upon their return to the Najāshī, they told him all they had learned and he, too, entered Islam and remained a believer until his death.[2] Subsequent *ḥadīth*s included in al-Ṭabarī's commentary flesh out this brief sketch.

One such from Mujāhid adds the fact that this Christian delegation formed part of the group that returned with Jaᶜfar b. Abī Ṭālib from Abyssinia. Another, more lengthy *ḥadīth* from Ibn ᶜAbbās fills in the background with an account of what occurred during the first Muslim emigration to Abyssinia. A synopsis of this *ḥadīth*, highlighting the main characters and events, will doubtless be useful in understanding both this and subsequent commentaries: Muḥammad, fearing the escalating persecution of his followers in Mecca, sent a group headed by Jaᶜfar b. Abī Ṭālib, Ibn Masᶜūd, and ᶜUthmān b. Maẓūn to seek the protection of the Najāshī, the king of Abyssinia.[3] When the Prophet's Meccan opponents, here tagged as the 'idolaters (*mushrikūn*)', discovered this scheme they quickly dispatched their own delegation, led by ᶜAmr b. al-ᶜĀṣ.[4] This group reached the Najāshī first. They addressed the king saying: "There is a man from among us who declares the minds and thoughts of the Quraysh to be stupid. He claims to be a prophet! He has sent a group (*rahṭ*) to you in order to alienate you from your people. We wanted to come and inform you about them."[5]

The Najāshī was not immediately persuaded and remained willing to give the Muslim deputation a hearing. When they finally arrived, the king questioned them about Muḥammad's thoughts on Jesus and Mary. The group's spokesman made this response: "He [Muḥammad] says that Jesus is the servant (*ᶜabd*) of God and the word (*kalimah*) of God, which God cast into Mary, and His spirit (*rūḥ*). About Mary he says that she is the virgin (*al-ᶜadhrāʾ al-batūl*)."[6] The Najāshī responded to this statement with

2 al-Ṭabarī, *Jāmiᶜ al-bayān*, 10:499.

3 Jaᶜfar b. Abī Ṭālib was Muḥammad's cousin and an older brother of ᶜAlī. L. Veccia Vaglieri, "Djaᶜfar b. Abī Ṭālib," *EI²* 2:372. For Ibn Masᶜūd see Chapter 1, notes 5 and 13. The *Sīrah* (1:243–44) of Ibn Isḥāq recounts the occasion on which the poet ᶜUthmān b. Maẓᶜūn renounced the protection of a Meccan opponent of Muḥammad's, al-Walīd b. al-Mughīrah.

4 ᶜAmr b. al-ᶜĀṣ (d. 42/663) is best remembered for his conquest of Egypt and founding of Fusṭāṭ, the forerunner of present-day Cairo. A.J. Wensinck, "ᶜAmr b. al-ᶜĀṣ," *EI²* 1:451.

5 al-Ṭabarī, *Jāmiᶜ al-bayān*, 10:500.

6 al-Ṭabarī, *Jāmiᶜ al-bayān*, 10:500. The closest Qurʾānic equivalent to Jaᶜfar's declaration would be *sūrat al-nisāʾ* (4):171, which both Muslim and Western scholars date as Medinan,

an illustrative command: "Pick up," he said, "a twig from the ground: between what your leader said about Jesus and Mary and what I believe there is not more than a twig's worth of difference."[7] Frustrated in their plans, the *mushrikūn* rivals left in disgust.

Among the group that later returned to the Prophet, according to a *ḥadīth* from al-Suddī, were a number of Abyssinian priests and monks. These were the ones who were so struck by the Qur'ānic verses that Muḥammad recited to them that they immediately converted. They then went back to the Najāshī and convinced him of the validity of this new religion so that he too converted and started back with them to Muḥammad. The *ḥadīth* closes with the statement that the king died on this trip and when the news reached Muḥammad, he prayed for him.[8]

Quite different is the second major interpretive theory advanced to identify these *Christians*. This one is far less specific or colorful. Rather it views the phrase *those who say "We are Christians"* as a general reference to those who in an earlier time believed in Jesus and followed his teaching. "However when God sent His Prophet, Muḥammad, they acknowledged him as a true prophet and believed in him, recognizing that what he brought was the truth."[9]

Al-Ṭabarī balances these two theories with a third that acknowledges the insufficiency of available information, a recognition to be found not infrequently in his commentary. He grounds himself in a very literal reading of the text, from which he seems loath to extrapolate. All that can be asserted, according to the exegete, is that God described a people who say "*We are Christians*" and whom the Prophet would find friendliest to the believers. "But," al-Ṭabarī emphatically asserts, "He did not name them for us."[10] It may be that the Najāshī and those around him were meant or perhaps the pre-Islamic followers of Jesus were intended. This exegete maintains that the text offers no real support for either option.

i.e., well after the Abyssinian emigration. On the use of the terms *kalimah* and *rūḥ* in association with Jesus see Thomas O'Shaughnessy, S.J., *The Koranic Concept of the Word of God* (Rome: Pontificio Istituto Biblico, 1948) and *The Development of the Meaning of Spirit in the Koran* (Rome: Pontificium Institutum Orientalium Studiorum, 1953), as well as Henninger, *Spuren*, 32–38.

7 al-Ṭabarī, *Jāmiʿ al-bayān*, 10:500.

8 al-Ṭabarī, *Jāmiʿ al-bayān*, 10:501. Other accounts of the Najāshī's death form a major part of the *asbāb al-nuzūl* for *sūrah Āl ʿImrān* (3):199, which was discussed in Chapter 5.

9 al-Ṭabarī, *Jāmiʿ al-bayān*, 10:501.

10 al-Ṭabarī, *Jāmiʿ al-bayān*, 10:501. Ahmad von Denffer presents only this episode (of the delegation sent by the Najāshī to Muḥammad) as the *sabab al-nuzūl* of the verse, adding that only such a carefully specified group of Christians is intended in this verse and, therefore, that "this verse, when seen in its historical context, does not seem to be meant as a general statement characterizing Christians as such as being nearest to Muslims." *Christians in the Qur'ān and the Sunna,* 13.

Two of these possible referents are accepted by al-Ṭūsī as well. The first, garnered from accounts of al-Suddī and Mujāhid, comprises the Abyssinian king and his followers who became Muslims, especially those who returned from Abyssinia with Jaᶜfar b. Abī Ṭālib. The alternative proposed by Qatādah is "a people of the *ahl al-kitāb* who lived in accord with the truth as strict adherents of the law of Jesus (*mutamassikūn bi-sharīᶜati ᶜĪsā*). When Muḥammad came, they believed in him."[11]

While al-Ṭabarī's only comment on the phrase *the Jews and the idolaters* (*al-mushrikūn*) is to explain the latter term as "the worshipers of idols (*al-awthān*) who take idols as gods to be worshiped rather than God," al-Ṭūsī explores the connection between the two terms. He attributes the association to political connivance between the two groups: "The Jews aided the *mushrikūn* against the believers despite the fact that the believers had faith in the prophethood of Moses and the Torah which he brought." The fact that the Muslim belief in Moses and the Torah has not resulted in Jewish congeniality clearly puzzles al-Ṭūsī. The dissonance he perceives is expressed in the following comment: "It would be more appropriate for them [the Jews] to be closest to those who agree with them by believing in their prophet and their scripture. Instead they helped the *mushrikūn* out of a grudge against the Prophet (*ḥasadan lil-nabī*)."[12]

This exegete then returns to the question of identifying *those who say "We are Christians*," examining it now in light of the Jewish-*mushrikūn* alliance. He cites the view of al-Zajjāj and al-Jubbāʾī that "perhaps it means *al-naṣārā* [Christians in general] because they were much less helpful to the idolaters."[13] However he immediately neutralizes this possibility with a counter-quotation from Ibn ᶜAbbās: "Whoever claims that it is about the Christians in general certainly lies. They [the ones to whom the phrase refers] are only the forty Christians whose eyes overflowed when the Prophet recited the Qurʾān to them, thirty-eight from Abyssinia and two from Syria. They hurried to become Muslims (*sāraᶜū ilā al-islām*) while the Jews did not."[14]

Then, at the very end of his commentary on this verse, al-Ṭūsī allies himself with one of the two major interpretations that seek to identify the groups mentioned in the verse. His affiliation with the specific rather than general identification is clearly stated: "God made an announcement about those Jews who were the Prophet's neighbors (*mujāwirū al-nabī*) and the friendship of the Najāshī and his followers who became Muslims."[15] Ap-

11 al-Ṭūsī, *al-Tibyān*, 3:614.
12 al-Ṭūsī, *al-Tibyān*, 3:614.
13 al-Ṭūsī, *al-Tibyān*, 3:614.
14 al-Ṭūsī, *al-Tibyān*, 3:614–15.
15 al-Ṭūsī, *al-Tibyān*, 3:616.

parently almost as an afterthought, al-Ṭūsī then connects these two groupings with the two major emigrations in the early history of Islam: "There was an emigration (*hijrah*) to Medina where the Jews lived, and to Abyssinia where the Najāshī and his followers lived, so an announcement was made about the hostility (*ᶜadāwah*) of the former and the friendship (*mawaddah*) of the latter."[16]

Given the divine descriptives of friendliness (in this verse) and weeping at hearing the Qur'ān read (in the next verse), al-Zamakhsharī finds the episode involving the Najāshī and his followers the only meaningful referent for *those who say "We are Christians."* Without attribution, al-Zamakhsharī sketches the scene played out in the Najāshī's audience chamber between the two delegations from Mecca. Responding to the ruler's query about Qur'ānic mention of Mary, Jaᶜfar recited selected portions of the *sūrah* that bears her name, *sūrah Maryam* (19), and of *sūrah Ṭā' Hā'* (20). The ruler recognized the truth and wept, as did the cohort of seventy whom he sent to the Prophet.[17]

Any notion that all Christians are intended by the divine praise recorded in this verse is forthrightly rejected by Abū al-Futūḥ Rāzī. His reason for such rejection is clear: "Christians (*tarsāyān*) are no less hostile to the Muslims than [are] the Jews."[18] Although he follows al-Ṭūsī in citing the identification proposed by Qatādah, Abū al-Futūḥ Rāzī clearly favors association of this verse with the emigration to Abyssinia.[19] This commentator recounts the story in considerably more detail than have previous commentators. He includes material about Muḥammad's proposal of marriage to Umm Ḥabībah, the daughter of Abū Sufyān, who, with her husband, had been among the immigrants to Abyssinia.[20] He also mentions the profession of faith in Muḥammad made by one of the Najāshī's slave girls. The Prophet's joy at the return of the immigrants, which coincided with the conquest of the Jewish oasis, Khaybar, in 7/628, is also recounted.[21]

16 al-Ṭūsī, *al-Tibyān*, 3:616.

17 al-Zamakhsharī, *al-Kashshāf*, 1:669. The passages recited were 19:1–33 and 20:1–8.

18 Abū al-Futūḥ Rāzī, *Rawḥ al-jinān*, 4:303.

19 Abū al-Futūḥ Rāzī, *Rawḥ al-jinān*, 4:305–06. The *ḥadīth* from Qatādah is appended, almost as an afterthought, to Abū al-Futūḥ Rāzī's lengthy description of the Abyssinian episode.

20 Abū al-Futūḥ Rāzī, *Rawḥ al-jinān*, 4:304. Abū Sufyān was among the most prominent of Muḥammad's Meccan opponents. He eventually submitted to the Prophet and one of his sons, Muᶜāwiyah, became the first Umayyad caliph. On the relations between Muḥammad and Abū Sufyān, particularly the legal issues surrounding the Prophet's marriage to Umm Ḥabībah, see M. J. Kister, "O God, Tighten Thy Grip on Muḍar . . . : Some Socio-economic and Religious Aspects of an early Ḥadith," *JESHO* 24 (1981): 258–67.

21 Abū al-Futūḥ Rāzī, *Rawḥ al-jinān*, 4:304–05. L. Veccia Vaglieri, "Khaybar," *EI*² 4:

This narrative of the Najāshī story differs from al-Ṭabarī's telling in the details of the Najāshī's conversion. According to Abū al-Futūḥ Rāzī, the Najāshī wrote to the Prophet a profession of faith and sent it by the hand of his son. In it he said: "I have come to believe in you and sworn allegiance to you (*man bi-tū īmān āvardam va tū-rā bayᶜat kardam*)." As his son crossed the sea to deliver this message to Muḥammad, the boat he was in foundered and sank.[22] He and part of his delegation of ascetics and pious worshipers (*zuhhād va ᶜubbād*) were drowned. The rest of the party finally reached Medina where they were presented to the Prophet in the company of a group of men from Syria, including Baḥīrā, the Christian monk who is said to have recognized the youthful Muḥammad as the last of the prophets.[23] The numbers and composition of this combined delegation is in dispute. Abū al-Futūḥ Rāzī cites several variants ranging from 40 to 80, and including men from Abyssinia, Byzantium, Syria, and the Yemenite district of Najrān.[24]

Ibn al-Jawzī repeats al-Ṭūsī's definition of *mushrikūn* and the charge that "the Jews helped the *mushrikūn* out of a grudge against the Prophet." He then poses the question about the phrase *those who say "We are Christians"* quite precisely: "Is this a generalization about all Christians or is it specific?" If the phrase means particular Christians then one of two groups could be intended. On the authority of Ibn ᶜAbbās and Ibn Jubayr the first possibility is, of course, the Christian king of Abyssinia and his followers who subsequently became Muslims. The second possible specification repeats al-Ṭūsī's and Abū al-Futūḥ Rāzī's use of an identification proposed by Qatādah: "they are a group of Christians who were strict adherents of the law of Jesus (*mutamassikūn bi-sharīᶜat i ᶜĪsā*)."[25] If the phrase is to be taken in a general sense, then Ibn al-Jawzī quotes, as did al-Ṭūsī, the

1137–43. For the relations of this incident to the development of *jizyah* legislation, see Albrecht Noth, "Minderheiten als Vertragspartner im Disput mit dem islamischen Gesetz," in *Studien zur Geschichte und Kultur des vorderen Orients: Festschrift für Bertold Spuler zum siebzigsten Geburtstag*, ed. by Hans R. Roemer and A. Noth (Leiden: E. J. Brill, 1981), 289–309. Gordon Newby provides information on the life of Ḥijāzī Jews with specific reference to Khaybar. *A History*, 49–77.

22 Abū al-Futūḥ Rāzī, *Rawḥ al-jinān*, 4:305. The episode of the shipwreck to which Abū al-Futūḥ Rāzī's account refers may be found in al-Ṭabarī's *Taʾrīkh al-rusul wa-al-mulūk*, ed. by M.J. de Goeje (1879–1901; reprint, Leiden: E.J. Brill, 1964), 1:1569 (Guillaume, *Life*, 657–58).

23 Abū al-Futūḥ Rāzī, *Rawḥ al-jinān*, 4:305.

24 Abū al-Futūḥ Rāzī, *Rawḥ al-jinān*, 4:305. The specifics of this enumeration are: (1) in Abū al-Futūḥ Rāzī's narrative the number is seventy, with sixty-two from Abyssinia and eight from Syria; (2) on the authority of Muqātil and al-Kalbī, the number is forty, with thirty-two from Abyssinia and eight from Byzantium; (3) ᶜAṭāʾ gives the figure of eighty, forty being of the Banū al-Ḥārith b. Kaᶜb from Najrān, thirty-two from Abyssinia, and eight from Byzantium.

25 Ibn al-Jawzī, *Zād al-masīr*, 2:408.

rationale offered by al-Zajjāj, that the Christians were less helpful to the *mushrikūn* than were the Jews. As noted above, this position had been strongly contradicted by Abū al-Futūḥ Rāzī.

Fakhr al-Dīn al-Rāzī begins his commentary on this verse by reinforcing the divine castigation of the Jews. He, too, sees in the close placement of the words *the Jews* and *the idolaters* a measure of the degree of Jewish belligerence. He repeats the Prophetic *ḥadīth* that brands all Jews as potential Muslim-killers and quotes those who speak of a generalized Jewish hostility. "Jewish teaching requires them to inflict evil (*īṣāl al-sharr*) by any means on those who oppose them in religion. If they can do so by killing, then they choose that way. Otherwise they act by forcible seizure of property or robbery or any sort of cheating, deception, and trickery."[26]

The Christians, on the other hand, are characterized as milder-mannered (*alyan ʿarīkatan*). Fakhr al-Dīn al-Rāzī contrasts their ethics with those of the Jews by saying that "in their religion causing harm is forbidden (*al-īdhāʾ fī dīnihim ḥarām*)."[27] Yet he is certainly unwilling to view all Christians in so flattering a light. Fakhr al-Dīn al-Rāzī cites Ibn ʿAbbās, Saʿīd b. Jubayr, ʿAṭāʾ, and al-Suddī as referents for the association of this verse with the Najāshī and his associates. It is the only specification that he proposes. He immediately follows it with the caution that certainly the verse does not mean all Christians (*jamīʿ al-naṣārā*), given the visible evidence of their animosity toward Muslims (*ẓuhūr ʿadāwatihim lil-muslimīn*).[28]

On the other hand, he does raise a question about the text that previous exegetes have not addressed in quite this fashion. He queries the purpose for which this verse was included in divine revelation, and finds his answer in the tension that developed between Muḥammad and his nascent Islamic community, on the one hand, and the Jewish groups with whom they came in contact. Fakhr al-Dīn al-Rāzī understands the verse as an instance of divine clarification for Muḥammad, meant "to alleviate the Jewish problem for the Messenger (*takhfīf amr al-yahūd ʿalā al-rasūl*)."[29] To highlight this

26 Fakhr al-Dīn al-Rāzī, *al-Tafsīr al-kabīr*, 12:66.

27 Fakhr al-Dīn al-Rāzī, *al-Tafsīr al-kabīr*, 12:66. The Christian promotion of such virtues as 'turning the other cheek' or forgiving one's enemies has often provoked puzzlement or ridicule from Muslim writers. A clear example may be found in the *al-Radd ʿalā al-naṣārā* of ʿAmr b. Baḥr al-Jāḥiẓ (d. 255/868–69), who mocks the Christians for "their ideas on forgiveness, their aimless spiritual wandering, their censure on meat-eating and their predilection for cereals." His derision is further prompted by their "preaching abstinence from marriage and reproduction" and their "venerating their leaders and praising their patriarchs and metropolitans, their bishops and monks, for practicing celibacy." These translations of al-Jāḥiẓ's are from an unpublished paper by G.M. Wickens entitled "Anti-Christian Polemic in Islam." Portions of al-Jāḥiẓ's essay have been translated by Joshua Finkel, "A Risāla of al-Jāḥiẓ," *JAOS* 47 (1927):311–34.

28 Fakhr al-Dīn al-Rāzī, *al-Tafsīr al-kabīr*, 12:66.

29 Fakhr al-Dīn al-Rāzī, *al-Tafsīr al-kabīr*, 12:66.

explanation he paraphrases the divine word: "I swear that you will find the Jews and *mushrikūn* the people most hostile to the believers. I have already made plain to you that this recalcitrance and disobedience (*al-tamarrud wa-al-maʿṣiyah*) is a long-standing habit with them. So put them out of your mind and pay no attention to their deception and treachery."[30]

While Ibn Kathīr, too, associates the verse with the Najāshī, he does so in a more discriminating fashion, noting both historical and source-critical discrepancies. On the grounds that the verse was revealed in Medina, he questions the plausibility of its being occasioned by an episode, that of Jaʿfar with the Najāshī, that took place before the *hijrah* to Medina.[31] Ibn Kathīr also notes the position of those, such as Saʿīd b. Jubayr and al-Suddī, who find the revelatory context to be the delegation that the Najāshī sent to Muḥammad.[32] Here, however, he takes issue with al-Suddī's assertion that the Najāshī, persuaded by the testimony of the returning delegation, himself goes to join the Prophet and dies on the way. Ibn Kathīr dismisses this as a view idiosyncratic to Suddī (*min afrād al-Suddī*) and counters it with the more generally accepted historical tradition that the Najāshī died in Abyssinia.[33] Although the increasingly general identifications of ʿAṭāʾ b. Abī Rabāḥ and then Qatādah are repeated, Ibn Kathīr concludes his survey of possible attributions with the position taken by al-Ṭabarī: "Ibn Jarīr's [i.e., al-Ṭabarī's] decision is that this verse was sent down to describe various groups of this sort (*fī ṣifah aqwām bi-hādhihi al-mathābah*) whether they be from Abyssinia or elsewhere."[34]

Kāshānī is adamant in his rejection of such a broad understanding. Expanding Abū al-Futūḥ Rāzī's position he states: "The number of Christians who kill Muslims, devastate countries, and destroy mosques is no less than the number of Jews."[35] Thus the only possible identification for *those who say "We are Christians"* would be the Abyssinians and their king. He, too, relates in considerable detail the story of the *hijrah* to Abyssinia and of the hospitality accorded the immigrants. While his account corresponds closely to that found in Abū al-Futūḥ Rāzī's commentary, certain embellishments are unique to it.

Kāshānī describes a fight that broke out among the Quraysh delegation

30 Fakhr al-Dīn al-Rāzī, *al-Tafsīr al-kabīr*, 12:66.

31 Ibn Kathīr, *Tafsīr al-Qurʾān al-ʿaẓīm*, 2:85. John Wansbrough has analyzed Jaʿfar b. Abī Ṭālib's speech before the Najāshī and decided that "the structure of the report suggests a careful rhetorical formulation of Quranic material generally supposed to have been revealed after the date of that event." *Quranic Studies*, 41.

32 Ibn Kathīr, *Tafsīr al-Qurʾān al-ʿaẓīm*, 2:85. While Ibn Kathīr repeats some of the enumerations given for this delegation, he does so without specific attributions.

33 Ibn Kathīr, *Tafsīr al-Qurʾān al-ʿaẓīm*, 2:85.

34 Ibn Kathīr, *Tafsīr al-Qurʾān al-ʿaẓīm*, 2:85.

35 Kāshānī, *Minhaj al-ṣādiqīn*, 3:291.

while en route to the Najāshī's court. ʿAmr b. al-ʿĀṣ was thrown overboard when he repulsed another man's drunken advances to his wife. He was able to swim to the front of the boat and hoist himself aboard but the whole incident is used to illustrate the sinful and contentious nature of the Quraysh group.[36] When this embassy appeared before the Najāshī they were bested by the debating skills of Jaʿfar b. Abī Ṭālib, in a debate that Kāshānī recounts in some detail. Muḥammad's proposal to Umm Ḥabībah, the return of Jaʿfar b. Abī Ṭālib, and the death of the king's son are all described. Also included is mention of the monk Baḥīrā as a member of the combined delegations that appeared before the Prophet. In almost every particular, Kāshānī accords with Abū al-Futūḥ Rāzī's account, but adds considerably more detail to the narrative.

Rashīd Riḍā takes as his first task the clarification of the terms here translated as 'hostility (*ʿadāwah*)' and 'friendship (*mawaddah*)'.[37] He next questions to whom this verse was directed, whether it be Muḥammad or a wider audience, such as all who might eventually hear the words. No immediate response is given because the answer to this is closely tied to the identification of the primary categories.

Here again the issue is whether that identification should be particular or general. Rashīd Riḍā begins by exploring the first option, which is especially compelling if the verse is considered to have been addressed chiefly to the Prophet. Briefly put, the referents would then be the Jews living in the Ḥijāz, the Arabic *mushrikūn*, and the Christians of Abyssinia who were alive during the time of Muḥammad.[38] This last group is praised for their friendliness "to the emigrants (*muhājirūn*) whom the Prophet sent at the beginning of Islam from Mecca to Abyssinia because he was afraid that the Meccan *mushrikūn*, who were causing them great trouble, would lure them from their religion."[39] Rashīd Riḍā also notes that this tripartite identification is the most commonly held view in the exegetical tradition.

But this commentator's interest in early Christian-Muslim contact does not stop with the Islamic *hijrah* to Abyssinia. He also brings into consideration the story of Muḥammad's missions to foreign rulers. The traditional accounts of this missionary activity record some interesting aspects of the Christian reaction to Islam. The first that Rashīd Riḍā mentions is the approach made to Heraclius, "the king of Byzantium (*Rūm*) in Syria." He is credited with an unsuccessful effort to persuade his subjects to accept

36 Kāshānī, *Minhaj al-ṣādiqīn*, 3:292.

37 Rashīd Riḍā, *Tafsīr al-Manār*, 7:2. For *ʿadāwah* Rashīd Riḍā offers as a synonym *bughḍ* (hatred) as it is expressed in word and deed. Likewise *mawaddah* is equated with *maḥabbah*, not absolutely but as manifested in speech and behavior.

38 Rashīd Riḍā, *Tafsīr al-Manār*, 7:3.

39 Rashīd Riḍā, *Tafsīr al-Manār*, 7:3.

Islam. Their refusal to do so is attributed to their persistence in following uncritically their old ways (*li-jumūdihim ʿalā al-taqlīd*) and to their inability to comprehend the true nature of the new religion (*ʿadam fiqhihim ḥaqīqat al-dīn al-jadīd*).[40]

The Muqawqis, the Coptic ruler of Egypt, is reputed to have been more successful and is praised for having sent a handsome offering to Muḥammad. As a historical footnote Rashīd Riḍā adds that "when Egypt and Syria were conquered and their two peoples recognized the superiority of Islam, they entered the religion of God in droves, the Copts being the quicker in accepting it."[41] Of particular interest is the debate he recounts between the Muqawqis and the Prophet's messenger, Ḥāṭib b. Abī Baltaʿah. When Ḥāṭib urges the Muqawqis to turn to Islam, the latter's first response is that he will not forsake his own religion unless shown something better. Ḥāṭib's rejoinder makes reference to the oft-repeated chronological analogy that Islamic theology draws between first the Jewish and Christian religions and then the Christian and Muslim religions: "There is no difference between Moses' foretelling (*bishārah*) of Jesus and Jesus' foretelling of Muḥammad; our inviting you to the Qurʾān is exactly like your inviting the people of the Torah to the Gospel." He then proceeds to explain that every prophet comes unexpectedly to his people, yet it is their duty to submit to his revelation. Ḥāṭib concludes his argument by saying "we are not prohibiting the religion of the Messiah for you; rather we are ordering you to it."[42] What this means – as Rashīd Riḍā hastens to clarify – is that Islam is the essence of Christianity itself (*al-islām ʿaynuhu*). The Muqawqis promises to consider the summons, assuring the Prophet's messenger that he suspects Muḥammad of no deviousness or sorcery. Rather he finds associated with him the sign of prophethood (*āyat al-nubūwah*), which consists in bringing forth hidden meanings and announcing what has been concealed.[43]

The description of the Prophet's mission to Oman brings to the fore certain figures previously mentioned. The first to appear is ʿAmr b. al-ʿĀṣ, who was the Muslims' adversary in the court of the Najāshī of Abyssinia. He has since offered allegiance to Muḥammad and been sent as the Prophet's

40 Rashīd Riḍā, *Tafsīr al-Manār*, 7:3. The disavowal of *taqlīd* is an important note in the thought of both Muḥammad ʿAbduh and Muḥammad Rashīd Riḍā. For a classical-period repudiation of this form of traditionalism see J.R.T.M. Peters's work on the Muʿtazilī Abū al-Ḥasan ʿAbd al-Jabbār (d. 415/1025), *God's Created Speech* (Leiden: E.J. Brill, 1976), 43–45. For Rashīd Riḍā's conjunction of the terms *jumūd* and *taqlīd* see Hourani, *Liberal Age*, 235.

41 Rashīd Riḍā, *Tafsīr al-Manār*, 7:3. A. Grohmann reviews the scholarship that denies the historicity of this incident in "al-Muḳawḳas," *EI*[1] 6:712–25.

42 Rashīd Riḍā, *Tafsīr al-Manār*, 7:4.

43 Rashīd Riḍā, *Tafsīr al-Manār*, 7:4.

emissary to the ruler of Oman, Jayfar b. Julandā. He first approaches the king's brother, ʿAbbād b. Julandā, who is reputed to be more accessible and more discerning. As a way of convincing this noble, he describes his own conversion and that of the Najāshī. His curiosity piqued, ʿAbbād b. Julandā questions him initially about the reaction of the Abyssinian people and then about the response of the bishops and monks (*al-asāqifah wa-al-ruhbān*).[44] When ʿAmr reports that they have all become Muslim, ʿAbbād accuses him of lying. ʿAmr protests that lying is not permitted in Islam and then goes on to tell him about how the Najāshī, once he was a Muslim, refused to continue paying tribute to Heraclius, the Christian king of Byzantium. When Heraclius was faced with the Najāshī's defection, his response was a model of tolerance: "A man's preference and choice in religion is personal (*li-nafsihi*), what can I do to him? By God, were I not so anxious to hold on to my kingdom, I would do what he did."[45] When ʿAbbād is then told the obligations and prohibitions that Islam imposes, his reply is reminiscent of Heraclius's words: "How fortunate is the one who is called to it [Islam]!"[46]

Rashīd Riḍā uses the accounts of these missionary deputations as well as the story of the *hijrah* to Abyssinia as evidence of the fact that Christians in the areas surrounding the Ḥijāz were particularly open to Islam and friendly to the Muslims. Those who did not actually accept Islam were held back by rulers jealous of their power. The commentator does remark that Islam did not spread in Abyssinia after the Najāshī's death nor was Muslim law instituted there as it was in Egypt and Syria. However he adds that this is a matter for historical research and not germane to the commentary on this verse.[47]

In this analysis of the views supporting a particular identification of the Christians, Rashīd Riḍā mentions the opinion of those who hold that geography determines amicability. That is, the more distant Christians could afford to be friendlier to the Muslims than the Jews and *mushrikūn* of Mecca and Medina. Those summoned to Islam from afar were less concerned about the consequences that their hostile response to the summons might provoke than those to whom that call was addressed orally. "Therefore the Jews in Syria and Spain were favorably disposed to the Muslims at the beginning and wanted to help them against the Christians of Byzantium and the Goths (*Qūṭ*)."[48] The hostility that eventually developed between the Muslims and

44 Rashīd Riḍā, *Tafsīr al-Manār*, 7:4.

45 Rashīd Riḍā, *Tafsīr al-Manār*, 7:4.

46 Rashīd Riḍā, *Tafsīr al-Manār*, 7:5. Accounts of these deputations to various rulers may be found in Ibn Isḥāq, *Sīrah*, 1:971–72 (Guillaume, *Life*, 652–59.) Guillaume's presentation of this incorporates material from al-Ṭabarī's *Ta'rīkh*.

47 Rashīd Riḍā, *Tafsīr al-Manār*, 7:5.

48 Rashīd Riḍā, *Tafsīr al-Manār*, 7:5. J. Sadan draws attention to this same geographical

these two groups of distant Christians, continues this commentator, was far more intense than that displayed by early-seventh-century Jews and *mushrikūn*. But, he adds, many instances of Muslim-Christian opposition and Muslim-Jewish opposition have nothing to do with religious matters but are rooted in struggles for earthly domination. Contemporary examples come immediately to mind: "This can be confirmed by the irritating effect that Christian propaganda has on contemporary Muslims, and by the outrage and enmity (*al-baghy wa-al-ʿudwān*) existing between Islamic and Christian nations which is nonexistent between Muslims and Jews."[49] A similar state of animosity is found between the Muslims and *mushrikūn* of India because their interests and advantages conflict there (*li-taʿāruḍ maṣāliḥihim wa-manāfiʿihim fīhā*).[50]

Thus Rashīd Riḍā's vision of his own contemporary situation appears to run counter to that of nascent Islam, with the descending order of hostility being Christians – *mushrikūn* – Jews, rather than the reverse. Rashīd Riḍā points out that recent warfare among the Christian Balkan states and between other Christian nations of Europe, such as England and Germany, confirms the fact that much international strife has no basis at all in religious matters. As a consequence, he feels, any particular identification of those groups mentioned in this verse is inappropriate and counter to the true meaning of the verse. The Qurʾān is not making a circumscribed but a general statement: "The real reason for the hostility of those who are hostile, and for the friendliness of those who are friendly, is the mental attitude (*al-ḥālah al-rūḥīyah*) which is the result of their religious and customary traditions (*taqālīduhum al-dīnīyah wa-al-ʿādīyah*) and their moral and social upbringing (*tarbiyatuhum al-adabīyah wa-al-ijtimāʿīyah*)."[51] He notes that while this verse does offer a rudimentary explanation for Christian friendship, it gives no explanation for the hostility exhibited by the Jews and the *mushrikūn*.

Although explanations are forthcoming elsewhere in the Qurʾān, Rashīd Riḍā ventures his own analysis. This amounts to little more than a list of unfortunate characteristics shared by the Jews and the *mushrikūn*: unbelief, insolence, injustice, love of preeminence (*ḥubb al-ʿulūw*), racial solidarity (*al-ʿaṣabīyah al-jinsīyah*), ethnic protectiveness (*al-ḥimāyah al-qawmīyah*), egoism, cruelty, and weakness of sympathetic and compassionate feeling (*ḍuʿf ʿāṭifat al-ḥanān wa-al-raḥmah*).[52] Despite these shared characteristics,

argument in the *al-Radd ʿalā al-naṣārā* of al-Jāḥiẓ. "Some Literary Problems," 354, note 5.

49 Rashīd Riḍā, *Tafsīr al-Manār*, 7:6. Rashīd Riḍā's remarks predate the partition of Palestine and establishment of the state of Israel.

50 Rashīd Riḍā, *Tafsīr al-Manār*, 7:6.

51 Rashīd Riḍā, *Tafsīr al-Manār*, 7:6.

52 Rashīd Riḍā, *Tafsīr al-Manār*, 7:6. The translation of *qawmīyah* as 'ethnic' has been

this exegete finds the *mushrikūn* less culpable than the Jews. Although they were religiously ignorant, they were more generous and altruistic, far more liberal in thinking and more independent.[53] He reiterates some of the Qurʾānic accusations against the Jews and dismisses any effort to rehabilitate their image based on their siding with the believers in the Holy Land, Syria, and Spain. This, he insists, was solely for financial and strategic motives: "They act solely for their own benefit."[54]

Ṭabāṭabāʾī takes the initial approach of contextual analysis and sees this verse as crowning the fifth *sūrah*'s treatment of the *ahl al-kitāb*. Earlier verses have detailed the errors of the *ahl al-kitāb*, both moral and doctrinal, so the revelation concludes with a more general statement about the various religious groups, relating them to the Muslims and their religion. The *mushrikūn* are included "so that the discussion of the impact of Islam on non-Muslims, relative to how near or far they are from accepting it, should be complete."[55]

In commenting upon the matter of the greater Christian amicability, this exegete takes issue with one stream of traditional exegesis on this verse. To think that the divine commendation is based on the response of a particular group of Christians does violence to the logic of the text.[56] "If the coming to believe of a group had authenticated it, then the Jews and *mushrikūn* would have to be reckoned like the Christians and credited with the same attributes, since a group of Jews became Muslims . . . and a number of *mushrikūn* from Arabia became Muslims; in fact, today they are the generality of Muslims."[57] The very specification of the Christians, then, is proof of their greater receptivity to Islam and more positive response to the Prophet.

Without actually using the term *dhimmah*, which is commonly used by Muslim authors to designate the legal status of the *ahl al-kitāb*, Ṭabāṭabāʾī describes the options available to the various groups of newly subject people

chosen in light of Bernard Lewis's remarks about the use of the cognate, *kavmiyet*, by Turkish-educated writers in the early years of this century "to denote identity and solidarity based on ethnic affinity." "On Modern Arabic Political Terms" in his *Islam in History* (London: Alcove Press, 1973), 285. For Rashīd Riḍā's application of *al-ʿaṣabīyah al-jinsīyah* to the *ahl al-kitāb* as a whole, see Chapter 6.

53 Rashīd Riḍā, *Tafsīr al-Manār*, 7:6.

54 Rashīd Riḍā, *Tafsīr al-Manār*, 7:7.

55 Ṭabāṭabāʾī, *al-Mīzān*, 6:79.

56 Ṭabāṭabāʾī repeats this in his comments on the *ḥadīth* material to which he makes reference for this verse, insisting that "the evident meaning (*ẓāhir*) of the verse is general not specific." *al-Mīzān*, 6:85.

57 Ṭabāṭabāʾī, *al-Mīzān*, 6:79–80. The author was apparently unaware of the vast demographic shift that has taken place in the Muslim world with the largest Muslim populations now to be found in south and southeast Asia.

at the dawn of Islamic history.[58] The Christians could choose between staying in their religion and paying a tax, the *jizyah*, or accepting Islam and fighting in its name. For the *mushrikūn* there was no choice other than accepting the Islamic summons. (Ṭabāṭabāʾī does not explain that the obvious reason for this is that the *mushrikūn*, as their designation indicates, were not considered monotheists by the Muslims, as were the Jews and Christians.) The fact that they had no choice makes their numerically greater conversion rate to Islam no particular factor in their favor. That many Christians, who did have a choice, chose to become Muslims is a strong argument for this divine commendation.[59]

To complete his argument, Ṭabāṭabāʾī must then ask why another group of the *ahl al-kitāb*, the Jews, are not accorded equal praise. After all, they, too, have the option of remaining in their religion and paying the *jizyah* or converting to Islam. What, then, differentiates them from the Christians? Ṭabāṭabāʾī finds his answer in those perennial accusations of arrogance (*nakhwah*) and racial solidarity. He adds to this the sins of treachery and scheming and claims that they "wait for disaster to befall the Muslims."[60]

Ṭabāṭabāʾī finds historical confirmation of this greater Christian receptivity to the message of Islam. The greater number of Jews and *mushrikūn* who became Muslims in the first years of Islam – due in large part to their geographical proximity – has given way to "Christian numerical superiority in acceptance of the Islamic summons (*daʿwah*) during past centuries."[61] So self-evident does this exegete find the argument for Christian receptiveness that his commentary on *you will find the people most intensely hostile to the believers are the Jews* consists of nothing more than citing two Qurʾānic passages (*sūrat al-māʾidah* [5]:62 and 80) that describe Jewish perfidy.

58 See Claude Cahen, "Dhimma," *EI²* 2:227–31. A standard source is Antoine Fattal, *Le statut légal des non-musulmans en pays d'islam* (Beirut: Imprimerie Catholique, 1958). The Islamic legal regulations pertinent to *dhimmīs* are presented in Adel Khoury, *Toleranz im Islam* (Munich: Kaiser, 1980) while a selection of translated legal and historical material has been collected by Bat Ye'or (pseud.), *The Dhimmi: Jews and Christians Under Islam*, trans. by David Maisel et al. (Rutherford, N.J.: Fairleigh Dickinson University Press, 1985). An earlier French edition carries the more polemical title *Le Dhimmi: Profil de l'opprimé en Orient et en Afrique du Nord depuis la conquête arabe* (Paris: Éditions Anthropos, 1980). Berthold Spuler presents a historical overview in "L'Islam et les minorités," in *Die Islamische Welt zwischen Mittelalter und Neuzeit: Festschrift für Hans Robert Roemer zum 65. Geburtstag* (Beirut: Orient-Institut der Deutschen Morgenländischen Gesellschaft, 1979), 609–19. For a recent historical study of the early classical period see André Ferré, "Chrétiens de Syrie et de Mésopotamie aux deux premiers siècles de l'Islam," *Islamo* 14 (1988): 71–106.

59 Ṭabāṭabāʾī, *al-Mīzān*, 6:80.

60 Ṭabāṭabāʾī, *al-Mīzān*, 6:80.

61 Ṭabāṭabāʾī, *al-Mīzān*, 6:80.

REASONS FOR CHRISTIAN AMICABILITY

Several themes raised in the modern commentaries of Rashīd Riḍā and Ṭabāṭabā'ī were anticipated in that part of the earlier exegetical tradition that sought to clarify and develop the basis for the contrast of the Jews and Christians in *sūrat al-mā'idah* (5):82. Such a concern moves beyond an interest in purely historical specification. Rather it seeks to understand the religio-cultural structures that buttress the varying relations among religious groups. The focus for such an investigation is to be found in the pivotal sentence *that is because among them are priests (qissīsīn) and monks (ruhbān) and because they are not arrogant.* Al-Ṭabarī does not, of course, ignore the need to determine historical context for these two categories. After a word study of the terms themselves, he proposes two possible referents for the individuals so designated.

The first theory is that the *priests and monks* are Jesus' disciples, those who answered when he summoned them and lived according to his law (*wa-ittabaʿūhu ʿalā sharīʿatihi*). The single supporting *ḥadīth* from Ibn ʿAbbās cited by this exegete is interesting for the terminology it uses: "They were sailors (*nawātī*) on the sea, i.e., mariners (*mallāḥūn*). Jesus, son of Mary, walked by them and called them to submission (*daʿāhum ilā al-islām*), so they responded to him."[62]

The second interpretation returns to the Abyssinian interlude described above, by identifying the *priests and monks* with the delegation that the Najāshī sent to Muḥammad. The *ḥadīth*s brought in support of this view on the authority of Abū Ṣāliḥ al-Miṣrī (d. 223/838) and Saʿīd b. Jubayr offer bits of information, sometimes contradictory. The number of delegates ranges from fifty to seventy. They are described as hermits (*ṣāḥib ṣawmaʿah*) and wool wearers (*ʿalayhim thiyāb al-ṣūf*) in one *ḥadīth*, while in another they are given the more general appellation of 'the elite (*khiyār*)'.[63]

Al-Ṭabarī, however, probes beyond these two identification theories to a more comprehensive concern. He moves from attempting to decide who exactly are these *priests and monks* to pointing out the explanatory nature

62 al-Ṭabarī, *Jāmiʿ al-bayān*, 10:504. The term that puzzles al-Ṭabarī, *nawātī* (sing. *nūtī*), and for which he offers the synonym *mallāḥīn*, is defined by Lane as "sailor upon the sea." He adds that according to Abū Naṣr Ismāʿīl al-Jawharī (d. 397/1006) it is derived from a Syriac word, while others (unnamed) consider it an Arabicized form of the Greek *nautēs*. *Arabic-English Lexicon*, 8:2863. Ibn Manẓūr mentions only a Syriac etymology. He quotes this same *ḥadīth* from Ibn ʿAbbās but in connection with 5:83 not 5:82. *Lisān al-ʿarab*, 3:101.

63 al-Ṭabarī, *Jāmiʿ al-bayān*, 10:505. In a final *ḥadīth* from Saʿīd b. Jubayr the *qissīsūn* and *ruhbān* are identified as "messengers from the Najāshī who brought word of his submission (*islāmuhu*) and the submission of his people (*islām qawmihi*)" and further equated with those referred to in *sūrat al-qaṣaṣ* (28):52–54, which will be discussed in Chapter 8.

of this whole phrase. It is because of the very presence of such individuals among the people who call themselves Christians – whoever they may be – that there is such friendliness with the believers. This divinely commended amicability on the part of the Christians is due to the presence among them of "a people diligent in worship (*ahl ijtihād fī al-ʿibādāt*), living monastically in cells and hermitages (*tarahhub fī al-diyārāt wa-al-ṣawāmiʿ*). They are not far from the believers because they assent to the truth when they recognize it, and they are not too proud to accept it when they see it clearly."[64] He then proceeds to refer to them as "people of a religion (*ahl dīnin*)," vastly different from "the Jews who habitually killed prophets and messengers, stubbornly opposed God's commands and prohibitions, and altered the revelation that He sent down in His books."[65] By implication, then, it is the very lack of a faithful remnant among the Jews that exacerbates their hostility to the Muslims and prevents the development of the concord that exists between Christians – at least a certain group of them – and Muslims.

Al-Ṭūsī's principal concern is also the logical connection between this phrase and what precedes it. He, too, reads *that is because among them are priests and monks and because they are not arrogant* as an explanation for the discrepancy between Muslim-Christian and Muslim-Jewish relations. It is a problem of inhibiting pride: "The Christians who believe are not too proud to follow the truth and submit to it (*ittibāʿ al-ḥaqq wa-al-inqiyād lahu*), as are the Jews and idol worshipers (*ʿubbād al-awthān*)."[66]

Al-Zamakhsharī confronts the basic issue of foundational perspective directly when he summarizes this verse by pitting Jewish recalcitrance (*ṣuʿūbah*) against Christian tractability (*līn*) and the ease with which the latter repent and incline toward submission to God (*suhūlat irʿawāʾihim wa-maylihim ilā al-islām*).[67] The association of the Jews with the *mushrikūn* is a gauge of the intensity of their hostility to the believers. Furthermore this commentator is another who finds significance in the relative placement of the terms *al-yahūd* and *alladhīna ashrakū*. The fact that the Jews are mentioned before the *mushrikūn* in this verse demonstrates the longer du-

64 al-Ṭabarī, *Jāmiʿ al-bayān*, 10:505. The basic study of the Qurʾānic understanding of monasticism, which examines the three relevant loci (*sūrat al-māʾidah* [5]:82–86, *sūrat al-tawbah* [9]:29–35, and *sūrat al-ḥadīd* [57]:27), is that by Edmund Beck, *Das christliche Mönchtum im Koran* (Helsinki: Societas Orientalis Fennica, 1946).

65 al-Ṭabarī, *Jāmiʿ al-bayān*, 10:506.

66 al-Ṭūsī, *al-Tibyān*, 3:616. In his note on the phrase *dhālika bi-anna minhum qissīsīna wa-ruhbānan wa-annahum lā-yastakbirūna*, Rudi Paret remarks that *istakbara* is found frequently in the Qurʾān and "er bedeutet in der Regel nicht Stolz gegen Menschen, sondern Hochmut in religiösem Sinn, nämlich mangelnde Ehrfurcht vor Gott und der göttlichen Offenbarung." *Kommentar und Konkordanz*, 128.

67 al-Zamakhsharī, *al-Kashshāf*, 1:668.

ration of Jewish hostility to the believers.[68] As a supporting verse he draws upon *sūrat al-baqarah* (2):96: "You will find them [the Jews] the most avid (*aḥraṣ*) of people for life [more so than] those who are idolaters (*alladhīna ashrakū*)." Al-Zamakhsharī adds his own rejoinder to this commentary-verging-on-anti-Jewish-polemic with the words: "By God, they are really like that and worse!" To cap it off he quotes a Prophetic *ḥadīth*: "No two Jews can be alone with a Muslim except with intent to kill."[69] By contrast, Christian pliability is to be explained in terms of the presence of priests and monks (*qissīsūn wa-ruhbān*). The synonyms al-Zamakhsharī has selected for these two words are 'people of learning (*ʿulamāʾ*)' and 'pious devotees (*ʿubbād*)'. He describes them as humble and submissive, devoid of arrogance and, as such, quite the opposite of the Jews.[70] However, his understanding of this phrase is not restricted by the designation of these two groups. Rather he finds in this reference a general laudation of learning, of which the Christian priests and monks are but a particular instance.

Semantic association of the term *qissīsūn* with connotations of 'learning' is continued by Abū al-Futūḥ Rāzī who also includes Ibn Zayd's gloss of the term as 'ascetics (*zuhhād*)'. He, however, adds to the developing tradition a curious bit of etymological lore on the authority of ʿUrwah b. al-Zubayr (d. 94/712). This begins with the statement that "the Christians ruined the Gospel by alteration and substitution (*tarsāyān injīl żāyiʿ kardand va ānrā taghyīr va tabdīl kardand*)."[71] There were five men involved: four of them altered and made substitutions in the Gospel. These four were Lūqās, Marqūs, Baljīs, and Mīmnūs. "The one who remained steadfast in the truth was [named] Qissīs. Therefore, anyone who imitated him by remaining truthful was called *qissīs*."[72] As further explanation for the term,

68 al-Zamakhsharī, *al-Kashshāf*, 1:668.

69 al-Zamakhsharī, *al-Kashshāf*, 1:668. The editor quotes a variant of this *ḥadīth* in which the word "Jew" is in the singular.

70 al-Zamakhsharī, *al-Kashshāf*, 1:668. Tor Andrae argues that the tenor of Muḥammad's religious experience, "the deep earnestness, the keen expectation of future life, the contrition and trembling before the Day of Judgment, fear as an actual proof of piety, the warning against the carelessness which forgets responsibility and retribution," show a close relationship to "the basic mood of *Christian ascetic piety* [Andrae's italics]." *Mohammed: The Man and His Faith (Mohammed, sein Leben und sein Glaube)*, trans. by Theophil Menzel (1936; reprint of revised edition, New York: Harper and Brothers, 1960), 83. This judgment is developed at length in Andrae's *Les Origines de l'Islam et le Christianisme*.

71 Abū al-Futūḥ Rāzī, *Rawḥ al-jinān*, 4:306.

72 Abū al-Futūḥ Rāzī, *Rawḥ al-jinān*, 4:306. The synonym that Abū al-Futūḥ Rāzī gives for *ruhbān* is the expected *ʿubbād* (devotees) while the root meaning noted for *RHB* is *khawf* (fear). Al-Ṣadūq Abū Jaʿfar Muḥammad b. Bābawayh's (d. 381/991) *Kitāb al-tawḥīd* offers another Shīʿī account of Gospel origins: after the *injīl* of Jesus was lost, Luke, Mark, John, and Matthew reproduced it from memory. David Thomas has trans-

Abū al-Futūḥ Rāzī quotes a *ḥadīth* from Salmān al-Fārisī in which the Prophet recites this verse to him and substitutes 'righteous men (*ṣiddīqīn*)' for *qissīsīn*.

The final segment of this sentence, *and because they are not arrogant,* is then understood to be intimately connected with these two foregoing categories, expressing a further praiseworthy qualification possessed by such individuals. Once again, it is the notion of priests and monks functioning as a kind of leaven or 'saving remnant' among the main body of Christians that comes strongly to the fore.[73]

According to Ibn al-Jawzī, who is here quoting al-Zajjāj, *qissīsūn* means 'leaders of the Christians (*ruʾasāʾ al-naṣārā*)'; on the authority of Abū ʿAlī Muḥammad al-Quṭrub (d. 206/821) the word comes from the Syriac where it means 'a learned man (*ʿālim*)'. As for *ruhbān*, while no etymology is given, the synonyms *ʿubbād* ('worshipers') and *arbāb al-ṣawāmiʿ* ('cell people') are proffered.[74] After these etymological considerations, Ibn al-Jawzī raises an interesting question, one that broadens the range of exegetical discussion on this verse. He asks "why the Christians are being praised *because among them are priests and monks* when that is no part of our law (*wa-laysa dhālika min amr sharīʿatinā*)?"[75] The question, of course, refers to the oft-mentioned prohibition against "monkery" in Islam. The answer this exegete proposes clearly distinguishes the difference between these two religious traditions in the matter of monasticism: "Monasticism (*rahbānīyah*) was well-regarded (*mustaḥsan*) in their [the Christians'] religion."[76] How-

lated the relevant portion of Ibn Bābawayh in "Two Muslim-Christian Debates from the Early Shīʿite Tradition," *JSS* 33 (1988): 74.

73 Abū al-Futūḥ Rāzī, *Rawḥ al-jinān*, 4:307.

74 Ibn al-Jawzī, *Zād al-masīr*, 2:408. Abraham Geiger, drawing as well upon Syriac etymologies, concludes that "*ruhbān* does not really mean the ordinary monks . . . but the clergy; whereas *qissīs* stands for the presbyter, the elder . . . ." *Judaism and Islam (Was hat Mohammed aus dem Judenthume aufgenommen?)*, trans. by F.M. Young (1898; reprint with Prolegomenon by Moshe Pearlman, New York: Ktav, 1970), 36.

75 Ibn al-Jawzī, *Zād al-masīr*, 2:408. In contrasting this verse's praise of priests and monks with the denunciation of rabbis and monks (*aḥbār wa-ruhbān*) in *sūrat al-tawbah* (9):31, Kenneth Cragg remarks that "it is hard to resist the impression that Muḥammad's attitude changed, when he discovered that his claims failed to receive the hospitable welcome he had first expected from the people of the earlier Book." *The Call of the Minaret*, 1st ed., 261. Geoffrey Parrinder finds a possible reference to "saint cults" in the phrase found in 9:31, "they take their scholars and monks (*aḥbār wa-ruhbān*) as lords apart from God." He then adds that "it is well known that legends and devotions grew up around the lives of some of the Christian martyrs and ascetics." *Jesus in the Qurʾān*, 157.

76 Ibn al-Jawzī, *Zād al-masīr*, 2:409. Louis Massignon counters those who would understand the *ḥadīth* "*lā rahbānīyah fī al-islām*" as a complete disavowal of celibacy with the reminder that temporary celibacy is one of the *ḥajj* requirements. *Essai sur les origines du lexique technique de la mystique musulmane*, 2nd ed. (Paris: Librairie Philosophique G.

ever, divine praise is not being offered for communal celibacy as such, but for learning and erudition. The Christians are praised, in Ibn al-Jawzī's paraphrase of the Qurʾānic citation, because "among them were men learned in what Jesus had enjoined about Muḥammad (*ʿulamāʾ bimā awṣā bihi ʿĪsā min amr Muḥammad*)."[77] This commentator thus maintains the chronological discrimination between what is expected of Christians before and after the advent of Muḥammad, but does so with greater specification. This makes the critical word in the following statement the conjunction "until": Christians "are being praised for adhering to the religion of Jesus *until* they act upon what their scripture enjoins upon them with respect to Muḥammad."[78]

Should any ignoramus, continues Ibn al-Jawzī, find in this verse praise for the Christians in general, he would be completely wrong. It is praise only for those among them who believe (*man āmana*), that is, who become Muslims. Lest there be any lingering doubt about pervasive Christian defectiveness this commentator contrasts Jewish and Christian doctrine (*maqālah*) to the grave detriment of the latter: "There is no doubt that Christian doctrine is more repugnant (*aqbaḥ*) than Jewish."[79] The only redeeming feature attributable to the Christians is the presence among them of men of learning whose scholarly ability has not been corrupted by arrogance. Verification of this is found in the Qurʾānic description *they are not arrogant* (*lā yastakbirūna*), which Ibn al-Jawzī explains as not being too proud to follow the truth.[80]

Rather than immediately involving himself in a philological analysis of the terms *qissīsūn* and *ruhbān*, as other commentators have, Fakhr al-Dīn al-Rāzī uses the phrase as the basis for a continued analysis of Jewish-Christian differences. This time he finds a contrast not between Jewish belligerence and Christian tractability, but between Jewish greed for worldly things and Christian renunciation of them. It is this latter polarity between avidity and renunciation that generates the resultant belligerent or compliant behavior. Fakhr al-Dīn al-Rāzī locates proof for this accusation of Jewish greed, as did al-Zamakhsharī, in *sūrat al-baqarah* (2):96. Greed (*ḥirṣ*), says this exegete, is the root and source of discord, because "the man who is greedy for worldly things discards his religious duty in pursuit

Vrin, 1968), 1:147. The Qurʾānic conception of monasticism is briefly contrasted with its variety of Christian forms in the chapter entitled "L'antinomie de la 'rahbaniyya' en Islam" in Jean-Paul Gabus, Ali Merad, and Youakim Moubarac, *Islam et Christianisme en dialogue* (Paris: Les Éditions du Cerf, 1982), 161–69.

77 Ibn al-Jawzī, *Zād al-masīr*, 2:409.

78 Ibn al-Jawzī, *Zād al-masīr*, 2:409.

79 Ibn al-Jawzī, *Zād al-masīr*, 2:409.

80 Ibn al-Jawzī, *Zād al-masīr*, 2:409. The central place of 'arrogance (*istikbār*)' within the semantic field of *kufr* is analyzed by Izutsu, *Ethico-Religious*, 142–52.

of worldly pleasures. He has the audacity to do any forbidden or abominable deed in the search for temporal goods. Naturally his hostility increases towards anyone who gains wealth and fame."[81]

The obverse of this stark picture of Jewish moral deformation is Fakhr al-Dīn al-Rāzī's idealistic depiction of Christian rectitude. He maintains that unlike the Jews (who are greedy for the world's goods), the Christians are a people who renounce temporal satisfactions (*muʿriḍūn ʿan al-dunyā*) and who turn to divine worship (*muqbilūn ʿalā al-ʿibādah*). As a result their behavior is devoid of self-aggrandizement, arrogance, and haughtiness; their inner virtue is reflected in outward action. Anyone whose eyes are diverted from worldly gain "does not envy people or hold grudges against them or quarrel with them; rather his is a nature open to the truth and prepared for compliant submission to it."[82]

Having said this, Fakhr al-Dīn al-Rāzī hastens to add a strong corrective to his complimentary portrayal of Christianity. The issue he raises is that of the nature of Christian unbelief: "The unbelief (*kufr*) of the Christians is cruder (*aghlaẓ*) than that of the Jews because the Christians dispute about matters theological-metaphysical and prophetical (*yunāziʿūna fī ilāhīyāt wa-fī al-nubūwāt*) while the Jews debate only about the latter."[83] Yet the Christian lack of worldly greed and inclination toward the Hereafter (*mayl ilā al-ākhirah*) partially redeems them in God's eyes, as the divine honor accorded them in this verse attests. Again, in contrast stands the divine denunciation of the Jews "whose belief is not as coarse as that of the Christians" but whose condemnation is occasioned by "their greed for worldly things."[84]

Fakhr al-Dīn al-Rāzī concludes his commentary on 5:82 with the postponed word study of *qissīsūn* and *ruhbān*. He closely follows the philological exegesis of Ibn al-Jawzī here, explicitly acknowledging the attribution to Quṭrub but not to al-Zajjāj. Then Fakhr al-Dīn al-Rāzī quotes on the authority of ʿUrwah b. al-Zubayr a condensed form of the curious bit of etymological lore first found in Abū al-Futūḥ Rāzī: "The Christians fabricated the Gospel (*ṣanaʿat al-naṣārā al-injīl*) and introduced extraneous material. But one of their learned men remained steadfast in the truth and

81 Fakhr al-Dīn al-Rāzī, *al-Tafsīr al-kabīr*, 12:66.

82 Fakhr al-Dīn al-Rāzī, *al-Tafsīr al-kabīr*, 12:66.

83 Fakhr al-Dīn al-Rāzī, *al-Tafsīr al-kabīr*, 12:67. For a more extended discussion of Fakhr al-Dīn al-Rāzī's various religious categories see the section on "Qurʾānic parallels" in Chapter 3.

84 Fakhr al-Dīn al-Rāzī, *al-Tafsīr al-kabīr*, 12:67. Rudi Paret highlights this reason for Jewish/Christian contrast in his remarks on 5:82. *Muhammed und der Koran: Geschichte und Verkündigung des arabischen Propheten*, 5th revised ed. (Stuttgart: W. Kohlhammer, 1980), 141.

his name was Qissīs. So whoever lives according to his guidance and religion is a *qissīs*.[85]

The questions of how to reconcile this phrase with the Qur᾿ānic rejection of monasticism found in *sūrat al-ḥadīd* (57):27 and the Prophet's denunciation of it is answered by Fakhr al-Dīn al-Rāzī again in terms of Christian-Jewish contrast. The point, he insists, is not that monasticism is praiseworthy in general. Rather it is something to be praised "in comparison with the Jewish way of harshness and ruthlessness (*al-qasāwah wa-al-ghilẓah*)."[86]

When Ibn Kathīr starts to probe the interreligious dynamics to which this verse testifies he intensifies the initial condemnation of the Jews by remarking upon the pervasive obstinacy and denial (*ᶜinād wa-juḥūd*) of the Jews and their defamation of the truth (*mubāhatah lil-ḥaqq*). These serious moral deficiencies are the cause of their killing previous prophets – a Qur᾿ānic charge repeated here by Ibn Kathīr. They are thus the cause of Jewish attempts on the life of Muḥammad: "They poisoned him and used sorcery against (*sammūhu wa-saḥarūhu*) and incited the like-minded *mushrikūn* against him."[87] Ibn Kathīr reinforces this accusatory exegesis by quoting two versions of the oft-mentioned Prophetic *ḥadīth* about general Jewish hostility to Muslims, both on the authority of Abū Hurayrah but one of which he characterizes as very uncommon.

When dealing with the phrase that refers to Christians, this commentator speaks of Christians as a whole and first proposes a sort of Christian self-definition: "Those who claim (*zaᶜamū*) to be Christians based on following the Messiah and living according to the ways of his Gospel (*manāhij injīlihi*)."[88] They are friendly both to Islam and its people, in the sense

85 Fakhr al-Dīn al-Rāzī, *al-Tafsīr al-kabīr*, 12:67.

86 Fakhr al-Dīn al-Rāzī, *al-Tafsīr al-kabīr*, 12:67. Fakhr al-Diñ al-Rāzī here repeats the famous *ḥadīth* that is usually translated as "There shall be no monkery in Islam" (*lā rahbānīyah fī al-islām*). For contrastive purposes, it is interesting to note the view found in the *tafsīr* often attributed to Ibn al-ᶜArabī. For this exegete the Jews represent a fairly primitive stage of spiritual development, for "they are veiled from the [divine] essence and attributes, having nothing but the *tawḥīd* of actions." Thus does he explain their affinity for the *mushrikūn*, "those who are absolutely veiled," completely beyond the range of God's self-revelation. In like manner is Christian-Muslim rapport understood. Since the Christians "have emerged from the veil of the [divine] attributes and nothing but the veil of the [divine] essence covers them, their relationship with the believers (*mu᾿minūn*) is stronger." This, says Ibn al-ᶜArabī, is what the idea of friendship connotes. Unlike other commentators, he does not go on to explore the nature of Muslim-Jewish hostility. Rather he emphasizes the Jewish-*mushrikūn* affinity which the density of their 'veils' ensures. (This final statement is based on reading the sentence *wa-al-mushrikūna al-yahūdu ashaddu ᶜadāwatan li-qūwati ḥijābihim* with a *wa* inserted between the first two nouns.) Ibn al-ᶜArabī, *Tafsīr al-Qur᾿ān al-karīm*, 1:340.

87 Ibn Kathīr, *Tafsīr al-Qur᾿ān al-ᶜaẓīm*, 2:85.

88 Ibn Kathīr, *Tafsīr al-Qur᾿ān al-ᶜaẓīm*, 2:86.

that this friendship is "in their hearts since kindliness and compassion (*al-riqqah wa-al-raʾfah*) are part of the religion of the Messiah."[89] Qurʾānic support for this description is found in *sūrat al-ḥadīd* (57):27: "We put compassion and mercy in the hearts of those who followed him [Jesus]."[90] Ibn Kathīr even goes beyond the Qurʾān to Christian scriptural sources. He observes that in "their book," the Gospel, the following dictum occurs: "Whoever strikes you on your right cheek, turn to him your left cheek."[91] This is clearly an almost verbatim citation of Matthew 5:39 (cf. Luke 6:29) from which Ibn Kathīr draws the conclusion that fighting is unlawful in Christianity (*wa-laysa al-qitāl mashrūʿ fī millatihim*).[92]

This exegete expands the usual definition offered for *qissīsūn* to include not only 'learned men (*ʿulamāʾ*)' but also 'preachers (*khuṭabāʾ*)'. For *ruhbān* he cites the single synonym of 'worshiper (*ʿābid*)'. Ibn Kathīr then moves beyond these etymological considerations to introduce several versions of a *ḥadīth*, earlier noted in Abū al-Futūḥ Rāzī, which is traced back to Salmān al-Fārisī. It begins with the explanation that *qissīsūn* live in churches and ruins (*al-biyaʿ wa-al-khirab*). (In another version this is given as hermit cells [*al-ṣawāmiʿ*] and ruins.)[93] Then Salmān records that when he recited to the Prophet *that is because among them are priests and monks* Muḥammad glossed the Qurʾānic phrase by adding "that is because among them are sincere and righteous men (*ṣiddīqīn*) and monks."[94] Ibn Kathīr concludes by recasting the terms of this verse's final phrase to create a laudatory catalogue of Christian attributes: among them are to be found knowledge (*ʿilm*), veneration (*ʿibādah*), and humility (*tawāḍuʿ*); they can be described as complying with truth (*inqiyād lil-ḥaqq*), adhering to it (*ittibāʿuhu*), and acting with equity (*al-inṣāf*).[95]

In commenting upon this verse's opening phrase, Kāshānī spends rather more time detailing the vices of the Jews than did Abū al-Futūḥ Rāzī. The now-familiar catalogue of accusations includes "the multiplication of their unbelief (*taẓāʿuf-i kufr-i īshān*)," "being slaves to their passions (*in-himāk-i īshān dar ittibāʿ-i-havā*)," and "obstinately refuting prophets (*ta-*

89 Ibn Kathīr, *Tafsīr al-Qurʾān al-ʿaẓīm*, 2:86. For Ibn Taymīyah the friendliness of Christians will not necessarily save them from punishment or merit eternal reward for them. His response to the arguments of Paul of Antioch also stresses the importance of reading 5:82 and 83 in tandem. T. Michel, *A Muslim Theologian's Response*, 243–46, and P. Khoury, *Paul d'Antioche*, 66–67 of Arabic text.

90 This verse will be the subject of Chapter 9.

91 Ibn Kathīr, *Tafsīr al-Qurʾān al-ʿaẓīm*, 2:86.

92 Ibn Kathīr, *Tafsīr al-Qurʾān al-ʿaẓīm*, 2:86.

93 Ibn Kathīr, *Tafsīr al-Qurʾān al-ʿaẓīm*, 2:86. The story of Salmān al-Fārisī forms one of the *asbāb al-nuzūl* for 2:62, which is treated in Chapter 3.

94 Ibn Kathīr, *Tafsīr al-Qurʾān al-ʿaẓīm*, 2:86. Arthur Jeffery finds *ṣiddīqīn* instead of *qissisīn* in the codex of Ubayy b. Kaʿb. *Materials*, 129.

95 Ibn Kathīr, *Tafsīr al-Qurʾān al-ʿaẓīm*, 2:86.

marrud-i īshān bar takzīb-i anbiyāʾ)."[96] The *mushrikūn* are treated as equivalent to the Jews in these offenses, and even the *ḥadīth* on the authority of Abū Hurayrah that portrays the Jews as an ever-present threat is applied to them also.

By contrast the phrase referring to the Christians occasions a listing of the virtues that may be found in this group. Christians are praised for "their soft and tender hearts, for their little interest in worldly things (*qillat-i ḥirṣ-i īshān bar dunyā*) and their great diligence in knowledge and action (*kasrat-i ihtimām-i īshān bi-ʿilm va ʿamal*)."[97] Since the *mushrikūn* do not share these qualities, an alliance between them and the Christians could not develop. Kāshānī understands the *that* in *that is because among them are priests and monks* to refer to the nearness of friendship (*qurb-i mawaddat*). He offers as a translation for *qissīsūn* 'truth-speaking sages (*dānāyān-i rāstgū*)'; that given for *ruhbān* is 'cell-dwelling worshipers (*ʿābidān-i ṣawmaʿa-nishīn*)'.[98] Chief of the Christian virtues, as attested to by the last phrase of this verse, is an absence of arrogance. Being open to the reception of truth, when it is heard and understood, is the meaning Kāshānī assigns to *they are not arrogant*. Once again praise of Christians is contrasted with condemnation of the Jews, who, Kāshānī insists, boast that they will always remain Jews.[99]

Rashīd Riḍā continues the tradition of finding an explanation for Christian amicability in the sentence *that is because among them are priests and monks and because they are not arrogant*. For this exegete the *qissīsūn* are the teachers, the ones responsible for religious education, while the *ruhbān* are concerned with world-renouncing and worshiping God.[100] Their willingness to submit to the truth is eased by their religion's insistence on humility (*al-tawāḍuʿ*), self-abasement (*al-tadhallul*), and the acceptance of any authority (*qabūl kulli sulṭatin*).[101] "Of particular note," says Rashīd Riḍā, echoing Ibn Kathīr, "is the admonition to love the enemy and to turn the left cheek to anyone who strikes the right cheek."[102] Although these exhortations were directed to all Christians, they were more seriously heeded

96 Kāshānī, *Minhaj al-ṣādiqīn*, 3:291.
97 Kāshānī, *Minhaj al-ṣādiqīn*, 3:291.
98 Kāshānī, *Minhaj al-ṣādiqīn*, 3:291.
99 Kāshānī, *Minhaj al-ṣādiqīn*, 3:291.
100 Rashīd Riḍā, *Tafsīr al-Manār*, 7:7. Although he does not divide these functions between the two groups, Beck takes a similar position by speaking of an "inner" and an "outer" basis for the Qurʾānic presentation of Muslim-Christian affinity. The inner basis would be that spiritual state which is characterized by the lack of religious arrogance, while the outer is the educational function of biblical exegesis correctly performed and thus conducive to the reception of God's final revelation. *Das christliche Mönchtum*, 5–7.
101 Rashīd Riḍā, *Tafsīr al-Manār*, 7:7.
102 Rashīd Riḍā, *Tafsīr al-Manār*, 7:7.

by the priests and monks, who act as a spiritual leaven within the whole community. It is their edifying presence, then, that accounts for greater Christian amicability.

The Jewish-Christian antithesis highlighted by the phrase *and because they are not arrogant* is given further explanation. Rashīd Riḍā locates the source of Christian tractability in the greater ease with which the authority of an adversary is accepted (*qabūl sulṭat al-mukhālif lahum*).[103] They have long acquaintance with the acceptance of submission to such authority and with showing themselves publicly and privately content with it. "The Jews, on the other hand, may publicly exhibit satisfaction under compulsion but secretly they conceal treachery and they delude with great cunning."[104]

Having followed the traditional exegetical schema of commenting on each phrase of the verse, Rashīd Riḍā then moves back for a macroscopic view and discusses some matters to which the verse as a whole gives rise. The first of these he prefaces with the remark that though "these are general descriptions of the two groups, they do not suffice to explain individual characters."[105] Thus, among the Jews there are good people and bad, and the Qurʾān makes this distinction in *sūrat al-aʿrāf* (7):159. Yet this commentator feels called upon to draw attention once more to Jewish racial exclusivity "upon which all its [Judaism's] statutes and stipulations are built."[106] He bases the historical explanation for this exclusivity within Israel's growth as a monotheistic community (*ummah muwaḥḥidah*) among idolatrous nations (*umam wathanīyah*). The exodus from Egypt and entrance into the Holy Land (*al-arḍ al-muqaddasah*) was overlaid with divine admonitions to avoid all contact with that land's original inhabitants.[107]

Rashīd Riḍā seeks to still the objections of those who doubt whether the Jewish religion can be at all connected with God. Given such wicked

103 Rashīd Riḍā, *Tafsīr al-Manār*, 7:7. Jomier has drawn attention to the difference between Christian and Islamic understandings of *istikbār*. In commenting upon *lā-yastakbirūna* he states: "L'orgueil, dans le Coran, ne s'applique point d'abord à ce sentiment que les auteurs spirituels chrétiens essaient de pourchasser partout où ils le trouvent, cet orgueil 'qui se glisse même dans les oeuvres bonnes pour les faire périr', comme l'écrivait saint Augustin dans la *Règle* qui porte son nom. L'orgueil, dans le Coran, est avant tout une attitude d'âme qui pousse à refuser l'Islam. N'être point orgueilleux signifie que l'on est prêt à se faire musulman." *Le commentaire coranique du Manār*, 303.

104 Rashīd Riḍā, *Tafsīr al-Manār*, 7:7. H. Zafrani draws upon a number of sources, including documents from the Cairo Geniza, to sketch some of the legal ramifications encountered by Jews under Muslim hegemony. "Les relations judéo-musulmanes dans la littérature juridique," in *Les relations entre juifs et musulmans en Afrique du Nord: actes du colloque international de l'Institut d'histoire des pays d'Outre-Mer* (Paris: Éditions du Centre national de la recherche scientifique, 1980), 32–48.

105 Rashīd Riḍā, *Tafsīr al-Manār*, 7:7.

106 Rashīd Riḍā, *Tafsīr al-Manār*, 7:7.

107 Rashīd Riḍā, *Tafsīr al-Manār*, 7:7.

behavior among the Jews, how could one say that their religion is from God? The commentator responds that "the answer to this doubt is easy for Muslims; it can be explained by the fact that this *sharīʿah* [that of the Jews] was temporary, not permanent."[108] It was a stage in the development of monotheism. Prophets would repeatedly exhort their people to reform. The Psalms of David (*zabūr Dāwūd*) and the Wisdom of Solomon (*ḥikam Sulaymān*) reflect these prophetic concerns, reaffirming spiritual values and cautioning against excessive materialism.[109]

Then came the greatest reformer of Israel (*muṣliḥ isrāʾīl al-aʿẓam*), Jesus the Messiah. Rashīd Riḍā expresses the extent of Jesus' reformation by juxtaposing Jewish defects with Christian virtues: "The Jews' extreme materialism was countered with extreme spirituality, their extreme selfishness with extreme altruism, which the Christians call self-denial (*inkār al-dhāt*), and their exaggerated inflexibility about the literal meanings of the law with careful attention to observing the law's intent."[110] Jesus directed his followers away from concern with temporal power and wealth and the enjoyment of earthly happiness. Rather he enjoined them to love their enemies and not to seek retaliation. "All that was a preparation for God's completing His religion by sending the Seal of the prophets and messengers, Muḥammad."[111] It was only with Muḥammad's arrival that God's religion achieved a proper balance. This prophet's reformation "combined for mankind those things beneficial to soul and body and enjoined both just action (*ʿadl*) and gratuitous charity (*iḥsān*), not just the latter."[112]

Of course, Rashīd Riḍā continues, few among the Jews took the Messianic reformation to heart and most were openly hostile to Jesus. Comparable was the reception accorded to the reformation initiated by Muḥammad. The most receptive and quickest to believe were the group of *qissīsūn* and *ruhbān*. This commentator equates them with the reference in *sūrat al-aʿrāf* (7):157 to "those who follow the Messenger, the *ummī* Prophet [whom they find written with them in the Torah and the Gospel]." Such individuals follow the Prophet whom they find foretold in the Torah and Gospel and he, by rightly guiding them, "relieves them of their burden and the fetters which bind." Identifying this weight and these shackles brings Rashīd Riḍā again to the element of balance which Islam introduced: "That 'burden' and those 'fetters' were none other than the severity (*shiddah*) of the Torah's prescriptions about food and drink and the civil and criminal statutes (*al-aḥkām al-madanīyah wa-al-jināʾīyah*), and the severity of the

108 Rashīd Riḍā, *Tafsīr al-Manār*, 7:8.
109 Rashīd Riḍā, *Tafsīr al-Manār*, 7:8.
110 Rashīd Riḍā, *Tafsīr al-Manār*, 7:8.
111 Rashīd Riḍā, *Tafsīr al-Manār*, 7:8.
112 Rashīd Riḍā, *Tafsīr al-Manār*, 7:8.

Gospel's precepts about asceticism (*al-zuhd*), self-abasement (*idhlāl al-nafs*), and self-deprivation (*ḥirmānuhā*)."[113]

Rashīd Riḍā then raises the issue of subsequent historical confirmation for this verse by remarking upon "the large number of Christians who embraced Islam in every age and the small number of Jews who did so."[114] Obstacles to Christian conversion to Islam in the present day are attributed to a number of factors. He parcels out the blame between Muslim and Christian defects. On the Islamic side Rashīd Riḍā lists such things as the general 'weakness (*ḍuʿf*)' of Muslims in this time, "their turning away from the guidance of the Qurʾān, and their neglecting to proselytize for Islam (*ihmāluhum al-daʿwah ilā al-islām*) and to present it in its correct form so as to disclose the corruption of their governments (*fasād ḥukūmātihim*) together with the impotence of their [the governments'] administrative officials in political/diplomatic affairs (*ʿajz rijālihā fī al-siyāsāt*), and their not keeping up with other nations in learning and culture (*takhallufuhum ʿan mujārāt al-uman fī al-ʿilm wa-al-haḍārah*)."[115] The most immediate obstacle to increased Christian conversion to Islam, according to Rashīd Riḍā, is the political disputes between Christian and Islamic nations. Were it not for these, "then the friendship between the two groups would be fuller and there would be a more general diffusion of Islam among them, because Islam is an amelioration of Christianity (*li-anna al-islām iṣlāḥ fī al-naṣrānīyah*) just as Christianity is an enhancement of Judaism."[116] Rashīd Riḍā then finds in the logic of this development another reason for Jewish-Muslim enmity. In instances of Jewish-Christian dispute, Muslims should take the Christian side, because Christianity is a closer stage to the perfection of religion, Islam.[117]

One historical event this commentator feels compelled to deal with is the Crusades, a war "whose fire the Christians ignited in the name of religion."[118] Nothing like it ever occurred between the Muslims and Jews or *mushrikūn*. Rashīd Riḍā deals with this problem from two perspectives. The first is that of the medieval Christian misunderstanding of Islam. Plainly stated, the Christians simply did not realize that Islam was an improvement on their religion. Christians had only the most distorted im-

113 Rashīd Riḍā, *Tafsīr al-Manār*, 7:9.

114 Rashīd Riḍā, *Tafsīr al-Manār*, 7:9. Richard Bulliet has used the quantitative analysis of data drawn from Muslim biographical dictionaries to graph the rates of conversion in selected areas of the medieval Islamic world. *Conversion to Islam in the Medieval Period* (Cambridge, Mass.: Harvard University Press, 1979).

115 Rashīd Riḍā, *Tafsīr al-Manār*, 7:9.

116 Rashīd Riḍā, *Tafsīr al-Manār*, 7:9.

117 Another argument Rashīd Riḍā offers for the closer proximity of Christianity to Islam is presented in Chapter 3.

118 Rashīd Riḍā, *Tafsīr al-Manār*, 7:10.

age of Islam, "an image [of something] pagan, wild and ugly – the most repulsive defacement."[119] This exegete even locates the source of this falsification "in the writing, letters and speeches which Peter the Monk (*Biṭrus al-rāhib*) and his like produced."[120] In fact, insists Rashīd Riḍā, so intimidating was the misrepresentation that had the Muslims themselves been summoned to fight a people so described they would have fled.

The second line of response that he takes on the problem of the Crusades contrasts the Gospel message of peace and love with the nationalistic thrust for power and temporal dominion. The Christian teaching never triumphed over European belligerence and aggressiveness: "These characteristics had already reached full maturity in the era of Byzantine sovereignty and were the reason for the annihilation of paganism in all of Europe as well as being the cause of the Crusades and the attempt to eliminate the Muslims from the Holy Land or the whole Eastern world."[121]

Lest the impression remain that Christian aggression is directed principally against Muslims, Rashīd Riḍā mentions the bitter wars that have been fought between various Christian groups themselves. These he attributes to differing religious beliefs and practice (*ikhtilāf al-madhāhib*) or nationalistic contention. Both derive from Satan (*shayṭān*), not from the Spirit of God (a Qurʾānic expression used in relation to Jesus), "even though it is reported that he said: 'I have not come to bring peace on earth, I have come only to bring the sword.' "[122] This quotation from Matthew 10:34, presented without explanation, of course undercuts the statement it was ostensibly intended to support.

Unlike the doctrinal disputes at the base of some intra-Christian wars, Muslim-Christian conflict is not commonly founded on religion, but occurs

119 Rashīd Riḍā, *Tafsīr al-Manār*, 7:10. The most comprehensive study to date of medieval Christian attitudes toward Islam is that of Norman Daniel, *Islam and the West: The Making of an Image* (Edinburgh: The University Press, 1960).

120 Rashīd Riḍā, *Tafsīr al-Manār*, 7:10. James Kritzeck published a study of this "major source of informed European Christian knowledge of Islam" (p. viii), including an interpretive translation of this *Summa totius haeresis Saracenorum*, entitled *Peter the Venerable and Islam* (Princeton: Princeton University Press, 1964). For a summary and critique of Kritzeck's work see Cutler, *The Jew as Ally of the Muslim*, 22–51.

121 Rashīd Riḍā, *Tafsīr al-Manār*, 7:10. Rashīd Riḍā's explanation of Muslim-Christian enmity as a failure of each side to act according to the best principles of its religion has captured the attention of Father Maurice Borrmans. He finds in the document *Nostra aetate* of the Second Vatican Council an echo of such sentiments: "Si, au cours des siècles, de nombreuses dissensions et inimitiés se sont élevées entre Chrétiens et Musulmans, le Concile les exhorte tous à oublier le passé, à s'efforcer sincèrement à la compréhension mutuelle, et à garder et promouvoir en commun, pour tous les hommes, la justice sociale, les valeurs morales, la paix et la liberté." "Le Commentaire du Manâr à propos du verset coranique sur l'amitié des musulmans pour les chrétiens (5,82)," *Islamo* 1 (1975): 72.

122 Rashīd Riḍā, *Tafsīr al-Manār*, 7:10.

beyond the guidance range of each religion. "No one but an ignorant man or a fool connects it to the nature of the two religions."[123] Yet the call to religion has certainly been used as a goad to incite nations to war. Rashīd Riḍā makes this point well in a statement that resounds with an ironical prophetic ring: "The deceptive political *imāms* of the two groups continue to use religion as a trick to deceive the masses into supporting their politics to a degree that is criminal both to the religion and its people."[124]

Taking another tack, this exegete now moves from historical to doctrinal objections. Could it not be said, he ponders, that Judaism is closer to Islam than Christianity because it is a monotheistic religion (*diyānah tawḥīd*) while Christianity is trinitarian (*diyānah tathlīth*)? After all, affirming the oneness of God (*tawḥīd*) is the essence of God's religion and the perfection of all religious teaching. "God pardons every sin except that of associating other gods with Him (*al-shirk*)."[125] Rashīd Riḍā responds to this query by denying the importance of the doctrine of the Trinity within Christianity (an unusual line of argument in Islam): "The doctrine of the Trinity which belongs to Christianity (*dākhil fī al-masīḥīyah*) is so unfathomable and incomprehensible that it has no effect on the souls of its people which would distance them from Islam; in fact it might be one of the reasons for accepting the summons to Islam."[126] With that, the exegete returns to his theme of the enduring friendship between Muslims and Christians, a friendship never achieved with the Jews and *mushrikūn*, a friendship "which has not weakened in any country except through administrative intrigue and the nationalistic strivings of those in power (*ʿaṣabīyah ahl al-riyāsah*)."[127]

In a curiously placed epilogue Rashīd Riḍā provides a word study of *qissīsūn* and *ruhbān* and comments upon the Christian institution of monasticism. A 'monk (*rāhib*)' is one who separates himself from the world by living in a monastery or hermitage in order to engage in divine worship. "He deprives himself of the enjoyment of wife and child and the delights of food and fine adornment."[128] A 'priest (*qissīs*)' is a religious leader "who is superior to the deacon (*al-shammās*) but inferior to the bishop (*al-usquf*)."[129] The *qissīsūn* are men learned in their religious traditions and scriptures, pastors of their people and authorized to deliver legal opinions (*ruʿāt wa-muftūn*). The words *ruhbān* and *qissīsūn* are used in this verse to mean 'worshipers' and 'scholars'.[130] Rashīd Riḍā's consideration of monasticism

123 Rashīd Riḍā, *Tafsīr al-Manār,* 7:10–11.
124 Rashīd Riḍā, *Tafsīr al-Manār,* 7:11.
125 Rashīd Riḍā, *Tafsīr al-Manār,* 7:11.
126 Rashīd Riḍā, *Tafsīr al-Manār,* 7:11.
127 Rashīd Riḍā, *Tafsīr al-Manār,* 7:11.
128 Rashīd Riḍā, *Tafsīr al-Manār,* 7:11.
129 Rashīd Riḍā, *Tafsīr al-Manār,* 7:11.
130 Rashīd Riḍā, *Tafsīr al-Manār,* 7:11.

as a religious institution is brief. He characterizes it as an innovation (*bidʿah*) in Christianity that had some influence on increasing Christian friendship for Muslims but is of no great importance.

Ṭabāṭabāʾī's etymological reflections are brief but include mention of the fact that the the root meaning of *RHB*, from which *rāhib* (pl. *ruhbān*) is notionally derived, is 'to fear'. Based on this consideration, Ṭabāṭabāʾī defines monasticism as "exaggerated devotional piety deriving from excessive fear (*ghulūw fī taḥammul al-taʿabbud min farṭ al-rahbah*)."[131] He is consonant with most of the exegetical tradition in treating the concluding phrase of the verse as an explanation for Christian-Muslim friendship. Among the Christians there are three characteristics that both the Jews and the *mushrikūn* lack: the presence of priests, the presence of monks, and the absence of arrogance.[132]

The mention of arrogance provides Ṭabāṭabāʾī the opportunity for an exhortatory digression on the need for eliminating bad attitudes in order to move from knowledge of the good to right action. "Attaining the truth does not suffice to prepare one to act in accordance with it;" the individual must first "pluck from himself the attitude that is holding him back from it (*al-hayʾah al-māniʿah ʿanhu*)."[133] The obstructive attitude to which Ṭabāṭabāʾī is referring is "haughty disdain for the truth because of racial pride and so forth (*al-istikbār ʿan al-ḥaqq bi-ʿaṣabīyah wa-mā yushābihuhā*)."[134] He realizes that such attitudes do not develop in a vacuum but are greatly influenced by one's society and culture. Right thinking flourishes with societal reinforcement as do right actions in an environment "in which it would be embarrassing for the individual to neglect them."[135]

The prerequisites, then, for a society's reception of the truth are the presence in that society of learned men who know and teach it, as well as the presence of men who act in accordance with it, so that people can see that it is both possible and right to do so. The people themselves must be accustomed to surrendering to the truth (*al-khuḍūʿ lil-ḥaqq*) and must lack haughty disdain for it (*ʿadam al-istikbār ʿanhu*).[136]

These prerequisites have been met by the Christians, as the final sentence of this verse manifests. Ṭabāṭabāʾī paraphrases this sentence in a way that makes completely clear how the Christians have satisfied the conditions he sets: "Among them are learned men who keep reminding them of the importance of truth and the things that must be known about religion,

131 Ṭabāṭabāʾī, *al-Mīzān*, 6:80.
132 Ṭabāṭabāʾī, *al-Mīzān*, 6:80–81.
133 Ṭabāṭabāʾī, *al-Mīzān*, 6:81.
134 Ṭabāṭabāʾī, *al-Mīzān*, 6:81.
135 Ṭabāṭabāʾī, *al-Mīzān*, 6:81.
136 Ṭabāṭabāʾī, *al-Mīzān*, 6:81.

by word; among them are ascetics (*zuhhād*) who keep reminding them of the greatness of their Lord and the significance of their earthly and heavenly fortune, by deed; and among them there is no sense of being too proud to accept the truth."[137] The exegete then catalogues the deficiencies of the Jews and *mushrikūn* that prevent them from fulfilling these divinely instituted requirements. The Jews, in spite of their learned rabbis (*aḥbār*), are disqualified because "the vice of obduracy and presumed superiority does not induce them to be ready to receive the truth."[138] The *mushrikūn* are found wanting on all three counts: not only are they bereft of learned men and of ascetics, but they too are guilty of the vice of arrogance.

TEARS AND TESTIMONY

The following verse, 5:83, is taken by most commentators as a continuation and specification of this Qurʾānic commendation of Christians. As such it shares, for the most part, the same 'occasion of revelation', that combination of incidents involving the Christian Abyssinian king and his subjects. Ibn al-Jawzī succinctly presents the two principal scenarios. In the first, on the authority of Ibn ʿAbbās, it is the emigrants from Mecca to Abyssinia who recite the Qurʾān aloud in the court of the Najāshī. The *qissīsūn* and *ruhbān* who were present heard this recitation and wept, for they recognized the truth in those utterances. The second depiction, from Saʿīd b. Jubayr, features a delegation sent by the Najāshī to Muḥammad. When the Prophet recited the Qurʾān, this group, which also contained priests and monks, wept in recognition of the truth and entered Islam.[139]

While Ibn al-Jawzī shows no preference for either of these two scenarios, Ibn Kathīr indicates a clear inclination for the second. Although he includes a *ḥadīth* from ʿAbdallāh b. al-Zubayr that locates the source of this revelation in the Najāshī and his followers, he pays far more attention to one from Ibn ʿAbbās that describes the Abyssinian delegation to Muḥammad. The account includes speculation by Muḥammad about the constancy of these new converts. The Prophet queries them: "Perhaps when you return to your country, you will return to your religion (*intaqaltum ilā dīnikum*)?" They respond, saying, "We will not turn from our religion (*lan nantaqila ʿan dīninā*)."[140]

137 Ṭabāṭabāʾī, *al-Mīzān*, 6:81–82.

138 Ṭabāṭabāʾī, *al-Mīzān*, 6:82.

139 Ibn al-Jawzī, *Zād al-masīr*, 2:409. Cf. al-Ṭabarī, *Jāmiʿ al-bayān*, 10:508–09. One *ḥadīth* cited by al-Ṭabarī on the authority of al-Suddī parallels that from Saʿīd b. Jubayr. While the remaining *ḥadīth*s that al-Ṭabarī mentions do not specify the incident, they all maintain the connection of this verse with the Najāshī.

140 Ibn Kathīr, *Tafsīr al-Qurʾān al-ʿaẓīm*, 2:86. The wording of this exchange is admittedly ambiguous and depends for its meaning on understanding the first use of *dīn* as a reference to Christianity and the second as a reference to Islam.

Ibn Kathīr then draws upon other Qurʾānic citations to specify further the identity of this group: "These sorts of Christians are the ones mentioned in *sūrah Āl ʿImrān* (3):199 and *sūrat al-qaṣaṣ* (28):52–53 [quoted in Ibn Kathīr's text]."[141] In conclusion he ties this verse to two that follow it, 5:85 and 5:86. The first decrees the rewards to be gained by the blessed "on account of their belief (*īmānuhum*), their attesting to the truth (*taṣdīquhum*), and their confessing the truth (*iʿtirāfuhum bi-al-ḥaqq*)."[142] That triad of laudable activities neatly parallels the three steps of the conversion process recorded in 5:83. In the first stage *they recognized . . . the truth*, that is, they came to belief. In the second stage they announced this belief by saying *"Our Lord, we believe."* In the third stage they asked to be placed in the category of those who witness to the faith, the *shāhidūn*. The second verse to which Ibn Kathīr alludes, 5:86, consigns those who reject belief to hellfire (*al-jaḥīm*).[143]

While Kāshānī locates 5:83 within the same cluster of incidents as have Ibn al-Jawzī and Ibn Kathīr, he does so in a novel way. In the narratives upon which he draws, revelation is prompted not by piety but by provocation. In the first briefly sketched situation, Kāshānī depicts Jewish taunting of the companions of Jaʿfar because they so quickly became believers: "Although they have been summoning us [to Islam] for a long time," the Jews are quoted as saying, "we do not accept."[144] The second, even briefer, suggestion is that the verse was revealed because the people of Abyssinia chided the Najāshī for believing in someone whom he had never seen (i.e., Muḥammad).

A citation by Abū al-Futūḥ Rāzī marks the only significant exception to this pattern of association. Drawing from ʿAmr b. Murrah he states: "In the time of Abū Bakr, a group arrived from the Yemen and said 'Recite something from the Qurʾān for us.' The Qurʾān was recited for them and they wept." Struck by this response, Abū Bakr remarks that "at first, we, too, were like this. When we heard the Qurʾān, we wept. But now our hearts have hardened."[145]

The weeping and tear-filled eyes to which this verse attests are explained by the phrase here translated as *because of what they recognized as the truth*. Al-Ṭabarī glosses this succinctly as "because of their recognition that what had been recited to them from the Book of God, which was sent down to the Messenger of God, was true," an understanding consonant with the

141 Ibn Kathīr, *Tafsīr al-Qurʾān al-ʿaẓīm*, 2:86. The verses mentioned are discussed in Chapter 5 (3:199) and Chapter 8 (28:52–53).
142 Ibn Kathīr, *Tafsīr al-Qurʾān al-ʿaẓīm*, 2:86.
143 Ibn Kathīr, *Tafsīr al-Qurʾān al-ʿaẓīm*, 2:87.
144 Kāshānī, *Minhaj al-ṣādiqīn*, 3:294.
145 Abū al-Futūḥ Rāzī, *Rawḥ al-jinān*, 4:307.

above translation. Al-Zamakhsharī, however, stresses the partitive nature of the Arabic preposition in the expression *as the truth (min al-ḥaqqi),* insisting that those involved "recognized [only] part of the truth (*annahum ʿarafū baʿḍ al-ḥaqq*)." To underscore this he appends this exclamation: "Imagine what it will be like when they have understood all [the truth], read the Qurʾān and become fully acquainted with the *sunnah*!"[146] Fakhr al-Dīn al-Rāzī, Kāshānī, and Rashīd Riḍā subsequently share this understanding and repeat a version of al-Zamakhsharī's exclamation.[147]

An issue that preoccupies virtually all of the commentators on this verse is the precise specification of *those who testify (al-shāhidūn).* Once again Ibn al-Jawzī proves to be a useful source of reference. He offers five choices for this phrase, one of his own and four from other exegetes. His own preference is for a broad definition, "those who testify to the truth." The four interpretations that he offers from earlier authorities are presented with no elaboration or explanation. The first two, both traced ultimately to Ibn ʿAbbās, are (1) Muḥammad and his community and (2) the Companions of Muḥammad. The third, on the authority of al-Ḥasan al-Baṣrī, is "those who testify to the faith (*bi-al-īmān*)," while the fourth, from al-Zajjāj, makes the phrase coextensive with "the prophets and the believers."[148]

Such breadth does not accurately mirror the spectrum of exegetical reflection on this phrase. Most commentators, such as al-Ṭabarī, al-Ṭūsī, Abū al-Futūḥ Rāzī, Ibn Kathīr, and Kāshānī, restrict the scope to the community of Muḥammad.[149] Fakhr al-Dīn al-Rāzī, on the other hand,

146 al-Zamakhsharī, *al-Kashshāf*, 1:670.

147 Fakhr al-Dīn al-Rāzī, *al-Tafsīr al-kabīr,* 12:68; Kāshānī, *Minhaj al-ṣādiqīn*, 3:294; Rashīd Riḍā, *Tafsīr al-Manār,* 7:12.

148 Ibn al-Jawzī, *Zād al-masīr,* 2:409. The term *shāhidūn* is semantically related to the word *shahādah*, commonly defined as the basic faith confession for Muslims, the first of the 'five pillars' of Islamic orthopraxis. M.J. Kister discusses a line of tradition that accepts an attenuated form of the *shahādah*, one that does not include testifying to the prophethood of Muḥammad, as sufficient to guarantee the legal and economic rights of a Muslim. ". . . *illā bi-ḥaqqihi* . . . : A Study of an Early Ḥadīth," *JSAI* 5 (1984): 33–52.

149 Al-Ṭabarī, *Jāmiʿ al-bayān*, 10:509–11; al-Ṭūsī, *al-Tibyān*, 4:3–4; al-Zamakhsharī, *al-Kashshāf*, 1:670; Abū al-Futūḥ Rāzī, *Rawḥ al-jinān*, 4:307; Ibn Kathīr, *Tafsīr al-Qurʾān al-ʿaẓīm*, 2:86; Kāshānī, *Minhaj al-ṣādiqīn*, 3:294. Al-Ṭabarī cites *ḥadīth*s on the authority of Ibn ʿAbbās in several versions and Ibn Jurayj in support of this restricted connotation. However his own rephrasing goes considerably beyond this: the *shāhidūn* are "those who bear witness on behalf of Your [God's] prophets on the Day of Resurrection that they had communicated Your messages to their communities." *Jāmiʿ al-bayān*, 5:110. This is a far broader definition of the term because it includes not only those who attest to the veracity of Muḥammad but also all who responded rightly to former prophets sent by God. However, in his concluding remarks on this phrase al-Ṭabarī agrees that in the present context the correct meaning of *shāhidūn* is those who testify to the truth of what God has sent down on Muḥammad in the Qurʾān. These

permits a more inclusive reading. He presents the more restricted meaning as one option, basing it – as have other commentators – on a Qurʾānic parallel in *sūrat al-baqarah* (2):143: "We have made you a community of the middle (*ummatan wasaṭan*) so that you may be witnesses (*shuhadāʾ*) for people." He is willing to consider, however, a much broader second reading, one that expands the definition of al-Zajjāj. *Those who testify (shāhidūn)* is rephrased as: "all those among Your prophets and mankind's believers who witness that there is no God but You."[150] Such a definition would apparently cover not only Muslims but all professing monotheists. As such it could include both Christians and Jews as well as any others who acknowledge that there is but one God.

While Ṭabāṭabāʾī does not comment upon this question, Rashīd Riḍā continues the tradition of a more restrictive understanding of *shāhidūn*. He does, however, combine with this something of the sequential nature of the conversion process first noted by Ibn Kathīr. Thus Rashīd Riḍā notes that although recognition of the truth is an essential element of faith, it is incomplete without verbal acknowledgment. The second phrase of this verse, *They say, "Our Lord, we believe, so write us with those who testify,"* is important. Rashīd Riḍā maintains that such a faith statement was possible only because of preparatory revelation and teaching about the nature of the final stage of religious evolution; those who wept "can say that only because they would know from their scriptures, or from what had been reported to them on the authority of their ancestors, that it is the followers of the last prophet – the one in whom God brings religion to perfection – who are witnesses to mankind."[151] Therefore asking to be "written among the witnesses" is equivalent to inclusion within the community of Muḥammad. In fact, for Rashīd Riḍā, the term *shāhidūn* is the most noble descriptive that can be applied to the community (*ummah*).

are the people eligible for divine reward and recompense. Al-Zamakhsharī continues this eschatological emphasis when he defines the *shāhidūn* as the community of Muḥammad "who will testify against all [other] peoples (*ʿalā sāʾir al-umam*) on the Day of Resurrection." *al-Kashshāf*, 1:670.

150 Fakhr al-Dīn al-Rāzī, *al-Tafsīr al-kabīr,* 13:68.

151 Rashīd Riḍā, *Tafsīr al-Manār,* 7:12. J. Chelhod contrasts the increasing use of the reference *Allāh* and the decreasing use of *rabb* (Lord) in the chronology of Qurʾānic revelation and suggests that attention to this phenomenon may be one contribution to the efforts to date particular passages. "Note sur l'emploi du mot *rabb* dans le Coran," *Arabica* 5 (1958): 159–67. Daniel Gimaret notes that in its more than 1000 Qurʾānic occurrences, the term *rabb* is always found in pronominal or nominal constructions. He also remarks upon the fact that, despite its Qurʾānic frequency, it is not to be found in the most well-known list of the divine names (*al-asmāʾ al-ḥusnā*). *Les noms divins en Islam* (Paris: Éditions du Cerf, 1988), 318–19.

CONCLUSION

Structurally, the first of these two verses is constituted as a declaration buttressed by reasons and justifications. The statement that Christians are *closest in friendship* to the Muslims reinforces the pervasive sense of group configuration and identification that permeates the exegesis of all the verses thus far examined. The unequivocal certitude of this declaration poses an urgent exegetical problem for the commentators. Several hasten to assert that the range of signification, the numbers of Christians to whom such praise is actually or potentially applicable, is indeed limited. An interesting division develops on this issue between the classical Sunnī and Shīʿī exegetes. Some of the former, such as al-Ṭabarī and Ibn Kathīr, are unwilling to condone a narrow reading. Arguing from the lack of divine specification in this verse, they both reject the notion that there is any explicit warrant for restricting the range of relevance to a particular group of Christians. In opposition to such latitude stand the Shīʿī scholars, al-Ṭūsī, Abū al-Futūḥ Rāzī, and Kāshānī. Each candidly contends that the verse does not intend *all* Christians. Each goes beyond the implicit limitation of positing a particular *sabab al-nuzūl* to insist squarely upon such restriction of signification. The modern commentator, Ṭabāṭabāʾī, represents the only break in this Shīʿī exegetical front.

Yet the stance taken by such Sunnī commentators as al-Ṭabarī and Ibn Kathīr makes no positive argument for unrestricted or universal applicability to all Christians. The degree of detail lavished on the episodes that center upon the Najāshī inevitably focuses attention upon a historically and geographically limited group of Christians. Nor are even these allowed to occupy center stage for long. Frequently the narratives express less interest in highlighting the Abyssinian Christians than the Muslim emigrants from Mecca. It is the fortitude and persistence of the latter that garner the most praise.

Additionally, the opening phrases of this verse group provide a lexical focus for that castigation of the Jews which often accompanies praise of Christians. At no other point in the Qurʾān does the one group stand so sharply contrasted to the other. Fakhr al-Dīn al-Rāzī even cites early Muslim-Jewish tension as a principal purpose for this revelation. Several of the commentators combine harsh denunciation of the Jews with their limited praise of Christians, repeating a pattern uncovered in the analysis of other verses in this study.

The need to understand the Qurʾānic reasons given for Christian-Muslim amicability produces the most persistent praise of Christians and of Christianity found in the exegesis of any of the verses examined for this work. The etymological consideration of *qissīsūn* and *ruhbān* elicits from the commentators sustained reflection upon those qualities in the religion and its adherents which could prompt divine approbation. Once again the description is frequently contrastive, Christian virtues being catalogued in tandem with Jewish vices. The specific points of praise mentioned by the exegetes manifest a closer knowledge of Christianity than has elsewhere been exhibited. Ibn Kathīr's reference to Christian pacifism draws upon a passage in the Gospel of Matthew. Al-Ṭabarī recognizes the seafaring vocation of some of Jesus' disciples. Distinctions are made between ecclesiastical categories represented by the terms *qissīsūn* and *ruhbān*. Yet misinformation about Christianity is certainly not lacking. One etymology for *qissīs* repeated by both Abū al-Futūḥ Rāzī and Fakhr al-Dīn al-Rāzī, which traces the word to a supposed Christian figure named Qissīs, is but the most obvious example.

Nevertheless a continuing chorus of commendation marks the treatment of Christianity in the exegetical history of this verse. Consistently but not exclusively this commendation is directed at two qualities that Christianity is perceived as promoting. These are a veneration of learning and an aptitude for ascetic disciplines. The first, associated with the eccelesiastical category of *qissīsūn*, finds unqualified acclaim among the commentators. The further Qurʾānic compliment, *and because they are not arrogant*, is regularly understood as a right-minded respect for the truth or as an openness to the truth that finds its heart-sought fulfillment in the embrace of Islam.

Praise for asceticism as embodied in the Christian institution of monasticism is somewhat more problematic for the commentators. Muḥammad's proscription of "monkery" casts a long shadow over the acknowledgment of any positive value in Christian asceticism. Ibn al-Jawzī, for one, decides that monks are being praised not for their celibacy but for their scholarship. Fakhr al-Dīn al-Rāzī allows only that Christian renunciation is a general improvement on Jewish avidity and self-aggrandizement. He is particularly anxious to refute any approval of Christian doctrine. While willing to admire the psychological and behavioral consequences of Christian ethical formation, Fakhr al-Dīn al-Rāzī underlines the abysmal crudity of Christian doctrine. Here comparison with the Jews is to the latter's advantage. In the chronology of this exegetical survey, however, that is a short-lived exception. Ibn Kathīr and Rashīd Riḍā replay the dominant theme – albeit in terms consonant with their respective exegetical agendas – commending Christianity as a higher stage of spiritual evolution than Judaism, a stage marked by deeper knowledge, more profound religious devotion, and greater humility. Those three qualities themselves summarize the results of the full exegetical search for the reasons underlying the divine praise that this verse records. They are nicely recast by Ṭabāṭabāʾī using sociological categories and configurations. In his view, a religious group guided by the truth must incorporate learned individuals who can know and convey it, devoted adherents who by their actions can witness to its efficacy and value, and, finally, a pervasive sense of humility and openness among all those who affiliate themselves with the group.

Such an attitude will sometimes manifest itself in fervent tears, as caught in the brief narrative scenario of 5:83. The affective response to revelation received is unabashedly conveyed in these few lines. A psychology of conversion deftly sketched captures the movement from reception to testimony. The commentators wonder, of course, about the moment that might be herein recorded and return to some of the now-familiar incidents, as well as noting other conversion scenes. The fulfillment of those qualities for which the Christians are lauded is that moment of recognition when the Qurʾānic message is apprehended. Yet even here a cautionary note is sounded, a final qualification is laid upon the words recorded. Fakhr al-Dīn al-Rāzī, Kāshānī, and Rashīd Riḍā all emphasize the partitive nature of this moment of recognition. Lest the Christians be applauded unreservedly, that ultimate circumscription prevails.

8

Christians as pre-Qur'ānic Muslims

The verse group that will be the subject of this chapter is perhaps the most allusive of those examined. There is no specific reference to the Christians either by name or designating phrase. Rather the clues to its import for the subject of this study must be sought in the exegetical tradition itself. From within the cluster of questions that confront the commentators as they address these verses there emerges a hermeneutical consensus, an orientation of meaning inclusive of Christians. The four consecutive verses to be discussed are from *sūrat al-qaṣaṣ* (28):52–55:

Those to whom We gave the book before it/him believe in it/him. (52)

And when it was recited to them they said, "We believe in it/him. Certainly it is the truth from our Lord; truly we were Muslims before it." (53)

These will be given their reward twice because of that in which they have persisted. They turn back evil with good. From what We have given them, they spend. (54)

When they hear idle chatter, they turn away from it and say, "To us, our deeds and to you, your deeds. Peace be upon you; we do not desire ignorant people." (55)

THE PROBLEM OF PRONOUNS

Matters of pronominal identification are of immediate concern, as even an English translation of these verses makes readily apparent. Verse 28:52 contains five uses of the pronoun *-hu* here translated first as *it*, as well as an implied pronominal subject for the verb *recited*. Although al-Ṭabarī does not address this issue specifically, he paraphrases the following verse in a way that makes retroactively clear that he considers the proper referent for the pronoun in *before it/him* to be the Qur'ān.[1] Al-Ṭūsī also understands this pronoun as a reference to the Qur'ān, yet he includes the possibility that *it/him* may be an allusion to Muḥammad. If this be the case, then the sense of the opening phrase would be for al-Ṭūsī "those to whom We gave

1 Abū Ja'far Muḥammad b. Jarīr al-Ṭabarī, *Jāmi' al-bayān 'an ta'wīl āy al-Qur'ān* (Beirut: Dār al-Fikr, 1405/1984), 20:89.

the book before Muḥammad are believers in Muḥammad because they found his description in the Torah."[2] The Torah is, in fact, the only prior scripture that al-Ṭūsī mentions as an explanation for the term *book* in this opening phrase. A reason may be found in the connection that he draws between this verse and 28:48, in which the Jews are chastised for their disbelief in the Mosaic revelation.[3]

Al-Zamakhsharī admits of no equivocation about the referent for the first pronominal usage in 28:52. The notion of its referring to Muḥammad is not raised. As al-Zamakhsharī tersely puts it: "The pronoun in *before it/him* refers to the Qurʾān."[4] Abū al-Futūḥ Rāzī's analysis of this same phrase directly contradicts that of al-Zamakhsharī. While the latter allows this to mean only the Qurʾān, Abū al-Futūḥ Rāzī suggests it refers only to Muḥammad. He does not, however, directly clarify the sense of the phrase in the following verse, *we believe in it/him.* That he takes it to refer to the Qurʾān may be assumed from his interpretation of *when it was recited to them,* which Abū al-Futūḥ Rāzī has paraphrased as "when they read Our verses to them from the Qurʾān."[5]

While returning to the univocal stance of al-Zamakhsharī in his identification of the pronoun in *before it/him* as a reference to the Qurʾān, Ibn al-Jawzī offers two alternatives for the subsequent phrase *believe in it/him.* The first anticipates – and, in fact, duplicates – his interpretation of the ensuing *truly we were Muslims before it.* That is to say, it is a reference to Muḥammad of whom mention has been made in antecedent scriptures.[6] The second alternative, not unexpectedly, is the Qurʾān.

The author of *al-Tafsīr al-kabīr* gives but one periphrastic interpretation for 28:52, "Those to whom We gave the book before the Qurʾān, believed in Muḥammad," while Ibn Kathīr does not gloss the first verse of this group to supply specific pronominal identification.[7] Kāshānī, however, does devote attention to this issue. He first mentions only the Torah as referent for the term *book* but later expands this to include the Gospel as well. For the pronominal object in the phrase *believe in it/him* he offers but one signification, the Qurʾān, apparently refusing to entertain the possibility of a reference to Muḥammad, which was tendered by his Shīʿī predecessor, al-Ṭūsī.[8] To conclude the survey of this issue, Ṭabāṭabāʾī, too, finds more persuasive those who argue that the two singular pronouns in *those to whom*

2 al-Ṭūsī, *al-Tibyān*, 8:161.
3 al-Ṭūsī, *al-Tibyān*, 8:161.
4 al-Zamakhsharī, *al-Kashshāf*, 3:421.
5 Abū al-Futūḥ Rāzī, *Rawḥ al-jinān*, 8:468.
6 Ibn al-Jawzī, *Zād al-masīr*, 6:229.
7 Fakhr al-Dīn al-Rāzī, *al-Tafsīr al-kabīr*, 24:262.
8 Kāshānī, *Minhaj al-ṣādiqīn*, 7:111.

We gave the book before it/him believe in it/him refer to the Qur'ān, not the Prophet.[9]

THE INDIVIDUALS INTENDED

The specific determination of pronominal referents depends, of course, upon the identification of those intended by these Qur'ānic statements. While al-Ṭabarī offers several possible explanations, all are but variations on the basic assertion that those intended by these verses are the *ahl al-kitāb*. Put more precisely this would encompass "a people of the *ahl al-kitāb* who believe in His messenger and attest to his authenticity."[10] These are more broadly distinguished from the illiterate, ignorant peoples to whom no divine scripture was sent. Yet refinements may also be made about the category of the *ahl al-kitāb*. One such is al-Ṭabarī's mention, on the authority of Mujāhid, of the term *maslamah*.[11] Another, taken from ʿAlī b. Rifāʿah, refers to "ten individuals who left the *ahl al-kitāb* (*kharaja ʿasharatun rahṭun min ahl al-kitāb*)" and who were subsequently injured, presumably by their former coreligionists. The one of this group to be named in the *ḥadīth* is Abū Rifāʿah, the father of the transmitter, of whom W. Montgomery Watt attempted an identification.[12] The final particularization of the *ahl al-kitāb* is drawn from a *ḥadīth* attributed to Qatādah that describes a group of them as ones "who adhered to an authentic code of conduct (*sharīʿah min al-ḥaqq*), by which they were obligated and restrained, up until the time of God's sending Muḥammad." Included among those thus described were both Salmān [al-Fārisī] and ʿAbdallāh b. Salām.[13]

Qatādah's association of the verse group with these last-named individuals is noted by al-Ṭūsī as well, who adds to the list both Tamīm al-Dārī and al-Jārūd al-ʿAbdī.[14] From an unnamed source al-Ṭūsī then notes an-

9 Ṭabāṭabāʾī, *al-Mīzān*, 16:54. (Rashīd Riḍā's *Tafsīr al-Manār* is not discussed in this or the subsequent chapter as it did not cover these verses.)

10 al-Ṭabarī, *Jāmiʿ al-bayān*, 20:88.

11 al-Ṭabarī, *Jāmiʿ al-bayān*, 20:89. The term *maslamah* is unvocalized in one instance of this *ḥadīth* and given the vocalization *muslimah* in another.

12 al-Ṭabarī, *Jāmiʿ al-bayān*, 20: 89; W. Montgomery Watt, *Muḥammad at Medina* (Oxford: Clarendon Press, 1956), 317, note 2. Watt's note is somewhat misleading. He mentions al-Ṭabarī's reference to "one Rifāʿah b. Quraẓī [sic]" (for whom Watt makes a possible identification with Rifāʿah b. Simwāl via Ibn al-Athīr's *Usd al-ghābah*) and associates this with al-Ṭabarī's subsequent mention of ʿAbdallāh b. Salām to support the contention that 28:52–54 refers to the Jews. However, al-Ṭabarī actually refers to Rifāʿah in connection with 28:51; al-Ṭabarī also names the Jewish convert ʿAbdallāh b. Salām in association with the Zoroastrian/Christian convert Salmān al-Fārisī and uses these two to sustain a more inclusive interpretation of this verse.

13 al-Ṭabarī, *Jāmiʿ al-bayān*, 20:89.

14 According to Ibn Isḥāq, Tamīm b. Aws was a member of the Banū al-Dār from the tribe of Lakhm, a nominally Christian group in southern Syria. *Sīrah*, 1:777 (Guil-

other list: "forty of the 'people of the Gospel' who were Muslims in the way of the Prophet (*kānū muslimīn bi-al-nabī*) before he was sent; thirty-two from Abyssinia who came forward with Jaᶜfar b. ᶜAbī Ṭālib at the time of his arrival; and eight who arrived from Syria, including Baḥīrā, Abrahah, al-Ashraf, ᶜĀmir, Amīn, Idrīs, and Nāfiᶜ." According to Qatādah again, all of these are subject to the divine promise of a twofold reward because of "their belief in both the first book [the Gospel] and the second [the Qurʾān]."[15]

Al-Zamakhsharī's efforts at identification first return to the figure of Rifāᶜah, previously cited by al-Ṭabarī. The general declaration that the verse was sent down about the *ahl al-kitāb* is supplemented with the statement of Rifāᶜah b. Qaraẓah: "It was sent down about ten persons of whom I am one."[16] He next cites the unattributed possibility just seen in the discussion of al-Ṭūsī, but in more compact form. In characteristic fashion, Ibn al-Jawzī presents the possible referents for *those to whom We gave the book* in a succinct and ordered sequence. They may be: (1) the believers of the *ahl al-kitāb*, as reported by Mujāhid, or (2) those of the *ahl al-injīl* who became Muslims, which the supporting *ḥadīth* from Ibn ᶜAbbās further identifies as "forty of those associated with the Najāshī who came before the Messenger of God as a unit and bore witness to him." The list concludes with the third and final element, a report from al-Suddī that it means those of the Jews, such as ᶜAbdallāh b. Salām, who became Muslims.[17]

Fakhr al-Dīn al-Rāzī combines efforts at identification found in both al-Ṭabarī and al-Zamakhsharī. From the former he repeats the *ḥadīth* from Qatādah and from the latter the suggestion (anonymous in both al-Ṭūsī and al-Zamakhsharī but here cited on the authority of Muqātil) about those who accompanied Jaᶜfar. From both he includes the comment of Rifāᶜah b. Qaraẓah.[18] Fakhr al-Dīn al-Rāzī does not stop, however, after this enu-

laume, *Life*, 523). Muḥammad b. Saᶜd records a vignette in which Tamīm is credited with the suggestion that the Prophet use a *minbar* (pulpit) "as I saw done in Syria." *al-Ṭabaqāt al-kubrā*, ed. by Iḥsān ᶜAbbās (Beirut: Dār Ṣādir, 1380–8/1960–68), 1:250. Trimingham refers to Tamīm al-Dārī as "a former monk according to tradition" but indicates no source for this. *Christianity Among the Arabs*, 124.

Jārūd b. al-Muᶜallā is mentioned as a member of the deputation from the ᶜAbd al-Qays tribe in al-Baḥrayn. Additionally, he is singled out as a Christian who answered Muḥammad's summons and made a sincere conversion (*fa-ḥasuna islāmuhu*) to Islam. Ibn Saᶜd, *Ṭabaqāt*, 2:314–15; 5:557.

15 al-Ṭūsī, *al-Tibyān*, 8:161. For the names associated with Baḥīrā in the commentary on 2:62, see Chapter 3, note 55.

16 al-Zamakhsharī, *al-Kashshāf*, 3:421.

17 Ibn al-Jawzī, *Zād al-masīr*, 6:228–29.

18 Fakhr al-Dīn al-Rāzī, *al-Tafsīr al-kabīr*, 24:262. The account from Muqātil refers to this group as those who came by boat (*aṣḥāb al-safīnah*) with Jaᶜfar b. Abī Ṭālib. See Ibn Isḥāq, *Sīrah*, 1:781–89 (Guillaume, *Life*, 526–30).

meration. He moves beyond it to a position in which all variants can be fused. What is important, he urges, is the general meaning of the words, not the particular individuals to whom they may first have been applied. "Therefore everyone to whom this description is applicable is included in this verse."[19]

Ibn Kathīr's consistent attention to possible Qur'ānic parallels is apparent in his treatment of these verses. He cites several references to the "holy and learned men (*al-ʿulamā' al-awliyā'*)" of the *ahl al-kitāb* who "believed in the Qur'ān," including *sūrah Āl ʿImrān* (3): 199 and *sūrat al-mā'idah* (5): 82–83, which have been discussed in Chapters 5 and 7.[20] For the latter citation he mentions as the occasion of revelation the incident in which seventy *qissīsūn* sent by the Najāshī come before Muḥammad who "recites to them *sūrah Yā' Sīn* (36) and *al-Qur'ān al-ḥakīm*."[21] They weep in recognition of the truth that they hear and become Muslims. Ibn Kathīr adds that not only 5:82–83 but also the verses under discussion were revealed about this occurrence.

Minhaj al-ṣādiqīn of Kāshānī adds nothing new to this survey of possible occasions of revelation (*asbāb al-nuzūl*) while Ṭabāṭabā'ī takes his cue from the contextual sequence of this verse. Given that the verse, which praises "a group of believers of the *ahl al-kitāb*," comes after a group of verses that censure the Meccan idolaters, it must refer to an equally specific group of the *ahl al-kitāb*. It is not to be understood in an unrestricted sense, a position that contradicts his more inclusive understanding of previously discussed verses.

PRE-QUR'ĀNIC MUSLIMS

The exegetical preoccupation that emerges in verse 53 of this pericope is the curious phrase *we were Muslims before it*. That declaration follows a statement that concisely sketches the confessional setting (*when it was recited to them*) and cites a preliminary profession of faith (*We believe in it/him. Certainly*

19 Fakhr al-Dīn al-Rāzī, *al-Tafsīr al-kabīr*, 24:262. In his discussion of a verse (*sūrah Āl ʿImrān* [3]:20) that also includes reference to "those who were given the Book," Toshihiko Izutsu explains that the Qur'ān divides humanity into two major categories: people with scripture (*ahl al-kitāb*) and people without scripture (*ummīyūn*). He then makes the important point that the latter cannot be equated with the unbelievers (*kuffār*), "because as yet they have never been admonished to open their eyes to the marvelous work of God. Real kâfirs are those who consciously show the most determined opposition to the Divine scheme, after the Revelation has made the truth clear to them." *God and Man in the Koran* (Tokyo: The Keio Institute of Cultural and Linguistic Studies, 1964), 79.

20 Ibn Kathīr, *Tafsīr al-Qur'ān al-ʿaẓīm*, 3:393. The other verses mentioned by Ibn Kathīr are *sūrat al-baqarah* (2): 121 and *sūrah Banī Isrā'īl* (17): 107–08.

21 Ibn Kathīr, *Tafsīr al-Qur'ān al-ʿaẓīm*, 3:393.

it is the truth from our Lord). Al-Ṭabarī expands the concluding phrase to read "we were Muslims before the sending down of this Qur'ān." Just what is meant by the term *muslimīn* in this context is then explained as belief in prior, divinely revealed scriptures that contained a description and characterization (*naʿt*) of Muḥammad. These *muslimūn*, or *muṣaddiqūn* (truth affirmers) to use al-Ṭabarī's synonym, believed in Muḥammad, in the fact that he would be sent, and in the book that would be revealed to him, on the basis of their own scriptures and before the revelation of the Qur'ān.[22]

Al-Ṭūsī concurs with this reading, but specifically identifies the previous scriptures as the Torah.[23] With al-Zamakhsharī the analysis takes a grammatical turn. He focuses upon the fact that verse 53 contains two clauses that begin with the Arabic particle *inna*. The first, *certainly it is the truth from our Lord (innahu al-ḥaqqu min rabbinā*), explains the reason for the previous assertion, *we believe in it/him*. The second, *truly we were Muslims before it (innā kunnā min qablihi muslimīna*), is also related to the basic faith statement by clarifying whether the believing occurred recently (*qarīb al-ʿahd*) or in the distant past.[24] The latter is, of course, the intent in this instance. Al-Zamakhsharī expands the Qur'ānic phraseology to explain that generations of yore found the truth in their scriptures and passed it from father to son, preserving it in the period before God's final revelation. Thus they merit the right to call themselves *muslimūn*. One of the most significant elements in al-Zamakhsharī's treatment of this verse is the way he defines that term, as "those in accordance with the religion of Islam, because the term *islām* is an attribute applied to each person who professes God's unity (*muwaḥḥid*) and affirms the truth of the revelation (*muṣaddiq lil-waḥy*)."[25]

In an explanation that echoes both al-Ṭabarī and al-Ṭūsī, Abū al-Futūḥ Rāzī understands the concluding declaration of verse 53 to be founded upon the recognition of the characterization and description of Muḥammad that was revealed in the Torah and Gospel.[26] There is no variation in this understanding to be discovered in Ibn al-Jawzī while Fakhr al-Dīn al-Rāzī follows the same exegetical pattern, repeating al-Zamakhsharī's analysis almost verbatim.[27]

Rather than stress the earlier scriptural attestations to Muḥammad's prophethood, Ibn Kathīr simply offers a definition of the term *muslimūn*: "professors of God's unity (*muwaḥḥidūn*), those whose devotion to God is

22 al-Ṭabarī, *Jāmiʿ al-bayān*, 20:89.
23 al-Ṭūsī, *al-Tibyān*, 8:161.
24 al-Zamakhsharī, *al-Kashshāf*, 3:421. Instances in which Jesus speaks as a Muslim prophet are treated by Henri Michaud in a section entitled "Jésus et ses disciples, parfaits musulmans avant la lettre?" *Jésus*, 41–43.
25 al-Zamakhsharī, *al-Kashshāf*, 3:421.
26 Abū al-Futūḥ Rāzī, *Rawḥ al-jinān*, 8:468.
27 Ibn al-Jawzī, *Zād al-masīr*, 6:228; Fakhr al-Dīn al-Rāzī, *al-Tafsīr al-kabīr*, 24:262.

pure (*mukhliṣūn lillāh*) and who are responsive to Him (*mustajībūn lahu*)."[28] With Kāshānī the established exegetical pattern is reasserted, with *truly we were Muslims before it* understood to be founded upon prior recognition of the Prophet based on allusions to him drawn from earlier scriptures. This exegete concurs with both al-Zamakhsharī and Fakhr al-Dīn al-Rāzī in finding grammatical support for this in the 'initiatory' use of the Arabic particle *inna*. Furthermore, Kāshānī cites Qatādah to support the view that places this verse and *sūrah* among the revelations of Medina because those to whom it applies, "Ibn Salām and his associates, had been in Medina not Mecca."[29] Ṭabāṭabā'ī, too, underscores the conventional understanding of this faith declaration, buttressing his position with two Qur'ānic cross-references: (1) "those who follow the Messenger, the *ummī* Prophet whom they find described in the Torah and Gospel at hand" (*sūrāt al-aʿrāf* [7]: 157), and (2) "Is it not a sign for them that the learned men of the Banū Isrā'īl know it?" (*sūrat al-shuʿarā'* [26]: 197).

THE PROMISE OF A DOUBLE REWARD

In a pattern frequently repeated in the Qur'ān, verses of description climax in the drama of a divine promise. In the present instance verses 52 and 53 reach their fulfillment in the initial statement of verse 54: *These will be given their reward twice because of that in which they have persisted.* Issues of identification and particularization achieve final focus as they define the subjects of this promised reward. But God's guarantee, in turn, specifies a further qualification, that of 'persistence' or 'endurance'. The pledge must be balanced by the proviso, as al-Ṭabarī's initiatory discussion makes clear.

The Arabic verb here translated as "have persisted (*ṣabarū*)" is drawn from the root *ṢBR*, which can carry connotations of 'steadfastness' and 'perseverance'. But for perseverance in what is the divine reward promised? Al-Ṭabarī offers three responses, with an additional variation on the first of them. The initial sense presented for this phrase, on the authority of Qatādah, is that it pertains to those who were steadfast in their adherence to the 'first book' and who then followed Muḥammad, remaining constant in this, too. The second possibility that al-Ṭabarī cites, which is derived from al-Ḍaḥḥāk, reflects the aforementioned belief in an antecedent revelation of the Prophet's 'description'. Those who recognized this description and believed were to be rewarded "for their perseverance in belief in Muḥammad before he was sent and for their following him when he was sent."[30]

28 Ibn Kathīr, *Tafsīr al-Qur'ān al-ʿaẓīm*, 3:393. While the terms *muwaḥḥid* and *mustajīb* are not found in the Qur'ān, the phrase *mukhliṣīn lahu al-dīn* occurs seven times from *sūrat al-aʿrāf* (7):29 to *sūrat al-bayyinah* (98):5.

29 Kāshānī, *Minhaj al-ṣādiqīn*, 7:112.

30 al-Ṭabarī, *Jāmiʿ al-bayān*, 20:90.

This exegete also includes in his commentary a variation on the first possible meaning that is remarkable for the clear connection it makes between the term *muslimūn* and the Christian religion. The exegetical *ḥadīth* from ʿAbd al-Raḥmān b. Zayd b. Aslam (d. 182/798) that this commentator quotes explains that *truly we were Muslims before it* means "according to the religion of Jesus. But when the Prophet came they submitted (*aslamū*); so they will have their reward twice – for their first adherence and for affiliating themselves with the Prophet."[31]

The third and final sense in which this phrase may be understood differs significantly from the first two. No longer is connection made to groups within the *ahl al-kitāb*. Rather, those intended, according to Mujāhid, are the ones termed 'idolaters (*mushrikūn*)' who became Muslims and then were made to suffer for their new affiliation by those whose views they had forsaken. The promised divine reward is to be recompense for this persecution.[32]

While al-Ṭabarī attributes *they turn back evil with good* solely to the good deeds (*ḥasanāt afʿālihim*) of those described in these verses, he explicates the subsequent phrase somewhat more fully. The "gift" in *from what We have given them, they spend* is worldly possessions (*al-amwāl*), which are 'spent' in a variety of ways: (1) in obedience to God, (2) in religiously motivated endeavor (*jihād fī sabīl Allāh*), and (3) in voluntary charity (*ṣadaqah*) based on need or compassion.[33]

As his initial contribution to this discussion, al-Ṭūsī defines the term here translated with connotations of 'persistence' negatively as "restraining the soul from its inclination to things impermissible in which it would be committing sin."[34] Those who succeed in such an effort are praised by God and eventually rewarded. Al-Ṭūsī has no illusions about the difficulty of such spiritual vigilance. "Perseverance in the truth," he says, "is bitter except for the fact that it leads to a reward which is sweeter than the effort."[35]

Obedience to the divine law, then, is the prime example of such perseverance. Al-Ṭūsī does, however, mention the notion that *they have persisted* implies enduring "injury while under God's protection (*fī janb allāh*)."[36]

31 al-Ṭabarī, *Jāmiʿ al-bayān*, 20:90.

32 al-Ṭabarī, *Jāmiʿ al-bayān*, 20:90. Although Izutsu stresses the pre-Islamic sense of *ṣabr* as physical endurance, he notes that within the Qur'ānic semantic field "the torment which the believers have to suffer is not in any way restricted to physical pains; it may also take the form of sneering, derision, and abuse on the part of the Kāfirs." *Ethico-Religious Concepts*, 103.

33 al-Ṭabarī, *Jāmiʿ al-bayān*, 20:90.

34 al-Ṭūsī, *al-Tibyān*, 8:161.

35 al-Ṭūsī, *al-Tibyān*, 8:161.

36 al-Ṭūsī, *al-Tibyān*, 8:161. Tilman Nagel connects this verse with the pragmatic concern expressed in 28:57 that conversion may entail loss of clan protection. *Der Koran: Einführung-Texte-Erläuterungen* (Munich: C.H. Beck, 1983), 127.

Yet he offers none of the supporting *ḥadīth*s utilized by al-Ṭabarī and returns again to this idea of continuous obedience by defining *they turn back evil with good* in like terms. Here the concept of repulsion is viewed from the perspective of penitence (*al-tawbah*) repelling sins (*al-maʿāṣī*).[37]

In anticipation of a subsequent phrase of verse 54, al-Ṭūsī also suggests that *they turn back* may mean "they repel the idle chatter of the unbelievers (*al-laghw min kalām al-kuffār*) with decent discourse (*al-kalām al-jamīl*)."[38] He also brings up a concern that will preoccupy succeeding commentators, the connection between this notion of repelling with good the evil occasioned by unbelievers and the divine injunction to fight these unbelievers. Although al-Ṭūsī notes the hypothesis that this verse preceded the Qurʾānic directives to fight (which are not specifically cited), he sees no real contradiction between the two. There is, for him, no incompatibility between their being ordered "to turn away from speaking with them [the unbelievers] together with the order to fight them."[39]

Concision marks al-Zamakhsharī's entry. He offers, without amplification, all the possibilities expressed thus far for the expression *they have persisted* (*ṣabarū*): that which was steadfastly maintained or endured was (1) belief in the Torah and in the Qurʾān, or (2) belief in the Qurʾān before and after its being sent down, or (3) injury from the *mushrikūn* and the *ahl al-kitāb*.[40] This exegete's only contribution is to draw attention to the Qurʾānic parallel, "He will give you two portions of His mercy" (*sūrat al-ḥadīd* [57]: 28), as another instance of the promised twofold reward. Equally compressed is al-Zamakhsharī's treatment of *they turn back evil with good*. What is rebuked is either disobedience by obedience or injury with forbearance (*al-ḥilm*).

While Abū al-Futūḥ Rāzī, too, maintains the notion of steadfastness in both prior and final revelation and the notion of withstanding the taunts and molestations that submission to the Prophet provokes, it is the latter idea that forms the context for his explanation of *they turn back evil with good*.[41] Faced with the hostility and jeers of those – here identified as the Jews – who do not share their belief, this group "returned the speech of these unbelievers with fair speech (*sukhun-i nīkū*)."[42] This commentator also offers a more novel view of this phrase, seeing in it an indication of superiority in apologetics. Returning good for evil is thus perceived as removing "all doubts in argument."[43]

37 al-Ṭūsī, *al-Tibyān*, 8:161.
38 al-Ṭūsī, *al-Tibyān*, 8:162.
39 al-Ṭūsī, *al-Tibyān*, 8:162. The issue of abrogation is discussed in Chapter 3.
40 al-Zamakhsharī, *al-Kashshāf*, 3:421.
41 Abū al-Futūḥ Rāzī, *Rawḥ al-jinān*, 8:468–69.
42 Abū al-Futūḥ Rāzī, *Rawḥ al-jinān*, 8:468.
43 Abū al-Futūḥ Rāzī, *Rawḥ al-jinān*, 8:469.

Their persistence, or endurance, for which a twofold reward is promised, is understood by Ibn al-Jawzī in a manner consonant with the previous commentators surveyed. For this interpretation of *they turn back evil with good* he refers the reader to his commentary on *sūrat al-raʿd* (13):22, a verse whose themes prefigure the present one: "Those who persevere in seeking the face of their Lord, who adhere to the prayer, who spend from what We have given them, in secret and overtly, who turn back evil with good, for them is the final end of the (heavenly) home." There he itemizes five possible connotations for the phrase, all of which are general enough to permit wide applicability. The five so listed are: they repulse (1) evil deeds with good, (2) the reprehensible (*al-munkar*) with the licit (*al-maʿrūf*), (3) iniquity with forgiveness, (4) insolence (*al-safah*) with forbearance (*al-ḥilm*), and (5) sin with repentance. It is only the fourth that he feels merits further elaboration. The example offered is the admirable behavior of those who respond to acts of impudence with forbearance.[44]

Drawing upon Muqātil, Fakhr al-Dīn al-Rāzī adds an interesting twist to those *ḥadīth*s that interpret *because of that in which they have persisted* as the physical and verbal abuse that new converts patiently suffered at the hands of the idolaters. Rather than retaliating, they forgave their tormentors "so they have two rewards, a reward for forgiving (*al-ṣafḥ*) and a reward for believing."[45] The idea of repelling evil with good, as expressed in the following phrase, is tied directly to this attitude of forbearance and forgiveness. In like manner does Fakhr al-Dīn al-Rāzī form a further connection with *from what We have given them, they spend*. In fact, this commentator sees the three sentences that constitute 28:54 as three distinct acts that provoked God's praise: "God praised them first for believing, then for physical acts of submission (*al-ṭāʿāt al-badanīyah*) . . . then for monetary acts of submission (*al-ṭāʿāt al-mālīyah*)."[46]

Ibn Kathīr identifies the pronominal referent of *these will be given their reward twice because of that in which they have persisted* as "those thus described who believed in the first book, then in the second" – effectively combining his identification and the explanation of *that in which they have persisted*.[47] He then introduces, as further explanation for the promise of a twofold

44 Ibn al-Jawzī, *Zād al-masīr*, 4:324–25. These five possibilities are offered on the authority of Ibn ʿAbbās, Saʿīd b. Jubayr, Juwaybir b. Saʿīd (d. 150/767), Ibn Quytabah, and Abū al-Ḥasan Muḥammad b. Aḥmad b. Kaysān (d. 299/911), respectively.

45 Fakhr al-Dīn al-Rāzī, *al-Tafsīr al-kabīr*, 24:262. The two instances cited are associated with Abū Jahl b. Hishām (d. 2/624) and ʿAbdallāh b. Salām. The former is remembered as a relentless opponent of the Prophet who died in the battle of Badr. The efforts he made to discourage Muslim converts are recorded by Ibn Isḥāq, *Sīrah*, 1:206–07 (Guillaume, *Life*, 145). See W. Montgomery Watt, "Abū Djahl," *EI*² 1:115.

46 Fakhr al-Dīn al-Rāzī, *al-Tafsīr al-kabīr*, 24:262.

47 Ibn Kathīr, *Tafsīr al-Qur'ān al-ʿaẓīm*, 3:393.

reward, two *ḥadīth*s that have not been encountered among the commentators discussed previously. The first recounts, on the authority of Abū Mūsā al-Ashʿarī, a statement by the Prophet: "Three are given their reward twice: a man of the *ahl al-kitāb* who believed in his prophet and then believes in me; a slave possessed by his master (*ʿabd mamlūk*) who performs what is due to God (*ḥaqq Allāh*) and what is due to his master; and a man who has a slave girl and has her trained (and did it well) and then frees her and marries her."[48] The second *ḥadīth*, from al-Qāsim b. Abī Imāmah, recounts the report of one who heard Muḥammad speak on the day of victory as saying, among other things, "whoever of the people of the two books [the Torah and the Gospel] becomes a Muslim will have his reward twice. There will count for him what counts for us, and against him what counts against us (*wa-lahu mā lanā wa-ʿalayhi mā ʿalaynā*)."[49]

While Ibn Kathīr adds nothing to the exegetical tradition of *they turn back evil with good,* he does offer a fuller explanation than have preceding commentators for the phrase that follows it. The kind of 'spending' intended by *from what We have given them, they spend* is both the obligatory expenses (*al-nafaqāt al-wājibah*) for family and relatives and statutory almsgiving (*al-zakāt al-mafrūḍah*) as well as nonobligatory but commendable almsgiving (*al-mustaḥabbah*). This latter can take the form of "voluntary acts (*al-taṭawwuʿāt*), charitable gifts of supererogation (*ṣadaqāt al-nafl*), and good works (*qurubāt*)."[50]

Kāshānī gives a very particular focus to 28:54, seeing it chiefly as a series of praises addressed to the *ahl al-kitāb*. He interprets *that in which they have persisted* as believing in the Torah and the Gospel, as well as believing in the Qurʾān both in anticipation of its revelation and after that event. He does add the now-familiar alternative possibilities for this phrase: (1) adhering to one's religion in the face of vituperation from the unbelievers, and (2) believing in both the former prophets and in Muḥammad.[51] Perhaps in anticipation of verse 55, this commentator explains *they turn back evil with good* first in terms of speech, juxtaposing discourse about *tawḥīd* with that which is an indication of *shirk* (*kih ān qāʾil shudan ast bi-shirk*).[52] He also includes the more general interpretations of warding off disobedience with obedience and that which is prohibited with that which is lawful.

48 Ibn Kathīr, *Tafsīr al-Qurʾān al-ʿaẓīm*, 3:393–94. The phrase *ʿabd mamlūk* occurs in *sūrat al-naḥl* (16):75 where it is contrasted with "one whom We have endowed from Our bounty (*man razaqnāhu minnā rizqan*)."

49 Ibn Kathīr, *Tafsīr al-Qurʾān al-ʿaẓīm*, 3:394.

50 Ibn Kathīr, *Tafsīr al-Qurʾān al-ʿaẓīm*, 3:394.

51 Kāshānī, *Minhaj al-ṣādiqīn*, 7:112.

52 Kāshānī, *Minhaj al-ṣādiqīn*, 7:112.

Kāshānī concludes this list of possibilities with one that again looks forward to the next verse. Here the scenario sketched is that of the taunts that unbelievers hurled at Christians or Jews who believed. Their mild and pacific response is an example of the way in which "they ward off with goodness (*nīkūʾī*) the talk of the unbelievers and the words of the foolish (*guftār-i sufahā*)."[53]

The justification for a divinely promised dual reward is what occupies Ṭabāṭabāʾī's attention in the first part of verse 54. While he recognizes this promise as a form of praise for "courteous dealings with the ignorant *mushrikūn*," the principal virtue to be highlighted by the reward is persistence and steadfastness, both in a prior scripture and in the final revelation.[54] That such persistence entails the endurance of persecution is made more explicit by the interpretation Ṭabāṭabāʾī prefers for the second phrase of this verse. He mentions two sets of contrarieties for the nouns in *they turn back evil with good,* namely, good and shameful speech and good and evil action, before expressing his own view. This exegete understands *good* and *evil* in terms of character or moral temper (*al-khulq*). The specific character traits herein contrasted are forbearance (*al-ḥilm*) and crude stupidity (*al-jahl*).[55] The former is the praiseworthy response to the aggressive antagonism motivated by the latter.

THE CONDUCT OF INTERRELIGIOUS DISCOURSE

Passivity and aggression figure prominently in the final verse of the Qurʾānic pericope under discussion, a verse that continues to cite those modes of behavior likely to prompt divine benefaction. Increasing specificity marks the conduct detailed by this and the preceding verse. The more general notions of 'persistence' and 'turning back evil with good' find clearer focus in the praise accorded spending *from what We have given them* and, finally, turning away from *idle chatter* with particular formulas of repudiation. Precisely what constitutes *idle chatter (al-laghw)* takes a central position on the exegetical agenda because that, in turn, defines the interpretive contours of the words of rebuttal.

Al-Ṭabarī first explains this term generally as any sort of false or useless speech (*al-bāṭil*) but then records the view of those who associate this term with the perennial charge of Christians' distortion or falsification of their scripture. The term thereby connotes "things that the *ahl al-kitāb* added to the book of God that were not part of it."[56] The scenario, as sketched

53 Kāshānī, *Minhaj al-ṣādiqīn*, 7:112.
54 Ṭabāṭabāʾī, *al-Mīzān*, 16:54.
55 Ṭabāṭabāʾī, *al-Mīzān*, 16:55.
56 al-Ṭabarī, *Jāmiʿ al-bayān* 20:91. See the discussion of *taḥrīf* in Chapter 5.

by the *ḥadīth* from Ibn Zayd that al-Ṭabarī records, is one in which individuals of the *ahl al-kitāb* give indiscriminate approval to both the genuine word of God and to "the falsehood that people have recorded with their own hands (*al-laghw alladhī kataba al-qawm bi-ayādihim*)."[57] Both are accorded the attention due only to the former. The Muslims, on the other hand, when confronted by the recitation of such spurious scripture "turn from it as if they had not heard it."[58] This *ḥadīth* concludes by noting that before those who act thus "believed in the Prophet, they were Muslims according to the religion of Jesus (*muslimūn ʿalā dīni ʿĪsā*)" – a phrase that echoes one quoted earlier in this discussion.[59]

The three short declarations that conclude this verse are explained by al-Ṭabarī as the responses of those persecuted Muslim converts to whom reference has already been made. However, unlike the former reference to only *mushrikūn* converts, mention is here made of converts from the *ahl al-kitāb* as well. In both instances, nevertheless, the tormentors remain the *mushrikūn*, to whom these words are directed: *they . . . say, "To us, our deeds and to you, your deeds. Peace be upon you; we do not desire ignorant people."*[60] In fact, this exegete ties the triple declaration to yet another interpretation of *al-laghw*, one that views it as the insults and abuse heaped upon Muslim converts by these very *mushrikūn*. The declarations may then be viewed as the Muslims' courteous rejoinder to verbal provocation. In particular, *peace be upon you* would then mean that you idolaters are "safe from our returning your insults" or saying things that you would be loath to hear.[61] Even the phrase *we do not desire ignorant people* is understood as the converts' efforts to explain that "we do not want to be near ignorant people or to exchange insults with them."[62]

Al-Ṭūsī broadens the connotation of *idle chatter* to include both vain talk (*laghw min al-kalām*) and senseless action (*laghw min al-fiʿl*).[63] In both cases the approved response is avoidance even to the point of shunning all argument. Such complete dissociation merits the right to proclaim *to us, our deeds and to you, your deeds,* which this exegete expands to mean "to us the recompense (*jazāʾ*) for our deeds and to you the recompense for yours."[64] Al-Ṭūsī then ties the penultimate and concluding phrases of this verse to the same dual sense of *al-laghw*. To say *we do not desire ignorant people (al-*

57 al-Ṭabarī, *Jāmiʿ al-bayān* 20:91.
58 al-Ṭabarī, *Jāmiʿ al-bayān* 20:91.
59 al-Ṭabarī, *Jāmiʿ al-bayān* 20:91.
60 al-Ṭabarī, *Jāmiʿ al-bayān* 20:91.
61 al-Ṭabarī, *Jāmiʿ al-bayān* 20:91.
62 al-Ṭabarī, *Jāmiʿ al-bayān* 20:91.
63 al-Ṭūsī, *al-Tibyān*, 8:162.
64 al-Ṭūsī, *al-Tibyān*, 8:162. The term *jazāʾ* is particularly apposite in this instance as it can convey a connotation of either reward or punishment.

jāhilūn) means, for al-Ṭūsī, "we do not seek them and we do not reward them for their idle talk and their useless activity in which there is no benefit. The one who acts thus does so only because of a corrupt imagination (*tawahhum fāsid*)."[65]

With this final group of phrases al-Zamakhsharī makes two points worth noting. The first is his identification of *peace be upon you* as a farewell (*tawdīʿ*) and leave-taking (*mutārakah*).[66] As such it constitutes an oral expression for *they turn away*. In like manner is his very practical interpretation of *we do not desire ignorant people:* "we do not want to mingle with them (*lā-nurīdu mukhālaṭatahum*) and associate with them (*ṣuḥbatahum*)."[67]

Aside from drawing attention to a Qurʾānic parallel in *sūrat al-furqān* (25):63, Abū al-Futūḥ Rāzī's brief remarks on the final verse of this group contain nothing of particular note beyond the interpretation he gives to *peace be upon you; we do not desire ignorant people*. He seems intent on disrupting any apparent causal connection between these two clauses when he insists that "in order to seek a good outcome (*salām*) it is not necessary to address the ignorant."[68]

Clemency in the face of abuse is the theme to which Ibn al-Jawzī returns in his interpretation of *when they hear idle chatter, they turn away from it*. In addition to this gloss on the authority of Mujāhid, however, he also proposes two other meanings for the term *al-laghw*. The first, from al-Ḍaḥḥāk, is any speech that attempts to deny or compromise God's oneness while the second is "the description of the Messenger of God [presumably in the

65 al-Ṭūsī, *al-Tibyān*, 8:162. In his study of the word *jāhilīyah* Toshihiko Izutsu has defined it in terms of its original meaning as "the keenest sense of tribal honor, the unyielding spirit of rivalry and arrogance, and all the rough and rude practices coming from an extremely passionate temper." In doing so, he follows the insights of Ignaz Goldziher who has offered the yet more controversial translation of 'barbarism'. *Muslim Studies*, 207. The opposite of *jahl*, then, as several of the commentators on this verse have noted, is *ḥilm*. Izutsu repeats R.A. Nicholson's definition of this latter term, "the moral reasonableness of a civilized man," and adds to this definition the remark that *ḥilm* includes "such characteristics as forbearance, patience, clemency, and freedom from blind passion." In a further stage of his analysis Izutsu then concludes that "the rise of Islām on its ethical side may very well be represented as a daring attempt to fight to the last extremity with the spirit of *jāhilīyah*, to abolish it completely, and to replace it once and for all by the spirit of *ḥilm*." In his analysis of the verse under consideration (28:55) this author notes that the policy advocated therein of "remaining indifferent and 'turning away' is recognized as the ideal attitude for all pious believers to adopt towards people of this kind [i.e., the *jāhilūn*]." He adds, however, that this was necessarily a temporary rather than a permanent policy "towards the infidels." *Ethico-Religious Concepts*, 28–34.

66 al-Zamakhsharī, *al-Kashshāf*, 3:442. Such an understanding may be prompted by the echo of *sūrat al-muzzammil* (73):10: "Patiently endure what they say and take leave of them courteously."

67 al-Zamakhsharī, *al-Kashshāf*, 3:442.

68 Abū al-Futūḥ Rāzī, *Rawḥ al-jinān*, 8:469.

Torah] as changed by the Jews."[69] For this second meaning, Ibn al-Jawzī repeats al-Ṭabarī's citation of a scene sketched by Ibn Zayd in which certain of the Jews who had come to believe in Muḥammad heard these distortions in their scripture and turned away in disgust.[70]

These various lines of interpretation are interwoven into this exegete's commentary on *they . . . say, "To us, our deeds and to you, your deeds."* He first rephrases it as a rejoinder appropriate to interreligious wrangling: "To us, our religion and to you, your religion."[71] (The curious resonance of this rephrasing with *sūrat al-kāfirīn* [109]:6, "to you, your religion and to me, my religion [*lakum dīnukum wa-liya dīnī*]," goes unremarked). Next, Ibn al-Jawzī draws upon the *safah/ḥilm* polarity introduced above to explain this statement, which is thereby perceived as yet another instance of religious forbearance.

Interestingly, this exegete, like al-Zamakhsharī, does not express such an attitude toward the penultimate phrase of this section of verses, *peace be upon you*. This, he maintains on the authority of al-Zajjāj, is not a greeting or salutation; it means only "between us and between you is a leave-taking (*al-mutārakah*)."[72] As such it marks a stage prior to the Qurʾānic injunction to fight the unbelievers (*sūrat al-tawbah* [9]:5, known as the 'verse of the sword [*āyat al-sayf*]'), which some commentators have held to be an abrogation of this verse.[73]

69 Ibn al-Jawzī, *Zād al-masīr*, 6:230.

70 Ibn al-Jawzī, *Zād al-masīr*, 6:230. Ibn al-Jawzī also notes that opinion is divided about whether this verse is abrogated (*mansūkh*). Although he does not specify the possible abrogating verse, probably it is one (such as 9:5, *āyat al-sayf*) that adjures a stronger reaction than clement passivity.

71 Ibn al-Jawzī, *Zād al-masīr*, 6:230.

72 Ibn al-Jawzī, *Zād al-masīr*, 6:230.

73 Ibn al-Jawzī, *Zād al-masīr*, 6:230. Issues of periodization and abrogation converge here. As has already been noted, a number of scholars subscribe to the theory that Muḥammad's relations with Christians and Jews evolved through several stages. Rudi Paret, for example, sees 2:62 (which is discussed in Chapter 3) as an indication of the Prophet's "high respect and sympathy for both the revealed religions in the beginning." After the Hijrah, Muḥammad's contacts with the Jews of Medina led to the kind of hostility exhibited in the remarks about the Jews in 5:82 (which is discussed in Chapter 7) and most strongly expressed in 9:29, known as *āyat al-jizyah*. Finally, according to Paret, "Muḥammad was to adopt an attitude of rejection and antagonism even towards the Christians. With that the independence of the new religion became complete." "Islam and Christianity," trans. by Rafiq Ahmad, *IS* 3 (1964):84–85. Anton Schall sketches the same sequence in his "Die Sichtung des Christlichen im Koran," *Mitteilungen und Forschungsbeiträge der Cusanus-Gesellschaft* 9 (1971):76–91. Johan Bouman, on the other hand, stresses the disjunction between the second and third stages, i.e., 5:82 and 9:29. *Gott und Mensch im Koran* (Darmstadt: Wissenschaftliche Buchgesellschaft, 1977) 249–51. Jacques Waardenburg's analysis is much fuller than the preceding. He adds details about the possible political motivations for Muḥammad's attack on Christianity and remarks that "contrary to the Qurʾānic texts directed against the polytheists and the

Ibn al-Jawzī includes more breadth and variety in his analysis of *we do not desire ignorant people* than have previous commentators. It may mean, he begins, "we do not desire the *religion* of the ignorant (*dīn al-jāhilīn*)." Alternatively, the sense could be "we do not seek proximity to them" or "*we* do not want to be ignorant."[74]

Fakhr al-Dīn al-Rāzī interprets the opening phrase of 28:55 in light of the one that concludes it. The idle chatter (*al-laghw*) that had once seemed attractive, they now refuse to countenance and politely (*iʿrāḍan jamīlan*) they turn from it.[75] Their saying *to us, our deeds and to you, your deeds* is but one more step in this progression, while *peace be upon you* can function as a greeting between believers or as a gesture of forbearance when addressed to the ignorant. Fakhr al-Dīn al-Rāzī, as did Abū al-Futūḥ Rāzī, refers the reader to *sūrat al-furqān* (25):63 for an example of this second use: "The servants of the Merciful are those who trod the earth unpretentiously and when the ignorant address them, they say 'Peace.' "

For the concluding phrase of this verse Fakhr al-Dīn al-Rāzī, echoing al-Ṭabarī, underlines the connection with its opening phrase by stating that the meaning of *we do not desire ignorant people* is "we do not repay their falsehood (*bāṭiluhum*) with falsehood."[76] While he acknowledges that some have said that this verse was abrogated by the command to fight, he himself finds this unlikely inasmuch as the two elements involved do not have the same legal status. He explains it thus: "To abstain from treating someone as foolish (*al-musāfahah*) is 'recommended' whereas fighting is 'obligatory.' "[77]

Once again Ibn Kathīr seeks a Qur'ānic parallel for the verse under discussion, finding it not in the same verse cited by Abū al-Futūḥ Rāzī and Fakhr al-Dīn al-Rāzī but one that shortly follows it, *sūrat al-furqān* (25):72, "when they walk by [people engaging in] idle chatter they walk by nobly." For the verse's concluding statement, Ibn Kathīr returns again to the occasion of revelation (*sabab al-nuzūl*) that he had previously adduced

Jews, which seem to reflect real debates in which Muḥammad used any argument he could find in the arsenal of the beliefs of the other party, the Qur'ānic texts against the Christians are rather wishy-washy and give the impression of a man shouting at an enemy who is far away." "Towards a Periodization of Earliest Islam According to its Relations with Other Religions," in *UEAI* 9, 313. For the modern period, J.J.G. Jansen draws attention to the importance that contemporary Muslim revolutionary groups attach to *āyat al-sayf* as well as to other Qur'ānic injunctions to fight. "Tafsîr, Ijmâʿ and Modern Muslim Extremism," *Orient* 27 (1986): 642–46.

74 Ibn al-Jawzī, *Zād al-masīr*, 6:230.

75 Fakhr al-Dīn al-Rāzī, *al-Tafsīr al-kabīr*, 24:263.

76 Fakhr al-Dīn al-Rāzī, *al-Tafsīr al-kabīr*, 24:263.

77 Fakhr al-Dīn al-Rāzī, *al-Tafsīr al-kabīr*, 24:263. Fakhr al-Dīn al-Rāzī is here employing terms, *mandūb* and *wājib* respectively, used in Islamic religio-legal literature to rank the moral value of actions.

for this verse group. This time he quotes the *Sīrah* of Ibn Isḥāq in recounting the episode of the Christian delegation that came to the Prophet from Abyssinia. The narrative is here expanded as follows: as the delegation rose to depart, having made a declaration of faith in God and His Prophet, a group of Quraysh led by Abū Jahl b. Hishām intercepted them to exclaim: "May God thwart the whole lot of you! Those of your coreligionists who stayed behind asked you to explore for them so that you could bring back news of the man. Yet you were barely seated in his presence before you had quit your own religion and acknowledged the truth of what he said. We know of no group as stupid as you!"[78]

Rather than flinging back an angry rejoinder, the Christian delegation – this is the point of note for the phrase under discussion – simply said: "Peace be to you; we will not exchange stupidities with you; to us, our business (*lanā mā naḥnu ʿalayhi*) and to you, yours. We ourselves do not neglect good."[79] Ibn Kathīr then interrupts the narrative portion of his citation from the *Sīrah* to broach the view of those who say the delegation was from Najrān (in Arabia), not Abyssinia. He returns, however, to the first referent when he quotes via Ibn Isḥāq the view from al-Zuhrī that both this verse (28:55) and 5:82–83 were sent down about the Najāshī and his associates, among whom the Christian delegation herein mentioned would certainly be numbered.

While the term *idle chatter* is understood conventionally, Kāshānī rephrases the dignified response (*takrimah*) of those thus bothered with three sets of antitheses: "(1) to us, our acts of forbearance (*ḥilm*) and pardoning (*ṣafḥ*) and to you, your acts of stupidity (*safāhat*) and vain talk (*laghw*); (2) to us, our religion and to you, your religion; or (3) to us, our knowledge (*ʿilm*) and to you, your insolence (*safah*)."[80] The point this exegete apparently wishes to emphasize is that of the inevitability of personal judgment. We will not be held accountable, he insists, for one another's actions; rather each of us will be judged for his own.

In *we do not desire ignorant people* Kāshānī finds a springboard from which to launch a short discourse on the unwholesome effects of association with the "ignorant." Association with them leads to a kind of spiritual contamination that can only result in both present and future divine punishment. Far better is it to be "seekers of wisdom and learned men."[81]

For Ṭabāṭabāʾī the connotation of *idle chatter* covers the whole range from idle talk (*hadhr*) to vituperation (*sabb*) to "anything that contains crudeness

78 Ibn Kathīr, *Tafsīr al-Qurʾān al-ʿaẓīm*, 3:394; Ibn Isḥāq, *Sīrah*, 1:259 (Guillaume, *Life*, 179).

79 Ibn Kathīr, *Tafsīr al-Qurʾān al-ʿaẓīm*, 3:394.

80 Kāshānī, *Minhaj al-ṣādiqīn*, 7:112.

81 Kāshānī, *Minhaj al-ṣādiqīn*, 7:113.

(*khushūnah*)."[82] The proper reaction is refusal to respond in kind, an awareness expressed by *to us, our deeds and to you, your deeds,* and reinforced by the courtesy of *peace be upon you.* The extent of such courtesy can be appreciated in this commentator's curious exegesis of the verse's concluding phrase, *we do not desire ignorant people.* This, he feels, must be understood as an interior pronouncement, "since if they said it aloud it would amount to countering evil with evil."[83] Only by saying such a thing silently to oneself could the discourtesy here abjured be avoided.[84]

CONCLUSION

From the exegetical tradition itself comes the association of these verses with Christians and their scriptural heritage. The bare Qurʾānic text remains elusive, subject to the transforming possibilities of specification and identification. Nowhere is this more obviously the case than in the exegetical attempt to wrest clarity from the pronominal confusion of the first two verses. The preponderant interpretation would paraphrase the first verse as "those to whom We gave the book before the Qurʾān believe in Muḥammad." The classical Shīʿī commentators, al-Ṭūsī and Abū al-Futūḥ Rāzī, allow for the possibility of "the book before Muḥammad," while Ibn al-Jawzī and Ṭabāṭabāʾī both permit the gloss, "believe in the Qurʾān."

This preponderant exegetical opinion rests, in turn, on that vision of Christian scripture which sees in it a prefiguration of the final Prophet. It is at precisely this point that identification with Christians is made most strongly. When the commentators begin to itemize those groups or individuals who might be the subject of this divine disclosure, the oft-repeated names of early Christian converts to Islam figure prominently in their lists. The generic term for such, *maslamah*, appears in the commentaries of both al-Ṭabarī and Ibn al-Jawzī. Ibn Kathīr draws this verse group into an ambient shared by the one discussed in the previous chapter, maintaining that both reflect the episode and the individuals surrounding the Najāshī. That each of these Qurʾānic pericopes includes a recitation scenario reinforces the connection that Ibn Kathīr makes. The only significant exception to this pattern of association is produced by Fakhr al-Dīn al-Rāzī and Ṭabāṭabāʾī. The former argues for broad applicability on the grounds that the text itself contains no marks of delimitation. Ṭabāṭabāʾī, on the other hand, uses a contextual argument to justify the opposite conclusion.

82 Ṭabāṭabāʾī, *al-Mīzān*, 16:56.
83 Ṭabāṭabāʾī, *al-Mīzān*, 16:56.
84 Although, in his customary fashion, Ṭabāṭabāʾī appends a list of *ḥadīth*s relevant to the exegesis of these verses, it includes nothing that has not appeared in the previous commentators treated.

The preceding censure of a specific group may logically only be followed with praise of an equally restricted group.

The initially puzzling phrase *truly we were Muslims before it* offers the exegetes an excellent opportunity to express an Islamic vision of salvation history with increasing refinement. Early attempts speak generally of attestations to the prophethood of Muḥammad that may be found in pre-Qur'ānic scriptures. The implicit assumption behind this perspective reaches greater clarity with al-Zamakhsharī. He fills in the background with a verbal depiction of faithful scriptural transmission. The passage of preserved truth from generation to generation stands in stark contrast to the usual Muslim charges of Christian scriptural deformation. Of course it must be borne in mind that only a minority merit the status of pre-Qur'ānic *muslimūn*. These form an elite whose religious sensitivity prevents their approving any adulteration of God's unicity and prompts their ready recognition of revelatory testimony to Muḥammad. Once again what is being praised is scriptural perceptivity, an attitude or spiritual aptitude that permits one to discern the forthcoming and final closure of revelation. Remaining faithful to that in pious anticipation of its fulfillment is the meaning of adherence/perseverance.

Missing from this and previous exegetical allusions to such pre-Qur'ānic attestation to Muḥammad is any sustained interest in specificity. Although it is repeatedly asserted that both the Torah and Gospel contain clear reference to the advent of Muḥammad, there is no attempt to cite particular passages from those scriptures. Christian rebuttals to this claim are dismissed on the grounds that current versions of the Gospel are corruptions of the original transmission or that Christians themselves have become so spiritually corrupt that they are unable to understand and to interpret the attestations enshrined in their own scripture. Only a few remained faithful to the Gospel as originally revealed or possess a religious sensibility sufficiently uncorrupted to permit their recognition of the textual foretelling of Muḥammad.

Although none of the commentators herein studied explains in such detail the understanding of Christian scriptural adherence (or the lack thereof) that underlies verses like the ones under discussion, it is presupposed in the more allusive and elliptical remarks that they make. It is also the basis upon which some of the exegetes make sense of the divine promise of a twofold reward. The praise for persistence, expressed in 28:54, echoes the idea of adherence in 5:66. For al-Ṭabarī, al-Zamakhsharī, Abū al-Futūḥ Rāzī, Ibn Kathīr, and Kāshānī, it is precisely this notion of a continuity of scriptural faithfulness that warrants such a pledge. Others have offered the notion of enduring the retaliation of a convert's former coreligionists as justification for the dual reward. Recompense for persecution can be a reward for suffering physical abuse and verbal sneers with dignity and restraint, refusing to retaliate or to debate or even to listen to the arguments of unbelievers. Alternatively, it can compensate the more aggressive convert, the one whose skills in intellectual combat best all opponents.

Both explanations for the dual reward, that for scriptural faithfulness and that for a convert's suffering, presuppose the expectation that steadfast adherence to the truth may involve social alienation. Those Christians who stayed faithful to their scripture as originally revealed did so in resistance to the others who deliberately falsified their scripture or inadvertently accepted the falsification. Similarly, Christians who affiliated themselves with the nascent Muslim community could expect to be treated with disdain by those whose beliefs they were rejecting.

Out of the final phrases of this verse group emerges an embryonic agenda for the conduct of unwelcome interreligious contact. Among the items on this agenda are various forms of appropriate and inappropriate response to such contact. Avoidance, physical and verbal restraint, courteous rejoinder, and simply taking one's leave of an antagonist are all mentioned by the commentators as suitable responses to the overtures of hostile or ignorant nonbelievers. What may be thought useless or improper behavior would be any attempt to match the rude or abusive assaults of nonbelievers. Staying above the loutish fray is the implicit prescription of these final phrases. The sense of individual responsibility before God's judgment that supports this stance Kāshānī makes explicit. This commentator also gives expression to a concern that lies beyond much of the exegetical interest in verse 28:55. There is a sense conveyed indirectly by many of the commentators that association with those who are inimical to one's religious belief poses not only a physical but a spiritual danger as well. The possibility of intellectual and moral contamination constitutes a grave threat, one best countered by avoiding all association or verbal interchange with non-Muslims. Where that is impossible, then a restrained courtesy is the recommended action. The notion that such restraint was but a temporary recommendation, one later abrogated by the command to fight, is noted but not conceded. Although both al-Ṭūsī and Fakhr al-Dīn al-Rāzī draw the connection between 28:55 and Qurʾānic injunctions to fight such as *āyat al-sayf*, neither places this in the category of abrogated verses. While al-Ṭūsī sees no incompatibility between 28:55 and verses such as 9:5, Fakhr al-Dīn al-Rāzī regards them as being of different legal status. In each case, this Qurʾānic approbation of withdrawal, restraint, and clemency is allowed to stand.

9

Compassion, mercy, and monasticism

The concluding verse of this study presents a particularly rich range of exegetical issues for consideration. Identification with the Christians is assured here, as it was in 3:55, by specific reference to the name ʿĪsā. Mention of the *injīl* further reinforces that association. A yet more precise focus is achieved with the verse's reference to that form of Christian behavior known as monasticism (*rahbānīyah*). Monasticism, in turn, raises a complex of questions for cross-traditional consideration, both legal and historical. As grammatical conundrums affect the hermeneutical perspective of some of the commentators, the following is but one possible rendering of *sūrat al-ḥadīd* (57):27:

> Then We caused Our messengers to follow in their footsteps. We sent Jesus, son of Mary, to follow and We gave him the Gospel. We placed in the hearts of those who followed him compassion and mercy and monasticism which they invented; We did not prescribe it for them except as the seeking of God's acceptance. But they did not observe it correctly. So We gave to those of them who believed their reward but many of them are sinners.

EXEGETICAL GLOSSING

Al-Ṭabarī's commentary on this verse begins periphrastically and includes but slight elaboration of the individual phrases. He adds precision to the general identification of the verse by glossing *We placed in the hearts of those who followed him* as "those who follow Jesus according to his path (*minhāj*) and his law (*sharīʿah*)."[1]

As did al-Ṭabarī, al-Ṭūsī makes explicit the contextual sequence within which this verse must be understood. Reference to Noah and Abraham in the immediately preceding verse forms the background against which the phrase *then We caused Our messengers to follow in their footsteps* may be explicated.

1 al-Ṭabarī, *Jāmiʿ al-bayān*, 27:238. Abdelmajid Charfi notes that al-Ṭabarī "hesitates between regarding the injīl as 'exhortation and warning' and as a scripture with its own legal rulings (*aḥkām*) and a particular code of conduct (*sharīʿah*)." "Christianity in the Qurʾān Commentary," 108.

His attention is captured, however, by the statement *We placed in the hearts of those who followed him compassion and mercy.* Here al-Ṭūsī makes some subtle distinctions about the sense in which God 'placed' mercy and compassion in their hearts. He admits of two possibilities. The verb may be used in the sense that God commanded it (*bi-al-amr bihi*) or aroused the desire for it (*al-targhīb fīhi*).[2] Alternatively the meaning might be that "God created (*khalaqa*) mercy and compassion in their hearts. He then praised them only because they gave careful attention (*taʿarraḍū*) to [the development of] these two qualities."[3]

Philological concerns, so pronounced in al-Zamakhsharī's commentary, occupy the opening lines of his treatment of the verse. He notes that the Arabic word for Gospel, *al-injīl*, is sometimes pronounced as *anjīl* but comments that the difference is of little concern as it is a foreign term to which the rules of Arabic do not apply.[4] This commentator finds a Qurʾānic parallel for *We placed in the hearts of those who followed him compassion and mercy* because of the direction that his interpretation of the phrase takes. He views it in terms of "showing compassion (*al-tarāḥum*) and affection (*al-taʿāṭuf*) for one another," and can therefore liken it to the Qurʾānic description of Muḥammad's Companions in *sūrat al-fatḥ* (48):29: "compassionate among themselves."[5]

In his Persian translation of the phrase *We placed in the hearts of those who followed him compassion and mercy,* Abū al-Futūḥ Rāzī adds a third term, forgiveness (*bakhshāyish*).[6] The two Qurʾānic terms mean, he says, the same thing. The repetition is simply for the sake of effect. Ibn al-Jawzī offers the most specific identification of those intended by the phrase *We placed in the hearts of those who followed him compassion and mercy* by stating that it means "the disciples (*al-ḥawārīyūn*) and others who followed him [Jesus] in his religion."[7] This exegete looks to *sūrat al-nūr* (24):2 for another use of the term compassion (*raʾfah*). Here, in a reference to the punishment necessary for sexual misconduct, it is the proscription of compassion that

2 al-Ṭūsī, *al-Tibyān*, 9:536. For a comparison of Sunnī and Muʿtazilī positions on the concept of the "creation" of human acts, see Daniel Gimaret, *Théories de l'acte humain en théologie musulmane* (Paris: Librairie Philosophique J. Vrin, 1980), 334–95, especially 388–91 which are specific to this verse. Among Gimaret's principal sources for this comparison are the *tafsīrs* of al-Ṭabarī, al-Zamakhsharī, and Fakhr al-Dīn al-Rāzī.

3 al-Ṭūsī, *al-Tibyān*, 9:536.

4 al-Zamakhsharī, *al-Kashshāf*, 4:481. For *injīl* see Chapter 6, note 1.

5 al-Zamakhsharī, *al-Kashshāf*, 4:481.

6 Abū al-Futūḥ Rāzī, *Rawḥ al-jinān*, 11:56.

7 Ibn al-Jawzī, *Zād al-masīr*, 8:175. The only Qurʾānic mentions of the term *ḥawārīyūn* are those in *sūrah Āl ʿImrān* (3):52, *sūrat al-māʾidah* (5):111–12, and *sūrat al-ṣaff* (61):14. Mustansir Mir provides a brief conspectus of these passages in *Dictionary of Qurʾānic Terms and Concepts* (New York: Garland, 1987), 53. For the Muslim analogues to such Christian disciples see A.J. Wensinck, "Ḥawārī," *EI*[2] 3:285, a reprint of *EI*[1] 3:292–93.

is mandated. He then cites the same Qur'ānic parallel as did al-Zamakhsharī, *sūrat al-fatḥ* (48):29, as explanation for the synonyms here translated as 'mercy' and 'compassion'.

Fakhr al-Dīn al-Rāzī spends more time than did al-Zamakhsharī on various theories for *anjīl* as an alternative spelling of *al-injīl*. He notes that attempts have been made to relate the word to the Arabic root *NJL*, which carries, among others, connotations of 'begetting' and 'producing'. By this line of reasoning the *injīl* is so designated because "he derives by it the religious ordinances (*yastakhriju bihi al-aḥkām*)."[8] Nevertheless Fakhr al-Dīn al-Rāzī finds no compelling justification for this alternative vocalization and attributes its currency to a particular received tradition. One possibility he suggests is that al-Ḥasan al-Baṣrī, to whom this reading is ascribed, "supposed *al-injīl* to be a non-Arabic word, so he perverted the pattern of it [i.e., to *anjīl*] to indicate its being non-Arabic."[9]

In contrast to some of the positions expressed by al-Ṭūsī, Fakhr al-Dīn al-Rāzī uses the phrase *We placed in the hearts of those who followed him compassion and mercy* as the springboard for a summary statement of Ashʿarī views on human volition: "Our colleagues advance this verse as an argument that the action of man is the creation of God but is attributed to man."[10]

Ibn Kathīr uses the more specific term adopted by both Ibn al-Jawzī and Fakhr al-Dīn al-Rāzī, *al-ḥawārīyūn*, as the referent for *those who followed him*, with Kāshānī following suit. The latter proposes, as Persian equivalents of the coordinates *compassion and mercy*, the terms 'kindness (*mihrbānī*)' and – in concert with al-Ṭūsī – 'forgiveness (*bakhshāyish*)'. He paraphrases the complete statement in this way: "We caused the followers (*mutābiʿān*) and those close to Jesus (*khavāṣṣ-i ʿĪsā*) to be kind and forgiving to one another."[11] The precise sense of *We placed* is identified as either the instigation of these qualities by promise of divine reward or the creation of them "in their hearts."

Ṭabāṭabāʾī, too, pays attention to the coordinate terms *compassion and mercy*. While conceding that they are usually understood as synonyms, he

8 Fakhr al-Dīn al-Rāzī, *al-Tafsīr al-kabīr*, 29:244. In his commentary on *sūrah Āl ʿImrān* (3):3, which contains the first Qur'ānic mention of *injīl* and *tawrāt*, Fakhr al-Dīn al-Rāzī cites al-Zamakhsharī's opinion that as the two are "foreign words, being concerned with their etymology is without benefit." *al-Tafsīr al-kabīr*, 7:171.

9 Fakhr al-Dīn al-Rāzī, *al-Tafsīr al-kabīr*, 29:244. Arthur Jeffery mentions the attempts of early authorities to find an Arabic origin for *injīl* as an *ifʿīl* form from *NJL* and also refers to al-Ḥasan's reading of *anjīl* in his *Foreign Vocabulary*, 71.

10 Fakhr al-Dīn al-Rāzī, *al-Tafsīr al-kabīr*, 29:244. By contrast, Gimaret presents an earlier view of ʿAbd al-Jabbār that disallows the notion that God could create 'mercy (*raʾfah*)' in human hearts because of His proscription of it in *sūrat al-nūr* (24):2 in the case of those convicted of adultery. *Théories*, 390.

11 Kāshānī, *Minhaj al-ṣādiqīn*, 9:194.

notes the view of those who maintain that the former (*al-raʾfah*) carries connotations of "having harm averted (*darʾ al-sharr*)" while *al-raḥmah* carries the more positive sense of "attracting the good (*jalb al-khayr*)."[12] Although Ṭabāṭabāʾī does not define *those who followed* Jesus with any specificity, he does draw the standard Qurʾānic parallel between the behavior of this group and the comportment of those who followed the Prophet. The former, he states, "lived by assisting each other (*al-muʿāḍadah*) and keeping peace with each other (*al-musālamah*)," just as did the latter whom God described in *sūrat al-fatḥ* (48):29 as "compassionate among themselves."[13]

THE PUZZLING PRAISE OF MONASTICISM

These preliminary considerations are but a backdrop to the principal exegetical focus of this verse, the reference to monasticism. Virtually all of the commentators herein discussed have made the phrases of this verse that pertain to monasticism their primary object of attention. Al-Ṭabarī's method of doing so is less systematic than usual, as he moves toward the topic from several angles. For him, the first issue of significance is determining the subject of *but they did not observe it correctly.* Al-Ṭabarī notes that some of the exegetes prior to him identify the subject of this sentence with that of a preceding phrase, *which they invented.* In other words, the same people who "invented" monasticism are the ones charged with incorrect or inadequate observance of it. In the very act of instituting it, "they altered and diverged from the religion of God which was sent down on Jesus and converted to Christianity (*tanaṣṣarū*) and to Judaism (*tahawwadū*)."[14] (This sentence makes very clear the oft-maintained distinction between the 'true' religion of Jesus and that falsely associated with him, i.e., that which Christians normally practice.)

The opposing viewpoint is that incorrect compliance arose not with the originators of monasticism but with subsequent adherents. Although this latter group claimed to be following the precepts laid down by their forerunners, "they were unbelievers (*kuffār*)." Among the *ḥadīth*s that al-Ṭabarī includes is one from Qatādah that characterizes monasticism as rejecting women and residing in hermitages (*al-ṣawāmiʿ*).[15] Another, from Ibn Zayd, supports the position just mentioned, namely, that monastic deterioration is the fault not of the initiators but of those who sought to emulate them, their disciples (*al-murīdūn*).[16]

12 Ṭabāṭabāʾī, *al-Mīzān*, 19:173.
13 Ṭabāṭabāʾī, *al-Mīzān*, 19:173.
14 al-Ṭabarī, *Jāmiʿ al-bayān*, 2:238. Tilman Nagel makes an interesting association of this verse with *sūrah Āl ʿImrān* (3):78–93, a strong denigration of those who deviate from the revelation granted to them. *Der Koran*, 131–33.
15 al-Ṭabarī, *Jāmiʿ al-bayān*, 27:238.
16 al-Ṭabarī, *Jāmiʿ al-bayān*, 27:238.

However, particular prominence is also given to a *ḥadīth* from Ibn ʿAbbās that finds this fault not in the followers, but the initiators. It is of additional interest for the distinctions it draws among the various forms of hermetic or cenobitic life. This account begins with the charge that after the time of Jesus certain secular (i.e., not specifically Christian) authorities made changes in the Torah and Gospel, while other rulers remained faithful to the original scriptures. Similarly there were some Christians who falsified the originals and others who remained true to them. Goaded by the taunts of the falsifiers, the faithful group sought redress from a sympathetic authority, demanding that he order their coreligionists to cease the altered recitation. When the king complied with this request, the falsifiers took umbrage and chose to exile themselves rather than return to the original scriptures.[17]

Their forms of self-exile correspond to three kinds of monastic life. One group said, "Build for us a column (*usṭuwānah*), then raise us up to it and give us something so that we can lift up our food and drink." Another group chose a different path, saying, "Let us roam about the land and wander, drinking what the wild beasts drink." Yet a third group demanded, "Build for us a dwelling in the desert and we will dig wells and cultivate herbs (*al-buqūl*)."[18]

While this *ḥadīth* is indeed interesting for the varieties of stylitic, nomadic, and settled monastic life that it presents, its chief importance lies in the light it sheds upon the question of the subject of *but they did not observe it correctly.* By the evidence of this account, monasticism was spiritually bankrupt from the moment of its inception because it was founded by those who had corrupted their own spiritual heritage. Given such roots, it is little wonder that the plant was diseased and withered. Yet others argue, reports al-Ṭabarī, that blight appeared not in the first but in subsequent generations of ascetics.

These followers attempted to model themselves on their precursors but "given their *shirk*, had no knowledge of the faith of those whom they emulated."[19] By the time of the Prophet's coming, the account continues, "there remained but a few" who had continued in the true observance of monasticism.[20] As this narrative so vividly puts it, they gathered around

17 Elements of this account find striking parallels in the reports that convey the process of Qurʾānic textual fixation. The notions of emergent diversity, of an effort to mandate uniformity, and of the resultant compliance and dissent may be compared with traditional views, presented in Chapter 1, of the Qurʾān's final codification.

18 al-Ṭabarī, *Jāmiʿ al-bayān*, 27:239.

19 al-Ṭabarī, *Jāmiʿ al-bayān*, 27:239.

20 al-Ṭabarī, *Jāmiʿ al-bayān*, 27:239. In his discussion of this verse Simon Jargy translates *fa-mā raʿawhā ḥaqqa riʿāyatihā* as "mais ils ne l'ont point (toujours) observé correctment."

Muḥammad thus: "A man descended from his cell (*ṣawmaʿah*) – no further mention is made of a column – a wanderer came forth from his wanderings, and the one who had a constructed dwelling (*ṣāḥib al-dār*) came from his abode."[21] They acknowledged belief in Muḥammad and were rewarded with the divine promise revealed in the verse that immediately follows the one under discussion, *sūrat al-ḥadīd* (57):28: "He will give you two portions (*kiflayn*) of His mercy." Consistent with the interpretation of a similar promise in the verses analyzed in the preceding chapter, the two rewards are here understood as recompense "for their believing in Jesus and attesting to the truth of the Torah and the Gospel and for believing in Muḥammad and their attesting to him."[22]

Al-Ṭabarī next recounts a Prophetic *ḥadīth* from ʿAbdallāh b. Masʿūd that examines the issue of monasticism's origin and preservation from yet another perspective. This begins with a quotation from the Prophet to the effect that those who preceded him had subdivided into seventy-one groups of which only three were saved (*najā*) while the rest perished (*halaka*).[23] The first of these actively opposed the persecution by unjust rulers but were killed fighting for "the religion of God and the religion of ʿĪsā b. Maryam."[24] The second, lacking the capacity to defend themselves, were slaughtered by the rulers, who "sawed them up with saws (*nasharathum bi-manāshīr*)."[25] The third group avoided even the possibility of martyrdom by clinging fast to their desert and mountain retreats while living as monks and hermits. The clear implication of lack of religious courage and fervor as the primary motivation of *rahbānīyah* is inescapable.

Yet another insight into the problem of monasticism's initial or subsequent corruption is provided by this commentator's use of a pair of nearly identical *ḥadīth*s, one from Ibn ʿAbbās and the other from al-Ḍaḥḥāk, which are more condemnatory in tone. Here the primary accusation is that of disobedience, outright refusal on the part of some of those who lived in the time between Jesus and Muḥammad to fight in the name of religion. Instead this recalcitrant contingent "segregated themselves and maintained

His parenthetical inclusion of "toujours" nicely signals the entire exegetical discussion of whether this criticism must be laid on those who initiated *rahbānīyah* or their successors. *Islam et chrétienté*, 59.

21 al-Ṭabarī, *Jāmiʿ al-bayān*, 27:239. Efforts to determine the kinds of religious practice known to Muḥammad are surveyed and critiqued by M.J. Kister, "Al-taḥannuth: An Inquiry into the Meaning of a Term," in *Studies in Jāhiliyya and Early Islam* (London: Variorum Reprints, 1980), reprinted from *BSOAS* 31 (1968): 223–36.

22 al-Ṭabarī, *Jāmiʿ al-bayān*, 27:239.

23 al-Ṭabarī, *Jāmiʿ al-bayān*, 27:239. For a variant of this tradition and its exegetical deployment see Chapter 6.

24 al-Ṭabarī, *Jāmiʿ al-bayān*, 27:239.

25 al-Ṭabarī, *Jāmiʿ al-bayān*, 27:239.

this segregation until a group of them renounced belief (*kafara*), ceased observing God's command (*tarakū amr Allāh*) and embraced innovation (*akhadhū bi-al-bidᶜah*), Christianity (*al-naṣrānīyah*) and Judaism (*al-yahūdīyah*)."[26] The second version of this *ḥadīth* substitutes for the closing phrase "they innovated (*ibtadaᶜū*) Christianity and Judaism." Both versions conclude, however, with mention of a group who "remained steadfast (*thabatat*)" in the religion of Jesus and believed in Muḥammad when he was sent.[27] They are those to whom the double reward is promised in the next verse, 57:28.

Before declaring his own position on this issue, al-Ṭabarī adds a final *ḥadīth*, one ascribed to Abū Imāmah al-Bāhilī (d. 231/855). This focuses not on *rahbānīyah* but on the fast of Ramaḍān, finding in the latter another instance of 'innovation'. This time, however, the term is not being used pejoratively. Abū Imāmah is reported as saying "God prescribed for you (*kataba ᶜalaykum*) the fast of Ramaḍān but did not prescribe for you the manner of its observance (*qiyāmuhu*). The latter is merely something that they invented."[28] He then draws the parallel with this verse's statement about monasticism and the accusation of innovation contained therein.

In his summary statement, this exegete unequivocally supports the position that from the beginning monasticism was not properly observed.[29] Yet he brings to the argument quite a different line of analysis from those that he has so faithfully reported. He treats those who "invented" monasticism not as a unit but as individuals or, at least, divergent groups. This permits him to acknowledge that while some are liable to the accusation of noncompliance, others are not. Al-Ṭabarī finds in the phrase *We gave to those of them who believed their reward* his principal justification for this line of reasoning. He feels that God indicated by that phrase that "among them are those who do indeed adhere (*qad raᶜā*) to it [i.e., monasticism] properly, for if there were not such as those among them, they would not be entitled to the reward."[30] On the other hand, his paraphrase of *but many of them are sinners* allows him to conclude that at any rate "many of them are a disobedient people who have stopped obeying or believing in Him."[31]

Interesting distinctions are also a feature of al-Ṭūsī's discussion of monasticism and the Qurʾānic statements about it. He first defines the term as

26 al-Ṭabarī, *Jāmiᶜ al-bayān*, 27:240.
27 al-Ṭabarī, *Jāmiᶜ al-bayān*, 27:240.
28 al-Ṭabarī, *Jāmiᶜ al-bayān*, 27:240. Abū Imāmah al-Bāhilī is briefly mentioned by Ibn Saᶜd in *Ṭabaqāt*, 1:415 and 7:416–17. In the latter instance, he is presented as responding to a request that he supply a physical description of Muḥammad.
29 al-Ṭabarī, *Jāmiᶜ al-bayān*, 27:241. Al-Ṭabarī does, however, admit that the alternative view is not inconsistent with the Qurʾānic Arabic usage here.
30 al-Ṭabarī, *Jāmiᶜ al-bayān*, 27:241.
31 al-Ṭabarī, *Jāmiᶜ al-bayān*, 27:241.

that quality of devotional activity (*al-khaṣlah min al-ʿibādah*) in which there is manifest a sense of fear (*al-rahbah*), a definition that draws upon etymological connections of the term *rahbānīyah* with the Arabic root *RHB*. This may take the form of the wearing of particular kinds of clothing or of withdrawal from the community (*infirād ʿan al-jamāʿah*) or of various other ascetic practices.[32] Then by juxtaposing the phrases *We did not prescribe it for them* and *except as the seeking of God's acceptance*, he discriminates between two ways of conceiving *rahbānīyah*. In the first, *rahbānīyah* is an activity lacking divine prescription, while in the second, it is a way of winning divine favor. The two things must be differentiated, insists al-Ṭūsī, for though the terminology is the same, the concepts and their implementation are different.[33]

Support for such a distinction is then garnered from an examination of the ideas of invention and innovation. Al-Ṭūsī defines invention (*al-ibtidāʿ*) more positively than innovation (*al-bidʿah*). The former is characterized as "beginning something that has no prior model" while the latter is deemed to be "establishing something contrary to the *sunnah*."[34] Varying descriptions of the invention known as monasticism may then be culled from the statements that this exegete includes. One such, repeating Qatādah's definition which al-Ṭabarī cited, views monasticism as "abandoning women (*rafḍ al-nisāʾ*) and occupying hermits' dwellings (*ittikhādh al-ṣawāmiʿ*)," while another, offered without specific attribution, perceives it in terms of "their betaking themselves to the deserts and the mountains."[35] A final perception emphasizes the motive for these various asceticisms: "Monasticism is being cut off from people in order to worship in solitude (*lil-infirād bi-al-ʿibādah*)."[36]

The distinction between the two referents for the term *rahbānīyah* is made even clearer when al-Ṭūsī, following al-Zajjāj, rephrases *We did not prescribe it for them* as "We did not decree it (*faraḍnāhā*), i.e., this monasticism, for them at all (*al-battata*)."[37] Yet once they have undertaken that monasticism which is a means of seeking God's favor, "its observance becomes incumbent upon them" just as one who has begun a voluntary fast is required to complete it.[38] A *ḥadīth* from al-Ḥasan goes even further and joins these two aspects of monasticism, which al-Ṭūsī has heretofore so rigorously sep-

32 al-Ṭūsī, *al-Tibyān*, 9:536. Ibn Manẓūr's etymological analysis incorporates exegetical remarks on this verse, including a description of monasticism as involving such practices as self-castration and self-enchainment. *Lisān al-ʿarab*, 1:437–38.

33 al-Ṭūsī, *al-Tibyān*, 9:536.

34 al-Ṭūsī, *al-Tibyān*, 9:536–37.

35 al-Ṭūsī, *al-Tibyān*, 9:537.

36 al-Ṭūsī, *al-Tibyān*, 9:537.

37 al-Ṭūsī, *al-Tibyān*, 9:537.

38 al-Ṭūsī, *al-Tibyān*, 9:537.

arated, by stating: "God made it incumbent on them after they invented it."[39]

Al-Ṭūsī explains this verse's charge of noncompliance, *but they did not observe it correctly*, in two different places in his commentary. In one place he quotes the verse and then provides a paraphrase by synonym substitution. In the other, however, he specifies the form that this noncompliance assumed and the source from which it sprang: "that is because of their calling Muḥammad a liar (*li-takdhībihim*)."[40]

What is most novel about al-Zamakhsharī's discussion of monasticism is the connection he forms with the concept of temptation (*al-fitnah*). He first defines monastic life as a retreat to the mountains, motivated by a desire to avoid worldly temptations. Put more positively, its goal is dedication to divine worship.[41] This commentator then connects the definition to a brief historical *excursus* reminiscent of some of the material used by al-Ṭabarī. One noteworthy feature of al-Zamakhsharī's version is its unequivocal use of the term 'believers (*mu'minūn*)' to designate the followers of Jesus. It begins by recounting how "tyrants overcame the believers after the death of Jesus," killing them until only a few were left.[42] The response of those remaining and its connection with temptation is then recorded: "They were afraid they would be tempted in their religion (*khāfū an yuftanū fī dīnihim*) so they chose monasticism."[43]

Al-Zamakhsharī uses a technical grammatical term to explain *except as the seeking of God's acceptance.* It is a "disconnected exclusion/exceptive (*istithnā' munqaṭi'*)," that is, its sense follows *monasticism which they invented* but its placement is interrupted by the phrase *We did not prescribe it for them.*[44] In other words, the intent of the revelation is "they invented monasticism out of a desire to please God" with the notion of God's not prescribing it for them as a completely separate idea. From such a perspective the word group *We did not prescribe it for them except as the seeking of God's acceptance* cannot mean something like "We did not prescribe it for them except insofar as they might use it as a means of pleasing Us." According to this exegete, there is no equivocation about the divine disinvolvement.

Nevertheless, like al-Ṭūsī, al-Zamakhsharī finds in the creation and acceptance of monasticism a self-imposed obligation for those involved. Even

39 al-Ṭūsī, *al-Tibyān*, 9:537.
40 al-Ṭūsī, *al-Tibyān*, 9:537.
41 al-Zamakhsharī, *al-Kashshāf*, 4:481.
42 al-Zamakhsharī, *al-Kashshāf*, 4:481.
43 al-Zamakhsharī, *al-Kashshāf*, 4:482.
44 al-Zamakhsharī, *al-Kashshāf*, 4:482. Louis Massignon has paraphrased the exegetical intent thus: "Quant à la vie monastique, ce sont eux qui l'ont instituée, par désir de complaire à Dieu; Nous ne leur en avions pas fait un devoir canonique." *Essai sur les origines*, 152.

though God has not prescribed monasticism, the one who vows himself to it must comply with his vow "because it is a contract made with God (*ʿahd maʿa Allāh*) which may not be violated."[45]

Al-Zamakhsharī defines *We gave to those of them who believed* more specifically than have the previous two exegetes. For him the phrase means the people of *compassion and mercy* who followed Jesus.[46] He does not here explicitly connect this phrase to the preceding one, *but they did not observe it correctly,* by understanding the reward promised to *those of them who believed* as a recompense for their faithful observance of monasticism. He does, however, interpret the concluding phrase, *but many of them are sinners,* as being in this connection. The *sinners* are those very ones who failed to keep their monastic contract with God.[47]

The matter does not end here for al-Zamakhsharī. Rather he completes his exegesis of this verse with the novel suggestion that *monasticism* is connected to *compassion and mercy* as the third object of *We placed.* The sense would then be: "We placed in their hearts compassion and mercy and monasticism, which they invented."[48] This exegete then goes on to rework the entire verse in light of this possibility. His paraphrase is interesting enough to merit quotation in its entirety: "We made them successful in dealing compassionately with each other (*waffaqnāhum lil-tarāḥum baynahum*) and in innovating monasticism and originating it (*istiḥdāthihā*). We did not prescribe it for them except so that they might seek by it the approval of God and might thereby be entitled to reward."[49] Al-Zamakhsharī continues: "It is as though He wrote it for them and imposed it on them so that they might be freed from temptations (*li-yatakhallaṣū min al-fitan*) and seek thereby the acceptance of God and His reward."[50] Given this possible perspective on the verse, the concluding distinction between those who will be rewarded and those who are *sinners* can only be understood in terms of monastic observance or neglect, as al-Zamakhsharī duly notes.

The possibility that *monasticism* can be understood in connection with the two preceding terms as a third accusative of *We placed* aroused considerable interest in the subsequent exegetical tradition on this verse. Abū al-Futūḥ Rāzī, for example, completely rejects it. To illustrate the grammatical connection that exists between *monasticism* and *which they invented,* Abū al-

45 al-Zamakhsharī, *al-Kashshāf*, 4:482.
46 al-Zamakhsharī, *al-Kashshāf*, 4:482.
47 al-Zamakhsharī, *al-Kashshāf*, 4:482.
48 al-Zamakhsharī, *al-Kashshāf*, 4:482. Louis Massignon has traced earlier instances of this interpretation among the Muʿtazilīs, such as al-Jubbāʾī, and found that the Muʿtazilī meaning of *jaʿalnā* in this verse would be: "Nous avons donné à l'homme le pouvoir de créer (par lui-même . . .)." *Essai sur les origines*, 151.
49 al-Zamakhsharī, *al-Kashshāf*, 4:482.
50 al-Zamakhsharī, *al-Kashshāf*, 4:482.

Futūḥ Rāzī refers to a similar Qur'anic instance in *sūrah Yā' Sīn* (36):39: "And the moon, We have decreed for it stages (*wa-al-qamara qaddarnāhu manāzila*)." Yet he agrees with al-Zamakhsharī in deeming *except as the seeking of God's acceptance* a "disconnected exclusion/exceptive."[51]

This exegete's interest in the theories surrounding the origin of monasticism is manifest by the variety of *ḥadīth*s he recounts. The first of those he has selected begins with a rhetorical question posed by the Prophet to ʿAbdallāh b. Masʿūd: "O Ibn Umm ʿAbd, do you know how the Christians invented monasticism?" The Prophetic response then repeats much of the now familiar scenario in which tyrants war against those who came after Jesus, severely reducing their number. Faced with the possibility of extinction, those few remaining decide to scatter into inaccessible areas "until Muḥammad, of whom Jesus gave us good tidings, comes forth."[52] They went to ground in mountain caves to avoid further persecution, but not all remained steadfast. "Some of them stood firm in their religion but some instituted innovations."[53] It is because of this discrepancy in behavior that the verse under discussion was revealed. The *ḥadīth* then concludes with a statement from the Prophet that will be found again in subsequent commentaries: "O Ibn Umm ʿAbd, do you know what is the monasticism of my community? . . . It is the *hijrah*, *jihād*, prayer (*namāz*), fasting, the *ḥajj*, the lesser *ḥajj* (*ʿumrah*), and doing *takbīr*s for God on elevated places."[54]

Abū al-Futūḥ Rāzī also follows al-Ṭabarī's lead in citing a version of the *ḥadīth* from Ibn Masʿūd in which Muḥammad speaks of the division of prior religions into seventy-two groups, of which only three are saved. One of these ceased to exist (*biraftand*) in the time of Jesus, while a second fought (presumably unjust) rulers and tyrants.[55] Of this latter group there was a contingent "who were persuaded to forsake their own religion (*kih dīn-i khvudrā az īshān bigurīzānīdand*)."[56] To these is attributed monasticism as described in this verse. The test that distinguishes those who observed

51 Abū al-Futūḥ Rāzī, *Rawḥ al-jinān*, 11:56.

52 Abū al-Futūḥ Rāzī, *Rawḥ al-jinān*, 11:56. R. Köbert has surveyed the views on monasticism of both Ibn Masʿūd and Ibn ʿAbbās in his article "Zur Ansicht des frühen Islam über das Mönchtum (*rahbānīya*)," *Orientalia* 42 (1973): 520–24.

53 Abū al-Futūḥ Rāzī, *Rawḥ al-jinān*, 11:56.

54 Abū al-Futūḥ Rāzī, *Rawḥ al-jinān*, 11:56. This list constitutes a catalogue of the major elements of Islamic orthopraxis. The *hijrah* is the nascent community's emigration from Mecca to Medina in 1/622. The term *jihād* is classically understood as 'religious striving', which can take a spiritual (*al-jihād al-akbar*, 'the greater struggle') or a military form (*al-jihād al-aṣghar*, 'the lesser struggle'). Prayer, fasting, and the Pilgrimage are three of the five principal religious duties incumbent upon Muslims, while *takbīr* is the technical term for the verbal heartbeat of the Islamic world, the frequently heard refrain, *Allāhu akbar* ('God is greater').

55 Abū al-Futūḥ Rāzī, *Rawḥ al-jinān*, 11:56.

56 Abū al-Futūḥ Rāzī, *Rawḥ al-jinān*, 11:56–57.

monasticism correctly and those who did not is, according to this *ḥadīth*, belief in the Prophet.

Quite a different account of monasticism's origins is offered by the next *ḥadīth*, which Abū al-Futūḥ Rāzī cites on the authority of ʿAbdallāh b. ʿAbbās. Here again the results of persecution are divisive, but in this case it is the faithful remnant, not those who abandoned their religion, who are credited with the institution of monasticism.[57] This latter group is the one promised a divine reward, while the former is identified by the verse's phrase, *but they did not observe it correctly.* Those to be divinely rewarded are then equated by this commentator with those "in whose hearts We put mercy and compassion."[58] He never specifies the referent of this phrase more directly.

Abū al-Futūḥ Rāzī takes a closer look at the connection of *We did not prescribe it for them* and the term *monasticism* before concluding his commentary on this verse. There are, he notes, two ways of understanding this connection. One is to see *We did not prescribe it for them* as an adjectival phrase (*ṣifah*) modifying *rahbānīyah* (monasticism). The second is to connect the phrase to what follows it, *except as the seeking of God's acceptance.* Abū al-Futūḥ Rāzī's Persian paraphrase develops this latter meaning: "We did not write this monasticism for them except by way of pleasing God; for this reason it was written for them – as a way of satisfying God (*ʿalā wajh riḍwān Allāh*)."[59] To make this distinction completely clear Abū al-Futūḥ Rāzī ends by saying: "According to the first view it is not written for them in any way at all."[60]

Ibn al-Jawzī, too, denies any connection between *rahbānīyah* and the two preceding nouns. Contrary to the possibility raised by al-Zamakhsharī, it is not one of the things that God placed in the hearts of those who followed Jesus. For the term itself he offers a conventional definition: "It is their intemperance in religious practices (*ghulūwuhum fī al-ʿibādah*), and taking hardship upon themselves (*ḥaml al-mashāqq ʿalā anfusihim*) by refraining from food, drink, dress, and marriage, and [by their] devotional activities in the mountains."[61]

57 Abū al-Futūḥ Rāzī, *Rawḥ al-jinān*, 11:57.
58 Abū al-Futūḥ Rāzī, *Rawḥ al-jinān*, 11:57.
59 Abū al-Futūḥ Rāzī, *Rawḥ al-jinān*, 11:57.
60 Abū al-Futūḥ Rāzī, *Rawḥ al-jinān*, 11:57.
61 Ibn al-Jawzī, *Zād al-masīr*, 8:176. Maurice Borrmans observes that Muslim estimations of such Christian "excess" continue to be an obstacle in the contemporary Muslim-Christian encounter. *Orientations pour un dialogue entre chrétiens et musulmans* (Paris: Les Éditions du Cerf, 1981) 121–23. The testimony of early traditions that authorize 'concessions (*rukhaṣ*)' in ritual practice is explored by M.J. Kister, "On 'Concessions' and Conduct: A Study in Early *Ḥadīth*," in *Studies in the First Century of Islamic Society*, ed. by G.H.A. Juynboll (Carbondale, Ill.: Southern Illinois University Press, 1982) 89–107.

This exegete clarifies the exegetical debate on the correct interpretation of *except as the seeking of God's acceptance* by outlining the various positions. According to one way of thinking, as transmitted from Zayd b. Aslam al-ʿAdawī (d. 136/753), it is connected to the statement about their invention of monasticism and conveys the idea that they invented it as a way of seeking God's acceptance. There are also those who maintain that the phrase is properly connected with *We did not prescribe it for them*, but they disagree about the implication of this connection. One view, on the authority of al-Ḥasan, assumes a seemingly chronological perspective whereby those who assume the burdens of monasticism subsequently receive a divine injunction to fulfill their self-imposed obligations. Ibn al-Jawzī quotes al-Zajjāj as saying, "When they enjoined on themselves that voluntary act (*al-taṭawwuʿ*), He enjoined on them its execution."[62] The standard example of the discretionary fast is then cited with supplementary remarks from al-Qāḍī Abū Yaʿlā b. al-Farrāʾ (d. 485/1066) about whether the obligation lies properly in the words or the actual deeds.

The alternative view on the connection of this phrase to *We did not prescribe it for them* is that it qualifies the force of the negative in that statement. It permits the exclusion of a limited range of meaning from the general negation. In the words quoted by Ibn al-Jawzī from Ibn Qutaybah, what God means is: "We did not command them concerning it except that they might seek to please God, but for no other reason (*lā ghayr dhālika*)."[63]

For the phrase *but they did not observe it correctly*, this commentator provides the most complete analysis of all the exegetes yet surveyed. Differences exist about both the subject of this accusation and the substance of it. If those accused are the ones who "invented" monasticism, as Ibn al-Jawzī feels most people have maintained, then their noncompliance could involve one of three things: (1) "changing and altering their religion," (2) "failing to do what they had imposed on themselves," or (3) "not believing in the Messenger of God when he was sent."[64] If, however, those so charged are the followers and spiritual descendants of these early founders, then Ibn al-Jawzī records, from Ibn ʿAbbās, but one reason for this imputation: "They did not observe it by traveling the path of their forerunners (*bi-sulūk ṭarīq awwalīhim*)."[65]

With the concluding phrases of this verse Ibn al-Jawzī offers three sets of interpretations but without specifically coordinating them with the foregoing exegetical schemata. The first is to take *those of them who believed* as

62 Ibn al-Jawzī, *Zād al-masīr*, 8:176.
63 Ibn al-Jawzī, *Zād al-masīr*, 8:177.
64 Ibn al-Jawzī, *Zād al-masīr*, 8:177. The first view is represented as that of ʿAṭīyah b. Saʿd al-ʿAwfī (d. 111/729), the second and third as those of al-Zajjāj.
65 Ibn al-Jawzī, *Zād al-masīr*, 8:177.

a reference to those who believe in Muḥammad. Its coordinate, *but many of them are sinners*, would, of course, be those who do not believe in him.[66] Another possibility is to find in the first phrase a reference to those who believe in Jesus and, in the second, a reference to the *mushrikūn*. The final suggestion ties this concluding phrase more tightly to what immediately precedes it in the verse: "*those who believed* are those who invented monasticism; the *sinners* are their followers without the true rule (*al-qānūn al-ṣaḥīḥ*)."[67]

Fakhr al-Dīn al-Rāzī presents the view of one who sees a chronological connection in *compassion and mercy and monasticism* taken as three objects of *We placed*: "Al-Qāḍī [ᶜAbd al-Jabbār] said what is meant by that is that God was gracious to them (*laṭafa bihim*) until their attempts to proselytize for monasticism (*dawāᶜīhim ilā al-rahbānīyah*) became too strong."[68] These attempts developed from the presumption that additions to what God has made obligatory are spiritually desirable. Such a chronological interpretation is, in Fakhr al-Dīn al-Rāzī's view, unsupported by the literal meaning of the text. Yet he does concede that such a perspective does no violence to his own metaphysics of human volition, a concession that he supports with a somewhat grandiose philosophical digression.

This commentator says nothing novel about the coordinate terms *compassion* and *mercy* and cites in explanation the same Qurʾānic text, *sūrat al-fatḥ* (48):29, as have some of his predecessors. Preceded by an extended etymological *excursus*, Fakhr al-Dīn al-Rāzī offers an expanded definition of *al-rahbānīyah* that includes most of the elements mentioned by previous exegetes. He also relates a condensed variant of the *ḥadīth* from Ibn ᶜAbbās that describes the early period of monasticism: "In the days of the interval (*al-fatrah*) between Jesus and Muḥammad, rulers altered the Torah and the Gospel but a group of people roamed about the land and wore wool (*al-ṣūf*)."[69]

In the version of the now-familiar *ḥadīth* from Ibn Masᶜūd about religious segmentation that Fakhr al-Dīn al-Rāzī recounts, the identification of the three groups (out of seventy) who are not doomed is somewhat different from the renderings recorded by al-Ṭabarī and Abū al-Futūḥ Rāzī. While the first group are those who suffered persecution and death in the name of Jesus, the second group are characterized as "those who lack the capacity for fighting but commanded what was right (*al-maᶜrūf*) and forbade what was wrong (*al-munkar*)."[70] The third, and clearly least praiseworthy, group

66 Ibn al-Jawzī, *Zād al-masīr*, 8:177.
67 Ibn al-Jawzī, *Zād al-masīr*, 8:177.
68 Fakhr al-Dīn al-Rāzī, *al-Tafsīr al-kabīr*, 29:244.
69 Fakhr al-Dīn al-Rāzī, *al-Tafsīr al-kabīr*, 29:244. The wearing of wool (*al-ṣūf*) is a commonly ascribed etymological justification for the term Ṣūfī.
70 Fakhr al-Dīn al-Rāzī, *al-Tafsīr al-kabīr*, 29:244. The injunction *al-amr bi-al-maᶜrūf*

are those who can neither fight nor adhere to the divinely ordained obligations and proscriptions "but wore the *ʿabāʾ* (a [woolen] cloak) and went out into the deserts and wastelands."[71] It is this final category to which the verse under discussion is deemed most applicable.

While al-Ṭūsī made a distinction between invention (*al-ibtidāʿ*) and innovation (*al-bidʿah*), Fakhr al-Dīn al-Rāzī states explicitly that God does not mean the phrase *which they invented* to be understood as a mode of condemnation (*ṭarīqat al-dhamm*). He only means that "they originated monasticism among themselves and vowed themselves to it. It is for this reason that God then added *We did not prescribe it for them.*"[72] Yet Fakhr al-Dīn al-Rāzī is not altogether consistent in maintaining this separation between divine and human activity, as might be expected given his views on the true origination of human action. As a result he takes a different view of the possible relation of *monasticism* to *We placed* than has hitherto been expressed.[73]

The point of contention, as he sees it, is the argument that *monasticism* cannot be the third consecutive accusative for *We placed* because it is qualified by the phrase *which they invented.* The reason commonly expressed for this is that something "invented" by human agency cannot be the same as something "placed" by God. Fakhr al-Dīn al-Rāzī's rebuttal is negative in form. While not insisting that *monasticism* is such a third accusative, he nevertheless maintains that those who deny the very possibility must prove that it is out of the question for one object, such as *monasticism,* to have two agents, human and divine.[74]

For the phrase *except as the seeking of God's acceptance,* this commentator

wa-al-nahy ʿan al-munkar, a form of which is first found in *sūrah Āl ʿImrān* (3):104, stands among the fundamental principles of Qurʾānic ethics. For further consideration of this see George Hourani, "Ethics in Classical Islam: A Conspectus," in his *Reason and Tradition in Islamic Ethics* (Cambridge: Cambridge University Press, 1985), 35–36, reprinted from *MW* 70 (1980): 1–28; and Izutsu, *Ethico-Religious Concepts*, 213–17. A treatment of this in classical *kalām* is offered by Louis Gardet, *Dieu et la destinée de l'homme* (Paris: Librairie Philosophique J. Vrin, 1967), 445–58.

71 Fakhr al-Dīn al-Rāzī, *al-Tafsīr al-kabīr*, 29:244. Ignaz Goldziher notes Fakhr al-Dīn al-Rāzī's variation on this familiar *ḥadīth* as well as the reservations that this exegete has expressed about the viability of its traditional interpretation. "Le dénombrement," 2:408–10.

72 Fakhr al-Dīn al-Rāzī, *al-Tafsīr al-kabīr*, 29:244.

73 For a thorough analysis of the various grammatical issues raised in the exegesis of this verse, see Beck, "Das christliche Mönchtum in Koran." A more recent discussion is to be found in Claus Schedl's *Muhammad und Jesus* (Vienna: Herder, 1978), in which he concludes that for Muḥammad, Christian monasticism was "keine unbekannte Grösse." He adds that since the triumph of Islam removed all trace of monasticism from Mecca and Medina, later commentators on the Qurʾān took no account of Muḥammad's likely acquaintance with it (pp. 491–92).

74 Fakhr al-Dīn al-Rāzī, *al-Tafsīr al-kabīr*, 29:245.

offers the now-standard distinction between reading it as logically connected to *which they invented* or as a specification of *We did not prescribe it for them.* In support of the second reading Fakhr al-Dīn al-Rāzī gives this expanded paraphrase: "We did not call them to devote themselves to it (*mā taʿabbadnāhum bihā*) except so that they might innovate it as a way of seeking God's pleasure."[75] The main point to be grasped, however, is that monasticism is not required (*laysat wājibatan*). Fakhr al-Dīn al-Rāzī then explains the motivational difference between required and recommended actions. The required (*al-wājib*) is done both to ward off divine punishment and in an effort to please God. The recommended (*al-mandūb*), on the other hand, is not motivated by the first consideration, only by the second.[76]

Fakhr al-Dīn al-Rāzī takes the concluding portion of this verse as one unit. He lists five reasons for the division between those to be rewarded and those considered evildoers, all of which are based on monasticism, its observance or lack thereof. The first interpretation draws the distinction between those who originated monasticism but then added to it the doctrine of "trinitarianism and unicity (*al-tathlīth wa-al-ittiḥād*)," and those who "persisted in the religion of Jesus until they came into the era of (*adrakū*) Muḥammad and then believed in him."[77]

The second reason refers back to the characterization of monasticism as not divinely prescribed but nevertheless practiced as a way of seeking God's acceptance. The *sinners* would then be those who lived a monastic life but for the wrong reasons, that is, "in pursuit of the world (*al-dunyā*), hypocritical motives (*al-riyāʾ*), and good repute (*al-sumʿah*)."[78] The third interpretation erases the distinction noted above between *al-wājib* and *al-mandūb* by declaring *sinners* those who neglected their monastic vows and deeming this neglect to be as blameworthy as the disregard of obligatory demands.[79] It does so by treating the *except* clause as so comprehensive a limitation to the negative scope of *We did not prescribe it for them* that the force of the negative is canceled.

With the fourth item on his list Fakhr al-Dīn al-Rāzī returns to the

75 Fakhr al-Dīn al-Rāzī, *al-Tafsīr al-kabīr*, 29:246.

76 Fakhr al-Dīn al-Rāzī, *al-Tafsīr al-kabīr*, 29:246.

77 Fakhr al-Dīn al-Rāzī, *al-Tafsīr al-kabīr*, 29:246. Jacques Jomier has written at length about Fakhr al-Dīn al-Rāzī's refutation of this Christian "deviation." Among his most interesting insights is that Fakhr al-Dīn al-Rāzī explains the development of such ideas among the Christians on hermeneutical grounds. Building upon the Qurʾānic distinction between the verses "dont le sens apparaît immédiatement et ceux qui sont volontairement évasifs" Fakhr al-Dīn al-Rāzī accuses the Christians of deliberate hermeneutical subversion. Rather than interpreting the ambiguous (*mutashābih*) in light of the unequivocal (*muḥkam*), the Christians neglect the latter and base their theological fancies on the former. "Unité de Dieu," 171–72.

78 Fakhr al-Dīn al-Rāzī, *al-Tafsīr al-kabīr*, 29:246.

79 Fakhr al-Dīn al-Rāzī, *al-Tafsīr al-kabīr*, 29:246.

issue of acceptance or rejection of Muḥammad, which was part of the first interpretation. Here the *sinners* are not those who introduce doctrinal aberration into the religion of Jesus but those who, while recognizing the importance of Muḥammad, refuse to believe in him. To support this Fakhr al-Dīn al-Rāzī quotes the following Prophetic *ḥadīth*: "Whoever believes in me, bears witness to me, and follows me, has observed it in its proper due (*fa-qad raʿāhā ḥaqq riʿāyatihā*); those who do not believe in me will perish (*al-hālikūn*)."[80]

The final interpretation suggested by this exegete follows the historical differentiation first proposed by al-Ṭabarī. In this case monasticism's foundation is attributed to "the virtuous, right-acting individuals among the people of Jesus."[81] Although they dutifully fulfilled their self-imposed obligations, those who succeeded them "imitated them by tongue but not by deed."[82] Fakhr al-Dīn al-Rāzī quotes ʿAṭāʾ b. Abī Rabāḥ in confirmation of this: "They did not observe it as the disciples (*al-ḥawārīyūn*) did."[83] In summation, this commentator describes all the *sinners* as those who "manifested depravity (*al-fisq*) and neglected this path both outwardly (*ẓāhiran*) and inwardly (*bāṭinan*)."[84]

While identifying the subject of *which they invented* as "the community of Christians," Ibn Kathīr paraphrases *We did not prescribe it for them* as "We did not make it law (*mā sharaʿnāhā*) for them; they took it on as a duty solely on their own accord."[85] For the clause *except as the seeking of God's acceptance,* this exegete gives a new turn to the standard twofold interpretation. Although he does not explicitly state the opinion of those who logically connect this phrase to *which they invented*, it is implied in the first interpretation that he proposes. It is, however, with the second explanation that Ibn Kathīr diverges from some of his predecessors. Rather than consider the phrase to be a limited restriction on the full negative force of *We did not prescribe it for them,* he allows the negation to stand unqualified: "We did not write that for them; We only wrote for them the seeking of God's acceptance."[86]

As for the condemnation *but they did not observe it correctly,* Ibn Kathīr

80 Fakhr al-Dīn al-Rāzī, *al-Tafsīr al-kabīr*, 29:246.
81 Fakhr al-Dīn al-Rāzī, *al-Tafsīr al-kabīr*, 29:246.
82 Fakhr al-Dīn al-Rāzī, *al-Tafsīr al-kabīr*, 29:246.
83 Fakhr al-Dīn al-Rāzī, *al-Tafsīr al-kabīr*, 29:246.
84 Fakhr al-Dīn al-Rāzī, *al-Tafsīr al-kabīr*, 29:246.
85 Ibn Kathīr, *Tafsīr al-Qurʾān al-ʿaẓīm*, 4:315.
86 Ibn Kathīr, *Tafsīr al-Qurʾān al-ʿaẓīm*, 4:315. Ibn Kathīr accords squarely with his teacher Ibn Taymīyah in this interpretation. The latter denies any validity to monastic observance in his reply to Paul of Antioch. Michel, *A Muslim Theologian's Response*, 251; Khoury, *Paul d'Antioche,* 68 (of the Arabic text).

insists that this is a censuring (*dhamm*) of them for two misdeeds: (1) "innovating in the religion of God what God did not order," and (2) "their nonadherence to what they imposed on themselves despite their claim that it is a propitiatory act that draws them closer (*qurbah yuqarribuhum*) to God."[87] He follows this with reproduction of the *ḥadīth* from Ibn Masᶜūd, about the religious divisions of the Banū Isrāʾīl, which was first encountered in al-Ṭabarī. In fact, Ibn Kathīr credits al-Ṭabarī with a further, variant recension of it not found in the published text of *Jāmiᶜ al-bayān*.[88]

For the concluding phrases of this verse Ibn Kathīr proposes but one set of identifications for *those of them who believed* and the *sinners*. The first are, in the words of the Prophet, "those who believe in me and bear witness to me," while the latter are "those who call me a liar and are opposed to me."[89] No effort is made this time to connect these identifications specifically to the issue of monasticism and its observance or neglect.

As is customary with this exegete, the remainder of his commentary is devoted to a selection of *ḥadīth* that have particular bearing on this verse. The first quoted is one from Ibn ᶜAbbās detailing the institution of various types of monastic life to which al-Ṭabarī gave prominence in the first part of his commentary on the verse. Since Ibn Kathīr does no more than duplicate the version of this *ḥadīth* found in al-Ṭabarī, no additional attention will be paid to it here.[90] Unique to Ibn Kathīr, among the commentators herein surveyed, is a *ḥadīth* from Saᶜīd b. ᶜAbd al-Raḥmān al-Makhzūmī (d. 249/863) that recounts the meeting of Sahl b. Abī Imāmah and his father with Anas b. Mālik in Medina during the caliphate of ᶜUmar b. ᶜAbd al-ᶜAzīz. When the two visitors came upon Anas b. Mālik saying an abbreviated form of the ritual prayer (*ṣalāt khafīfah*) "which he performed as if it were the prayer of a traveler or some such," they asked him whether he considered that to be the prayer as prescribed or whether he was performing it as an act of supererogation.[91] He answered that it was prescribed and was, in fact, the prayer of the Messenger of God. Moreover, he said, "you sin only in neglecting something" (i.e., not in merely shortening it).[92] Furthermore, to emphasize the danger of spiritual presumption so often manifest in acts of immoderate asceticism and exorbitant devotional exercises, Ibn Mālik quotes a statement by the Prophet: "Do not be hard

87 Ibn Kathīr, *Tafsīr al-Qurʾān al-ᶜaẓīm*, 4:315.

88 Ibn Kathīr, *Tafsīr al-Qurʾān al-ᶜaẓīm*, 4:315. While Ibn Kathīr quotes al-Ṭabarī's version as mentioning seventy-three groups, the published text of al-Ṭabarī's *tafsīr* used in this study says seventy-one. See al-Ṭabarī, *Jāmiᶜ al-bayān*, 27:239.

89 Ibn Kathīr, *Tafsīr al-Qurʾān al-ᶜaẓīm*, 4:316.

90 al-Ṭabarī, *Jāmiᶜ al-bayān*, 27:239.

91 Ibn Kathīr, *Tafsīr al-Qurʾān al-ᶜaẓīm*, 4:316.

92 Ibn Kathīr, *Tafsīr al-Qurʾān al-ᶜaẓīm*, 4:316.

on yourselves (*lā tushaddidū ʿalā anfusikum*) lest God be hard on you, for if a people are hard on themselves, then God is hard on them."[93]

The statement then concludes with a reference to monastic remains and a citation from this verse. Bowing to the entreaties of Sahl b. Abī Imāmah and his father, Ibn Mālik therefore agrees to take them to see one of these monastic ruins, "fallen in upon its foundations" (*sūrat al-baqarah* [2]:259, *sūrat al-kahf* [18]:42, and *sūrat al-ḥajj* [22]:45).[94] The sight of it prompts him to declaim against the spiritually debilitating effects of insolence (*al-baghy*) and envy (*al-ḥasad*). The final group of *ḥadīth*s that Ibn Kathīr includes are variations of the Prophetic statement about Islamic "monasticism," such as: "For every prophet there is a monasticism and the monasticism of this community is striving in the way of God (*al-jihād fī sabīl Allāh*)."[95]

In defining *rahbānīyah* (monasticism) Kāshānī follows al-Ṭūsī in stressing its connection to the Arabic root *RHB*, whose semantic range covers such notions as "to fear" or "to dread." Consequently a *rāhib* (pl. *ruhbān*, monk) is "one who goes to extremes of fearfulness and abstinence," while *rahbānīyah* involves "excess in fear [of God's judgment], devotional activity, asceticism, and self-isolation."[96] For the origin of such practices Kāshānī looks to the divisiveness rampant in the community of Jesus after his resurrection (*baʿd az rafʿ-i vay*). Some had ceased to follow the ordinances of the Gospel while others remained faithful. Of this latter group, a contingent

93 Ibn Kathīr, *Tafsīr al-Qur'ān al-ʿaẓīm*, 4:316. Presenting the view of *rahbānīyah* revealed in the *Tafsīr* of Muqātil b. Sulaymān, Paul Nwyia notes that Muqātil's position is based upon his interpretation of *sūrat al-mā'idah* (5):87, a basic text in the Qur'ānic rejection of illicit supererogation. Muqātil explained 5:87 ("Do not make unlawful [*lā tuḥarrimū*] the good which God has made lawful for you [*mā aḥalla Allāhu lakum*]") as a specific rejoinder to the various forms of monastic renunciation. On the basis of this Nwyia feels confident in claiming that the Islamic interdiction of monasticism is founded upon the Qur'ān and not, as Louis Massignon thought, on the much later *ḥadīth, lā rahbānīyah fī al-islām. Exégèse coranique,* 55–56.

94 Ibn Kathīr, *Tafsīr al-Qur'ān al-ʿaẓīm*, 4:316. None of the Qur'ānic uses of this phrase refers to a monastic establishment. In 2:259 and 22:45 the devastation of a village (*qaryah*) is described, while 18:42 depicts fruit (*thamar*) that has been ruined on its trellises. For an overview of Islamic law with regard to Christian ecclesiastical buildings see Khoury, *Toleranz*, 147–49.

95 Ibn Kathīr, *Tafsīr al-Qur'ān al-ʿaẓīm*, 4:316–17. This is the version Ibn Kathīr quotes from Anas b. Mālik. The wording from ʿAbdallāh b. al-Mubārak (d. 181/797) begins "For every *community* there is a. . . . " Ibn Kathīr embellishes this with a *ḥadīth* from Abū Saʿīd al-Khudrī (d. 74/693) that also identifies *jihād* as the *rahbānīyah* of Islam but joins with it fear of God (*taqwā Allāh*), remembrance of God (*dhikr Allāh*), and recitation (*tilāwah*) of the Qur'ān, "wherein lies your refreshment (*rawḥ*) in heaven and your remembrance [of God] (*dhikr*) on earth."

96 Kāshānī, *Minhaj al-ṣādiqīn*, 9:194.

"escaped into the mountains where they became aspirants (*mutarahhib*) and put barriers around themselves (*mutaḥaṣṣin*)."[97]

This exegete quotes from al-Zamakhsharī the *ḥadīth* that attributes the origin of monasticism to the survivors of relentless persecution. Kāshānī concludes his version by saying that some of those who remained became monks in the mountains and applied themselves with complete devotion to the worship of God. "They vowed themselves to thoroughgoing austerities (*mashaqqathā-ī*) and the considerable mortifications of abstaining from food, drink, clothing, and sexual intercourse."[98] He then refers to the twelfth-century Shīʿī exegete, al-Faḍl b. al-Ḥasan al-Ṭabarsī, for the connection between *We did not prescribe it for them* and *except as the seeking of God's acceptance.* The result is a paraphrase that keeps the two elements of this statement separate: "We did not impose monasticism on them; however We did impose upon them seeking the satisfaction of God."[99]

Kāshānī gives fuller consideration to the possibility of reading the *except* clause as logically connected to what precedes it and understands *monasticism* as the third of three accusatives after *We placed.* He then provides a full elaboration that takes into consideration these two exegetical decisions: "We placed in their hearts compassion and mercy and monasticism, which is innovated on their part and newly invented, that is, We gave them the grace to be compassionate to one another and to innovate and invent monasticism, which We did not ordain (*farḍ nakardah būdīm*) for them. On the other hand, they followed that as something commended (*bar sabīl-i nadbīyat*) not as something [to be] newly invented (*bar wajh-i ikhtirāʿ*), in order to satisfy God, merit reward, and save themselves from the depredations of tyrants."[100] In an effort to clarify further the sense of *We did not prescribe it for them,* Kāshānī explains that those who took this on as a way of life may appear to be assuming a divinely imposed obligation but, in fact, their activities are not mandatory (*mafrūḍ*) but only recommended (*mandūb*).[101]

With yet another version of the report (here unattributed) that traces the origins of monasticism to the reactions of a group that survived the repeated abuse of tyrants, Kāshānī seeks to explain the significance of *but they did not observe it correctly.* This recension bases the distinction between proper and improper observance on the acceptance or rejection of the

97 Kāshānī, *Minhaj al-ṣādiqīn*, 9:194.
98 Kāshānī, *Minhaj al-ṣādiqīn*, 9:195.
99 Kāshānī, *Minhaj al-ṣādiqīn*, 9:195.
100 Kāshānī, *Minhaj al-ṣādiqīn*, 9:195.
101 The terms *mafrūḍ* (or *wājib* – see Fakhr al-Dīn al-Rāzī above) and *mandūb* are among the five legal/moral classifications (*al-aḥkām al-khamsah*) by which every human act is graded within Islamic law: required, recommended, indifferent, blameworthy, forbidden.

Prophet, once he has been revealed. Those to whom the accusation applied "became adherents to the doctrine of the Trinity (*bi-tathlīth qā'il gashtah*) and denied Muḥammad and the Qur'ān." [102] To compensate for the faithlessness of the many, however, there was the constancy of the few "who did not swerve from following the Messiah. They lived into the age of the Prophet and witnessed the beginning of Islam. They were exalted by the honor of being followers of that Lord of mankind."[103]

Although Kāshānī acknowledges the interpretation that understands *but they did not observe it correctly* as a reference to those who were not faithful to their self-imposed monastic obligations, he finds reinforcement for the alternative view detailed above in the verse itself. The reward promised to *those of them who believed* is tied to belief in the Prophet. Therefore "observant" monks are those who may be characterized by their belief in Muḥammad.[104] For their opposite number, the *many of them* who are *sinners,* Kāshānī notes that these are the Christians "who left the sphere of belief (*dā'irat-i īmān*)."[105]

Two Prophetic *ḥadīth*s, both encountered in several earlier commentaries, conclude Kāshānī's treatment of this verse. The first, a version of that *ḥadīth* which seeks to explain the many divisions among the *ahl al-kitāb*, is noteworthy only because it speaks of two, rather than the usual three, groups who are "saved." The second is the repetition of a statement by Muḥammad last found in the commentary of Ibn Kathīr, which details what constitutes the "monasticism" of Islam.[106]

In the modern commentary of Ṭabāṭabā'ī, the tripartite sense of *We placed* is expressed as an instance of divine psychology: God placed mercy and compassion in their hearts by "commanding the two, arousing desire for them and promising the reward for them."[107] Ṭabāṭabā'ī's treatment of the controversial phrases of this verse is brief and concise. *Monasticism,* whose etymological relationship to the Arabic root meaning "to fear" or "to dread" is acknowledged in concert with al-Ṭūsī and Kāshānī, is defined as the state of "man's being cut off from human society to worship God out of fear of Him."[108] The concept of "invention" is also treated by way of definition and characterized as "producing that for which there is no precedent

102 Kāshānī, *Minhaj al-ṣādiqīn*, 9:195.
103 Kāshānī, *Minhaj al-ṣādiqīn*, 9:195.
104 Kāshānī, *Minhaj al-ṣādiqīn*, 9:195–96.
105 Kāshānī, *Minhaj al-ṣādiqīn*, 9:196.
106 Kāshānī, *Minhaj al-ṣādiqīn*, 9:196. The elements included in the version that Kāshānī reports are the emigration (*hijrah*), *jihād*, prayer (*namāz*), mandatory almsgiving (*zakāt*), the greater and lesser Pilgrimage (*ḥajj va 'umrah*), and exclamations of *Allāhu akbar* when entering sacred sanctuaries.
107 Ṭabāṭabā'ī, *al-Mīzān*, 19:173.
108 Ṭabāṭabā'ī, *al-Mīzān*, 19:173.

in religion, *sunnah*, or skilled craft (*ṣanʿah*)."[109] The fact of monasticism's human origin as expressed by *We did not prescribe it for them* is further reinforced by Ṭabāṭabāʾī's approach to the phrase that follows it. All connection between the two statements is disavowed, as this commentator's paraphrase makes clear: "We did not decree it for them; nevertheless they imposed it on themselves out of a desire to please God (*ibtighāʾan li-riḍwān Allāh*) and as a way of seeking to satisfy Him (*ṭalaban li-marḍātihi*)."[110] However, Ṭabāṭabāʾī feels that implicit in the verse is still the idea that *monasticism* is a way of finding favor in God's eyes even if He did not decree it.

Ṭabāṭabāʾī's comments on the closing section of the verse are general and without particular reference to monastic adherence or backsliding. He appears to tie the categories of *those of them who believed* and *sinners* to the ones intended by *those who followed him*, for he remarks that they are like the communities to whom former messengers were sent: "Among them are believers rewarded for their believing but many of them are evildoers."[111]

CONCLUSION

Christian asceticism as institutionalized in various forms of monasticism captures most of the exegetical interest focused upon this verse. A prelude to the multifaceted discussion of this phenomenon is provided by the attention paid to the verse's initial phrases. Here in brief glosses, a number of the commentators express a somewhat more insightful understanding of certain elements of the Christian tradition. The efforts at identification demonstrate a greater degree of specific knowledge about matters of philology and ethics than is usually displayed. Both al-Ṭūsī and Fakhr al-Dīn al-Rāzī puzzle over alternate spellings of the Arabic term for "Gospel." Al-Ṭabarī draws an implicit analogy between Islam and Christianity by referring to the latter's adherents as "followers of Jesus according to his *sharīʿah* (law)," *sharīʿah* being a term of foundational connotations within the Islamic context.

Analogies multiply with the repeated use of a Qurʾānic citation to characterize the behavior of Jesus' disciples. Ibn al-Jawzī, Fakhr al-Dīn al-Rāzī, Ibn Kathīr, Kāshānī, and Ṭabāṭabāʾī all use the term *ḥawārīyūn* to designate this group, a word that the Qurʾān itself applies to the Companions of Muḥammad. In *sūrat al-fatḥ* (48):29 these early followers of the Prophet are praised for being "compassionate among themselves" and for their faithful persistence in prayerful prostration. A subsequent reference in the verse

109 Ṭabāṭabāʾī, *al-Mīzān*, 19:173. In his appended collection of relevant *ḥadīths*, Ṭabāṭabāʾī includes a familiar account of monasticism's origins on the authority of Ibn Masʿūd. *al-Mīzān*, 9:175.

110 Ṭabāṭabāʾī, *al-Mīzān*, 19:173.

111 Ṭabāṭabāʾī, *al-Mīzān*, 19:173.

to both the Torah and the Gospel prompts the exegetical transference of such praise to Jesus' companions. The combined associations echo between these two Qur'ānic loci, allowing the commentators to credit Christianity with equivalent virtues. Christians, too, are portrayed as practicing mutual assistance and forgiveness. The social bonds among them are strengthened by compassionate reciprocity.

The commentators replicate their own ethical orientation by circumscribing the arena within which such Christian behavior is seen to operate. The compassion and mercy that God 'placed' in their hearts is not given universal extension but contained within the community. Just as Muḥammad's Companions were "compassionate among themselves" so, too, are their Christian analogues perceived as operating within the confines of a religiously delimited group.

Some of the commentators pause to consider the sense in which such qualities can be divinely 'placed' within the individual. Their comments on this constitute an embryonic apperception of what would now be termed the psychology of religious development. Reference to Ashʿarī occasionalism surfaces here, particularly in the thought of Fakhr al-Dīn al-Rāzī. The Shīʿī exegetes, al-Ṭūsī, Kāshānī, and Ṭabāṭabāʾī, however, raise questions about the interior movements of the heart that God instigates or arouses by His promise of divine reward.

The focal discussion of monasticism that emerges from the commentaries on this verse is a study of exegetical ambivalence. The often unexpressed background to this discussion is shaped by Qur'ānic statements that encourage marriage, such as that in *sūrat al-nūr* (24):32, and by Prophetic *ḥadīth*s that repudiate *rahbānīyah*. Yet there are hints in 57:27 that such a form of life is able to prompt divine favor. While most of the commentators strongly reject the kind of overt divine approval entailed in making monasticism the third object of *We placed*, they are less willing to pronounce favorably upon the contrary position. Proceeding from a judgment that monasticism was corrupt in its origins, this latter view would maintain that it has always remained totally divorced from any divine approbation. Thus, even if its originators and adherents thought that they were trying to seek God's approval, He did not look kindly upon their efforts.

Nevertheless, the subject of monasticism remains a source of fascination for the exegetes herein examined. In their analysis of this verse each has fastened upon one or more aspects of the monastic puzzle to explore the tensions expressed in this Qur'ānic ambivalence. Al-Ṭabarī was particularly intrigued by the perception of monastic deterioration as it is depicted in the various *ḥadīth*s that his commentary includes. Could that be seen as the fault of those who initiated such practices or of those who attempted to follow in their footsteps? To this question, al-Ṭabarī refuses to give a categorical response. Rather he finds within this verse's reference to a promised reward a necessary nuance. Some, at least, must be entitled to the recompense cited at the verse's conclusion.

For al-Ṭūsī the preoccupying question is that of the perspective from which the moral value of monasticism may be assessed. The extent to which monasticism must be considered an 'innovation' and thus by definition beyond the range of acceptable religious behavior enters this exegete's considerations. Like al-Ṭabarī he draws upon the example of religiously motivated fasting for an apt analogy. While al-Ṭabarī's comparison concentrated upon the evolved particulars of the Ramaḍān fast, al-Ṭūsī takes the obligation assumed in commencing a voluntary fast as correlative to that accepted by entrance into monastic life. It is worth noting, however, that neither with these two commentators nor with the others examined is any sense of the duration of this latter obligation expressed. That within Christianity monastic vows are traditionally understood to be a lifetime commitment is never mentioned.

Quite a number of the commentators press the preoccupation with monastic origins that finds first expression in al-Ṭabarī's assemblage of *ḥadīth*s on this subject. Al-Zamakhsharī, for one, detects the genesis of monasticism in the desire of an early, persecuted minority to maintain religious purity and avoid the dangers posed by worldly temptations. His suggestion that the term *rahbānīyah* be construed as the third object of *We placed* is phrased in light of this understanding of original motivation.

For most of the commentators, however, it is not temptation that the founders of monasticism fled but persecution. While al-Ṭabarī cites an account that traces the origin of this institution to those who accepted self-exile rather than amend their falsified scriptures, he also recounts that testimony of Ibn Masʿūd which becomes the predominant explanation of monastic origins. This *ḥadīth*, variants of which are repeated by Abū al-Futūḥ Rāzī, Fakhr al-Dīn al-Rāzī, Ibn Kathīr, and Kāshānī, traces the initiatory impulse of monastic observance to fear of persecution. Although the contrast between the seventy (or seventy-one or seventy-two) condemned groups and the three (or two) groups that are saved is reminiscent of the *ḥadīth* that figured conspicuously in Chapter 6, the general scenario depicted is not a religiously flattering one. The clear sense conveyed is that monks were those who lacked the courage to withstand persecution. Rather than fight the abuse of tyrants, these people retreated, hiding themselves in the inaccessible regions of mountain and desert.

Ibn Kathīr highlights the judgment passed upon such religious cowardice when he includes that portion of the *ḥadīth* from Ibn Masʿūd which quotes the Prophetic declaration of what constitutes the "monasticism" of Islam. Both Abū al-Futūḥ Rāzī and Kāshānī include the fuller text which notes a wide range of orthopraxis, such as the *ḥajj*, prayer, fasting, and almsgiving. Ibn Kathīr, however, restricts the declaration to the terse definition that "the monasticism of this community is *jihād* in the way of God." While the term *jihād* carries the broad signification of spiritual striving in a variety of ways, it also connotes defensive warfare against those who would interfere with the religion of God. Certainly what is being enjoined is not flight or retreat from persecution.

The idea of fear also marks the definition of monasticism offered by several of the Shīʿī commentators. Al-Ṭūsī, Kāshānī, and Ṭabāṭabāʾī note an etymological link to this sentiment in the Arabic term itself, and this, in turn, forms the basis of their definitions. The second theme heard in the various exegetical attempts to define monasticism is that of "intemperance" or "excess." Several of the exegetes specify the particular ascetic practices of abstinence and self-isolation that have characterized traditional forms of monasticism. As they do so, definition dips toward judgment with the use of such qualifiers as those just cited.

Nevertheless, assumption of such intemperate or fear-laden religious activity can, for some of the commentators, represent a valid attempt to win divine favor. It may, in their eyes, appear misguided or perverse but simply as a religiously motivated human initiative it does possess a potential for divine approval. Once undertaken, however, it constitutes a contractual obligation with the divine. That obligation, in turn, has both synchronic and diachronic consequences. Synchronically viewed it would be the responsibility of each individual to be faithful to the vows made within this lifetime. Diachronically, the obligation would be one of communal faithfulness to the right practice, the *sunnah* of one's predecessors. Since such can only be accomplished within the framework of right belief, attestation to the authentic prophethood of Muḥammad stands, for at least some of the commentators, as a necessary requisite of praiseworthy Christian monasticism.

Conclusion

Completing the close textual analysis of these seven verse groups now permits the reassertion of a more comprehensive perspective. Broadly considered, persistent patterns and themes emerge, allowing these passages to intersect at several hermeneutical levels. Prominent among such patterns stands the sheer proliferation of categories. These verses continuously classify and catalogue humankind. The typologies merge and overlap, moving from formal religious designations (Jews, Christians, Ṣābiʾūn, Majūs) to particularization within one of those groups, such as Christian priests and monks. Formal designation then shades into less clearly defined but nevertheless descriptive phrases such as *those who follow you [Jesus], those to whom We gave the book before,* and *the idolaters.* Positive and negative moral categorization pits the ones specified as *a balanced people* and *those who testify* against the *evildoers* and the *sinners.* But the overriding classification remains the great divide between *those who believe* (or *whoever believes in God and the Last Day*) and *those who disbelieve.* Consistently people are grouped, pervasively they are catalogued on dogmatic, on moral, on religio-sociological grounds.

Within these convergent systems of classification appears an enduring pattern of praise. Specific qualities are honored and extolled. Those intended are lauded for being *submissive before God,* for being respectful of His revelation (*they do not sell the verses of God for a small price*), for being steadfast (*they have persisted*). Their hearts hold *compassion and mercy*; they are *not arrogant* but *turn away from [idle chatter].* They *recognized . . . the truth* and *turn back evil* as qualities of heart and mind find expression in praiseworthy action.

Energizing both classification and characterization are dramatic elements of narrative voice and promissory climax. The voice of God animates some of these verses, while others are cast in the Prophet's address. Still another group moves between these foci as descriptive declaration culminates in divine promise. Promise pervades these verses. Human categories and qualities prompt a judgment that issues in reward or retribution. One verse, structured as a series of guarantees to Jesus, concludes with the pledge of decisive, and divisive, divine adjudication. In another, those judged favorably will reap both spiritual and psychological benefits; *they will have no fear, neither will they grieve.* Confidently may they anticipate the consistent, consummative promise of reward. Four of the seven verse groups repeat this divine avowal. Reference to *their reward (ajruhum)* beats a reassuring refrain through these passages. Sometimes a twofold recompense is promised, a divine recognition of the difficulties attendant upon human response to revelation.

Such recurrent patterns confirm the textual coherence of these seven passages, a coherence buttressed by the centuries of exegetical effort that they have sustained. From this combination of text and interpretive testimony emerges the developed comprehension of that category here termed Qurʾānic Christians. Because every approach to the text is fundamentally an act of interpretation, no effort has been made in this study to isolate meaning within the text of the Qurʾān itself apart from the exegetical investigation that it has generated. Text and receptive community interpenetrate permanently and inescapably. Hermeneutical levels coalesce within that interpenetration to present a clear but complex depiction of Christians as a religio-social group. Elements of this presentation Biblical Christians can themselves recognize because these collective characterizations reflect facets of Christian self-understanding.

The qualities commended can be readily acknowledged as Christian virtues, ideals of behavior exemplified in the life of Jesus. Submission to God, reverence for what He has revealed, acknowledging and acting upon the truth consistently and compassionately – all represent aspects or aspirations of an estimable Christian existence. Those who call themselves Christians find no difficulty in accepting such attitudes and actions as praiseworthy when viewed from within their own religious context. Certainly the culminating promise of divine reward constitutes a fundamental element of Christian expectation. Much within these verses, therefore, warrants Christian affirmation and approbation.

Yet ultimately exegetical circumscription prevails. Within the commentary tradition on these seven verse groups, delimitation and specification clearly control the emerging depiction. The centuries-long testimony of commentary sunders the category of Christians, reserving to but a very limited number the application of divine approval and award. In one verse only a group "among them" may be counted as those who believe and act rightly. The commentators understand the Qurʾān to make a clear distinction between true Christians, a tiny minority, and those who have appropriated and propagated a corrupted form of the religion of Jesus. In a judgment tied to the tension between *islām* as the rightful human attitude before God and Islam as the institutional realization of His final revelation, the Christian community has been assessed and divided into two unequal components. Of the two, the larger is excoriated, subjected to a broad range of religious accusation and denunciation. Only a small fraction escape the charges and reap the compliments of the commentators.

Briefly put, these are the Christians whose scripture is the uncorrupted *injīl*. These are the Christians whose persistence in the truth allowed the proper response to the historical appearance of Muḥammad's prophethood. These are the Qurʾānic Christians – or to use appellations perhaps more suited to that scripture's sensibilities – the Qurʾānic Nazarenes, the Qurʾānic Jesus-Followers. The qualities lauded belong to them; the promised reward will be theirs. As culled from a close study of the exegetical literature, the Qurʾānic view of praiseworthy Christians presents itself as a coherent theological construct. Qurʾānic Christians, those Christians whom the Qurʾān is understood to commend, are neither the historical nor the living community of people who call themselves Christians. As a conceptual idealization, the notion of Qurʾānic Christians bears very little relation to present or past sociological configurations of the Christian community.

Created in the interplay of text and interpretation, Qurʾānic Christians are those whose fundamental submission to God, whose *islām*, was undertaken within the context of following the prophet Jesus. To him had God vouchsafed a revelation that, given its divine origins, obviously could not be inconsistent with God's culminating revelation in the Qurʾān. Qurʾānic Christians guarded this revelation in its pristine purity, keeping themselves free from the eventual dogmatic aberrations of their coreligionists. Scripturally anticipating the advent of God's final prophet, they stood ready to acknowledge him as the fulfillment of that same divine graciousness that had sent their earlier prophet, Jesus. For Qurʾānic Christians there was not, nor could there be, any incongruity between the two prophets, Jesus and Muḥammad. Those who had faithfully followed the former would necessarily be eager to welcome the latter. Qurʾānic Christians, then, are Christians who either accepted the prophethood of Muḥammad and the revelation entrusted to him or would have done so had their historical circumstances permitted.

Various conversion scenarios support this assessment. Such figures as Salmān al-Fārisī function as paradigmatic embodiments of the requisite virtues and attitudes. Salmān's own spiritual pilgrimage from Christian convert to Muslim convert dramatically exemplifies the judgment that Christianity is but one possible, penultimate stage prior to the final manifestation of God's will. Even when the Qurʾānic text itself does not clearly insist upon the conclusive necessity of belief in the prophethood of Muḥammad, the bulk of the classical exegetical tradition has included this as an explicit requirement. The Muslim emigrants to Abyssinia skillfully transform a confrontation into a conversion opportunity, prompting the Najāshī to recognize publicly the congruities of Muslim and Christian belief. His ability to trace such theological continuity and his willingness to act upon its implications both testify to his status as a preeminent Qur'ānic Christian.

The geography of such conversion accounts is territorially confined. A circle centered at Mecca need circumscribe no very large area to enclose the few places in Abyssinia, Byzantium, and the Arabian peninsula that the early commentators actually mention. Subsequent exegesis largely restricts itself to this circumference, repeating and refining a limited number of representative scenarios. Classical commentators also exhibit virtually no interest in the Christians of whom they must have had some contemporary knowledge. Reference to the historical vicissitudes of particular Christian communities, to the changing status of Christians under various forms of Muslim hegemony, or to the evolving varieties of Christian belief and practice simply find no place on the exegetical agenda. Consequently, remarkably little development occurs in the depiction of Christians throughout the classical period of Qur'ānic commentary. While modern commentators demonstrate somewhat more awareness of particularity and historical specificity, even they do not address these matters in any sustained or systematic way. For Qur'ānic commentators generally the understanding of Christians remains at the level of theoretical construct, largely divorced from the realities of time and place yet subject to judgment on theological and moral grounds.

Qur'ānic statements that relate Jesus to his "followers" offer additional examples of this pattern of exegetical circumscription and specification. Alluding to both his disciples and subsequent generations of adherents, commentators have characterized Jesus' followers as 'believers (*mu'minūn*)' or even as 'muslims (*muslimūm*)'. Such characterization rests, of course, upon the distinction between "true" and "false" followers – those who have an unsullied comprehension of Jesus' nature and mission versus those who do not. Faithful followers "spoke the truth" about Jesus, having preserved his message from doctrinal degeneration. When Muḥammad did come, those who had held fast to the "true" message of Jesus – the authentic, Qur'ānic Christians – welcomed him and readily submitted to the final divine disclosure of which he was the bearer. Those who did not become *muslimūn*, that is, did not remain *mu'minūn* in this latest manifestation of God's guidance, ceased thereby to be "true" followers of Jesus, to be "true" Christians.

Qur'ānic Christians before the time of Muḥammad, then, are those who kept their revelation undefiled and, therefore, their belief pure – *truly we were Muslims before it* – embracing that vision of Christian scripture that sees in it a prefiguration of the final Prophet. At the time of Muḥammad, they were those who acknowledged his prophethood and the preeminence of the revelation accorded him, whose Christianity was but a temporary, intermediate stage on the way to Islam. Such are the ones praised for persisting in their recognition of the truth even in the face of physical retaliation and social alienation on the part of their former coreligionists. Such are the ones exegetically reassured that the continuing unbelief of these latter affects neither their own present status nor future reward.

Foundational to this depiction stands the assertion, always latent in Islamic apologetics, of one consistent stream of divine revelation, the Qurʾān being but its most recent, and final, manifestation. Evaluation of antecedent revelations, such as that accorded Jesus, necessarily remains somewhat ambivalent. While charging that its present textual embodiment does not conform completely with the original *injīl*, the accusation of scriptural alteration is not so absolute as to preclude the possibility of precursive reference to Muḥammad. Similarly, although acknowledging the incompatibility between the Qurʾān and the *injīl*, some Muslim commentators insist that the latter remains a source for guidance sufficient to ensure in those of pure heart a spiritual susceptibility to the message of Muḥammad.

The charge of scriptural corruption expands to cover such ancillary effects as spiritual perversion and arrogance. Often these accusations and consequent defamations are levied against religious leaders. In fact, a primary subdistinction made within the Qurʾānic assessment of Christians is that between good and bad religious functionaries. Where Christian leaders are apparently praised, as in the references to *qissīsūn* and *ruhbān*, the designated categories are scoured for clues to the spiritual sensitivities that could warrant such possible divine commendation. In this instance the commentators take special note of what they perceived to be a pronounced veneration of learning and a manifest aptitude for ascetic disciplines.

Ordinary adherents also elicit a mixed exegetical appraisal. Loyalty to religious leaders, for example, does not always merit commendation. Particularly reproached are the degenerative effects of uncritical allegiance (*taqlīd*) to a system of thought, bolstered – as this frequently is – by an entrenched social status. The inevitable spiritual deformation that this engenders partially explains Christian recalcitrance when confronted with Islamic missionary activity. The key compliment, *a balanced people,* offsets such censure when applied to those whose doctrinal and behavioral moderation reflects their status as Qurʾānic, not Biblical, Christians. Such uncorrupted individuals provide ballast in a community top heavy with *taqlīd*; they serve as a spiritual leaven for the regeneration and growth of the entire body. When addressed within the more restricted class of Christian monastics, this tribute to moderation transmutes to a rejection of ascetic intemperance and to an equation of social seclusion with spiritual cowardice.

Frequently such praise of Christian balance is simply contrastive, prompted by comparison with perceived Jewish vices. In some cases Christians are then credited with a higher stage of religious evolution than Judaism, a stage marked by more profound knowledge, more absorbing religious devotion, and more heartfelt humility. This perspective comprehends the Christian "reformation" of Judaism as a movement beyond externals of the law to a greater spiritual depth. But even this progression is never understood as more than an intermediate stage, a viaduct to the final fullness of religious truth and behavior.

In no way, then, does Biblical Christianity remain a fully valid 'way of salvation' after the advent of Muḥammad. It is inconceivable under the Qurʾānic definition of authentic Christianity, as interpreted by these ten commentators, that a "true" Christian who had been exposed to the Prophet's message would refuse to become a Muslim. Not to acknowledge the prophethood of Muḥammad, which has been clearly foretold in the untainted version of the *injīl*, would itself constitute a betrayal of "true" Christianity. The one possible exception to this concerted exegetical response may be the few allusions in modern commentaries to the overriding importance of belief in God and of right action under whatever label such faith and action are sustained.

Ultimately, therefore, Christian self-definition and Muslim comprehension of praiseworthy Christians must diverge. Biblical Christians as both a sociological and theological category can no longer recognize themselves in the exegetical elaboration of these verses. Qurʾānic commentary has shaped and molded this material within a particular hermeneutical configuration. Consequently these seven passages have generated a tradition of interpretation that simply does not accord with the many instances of their uncritical reading and reception. To use the verses herein analyzed as prooftexts to demonstrate unrestricted Muslim toleration of Christians would be to ignore the decisive religious impact of both classical and modern *tafsīr*.

In a generation that has witnessed an extraordinary increase in the number and intensity of exchanges intended to promote mutual understanding between Muslims and Christians the practical implications of such mistaken perception should be apparent. Christians involved in these collaborations cannot expect that Muslims deeply schooled in their tradition will understand the Qurʾānic passages of praise to apply indiscriminately to the individuals sitting across the table. Christians may wish for such an interpretation, welcoming it as a textual entrée to greater interreligious appreciation. Muslim participants may even choose to venture such an interpretation. Those who do so, however, will be compelled by the exegetical history of their tradition to acknowledge that they are creating new interpretive strategies. But that, of course, is precisely what the perennial tension between text and hermeneutical possibilities promotes.

While the Qur'ān is morphologically immutable, it is semantically alive. The invariant structure of the pronounced text perdures but the signification conveyed lives anew through generation after generation of painstaking commentary. The exegetical chorus on these seven verse groups, therefore, combines many voices. The ten commentators whose lives were sketched in Chapter 2 and whose thoughts were analyzed in the subsequent chapters have contributed significantly to that full chorus. Taken together they offer a broad and representative spectrum of Islamic exegetical activity. Chronologically spanning ten centuries, their work bears witness to the formative power of the tradition to which they have pledged themselves. Each has undertaken the analysis of a verse with the accumulated wisdom of his exegetical predecessors at the forefront of his consciousness.

This accumulated wisdom is given primacy and pride of place. Any suggestion not carefully placed within that total context may well be dismissed by others in the exegetical community as irresponsible innovation. Certainly some of what these ten have produced could be characterized as variations on a set theme. As such, it is ever liable to the dismissive gesture of premature summarization. Yet each, in turn, has reshaped and elaborated the traditional core of material, giving rise to new insights drawn from the inexhaustible sources of scriptural signification. Accordingly there is simply no way to convey the relative weights of old and new within each commentator without presenting the full exegetical discussion for a verse. Without detailed exposure to the entire range of concerns which a particular verse provokes, there is no way to evaluate the contributions and the exegetical decisions of an individual commentator. His subtle reshaping of the tradition only stands forth if that tradition itself is clearly presented. Artificially to extract what is novel in a particular commentator does violence to the integrity of this cumulative discipline.

Contrary to some contemporary expectations, the faithful reproduction of earlier interpretive conclusions represents a necessary and valued element of the hermeneutical quest. The new may only be validly expressed against the backdrop of the consensually accepted tradition, the manner in which it legitimately connects with that tradition and grows from it being clearly displayed. With willing acceptance of such methodological mandates, these ten commentators from Ṭabarī to Ṭabāṭabā'ī have functioned as creators and sustainers of the living Qur'ān. From the tenth to the twentieth century, their voices have brought the text alive in the minds of their own and subsequent generations. As a guild of exegetical artisans, they have taken upon themselves the task of continuing, refining, and redirecting the semantic universe of Qurʾānic discourse. The tradition that they have inherited, the configurations within which they operate, continue to shape the contours of that discourse, for it is only within this framework of accepted lines of interpretation that new exegetical channels may be charted.

The tradition suggests but does not determine. No exegetical agenda is ever finally fixed. The last word has yet to be spoken. Invariably, the protean nature of the commentator's charge allows it to serve as an ever-present source of renewal. The Qurʾānic text remains malleable to the interpretive touch, ready to reveal new insights and intimations, ready to generate renewed understandings of these scriptural sources of Muslim-Christian rapprochement. Nor need that resumed task refute the results of its tradition. Careful analysis of a representative range of *tafāsīr* has clearly demonstrated the multiple trajectories of traditional exegesis. The commentators, both classical and modern, do not speak with one voice. While the formative power of intellectual conservatism is undeniable, it is not inescapable. As with the Muslim religious sciences generally, the Qurʾānic scholars may be more shaped by their enterprise than able or willing to reshape it. Yet within the inherited contours a healthy profusion of interpretive perspectives has flourished. Those multiple tones and notes sound the necessary prelude for new exegetical voices, voices that can again recast the traditional refrains with both fidelity and freedom.

Works cited

Abbott, Nabia. *Studies in Arabic Literary Papyri*. Vol. 2: *Qurʾānic Commentary and Tradition*. Chicago: University of Chicago Press, 1967.

ʿAbd al-ʿĀl, Ismāʿīl Sālim. *Ibn Kathīr wa-manhajuhu fī al-tafsīr.* Cairo: Maktabat al-Malik Fayṣal al-Islāmīyah, 1404/1984.

ʿAbd al-Bāqī, Muḥammad Fuʾād. *al-Muʿjam al-mufahras li-alfāẓ al-Qurʾān al-karīm*. Beirut: Dār Iḥyāʾ al-Turāth al-ʿArabī, n.d.

ʿAbdallāh, ʿAbd al-Raḥmān Ṣāliḥ. *Ibn al-Jawzī wa-tarbiyat al-ʿaql*. Mecca: Sharikah Makkah lil-Ṭibāʿah wa-al-Nashr, 1406/1986.

Abd el-Jalil, Jean. *Marie et l'Islam*. Paris: Beauchesne, 1950.

Abdul, M.O.A. "The Historical Development of Tafsīr." *Islamic Culture* 50 (1976): 141–53.

Abel, A. "Baḥīrā." In *The Encyclopedia of Islam*, 1:922–23. New Edition. Leiden: E.J. Brill, 1954–.

Abū al-Futūḥ Rāzī, Ḥusayn b. ʿAlī. *Rawḥ al-jinān wa-rūḥ al-janān*. 12 vols. Tehran: Kitābfurūshī-yi Islāmīyah, 1382–87/1962–65.

Rawḥ al-jinān wa-rūḥ al-janān. 5 vols. Qum: Intishārāt-i Kitāb, n.d.

Abū Dhuʾayb, Isrāʾīl. *Kaʿb al-Aḥbār.* Jerusalem: Maṭbaʿat al-Sharq al-Taʿāwunīyah, 1976.

Abū Mūsā, Muḥammad Ḥusayn. *al-Balāghah al-Qurʾānīyah fī tafsīr al-Zamakhsharī*. Cairo: Dār al-Fikr al-ʿArabī, n.d.

Adams, Charles C. *Islam and Modernism in Egypt*. London: Oxford University Press, 1933.

Adams, Charles J. "Islamic Religious Tradition." In *The Study of the Middle East: Research and Scholarship in the Humanities and Social Sciences*, edited by Leonard Binder, 29–95. New York: John Wiley, 1976.

al-ʿAdawī, Ibrāhīm Aḥmad. *Rashīd Riḍā al-imām al-mujāhid*. Cairo: al-Muʾassasah al-Miṣrīyah al-ʿĀmmah lil-Taʾlīf, n.d.

Āghā Buzurg al-Ṭihrānī, Muḥammad Muḥsin. "Ḥayāt al-Shaykh Ṭūsī." In Abū Jaʿfar Muḥammad b. al-Ḥasan al-Ṭūsī's *al-Tibyān fī tafsīr al-Qurʾān*, 1:*alif – alif-bāʾ-qāf*. Najaf: al-Maṭbaʿah al-ʿIlmīyah, 1376/1957.

Zindagīnāmah-i Shaykh Ṭūsī. Translated by ʿAlī Riḍā Mīrzā Muḥammad and Sayyid Ḥamīd Ṭabībīyān. Tehran: Jumhūr-i Islamī-yi Irān, 1360 (solar)/1982.

Agius, Dionisius A. "Some Bio-bibliographical Notes on Abū 'l-Qāsim Maḥmūd b. ʿUmar al-Zamakhsharī." *Al-ʿArabiyya* 15 (1982): 108–30.

Ahmad, Rashid (Jullandri). "Qurʾānic Exegesis and Classical Tafsīr." *Islamic Quarterly* 12 (1968): 71–119.

Al-Assiouty, Sarwat Anis. *Théorie des sources: évangiles et corans apocryphes, logia et hadîths forgés.* Paris: Letouzey et Ané, 1987.

Ali, Abdul. "Tolerance in Islam." *Islamic Culture* 56 (1982): 110.

Allard, Michel. *Analyse conceptuelle du Coran sur cartes perforées.* 2 vols. and cards. Paris: Mouton, 1963.

Textes apologétiques de Juwainī. Beirut: Dar El-Machreq, 1968.

Almagor, Ella. "The Early Meaning of *majāz* and the Nature of Abū ʿUbayda's Exegesis." In *Studia Orientalia Memoriae D.H. Baneth Dedicata,* edited by J. Blau et al., 307–26. Jerusalem: Magnes Press, 1979.

ʿAmāyrah, Ismāʿīl Aḥmad, and ʿAbd al-Ḥamīd Muṣṭafā al-Sayyid. *Muʿjam al-adawāt wa-al-ḍamāʾir fī al-Qurʾān al-karīm.* Beirut: Muʾassasat al-Risālah, 1407/1986.

al-Amīn, Muḥsin b. ʿAbd al-Karīm. *Aʿyān al-shīʿah.* 56 vols. Beirut: Maṭbaʿat al-Inṣāf, 1378–82/1959–63.

Amin, Osman. *Muhammad ʿAbduh.* Translated by Charles Wendell. Washington, D.C.: American Council of Learned Societies, 1953.

Anawati, Georges. "Fakhr al-Dīn al-Rāzī." In *The Encyclopedia of Islam,* 3:751–55. New Edition. Leiden: E.J. Brill, 1954–.

"ʿĪsā." In *The Encyclopedia of Islam,* 4: 81–86. New Edition. Leiden: E.J. Brill, 1954–.

al-Anbārī, Abū al-Barakāt ʿAbd al-Raḥmān. *Nuzhāt al-alibbāʾ fī ṭabaqāt al-udabāʾ*. Edited by ʿAṭīyah ʿĀmir. Stockholm: Almquist and Wiksell, 1963.

Andrae, Tor. *Mohammed: The Man and His Faith* (*Mohammed, sein Leben und sein Glaube*). Translated by Theophil Menzel. 1936. Reprint of revised edition, New York: Harper and Brothers, 1960.

Les Origines de l'Islam et le Christianisme. Translated by Jules Roche. Paris: Adrien-Maisonneuve, 1955. Originally published as "Der Ursprung des Islams und das Christentum." *Kyrkohistorisk Arsskrift* 23 (1923): 149–206, 24 (1924): 213–92, 25 (1925): 45–112.

Antes, Peter. "Relations with Unbelievers in Islamic Theology." In *We Believe in One God: The Experience of God in Christianity and Islam,* edited by Annemarie Schimmel and Abdoldjavad Falatūri, 101–11. New York: Seabury, 1979.

"Schriftverständnis im Islam." *Theologische Quartalschrift* 161 (1981): 179–91.

Arkoun, Mohammed. *Lectures du Coran*. Paris: Éditions Maisonneuve et Larose, 1982.

"Logocentrisme et vérité religieuse dans la pensée islamique d'après *al-Iʿlām bi-manāqib al-Islām* d'al-ʿĀmirī." In his *Essais sur la pensée islamique*, 185–231. 3rd ed. Paris: Editions Maisonneuve et Larose, 1984. Reprinted from *Studia Islamica* 35 (1972): 5–51.

"The Notion of Revelation: From Ahl al-Kitāb to the Societies of the Book." *Die Welt des Islams* 28 (1988): 62–89.

Pour une critique de la raison islamique. Paris: Éditions Maisonneuve et Larose, 1984.

Arnaldez, Roger. *Jésus: fils de Marie, prophète de l'Islam*. Paris: Desclée, 1980.

"L'oeuvre de Fakhr al-Dīn al-Rāzī, commentateur du Coran et philosophe." *Cahiers de civilisation médiévale* 3 (1960): 307–23.

"Trouvailles philosophiques dans le commentaire coranique de Fakhr al-Dīn al-Rāzī." *Études philosophiques et littéraires* 3 (1968): 11–24.

Ashtiyānī, Sayyid Jalāl al-Dīn. "Chihrahā-yi dirakhshān." *Maʿārif-i islāmī* 5 (1347 [solar]/1969): 48–50.

Asín Palacios, Miguel. "Logia et Agrapha Domini Jesu apud Moslemicos Scriptores." *Patrologia Orientalia* 13 (1919): 332–432 and 19 (1926): 529–624.

Audebert, Claude-France. *Al-Khaṭṭābī et l'inimitabilité du Coran: traduction et introduction au Bayān iʿjāz al-Qurʾān*. Damascus: Institut Français de Damas, 1982.

Awn, Peter J. *Satan's Tragedy and Redemption: Iblīs in Sufi Psychology,* Leiden: E.J. Brill, 1983.

Awsī, ʿAlī. *al-Ṭabāṭabāʾī wa-manhajuhu fī tafsīrihi al-mīzān*. Tehran: al-Jumhūrīyah al-Islāmīyah fī Īrān, 1985.

Aydin, Mehmet. "Rapporti islamo-cristiani all'epoca di Muhammad." *Islam, storia e civiltà* 5 (1986): 11–23.

Ayoub, Mahmoud. *The Qurʾan and Its Interpreters*. Albany: State University of New York Press, 1984.

"Roots of Muslim-Christian Conflict." *The Muslim World* 79 (1989): 31.

"The Speaking Qurʾān and the Silent Qurʾān: A Study of the Principles and Development of Imāmī Shīʿī *tafsīr*." In *Approaches to the History of the Interpretation of the Qurʾān*, edited by Andrew Rippin, 177–98. Oxford: Clarendon Press, 1988.

"Towards an Islamic Christology, II: The Death of Jesus, Reality or Delusion." *The Muslim World* 70 (1980): 91–121.

Badawi, Zaki. *The Reformers of Egypt – A Critique of al-Afghani, ʿAbduh and Ridha*. Slough, Berkshire, England: The Open Press, 1976.

Baffioni, Carmela. "L'esegesi coranica di Mohammed Arkoun." *Islam, storia e civiltà* 3 (1984): 17–21.

Bakker, Dirk. *Man in the Qur'ān.* Amsterdam: Drukkerij Holland, 1965.
Baljon, J.M.S. *Modern Muslim Koran Interpretation, 1880–1960.* Leiden: E.J. Brill, 1961.
al-Bāqillānī, Abū Bakr Muḥammad b. al-Ṭayyib. *Iʿjāz al-Qurʾān.* Edited by Aḥmad Ṣaqr. Cairo: Dār al-Maʿārif, 1401/1981.
Bat Ye'or (pseud.). *The Dhimmi: Jews and Christians Under Islam (Le Dhimmi: Profil de l'opprimé en Orient et en Afrique du Nord depuis la conquête arabe).* Translated by David Maisel et al. Rutherford, N.J.: Fairleigh Dickinson University Press, 1985.
al-Bayḍāwī, ʿAbdallāh b. ʿUmar. *Anwār al-tanzīl wa-asrār al-taʾwīl.* 2 vols. Edited by H.O. Fleischer. 1846–48. Reprint, Osnabrück: Biblio Verlag, 1968.
Beck, Edmund. *Das christliche Mönchtum im Koran.* Helsinki: Societas Orientalis Fennica, 1946.
Bell, Richard. *Introduction to the Qurʾān.* Edinburgh: The University Press, 1953.
The Origin of Islam in its Christian Environment. London: Macmillan, 1926.
trans. *The Qurʾan.* 2 vols. Edinburgh: T. and T. Clark, 1939.
Bergsträsser, Gotthelf. "Koranlesung in Kairo." *Der Islam* 20 (1932): 1–42.
Verneinungs und Fragepartikeln und Verwandtes im Ḳurʾān. Leipzig: J.C. Hinrichs, 1914.
Bijlefeld, Willem A. "Some Recent Contributions to Qurʾānic Studies: Selected Publications in English, French, and German, 1964–1973." *The Muslim World* 64 (1974): 79–102.
Birkeland, Harris. *The Lord Guideth: Studies on Primitive Islam.* Oslo: I Kommisjon Hos H. Aschehoug, 1956.
Old Muslim Opposition Against Interpretation of the Koran. Oslo: I Kommisjon Hos Jacob Dybwad, 1955.
Björkman, W. "Kufr." In *The Encyclopedia of Islam,* 4:407–09. New Edition. Leiden: E.J. Brill, 1954–.
Blachère, Régis. *Le Coran: Traduction selon un essai de reclassement des sourates.* 3 vols. Paris: G.P. Maisonneuve, 1947–51.
Introduction au Coran. 1st ed. Paris: G.P. Maisonneuve, 1947.
Introduction au Coran. 2nd ed. Paris: Éditions Besson et Chantemerle, 1959.
Borrmans, Maurice. "Le Commentaire du Manâr à propos du verset coranique sur l'amitié des musulmans pour les chrétiens (5,82)." *Islamochristiana* 1 (1975): 71–86.
Orientations pour un dialogue entre chrétiens et musulmans. Paris: Les Éditions du Cerf, 1981.

Bosworth, Clifford E. "Khwārazm." In *The Encyclopedia of Islam,* 4:1060–65. New Edition. Leiden: E.J. Brill, 1954–.

Bouman, Johan. *Gott und Mensch im Koran.* Darmstadt: Wissenschaftliche Buchgesellschaft, 1977.

Das Wort vom Kreuz und das Bekenntnis zu Allah: Die Grundlehren des Korans als nachbiblische Religion. Frankfurt-am-Main: Otto Lembeck, 1980.

Böwering, Gerhard. "Miʿrāj." In *The Encyclopedia of Religion*, edited by Mircea Eliade et al., 9:552–56. New York: Macmillan, 1987.

The Mystical Vision of Existence in Classical Islam: The Qurʾānic Hermeneutics of the Ṣūfī Sahl At-Tustarī. Berlin: Walter de Gruyter, 1980.

Bowman, John. "Banū Isrāʾīl in the Qurʾān." *Islamic Studies* 2 (1963): 447–55.

Boyle, J.A. "The Death of the Last ʿAbbasid Caliph: A Contemporary Muslim Account." *Journal of Semitic Studies* 6 (1961): 145–61.

Bravmann, Meïr M. "A propos de Qurʾān IX-29: ḥattā yuʿṭū l-jizyata [. . .] wa-hum ṣāghirūna." *Arabica* 10 (1963): 94–95.

Brockelmann, Carl. *Geschichte der arabischen Litteratur.* 2nd ed. of 2 vols. and 3-vol. supplement. Leiden: E.J. Brill, 1943–49 and 1937–42.

"Ibn Kathīr." In *The Encyclopedia of Islam*, 3:393–94. 8 vols. and supplement. 1913–38. Reprint, Leiden: E.J. Brill, 1987.

"al-Murtaḍā al-Sharīf." In *The Encyclopedia of Islam*, 6:736. 8 vols. and supplement. 1913–38. Reprint, Leiden: E.J. Brill, 1987.

"al-Zamakhsharī." In *The Encyclopedia of Islam*, 8:1205–07. 8 vols. and supplement. 1913–38. Reprint, Leiden: E.J. Brill, 1987.

Brockett, Adrian. "The Value of the Ḥafṣ and Warsh Transmissions for the Textual History of the Qurʾān." In *Approaches to the History of the Interpretation of the Qurʾān*, edited by Andrew Rippin, 31–45. Oxford: Clarendon Press, 1988.

Buck, Christopher. "The Identity of the Ṣābiʾūn: An Historical Quest." *The Muslim World* 74 (1984): 172–86.

Bulliet, Richard. *Conversion to Islam in the Medieval Period.* Cambridge, Mass.: Harvard University Press, 1979.

Burton, John. *The Collection of the Qurʾan.* Cambridge: Cambridge University Press, 1977.

"The Interpretation of Q. 87, 6–7 and the Theories of *Naskh.*" *Der Islam* 62 (1985): 5–19.

"Introductory Essay." In *Abū ʿUbaid al-Qāsim b. Sallām's K. al-nāsikh wa-l-mansūkh*, edited by John Burton, 1–45. Cambridge: E.J.W. Gibb Memorial Trust, 1987.

"Linguistic Errors in the Qurʾān." *Journal of Semitic Studies* 33 (1988): 181–96.

"*Mutʿa, tamattuʿ* and *istimtāʿ* – a Confusion of *tafsīr*s." In *Proceedings of* *the Tenth Congress of the Union Européenne des Arabisants et Islamisants, Edinburgh 1980*, edited by Robert Hillenbrand, 1–11. Edinburgh: n.p., 1982.

"Those Are the High-flying Cranes." *Journal of Semitic Studies* 15 (1970): 246–65.

Cahen, Claude. "Coran IX-29: ḥattā yuʿṭū l-jizyata ʿan yadin wa-hum ṣāghirūna." *Arabica* 9 (1962): 76–79.

"L'historiographie Arabe des origines au viie s.H." *Arabica* 33 (1986): 133–78.

"Dhimma." In *The Encyclopedia of Islam*, 2:227–31. New Edition. Leiden: E.J. Brill, 1954–.

"Djizya." In *The Encyclopedia of Islam*, 2:559–62. New Edition. Leiden: E.J. Brill, 1954–.

La Syrie du Nord à l'époque des Croisades. Paris: Librairie Orientaliste Paul Geuthner, 1940.

Calasso, G. "La 'sura degli uomini' nel commento di Fakhr ad-Din ar-Razi." *Egitto e Vicino Oriente* 2 (1979): 231–52.

Carter, Michael G. "Remarks on M.B. Schub: 'A Sublime Subtlety?' " *Zeitschrift für arabische Linguistik* 7 (1982): 79–81.

Caspar, Robert, et al. "Bibliographie du dialogue islamochrétien." *Islamochristiana* 1 (1975): 125–81; 2 (1976): 187–249; 3 (1977): 255–86; 4 (1978): 247–67; 5 (1979): 299–317; 6 (1980): 259–99; 7 (1981): 299–307; 10 (1984): 273–92.

Charfi, Abdelmajid. "Christianity in the Qurʾan Commentary of Ṭabarī." *Islamochristiana* 6 (1980): 105–48. Translated from Arabic by Penelope C. Johnstone from *Revue Tunisienne des Sciences Sociales* 58/59 (1979): 53–96; French translation by Robert Caspar in *Mélanges de l'Institut Dominicain d'Études Orientales du Caire* 16 (1983): 117–61.

Chelhod, J. "Note sur l'emploi du mot *rabb* dans le Coran." *Arabica* 5 (1958): 159–67.

Cleveland, William. *Islam Against the West, Shakib Arslan and the Campaign for Islamic Nationalism.* Austin: University of Texas Press, 1985.

Cole, Juan R. "Rashid Rida on the Bahaʾi Faith: A Utilitarian Theory of the Spread of Religions." *Arab Studies Quarterly* 5 (1983): 276–91.

Cook, Michael. *Early Muslim Dogma: A Source-critical Study.* Cambridge: Cambridge University Press, 1981.

Corbin, Henri. *Histoire de la philosophie islamique.* Paris: Gallimard, 1964.

"La philosophie islamique depuis la mort d'Averroës jusqu'à nos jours." *Histoire de la philosophie (Encyclopédie de la Pléiade)*, vol. 3. Edited by Yvon Belaval. Paris: Gallimard, 1974.

Cornell, Vincent. "*Ilm al-qurʾan* in al-Andalus: the *tafsir muharrar* in the Works of Three Authors." *Jusūr* 2 (1986):, 63–81.

Coulson, N.J. "European Criticism of *Ḥadīth* Literature." In *Arabic Literature to the End of the Umayyad Period*, edited by A.F.L. Beeston, T.M. Johnstone, R.B. Serjeant, and G.R. Smith, 317–21. Cambridge: Cambridge University Press, 1983.

Cragg, Kenneth. *The Call of the Minaret*. New York: Oxford University Press, 1956. 2nd ed. Maryknoll: Orbis, 1985.

"How Not Islam?" *Religious Studies* 13 (1977): 387–94.

Jesus and the Muslim: An Exploration. London: George Allen and Unwin, 1985.

The Pen and the Faith: Eight Modern Muslim Writers and the Qurʾān. London: George Allen and Unwin, 1985.

Crapon de Caprona, Pierre. *Le Coran: Aux sources de la parole oraculaire*. n.p.: Publications Orientalistes de France, 1981.

Cutler, Allan Harris, and Helen Elmquist Cutler. *The Jew As Ally of the Muslim: Medieval Roots of Anti-Semitism*. Notre Dame, Ind.: University of Notre Dame Press, 1986.

Ḍanāwī, Ḥusayn. *al-Sayyid Rashīd Riḍā fikruhu wa-niḍāluhu al-siyāsī*. Tripoli: Dār al-Inshāʾ, 1983.

Daniel, Norman. *Islam and the West: The Making of an Image*. Edinburgh: The University Press, 1960.

al-Dāwūdī, Muḥammad b. ʿAlī b. Aḥmad. *Ṭabaqāt al-mufassirīn*. Edited by ʿAlī Muḥammad ʿUmar. 2 vols. Cairo: Maktabah Wahbah, 1392/1972.

Denffer, Ahmad von. *Christians in the Qurʾan and Sunna: An Assessment from the Sources to Help Define Our Relationship*. Leicester: The Islamic Foundation, 1399/1979.

Denny, Frederick M. "The *Adab* of Qurʾan Recitation." In *International Congress for the Study of the Qurʾān, Australian National University, Canberra, 8–13 May 1980*, edited by A.H. Johns, 143–60. 2nd ed. Canberra: Australian National University, n.d.

"Exegesis and Recitation: Their Development as Classical Forms of Qurʾānic Piety." In *Transition and Transformations in the History of Religion*, edited by Frank E. Reynolds and Theodore M. Ludwig, 91–123. Leiden: E.J. Brill, 1980.

"The Problem of Salvation in the Quran: Key Terms and Concepts." In *In Quest of an Islamic Humanism: Arabic and Islamic Studies in Memory of Mohamed al-Nowaihi*, edited by A.H. Green, 196–210. Cairo: The American University in Cairo Press, 1984.

"Qurʾān Recitation Training in Indonesia: A Survey of Contexts and Handbooks." In *Approaches to the History of the Interpretation of the Qurʾān*, edited by Andrew Rippin, 288–306. Oxford: Clarendon Press, 1988.

al-Dhahabī, Muḥammad Ḥusayn. *al-Tafsīr wa-al-mufassirūn*. 2 vols. Cairo: Maktabah Wahbah, 1405/1985.

al-Dhahabī, Shams al-Dīn Abū ᶜAbdallāh Muḥammad. *Siyar aᶜlām al-nubalāʾ*. Edited by Shuᶜayb al-Arnaʾūt. 23 vols. Beirut: Muʾassasat al-Risālah, 1403/1983.

Tadhkirat al-ḥuffāẓ. 4 vols. Hyderabad: Dāʾirat al-Maᶜārif al-ᶜUthmānīyah, 1375/1955.

Di Matteo, Ignazio. "Le pretese contraddizioni della S. Scrittura secondo Ibn Hazm." *Bessarione* 27 (1923): 77–127.

"Il 'taḥrīf' od alterazione della Bibbia secondo i musulmani." *Bessarione* 26 (1922): 64–111 and 223–60. Translated by M.H. Ananikian for *The Muslim World* 14 (1924): 61–84.

Donaldson, Dwight M. *The Shīᶜite Religion*. London: Luzac, 1933.

Dozy, Reinhart. *Supplément aux dictionnaires arabes*. 2 vols. 1881. Reprint, Beirut: Librairie du Liban, 1968.

Duri, A.A. "Baghdad." In *The Encyclopedia of Islam*, 1:894–908. New Edition. Leiden: E.J. Brill, 1954–.

Eklund, Ragnar. *Life Between Death and Resurrection According to Islam*. Uppsala: Almqvist and Wiksells, 1941.

Eliash, J. " 'The Shīᶜite Qurʾān': A Reconsideration of Goldziher's Interpretation." *Arabica* 16 (1969): 15–24.

Endress, Gerhard. *An Introduction to Islam (Einführung in die islamische Geschichte)*. Translated by Carole Hillenbrand. New York: Columbia University Press, 1988.

Ess, Josef van. "Islamic Perspectives." In *Christianity and the World Religions: Paths of Dialogue with Islam, Hinduism, and Buddhism (Christentum und Weltreligionen)*, edited by Hans Küng et al., 97–108. Translated by Peter Heinegg. Garden City, N.Y.: Doubleday and Company, 1986.

"Muᶜtazilah." In *The Encyclopedia of Religion*, edited by Mircea Eliade et al., 10:220–29. New York: Macmillan, 1987.

"Some Fragments of the *Muᶜāraḍat al-Qurʾān* Attributed to Ibn al-Muqaffaᶜ." In *Studia Arabica et Islamica: Festschrift for Iḥsān ᶜAbbās on his Sixtieth Birthday*, edited by Wadād Qāḍī, 151–63. Beirut: American University of Beirut, 1981.

Expert-Bezancon, Hélène. "Regard d'un humaniste égyptien, le Dr. Kāmil Ḥusayn sur les religions non-musulmans." *Islamochristiana* 14 (1988): 17–49.

Fakhry, Majid. *A History of Islamic Philosophy*. New York: Columbia University Press, 1940.

Fattal, Antoine. *Le statut légal des non-musulmans en pays d'islam*. Beirut: Imprimerie Catholique, 1958.

Ferré, André. "Chrétiens de Syrie et de Mésopotamie aux deux premiers siècles de l'Islam." *Islamochristiana* 14 (1988): 71–106.

Finkel, Joshua. "A Risāla of al-Jāḥiẓ." *Journal of the American Oriental Society* 47 (1927): 311–34.

Fischer, Michael. *Iran: From Religious Dispute to Revolution.* Cambridge, Mass.: Harvard University Press, 1980.

Flügel, Gustav. *Concordantiae Corani Arabicae.* Leipzig: C. Tauchnit, 1842.

Foster, Frank H. *A Brief Doctrinal Commentary on the Arabic Koran.* London: Sheldon Press, 1932.

Frank, Richard. "Knowledge and *Taqlīd*: The Foundations of Religious Belief in Classical Ashᶜarism." *Journal of the American Oriental Society* 109 (1989): 37–62.

Gabrieli, Giuseppe. "Fakhr al-Din al-Razi." *Isis* 7 (1925): 9–13.

Gabus, Jean-Paul, Ali Merad, and Youakim Moubarac. *Islam et Christianisme en dialogue.* Paris: Les Éditions du Cerf, 1982.

Galli, Ahmad Mohmed Ahmad. "Some Aspects of al-Māturīdī's Commentary on the Qurʾān." *Islamic Studies* 21 (1982): 3–21.

Gardet, L. *Dieu et la destinée de l'homme.* Paris: Librairie Philosophique J. Vrin, 1967.

"al-Djubbāʾī." In *The Encyclopedia of Islam*, 2:569–70. New Edition. Leiden: E.J. Brill, 1954–.

Gätje, Helmut. *The Qurʾān and Its Exegesis (Koran and Koranexegese).* Translated and edited by Alford T. Welch. London: Routledge and Kegan Paul, 1976.

Gaudeul, Jean Marie, and Robert Caspar. "Textes de la tradition musulmane concernant le *taḥrīf* (falsification) des écritures." *Islamochristiana* 6 (1980): 61–104.

Geagea, Nilo. *Mary of the Koran: A Meeting Point Between Christianity and Islam.* Translated and edited by Lawrence T. Fares. New York: Philosophical Library, 1984.

Geiger, Abraham. *Judaism and Islam (Was hat Mohammed aus dem Judenthume aufgenommen?).* Translated by F.M. Young. 1898. Reprint with Prolegomenon by Moshe Pearlman, New York: Ktav, 1970.

Gibb, H.A.R. *Modern Trends in Islam.* Chicago: University of Chicago Press, 1947.

Gilliot, Claude. "Parcours exégétiques: de Ṭabarī à Rāzī (Sourate 55)." *Analyses, théorie* n.v. (1983): 87–116.

"Portrait 'mythique' d'Ibn ᶜAbbās." *Arabica* 32 (1985): 127–83.

"Les sept 'lectures', corps social et écriture révélée." *Studia Islamica* 61 (1985): 5–25 and 63 (1986): 49–62.

"Traduire ou trahir at-Ṭabarī?" *Arabica* 34 (1987): 366–70.

Gilsenan, Michael. "Sacred Words." In *The Diversity of the Muslim Com-*

munity: Anthropological Essays in Memory of Peter Lienhardt, edited by Ahmed Al-Shahi, 92–98. London: Ithaca Press, 1987.

Gimaret, Daniel. "Matériaux pour une bibliographie de Jubbā'ī." *Journal asiatique* 257 (1976): 277–332.

Les noms divins en Islam. Paris: Éditions du Cerf, 1988.

Théories de l'acte humain en théologie musulmane. Paris: Librairie Philosophique J. Vrin, 1980.

and Guy Monnot, trans. *Livre des religions et des sectes.* Paris: Peeters/UNESCO, 1986.

Givony, Joseph. " 'Wa 'ākharūna murjawna li'amri 'llāhi': An Inquiry into the Alleged Qur'ānic Origin of the Idea of Irjā'." *Die Welt des Orients* 12 (1981): 73–80.

Goldfeld, Isaiah. "Muqātil Ibn Sulaymān." *Arabic and Islamic Studies (Bar-Ilan)* 2 (1978): xiii–xxx.

"The *Tafsīr* of Abdallāh b. ʿAbbās." *Der Islam* 59 (1982): 125–35.

Goldziher, Ignaz. "Aus der Theologie des Fachr al-dīn al-Rāzī." *Der Islam* 3 (1912): 213–47.

"Le dénombrement des sectes mohamétanes." In *Gesammelte Schriften*, edited by Joseph Desomogyi, 2:406–14. Hildesheim: Georg Olms, 1968.

Introduction to Islamic Theology and Law (Vorlesungen über den Islam). Translated by Andras and Ruth Hamori; introduction and notes by Bernard Lewis. Princeton: Princeton University Press, 1981.

Muslim Studies (Muhammedanische Studien). Edited by S.M. Stern, translated by C.R. Barber and S.M. Stern. 2 vols. London: George Allen and Unwin, 1971.

Die Richtungen der islamischen Koranauslegung. Leiden: E.J. Brill, 1920.

Götz, M. "Māturīdī und sein *Kitāb Ta'wīlāt al-Qur'ān*." *Der Islam* 41 (1965): 27–70.

Graham, William A. *Beyond the Written Word: Oral Aspects of Scripture in the History of Religion.* Cambridge: Cambridge University Press, 1987.

Divine Word and Prophetic Word in Early Islam: A Reconsideration of the Sources with Special Reference to the Divine Saying or Ḥadīth Qudsī. The Hague: Mouton, 1977.

"Those Who Study and Teach the Qur'ān." In *International Congress for the Study of the Qur'ān, Australian National University, Canberra, 8–13 May 1980*, edited by A.H. Johns, 9–28. 2nd ed. Canberra: Australian National University, n.d.

Gramlich, Richard. "Fakhr ad-Dīn ar-Rāzī's Kommentar zu Sure 18, 9–12." *Asiatische Studien/Études asiatiques* 33 (1979): 99–152.

Griffiths, Sidney. "The Monks of Palestine and the Growth of Christian Literature in Arabic." *The Muslim World* 78 (1988): 1–28.

Grohmann, A. "al-Muḳawḳas." In *The Encyclopedia of Islam*, 6:712–25. 8 vols. and supplement. 1913–38. Reprint, Leiden: E.J. Brill, 1987.

Guillaume, A. *The Life of Muhammad: A Translation of Ibn Isḥāq's Sīrat Rasūl Allāh*. London: Oxford University Press, 1955.

"The Version of the Gospels Used in Medina Circa 700 A.D." *al-Andalus* 15 (1950): 289–96.

Guthrie, A., and E.F. Bishop. "The Paraclete, Almunhamanna and Aḥmad." *The Muslim World* 41 (1951): 251–56.

Gwynne, Rosalind. "Al-Jubbā'ī, al-Ashʿarī and the Three Brothers: The Uses of Fiction." *The Muslim World* 75 (1985): 132–61.

Haddad, Yvonne Yazbeck. *Contemporary Islam and the Challenge of History.* Albany: State University of New York Press, 1982.

al-Ḥakīm, Ḥasan ʿĪsā. *al-Shaykh al-Ṭūsī, Abū Jaʿfar Muḥammad b. al-Ḥasan.* Najaf: Maṭbaʿat al-Ādād, 1975.

Halperin, David J., and Gordon D. Newby. "Two Castrated Bulls: A Study in the Haggadah of Kaʿb al-Aḥbār." *Journal of the American Oriental Society* 102 (1982): 631–38.

Hamzaoui, Rachad. "Idéologie et langue ou l'emprunt linguistique d'après les exégètes du Coran et les théologiens: interprétation socio-linguistique." *Atti 2 congresso internazionale di linguistica camito-semitica, 1974*, 157–71. Florence: Istituto di Linguistica et di Lingue Orientale, 1978.

Haq, Mahmudul. *Muhammad ʿAbduh: A Study of a Modern Thinker of Egypt.* Aligarh: Institute of Islamic Studies, Aligarh Muslim University, 1970.

al-Hasan, Sharif. "A Fresh Look at Ancient Christians of Najrān and Present Religious Dialogues." *Islamic Studies* 16 (1977): 367–75.

Haussleiter, Hermann. *Register zum Qorankommentar des Ṭabarī.* Strassburg: Karl J. Trübner, 1912.

Ḥaydar, ʿAlī. *Iʿrāb sūrah Āl ʿImrān.* Damascus: Manshūrāt Dār al-Ḥikmah, 1392/1973.

Haywood, John. "Fakhr al-Dīn al-Rāzī's Contribution to Ideas of Ultimate Reality and Meaning." *Ultimate Reality and Meaning* 2 (1979): 264–91.

Henninger, Josef, S.V.D. *Spuren christlicher Glaubenswahrheiten im Koran.* Schöneck: Administration der neuen Zeitschrift für Missionswissenschaft, 1951.

Hidayet Hosain, M. "al-Ṭūsī." In *The Encyclopedia of Islam*, 8: 982. 8 vols. and supplement. 1913–38. Reprint, Leiden: E.J. Brill, 197.

Hilāl, Māhir Mahdī. *Fakhr al-Dīn al-Rāzī balāghīyan.* Baghdad: Wizārat al-Iʿlām fī al-Jumhūrīyah al-ʿIrāqīyah, 1397/1977.

Hodgson, Marshall G.S. *The Venture of Islam.* 3 vols. Chicago: University of Chicago Press, 1974.

Horovitz, Joseph. "ᶜAbd Allāh b. Salām." In *The Encyclopedia of Islam*, 1: 52. New Edition. Leiden: E.J. Brill, 1954–.

Koranische Untersuchungen. Berlin: Walter de Gruyter, 1926.

"Salmān al-Fārisī." *Der Islam* 12 (1922): 178–83.

"Zabūr." In *The Encyclopedia of Islam*, 8: 1184–85. 8 vols. and supplement. 1913–38. Reprint, Leiden: E.J. Brill, 1987.

Horst, Heribert. "Zur Überlieferung im Korankommentar aṭ-Ṭabarīs." *Zeitschrift der Deutschen Morgenländischen Gesellschaft* 103 (1953): 290–307.

Hourani, Albert. *Arabic Thought in the Liberal Age, 1789–1939*. 1962. Corrected reprint, London: Oxford University Press, 1967.

Moh'ammed ᶜAbduh (1849–1905) ou les voies contemporaines du réformisme musulman. Paris: Éditions J.A., 1977.

"Preface." In Jamal Mohammed Ahmed's *The Intellectual Origins of Egyptian Nationalism*. London: Oxford University Press, 1960.

Hourani, George. "Ethics in Classical Islam: A Conspectus." In his *Reason and Tradition in Islamic Ethics*, 15–22. Cambridge: Cambridge University Press, 1985. Reprinted from *The Muslim World* 70 (1980): 1–28.

al-Ḥūfī, Aḥmad Muḥammad. *al-Zamakhsharī*. Cairo: Dār al-Fikr al-ᶜArabī, 1386/1966.

Hughes, Thomas. "Ḥujrah." In *Dictionary of Islam*. 1885. Reprint, New Delhi: Cosmo, 1977.

Humphreys, Stephen. *Islamic History: A Framework for Inquiry*. Minneapolis: Bibliotheca Islamica, 1988.

Ḥuqūqī, ᶜAskar. *Taḥqīq dar tafsīr-i Abū al-Futūḥ Rāzī*. 3 vols. Tehran: Dānishgāh-i Ṭihrān, 1346 (solar)/1968.

Ibn Abī ᶜUṣaybiᶜah, Aḥmad b. al-Qāsim. *ᶜUyūn al-anbāʾ fī ṭabaqāt al-aṭibbāʾ*. Edited by August Müller. 2 vols. in 1. 1884. Reprint, Farnborough: Gregg International, 1972.

Ibn [al-]ᶜArabī, Muḥyī al-Dīn. *Tafsīr al-Qurʾān al-karīm*. 2 vols. Beirut: Dār al-Yaqẓah al-ᶜArabīyah, 1387/1968.

Ibn ᶜĀshūr, Muḥammad al-Fāḍil. *al-Tafsīr wa-rijāluhu*. Tunis: Dār al-Kutub al-Sharqīyah, 1966.

Ibn al-Athīr, ᶜIzz al-Dīn. *al-Kāmil fī al-taʾrīkh*. Edited by C.J. Tornberg. 12 vols. 1851–74. Reprint, Beirut: Dār Ṣādir lil-Ṭibāᶜah wa-al-Nashr, 1965–67.

Ibn Ḥajar al-ᶜAsqalānī, Shihāb al-Dīn Abū al-Faḍl Aḥmad b. ᶜAlī. *Lisān al-mīzān*. 7 vols. Beirut: Muʾassasat al-Aᶜlāmī lil-Maṭbūᶜāt, 1390/1971.

Ibn al-ᶜImād, ᶜAbd al-Ḥayy. *Shadharāt al-dhahab fī akhbār man dhahab*. 8 vols. Cairo: Maktabat al-Qudsī, 1350–51/1931–32.

Ibn Isḥāq, Muḥammad. *Sīrah rasūl Allāh* (recension of ʿAbd al-Malik b. Hishām). Edited by Ferdinand Wüstenfeld. 2 vols. 1858. Reprint, Frankfurt-am-Main: Minerva, 1961.

Ibn al-Jawzī, Abū al-Faraj ʿAbd al-Raḥman. *Zād al-masīr fī ʿilm al-tafsīr.* 9 vols. Beirut: al-Maktab al-Islāmī lil-Ṭibāʿah wa-al-Nashr, 1384–88/1964–68.

Ibn Jubayr, Abū al-Ḥusayn Muḥammad b. Aḥmad. *Riḥlah.* Edited by William Wright. Leiden: E.J. Brill, 1907.

Ibn Kathīr, Ismāʿīl b. ʿUmar. *al-Bidāyah wa-al-nihāyah.* 14 vols. Beirut: Maktabat al-Maʿārif, 1386/1966.

Tafsīr al-Qurʾān al-ʿaẓīm. 4 vols. Cairo: Maṭbaʿah Muṣṭafā Muḥammad, 1356/1937.

Ibn Khaldūn, [ʿAbd al-Raḥmān b. Muḥammad]. *The Muqaddimah.* 2nd revised ed. Translated by Franz Rosenthal. Princeton: Princeton University Press, 1967.

Ibn Khallikān, Shams al-Dīn Aḥmad b. Muḥammad b. Abī Bakr. *Wafayāt al-aʿyān wa-anbāʾ al-zamān.* Edited by Iḥsān ʿAbbās. 8 vols. Beirut: Dār al-Thaqāfah, 1968.

Ibn Manẓūr, Muḥammad b. Mukarram. *Lisān al-ʿarab.* 15 vols. Beirut: Dār Ṣādir, 1375/1957.

Ibn al-Qifṭī, Jamāl al-Dīn Abū al-Ḥasan ʿAlī b. Yūsuf. *Taʾrīkh al-ḥukamāʾ.* Edited by Julius Lippert. 1903. Reprint, Baghdad: Maktabat al-Muthannā, 1967.

Ibn Rajab, ʿAbd al-Raḥmān b. Aḥmad. *Dhayl ʿalā ṭabaqāt al-ḥanābilah.* Cairo: Dār al-Maʿārif, n.d.

Ibn Saʿd, Muḥammad. *al-Ṭabaqāt al-kubrā.* Edited by Iḥsān ʿAbbās. 9 vols. Beirut: Dār Ṣādir, 1380–88/1960–68.

Ibn al-Sāʿī al-Khāzin, ʿAlī b. Anjab. *al-Jāmiʿ al-mukhtaṣar, Part Nine.* Edited by Muṣṭafā Jawād and Père Anastase-Marie de St. Elie. Baghdad: Imprimerie Syrienne Catholique, 1934.

Ibn Ṣaṣrā, Muḥammad b. Muḥammad. *A Chronicle of Damascus, 1389–1397.* Translated and edited by William M. Brinner. 2 vols. Berkeley: University of California Press, 1963.

Ibn Taymīyah, Taqī al-Dīn. *al-Jawāb al-ṣaḥīḥ li-man badala dīn al-masīḥ.* 4 vols. Cairo: Maṭbaʿat al-Nīl, 1322/1905.

Ibrahim, Lutpi. "Az-Zamakhsharī: His Life and Works." *Islamic Studies* 19 (1980): 95–110.

Ihsanoglu, Ekmeleddin, ed. *World Bibliography of Translations of the Meanings of the Holy Qurʾān: Printed Translations 1515–1980.* Istanbul: Research Centre for Islamic History, Art and Culture, 1406/1986.

Izutsu, Toshihiko. *The Concept of Belief in Islamic Theology.* 1965. Reprint, New York: Books for Libraries, 1980.

Ethico-Religious Concepts in the Qur'ān. Montreal: McGill University Press, 1966.

God and Man in the Koran. Tokyo: The Keio Institute of Cultural and Linguistic Studies, 1964.

The Structure of the Ethical Terms in the Koran. Tokyo: Keio University, 1959.

Jansen, J.J.G. *The Interpretation of the Koran in Modern Egypt.* Leiden: E.J. Brill, 1974.

" 'I suspect that my friend Abdu (. . .) was in reality an agnostic.' " In *Acta Orientalia Neerlandica: Proceedings of the Congress of the Dutch Oriental Society, 1970*, edited by P.W. Pestman. Leiden: E.J. Brill, 1971.

"Polemics on Mustafa Mahmud's Koran Exegesis." In *Proceedings of the Ninth Congress of the Union Européenne des Arabisants et Islamisants, Amsterdam 1978*, edited by Rudolph Peters, 110–22. Leiden: E.J. Brill, 1981.

"Shaikh al-Shaʿrāwī's Interpretation of the Qur'ān." In *Proceedings of the Tenth Congress of the Union Européenne des Arabisants et Islamisants, Edinburgh 1980*, edited by Robert Hillenbrand, 22–28. Edinburgh: n.p., 1982.

"Tafsîr, Ijmâʿ and Modern Muslim Extremism." *Orient* 27 (1986): 642–46.

Jargy, Simon. *Islam et chrétienté: les fils d'Abraham entre la confrontation et le dialogue.* Geneva: Labor et Fides, 1981.

Jeffery, Arthur. *The Foreign Vocabulary of the Qur'ān.* Baroda: Oriental Institute, 1938.

Index of Qur'ānic Verses to the English Part of 'Materials for the History of the Text of the Qur'ān'. Leiden: E.J. Brill, 1951.

Materials for the History of the Text of the Qur'ān. Leiden: E.J. Brill, 1937.

"The Present Status of Qur'ānic Studies." In *Report on Current Research on the Middle East*, 1–16. Washington, D.C.: The Middle East Institute, 1957.

The Qur'ān as Scripture. New York: Russel F. Moore, 1952.

Two Muqaddimas to the Qur'anic Sciences. 2nd ed. Cairo: Brothers al-Khaniji, 1972.

Jin Yijiu. "The Qur'ān in China." *Contributions to Asian Studies* 17 (1983): 95–101.

Johns, Anthony H. "Al-Rāzī's Treatment of the Qur'ānic Episodes Telling of Abraham and His Guests: Qur'ānic Exegesis with a Human Face." *Mélanges de l'Institut Dominicain d'Études Orientales du Caire* 17 (1986): 81–114.

"Solomon and the Queen of Sheba: Fakhr al-Dīn al-Rāzī's Treatment of the Qurʾānic Telling of the Story." *Abr-Nahrain* 24 (1986): 58–82.

Jomier, Jacques. *Le commentaire coranique du Manār: tendances modernes de l'exégèse coranique en Égypte.* Paris: G.-P. Maisonneuve, 1954.

"Fakhr al-Dīn al-Rāzī et les commentaires du Coran les plus anciens." *Mélanges de l'Institut Dominicain d'Études Orientales du Caire* 15 (1982): 145–72.

Les grandes thèmes du Coran. Paris: Centurion, 1978.

"Les *Mafātīḥ al-ghayb* de l'Imām Fakhr al-Dīn al-Rāzī: quelques dates, lieux, manuscrits." *Mélanges de l'Institut Dominicain d'Études Orientales du Caire* 13 (1977): 253–90.

"Qui a commenté l'ensemble des sourates al-ʿankabūt à Yāsīn (29–36) dans le 'Tafsīr al-kabīr' de l'Imām Fakhr al-Dīn al-Rāzī?" *International Journal of Middle East Studies* 11 (1980): 467–85.

"The Qurʾānic Commentary of Imām Fakhr al-Dīn al-Rāzī: Its Sources and Its Originality." In *International Congress for the Study of the Qurʾān, Australian National University, Canberra, 8–13 May 1980*, edited by A.H. Johns, 93–111. 2nd ed. Canberra: Australian National University, n.d.

"La revue 'al-orwa al-wothqa' (13 mars–16 octobre 1884) et l'autorité du Coran." *Mélanges de l'Institut Dominicain d'Études Orientales du Caire* 17 (1986): 9–36.

"Unité de Dieu, Chrétiens et Coran selon Fakhr al-Dīn al-Rāzī." *Islamochristiana* 6 (1980): 149–77.

Jones, L. Bevan. "The Paraclete or Mohammed." *The Muslim World* 10 (1920): 112–25.

al-Jundī, Darwīsh. *al-Naẓm al-Qurʾānī fī Kashshāf al-Zamakhsharī.* Cairo: Dār Nahḍah Miṣr lil-Ṭabʿ wa-al-Nashr, 1969.

al-Juwaynī, Muṣṭafā al-Sāwī. *Minhaj al-Zamakhsharī fī tafsīr al-Qurʾān wa-bayān iʿjāzihi.* Cairo: Dār al-Maʿārif, 1379/1959.

Juynboll, G.H.A. *The Authenticity of the Tradition Literature: Discussions in Modern Egypt.* Leiden: E.J. Brill, 1969.

Muslim Tradition: Studies in Chronology, Provenance and Authorship of Early Ḥadīth. Cambridge: Cambridge University Press, 1983.

"The position of Qurʾan Recitation in Early Islam." *Journal of Semitic Studies* 19 (1974): 240–51.

"The Qurrāʾ in Early Islamic History." *Journal of the Economic and Social History of the Orient* 16 (1973): 13–29.

Kalāntarī, Ilyās. *Rāhnamā-yi mawḍūʿāt-i tarjumah-i al-mīzān fī tafsīr al-Qurʾān.* Tehran: Intishārāt-i Wafā, 1361 (solar)/1983.

Kāshānī, Mullā Fatḥ Allāh. *Minhaj al-ṣādiqīn fī ilzām al-mukhālifīn.* 10 vols. Tehran: Kitābfurūshī-yi Islāmīyah, 1347 (solar)/1969.

Tanbīh al-ghāfilīn va taẕkirat al-ʿārifīn: tarjumah va sharḥ-i fārsī-yi nahj al-balāghah. Edited by Manṣūr Pahlavān. Tehran: Mīqāt, 1364–66 (solar)/1985–87.

Kassis, Hanna E. *A Concordance of the Qurʾān.* Berkeley: University of California Press, 1983.

Kazi, A.K., and J.G. Flynn, trans. *Muslim Sects and Divisions: The Section on Muslim Sects in Kitāb al-Milal wa'l-Niḥal.* London: Routledge and Kegan Paul, 1984.

Kedourie, Elie. *Afghani and ʿAbduh: An Essay on Religious Unbelief and Political Activism in Modern Islam.* New York: The Humanities Press, 1966.

Kerr, David. "Mary, Mother of Jesus, in the Islamic Tradition: A Theme for Christian-Muslim Dialogue." *Newsletter of the Office on Christian-Muslim Relations* 39 (1988): 1–9.

Kerr, Malcolm H. *Islamic Reform: The Political and Legal Theories of Muhammad ʿAbduh and Rashid Rida.* Berkeley: University of California Press, 1966.

Kholeif, Fathalla. *Fakhr al-Dīn al-Rāzī.* Cairo: Dār al-Maʿārif bi-Miṣr, 1389/1969.

Falāsifat al-islām: Ibn Sīnā, al-Ghazālī, Fakhr al-Dīn al-Rāzī. Alexandria: Dār al-Jāmiʿāt al-Miṣrīyah, 1976.

A Study on Fakhr al-Dīn al-Rāzī and His Controversies in Transoxiana. Beirut: Dār El-Machreq, 1966.

Khoury, Adel. *Toleranz im Islam.* Munich: Kaiser, 1980.

Khoury, Paul. *Paul d'Antioche.* Beirut: Imprimerie Catholique, 1964.

Khoury, R.G. "Pour une nouvelle compréhension de la transmission des textes dans les trois premiers siècles islamiques." *Arabica* 34 (1987): 181–96.

"Quelques réflexions sur les citations de la Bible dans les premières générations islamiques du premier et du deuxième siècles de l'Hégire." *Bulletin d'études orientales* 29 (1977): 269–78.

Wahb B. Munabbih. Wiesbaden: Otto Harrassowitz, 1972.

al-Khw̱ānsārī, Muḥammad Bāqir al-Mūsawī. *Rawḍāt al-jannāt.* Edited by Asadallāh Ismāʿīlīyān. 8 vols. Tehran: Maktabat-i Ismāʿīlīyān, 1392/1972.

Kimball, Charles. "Striving Together in the Way of God: Muslim Participation in Christian-Muslim Dialogue." Ph.D. thesis, Harvard Divinity School, 1987.

Kister, M.J. " 'ʿAn yadin' (Qurʾān, IX/29): An Attempt at Interpretation." *Arabica* 11 (1964): 272–78.

"Ḥaddithū ʿan banī isrāʾīla wa-lā-ḥaraja." *Israel Oriental Studies* 2 (1972): 215–39.

"... *illā bi-ḥaqqihi....*: A Study of an Early Ḥadīth." *Jerusalem Studies in Arabic and Islam* 5 (1984): 33–52.

"The Massacre of the Banû Qurayẓa: A Re-examination of a Tradition." *Jerusalem Studies in Arabic and Islam* 8 (1986): 61–96.

"O God, Tighten Thy Grip on Muḍar ...: Some Socio-economic and Religious Aspects of an Early Ḥadith." *Journal of the Economic and Social History of the Orient* 24 (1981): 242–73.

"On 'Concessions' and Conduct: A Study in Early *Ḥadīth*." In *Studies in the First Century of Islamic Society*, edited by G.H.A. Juynboll, 89–107. Carbondale, Ill.: Southern Illinois University Press, 1982.

"On the Papyrus of Wahb b. Munabbih." *Bulletin of the School of Oriental and African Studies* 37 (1974): 545–71.

"Al-taḥannuth: An Inquiry into the Meaning of a Term." In *Studies in Jāhiliyya and Early Islam*. London: Variorum Reprints, 1980. Reprinted from *Bulletin of the School of Oriental and African Studies* 31 (1968): 223–36.

Köbert, R. "Zur Ansicht des frühen Islam über das Mönchtum." *Orientalia* 42 (1973): 520–24.

Kohlberg. E. "Some Notes on the Imāmite Attitude to the Qur'ān." In *Islamic Philosophy and the Classical Tradition* (R. Walzer *Festschrift*), edited by S.M. Stern, Albert Hourani, and Vivian Brown, 209–24. Columbia, S.C.: University of South Carolina Press, 1972.

Kraemer, Joel L. *Humanism in the Renaissance of Islam: The Cultural Revival During the Buyid Age*. Leiden: E.J. Brill, 1986.

Kramers, J.H. "al-Rāzī." In *Shorter Encyclopaedia of Islam*, 470–71. E.J. Brill, 1953.

Kraus, Paul. "The 'Controversies' of Fakhr al-Dīn Rāzī." *Islamic Culture* 12 (1938): 131–53.

Kritzeck, James. *Peter the Venerable and Islam*. Princeton: Princeton University Press, 1964.

Kronholm, Tryggve. "Akhbaranā jaddī: Preliminary Observations on the Dependence of Sibṭ b. al-Jauzī in his *Kitāb al-Jalīs aṣ-ṣāliḥ wal-anīs an-nāṣiḥ* on the Works of His Grandfather." *Orientalia Suecana* 33–35 (1984–86): 241–56.

Künstlinger, David. " 'Kitāb' und 'ahlu l-kitābi' im Kurān." *Rocznik Orientalistyczny* 4 (1926): 238–47.

Lagarde, Michel. "Un index en préparation pour le *Grand Commentaire* de Fakhr al-Dīn al-Rāzī." *Arabica* 33 (1986): 383–84.

al-Laknawī, Abū al-Ḥasanāt Muḥammad. *Kitāb al-fawā'id al-bahīyah fī tarājim al-Ḥanafīyah*. Edited by Abū Firās al-Naʿsānī. Beirut: Dār al-Maʿrifah, n.d.

Lane, Edward William. *Arabic-English Lexicon*. 1 vol. in 8 parts. Parts 6–

8 edited by Stanley Lane-Poole. 1872. Reprint, New York: Frederick Ungar, 1956.

Laoust, H. "Ibn al-Djawzī." In *The Encyclopedia of Islam,* 3:751–52. New Edition. Leiden: E.J. Brill, 1954–.

"Ibn Kathīr." In *The Encyclopedia of Islam,* 3:817–18. New Edition. Leiden: E.J. Brill, 1954–.

"Ibn Kathīr, historien." *Arabica* 2 (1955): 42–88.

La Profession de foi d'Ibn Baṭṭa. Damascus: Institut Français de Damas, 1958.

"Renouveau de l'apologétique missionnaire traditionnelle au xxe siècle dans l'oeuvre de Rashīd Riḍā." In *Prédication et propagande au Moyen Age*, 271–92. Paris: Presses Universitaires de France, 1983.

Lapidus, Ira. *A History of Islamic Societies.* Cambridge: Cambridge University Press, 1988.

Laroussi, G. "Enonciation et stratégies discursives dans le Coran." *Analyses, théorie* 2/3 (1982): 121–71.

Layish, Aharon. "Notes on Joseph Schacht's Contribution to the Study of Islamic Law." *British Society for Middle Eastern Studies Bulletin* 9 (1982): 132–40.

Lazarus-Yafeh, Hava. "Is There a Concept of Redemption in Islam?" In her *Some Religious Aspects of Islam*, 48–57. Leiden: E.J. Brill, 1981. Reprinted from *Types of Redemption*, edited by R.I.Z. Werblowsky and C.J. Bleeker, 168–80. Leiden: E.J. Brill, 1970.

"*Tajdīd al-Dīn*: A Reconsideration of Its Meaning, Roots and Influences in Islam." In *Studies in Islamic and Judaic Traditions*, edited by William M. Brinner and Stephen D. Ricks, 99–108. Atlanta: Scholars Press, 1986.

Lecomte, Gérard. "Les citations de l'Ancien et du Nouveau Testament dans l'oeuvre d'Ibn Qutayba." *Arabica* 5 (1958): 34–46.

"Sufyān al-Thawrī: quelques remarques sur le personnage et son oeuvre." *Bulletin d'études orientales* 30 (1978): 51–60.

Leder, Stefan. *Ibn al-Jauzī und seine Kompilation wider die Leidenschaft: der Traditionalist in gelehrter Überlieferung und originärer Lehre.* Beirut: Orient-Institut der Deutschen Morgenländischen Gesellschaft; Wiesbaden: Franz Steiner, 1984.

Leemhuis, Fred. *The D and H Stems in Koranic Arabic.* Leiden: E.J. Brill, 1977.

"MS. 1075 Tafsīr of the Cairene Dār al-Kutub and Mujāhid's *Tafsīr.*" In *Proceedings of the Ninth Congress of the Union Européenne des Arabisants et Islamisants, Amsterdam 1978*, edited by Rudolph Peters, 169–80. Leiden: E.J. Brill, 1981.

"Origins and Early Development of the *tafsīr* Tradition." In *Approaches to the History of the Interpretation of the Qurʾān*, edited by Andrew Rippin, 13–30. Oxford: Clarendon Press, 1988.

Le Strange, Guy. *Baghdad during the Abbasid Caliphate*. Oxford: Clarendon Press, 1900.

Levi Della Vida, G. "Salmān al-Fārisī." In *The Encyclopedia of Islam*, 7: 116–17. 8 vols. and supplement. 1913–38. Reprint, Leiden: E.J. Brill, 1987.

Lewis, Bernard. "ʿAyn Djālūt." In *The Encyclopedia of Islam*, 1:786–87. New Edition. Leiden: E.J. Brill, 1954–.

"On Modern Arabic Political Terms." In his *Islam in History*. London: Alcove Press, 1973.

Lichtenstädter, Ilse. "Quran and Quran Exegesis." *Humaniora Islamica* 2 (1974): 3–28.

Lings, Martin. *Muḥammad: His Life Based on the Earliest Sources*. London: George Allen and Unwin, 1983.

LoJacono, Claudio. "Ṭàbari [*sic*], storiografo del primo Islàm." *Islam, storia e civiltà* 4 (1985): 91–99.

Lory, Pierre. *Les commentaires ésotériques du Coran d'après ʿAbd ar-Razzāq al-Qāshānī*. Paris: Les Deux Océans, 1980.

Loth, O. "Ṭabarī's Korankommentar." *Zeitschrift der Deutschen Morgenländischen Gesellschaft* 35 (1881): 588–628.

Lüling, Gunter. *Über den Ur-Qurʾān: Ansätze zur Rekonstruktion vorislamischer christlicher Strophenlieder im Qurʾān*. Erlangen: H. Lüling, 1974.

Ma'ayergi, Hassan A. "History of the Works of Qurʾānic Interpretation (*Tafsir*) in the Kurdish Language." *Journal: Institute of Muslim Minority Affairs* 7 (1986): 268–74.

Macdonald, Duncan B. "The Development of the Idea of Spirit in Islam." *The Muslim World* 22 (1932): 25–42 and 153–68. Reprinted from *Acta Orientalia* 9 (1931): 307–51.

Madelung, Wilferd. "The Early Murjiʾa in Khurāsān and Transoxania and the Spread of Ḥanafism." *Der Islam* 59 (1982): 32–39.

al-Majdūb, ʿAbd al-ʿAzīz. *al-Imām al-ḥakīm Fakhr al-Dīn al-Rāzī min khilali tafsīrihi*. Tunis: al-Dār al-ʿArabīyah lil-Kitāb, 1400/1980.

Majmaʿ al-lughah al-ʿarabīyah. *Muʿjam alfāẓ al-Qurʾān al-karīm*. 6 vols. Cairo: al-Maṭbaʿah al-Thaqāfīyah, 1380/1960.

Makdisi, George. "Interaction between Islam and the West." In *Colloques Internationaux de la Napoule (1976): L'enseignement en islam et en occident au moyen age*, edited by G. Makdisi, D. Sourdel, and J. Sourdel-Thomine, 287–309. Paris: Librairie Orientaliste Paul Geuthner, 1977. *Revue des études islamiques* hors série 13.

The Notebooks of Ibn ʿAqīl: Kitāb al-funūn, Part One. Beirut: Dar El-Machreq, 1970.

The Rise of Colleges: Institutions of Learning in Islam and the West. Edinburgh: Edinburgh University Press, 1981.

"The Scholastic Method in Medieval Education: An Inquiry into its Origins in Law and Theology." *Speculum* 49 (1974): 640–61.

al-Marʿashlī, Yūsuf ʿAbd al-Raḥmān, Muḥammad Salīm Ibrāhīm Samārah, and Jamāl Ḥamdī al-Dhahabī. *Fihris aḥādīth tafsīr al-Qurʾān al-ʿaẓīm.* Beirut: Dār al-Maʿrifah, 1406/1986.

Martin, Richard C. "The Role of the Basrah Muʿtazilah in Formulating the Doctrine of the Apologetic Miracle." *Journal of Near Eastern Studies* 39 (1980): 175–89.

"Text and Contextuality in Reference to Islam." *Semeia* 40 (1987): 125–45.

"Understanding the Qurʾān in Text and Context." *History of Religions* 21 (1982): 361–84.

Massé, Henri. "Abū 'l-Futūḥ al-Rāzī." In *The Encyclopedia of Islam,* 1:120. New Edition. Leiden: E.J. Brill, 1954–.

"Le *tafsīr* d'Abū 'l-Futūḥ Rāzī." In *Mélanges offerts à William Marçais*, edited by Institut d'Études Islamiques de l'Université de Paris, 243–49. Paris: G.P. Maisonneuve, 1950.

Massignon, Louis. *Essai sur les origines du lexique technique de la mystique musulmane.* 2nd ed. Paris: Librairie Philosophique J. Vrin, 1968.

"La Mubahala de Médine et l'hyperdulie de Fatima." In his *Opera Minora*, edited by Y. Moubarac, 1:550–72. 3 vols. Beirut: Dar al-Maareef, 1963. Reprinted from *Annuaire de l'École des Hautes Études*, 1943.

"Salman Pak et les prémices spirituelles de l'islam iranien." In his *Opera Minora*, edited by Y. Moubarac, 1:443–83. 3 vols. Paris: Presses Universitaires de France, 1969. Reprinted from *Société d'études iraniennes* 7 (1934).

Masson, Denise. *Monothéisme coranique et monothéisme biblique.* 2nd ed. Paris: Desclée de Brouwer, 1976. (First edition entitled *Le Coran et la révélation judéo-chrétienne* [Paris: Adrien Maisonneuve, 1958].)

al-Māturīdī, Abū Manṣūr. *Taʾwīlāt ahl al-sunnah.* Edited by Ibrāhīm and al-Sayyid ʿAwadayn. Cairo: Lajnat al-Qurʾān wa-al-sunnah, 1391/1971.

McAuliffe, Jane Dammen. "Chosen of All Women: Mary and Fāṭima in Qurʾānic Exegesis." *Islamochristiana* 7 (1981): 19–28.

"Exegetical Identification of the Ṣābiʾūn." *The Muslim World* 72 (1982): 95–106.

"Fakhr al-Dīn al-Rāzī on *āyat al-jizyah* and *āyat al-sayf.*" In *Conversion and Continuity: Indigenous Christian Communities in Islamic Lands, Eighth to Eighteenth Centuries*, edited by Michael Gervers and Ramzi J. Bik-

hazi, 103–19. Toronto: Pontifical Institute of Mediaeval Studies, 1990.
"Ibn al-Jawzī's Exegetical Propaedeutic: Introduction and Translation." *Alif: Journal of Comparative Poetics* 8 (1988): 101–13.
"Quranic Hermeneutics: The Views of al-Ṭabarī and Ibn Kathīr." In *Approaches to the History of the Interpretation of the Qurʾān*, edited by Andrew Rippin, 46–62. Oxford: Clarendon Press, 1988.
"The Wines of Earth and Paradise: Qurʾānic Proscriptions and Promises." In *Logos Islamikos: Studia Islamica in Honorem Georgii Michaelis Wickens*, edited by Roger M. Savory and Dionisius A. Agius, 160–74. Toronto: Pontifical Institute of Mediaeval Studies, 1984.
McDermott, Martin J. *The Theology of al-Shaikh al-Mufīd*. Beirut: Dar El-Machreq, 1978.
Mez, Adam. *Die Renaissance des Islams*. 1922; reprint, Hildesheim: G. Olms, 1968. English translation, *The Renaissance of Islam*, translated by Salahuddin Khuda Bukhsh and D.S. Margoliouth. London: Luzac, 1937.
Michaud, Henri. *Jésus selon le Coran*. Neuchatel: Éditions Delachaux et Niestlé, 1960.
Michel, Thomas F., S.J. *A Muslim Theologian's Response to Christianity*. Delmar, N.Y.: Caravan Books, 1984.
Mir, Mustansir. *Coherence in the Qurʾān*. Indianapolis: American Trust Publications, 1986.
Dictionary of Qurʾānic Terms and Concepts. New York: Garland, 1987.
Moberg, A. "Nadjrān." In *The Encyclopedia of Islam*, 6:823–25. New Edition. Leiden: E.J. Brill, 1954–.
Monnot, Guy. "L'histoire des religions en Islam, Ibn al-Kalbī et Rāzī." *Revue de l'histoire des religions* 187 (1975): 23–34.
"Le panorama religieux de Fakhr al-Dīn al-Rāzī." *Revue de l'histoire des religions* 203 (1986): 263–79.
"Le verset du Trône." *Mélanges de l'Institut Dominicain d'Études Orientales du Caire* 15 (1982): 119–44.
Morris, James. "Ibn ʿArabī and His Interpreters: Part II (Conclusion): Influences and Interpretations." *Journal of the American Oriental Society* 107 (1987): 101–19.
Mottahedeh, Roy. *Loyalty and Leadership in an Early Islamic Society*. Princeton: Princeton University Press, 1980.
The Mantle of the Prophet: Religion and Politics in Iran. New York: Pantheon, 1985.
al-Muḥtasib, ʿAbd al-Majīd ʿAbd al-Salām. *Ittijāhāt al-tafsīr fī al-ʿaṣr al-ḥadīth*. Beirut: Dār al-Fikr, 1973.
Mujāhid b. Jabr. *Tafsīr Mujāhid*. Edited by ʿAbd al-Raḥmān al-Ṭāhir b.

Muḥammad al-Sūrtī. 2 vols. Islamabad, n.d. Reprint, Beirut: al-Manshūrāt al-ʿIlmīyah, n.d.

Muqātil b. Sulaymān. *Tafsīr al-khams miʾat āyah min al-Qurʾān.* Edited by Isaiah Goldfeld. Shefarʿam: Dār al-Mashriq, 1980.

Tafsīr Muqātil b. Sulaymān. Edited by ʿAbdallāh Maḥmūd Shiḥātah. Cairo: al-Hayʾah al-Miṣrīyah al-ʿĀmmah lil-Kitāb, n.d.

Muth, Franz-Christoph. *Die Annalen von at-Ṭabarī im Spiegel der europäischen Bearbeitungen.* Frankfurt-am-Main: Peter Lang, 1983.

Nagel, Tilman. "Gedanken über die europäische Islamforschung und ihr Echo im Orient." *Zeitschrift für Missionswissenschaft und Religionswissenschaft* 62 (1978): 21–39.

"Ḳiṣaṣ al-anbiyāʾ." In *The Encyclopedia of Islam*, 5: 180–81. New Edition. Leiden: E.J. Brill, 1954–.

Der Koran: Einführung-Texte-Erläuterungen. Munich: C.H. Beck, 1983.

"Ḳurrāʾ." In *The Encyclopedia of Islam*, 5:499–500. New Edition. Leiden: E.J. Brill, 1954–.

Naṣīr, Āminah Muḥammad. *Abū al-Faraj b. al-Jawzī, ārāʾuhu al-kalāmīyah wa-al-akhlāqīyah.* Cairo: Dār al-Shurūkh, 1407/1987.

Nasr, Seyyed Hossein. "Foreword." In M.H. Ṭabāṭabāʾī's *The Qurʾan in Islam: Its Impact and Influence on the Life of Muslims.* London: Zahra, 1987.

"Introduction." In M.H. Ṭabāṭabāʾī's *A Shiʿite Anthology.* Albany: State University of New York Press, 1981.

"Preface." In M.H. Ṭabāṭabāʾī's *Shiʿite Islam.* London: George Allen and Unwin, 1975.

"Ṣadr al-Dīn Shīrāzī (Mullā Ṣadrā)." In *A History of Muslim Philosophy*, edited by M.M. Sharif. 2 vols. Wiesbaden: Otto Harrassowitz, 1966.

Nelson, Kristina. *The Art of Reciting the Qurʾān.* Austin: University of Texas Press, 1985.

Neuwirth, Angelika. "Koranlesung zwischen islamischem Ost und West." *Islamo e arabismo na península ibérica: actas do XI congresso da União europeia de arabistas e islamólogos (Évora-Faro-Silves, 29 set.–6 out. 1982).* Évora: Universidade de Évora, 1986.

Studien zur Komposition der mekkanischen Suren. Berlin: Walter de Gruyter, 1981.

Newby, Gordon. *A History of the Jews of Arabia.* Columbia, S.C.: University of South Carolina Press, 1988.

The Making of the Last Prophet. Columbia, S.C.: University of South Carolina Press, 1989.

"Tafsir Israʾiliyat." *Studies in Qurʾan and Tafsir: Journal of the American Academy of Religion*, Thematic Issue 47 (1979): 685–97.

Nöldeke, Theodor, et al. *Geschichte des Qorans.* 2nd revised ed.; vols. 1 and

2 revised by Friedrich Schwally; vol. 3 revised by G. Bergsträsser and O. Pretzl. Leipzig: Dieterich'sche Verlagsbuchhandlung, 1909–26.

Noth, Albrecht. "Minderheiten als Vertragspartner im Disput mit dem islamischen Gesetz." In *Studien zur Geschichte und Kultur des vorderen Orients: Festschrift für Bertold Spuler zum siebzigsten Geburtstag*, edited by Hans R. Roemer and A. Noth, 289–309. Leiden: E.J. Brill, 1981.

Noury, R.P. Pierre. "Le commentaire 'scientifique' du Coran: une innovation absurde." *Mélanges de l'Institut Dominicain d'Études Orientales du Caire* 16 (1983): 293–300.

Nwyia, Paul. *Exégèse coranique et langage mystique: Nouvel essai sur le lexique technique des mystiques musulmans*. Beirut: Dar El-Machreq, 1970.

O'Shaughnessy, Thomas, S.J. *The Development of the Meaning of Spirit in the Koran*. Rome: Pontificium Institutum Orientalium Studiorum, 1953.

The Koranic Concept of the Word of God. Rome: Pontificio Istituto Biblico, 1948.

Muhammad's Thoughts on Death: A Thematic Study of the Qurʾanic Data. Leiden: E.J. Brill, 1969.

Paret, Rudi. "Furḳān." In *The Encyclopedia of Islam*, 2:949–50. New Edition. Leiden: E.J. Brill, 1954–.

Grenzen der Koranforschung. Stuttgart: W. Kohlhammer, 1950.

"Islam and Christianity." Translated by Rafīq Ahmad. *Islamic Studies* 3 (1964): 83–95.

Der Koran: Kommentar und Konkordanz. 2nd ed. 1971. Reprint, Stuttgart: W. Kohlhammer, 1980.

Muhammed und der Koran: Geschichte und Verkündigung des arabischen Propheten. 5th revised ed. Stuttgart: W. Kohlhammer, 1980.

"al-Ṭabarī." In *The Encyclopedia of Islam*, 7:578–79. 8 vols. and supplement. 1913–38. Reprint, Leiden: E.J. Brill, 1987.

"Ummī." In *The Encyclopedia of Islam*, 4:1016. 8 vols. and supplement. 1913–38. Reprint, Leiden: E.J. Brill, 1987.

ed. *Der Koran*. Darmstadt: Wissenschaftliche Buchgesellschaft, 1975.

Parrinder, Geoffrey. *Jesus in the Qurʾān*. New York: Barnes and Noble, 1965.

Pedersen, J. "The Islamic Preacher: *wāʿiẓ, mudhakkir, qāṣṣ*." In *Ignace Goldziher Memorial Volume*, edited by Samuel Löwinger and Joseph Somogyi, 1:226–51. Budapest: n.p., 1948.

Pellat, Charles. "Fatra." In *The Encyclopedia of Islam*, 2:865. New Edition. Leiden: E.J. Brill, 1954–.

"Ḳuss b. Sāʿida." In *The Encyclopedia of Islam*, 5:528–29. New Edition. Leiden: E.J. Brill, 1954–.

Penrice, John. *A Dictionary and Glossary of the Kor-ân*. 1873. Reprint, London: Curzon Press, 1971.

Perlmann, M. "Another Kaᶜb al-Aḥbār Story." *The Jewish Quarterly Review* 45 (1954): 48–51.

"A Legendary Story of Kaᶜb al-Aḥbār's Conversion to Islam." In *The Joshua Starr Memorial Volume: Studies in History and Philology*, 85–99. New York: Conference on Jewish Relations, 1953.

Peters, J.R.T.M. *God's Created Speech*. Leiden: E.J. Brill, 1976.

"In the Fullness of Time: An Exegetical Analysis of *sūra* 97 of the Qurʾān." In *Von Kanaan bis Kerala: Festschrift für Prof. Mag. Dr. Dr. J.P.M. van der Ploeg O.P. zur Vollendung des siebzigsten Lebensjahres am 4. Juli 1979*, edited by W.C. Delsman et al., 389–409. Kevelaer: Butzon und Bercker, 1982.

Pinault, David. "Images of Christ in Arabic Literature." *Die Welt des Islams* 17 (1987): 103–25.

Plessner, M. "Sufyān al-Thawrī." In *The Encyclopedia of Islam*, 7:500–02. 8 vols. and supplement. 1913–38. Reprint, Leiden: E.J. Brill, 1987.

Powers, David S. "The Exegetical genre *nāsikh al-Qurʾān wa mansūkhuhu*." In *Approaches to the History of the Interpretation of the Qurʾān*, edited by Andrew Rippin, 117–38. Oxford: Clarendon Press, 1988.

"The Islamic Law of Inheritance Reconsidered: A New Reading of Q. 4:12B." *Studia Islamica* 55 (1982): 61–94.

"On Bequests in Early Islam." *Journal of Near Eastern Studies* 48 (1989): 185–200.

al-Qāḍī, Wadād. "The Term 'Khalīfa' in Early Exegetical Literature." *Die Welt des Islams* 28 (1988): 393–411.

Qassmi, Maulana Ghulam Mustafa. "Sindhi Translations and Tafsirs of the Holy Quran." Translated by Sayid Ghulam Mustafa Shah. *Sind Quarterly* 5 (1977): 33–49.

al-Qaysī, Qāsim. *Taʾrīkh al-tafsīr.* Baghdad: Maṭbūᶜāt al-Majmaᶜ al-ᶜIlmī al-ᶜIrāqī, 1966.

al-Qummī, ᶜAbbās b. Muḥammad Riḍā. *Mashāhīr-i dānishmandān-i islām.* 4 vols. Tehran: Kitābfurūshī-yi Islāmīyah 1350–51 (solar)/1972–73.

al-Qurʾān. Cairo (Būlāq): al-Maṭbaᶜah al-ᶜAmīrīyah, 1344/1925.

Rabin, C. "al-Fārisī." In *The Encyclopedia of Islam*, 2:802–03. New Edition. Leiden: E.J. Brill, 1954–.

al-Rāghib al-Iṣfahānī, Abū al-Qāsim al-Ḥusayn. *Muᶜjam mufradāt alfāẓ al-Qurʾān.* Beirut: Dār al-Kitāb al-ᶜArabī, 1392/1972.

Rahbar, Daud. "Aspects of the Qurʾān Translation." *Babel: International Journal of Translation* 9 (1963): 60–68.

"Reflections on the Tradition of Qurʾanic Exegesis." *The Muslim World* 52 (1962): 296–307.

Rahman, Fazlur. *Islam.* Chicago: University of Chicago Press, 1966.

Islam and Modernity: Transformation of an Intellectual Tradition. Chicago: University of Chicago Press, 1982.
Major Themes of the Qur'ān. Minneapolis: Bibliotheca Islamica, 1980.
"Sunnah and Ḥadīth." *Islamic Studies* 1 (1962): 1–36.
Räisänen, Heikki. *Das Koranische Jesusbild: ein Beitrag zur Theologie des Korans.* Helsinki: Missiologian ja Ekumeniikan, 1971.
Rashīd Riḍā, Muḥammad. *Tafsīr al-Qur'ān al-ḥakīm al-shahīr bi-tafsīr al-Manār.* 12 vols. Beirut: Dār al-Maᶜrifah lil-Ṭibāᶜah wa-al-Nashr, n.d.
and Muḥammad Aḥmad Kanᶜān. *Mukhtaṣar tafsīr al-Manār.* Edited by Zuhayr al-Shāwīsh. 3 vols. Beirut: al-Maktab al-Islāmī, 1404/1984.
Raven, Wim. "Some Early Islamic Texts on the Negus of Abyssinia." *Journal of Semitic Studies* 33 (1988): 197–218.
al-Rāzī, [Muḥammad b. ᶜUmar] al-Fakhr [al-Dīn]. *al-Tafsīr al-kabīr.* 32 vols. Cairo: al-Maṭbaᶜah al-Bahīyah al-Miṣrīyah, n.d.
Razzāqī, Abū al-Qāsim. "Bā ᶜAllāmah Ṭabāṭabā'ī dar al-mīzān." In *Yādnāmah-i mufassir-i kabīr ustād ᶜAllāmah-i Ṭabāṭabā'ī,* 209–47. Qum: Intishārāt-i Shafaq, 1361 (solar)/1983.
Richard, Yann. *Le Shi'isme en Iran.* Paris: Jean Maisonneuve, 1980.
Rickards, Donald Roland. "A Study of the Quranic References to ᶜĪsā in the Light of *Tafsīr* and *Ḥadīth.*" Ph.D. diss., Hartford Seminary Foundation, 1969.
Ringgren, Helmer. *Studies in Arabian Fatalism.* Uppsala: A.-B. Lundequistske Bokhandeln, 1955.
Rippin, Andrew. "The Exegetical Genre *asbāb al-nuzūl*: A Bibliographical and Terminological Study." *Bulletin of the School of Oriental and African Studies* 48 (1985): 1–15.
"The Function of *asbāb al-nuzūl* in Qur'ānic Exegesis." *Bulletin of the School of Oriental and African Studies* 51 (1988): 1–20.
"Ibn ᶜAbbās's *al-Lughāt fī'l-Qur'ān.*" *Bulletin of the School of Oriental and African Studies* 44 (1981): 15–25.
Ibn ᶜAbbās's *Gharīb al-Qur'ān.*" *Bulletin of the School of Oriental and African Studies* 46 (1983): 332–33.
"Lexicographical Texts and the Qur'ān." In *Approaches to the History of the Interpretation of the Qur'ān,* edited by Andrew Rippin, 158–74. Oxford: Clarendon Press, 1988.
"Literary Analysis of *Qur'ān*, *Tafsīr* and *Sīra*: The Methodologies of John Wansbrough." In *Approaches to Islam in Religious Studies,* edited by Richard C. Martin, 151–63. Tucson: The University of Arizona Press, 1985.
"The Present Status of *Tafsīr* Studies." *The Muslim World* 72 (1982): 224–38.
"Saᶜadya Gaon and Genesis 22: Aspects of Jewish-Muslim Interaction

and Polemic." In *Studies in Islamic and Judaic Tradition*, edited by William M. Brinner and Stephen D. Ricks, 33–46. Atlanta: Scholars Press, 1986.

"al-Zuhrī, *Naskh al-Qurʾān* and the Problem of Early *Tafsīr* Texts." *Bulletin of the School of Oriental and African Studies* 47 (1984): 22–43.

Rizzardi, Giuseppe. *Il Problema della cristologia coranica.* Milan: Istituto Propaganda Libraria, 1982.

Robson, J. "Abū Dharr." In *The Encyclopedia of Islam*, 1:114–15. New Edition. Leiden: E.J. Brill, 1954–.

"al-Bayḍāwī." In *The Encyclopedia of Islam*, 1:1129. New Edition. Leiden: E.J. Brill, 1954–.

"Ibn al-Ṣalāḥ." In *The Encyclopedia of Islam*, 3:927. New Edition. Leiden: E.J. Brill, 1954–.

Rodwell, J.M., trans. *The Koran.* London: J.M. Dent, 1909.

Roest Crollius, Ary A., S.J. *Thus Were They Hearing: The Word in the Experience of Revelation in Qurʾān and Hindu Scriptures.* Rome: Università Gregoriana, 1974.

Rosenthal, Franz. *General Introduction: From the Creation to the Flood, Volume 1 of The History of al-Ṭabarī.* Albany: State University of New York Press, 1989.

"Some Minor Problems in the Qurʾān." In *The Joshua Starr Memorial Volume: Studies in History and Philology*, 67–84. New York: Conference on Jewish Relations, 1953.

Rudolph, Wilhelm. *Die Abhängigkeit des Korans von Judentum und Christentum.* Stuttgart: W. Kohlhammer, 1922.

al-Ṣabbāgh, Muḥammad. *Lamaḥāt fī ʿulūm al-Qurʾān wa-ittijāhāt al-tafsīr.* Beirut: al-Maktabah al-Islāmīyah, 1974.

Sabbagh, T. *La Métaphore dans le Coran.* Paris: Adrien-Maisonneuve, 1943.

Sachedina, Abdulaziz. "Jews, Christians and Muslims According to the Qurʾān." *The Greek Orthodox Theological Review* 31 (1986): 105–20.

Sadan, J. "Some Literary Problems Concerning Judaism and Jewry in Medieval Arabic Sources." In *Studies in Islamic History and Civilization in Honour of Professor David Ayalon*, edited by M. Sharon, 353–98. Jerusalem, Cana/Leiden: E.J. Brill, 1986.

al-Ṣadr, Ḥasan. *Taʾsīs al-shīʿah li-ʿulūm al-islām.* Baghdad: Sharikat al-Nashr wa-al-Ṭibāʿah al-ʿIrāqīyah al-Maḥdūdah, n.d.

al-Ṣafadī, Khalīl b. Aybak. *al-Wāfī bi-al-wafayāt.* Edited by Sven Dedering et al. 22 vols. Damascus: Druckerei al-Hāshimīyah, 1959– .

al-Saʿīd, Labīb. *Difāʿ ʿan al-qirāʾāt al-mutawātirah fī muwājahat al-Ṭabarī al-mufassir.* Cairo: Dār al Maʿārif, 1978.

[as-Said, Labib]. *The Recited Koran.* Translated and adapted by Bernard

Weiss, M.A. Rauf, and Morroe Berger. Princeton: The Darwin Press, 1975.

al-Ṣaʿīdī, ʿAbd al-Mutaʿālī. *al-Mujaddidūn fī al-islām min al-qarn al-awwal ilā al-rābiʿ ʿashar.* Cairo: Maktabat al-Ādāb, n.d.

al-Ṣāliḥ, Ṣubḥī. *Mabāḥith fī ʿulūm al-Qurʾān.* Beirut: Dār al-ʿIlm lil-Malāyīn, 1969.

Salmon, P., ed. *Mélanges d'islamologie dédiés à la mémoire d'A. Abel.* Leiden: E.J. Brill, 1974.

al-Sāmarrāʾī, Ḥasīb. *Rashīd Riḍā al-mufassir.* Baghdad: Dār al-Risālah lil-Ṭibāʿah, 1396/1976.

Samir, Khalil. "Le commentaire de Ṭabarī sur Coran 2/62 et la question du salut des non-musulmans." *Annali: Istituto Orientale de Napoli* 40/n.s. 30 (1980): 555–617.

Sauvaire, Henri. "Description de Damas." *Journal asiatique* 9th series, 3–7 (1894–96).

Savory, Roger. *Iran Under the Safavids.* Cambridge: Cambridge University Press, 1980.

Schacht, Joseph. *An Introduction to Islamic Law.* Oxford: Clarendon Press, 1964.

"Muḥammad ʿAbduh." In *The Encyclopedia of Islam*, 6:678–80. 8 vols. and supplement. 1913–38. Reprint, Leiden: E.J. Brill, 1987.

The Origins of Muhammadan Jurisprudence. 3rd corrected impression. Oxford: Clarendon Press, 1959.

"A Revaluation of Islamic Traditions." *Journal of the Royal Asiatic Society of Great Britain and Ireland*, n.v. (1949): 143–54.

and W. Heffening. "Ḥanafiyya." In *The Encyclopedia of Islam*, 3:162–64. New Edition. Leiden: E.J. Brill, 1954– .

Schall, Anton. "Die Sichtung des Christlichen im Koran." *Mitteilungen und Forschungsbeiträge der Cusanus-Gesellschaft* 9 (1971): 76–91.

Schedl, Claus. "Die 144 Suren des Koran und die 114 Logien Jesu im Thomas-Evangelium." *Der Islam* 64 (1987): 261–64.

Muhammad und Jesus. Vienna: Herder, 1978.

Schleifer, J. "Banu'l-Ḥārith b. Kaʿb." In *The Encyclopedia of Islam*, 3:268–69. 8 vols. and supplement. 1913–38. Reprint, Leiden: E.J. Brill, 1987. Unrevised reprint in *The Encyclopedia of Islam*, 3:223. New Edition. Leiden: E.J. Brill, 1954–.

Schmitz, M. "Kaʿb al-Aḥbār." In *The Encyclopedia of Islam*, 4:316–17. New Edition. Leiden: E.J. Brill, 1954–.

Schoeler, Gregor. "Die Überlieferung der Wissenschaften im frühen Islam." *Der Islam* 62 (1985): 210–30.

Schreiner, Martin. "Beiträge zur Geschichte der theologischen Bewegungen im Islām." *Zeitschrift der Deutschen Morgenländischen Gesellschaft* 52 (1898): 463–510.

Schub, Michael. "A Sublime Subtlety?" *Zeitschrift für arabische Linguistik* 6 (1981): 72–73.

Schumann, Olaf H. *Der Christus der Muslime: christologische Aspekte in der arabisch-islamischen Literatur.* Gütersloh: Gütersloher Verlagshaus Gerd Mohn, 1975.

Schwarzbaum, Haim. *Biblical and Extra-Biblical Legends in Islamic Folk-Literature.* Walldorf-Hessen: Verlag für Orientkunde Dr. H. Vorndran, 1982.

Sezgin, Fuat. *Geschichte des arabischen Schrifttums, Band 1: Qurʾān wissenschaften, Ḥadīth, Geschichte, Fiqh, Dogmatik, Mystik bis ca. 430 H.* Leiden: E.J. Brill, 1967.

Shafīʿī, Muḥammad. *Mufassirān-i shīʿah.* Shiraz: Dānishgāh-i Pahlavī, 1349 (solar)/1970.

Shahābī, ʿAlī Akbar. *Aḥvāl va āthār-i Muḥammad Jarīr Ṭabarī.* Tehran: Intishārāt Dānishgāh-i Ṭihrān, 1335 (solar)/1957.

Shahid, Irfan. "A Contribution to Koranic Exegesis." In *Arabic and Islamic Studies in Honor of Hamilton A.R. Gibb*, edited by George Makdisi. Leiden: E.J. Brill, 1965.

"Two Qurʾānic Sūras: al-Fīl and Quraysh." In *Studia Arabica et Islamica: Festschrift for Iḥsān ʿAbbās on his Sixtieth Birthday*, edited by Wadād Qāḍī, 429–36. Beirut: American University of Beirut, 1981.

The Martyrs of Najrān: New Documents. Brussels: Société des Bollandistes, 1971.

Shahin, Emad Eldin. "Muḥammad Rashīd Riḍā's Perspectives on the West as Reflected in *al-Manār*." *The Muslim World* 79 (1989): 113–32.

al-Shahrastānī, Muḥammad b. ʿAbd al-Karīm. *al-Milal wa-al-niḥal.* Edited by Muḥammad Sayyid Kīlānī. Beirut: Dār al-Maʿrifah, 1402/1982.

al-Sharabāṣī, Aḥmad. *Rashīd Riḍā al-ṣiḥāfī al-mufassir al-shāʿir al-lughawī.* Cairo: al-Hayʾah al-ʿĀmmah li-Shuʾūn al-Maṭābiʿ al-Amīrīyah, 1977.

Rashīd Riḍā ṣāḥib al-Manār ʿaṣruhu wa-ḥayātuhu wa-maṣādir thaqāfatihi. Cairo: n.p., 1369/1970.

Shaʿrānī, Abū al-Ḥasan. "Muqaddimah." In Abū al-Futūḥ Rāzī's *Rawḥ al-jinān wa-rūḥ al-janān.* Tehran: Kitābfurūshī-yi Islāmīyah, 1382–85/1962–65.

"Tarjamah-i muʾallif." In Mullā Fatḥ Allāh Kāshānīʾs *Minhaj al-ṣādiqīn fī ilzām al-mukhālifīn.* Tehran: Kitābfurūshī-yi Islāmīyah, 1347 (solar)/1969.

al-Shāwīs, Muḥammad Zuhayr. "Tarjamat al-muʾallif." In Abū al-Faraj b.

al-Jawzī's *Zād al-masīr fī ʿilm al-tafsīr.* Beirut: al-Maktab al-Islāmī lil-Ṭibāʿah wa-al-Nashr, 1384/1964.

Shboul, Ahmad M.H. *Al-Masʿūdī and His World.* London: Ithaca Press, 1979.

Shiḥātah, ʿAbdallāh Maḥmūd. *Manhaj al-Imām Muḥammad ʿAbduh fī tafsīr al-Qurʾān al-karīm.* 1960. Reprint, Cairo: Maṭbaʿah Jāmiʿat al-Qāhirah, 1984.

Taʾrīkh al-Qurʾān wa-al-tafsīr. Cairo: al-Hayʾah al-Miṣrīyah al-ʿĀmmah lil-Kitāb, 1392/1972.

al-Shushtarī, Nūr Allāh. *Kitāb mustaṭāb majālis al-muʾminīn.* 2 vols. Tehran: Kitābfurūshī-yi Islāmīyah, 1375/1956.

Siddiqi, Mazher ud-Din. "Some Aspects of the Muʿtazilī Interpretation of the Qurʾān." *Islamic Studies* 3 (1963): 95–120.

Siddiqi, Muzammil H. "Muslim and Byzantine Christian Relations: Letter of Paul of Antioch and Ibn Taymīyah's Response." *The Greek Orthodox Theological Review* 31 (1986): 33–45.

Smith, Jane I. *An Historical and Semantic Study of the Term 'Islām' As Seen in a Sequence of Qurʾān Commentaries.* Missoula, Mont.: Scholars Press, 1975.

and Yvonne Yazbeck Haddad. *The Islamic Understanding of Death and Resurrection.* Albany: State University of New York Press, 1981.

Smith, Wilfred Cantwell. *Belief and History.* Charlottesville, Va.: University Press of Virginia, 1977.

Faith and Belief. Princeton: Princeton University Press, 1979.

Sourdel, Dominique. *L'Imamisme vu par le Cheikh al-Mufīd.* Paris: Librairie Orientaliste Paul Guethner, 1974. *Revue des études islamiques* hors série 7.

"Une profession de foi de l'historien al-Ṭabarī." *Revue des études islamiques* 2 (1968): 177–99.

Speyer, Heinrich. *Die biblischen Erzählungen im Qoran.* 1931. Reprint, Hildesheim: Georg Olms, 1961.

Spuler, Berthold. "The Disintegration of the Caliphate in the East." In *The Cambridge History of Islam*, Vol. IA: *The Central Islamic Lands from Pre-Islamic Times to the First World War*, edited by P.M. Holt, Ann K.S. Lambton, and Bernard Lewis. Cambridge: Cambridge University Press, 1970.

"L'Islam et les minorités." In *Die Islamische Welt zwischen Mittelalter und Neuzeit: Festschrift für Hans Robert Roemer zum 65. Geburtstag*, 609–19. Beirut: Orient-Institut der Deutschen Morgenländischen Gesellschaft, 1979.

Stauth, G. "Die Überlieferung des Korankommentars Mujāhid b. Jabrs. zur Frage der Rekonstruktion der in den Sammelwerken des 3. Jh.

D. H. benutzten frühislamischen Quellenwerke." Ph.D. diss., Justus-Liebig-Universität, Giessen, 1969.

Stern, S.M. "ʿAbd al-Jabbār's Account of How Christ's Religion was Falsified by the Adoption of Roman Customs." *Journal of Theological Studies* 19 (1968): 129–76. Reprinted in S.M. Stern's *History and Culture of the Medieval Muslim World.* London: Variorum, 1984.

Stetkevych, Jaroslav. "Arabic Hermeneutical Terminology: Paradox and the Production of Meaning." *Journal of Near Eastern Studies* 48 (1989): 81–96.

Stoddart, William. *Sufism: The Mystical Doctrines and Methods of Islam.* Wellingborough, England: Thorsons Publishers, 1976.

Storey, C.A. *Persian Literature: A Bio-bibliographical Survey.* 2 vols. in 5. London: Luzac, 1927–71.

Strothmann, R. "al-Mufīd." In *The Encyclopedia of Islam*, 6:625–26. 8 vols. and supplement. 1913–38. Reprint, Leiden: E.J. Brill, 1987.

al-Subkī, Tāj al-Dīn Abū Naṣr ʿAbd al-Wahhāb. *Ṭabaqāt al-shāfiʿīyah al-kubrā.* 10 vols. Cairo: ʿĪsā al-Bābī al-Ḥalabī, 1384–96/1964–76.

Sufyān al-Thawrī. *Tafsīr Sufyān al-Thawrī.* Edited by Imtiyāz ʿAlī ʿArshī. Beirut: Dār al-Kutub al-ʿIlmīyah, 1403/1983.

Sufyān b. ʿUyaynah. *Tafsīr Sufyān b. ʿUyaynah.* Edited by Aḥmad Ṣāliḥ Maḥāyirī. Riyadh: Maktabah Asāmah, 1403/1983.

al-Suyūṭī, Jalāl al-Dīn ʿAbd al-Raḥmān. *Bughyat al-wuʿāh fī ṭabaqāt al-lughawīyīn wa-al-nuḥāh.* Edited by Muḥammad Abū al-Faḍl Ibrāhīm. Cairo: Maṭbaʿah ʿĪsā al-Bābī al-Ḥalabī, 1384/1965.

al-Itqān fī ʿulūm al-Qurʾān. Edited by Muḥammad Abū al-Faḍl Ibrāhīm. 4 vols. in 2. Cairo: Dār al-Turāth, 1405/1985.

Ṭabaqāt al-mufassirīn. Edited by A. Meursinge. 1839. Reprint, Tehran: M.H. Asadi, 1960.

Swartz, Merlin, ed. *Kitāb al-quṣṣāṣ wa'l-mudhakkirīn.* Beirut: Dar El-Machreq, 1971.

"The Rules of Popular Preaching in Twelfth-Century Baghdād, According to Ibn al-Jawzī." In *Prédication et propagande au Moyen Age: Islam, Byzance, Occident*, 223–39. Paris: Presses Universitaires de France, 1983.

al-Ṭabarī, Abū Jaʿfar Muḥammad b. Jarīr. *Commentaire du Coran.* Abridged, translated, and annotated by Pierre Godé. 3 vols. Paris: Éditions d'Art Les Heures Claires, 1983–.

The Commentary on the Qurʾan. Abridged, translated, and annotated by J. Cooper. Oxford: Oxford University Press, 1987.

Jāmiʿ al-bayān ʿan taʾwīl āy al-Qurʾān. Edited by Maḥmūd Muḥammad Shākir and Aḥmad Muḥammad Shākir. 16 vols. Cairo: Dār al-Maʿārif,

1374–/1954–. References in Chapters 1–7 are to this edition, except where noted.

Jāmiʿ al-bayān ʿan taʾwīl āy al-Qurʾān. 30 vols. in 15. Beirut: Dār al-Fikr, 1405/1984. References in Chapters 8–9 are to this edition.

Jāmiʿ al-bayān fī tafsīr al-Qurʾān. 30 vols. Cairo: Maṭbaʿat al-Yamīnīyah, n.d.

Taʾ rīkh al-rusul wa-al-mulūk. 16 vols. Edited by M.J. de Goeje. 1879 – 1901. Reprint. Leiden: E.J. Brill, 1964. 5 vols.

al-Ṭabāṭabāʾī, Muḥammad Ḥusayn. *Al-Mīzān: An Exegesis of the Qurʾān*. Translated by Sayyid Saeed Akhtar Rizvi. 5 vols. Tehran: World Organization for Islamic Services, 1403/1983– .

al-Mīzān fī tafsīr al-Qurʾān. 20 vols. Beirut: Muʾassasat al-Aʿlāmī lil-Maṭbūʿat, 1394/1974.

The Qurʾan in Islam: Its Impact and Influence on the Life of Muslims. Translated by Assadullah ad-Dhaakir Yate. London: Zahra, 1987.

A Shiʿite Anthology. Edited and translated by William C. Chittick. London: Muḥammadi Trust of Great Britain and Northern Ireland, 1980.

Shiʿite Islam. Edited and translated by Seyyed Hossein Nasr. London: George Allen and Unwin, 1975.

Tarjumah-i tafsīr-i al-mīzān. Translated by Nāṣir Makārim Shīrāzī et al. Qum: Chāpkhānah-i Dār al-ʿIlm, 1337–54/1959–78.

Talbi, Mohamed. "Islam and Dialogue: Some Reflections on a Current Topic." In *Christianity and Islam: The Struggling Dialogue*, edited by Richard W. Rousseau, S.J., 53–73. Montrose, Pa.: Ridge Row Press, 1985.

Tardieu, Michel. "Ṣabiens coraniques et 'ṣabiens' de Ḥarrān." *Journal asiatique* 274 (1986): 1–44.

Thackston, W.M., Jr. *The Tales of the Prophets of al-Kisaʾi*. Boston: Twayne, 1978.

Thomas, David. "Two Muslim-Christian Debates from the Early Shīʿite Tradition." *Journal of Semitic Studies* 33 (1988): 53–80.

Torrey, Charles C. *The Commercial-Theological Terms in the Koran*. Leiden: E.J. Brill, 1892.

Trimingham, J. Spencer. *Christianity Among the Arabs in Pre-Islamic Times*. London: Longman, 1979.

Tritton, A.S. "Naṣārā." In *The Encyclopedia of Islam*, 6:848–51. 8 vols. and supplement. 1913–38. Reprint, Leiden: E.J. Brill, 1987.

Troll, Christian W., ed. *Islam in India: Studies and Commentaries*. New Delhi: Vikas, 1982.

Tropeau, Gérard. "Les fêtes des Chrétiens vues par un juriste musulman." In *Mélanges offerts à Jean Dauvillier*, 795–802. Toulouse: Centre d'Histoire Juridique Méridionale, 1979.

al-Tujībī, Abū Yaḥyā Muḥammad b. Ṣumādiḥ. *Mukhtaṣar min tafsīr al-Imām al-Ṭabarī.* Edited by Muḥammad Ḥasan Abū al-ʿAzm al-Zufaytī. 2 vols. Cairo: al-Hayʾah al-Miṣrīyah al-ʿĀmmah lil-Taʾlīf wa-al-Nashr, 1390–91/1970–71.

al-Ṭūsī, Abū Jaʿfar Muḥammad b. al-Ḥasan. *al-Tibyān fī tafsīr al-Qurʾān.* 10 vols. Najaf: al-Maṭbaʿah al-ʿIlmīyah, 1376–83/1957–63.

Ṭūsī, Naṣīr al-Dīn. *The Nasirean Ethics.* Translated by G.M. Wickens. UNESCO Collection of Representative Works: Persian Series. London: George Allen and Unwin, 1964.

ʿUmayrah, ʿAbd al-Raḥmān. *Rijāl anzala Allāh fīhim Qurʾānan.* 7 vols. Riyadh: Dār al-Liwāʾ lil-Nashr wa-al-Tawzīʿ, 1397/1977.

Vacca, V. "Waraḳa." In *The Encyclopedia of Islam*, 8:1121–22. 8 vols. and supplement. 1913–38. Reprint, Leiden: E.J. Brill, 1987.

"Zaid B. ʿAmr B. Nufail." In *The Encyclopedia of Islam*, 8:1194. 8 vols. and supplement. 1913–38. Reprint, Leiden: E.J. Brill, 1987.

Vadet, J.-C., trans. *Les dissidences de l'Islam.* Paris: Librairie Orientaliste Paul Geuthner, 1984.

"Ibn Masʿūd." In *The Encyclopedia of Islam*, 3:873–75. New Edition. Leiden: E.J. Brill, 1954–.

Vajda, G. "Ahl al-kitāb." In *The Encyclopedia of Islam*, 1:264–66. New Edition. Leiden: E.J. Brill, 1954–.

"Ḥabīb al-Nadjdjār." In *The Encyclopedia of Islam*, 3:12–13. New Edition. Leiden: E.J. Brill, 1954–.

"Isrāʾīliyyāt." In *The Encyclopedia of Islam*, 4:211–12. New Edition. Leiden: E.J. Brill, 1954–.

Vasiliev, A.A. *Byzance et les Arabes.* Edited and translated by Henri Grégoire and Marius Canard. 2 vols. Brussels: Éditions de l'Institut de Philologie et d'Histoire Orientales et Slaves, 1950.

Vatikiotis, P.J. "Muḥammad ʿAbduh and the Quest for Muslim Humanism." *Arabica* 4 (1957): 55–72.

Veccia Vaglieri, L. "Djaʿfar b. Abī Ṭālib." In *The Encyclopedia of Islam*, 2: 372. New Edition. Leiden: E.J. Brill, 1954–.

"Khaybar." In *The Encyclopedia of Islam*, 4:1137–43. New Edition. Leiden: E.J. Brill, 1954–.

Vernet, Juan. "Le *tafsīr* au service de la polémique antimusulmane." *Studia Islamica* 32 (1970): 305–09.

Waardenburg, Jacques. "Towards a Periodization of Earliest Islam According to its Relations with Other Religions." In *Proceedings of the Ninth Congress of the Union Européenne des Arabisants et Islamisants, Amsterdam 1978*, edited by Rudolph Peters, 305–26. Leiden: E.J. Brill, 1981.

"Twentieth-century Muslim Writings on Other Religions: A Proposed Typology." In *Proceedings of the Tenth Congress of the Union Européenne des*

Arabisants et Islamisants, Edinburgh 1980, edited by Robert Hillenbrand, 107–115. Edinburgh: n.p., 1982.

"Types of Judgment in Islam About Other Religions." In *Middle East: 30th International Congress of Human Sciences in Asia and North Africa, Mexico City 1976*, edited by Graciela de la Lama, 135–44. Mexico City: El Colegio de México, 1982.

Wagtendonk, K. *Fasting in the Qur'ān*. Leiden: E.J. Brill, 1968.

al-Wāḥidī, ʿAlī b. Aḥmad. *Asbāb al-nuzūl*. Beirut: Dār wa-Maktabat al-Hilāl, 1983.

Waines, David. "Cereals, Bread and Society: An Essay on the Staff of Life in Medieval Iraq." *Journal of the Economic and Social History of the Orient* 30 (1987): 255–85.

Waldman, Marilyn. "The Development of the Concept of *Kufr* in the Qur'ān." *Journal of the American Oriental Society* 88 (1968): 442–55.

Wansbrough, John. "Majāz al-Qur'ān: Periphrastic Exegesis." *Bulletin of the School of Oriental and African Studies* 33 (1970): 247–66.

Quranic Studies: Sources and Methods of Scriptural Interpretation. Oxford: Oxford University Press, 1977.

The Sectarian Milieu: Content and Composition of Islamic Salvation History. Oxford: Oxford University Press, 1978.

Wasserstein, David. "An Arabic Version of *Abot* 1:3 from Umayyad Spain." *Arabica* 34 (1987): 370–74.

Watt, William Montgomery. "Abū Djahl." In *The Encyclopedia of Islam*, 1:115. New Edition. Leiden: E.J. Brill, 1954–.

"The Arabian Background of the Qur'ān." In *Sources for the History of Arabia: Proceedings of the First International Symposium on Studies in the History of Arabia, 1977*, 3–13. Riyadh: University of Riyadh Press, 1979.

Bell's Introduction to the Qur'an. Edinburgh: The University Press, 1970.

"The Condemnation of the Jews of Banū Qurayẓah: A Study in the Sources of the *Sīrah*." *The Muslim World* 42 (1952): 160–71.

"The Early Development of the Muslim Attitude to the Bible." *Transactions of the Glasgow University Oriental Society* 16 (1955–56): 50–62.

"Ḥanīf." In *The Encyclopedia of Islam*, 3:165–66. New Edition. Leiden: E.J. Brill, 1954–.

"His Name is Aḥmad." *The Muslim World* 43 (1953): 110–17.

"Kaʿb b. al-Ashraf." In *The Encyclopedia of Islam*, 4:315. New Edition. Leiden: E.J. Brill, 1954–.

Muḥammad at Medina. Oxford: Clarendon Press, 1956.

"Review of Ṭabāṭabā'ī's *Shīʿite Islam*." *Religious Studies* 13 (1977): 377–78.

Weisheipl, James A., O.P. *Friar Thomas D'Aquino: His Life, Thought and Works.* Garden City, N.Y.: Doubleday and Company, 1974.

Weiss, Bernard. "Language and Law: The Linguistic Premises of Islamic Legal Science." In *In Quest of an Islamic Humanism: Arabic and Islamic Studies in Memory of Mohamed al-Nowaihi*, edited by A.H. Green, 15–21. Cairo: The American University in Cairo Press, 1984.

Welch, Alford. "Death and Dying in the Qurʾān." In *Religious Encounters with Death: Insights from the History and Anthropology of Religions*, edited by Frank E. Reynolds and Earle H. Waugh, 183–99. University Park, Pa.: Pennsylvania State University Press, 1977.

"Introduction: Qurʾanic Studies – Problems and Prospects." *Studies in Qurʾan and Tafsir: Journal of the American Academy of Religion*, Thematic Issue 47 (1979): 620–34.

"al-Ḳurʾān." In *The Encyclopedia of Islam*, 5:400–29. New Edition. Leiden: E.J. Brill, 1954–.

Wensinck, Arent Jan. "ʿAmr b. al-ʿĀṣ." In *The Encyclopedia of Islam*, 1:451. New Edition. Leiden: E.J. Brill, 1954–.

"Ḥawārī." In *The Encyclopedia of Islam*, 3:285. New Edition. Leiden: E.J. Brill, 1954–. Reprinted from *The Encyclopedia of Islam*, 3:292–93. 8 vols. and supplement. 1913–38. Reprint, Leiden: E.J. Brill, 1987.

Muhammad and the Jews of Medina (Mohammed en de Joden te Medina). 2nd ed. Translated by Wolfgang H. Behn. Berlin: Adiyok, 1982.

"al-Nadjāshī." In *The Encyclopedia of Islam*, 3:817–18. 8 vols. and supplement. 1913–38. Reprint, Leiden: E.J. Brill, 1987.

Wickens, G.M. "Nasir al-Din Tusi on the Fall of Baghdad." *Journal of Semitic Studies* 7 (1962): 23–35.

"Notional Significance in Conventional Arabic 'Book' Titles: Some Unregarded Potentialities." In *The Islamic World, from Classical to Modern Times: Essays in Honor of Bernard Lewis*, edited by C.E. Boswoth, Charles Issawi, Roger Savory, and A.L. Udovitch. Princeton: Darwin Press, 1989.

Widengren, Geo. *Muhammad, the Apostle of God, and his Ascension.* Uppsala: A.-B. Lundequistska, 1955.

Wismer, Don. *The Islamic Jesus: An Annotated Bibliography of Sources in English and French.* New York: Garland Publishing, 1977.

Yādnāmah-i mufassir-i kabīr ustād ʿAllāmah-i Ṭabāṭabāʾī. Qum: Intishārāt-i Shafaq, 1361 (solar)/1983.

Yāqūt b. ʿAbdallāh al-Ḥamawī al-Rūmī. *Irshād al-arīb ilā maʿrifat al-adīb.* Edited by D.S. Margoliouth. 7 vols. Cairo: Maṭbaʿah Hindīyah, 1925.

Zaehner, R.C. "Why Not Islam?" *Religious Studies* 11 (1975): 167–79.

Zafrani, H. "Les relations judéo-musulmanes dans la littérature juridique."

In *Les relations entre juifs et musulmans en Afrique du Nord: actes du colloque international de l'Institut d'histoire des pays d'Outre-Mer*, 32–48. Paris: Éditions du Centre national de la recherche scientifique, 1980.

Zahniser, A.H. Mathias. "The Forms of Tawaffā in the Qur'ān: A Contribution to Christian-Muslim Dialogue." *The Muslim World* 79 (1989): 14–24.

al-Zamakhsharī, Maḥmūd b. ʿUmar. *al-Kashshāf ʿan ḥaqāʾiq ghawāmiḍ al-tanzīl wa-ʿuyūn al-aqāwīl fī wujūh al-taʾwīl*. 4 vols. Beirut: Dār al-Kitāb al-ʿArabī, 1366/1947.

al-Zarkashī, Badr al-Dīn Muḥammad b. ʿAbdallāh. *al-Burhān fī ʿulūm al-Qurʾān*. Edited by Muḥammad Abū al-Faḍl Ibrāhīm. Cairo: Dār al-Turāth, n.d.

al-Zurkān, Muḥammad Ṣāliḥ. *Fakhr al-Dīn al-Rāzī wa-ārāʾuhu al-kalāmīyah wa-al-falsafīyah*. Beirut: Dār al-Fikr, 1383/1963.

Zwettler, Michael. *The Oral Tradition of Classical Arabic Poetry: Its Character and Implications*. Columbus: Ohio State University Press, 1978.

Zyson, Aron. "Two Unrecognized Karrāmī Texts." *Journal of the American Oriental Society* 108 (1988): 577–87.

Index of Qurʾānic verses

Index of names and subjects